INTERCULTURAL
COMMUNICATION
IN CONTEXTS

INTERCULTURAL COMMUNICATION IN CONTEXTS

SIXTH EDITION

Judith N. Martin
Arizona State University

Thomas K. Nakayama
Northeastern University

The McGraw·Hill Companies

Mc Graw Hill

Connect
Learn
Succeed™

INTERCULTURAL COMMUNICATION IN CONTEXTS, SIXTH EDITION

Published by McGraw-Hill, a business unit of The McGraw-Hill Companies, Inc., 1221 Avenue of the Americas, New York, NY 10020. Copyright © 2013 by The McGraw-Hill Companies, Inc. All rights reserved. Printed in the United States of America. Previous editions © 2010, 2006 and 2003. No part of this publication may be reproduced or distributed in any form or by any means, or stored in a database or retrieval system, without the prior written consent of The McGraw-Hill Companies, Inc., including, but not limited to, in any network or other electronic storage or transmission, or broadcast for distance learning.

Some ancillaries, including electronic and print components, may not be available to customers outside the United States.

This book is printed on acid-free paper.

1 2 3 4 5 6 7 8 9 0 DOC/DOC 1 0 9 8 7 6 5 4 3 2

ISBN 978-0-07-803677-4
MHID 0-07-803677-1

Vice President & Editor-in-Chief: *Michael Ryan*
Vice President of Specialized Publishing: *Janice M. Roerig-Blong*
Publisher: *David Patterson*
Senior Sponsoring Editor: *Debra B. Hash*
Marketing Coordinator: *Angela R. FitzPatrick*
Senior Project Manager: *Joyce Watters*
Design Coordinator: *Brenda A. Rolwes*
Cover Designer: *Studio Montage, St. Louis, Missouri*
Cover Image: © *Getty Images RF*
Buyer: *Sandy Ludovissy*
Media Project Manager: *Sridevi Palani*
Compositor: *Laserwords Private Limited*
Typeface: *10/12 JansonLTStd*
Printer: *R. R. Donnelley*

All credits appearing on page or at the end of the book are considered to be an extension of the copyright page.

Library of Congress Cataloging-in-Publication Data

Martin, Judith N.
    Intercultural communication in contexts / Judith N. Martin, Thomas K. Nakayama.—6th ed.
        p. cm.
    ISBN 978-0-07-803677-4 (alk. paper)
    1. Intercultural communication. I. Nakayama, Thomas K. II. Title.
HM1211.M373 2012
303.48'2—dc23   2011050486

www.mhhe.com

About the Authors

The two authors of this book come to intercultural communication from very different backgrounds and very different research traditions. Yet we believe that these differences offer a unique approach to thinking about intercultural communication. We briefly introduce ourselves here, but we hope that by the end of the book you will have a much more complete understanding of who we are.

Judith Martin grew up in Mennonite communities, primarily in Delaware and Pennsylvania. She has studied at the Université de Grenoble in France and has taught in Algeria. She received her doctorate at the Pennsylvania State University. By background and training, she is a social scientist who has focused on intercultural communication on an interpersonal level and has studied how people's communication is affected as they move or sojourn between international locations. More recently, she has studied how people's cultural backgrounds influence their online communication. She has taught at the State University of New York at Oswego, the University of Minnesota, the University of New Mexico, and Arizona State University. She enjoys gardening, hiking, and traveling, and she does not miss the harsh Midwestern winters.

Tom Nakayama grew up mainly in Georgia, at a time when the Asian American presence was much less than it is now. He has studied at the Université de Paris and various universities in the United States. He received his doctorate from the University of Iowa. By background and training, he is a critical rhetorician who views intercultural communication in a social context. He has taught at the California State University at San Bernardino and Arizona State University. He has done a Fulbright at the Université de Mons in Belgium. He is now professor of communication studies at Northeastern University in Boston. He lives in Providence, Rhode Island and loves taking the train to campus. He loves the change of seasons in New England, especially autumn.

The authors' very different life stories and research programs came together at Arizona State University. We have each learned much about intercultural communication through our own experiences, as well as through our intellectual pursuits. Judith has a well-established record of social science approaches to intercultural communication. Tom, in contrast, has taken a nontraditional approach to understanding intercultural communication by emphasizing critical perspectives. We believe that these differences in our lives and in our research offer complementary ways of understanding intercultural communication.

For almost 20 years, we have engaged in many different dialogues about intercultural communication—focusing on our experiences, thoughts, ideas, and analyses—which led us to think about writing this textbook. But our interest was not primarily sparked by these dialogues; rather, it was our overall interest in improving intercultural relations that motivated us. We believe that communication is an important arena for improving those relations. By helping people become more aware as intercultural communicators, we hope to make this a better world for all of us.

Brief Contents

Contents

THE INCREASING IMPORTANCE OF INTERCULTURAL COMMUNICATION IN A RAPIDLY CHANGING WORLD

The economic crisis facing the European Union has some experts questioning the future of the euro. The continued weakness in the U.S. economy and the rapid rise of other economies has the International Monetary Fund predicting that China will overtake the United States in 2016 to become the world's largest economy (Weisbrot, 2011). How will the expansion of globalization be affected? If the euro fails, what happens to Europe's economy, and what kind of impact will there be on the exchange of products and movement of people around the world? How will economic changes influence where tourists, businesspeople, students, immigrants, and refugees come from and where they go? What languages will be studied, and what is the future role of English in the world? Changes such as these are likely to influence the shape of intercultural communication.

When we look back upon the international and intercultural situation at the time we first began writing this book, we recognize how rapidly the world has changed and how, as a result, these changes have raised even more pressing issues for intercultural communication scholars and practitioners. We could not have predicted that the number of millionaires in Asia would surpass that of Europe so rapidly (Murray, 2011), nor could we have predicted the demonstrations and uprisings in the Arab world (dubbed the "Arab Spring"), 9/11 and the "war on terror," or the independence of South Sudan. The world will continue to change in ways that we cannot predict, but we must face this dynamic world open to new challenges, rather than retreating to ways of life that are rapidly disappearing.

Natural disasters such as the devastating earthquakes in Haiti and Japan; droughts in East Africa, China, and Texas; and record flooding in the United States, Australia, Brazil, and elsewhere have summoned a variety of positive responses, including tremendous caring and compassion across intercultural and international divides. In addition, the Internet, social media, texting, and people cell phones have made intercultural interactions that once may have seemed distant or peripheral to our lives now far more immediate. Regional identities continue to challenge national identities, such as is the case in Belgium, which appears closer than ever to dissolution along the lines of linguistic identities.

In this climate, the study of intercultural communication takes on special significance, because it offers tools to help us as we grapple with questions about religious and ethnic differences, hate crimes, and many other related issues. Those who study, teach, and conduct research in intercultural communication face an increasing number of challenges and difficult questions: Is it enough to identify differences among people? Are we actually reinforcing stereotypes in emphasizing differences? Is there a way to understand the dynamics of intercultural communication without resorting to lists of instructions? Don't we have to talk about the broader social, political, and historical contexts when we teach intercultural communication? How can we use our intercultural communication skills to help enrich our lives and the lives of those around us? Can intercultural communication scholars promote a better world for all?

Such questions are driven by rapidly changing cultural dynamics—both within the United States and abroad. On the one hand, attempts to establish peace between Israel and Palestine by withdrawing Israeli settlements from Gaza, as well as the continued expansion of the European Union, CAFTA (Central American Free Trade Agreement), and the African Union (formerly the Organization of African States), reflect some global movement toward unity. On the other hand, the increase in nuclear armaments, continuing clashes between India and Pakistan over Kashmir, and the tribal and religious struggles within Iraq and Pakistan exemplify continuing intergroup conflict. These extremes demonstrate the dynamic nature of culture and communication.

We initially wrote this book in part to address questions and issues such as these. Although the foundation of intercultural communication theory and research has always been interdisciplinary, the field is now informed by three identifiable and competing *paradigms*, or "ways of thinking." In this book, we attempt to integrate three different research approaches: (1) the traditional social-psychological approach that emphasizes cultural differences and how these differences influence communication, (2) the interpretive approach that emphasizes understanding communication in context, and (3) the more recent critical approach that underscores the importance of power and historical context to understanding intercultural communication, including postcolonial approaches.

We believe that each of these approaches has important contributions to make to the understanding of intercultural communication and that they operate in interconnected and sometimes contradictory ways. In this sixth edition, we have further strengthened our *dialectical* approach, which encourages students to think critically about intercultural phenomena as seen from these various perspectives.

Throughout this book, we acknowledge that there are no easy solutions to the difficult challenges of intercultural communication. Sometimes our discussions raise more questions than they answer. We believe that this is perfectly reasonable. The field of intercultural communication is changing, but the relationship between culture and communication is as well—because that relationship is, and probably always will be, complex and dynamic. We live in a rapidly changing world where intercultural contact will continue to increase, creating an increased potential for both conflict and cooperation. We hope that this book provides the tools needed to think about intercultural communication, as a way of understanding the challenges and recognizing the advantages of living in a multicultural world.

References

Murray, M. (2011, June 22). More wealthy people in Asia than in Europe, new report says. *ABC News*. Retrieved September 12, 2011, from http://abcnews .go.com/Business/millionaires-asia-europe-closing-number-wealthy-americans/ story?id=13905440.

Weisbrot, M. (2011, April 27). 2016: When China overtakes the U.S. *The Guardian*. Retrieved September 12, 2011, from http://www.guardian .co.uk/commentisfree/cifamerica/2011/apr/27/china-imf-economy-2016.

SIGNATURE FEATURES OF THE BOOK

Students usually come to the field of intercultural communication with some knowledge about many different cultural groups, including their own. Their understanding often is based on observations drawn from television, movies, the Internet, books, personal experiences, news media, and other sources. But many students have a difficult time assimilating information that does not readily fit into their preexisting knowledge base. In this book, we hope to move students gradually to the notion of a *dialectical framework* for thinking about cultural issues. That is, we show that knowledge can be acquired in many different ways— through social scientific studies, experience, media reports, and so on—but these differing forms of knowledge need to be seen dynamically and in relation to each other. We offer students a number of ways to begin thinking critically about intercultural communication in a dialectical manner. These include:

- An explicit discussion of differing research approaches to intercultural communication, focusing on both the strengths and limitations of each
- Ongoing attention to history, popular culture, and identity as important factors in understanding intercultural communication
- Student Voices boxes in which students relate their own experiences and share their thoughts about various intercultural communication issues
- Point of View boxes in which diverse viewpoints from news media, research studies, and other public forums are presented
- Incorporation of the authors' own personal experiences to highlight particular aspects of intercultural communication

NEW TO THE SIXTH EDITION

- To reflect the increasing influence of globalization, we continue to emphasize its importance to intercultural communication. For example, in Chapter 1, we discuss how globalization and related economic recessions influence intercultural communication. In Chapter 8, we provide new examples of the impact of globalization on the continuing worldwide migration and the resulting intercultural encounters.

- The continuing and expanding influence of communication technology in our daily lives is addressed by new material in Chapter 10 acknowledging the increasing role of social networking sites (SNS) in intercultural relationships.
- Our expanded discussion of the implications of religious identity and belief systems in Chapters 1 and 11 is prompted by continued awareness of the important role religion plays in intercultural communication.
- We continue to emphasize the important roles that institutions play in intercultural contact. In Chapter 10, we address the role of institutions in supporting or discouraging intercultural relationships.

SUPPLEMENTAL RESOURCES

The Online Learning Center at www.mhhe.com/martinnakayama6 provides interactive resources to fit the needs of a variety of teaching and learning styles. For instructors specifically, the OLC offers an online *Instructor's Resource Manual* with sample syllabi, discussion questions, and general pedagogical tips for teaching the course and to help meet the special challenges arising from the controversial nature of much of the material. In addition, a computerized test bank that allows instructors to edit and add their own questions is available in both Windows and Macintosh formats.

CHAPTER-BY-CHAPTER OVERVIEW

Intercultural Communication in Contexts is organized into three parts: Part I, "Foundations of Intercultural Communication"; Part II, "Intercultural Communication Processes"; and Part III, "Intercultural Communication Applications."

Part I, "Foundations of Intercultural Communication," explores the history of the field and presents various approaches to this area of study, including our own.

We begin Chapter 1 with a focus on the dynamics of social life and global conditions as a rationale for the study of intercultural communication. We introduce ethics in this chapter to illustrate its centrality to any discussion of intercultural interaction. In this edition, we have emphasized the importance of social justice and engagement with communities like the homeless as an important element in intercultural effectiveness and have also updated our discussion of the impact of globalization and immigration policies on intercultural encounters.

In Chapter 2, we introduce the history of intercultural communication as an area of study as well as the three paradigms that inform our knowledge about intercultural interactions. We establish the notion of a dialectical approach so that students can begin to make connections and form relationships among the paradigms. The popular Hurricane Katrina case study has been revamped to explore New Orleans six years later, examining the lasting effect of the hurricane on intercultural encounters, including the impacts on the various cultural groups who have left New Orleans versus those who stayed and the related long-term political implications.

In Chapter 3, we focus on four basic intercultural communication components—culture, communication, context, and power. In this edition, we've included updated examples of cultural struggles in political contexts (e.g., the DREAM Act) and a new example of interpretive research—Latino/Latina scholarship describing the performance of ethnic identity.

Chapter 4 focuses on the importance of historical forces in shaping contemporary intercultural interaction. We have provided additional information and examples of family histories and expanded the notion of hidden histories.

Part II, "Intercultural Communication Processes," establishes the factors that contribute to the dynamics of intercultural communication: identity, language, and nonverbal codes.

Chapter 5, on identity, has extended coverage of religious identity, multicultural identity, and sexual identity (in addition to gender identity). This chapter now includes a deeper exploration of sexual identity, including discussions of transgender, intolerance, and how one's sexuality contributes to development of ethnic and cultural identity.

Chapter 6 addresses language issues, with new examples of language barriers to intercultural communication—including slang, humor, and different types of communication styles—and a new discussion of the role of texting in online intercultural communication.

Chapter 7 focuses on nonverbal codes and cultural spaces and includes new examples of cultural variations in nonverbal behavior; a new section on cultural variations in physical appearance and attractiveness; and a discussion on the prohibition of the burqa/hijab (covering worn by some Muslim women) in Europe and the United States, along with its implications for intercultural communication.

Part III, "Intercultural Communication Applications," helps students apply the knowledge of intercultural communication presented in the first two parts.

Chapter 8 addresses intercultural transitions. In this edition, we introduce a revamped discussion on the migrant–host relationship to emphasize differences among assimilation, separation, and segregation.

In Chapter 9, we focus on popular and folk culture and their impact on intercultural communication. We have included new updated examples and an enhanced discussion of how popular culture influences body image of men and women in various cultural contexts.

Chapter 10 explores intercultural relationships. In this edition, we expand our discussion of sexuality and intimate relationships in multicultural environments, and new material on online relationships has been added.

Chapter 11 is reorganized in this edition. We have eliminated the emphasis on two distinct orientations to conflict and instead emphasize an integrated approach to intercultural conflict, using the recent riots in London and Paris as case studies. We have also updated the discussion on conflict styles, incorporating Hammer's 2005 framework of intercultural conflict styles.

Chapter 12 includes new examples of community coalition building and continues to emphasize practical experience in striving for intercultural competence in everyday encounters.

ACKNOWLEDGMENTS

The random convergence of the two authors in time and place led to the creation of this textbook. We both found ourselves at Arizona State University in the early 1990s. Over the course of several years, we discussed and analyzed the multiple approaches to intercultural communication. Much of this discussion was facilitated by the ASU Department of Communication's "culture and communication" theme. Department faculty met to discuss research and pedagogical issues relevant to the study of communication and culture; we also reflected on our own notions of what constituted intercultural communication. This often meant reliving many of our intercultural experiences and sharing them with our colleagues.

Above all, we must recognize the fine work of the staff at McGraw-Hill: sponsoring editor Debra Hash, media project manager Sridevi Palani, marketing Coordinator Angela R. FitzPatrick, and project manager Joyce Watters, and especially developmental editor Craig Leonard, who so effectively guided us through yet another project.

In addition, we want to thank all the reviewers of this and previous editions of *Intercultural Communication in Contexts*, whose comments and careful readings were enormously helpful. They are:

First Edition Reviewers

Rosita D. Albert, *University of Minnesota*
Carlos G. Aleman, *University of Illinois, Chicago*
Deborah Cai, *University of Maryland*
Gail Campbell, *University of Colorado, Denver*
Ling Chen, *University of Oklahoma*
Alberto Gonzalez, *Bowling Green State University*
Bradford "J" Hall, *University of New Mexico*
Mark Lawrence McPhail, *University of Utah*
Richard Morris, *Northern Illinois University*
Catherine T. Motoyama, *College of San Mateo*
Gordon Nakagawa, *California State University, Northridge*
Joyce M. Ngoh, *Marist College*
Nancy L. Street, *Bridgewater State College*
Erika Vora, *St. Cloud State University*
Lee B. Winet, *State University of New York, Oswego*
Gust A. Yep, *San Francisco State University*

Second Edition Reviewers

Eric Akoi, *Colorado State University*
Jeanne Barone, *Indiana/Purdue University at Fort Wayne*
Wendy Chung, *Rider University*
Ellen Shide Crannell, *West Valley College*

Patricia Holmes, *University of Missouri*
Madeline Keaveney, *California State University, Chico*
Mark Neumann, *University of South Florida*
Margaret Pryately, *St. Cloud State University*
Kara Shultz, *Bloomsburg University*

Third Edition Reviewers

Marguerite Arai, *University of Colorado at Colorado Springs*
Rona Halualani, *San José State University*
Piper McNulty, *De Anza College*
Karla Scott, *St. Louis University*
Candace Thomas-Maddox, *Ohio University, Lancaster*
Susan Walsh, *Southern Oregon University*
Jennifer Willis-Rivera, *Southern Illinois State University*

Fourth Edition Reviewers

Sara DeTurk, *University of Texas, San Antonio*
Christopher Hajek, *University of Texas, San Antonio*
Mary M. Meares, *Washington State University*
Kimberly Moffitt, *DePaul University*
James Sauceda, *California State University, Long Beach*
Kathryn Sorrells, *California State University, Northridge*
David Zuckerman, *Sacramento State University*

Fifth Edition Reviewers

Shirene Bell, *Salt Lake Community College*
Lisa Bradford, *University of Milwaukee-Wisconsin*
John Chiang, *State University of New York Oneonta*
Susan DeTurk, *University of Texas at San Antonio*
Charles Elliott, *Cedarville University*
Gayle Houser, *Northern Arizona University*
Tema Oliveira Milstein, *University of New Mexico*
Marc Rich, *California State University, Long Beach*

Sixth Edition Reviewers

Nader Chaaban, *Northern Virginia Community College*
Jenny Gardner, *Bay Path College*
Rachel Alicia Griffin, *Southern Illinois University-Carbondale*
Julia Hagemann, *Drexel University*
Amy N. Heuman, PhD, *Texas Tech University*

Kumi Ishii, *Western Kentucky University*
Meina Lui, *University of Maryland*
Dr. Nina-Jo Moore, *Appalachian State University*
Craig VanGeison, *Saint Charles County Community College*
Nadene Vevea, *North Dakota State University*
MJ Woeste, *University of Cincinnati*

Our colleagues and students have provided invaluable assistance. Thanks to our colleagues for their ongoing moral support and intellectual challenges to our thinking. Thanks to our editorial assistants, Robert Carlsen and Christopher McRae, both graduate students in the Speech Communication Department at Southern Illinois University. They conducted productive library research, finding relevant scholarship and interesting examples to support and liven up our writing. They were also always cooperative and responsive even when they had their own research projects to complete and academic deadlines to meet. And as always, we owe thanks to our undergraduate students, who continue to challenge us to think about intercultural communication in ways that make sense to their lives.

We thank our families and friends for once again allowing us absences and silences as we directed our energies toward the completion of this revision. We want to acknowledge both Ronald Chaldu and David L. Karbonski, who continue to be supportive of our academic writing projects.

Our international experiences have enriched our understanding of intercultural communication theories and concepts. We thank all of the following people for helping us with these experiences: Tommy and Kazuko Nakayama; Michel Dion and Eliana Sampaïo of Strasbourg, France; Jean-Louis Sauvage and Pol Thiry of the Université de Mons-Hainaut, Belgium; Christina Kalinowska and the Café "Le Ropieur" in Mons, Belgium; Scott and the others at Le BXL in Brussels, Belgium; Emilio, Vince, Jimmy, Gene and the others at the Westbury Bar in Philadelphia; Jerzy, Alicja, Marek, and Jolanta Drzewieccy of Bedzin, Poland; as well as Margaret Nicholson of the Commission for Educational Exchange between Belgium, Luxembourg, and the United States; and Liudmila Markina from Minsk, Belarus. Some research in this book was made possible by a scholarship from the Fulbright Commission and the Fonds National de la Recherche Scientifique in Brussels. In addition, we thank the countless others we have met in cafés, train stations, bars, and conferences, if only for a moment of international intercultural interaction.

Other people helped us understand intercultural communication closer to home, especially the staff and students at the Guadalupe Center at South Mountain Community College, and also Dr. Amalia Villegas, Laura Laguna, Cruzita Mori, and Lucia Madril and family.

In spirit and conceptualization, our book spans the centuries and crosses many continents. It has been shaped by the many people we have read about and encountered. It is to these guiding and inspiring individuals—some of whom we had the good fortune to meet and some of whom we will never encounter—that we dedicate this book. It is our hope that their spirit of curiosity, openness, and understanding will be reflected in the pages that follow.

Many textbooks emphasize in their introductions how you should use the text. In contrast, we begin this book by introducing ourselves and our interests in intercultural communication. There are many ways to think about intercultural interactions. One way to learn more about intercultural experiences is to engage in dialogue with others on this topic. Ideally, we would like to begin a dialogue with you about some of the ways to think about intercultural communication. Learning about intercultural communication is not about learning a finite set of skills, terms, and theories. It is about learning to think about cultural realities in multiple ways. Unfortunately, it is not possible for us to engage in dialogues with our readers.

Instead, we strive to lay out a number of issues to think about regarding intercultural communication. In reflecting on these issues in your own inter-actions and talking about them with others, you will be well on your way to becoming both a better intercultural communicator and a better analyst of intercultural interactions. There is no endpoint from which we can say that we have learned all there is to know. Learning about communication is a lifelong process that involves experiences and analysis. We hope this book will generate many dialogues that will help you come to a greater understanding of different cultures and peoples and a greater appreciation for the complexity of intercultural communication.

COMMUNICATING IN A DYNAMIC, MULTICULTURAL WORLD

We live in rapidly changing times. Although no one can foresee the future, we believe that changes are increasing the imperative for intercultural learning. In Chapter 1, you will learn more about some of these changes and their influence on intercultural communication.

You stand at the beginning of a textbook journey into intercultural communication. At this point, you might take stock of who you are, what your intercultural communication experiences have been, how you responded in those situations, and how you tend to think about those experiences. Some people respond to intercultural situations with amusement, curiosity, or interest; others may respond with hostility, anger, or fear. It is important to reflect on your experiences and to identify how you respond and what those reactions mean.

We also think it is helpful to recognize that in many instances people do not want to communicate interculturally. Sometimes people see those who are culturally different as threatening, as forcing them to change. They may believe that such people require more assistance and patience, or they may simply think of them as "different." People bring to intercultural interactions a variety of emotional states and attitudes; further, not everyone wants to communicate interculturally. Because of this dynamic, many people have had negative intercultural experiences that influence subsequent intercultural interactions. Negative experiences can range from simple misunderstandings to physical violence. Although it may be unpleasant to discuss such situations, we believe that it is necessary to do so if we are to understand and improve intercultural interaction.

Intercultural conflict can occur even when the participants do not intentionally provoke it. When we use our own cultural frames in intercultural settings, those hidden assumptions can cause trouble. For example, when renting a small apartment in a private home in Grenoble, France, coauthor Judith Martin invited a number of her U.S. friends who were traveling in Europe to stop by and stay with her. The angry and frustrated response that this drew from her landlady came as a surprise. She told Judith that she would have to pay extra for all of the water they were using, that the apartment was not a motel, and that Judith would have to move out if the practice of having overnight guests continued. Differing notions of privacy and appropriate renter behavior contributed to the conflict. Intercultural experiences are not always fun. Sometimes they are frustrating, confusing, and distressing.

On a more serious level, we might look at the U.S. military's continued engagement in Iraq and Afghanistan as yet another example of intercultural communication. The subsequent interpretations of and reactions to this presence by different communities of people reflect important differences in our society and in the world at large. Although some people in the United States and abroad see these efforts as attempts to liberate oppressed people and establish democratic governments, others view them as imperialist intervention on the part of the United States. These differing views highlight the complexity of intercultural communication. We do not come to intercultural interactions as blank slates; instead, we bring our identities and our cultures.

IMPROVING YOUR INTERCULTURAL COMMUNICATION

Although the journey to developing awareness in intercultural communication is an individual one, it is important to recognize the connections we all have to many different aspects of social life. You are, of course, an individual. But you have been influenced by culture. The ways that others regard you and communicate with you are influenced largely by whom they perceive you to be. By enacting cultural characteristics of masculinity or femininity, for example, you may elicit particular reactions from others. Reflect on your social and individual characteristics; consider how these characteristics communicate something about you.

Finally, there is no list of things to do in an intercultural setting. Although prescribed reactions might help you avoid serious faux pas in one setting or culture, such lists are generally too simplistic to get you very far in any culture and may cause serious problems in other cultures. The study of communication is both a science and an art. In this book, we attempt to pull the best of both kinds of knowledge together for you. Because communication does not happen in a vacuum but is integral to the many dynamics that make it possible—economics, politics, technology—the ever-changing character of our world means that it is essential to develop sensitivity and flexibility to change. It also means that you can never stop learning about intercultural communication.

PART I

Foundations of Intercultural Communication

CHAPTER

1

WHY STUDY INTERCULTURAL COMMUNICATION?

CHAPTER OBJECTIVES

After reading this chapter, you should be able to:

1. Identify six imperatives for studying intercultural communication.
2. Describe how technology can impact intercultural interaction.
3. Describe how global and domestic economic conditions influence intercultural relations.
4. Explain how understanding intercultural communication can facilitate resolution of intercultural conflict.
5. Explain how studying intercultural communication can lead to increased self-understanding.
6. Understand the difference among a universalistic, a relativist, and a dialogic approach to the study of ethics and intercultural communication.
7. Identify and describe three characteristics of an ethical student of culture.

When I was back home [Kuwait], before I came to the United States to go to college, I knew all about my culture and about my religion. However, I did not really know what other people from the other world [United States] think of Middle Eastern people or Muslims in general. So, what I have witnessed is a lot of discrimination in this country, not only against my race but against other groups. . . . Yet I under-stand that not all Americans hate us. I met a lot of Americans who are cooperative with me and show me love and are interested to know about my country and culture.

—Mohamad

My longest relationship was an intercultural relationship with a guy from Colombia. We didn't run into very many problems because we were both culturally open and enthusiastic to learn about each other's traditions and values. We talked a lot about our backgrounds and really learned to embrace our differences, as we grew close with each other's families. We both learned a lot about each other's culture and different philosophies on life. Overall, it was an extremely rewarding experience.

—Adrianna

Both Mohamad's and Adrianna's experiences point to the benefits and challenges of intercultural communication. Through intercultural relationships, we can learn a tremendous amount about other people and their cultures, and about ourselves and our own cultural background. At the same time, there are many challenges. Intercultural communication can also involve barriers like stereotyping and discrimination. And these relationships take place in complex historical and political contexts. Mohamad's experience in the United States is probably more challenging today than it would have been several years ago because of recent political events. An important goal in this book is how to increase your understanding of the dynamics at work in intercultural interaction.

This book will expose you to the variety of approaches we use to study intercultural communication. We also weave into the text our personal stories to make theory come alive. By linking theory and practice, we hope to give a fuller picture of intercultural communication than either one alone could offer.

We bring many intercultural communication experiences to the text. As you read, you will learn not only about both of us as individuals but also about our views of intercultural communication. Don't be overwhelmed by the seeming complexity of intercultural communication. Not knowing everything that you would like to know is very much a part of this process.

Why is it important to focus on intercultural communication and to strive to become better at this complex pattern of interaction? We can think of at least six reasons; perhaps you can add more.

THE SELF-AWARENESS IMPERATIVE

One of the most important reasons for studying intercultural communication is the awareness it raises of our own cultural identity and background. This is also one of the least obvious reasons. Peter Adler (1975), a noted social psychologist, observes that the study of intercultural communication begins as a journey into another culture and reality and ends as a journey into one's own culture.

We gain insights in intercultural experiences overseas. When Judith was teaching high school in Algeria, a Muslim country in North Africa, she realized something about her religious identity as a Protestant. December 25 came and went, and she taught classes with no mention of Christmas. Judith had never thought about how special the celebration of Christmas was or how important the holiday was to her. She then recognized on a personal level the uniqueness of this particular cultural practice. Erla, a graduate student from Iceland, notes the increased knowledge and appreciation she's gained concerning her home country:

> *Living in another country widens your horizon. It makes you appreciate the things you have, and it strengthens the family unit. You look at your country from a different point of view. We have learned not to expect everything to be the same as "at home," but if we happen to find something that reminds us of home, we really appreciate it and it makes us very happy. Ultimately we are all very thankful that we had the opportunity to live in another country.*

However, it is important to recognize that intercultural learning is not always easy or comfortable. Sometimes intercultural encounters makes us aware of our own **ethnocentrism**—a tendency to think that our own culture is superior to other cultures. This means that we assume, subconsciously, that the way we do things is the only way. For example, when Tom first visited France he was surprised to discover that shoppers are expected to greet shopkeepers when entering a small store. Or that French people sometimes ate horsemeat, snails, and very fragrant cheeses. Sometimes Americans think that these foods shouldn't be eaten. This attitude that foods we eat are somehow normal and that people shouldn't eat these other foods is a kind of ethnocentrism. To be surprised or even taken aback by unfamiliar customs is not unexpected; however, a refusal to expand your cultural horizons or to acknowledge the legitimacy of cultural practices different from your own can lead to intergroup misunderstandings and conflict.

ethnocentrism A tendency to think that our own culture is superior to other cultures.

What you learn depends on your social and economic position in society. Self-awareness through intercultural contact for someone from a racial or minority group may mean learning to be wary and not surprised at subtle slights by members of the dominant majority—and reminders of their place in society. For example, a Chinese American colleague is sometimes approached at professional meetings by white communication professors who ask her to take their drink order.

If you are white and middle class, intercultural learning may mean an enhanced awareness of your privilege. A white colleague tells of feeling uncomfortable staying in a Jamaican resort, being served by blacks whose ancestors were brought there as slaves by European colonizers. On the one hand, it is privilege that allows travelers like our colleague to experience new cultures and places. On the other hand, one might wonder if we, through this type of travel, are reproducing those same historical postcolonial economic patterns.

Self-awareness, then, that comes through intercultural learning may involve an increased awareness of being caught up in political, economic, and historical systems—not of our own making.

THE DEMOGRAPHIC IMPERATIVE

You have probably observed that your world is increasingly diverse. You may have classes with students who differ from you in ethnicity, race, religion, and/or nationality. College and university student bodies are becoming increasingly diverse. According to a recent report, minority students are a growing percentage of all undergraduates. There are currently 37% minority and foreign-born students (compared to 33% in 1998). Conversely, the share of white students on campuses declined from 70% to 63% during the same time period. Women now receive the majority of degrees (Undergraduate diversity, 2010).

Sports are a very visible part of this increasing diversity. A 2011 report on diversity in Major League Baseball shows that almost 30% of players were born outside the United States and almost 40% are people of color (Latino, Asian, Native American, and Native Hawaiian or Pacific Islander); all together, they "make the playing field look more like America" (Lapchick, 2011, p. 2). In addition, 33 percent of the MLB Central Office workers are people of color, and 38% are women. This increasing diversity extends to women's sports as well, including the LPGA where "Sixteen of the top-20 current money earners were born outside of the United States. Eight of those women are South Korean followed by two Swedes, two Australians, a Mexican, a Norwegian, a Brazilian and a Taiwanese" (The Canadian Press, 2008). This increasing diversity comes from changing U.S. demographics and more global interaction of people. (See Figure 1-1.)

Changing U.S. Demographics

demographics The characteristics of a population, especially as classified by race, ethnicity, age, sex, and income.

U.S. **demographics** are projected to change dramatically during your lifetime—the next 50 years. Another source of increased opportunity for intercultural contact exists because of the increasing cultural diversity in the United States. The 2010 census revealed a dramatic increase in ethnic/racial diversity, and this trend is expected to continue, as shown in Figure 1-2 (Passel & Cohn, 2008). The Hispanic population will triple in size and constitute approximately 30% of the population by 2050; in the same time period, the Asian American population will double in size and will constitute about 10% of the total population. African Americans will remain approximately the same in numbers and comprise 13% of the population; whites will continue to be a smaller majority as minority populations increase in number.

The nation's elderly population will more than double in size from 2005 through 2050, as the baby boom generation enters the traditional retirement years. The number of working-age Americans and children will grow more slowly than the elderly population and will shrink as a share of the total population (Passel & Cohn, 2008).

What is also interesting is the racial distribution in the various geographical regions. The Population Reference Bureau (PRB) computed a "diversity index" showing that the highest ethnic diversity is concentrated in the southeastern and southwestern regions of the United States. Minority concentrations are projected to increase especially in the South, Southwest, and West. The PRB

FIGURE 1-1   Rapid changes in technology, demographics, and economic forces mean that you are likely to come into contact with many people with diverse backgrounds and experiences. Although many of these communication experiences will be in professional and work situations, many other interactions will be in public and social settings. (© Esbin-Anderson/The Image Works)

estimates that, by 2025, minority groups will account for more than 50% of the population in four states (Hawaii, California, New Mexico, Texas) (www.prb .org/AmeristatTemplate.cfm?Section=Estimates).

There is increasing diversity in the U.S. workforce as well. The workforce is expected to continue to get older, and there will also be proportionately more women working. What accounts for these changes? The workforce will be older because the baby boomers are aging. More women are in the workforce for several reasons. First, economic pressures have come to bear; more women are single parents, and even in two-parent families, it often takes two incomes to meet family expenses. Second, the women's movement of the 1960s and 1970s resulted in more women seeking careers and jobs outside the home. In addition,

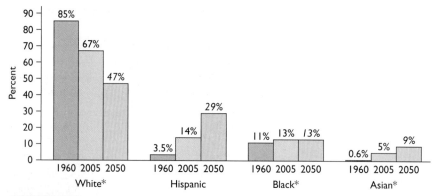

FIGURE 1-2   Population by race and ethnicity, actual and projected: 1960, 2005, and 2050 (% of total)

Source: From Jeffrey S. Passel and D'Vera Cohn, U.S. Population Projections: 2005–2050, Pew Research Center, 2008, p. 9.

Note: All races modified and not Hispanic (*); American Indian/Alaska Native not shown. See "Methodology." Projections for 2050 indicated by light gray bars.

the workforce is more ethnically and racially diverse—in part, simply because there are more minorities now than before, but also because of civil rights efforts, which led to more opportunities for minorities in business and industry.

Changing Immigration Patterns

The second source of demographic change is different immigration patterns. Although the United States has often been thought of as a nation of immigrants, it is also a nation that established itself by subjugating the original inhabitants and that prospered to some extent as a result of slave labor. These aspects of national identity are important in understanding contemporary society. Today, immigration has changed the social landscape significantly. First, the foreign-born population continues to rise as a percentage of the total population, up from almost 5% in 1970 to more than 13% in 2010. However, this is still lower than it was during the great migrations of the 1800s and 1900s when most Europeans came to the United States.

A second change concerns the origin of the immigrants. Prior to the 1970s, most of the immigrants to the United States came from Europe; now, 80% of the immigrants are from Latin America and Asia (Grieco & Trevelyan, 2010). These shifts in patterns of immigration have resulted in a much more racially and ethnically diverse population. It's not hard to see that the United States is becoming more heterogeneous. We address the issue of whites losing majority status in Chapter 5.

heterogeneous Difference(s) in a group, culture, or population.

homogeneous Similarity in a group, culture, or population.

Sometimes more **heterogeneous** cultures are contrasted to more **homogeneous** cultures. Instead of thinking of cultures as either heterogeneous or homogeneous, it is more useful to think about cultures as more or less heterogeneous (or more or less homogeneous). Cultures can change over time and become more or less homogeneous. They can also be more heterogeneous than another culture.

This heterogeneity presents many opportunities and challenges for students of intercultural communication. Sometimes, tensions can be created by (and be the result of) proposed legislation (Flores, Moon, & Nakayama, 2006). For example, in the 1990s, California passed several laws that prohibited undocumented immigrants from receiving public health and social services. In 2006, Arizona passed four propositions similarly limiting undocumented immigrants' rights: no right to bail, no right to collect any award from civil lawsuits, no right to in-state tuition or to taxpayer-funded adult education or child care. The same year, Arizona voted to declare English as the official language. 2008 was a particularly divisive year for immigration policies (see Point of View, p. 13). More recently, Arizona's Senate Bill 1070—signed by the governor but challenged in court—makes it a state crime to not carry immigration papers, gives the police broad powers to detain anyone suspected of being in the country illegally, and allows people to sue local government agencies if they believe the state immigration law is not being enforced. Other states are considering similar legislation. While some feel that these are reasonable measures, others feel that it paves the way for increased harassment by police and increased discrimination against Latinos (or people who look Latino), regardless of their citizenship status (Archibold, 2010).

We should also note the potential opportunities in a culturally diverse society. **Diversity** can expand our conceptions of what is possible—linguistically, politically, socially—as various lifestyles and ways of thinking converge. However, increased opportunity does not always lead to increased interaction. A recent "freshman survey" conducted by a research institute at UCLA reported that "a growing number of students appeared unlikely to have a diverse set of friends in college" (Farrell, 2005). This may be because these students are graduating from high schools that are becoming increasingly more segregated (see Point of View).

diversity The quality of being different.

To get a better sense of the situation in the United States today, let's take a look at our history. As mentioned previously, the United States has often been referred to as a nation of **immigrants**, but this is only partly true. When Europeans began arriving on the shores of the New World, an estimated 8 to 10 million Native Americans were already living here. Their ancestors probably began to arrive via the Bering Strait at least 40,000 years earlier. The outcome of the encounters between these groups—the colonizing Europeans and the native peoples—is well known. By 1940, the Native American population of the United States had been reduced to an estimated 250,000. Today, about 2.9 million Native Americans (from 565 recognized tribes) live in the United States (American Indians by the Numbers, 2011).

immigrants People who come to a new country, region, or environment to settle more or less permanently. (Compare with **sojourners**, see Chapter 8)

African American Immigrants   African Americans represent a special case in the history of U.S. immigration. African Americans did not choose to emigrate but were brought here involuntarily, mainly as slave labor. Many Europeans also emigrated as indentured servants. However, the system of contract servitude was gradually replaced by perpetual servitude, or slavery, almost wholly of Africans. Many landowners wanted captive workers who could not escape and who could not become competitors. They turned to slave labor.

POINT *of* VIEW

In this article, Harinder Bahra tackles some problems relating to race in university education in the United Kingdom. Do you think this article could apply to the United States as well?

Far from celebrating the growing diversity of UK university staff and students, the higher education sector is almost doing the opposite. There has been a collective failure of employers in the university sector to tackle race discrimination and racism, or even accept it exists.

Like football clubs, universities are descending on developing countries, picking up cheaper black and minority ethnic (BME) researchers and lecturers in response to the transatlantic brain drain and continued pressure on operating costs. BME staff are often on part-time or fixed-term contracts with lower salaries and have difficulty in progressing through to senior positions. Meanwhile, BME students are increasingly being stereotyped as "extremists" in addition to being seen as academically less able.

As the University and College Union today launches a race equality campaign it is high time to ask what is being done.

Some universities, like the trade union sector, have appointed BME chancellors or presidents in voluntary, unpaid roles, but without corresponding changes in senior paid positions. This window dressing presents a diverse public profile, but still preserves the status quo.

Source: From H. Bahra, "Time to kick racism out of university." *The Guardian*, November 16, 2008. Retrieved May 13, 2008, from http://education.guardian.co.uk/racism/comment/0,1949487,00.html.

The slave trade, developed by European and African merchants, lasted about 350 years, although slavery was outlawed in Europe long before it was outlawed in the United States. Roughly 10 million Africans reached the Americas, although many died in the brutal overseas passage (Curtin, 1969). Slavery is an important aspect of U.S. immigration history. As James Baldwin (1955) suggested, the legacy of slavery makes contemporary interracial relations in the United States very different from interracial relations in Europe and other regions of the world.

Slavery presents a moral dilemma for many whites even today. A common response is simply to ignore history. Many people assert that because not all whites owned slaves we should forget the past and move on. For others, forgetting the past is not acceptable. In fact, some historians, like James Loewen, maintain that acknowledging and understanding the past is the only viable alternative in moving forward. In his book *Lies My Teacher Told Me*, Loewen (1995) analyzes the content in contemporary high school history books and acknowledges that they do present the horrors of slavery. What is missing, however, is the connection of slavery to the current racial tensions in the United States:

Perhaps telling realistically what slavery was like for slaves is the easy part. After all, slavery as an institution is dead. We have progressed beyond it, so we can acknowledge its evils. . . . Without explaining its relevance to the present, however, extensive coverage of slavery is like extensive coverage of the Hawley-Smoot Tariff—just more facts for hapless eleventh graders to memorize. Slavery's twin legacies to the present are the social and economic inferiority it conferred upon blacks and the cultural racism it instilled in whites. Both continue to haunt our society. Therefore, treating slavery's enduring legacy is necessarily controversial. Unlike slavery, racism is not over yet. To function adequately in civic life in our troubled times, students must learn what causes racism. (p. 143)

Scholar and theologian Cornel West (1993) agrees that we should begin by acknowledging the historical flaws of U.S. society and recognizing the historical consequences of slavery. For instance, the United States has several Holocaust museums but no organized, official recognition of the horrors of slavery. Perhaps it is easier for us to focus on the negative events of another nation's history than on those of our own. On the other hand, many U.S. Americans feel that the election of Barack Obama, the first African American president, shows some progress in U.S. race relations. In Chapter 4, we explore the importance of history in understanding the dynamics of intercultural communication.

Relationships with New Immigrants   Relationships between residents and immigrants—between oldtimers and newcomers—have often been filled with tension and conflict. In the 19th century, Native Americans sometimes were caught in the middle of European rivalries. During the War of 1812, for example, Indian allies of the British were severely punished by the United States when the war ended. In 1832, the U.S. Congress recognized the Indian nations' right to self-government, but in 1871, a congressional act prohibited treaties between the U.S. government and Indian tribes. In 1887, Congress passed the Dawes Severalty Act, terminating Native Americans' special relationship with the U.S. government and paving the way for their removal from their homelands.

As waves of immigrants continued to roll in from Europe, the more firmly established European—mainly British—immigrants tried to protect their way of life, language, and culture. As one citizen lamented in 1856,

Four-fifths of the beggary and three-fifths of the crime spring from our foreign population; more than half the public charities, more than half the prisons and almshouses, more than half the police and the cost of administering criminal justice are for foreigners. (quoted in Cole, 1998, p. 126)

The foreigners to which this citizen was referring were mostly from Ireland, devastated by the potato famines, and from Germany, which had fallen on hard economic and political times. Historian James Banks (1991) identifies other anti-immigrant events throughout the nation's history. As early as 1729, an English mob prevented a group of Irish immigrants from landing in Boston. A few years later, another mob destroyed a new Scots-Irish Presbyterian church in Worcester,

Anglocentrism Using Anglo or white cultural standards as the criteria for interpretations and judgments of behaviors and attitudes.

melting pot A metaphor that assumes that immigrants and cultural minorities will be assimilated into the U.S. majority culture, losing their original cultures.

nativistic Extremely patriotic to the point of being anti-immigrant.

Massachusetts. In these acts, we can see the **Anglocentrism** that characterized early U.S. history. Later, northern and western European (e.g., German and Dutch) characteristics were added to this model of American culture. Immigrants from southern, central, and eastern Europe (e.g., Italy and Poland) were expected to assimilate into the so-called mainstream culture—to jump into the **melting pot** and come out "American."

In the late 19th and early 20th centuries, a **nativistic** (anti-immigrant) movement propagated violence against newer immigrants. In 1885, 28 Chinese were killed in an anti-Chinese riot in Wyoming; in 1891, a white mob attacked a Chinese community in Los Angeles and killed 19 people; also in 1891, 11 Italian Americans were lynched in New Orleans.

Nativistic sentiment was well supported at the government level. In 1882, Congress passed the Chinese Exclusion Act, officially prohibiting anyone who lived in China from immigrating to this country. In 1924, the Johnson-Read Act and the Oriental Exclusion Act established extreme quotas on immigration, virtually precluding the legal immigration of Asians. According to Ronald Takaki (1989), these two laws "provided for immigration based on nationality quotas: the number of immigrants to be admitted annually was limited to 2% of the foreign-born individuals of each nationality residing in the United States in 1890" (p. 209). The nativistic sentiment increasingly was manifested in arguments that economic and political opportunities should be reserved solely for whites, and not just for native-born Americans.

By the 1930s, southern and eastern European groups were considered "assimilatable," and the concept of race assumed new meaning. All of the so-called white races were now considered one, so racial hostilities could focus on ethnic (nonwhite) groups, such as Asian Americans, Native Americans, and Mexican Americans (Banks, 1991). Sociologist David Roediger (1991) traces how devastating this racialization was, particularly for African Americans. In the growing, but sometimes fragile, economy of the first half of the 20th century, white workers had an advantage. Although white immigrants received low wages, they had access to better schools and to public facilities, and they were accorded greater public acceptance. People of color often were considered less fit to receive economic benefits and, to some extent, to be not truly American (Foner, 1998).

The notion of the melting pot began to break down as immigrants came in larger numbers from outside of Europe. Although European immigrants were able to melt into white society, other immigrants were barred from doing so. In order to melt into white society, European immigrants were encouraged to assimilate by speaking English only and dropping their culturally specific customs. As part of this melting pot experience, many Americans of European ancestry today do not speak their forebearers' languages, such as German, Dutch, Norwegian, Polish, or Hungarian.

Although the notion of the melting pot could explain European immigrant experiences, the metaphor did not explain other immigrant experiences. Immigrants from Asia, Latin America, and Africa did not simply blend into white

The politics of immigration are always a topic of interest in America. An especially divisive year for immigration policy, 2008, highlighted the remarkably different approaches of various regions of the United States.

	Arizona's Employer Sanctions Law	Bay Area Day Laborer Policies
Policy	A statewide effort to punish employers who knowingly hire illegal immigrants	A San Francisco area effort to benefit the working conditions of day laborers, many of whom are undocumented immigrants
Specifics	Employers who violate the law will potentially have their business licenses revoked	Laborers in specific areas are eligible for English classes, a variety of free health clinics, and other services
Results	Many illegal immigrants are leaving Arizona for other areas or for their home countries (CNN, 2007)	Workers show up at the day labor centers even when the economy is slow to commune and learn. (Nieves, 2008)

Sources: From Evelyn Nieves, "Housing Slowdown Puts Day Laborers in Limbo," *USA Today*, February 17, 2008. Retrieved from http://www.usatoday.com/money/economy/housing/2008-02-17-day-laborers_N.htm; CNN, "Illegal immigrants packing up and leaving Arizona," December 22, 2007. Retrieved from http://www.cnn.com/2007/US/12/22/immigrants.leave.ap/.

society. As we will see in Chapter 4, there are many legal and historical reasons why this did not happen. Some people are critical of the melting pot metaphor, not only because it does not explain the experiences of non-European immigrants but also because it implies that immigrants should give up their unique cultural backgrounds to become white and American.

Economic conditions make a big difference in attitudes toward foreign workers and immigration policies. During the Depression of the 1930s, Mexicans and Mexican Americans were forced to return to Mexico to free up jobs for white Americans. When prosperity returned in the 1940s, Mexicans were welcomed back as a source of cheap labor. This type of situation is not limited to the United States, but occurs all over the world. For example, Algerian workers are alternately welcomed and rejected in France, depending on the state of the French economy and the demand for imported labor. Guest workers from Turkey have been subjected to similar uncertainties in Germany. Indian workers in Kenya, Chinese immigrants in Malaysia, and many other workers toiling outside their native lands have suffered the vagaries of fluctuating economies and immigration policies. In Chapter 8, we discuss the implications of these migration patterns for intercultural communication.

The tradition of tension and conflict among cultures continues to this day. The conflicts that arise in Southern California exemplify many aspects of the demographic changes in the United States. We can examine on a variety of levels the tensions in Los Angeles among Latinos/as, African Americans, Korean Americans, and European Americans. Some of the conflict is related to different languages, values, and lifestyles. Some African Americans resent the economic success of recent Korean immigrants—a reaction that reflects a typical historical pattern. The conflict may also be due to the pattern of settlement that results in cultural enclaves.

Immigration and Economic Classes   Some of the conflict may be related to the economic disparity that exists among these different groups. To understand this disparity, we need to look at issues of economic class. Most Americans are reluctant to admit that a class structure exists and even more reluctant to admit how difficult it is to move up in this structure. Indeed, most people live their lives in the same economic class into which they were born. And there are distinct class differences in clothing, housing, recreation, conversation, and other aspects of everyday life (Fussell, 1992). For example, the driveways to the homes of the very rich are usually obscured, whereas those of upper-class homes usually are long and curved and quite visible. Driveways leading to middle-class homes, in contrast, tend to go straight into garages.

The myth of a classless society is hardly benign. It not only reinforces middle- and upper-class beliefs in their own superior abilities but also promotes a false hope among the working class and the poor that they can get ahead. Whereas real-life success stories of upward mobility are rare, fictitious ones abound in literature, film, and television. But all such accounts perpetuate the myth. The reality is that the income gap between rich and poor in the United States is more extreme than in any other industrialized country (Yen, 2010). This gap continues to widen, particularly since the recent recession (December 2007–June 2009)—the longest recession since the Great Depression. While the recession is officially over, experts point out that the recovery has taken two tracks—one for typical workers and families and another for the wealthiest. While many U.S. families are still struggling with unemployment and foreclosures, the wealthiest have seen their incomes and assets increase dramatically—as they benefit from significant gains in the stock market and record corporate profits. In fact, in 2009, the top fifth of households held 87% of the wealth, the middle fifth had 3.3% (the lowest recorded share), and the lowest fifth actually had negative wealth (they owed more than they owned).

The staggering gap between the wealthy and the rest cannot be underestimated; it is now the largest ever recorded. That is, the wealthiest 1% of U.S. households now has a net worth 225 times greater than the median or typical household's net worth (Allegretto, 2011). And the recent census data show that the poorest of the poor (those that live at half the official poverty level) are now at a record high, rising from 5.7% in 2008 to 6.3% today. Child poverty is now at 21%, compared to 16% in 2000 (Yen, 2010). This widening gap is partly due to the loss of stable industrial jobs as companies move to cheaper labor markets within the United States and abroad and to declining home values. Class and demographic issues also play a role, with racial and ethnic minorities typically hardest hit by economic downturns. In 2009, the median net worth (what you have if you subtract your debt from what you own) of black households was the lowest ever recorded, $2,200; the median among white households was $97,000 (Allegretto, 2011).

Religious Diversity   Immigration also contributes to religious diversity, bringing increasing numbers of Muslims, Buddhists, Confucians, Catholics, and others to the United States. The religious composition of the United States is rapidly changing due to a number of factors. According to the U.S. Religious Landscape Survey (2008) done by the Pew Forum on Religion and Public Life, 28% of adults have left the religion they were raised in (some choosing another religion, some choosing no religion). Catholics have lost the greatest number of members, but they also gained the most from immigration. The greatest growth has been among adults who are unaffiliated with any religion. What do these changes mean to the role of religion in a diverse society? What is the future of religion in the United States? Religious beliefs and practices often play an important role in everyday cultural life. One example is the very different views on abortion, described by our student Tanya:

> *Pro-choice and pro-lifers have incredibly different worldview lenses. These different lenses they see through are most of the time influenced by religion and social upbringing. The values are different, yet no side is wrong and cannot see through the same worldview lens as their opponents.*

These different worldviews can sometimes lead to prejudices and stereotypes. Stereotypes about Islam are widespread in the United States, and some religious and political leaders seem to use these stereotypes in ways that increase prejudice and discrimination. For example, Pastor Terry Jones of the Dove World Outreach Center in Florida expressed his anti-Islamic views by soaking a copy of the Qur'an in kerosene and then lighting it on fire. These images of the burning Qur'an were streamed live over the Internet and seemed to lead to violence against Americans in Afghanistan and Pakistan (Harris & Gallagher, 2011). The battle over plans to build a Muslim community center near the site of the 9/11 attacks in New York City have revealed similar anti-Muslim sentiment—leading some to say that Americans seem less inclined to show restraint in expressing hostility toward Islam (see Figure 1.3). Some religious leaders and civil rights activist say that these and similar actions are fueling a tide of "Islamophobia" in the United States and that politicians use the issue to garner votes (McGreal, 2010). Political scientist Ali Muzrui (2001) describes Islam as the "ultimate negative 'Other' to the Christian tradition" and laments the rising tide of Islamophobia (fear of Islam and the hostility toward it). He lists the contrasting stereotypes:

> *Whereas Christianity is supposed to be peace loving, Islam is portrayed as fostering holy war (Jihad). Whereas Christianity liberates women, Islam enslaves them. Whereas Christianity is modern, Islam is medieval. Whereas Christianity is forward looking, Islam is backward looking. Whereas Christians prefer nonviolence, Muslims easily resort to terrorism. (p. 110)*

FIGURE 1-3   Protesters against the construction of an Islamic Cultural Center in lower Manhattan, four blocks from Ground Zero on Park Place, in New York, on Sept. 11, 2010. The project has inflamed and polarized people supporting the project and those against it, and at times the dialogue has turned into that of racism, xenophobia, and hate. (© Ashley Gilbertson/VII Network/Corbis)

Muzrui goes on to present evidence to debunk each of these stereotypes. Religious diversity is part of the demographic imperative that challenges us to learn more about intercultural communication.

These increasingly diverse ethnic, racial, economic, and religious groups come into contact mostly during the day in schools, businesses, and other settings, bringing to the encounters different languages, histories, and economic statuses. This presents great challenges for us as a society and as individuals. The main challenge is to look beyond the stereotypes and biases, to recognize the disparities and differences, and to try to apply what we know about intercultural communication. Perhaps the first step is to realize that the melting pot metaphor probably was never viable, that it was not realistic to expect everyone to assimilate into the United States in the same way. Today we need a different metaphor, one that reflects the racial, ethnic, and cultural diversity that truly exists in our country. Perhaps we should think of the United States as a "salad," in which each group retains its own flavor and yet contributes to the whole. Or we might think of it as a "tapestry," with many different strands contributing to a unified pattern.

In any case, the United States is hardly a model of diversity; many countries are far more diverse ethnically. For example, Nigeria has some 200 ethnic groups, and Indonesia has a similar number. Nigeria was colonized by the British, and artificially drawn boundaries forced many different groups into one nation-state, which caused many conflicts. The diverse groups in Indonesia, in contrast, have

The U.S. Religious Landscape Survey points to some interesting religious demographic information. Note how religion intersects with other social categories. Here are some interesting findings:

- Among people who are married, nearly 4 in 10 (37%) are married to a spouse with a different religious affiliation. (This figure includes Protestants who are married to another Protestant from a different denominational family, such as a Baptist who is married to a Methodist.) Hindus and Mormons are the most likely to be married (78% and 71%, respectively) and to be married to someone of the same religion (90% and 83%, respectively).

- The Midwest most closely resembles the religious makeup of the overall population. The South, by a wide margin, has the heaviest concentration of members of evangelical Protestant churches. The Northeast has the greatest concentration of Catholics, and the West has the largest proportion of unaffiliated people, including the largest proportion of atheists and agnostics.

- Of all the major racial and ethnic groups in the United States, black Americans are the most likely to report a formal religious affiliation. Even among those blacks who are unaffiliated, three in four belong to the "religious unaffiliated" category (i.e., they say that religion is either somewhat or very important in their lives), compared with slightly more than one-third of the unaffiliated population overall.

- Nearly half of Hindus in the United States, one-third of Jews, and a quarter of Buddhists have obtained postgraduate education, compared with only about one in ten of the adult population overall. Hindus and Jews are also much more likely than other groups to report high income levels.

- People not affiliated with any particular religion stand out for their relative youth compared with other religious traditions. Among the unaffiliated, 31% are under age 30 and 71% are under age 50. Comparable numbers for the overall adult population are 20% and 59%, respectively.

- By contrast, members of mainline Protestant churches and Jews are older, on average, than members of other groups. Roughly half of Jews and members of mainline churches are age 50 and older, compared with approximately four in ten American adults overall.

- Members of Baptist churches account for one-third of all Protestants and close to one-fifth of the total U.S. adult population. Baptists also account for nearly two-thirds of members of historically black Protestant churches.

Source: From U.S. Religious Landscape Survey (2008), *Pew Forum on Religion and Public Life*, http://religions.pewforum.org/reports.

I am involved in many different intercultural relationships. The main benefit of these relationships is that it shows other people that there is no reason to fear intercultural relationships. My generation, while more open to intercultural relationships than previous ones, is still hesitant, and I am often the recipient of dirty looks from strangers who disapprove. It is disheartening that people believe there is a difference in races, but the best way to change people's minds is to show them firsthand, which is what I hope to do.
    —Katie

largely coexisted amiably for many years. Diversity, therefore, does not necessarily lead to intercultural conflicts.

Fortunately, most individuals are able to negotiate day-to-day activities in spite of cultural differences. Diversity can even be a positive force. Demographic diversity in the United States has given us tremendous linguistic richness and culinary variety, varied resources to meet new social challenges, as well as domestic and international business opportunities.

THE ECONOMIC IMPERATIVE

The idea of globalization—the creation of a world market in goods, services, labor, capital, and technology—is shown dramatically in the account of a journalist who asks a Dell computer manager where his laptop is made. The answer? It was codesigned by engineers in Texas and Taiwan; the microprocessor was made in one of Intel's factories in the Philippines, Costa Rica, Malaysia, or China; the memory came from factories in Korea, Germany, Taiwan, or Japan. Other components (keyboard, hard drive, batteries, etc.) were made by Japanese, Taiwanese, Irish, Israeli, or British firms with factories mainly in Asia, and finally, the laptop was assembled in Taiwan (Friedman, 2005).

What is the ultimate impact of globalization on the average person? Some economists defend it, saying the losses are always offset by the gains in cheaper consumer prices. However, many working people, seeing their jobs outsourced to cheap labor in India, China, and Malaysia, feel threatened. An increasing number of economists agree (Rachman, 2011). What does the current global economy look like, and how does it relate to intercultural communication issues? Currently, U.S. retail sales are growing at 2.4%—faster than Europe and Japan but slower than many other countries. Consumer spending in China, for example, is expanding by 22%, including a big increase in the online sale of luxury goods. Spending in India and Russia is also increasing (The world in figures, 2011). Economies in many of the lesser industrialized countries are also doing well. Brazil, India, and China account for more than 50% of global growth, and countries in Africa (South Africa, Algeria, Botswana) and the Middle East (Turkey and Saudi Arabia) are also showing strong growth (Spread the wealth, 2011).

Americans, including myself, sometimes have this belief that what we do here in the United States is the best and only way to do things. We put these "cultural blinders" on and are oblivious to any other cultures and/or values. Although American tradition has been and can be a big influence on other markets and business sectors, we are failing to realize that the way we do business is not the basis for all businesses. Most of our international business ventures are failing due to our stubbornness. In the past we felt that we could send someone to Mexico or Japan without any intercultural training and still show them how to do business. How wrong were we?

Today we realize it takes an understanding of others and their beliefs and values to truly gain respect and further our business and personal relationships. Businesses are taking the time and money to train their employees about the new culture that they will be submerged in. People in the past failed because we did not take into account that companies' attitudes and beliefs differed from ours. Good relations with other international businesses can produce a lifelong bond that can create great economic wealth for each country. The companies are not only training their employees for this culture shock but are training their families as well, because they know that without family support, this venture will surely fail. The United States has taken strides to correct their errors of the past and are continuing their efforts to produce intercultural employees, and I hope this trend continues.

—Luis

The point is that, to compete effectively in this global market, Americans must understand how business is conducted in other countries (Varner & Beamer, 2011). American businesspeople should be able to negotiate deals that are advantageous to the U.S. economy. However, they are not always willing to take the time and effort to do this. For example, most U.S. automobile manufacturers do not produce automobiles that have right-hand drive, which prevents them from penetrating markets in nations like Japan. Stories abound of U.S. marketing slogans that were inaccurately translated, like Pepsi's "Come alive with the Pepsi Generation," which was translated into Chinese as "Pepsi brings your ancestors back from the grave" or had culturally inappropriate meanings like Ford's marketing the Pinto in Brazil (slang for "small male genitals") or General Motors marketing the Nova in South America (*no va* is Spanish for "*no go*") (Branding so much more, 2011).

Cross-cultural trainers in the United States report that Asian business personnel often spend years in the United States studying English and learning about the country before they decide to establish operations here or invest money. In contrast, many American companies provide little or no training before sending their workers overseas and expect to close business deals quickly, with little regard for cultural idiosyncrasies.

Many management experts have examined other countries' practices for ways to increase U.S. productivity. One such idea was "quality circles," borrowed from the Japanese and now popular in the United States. Another strength demonstrated in many Asian (and European) companies is the belief in effort for its own sake. Employees in many Asian countries work longer hours and sometimes produce better products simply as a result of persistance. This trait also pays off in schools where Asian and European students score higher on standardized math and science exams than do American students (Dillon, 2010).

It will also behoove Americans to research how to do business in the huge emerging market that is 21st-century China. As shown in the Point of View box (see page 21), a gaffe by Nike reflects the general lack of cultural understanding about the Chinese. In contrast, Starbucks' decision to change its logo when it entered the Asian markets seems to be successful. Starbucks decided to drop the Starbucks name and the word "coffee" from its logo, giving it a more rounded appearance, which seems to appeal to collectivist consumers—found in China and other Asian countries (Walsh, Winterich, & Mittal, 2010).

Why do so many businesspeople have difficulty succeeding in Chinese and other Asian markets? The reasons involve both differences in business practices and cultural differences between East and West. For example, business dealings in China, as in many Eastern countries, are relationship oriented, and business relationships cannot succeed without respect and harmony. Specifically, in China, three concepts are crucial:

- *Qingmian* (human feelings), which involves respect for the feelings of others
- *He* (harmony), which emphasizes the smooth functioning of a group or society
- *Guanxi* or *Kuan-hsi* (relationship or connection), which underscores the importance of relationships in Chinese business

The high value placed on these concepts highlights other differences as well. For example, contract law is practiced very differently in China. Whereas in the West the law is the essential set of rules of conduct, the "rules of conduct" in China are the ethics and standards of behavior required in a Confucian society. This means that social pressures rather than legal instruments are used to ensure compliance. Thus, what we might conceptualize as a legal issue may be seen in China as a relationship issue (Varner & Beamer, 2011).

Sometimes there are cultural differences in work ethics. One of our students, Vincent, describes a difference he observed while working as an intern in a manufacturing company:

> When looking back at this internship I can easily see that Mexican workers were more loyal to the company. I constantly noticed that American workers at this company would be walking around talking or smoking while they were supposed to be at their work stations, but the Mexican workers would never leave their stations until it was time for break. This sometimes created problems between Mexicans and other employees because of the differences in work ethics.

We discuss the implications of these types of cultural differences for relationships (Chapter 10) and conflicts (Chapter 11).

Cultural differences in business practices have implications not only when people from different companies do business with each other but also when people

CHINA CHOPS NIKE AD

The U.S. sportswear firm Nike has apologized for running a commercial in China which has been banned by popular demand for offending the country's national dignity.

The 90-second advertisement was meant to combine Kill Bill–*style martial arts with sassy basketball bravado. U.S. National Basketball Association star LeBron James is shown running rings around the animated figure of a wizened and bearded kung fu master, who resembles the martial arts teacher from Quentin Tarantino's latest movie.*

In the commercial, the American athlete also gets the better of two women in traditional Chinese attire, and a pair of dragons—considered to be a symbol of China.

In a sign of the growing influence of Internet opinion, the government has pulled the "Chamber of Fear" advertisement off the airwaves, after protests in online chat rooms overturned the initial approval by state censors.

According to the U.S. company, the commercial was designed by its advertising agent, Wieden and Kennedy, to encourage teenagers to overcome temptation, envy, complacency and self-doubt. But it has only managed to stir up irritation in China.

The state administration for radio, television, and film posted a statement saying that Nike had violated the condition that all advertisements in China should uphold national dignity.

"This ad shows Chinese characters losing again and again. It makes our country look helpless against America," said one chat room contributor.

Faced with the loss of business from a market in which its sales have nearly doubled in the past year, Nike meekly accepted the government's decision.

"We had no intention of hurting the emotions of Chinese consumers," the company said in a statement.

"We place much attention on the Chinese market and there was a lot of careful consideration before launching the advertisement," they said.

Source: From J. Watts, "China Chops Nike Ad; Multinational Apologizes After Outcry," *The Guardian* (London), December 8, 2004, p. 15.

from different cultures work on the same team. One effect of globalization is increasing numbers of international teams—sometimes working as virtual teams and rarely meeting face-to-face. These teams present large challenges in intercultural communication. A recent Hewlett-Packard project involved a 16-country multilingual virtual team that operated on both sides of the international dateline. The leaders describe the challenges: "Relatively routine tasks, such as scheduling a meeting, become complex and fraught with interpersonal friction when one person's work day begins as another is sitting down to dinner or sound asleep. A simple e-mail exchange frazzles nerves because of cultural misunderstandings" (Snyder, 2003).

Even when employees have good language skills, they naturally interpret written and verbal communication through the filter of their own culture. For example, Israeli workers in the project just described wondered why their U.S. counterparts would sometimes seem upset by e-mail exchanges. It turned out that Israelis, who tend to be rather direct and sometimes blunt, were sending e-mails that seemed rude to their American counterparts. And Americans' e-mails seemed "wishy-washy" to the Israelis. The Americans' requests, with phrases like "Thanks in advance for sending me . . . ," mystified the Israelis who would say, "Thanks for what? I haven't done anything yet." After some cultural training, both sides adapted to the other (Snyder, 2003). In later chapters, we explore the implications of these and other cultural differences in communication practices.

Globalization presents many new issues. Increasingly, **multinational corporations** are moving operations to new locations, often overseas, because of lower labor costs. These business moves have far-reaching implications, including the loss of jobs at closed facilities. Many U.S.-owned companies have established production facilities, known as *maquiladoras,* along the U.S.–Mexican border, where workers produce goods bound mainly for U.S. markets. These companies benefit from lower labor costs, tax breaks, and relaxed environmental regulations. Although Mexican laborers profit from the jobs, there is a cost in terms of environmental hazards. *Maquiladoras* thus present intercultural challenges for Mexicans and U.S. Americans.

Domestic diversity also requires businesses to be attentive to cultural differences. As the workforce becomes more diverse, many businesses are interested in capitalizing on these differences for economic gain. As trainers Bernardo M. Ferdman and Sara Einy Brody (1996) suggest, "Once organizations learn to adopt an inclusive orientation in dealing with their members, this will also have a positive impact on how they look at their customer base, how they develop products and assess business opportunities, and how they relate to their communities" (p. 289).

Understanding cultural differences involves not only working with diverse employees but also recognizing new business markets, developing new products, and so on. From this perspective, diversity is a potentially powerful economic resource if organizations view the challenge as an opportunity. In this sense, then, business can capitalize on diversity.

THE TECHNOLOGICAL IMPERATIVE

Today, with the explosion of computers and other communication technologies, we truly live in the **global village** envisioned by media expert Marshall McLuhan (1967). Communication technology links us to events from the most remote parts of the world and connects us to persons we may never meet face-to-face from around the world.

multinational corporations Companies that have operations in two or more nations.

maquiladoras Assembly plants or factories (mainly of U.S. companies) established on the U.S.–Mexican border and using mainly Mexican labor.

global village A term coined by Marshall McLuhan in the 1960s that refers to a world in which communication technology unites people in remote parts of the world.

Technology and Human Communication

The impact of technology on our everyday communication is staggering. Think of how often you use technology to communicate in any given day: You may text-message friends about evening plans, post a Facebook message with your latest news, participate in a discussion board for one of your courses, and check your cell phone website to see how many more minutes you can use this month without getting charged. And you are not alone. A recent survey showed that young people spent almost 8 hours a day on some electronic communication device, smartphone, computer, or the like (Rideout, Foehr, & Roberts, 2010). The effect of social media like Facebook and Twitter have far-reaching consequences, and it is important to understand that these technologies can have positive and negative impacts on intercultural encounters. For example, through social media like Twitter and Facebook, people were able to receive up-to-the-minute information and connect with friends and family in the immediate aftermath of the devastating Japanese tsunami in January 2011 (Smith, 2011). On the other hand, a recent viral YouTube video posted by a UCLA undergraduate offended thousands who saw and heard the vicious anti-Asian rant. This video, and others like it, illustrate the far-reaching negative potential of communication technologies (Internet uproar, 2011).

More and more people around the world are using technology to communicate with each other. Consider these statistics:

- The rate of Internet usage in Africa increased more than 2000% in the past 10 years (2000–2010) (www.internetworldstats.com/stats.htm).

- As of December 2011, Facebook had more than 800 million active users; 70% of users are outside the United States (www.facebook.com/press/info.php?statistics).

- As of March, 2011, there were 1 billion tweets sent each week (http://blog.kissmetrics.com/twitter-statistics/).

- 60% of the world's population owns a mobile phone, and Russia has the highest percentage of cell phones per capita in the world (121%)—Russia actually has more cell phones than people (www.associatedcontent.com/article/1764228/top_5_countries_with_most_cell_phone.html?cat=15).

These communication technologies have tremendous implications for intercultural communication. We will focus on five aspects of culture and technology: (1) increased information about peoples and cultures; (2) increased contact with people who are different from us; (3) increased contact with people who are similar to us who can provide communities of support; (4) identity, culture, and technology; ansd (5) differential access to communication technology.

Increase in Information   You may have found that the Internet provides access to information about other cultures and other peoples. We can now instantaneously find out almost anything about any group in the world simply by searching the Internet. This *should* give us a better understanding of our global neighbors and perhaps some motivation to coexist peacefully in our global village; however, the evidence seems to be to the contrary. According to the Center for Systemic Peace, of the approximately 95 armed conflicts in the world between 2004 and 2009, only 10 have been traditional international conflicts. The rest have arisen between ethnic or political groups within a country—for example, in Turkey, Pakistan, Chad, Nigeria, Ethiopia, Kenya, Thailand, Mexico, Lebanon, Sudan, and Russia (www.systemicpeace.org/warlist.htm). Apparently, knowledge about others does not necessarily lead to better communication or heightened understanding. We will tackle issues like this in later chapters.

Through communication technologies like the World Wide Web, people also have access to increasing amounts of information about what is happening in their own and other countries. This is especially important in countries where media are government controlled. For example, people in Pakistan and Afghanistan learn more about military actions in their countries by accessing CNN.com than through their local newspapers. In some ways, the Internet has democratized information, in that more people control and disseminate information than ever before. For this reason, leaders in some countries try to limit their citizens' access to information. The Chinese government censored Internet searches for years, resulting in Google threatening to shut down its China office; Egyptian leaders, faced with a major antigovernment uprising, suspended Internet and cell phone service in January 2011, practically shutting down Internet traffic and severely limiting the protesters' ability to organize and spread their message (Richtel, 2011).

In spite of this and other governments' attempts to limit their citizens' access to computer-mediated communication (CMC), the Internet is providing information, world news, and possibilities for interpersonal communication that were not available previously.

Increased Contact with People Who Differ   Communication technology brings us in contact with people we might never have the opportunity to know otherwise. And many of these people are from different cultural backgrounds. The Internet/e-mail allows us to have "pen pals" from different cultures and to carry on discussions with these people in virtual chat rooms and on discussion boards.

However, such mediated communication across cultures does present unique challenges. Unlike face-to-face communication, mediated communication filters out important nonverbal cues. One of our students, Val, described the challenges of intercultural e-mails:

> *I met a girl from Korea my junior year of college, and we became good friends. When it came time for her to go back to Korea we decided we would stay friends and become pen pals via e-mail. I found it much more difficult to communicate with her because she didn't always understand what I was writing and I couldn't repeat my sentences like I could if I were speaking to her, and the same applied to her. It definitely puts a strain on our relationship.*

When we are talking to individuals face-to-face, we use nonverbal information to help us interpret what they are *really* saying—tone of voice, facial expressions, gestures, and so on. The absence of these cues in some mediated contexts (e.g., e-mail, text messages, tweets) makes communication more difficult and can lead to misunderstandings. And these misunderstandings can be compounded when communicating across cultures. For example, a U.S. colleague reports that she was offended when the e-mails she received from colleagues overseas seemed too brief and to the point. She has since discovered that her colleagues overseas are charged computer time by the minute and so have learned to be very concise in their e-mail messages. What she interpreted as rudeness had more to do with the economic context in which the interaction took place than with the communicators themselves. If she had been able to observe their nonverbal cues while communicating, she probably would have known that they were not being rude.

Also, language may be a factor. The people we talk to on e-mail networks may speak languages different from our own. An interesting situation arose recently for one of the authors of this book. Tom was using an electronic bulletin board when someone posted a message in Dutch. It was met with a flurry of hostile responses from people protesting the use of an exclusionary language, one most people couldn't read. A discussion ensued about which languages might be acceptable on the network.

The decision reached was that subscribers could post messages in any language as long as there was an English translation. In a subsequent posting, someone from a university in South Africa recommended a book "for those of you who can read Dutch (heh-heh, all four of us)"—an apparent reaction to the exclusionary sentiments of other subscribers. Machine and other translation techniques are new ways to facilitate online intercultural communication, as seen in the Point of View box on page 26. The use of some languages is given even more privilege in the high-tech communication world, where we are likely to encounter many more people. Although many experts think that the Internet is dominated by English, there are indications that Chinese is becoming a formidable linguistic player in the Internet world. According to one source, the first day that registration opened for Chinese language domain names, 360,000 applications were filed (english1.e21times.com/asp/sacd.asp?r=880&p=0). Surprisingly, the most recent research suggests that the move is actually toward more multilingualism on the Net—rather than toward a global English Internet (Dor, 2004). Some speculate that this is because global businesses need to adapt to local languages to sell their products and also that learning a language is an awesome task and it is not feasible to think of the entire world learning a second language to accommodate.

Increased Contact with People Who Are Similar Communication technology also allows us to have more contact with people who are very similar to ourselves. Perhaps you participate in chat rooms or discussion boards with people who share your interests and opinions. Perhaps you turn to Internet groups for support and community. For example, international students can stay in touch with their local communities, keep up with what's going on at home, and receive emotional support during difficult times of cultural adaptation.

The Internet can also be used to strengthen a sense of identity, as is the case for some **diasporic groups**—ethnic and/or national groups that are geographically

diasporic groups Ethnic and/or national groups that are geographically dispersed throughout the world.

New techniques and technologies of translation have helped to bring different bodies of literature to English audiences. Remember from earlier that the Middle East has seen a sharp increase in Internet usage since 2008. In this article, the topic of Arabic literature is explored.

> *Saudi author Raja Alsanea spoke on topic [of Arabic literature in the English language], talking interestingly about her successful novel* Girls of Riyadh *and receiving the lion's share of questions from the audience.*
>
> *Translated into 23 languages and started when the author was only 18, this novel, Alsanea explained, could be seen as having captured the experience of a generation of young Saudi women who have used the Internet—blogs, forums, and chat sites—to create a "virtual liberating space" allowing freedom of expression. A new language, "Arabish," had been invented for use in this space, consisting of a mix of English and colloquial Arabic written in the Latin alphabet.*
>
> *Asked whether the success of* Girls of Riyadh *in translation had surprised her, Alsanea said that she had collaborated on the English translation and was aware that "western readers are more interested in Saudi Arabia than they are in Saudi literature." She was not "a feminist or an activist," though the novel did show up the "confused boundary" between "freedom in virtual space and the traditions that dominate the non-virtual space of family and society."*

Source: From David Tresilian, "The fun of the fair." Retrieved May 13, 2008, from http://weekly.ahram.org.eg/2008/894/cu21.htm.

dispersed throughout the world, sometimes as refugees fleeing from war, sometimes as voluntary emigrants. A recent study of children of South Asian immigrants found that the Internet plays a major role in creating a sense of community and ethnic identity for these young people. Whereas earlier generations of immigrants were expected to assimilate as quickly as possible into the host culture, the Internet now allows these children of immigrants to connect with other Indian adolescents, discussing religion and issues concerning Indian and immigrant identity. Similar diasporic discussions are held in the *Kava Bowl* and the *Kamehameha Roundtable*, online meeting places for the Polynesian diaspora and other people from the Pacific Islands who live in the United States, Australia, and New Zealand (Franklin, 2003). Similarly, discussion boards can provide virtual communities of support for cultural minorities (e.g., Planetout.com, a discussion board for gays and lesbians). However, the Internet can also provide a venue for like-minded people to promote prejudice and hatred. A British e-mail filtering company has been monitoring websites that were categorized as hate and violence sites. In 2000, there were about 2,500 such sites. However, the number of sites that promote hatred against Americans, Muslims, Jews, homosexuals, and people of non-European ancestry, as well as graphic violence, continues to rise. In fact, a recent report by the Simon Wiesenthal Center for Tolerance estimates that there are now more than 11,500 online hate groups. Social networking is where the biggest growth is happening, particularly on Facebook and YouTube, where hate-filled messages are often packaged in very creative ways. Experts point out that young people are especially vulnerable to racist online flash games, jokes, and general hate-filled information on social networking sites, blogs, and web pages (www.wiesenthal.com/site/apps/s/content.asp?c=lsKWLbPJLnF&b=4442915&ct=8430507).

Identity, Culture, and Technology   Advances in communication technology lead us to think differently about ourselves and our **identity management.** For example, communication technologies gives us more choices in how we express our identities than we typically have in face-to-face interaction. As noted previously, many of the identity cues individuals use to figure out how to communicate with others—such as age, gender, and ethnicity—are filtered out on the Internet. For instance, when you send an e-mail message or post a message, you can choose whether to reveal certain aspects of your identity. The recipients won't know if you are male or female, young or old, and so on—unless you tell them. You can choose which aspects, if any, of your identity you want to reveal. In fact, you can even give false information about your identity.

> **identity management**
> The way individuals make sense of their multiple images concerning the sense of self in different social contexts.

This capability has resulted in the opportunity for **identity tourism**—taking on the identities of other races, gender, classes, or sexual orientations for recreational purposes. And some online contexts (e.g., online games like *Dungeons and Dragons*) *require* users to take on new identities. How is this related to intercultural communication? One of the oft-touted skills of intercultural communication is empathy, the ability to understand what it's like to "walk in someone's shoes." Communication technology now affords an opportunity to do this—virtually. Thus, for instance, by taking on the virtual identity of a male, by participating in male-only online discussions, females might come to understand better what it feels like to be a male. The same might be true for other identities as well.

> **identity tourism**
> A concept that refers to people taking on the identities of other races, genders, classes, or sexual orientations for recreational purposes.

Although identity tourism provides intriguing possibilities for improving intercultural understanding, it also raises some important ethical questions. In one celebrated example, a male psychiatrist participated in online discussions as a disabled female. Ostensibly, he did so because he wanted to understand something of what it felt like to be a woman and to be disabled. The project backfired, however, as other chat room participants responded to him as a woman and, over time, even fell in love with him. Ultimately, many of the women suffered severe psychological problems as a result of their experiences with him (Turkle, 1995).

The idea of identity tourism may seem somewhat scary, but the same lack of nonverbal cues can result in less prejudice and stereotyping in mediated intercultural interaction. Some of these same nonverbal cues that are filtered out (indicators of age, gender, ethnicity, race) are often the basis for stereotyping and prejudice in initial interactions. When these cues are absent, communication may be more open because people cannot use the information to form impressions that often negatively impact communication.

Access to Communication Technology

As we've seen, technology plays a huge role in our everyday lives and often has a lot to do with our success as students and professionals. What would you do if you had no access to communication technology? If you were not able to text-message your friends or could not use your cell phone? Could not e-mail your family? How might you feel in our technology-dominated world? Although communication technologies are a fact of life for millions of people around the world, lack of access to these technologies is a reality for many people. Consider that

- As of 2010, only 56% of African Americans, only 45% of adults with a household income of under $30,000, and 33% of people who have less than a high school education use high-speed Internet at home.

- The rates of broadband adoption in rural areas trail those in urban areas by about five years. Meaning, the 2010 rate of Internet use in rural areas equates to the 2005 rate of use in cities.

- Even when education and income are the same, blacks and Latinos are less likely to have broadband access than whites.

Even larger inequalities exist outside the United States:

- Africa contains more than 14% of the world's population, but just 3% of the world's Internet users, while North America contains only 5% of the world's population, but accounts for 17.5% of the world's Internet users.

- There are more Internet users in Germany than there are in the entire continent of Africa.

Sources: A. Smith (2010, August 11). *Home broadband 2010.* Pew Internet & American Life Project. Retrieved April 29, 2011, from www.pewinternet.org/~/media//Files/Reports/2010/Home%20broadband%202010.pdf; www.internetworldstats.com/stats.htm.

These inequities are called the "digital divide" and have enormous implications for intercultural communication. In the global information society, information is an important commodity. Everybody needs it to function. This ability is especially important in an increasingly "networked" society. It is easy to see how without these skills and knowledge one can feel marginalized and disconnected from the center of society (Rojas, Straubhaar, Roychowdhury, & Okur, 2004; van Dijk, 2004).

The implications for intercultural communication are enormous. How do people relate to each other when one is information technology rich and the other is not? When there is increasing use of English on the Internet, what happens to those who don't speak English? Can this lead to resentment? Will the increase in communication technology lead to increasing gaps between haves and have-nots? To more misunderstandings?

Recent communication technology has impacted our lives in ways our grandparents could not have imagined and requires that we reexamine even our most basic conceptions of self, others, and culture. As Sherry Turkle (1995) observes, once we take virtuality seriously as a way of life, we need to consider who we are in these virtual relationships and what the connection is between our physical and virtual bodies. What kind of society or societies are we creating when we are so connected in cyberspace but not really present in physical spaces? We check our phones for text messages when eating a meal with friends, for example, not really relationally present with them (Turkle, 2008). We might also examine our own technological use: Who are we in contact with? People who are like ourselves? People who are different? Do we use technology to increase our contact with and understanding of other cultures or merely to hang out with people who are like us? What does this say about us and our identities?

THE PEACE IMPERATIVE

The bottom line seems to be this: Can individuals of different genders, ages, ethnicities, races, languages, socioeconomic statuses, and cultural backgrounds coexist on this planet? (See Figure 1-4.) Both the history of humankind and recent world events lead us not to be very optimistic on this point. And this imperative is even more evident after the events of September 11, 2001. Contact among different cultural groups—from the earliest civilizations until today— often has led to disharmony. For example, consider the ethnic/religious strife between Muslims and the Western world; the ethnic struggles in Bosnia and the

FIGURE 1-4   This Iraqi boy looks at shoes and clothes of victims of a car bomb explosion in Baghdad on March 1, 2006. The causes of this violence stem from long histories of intercultural conflict and are likely to influence intercultural relations in the future. (© Akram Saleh/Getty Images)

STARBUCKS' LOGO REDESIGN COULD PROVE BENEFICIAL TO COMPANY

A recent press release describes why Starbucks' decision to change its logo could be a good move as it expands into Asian markets. It recently dropped both its name and the word "coffee" from its 40-year-old logo in preparation for tripling its locations in China from about 400 to 1,500.

In this release, Rice University Professor of Marketing Vikas Mittal described the interesting results of several studies investigating customers, logos, and brand commitment. He and his co-researchers found that, while Starbucks may have alienated some of their loyal U.S. customers, the redesign will probably attract new consumers in Asian countries like China, India, Taiwan, and Singapore, where consumers tend to be culturally collectivist and interdependent.

Mittal said that removing the lettering gives the logo a more rounded appearance, and his research found that people with collectivistic values, like those in Asia, prefer rounded shapes. In fact, brands in collectivistic countries tend to have a higher percentage of rounded logos when compared to logos in individualistic countries (e.g., the United States), and logos and product shapes that are rounded are more acceptable and embraced in those cultures. The researchers' explanation for Asians' preference for rounded shapes is that these shapes represent harmony, which is consistent with an interdependent view of the world.

Source: J. Stark, "Rice Research Shows Starbucks Logo Redesign Could Prove Beneficial to Company," Press Release, Rice University, January 6, 2011. Retrieved May 25, 2011, from www.media.rice.edu/media/NewsBot.asp?MODE=VIEW&ID=15215&SnID=1521497554.

colonialism (1) The system by which groups with diverse languages, cultures, religions, and identities were united to form one state, usually by a European power; (2) the system by which a country maintains power over other countries or groups of people to exploit them economically, politically, and culturally.

former Soviet Union; the war between Hutus and Tutsis in Rwanda (Africa); the continued unrest in the Middle East; and the racial and ethnic struggles and tensions in neighborhoods in Boston, Los Angeles, and other U.S. cities.

Some of these conflicts are tied to histories of **colonialism** around the world, whereby European powers lumped diverse groups—differing in language, culture, religion, or identity—together as one state. For example, the division of Pakistan and India was imposed by the British; eventually, East Pakistan declared its independence to become Bangladesh. Nevertheless, ethnic and religious differences in some areas of India and Pakistan continue to cause unrest. And the acquisition of nuclear weapons by both India and Pakistan makes these antagonisms of increasing concern. The tremendous diversity—and accompanying antagonisms—within many former colonies must be understood in the context of histories of colonialism.

Some of the conflicts are also tied to economic disparities and influenced by U.S. technology and media. Many people in the United States see these influences as beneficial, but they also stimulate resistance. Communication scholar Fernando Delgado (2002) explains:

> *Such cultural dominance, though celebrated at home, can spark intercultural conflicts because it inhibits the development of other nations' indigenous popular culture products, stunts their economic development and foists U.S. values and perspectives on other cultures. These effects, in turn, often lead to resentment and conflict. (p. 353)*

For example, according to many Canadians, a Canadian cultural identity is almost impossible because of the dominance of U.S. media. This type of cultural domination is very complex. Delgado recalls that he noticed anti-American sentiments in graffiti, newspapers, and TV programs during a recent trip to Europe, but that he also saw U.S. influence everywhere—in music, television, film, cars, fast food, and fashion. He notes that "resentment, frustration, and disdain among the locals coexisted with an amazement at the penetration of U.S. popular culture" (p. 355).

Some of the conflicts have roots in past foreign policies. For example, the attacks in September 2001 were partly related to the confusing and shifting alliances among the United States, Afghanistan, and Arab and Muslim countries. In Afghanistan in the early 1990s, the Taliban seized power in response to the destructive rule of the Northern Alliance, a loose coalition of warlords. The United States had supported the Taliban in the fight against Soviet aggression in the late 1980s and had promised aid in rebuilding their country after the hostilities were over. However, with the withdrawal of Soviet forces and the fall of the Soviet Union, the United States wasn't as concerned about fulfilling its promises to the Afghan nation, leaving the Afghan people at the mercy of the Taliban. In addition, U.S. foreign policies toward many Arab countries in the last half century, coupled with open support for Israel, have caused widespread resentment (Kirkpatrick, 2011). Although there is no simple explanation for why terrorists attacked the United States, the attacks clearly did not happen in a vacuum. They need to be understood in historical, political, religious, and economic contexts.

It would be naive to assume that simply understanding the issues of intercultural communication would end war and intercultural conflict, but these problems do underscore the need for individuals to learn more about social groups other than their own. (See Figure 1-5.) Ultimately, people, and not countries, negotiate and sign peace treaties. An example of how individual communication styles may influence political outcomes can be seen in the negotiations between Iraqi president Saddam Hussein and representatives of the United States and the United Nations just prior to the Gulf War, in 1990. Many Middle East experts assumed that Hussein was not ready to fight, that he was merely bluffing, using an Arabic style of communication (see Chapter 6). This style emphasizes the importance of animation, exaggeration, and conversational form over content (Slackman, 2006). Communication specialists note that in conflict situations Arabic speakers may threaten the life and property of their opponents but have no intention of actually carrying out the threats. Rather, they use threats to buy time and intimidate their opponents. Thus, declaratory statements by U.S. leaders, such as "We will find the cancer and cut it out," seemed mundane and

FIGURE 1-5 Although this sign is an attempt to reach out to many cultural groups in Boston Harbor by posting in many languages, it does not explain the rationale for the ban and differing views on who "owns" natural resources, health concerns, and other issues facing shellfishing may lead to misunderstanding and conflicts among cultural groups. (*Courtesy T. K. Nakayama*)

unintimidating to Arab listeners. Verbal exchanges, regardless of the different speech styles, often take the place of physical violence (Griefat & Katriel, 1989).

However, we always need to consider the relationship between individual and societal forces in studying intercultural communication. Although communication on the interpersonal level is important, we must remember that individuals often are born into and are caught up in conflicts that they neither started nor chose.

THE ETHICAL IMPERATIVE

ethics Principles of conduct that help govern behaviors of individuals and groups.

Living in an intercultural world presents ethical challenges as well. **Ethics** may be thought of as principles of conduct that help govern the behavior of individuals and groups. These principles often arise from communities' consensus on what is good and bad behavior. Cultural values tell us what is "good" and what "ought" to be good. Ethical judgments focus more on the degrees of rightness and wrongness in human behavior than do cultural values (Johannesen, 1990).

Some judgments are stated very explicitly. For example, the Ten Commandments teach that it is wrong to steal, tell a lie, commit murder, and so on. Many other identifiable principles of conduct that arise from our cultural experience may be less explicit—for instance, that people should be treated equally and should work hard. Several issues come to mind in a discussion of ethics in intercultural communication. For example, what happens when two ethical systems collide? Although an individual may want to "do the right thing" to contribute to a better society, it is not always easy to know what is "right" in specific situations. Ethical principles are often culture bound, and intercultural conflicts arise from various notions of what is ethical behavior.

One common cross-cultural ethical dilemma involves standards of conducting business in multinational corporations. The U.S. Congress and the Securities and Exchange Commission consider it unethical to make payments to government officials of other countries to promote trade. (Essentially, such payments smack of bribery.) However, in many countries, like China, government officials are paid in this informal way instead of being supported by taxes (Ambler & Witzel, 2000). What, then, is ethical behavior for personnel in multinational subsidiaries?

Relativity versus Universality

In this book, we stress the relativity of cultural behavior—that no cultural pattern is inherently right or wrong. So, is there any universality in ethics? Are any cultural behaviors always right or always wrong? The answers depend on one's perspective. A universalist might try, for example, to identify acts and conditions that most societies think of as wrong, such as murder, theft, or treason. Someone who takes an extreme universalist position would insist that cultural differences are only superficial, that fundamental notions of right and wrong are universal. Some religions take universal positions—for example, that the Ten Commandments are a universal code of behavior. But Christian groups often disagree about the universality of the Bible. For example, are the teachings of the New Testament mainly guidelines for the Christians of Jesus's time, or can they be applied to Christians in the 21st century? These are difficult issues for many people searching for ethical guidelines (Johannesen, 1990). The philosopher Immanuel Kant (1949) believed in the universality of moral laws. His well-known "categorical imperative" states that people should act only on maxims that apply universally, to *all* individuals.

The extreme relativist position holds that any cultural behavior can be judged only within the cultural context in which it occurs. This means that only those members of a community can truly judge the ethics of their own members. According to communication scholar William S. Howell (1982),

> *The environment, the situation, the timing of an interaction, human relationships, all affect the way ethical standards are applied. . . . The concept of universal ethics, standards of goodness that apply to everyone, everywhere, and at all times, is the sort of myth people struggle to hold onto. (pp. 182, 187)*

And yet, to accept a completely relativistic position seems to tacitly accept the horrors of Nazi Germany, South African apartheid, or U.S. slavery. In each case, the larger community developed cultural beliefs that supported persecution and discrimination in such extreme forms that worldwide condemnation ultimately resulted (Hall, 1997, p. 23).

Philosophers and anthropologists have struggled to develop ethical guidelines that seem universally applicable but that also recognize the tremendous

This writer decries a certain kind of intercultural learning—the learning that some study-abroad students pursue—whereby people in other countries are objectified and viewed as exotic and strange. The real problem arises when these students are hired to write television commercials and to present ideas about other cultures.

One type of commercial model shows us exotic humans in all their tribal finery, but, in a multicultural twist, they—Masai warriors, Sicilian matrons, Tibetan monks, Irish fishermen—are revealed as strangely prescient consumers with a quirky knowledge of luxury cars or Internet stock trading. In one commercial, we witness an Inuit elder teaching his grandson about tracking by identifying marks in the snow. "That," he says, "is a caribou." Then, after a pause, during which the wise man stares at the snow, he reverentially intones the single word "Audi." From ads like those, astute students learn that foreigners are obsessed with us—our commodities and displays. What we may learn from them pales in comparison with the glories that they see in our consumer lifestyle.

Other commercials reduce distant lands to images of animals or nature and imply that nature can be thoroughly dominated by SUVs or swaggering, extreme-sports youths. Athletes and Nissan Pathfinders fight bulls in a ring, giant outdoorsmen tap the miniaturized Rockies, a hiker butts heads with a bighorn sheep. And, of course, sophisticated viewers know that all those animals are the creation of technology.

In one commercial, a driver—insulated in his fully self-sufficient cocoon—is able to program both the road and the various beautiful and exotic settings it passes through. Not only is the technologically empowered American greater than nature, we create nature to suit our whims. There is no outside world anymore, no dark places of mystery, yet to be seen. Our SUVs do not travel to an unknown world so much as create different options from a well-known list. Television's emphasis is on how the actor—whether a contestant on a reality-TV show or the driver in a car ad—is seen and manipulates how she is seen. Even when outsiders exist, everyone is looking at us.

When a promotional piece for the reality-TV show The Amazing Race *shows an American woman in a clearly foreign space—perhaps India—she is not troubled, confused, or interested in her environment. Instead she strips*

cultural variability in the world. And many ethical relativists appeal to more natural, humanitarian principles. This more moderate position assumes that people can evaluate cultures without succumbing to ethnocentrism, that all individuals and cultural groups share a fundamental humanistic belief in the sanctity of the human spirit and the goodness of peace, and that people should respect the well-being of others (Kale, 1994).

Communication scholar Bradford J. Hall (1997) reminds us that relativistic and universalistic approaches to ethics should be viewed not as a dichotomy, but down to a bikini emblazoned with a U.S. flag to get directions to the next challenge from a bug-eyed and eager native. "Will I wear this if it helps me get home?" she says. "Hell, yeah!" The young woman clearly did not travel to broaden her horizons. For her, India becomes, as much as Salt Lake City or Kandahar, a place for aggressive performance of her American identity— unwrapping herself in the flag, so to speak.

We now are the world, to be looked at, admired, or despised; what is important about the activity of others is their response to our display. . . . [Study-abroad students] talk about interactions with outsiders only in vague abstractions, while expostulating brilliantly about the nuances of American students' interactions with one another. The few individuals who left their peers to engage the outside world explained that move as an individual rejection of the group and still found it easier to discuss their fellow students than the generically defined "friends" they met at bars.

One young American who traveled to Guatemala bragged that "I have a surprising ability to relate to almost everyone," but "everyone" turned out to mean members of preconceived categories of human-rights workers, Indians, and children, whom she described as objects of more first-person sentences. She specifically excluded less exotic, fast-talking city folk who were "just different" and not worth mentioning.

Students return from study-abroad programs having seen the world, but the world they return to tell tales about is more often than not the world they already knew, the imaginary world of globalized, postmodern capitalism where everything is already known, everyone speaks the same language, and the outside world keeps its eyes on those of us who come from the center.

. . . we should avoid pre- and post-travel orientation sessions that focus on group dynamics and individual growth. Instead, those sessions could be used as opportunities for students to learn how to question the way that we tell stories about our travels, and to discover for themselves how those stories share features with commercials about men who play football with lions and reality shows where contestants dare each other to swallow centipedes.

Source: From B. Feinberg, "What Students Don't Learn Abroad," *The Chronicle Review*, May 2, 2000, p. B20.

rather as a compound of universalism and relativism. All ethics systems involve a tension between the universal and the relative. So, although we recognize some universal will toward ethical principles, we may have to live with the tension of not being able to impose our "universal" ethic on others.

A recent suggestion for meeting the ethical imperative is to employ a **dialogical approach** (Evanoff, 2004). The dialogical approach emphasizes the importance of relationships and dialogues between individuals and communities in wrestling with ethical dilemmas. Communication scholars Stanley Deetz,

dialogical approach
Focuses on the importance of dialogue in developing and maintaining relationships between individuals and communities.

Deborah Cohen, and Paige P. Edley (1997) suggest that even in international business contexts, a dialogical approach can work. As an example, they cite the ethical challenges that arise when a corporation relocates its operations overseas. Although this relocation may make good business sense, the move often has difficult personal and social (and therefore ethical) ramifications. The move may cause a wave of unemployment in the old location and raise issues of exploitation of the workforce and harm to the environment in the new location (especially where poverty is a problem).

Deetz and colleagues (1997) suggest that moving from an owner/manager model to a dialogical stakeholder model can help clarify some of the ethical issues. The dialogical approach emphasizes the importance of the relationship and dialogue between the company and the various communities and stakeholders. They propose forums for discussion even while acknowledging that sometimes discussions and forums are used by management to suppress or diffuse conflict rather than to promote genuine debate for the sake of company improvement. In this case, a dialogical approach

> does not rest in agreement or consensus but in the avoidance of the suppression of alternative conceptions and possibilities . . . the heterogeneity of the international community and the creative possibilities residing in intercultural communication provide possibilities that may have been overlooked in national cultures. (Deetz, et al., 1997, pp. 222–223)

The study of intercultural communication not only provides insights into cultural patterns but also helps us address the ethical issues involved in intercultural interaction. Specifically we should be able to (1) judge what is ethical and unethical behavior given variations in cultural priorities and (2) identify guidelines for ethical behavior in intercultural contexts in which ethics clash.

Being Ethical Students of Culture

Related to the issue of judging cultural patterns as ethical or unethical are the issues surrounding the study of culture. Part of learning about intercultural communication is learning about cultural patterns and cultural identities—our own and others. There are three issues to address here: developing self-reflexivity, learning about others, and acquiring a sense of social justice.

self-reflexivity A process of learning to understand oneself and one's position in society.

Developing Self-Reflexivity   In studying intercultural communication, it is vital to develop **self-reflexivity**—to understand ourselves and our position in society. In learning about other cultures and cultural practices, we often learn much about ourselves. Immigrants often comment that they never felt so much like someone of their own nationality until they left their homeland.

Think about it: Many cultural attitudes and ideas are instilled in you, but these can be difficult to unravel and identify. Knowing who you are is never simple; rather, it is an ongoing process that can never fully capture the ever-emerging person. Not only will you grow older but your intercultural experiences will change who you are and who you think you are. It is also important

I have spent three years in the United States seeking an education. I am from Singapore, and I believe that in many ways both countries are similar. They are both multicultural. They both have a dominant culture. In the United States the dominant culture is white, and in Singapore it is Chinese.

Coming to the United States has taught me to be more aware of diversity. Even though in Singapore we are diverse, because I was part of the majority there, I didn't feel the need to increase my level of intercultural awareness. In the United States I became a minority, and that has made me feel the need to become more culturally competent.
—Jacqueline

to reflect on your place in society. By recognizing the social categories to which you belong, and the implications of those categories, you will be in a better position to understand how to communicate. For example, being an undergraduate student positions you to communicate your ideas on specific subjects and in particular ways to various members of the faculty or staff at your school. You might want to communicate to the registrar your desire to change majors—this would be an appropriate topic to address to that person. But you would not be well positioned during an exam to communicate to your chemistry professor your problems with your girl- or boyfriend.

Learning About Others   It is important to remember that the study of cultures is actually the study of other people. Never lose sight of the humanity at the core of the topic. Try not to observe people as if they are zoo animals. Communication scholar Bradford Hall (1997) cautions against using the "zoo approach" to studying culture:

> *When using such an approach we view the study of culture as if we were walking through a zoo admiring, gasping and chuckling at the various exotic animals we observe. One may discover amazing, interesting and valuable information by using such a perspective and even develop a real fondness for these exotic people, but miss the point that we are as culturally "caged" as others and that they are culturally as "free" as we are. (p. 14)*

Remember that you are studying real people who have real lives, and your conclusions about them may have very real consequences for them and for you. Cultural studies scholar Linda Alcoff (1991/1992) acknowledges the ethical issues involved when students of culture try to describe the cultural patterns of others; she recognizes the difficulty of speaking "for" and "about" others who have different lives. Instead, she suggests, students of culture should try to speak "with" and "to" others. Rather than merely describe others from a distance, it's better to engage others in a dialogue about their cultural realities.

Learn to listen to the voices of others, to cultivate experiential knowledge. Hearing about the experiences of people who are different from you can broaden your ways of viewing the world. Many differences—based on race, gender, sexual orientation, nationality, ethnicity, age, and so on—deeply affect people's everyday lives. Listening carefully as people relate their experiences and their ways of knowing will help you learn about the many aspects of intercultural communication.

Developing a Sense of Social Justice   A final ethical issue involves the responsibility that comes with the acquisition of intercultural knowledge and insights—that this educational experience is not just transformative for the individual but should also benefit the larger society and other cultural groups in the increasingly interdependent world.

Everett Kleinjans (1975), an international educator, stresses that intercultural education differs from some other kinds of education: Although all education may be potentially transformative, learning as a result of intercultural contact is particularly so in that it deals with fundamental aspects of human behavior. Learning about intercultural communication sometimes calls into question the core of our basic assumptions about ourselves, our culture, and our worldviews and challenges existing and preferred beliefs, values, and patterns of behavior. Liliana, a Colombian student, describes such a transformation:

> *When I first came to the States to study and live I was surprised with all the diversity and different cultures I encountered. I realized I came from a country, society, school and group of friends with little diversity. During all the years I lived in Colombia I did not meet more than five people from other countries. Even at my school, there was little diversity—only two students of color among three thousand students. I realized that big difference when I was suddenly sharing a college classroom with students from all over the world, people of all colors and cultures. At the beginning it was difficult getting used to it because of the wide diversity, but I like and enjoy it now and I wish my family and friends could experience and learn as much as I have.*

As you learn about yourself and others as cultural beings, as you come to understand the larger economic, political, and historical contexts in which interaction occurs, is there an ethical obligation to continue learning? We believe that as members of an increasingly interdependent global community, intercultural communication students have a responsibility to educate themselves, not just about interesting cultural differences but also about intercultural conflicts, the impacts of stereotyping and prejudice, and the larger systems that can oppress and deny basic human rights—and to apply this knowledge to the communities in which they live and interact. This is the basis of social justice.

For example, how could you apply intercultural communication concepts in situations where gay and lesbian young people are the targets of bullying? Statistics show that these adolescents get bullied two to three times more than their heterosexual peers (Berlan, Corliss, Field, Goodman, & Austin, 2010). Why does this happen? What can be done to reduce harassment of this particular cultural group? In the following chapters, you will learn about the causes and patterns of conflict between various cultural groups, the origins and expressions of prejudice and discrimination, as well as strategies for reducing conflict and discrimination.

Consider the homeless—another cultural group rarely mentioned by cultural communication scholars—often the target of prejudice and violence. Perhaps increased knowledge about this group and ethical application of intercultural communication principles could lead to better understanding of these individuals and ultimately to less discrimination and prejudice. After working as an advocate for homeless people in Denver, one communication scholar, Professor Phil Tompkins, describes the link between communication skills and social justice. He defines social justice as the "process of communicating, inspiring, advocating, organizing and working with others of similar and diverse organizational affiliations to help all people gain respect and participate fully in society in a way that benefits the community as well as the individual" (Tompkins, 2009). This definition has three important components: (1) communication is central; (2) the outcome of social justice must be beneficial to society, not just the individuals involved; and (3) respect for and participation by all is important. We hope that as you read the following chapters, you will agree with us that learning about intercultural communication also involves ethical application of that knowledge.

What are unethical applications of intercultural communication knowledge? One questionable practice involves people who study intercultural communication in order to proselytize others without their consent. (Some religious organizations conduct Bible study on college campuses for international students under the guise of English language lessons.) Another questionable practice is the behavior of cross-cultural consultants who misrepresent or exaggerate their ability to deal with complex issues of prejudice and racism in brief, one-shot training sessions (Paige & Martin, 1996).

A final questionable practice concerns research on the intercultural communication of U.S. minority groups. A common approach in the United States is for a white tenured faculty member to conduct such research employing graduate and undergraduate students from the minority groups being studied:

> *Minority students are sometimes used as a way to gain immediate access to the community of interest. These students go into communities and the (usually white) professors are spared the intense, time-consuming work of establishing relationships in the community. (Martin & Butler, 2001, p. 291)*

These students are then asked to report their findings to and interpret their community for the faculty member. Unfortunately, doing so can jeopardize their relationship to their community, which may be suspicious of the academic community. The faculty member publishes articles and reaps the tangible rewards of others' hard work—promotions, pay raises, and professional visibility. Meanwhile, the community and the students may receive little for their valuable contributions to this academic work.

We feel there is a concomitant responsibility that goes along with this intercultural knowledge: to work toward a more equitable and fair society and world. We want you to keep in mind this ethical issue as you study the various topics covered in this book. In the final chapter, we'll address this issue again with practical suggestions for meeting this ethical challenge.

INTERNET RESOURCES

www.intercultural.org/
This is the website of a nonprofit organization dedicated to improving intercultural communication. It contains a lot of valuable information aimed at a broad audience, including businesses. The most interesting aspect of the website is that it is full of actual training materials used by intercultural practitioners in helping their clients develop a greater intercultural proficiency.

www.refintl.org/
This website explores the topic of refugees. Many people consider intercultural communication in the business setting, but intercultural communication due to refugee migrations is actually rather common. This site estimates that there are more than 34 million refugees around the world. What special intercultural issues are present when considering refugees?

www.kwintessential.co.uk/cultural-services/articles/intercultural-communication-tips.html
This is a "quick-tip" guide to intercultural communication. There are some good tips on this page, like encouragement to reflect on the practices you engage in while communicating in an intercultural context. It is worth considering that this is the type of information many people use when engaging in intercultural business, and so forth. What types of information or analysis are missing from its list of tips?

SUMMARY

There are six reasons or imperatives for studying intercultural communication:

- The self-awareness imperative involves increasing understanding of our own location in larger social, political, and historical contexts.
- The demographic imperative includes the changing domestic and international migration—raising questions of class and religious diversity.
- The economic imperative highlights issues of globalization and the challenges for increased cultural understanding needed to reach the global market.
- The technological imperative gives us increasing information and increased contact with people who are similar and different from us. Increased use of communication technology also raises questions about identity and access to these technologies.
- The peace imperative involves working through issues of colonialism, economic disparities, and racial, ethnic, and religious differences.
- The ethical imperative calls for an understanding of the universalist, relativist, and dialogic approach to ethical issues.

Being an ethical student of culture involves developing self-reflexivity, learning about others, and developing a sense of social justice and responsibility.

DISCUSSION QUESTIONS

1. How do electronic means of communication (e-mail, the Internet, fax, and so on) differ from face-to-face interactions?
2. How do these communication technologies change intercultural communication interaction?
3. What are some of the potential challenges organizations face as they become more diverse?
4. Why is it important to think beyond ourselves as individuals in intercultural interaction?
5. How do economic situations affect intergroup relations?

 Go to the self-quizzes on the Online Learning Center at www.mhhe.com/martinnakayama6 to further test your knowledge.

ACTIVITIES

1. *Family Tree.* Interview the oldest member of your family you can contact. Then answer the following questions:
   a. When did your ancestors come to the United States?
   b. Where did they come from?
   c. What were the reasons for their move? Did they come voluntarily?
   d. What language(s) did they speak?
   e. What difficulties did they encounter?
   f. Did they change their names? For what reasons?
   g. What were their occupations before they came, and what jobs did they take on their arrival?
   h. How has your family status changed through the generations?

   Compare your family experience with those of your classmates. Did most immigrants come for the same reasons? What are the differences in the various stories?

2. *Intercultural Encounter.* Describe and analyze a recent intercultural encounter. This may mean talking with someone of a different age, ethnicity, race, religion, and so on.
   a. Describe the encounter. What made it "intercultural"?
   b. Explain how you initially felt about the communication.
   c. Describe how you felt after the encounter, and explain why you think you felt as you did.
   d. Describe any challenges in trying to communicate. If there were no challenges, explain why you think it was so easy.
   e. Based on this experience, identify some characteristics that may be important for successful intercultural communication.

KEY WORDS

Anglocentrism (12)	ethnocentrism (5)	immigrants (9)
colonialism (30)	global village (22)	*maquiladoras* (22)
demographics (6)	heterogeneous (8)	melting pot (12)
dialogical approach (35)	homogeneous (8)	multinational
diasporic groups (25)	identity	corporations (22)
diversity (9)	management (27)	nativistic (12)
ethics (32)	identity tourism (27)	self-reflexivity (36)

 The Online Learning Center at www.mhhe.com/martinnakayama6 features flashcards and crossword puzzles based on these terms and concepts.

REFERENCES

Adler, P. S. (1975). The transition experience: An alternative view of culture shock. *Journal of Humanistic Psychology, 15*, 13–23.

Alcoff, L. (1991/1992). The problem of speaking for others. *Cultural Critique, 20*, 5–32.

Allegretto, S. A. (2011, March 23). The state of working America's wealth, 2011. Economic Policy Institute State of Working America Briefing Paper #292, retrieved April 26, 2011 from HYPER-LINK "http://epi.3cdn.net/002c5fc0fda0ae9cce_aem6idhp5.pdf"http://epi.3cdn.net/00p.2c5fc0fda0ae9cce_aem6idhp5.pdf.

Ambler, T., & Witzel, M. (2000). *Doing business in China*. New York: Routledge.

American Indians by the Number, US Census Bureau, retrieved December 26, 2011 from www.infoplease.com/spot/aihmcensus1.html.

Archibold, R. (2010, April 24). Arizona enacts stringent law on immigration. *The New York Times*, p. 1.

Baldwin, J. (1955). *Notes of a native son*. Boston: Beacon Press.

Banks, J. (1991). *Teaching strategies for ethnic studies*. Needham, MA: Allyn & Bacon.

Berlan, E. D., Corliss, H. L., Field, A. E., Goodman, E. & Austin, S. B. (2010). Sexual orientation and bullying among adolescents in the Growing Up Today study. *Journal of Adolescent Health, 46*(4), 366–371.

Branding so much more than a name (2011). *Strategic Direction, 27*(3), 6–8.

Canadian Press. (2008, August 27). Tour requires foreign golfers to speak English by next year. *Toronto Star*. Retrieved August 28, 2008 from www.thestar.com/Sports/Golf/article/486172.

Cole, D. (1998). Five myths about immigration. In P. S. Rothenberg (Ed.), *Race, class, and gender in the United States: An integrated study* (4th ed., pp. 125–129). New York: St. Martin's Press.

Curtin, P. D. (1969). *The Atlantic slave trade: A census*. Madison: University of Wisconsin Press.

Deetz, S., Cohen, D., & Edley, P. P. (1997). Toward a dialogic ethic in the context of international business organization. In F. L. Casmir (Ed.), *Ethics in intercultural and international communication* (pp. 183–226). Mahwah, NJ: Lawrence Erlbaum.

Delgado, F. (2002). Mass-mediated communication and intercultural conflict. In J. N. Martin, T. K. Nakayama, & L. A. Flores (Eds.), *Readings in intercultural communication* (pp. 351–359). Boston: McGraw-Hill.

Dillon, S. (2010, December 7). Top test scores from Shanghai stun educators. *The New York Times*, p. 1A.

Dor, D. (2004). From Englishization to imposed multilingualism: Globalization, the Internet, and the political economy of the linguistic code. *Public Culture, 16*, 97–118.

Evanoff, R. J. (2004). Universalist, relativist, and constructivist approaches to intercultural ethics. *International Journal of Intercultural Relations, 28*, 439–458.

Ferdman, B. M., & Brody, S. E. (1996). Models of diversity training. In D. Landis & R. Bhagat (Eds.), *Handbook of intercultural training* (2nd ed., pp. 282–303). Thousand Oaks, CA: Sage.

Flores, L. A., Moon, D. G., & Nakayama, T. K. (2006). Dynamic rhetorics of race: California's Racial Privacy Initiative and the shifting grounds of racial politics. *Communication and Critical/Cultural Studies*.

Foner, E. (1998). Who is an American? In P. S. Rothenberg (Ed.), *Race, class, and gender in the United States: An integrated study* (4th ed., pp. 84–92). New York: St. Martin's Press.

Fox, S. (2011, January 21). *Americans living with disability and their technology profile*. Pew Internet & American Life Project. Retrieved April 29, 2011, from www.pewinternet.org/~/media//Files/Reports/2011/PIP_Disability.pdf.

Franklin, M. I. (2003). I define my own identity: Pacific articulations of 'race' and 'culture' on the Internet. *Ethnicities, 3*, 465–490.

Friedman, T. L. (2005). *The world is flat: A brief history of the twenty-first century.* New York: Farrar, Straus & Giroux.

Fussell, P. (1992). *Class: A guide through the American status system.* New York: Touchstone Books.

Grieco, E. M. & Trevelyan, E. N. (2010, October). *Place of birth of the foreign-born population: 2009.* U.S. Census Bureau: American Community Survey Briefs, ACSBR/09-15. Retrieved May 5, 2011, from www.census.gov/prod/2010pubs/acsbr09-15.pdf.

Griefat, Y., & Katriel, T. (1989). Life demands *musayara:* Communication and culture among Arabs in Israel. In S. Ting-Toomey & F. Korzenny (Eds.), *Language, communication and culture: International and intercultural communication annual* (Vol. 13, pp. 121–138). Newbury Park, CA: Sage.

Griffin, G. (2011, April 20). Egypt's uprising: Tracking the social media factor. *PBS Newshour.* Retrieved May 7, 2011, from www.pbs.org/newshour/updates/middle_east/jan-june11/revsocial_04-19.html.

Hacker, K. L., & Steiner, R. (2002). The digital divide for Hispanic Americans. *Howard Journal of Communications, 13,* 267–283.

Hall, B. J. (1997). Culture, ethics and communication. In F. L. Casmir (Ed.), *Ethics in intercultural and international communication* (pp. 11–41). Mahwah, NJ: Lawrence Erlbaum.

Harris, P., & Gallagher, P. (2011, April 2). Terry Jones defiant despite murders in Afghanistan over Qur'an burning. *guardian.co.uk.* Retrieved April 22, 2011, from www.guardian.co.uk/world/2011/apr/02/pastor-terry-jones-burning-koran?.

Hochman, (2004, June 21). NBA teams continue to look outside U.S. *Times-Picayune* (New Orleans), p. 2.

Howell, W. S. (1982). *The empathic communicator.* Belmont, CA: Wadsworth.

Internet rant causes uproar at UD university (2011, March 27). *VOANews.com.* Retrieved May 6, 2011, from www.voanews.com/english/news/usa/Internet-Rant-Causes-Uproar-at-US-University-118747924.html.

Jackson, L. A., Barbatsis, G., Biocca, F. A., von Eye, A., Zhao, Y., & Fitzgerald, H. E. (2004). Home Internet use in low-income families: Is access enough to eliminate the digital divide? In E. P. Bucy & J. E. Newhagen (Eds.), *Media access: Social and psychological dimensions of new technology use* (pp. 155–186). Mahwah, NJ: Lawrence Erlbaum.

Jiménez, Tomás R. (2010). *Replenished ethnicity: Mexican Americans, immigration, and identity.* Berkeley: University of California Press.

Johannesen, R. L. (1990). *Ethics in human communication* (3rd ed.). Prospect Heights, IL: Waveland Press.

Kale, D. W. (1994). Peace as an ethic for intercultural communication. In L. Samovar & R. E. Porter (Eds.), *Intercultural communication: A reader* (7th ed., pp. 435–441). Belmont, CA: Wadsworth.

Kant, I. (1949). *Fundamental principles of the metaphysics of morals* (T. Abbott, Trans.). Indianapolis, IN: Library of Liberal Arts/Bobbs-Merrill.

Kirkpatrick, D. D. (2011, May 20). Many in Arab world say Obama's speech doesn't dispel grievances against U. S. *The New York Times,* p. A10.

Kleinjans, E. (1975). A question of ethics. *International Education and Cultural Exchange, 10,* 20–25.

Lapchick, R. (2011, April 21). The 2011 racial and gender report card: Major League Baseball. The Institute for Diversity and Ethics in Sport, University of Central Florida. Retrieved May 5, 2011, from www.tidesport.org/RGRC/2011/2011_MLB_RGRC_FINAL.pdf.

Lenhart, A., Horrigan, J., Rainie, L., Allen, K., Boyce, A., Madden, M., & O'Grady, E. (2003, April 16). *The ever-shifting Internet population: A new look at Internet access and the digital divide.* Washington, DC: Pew Internet & American Life Project (www.pewinternet.org).

Loewen, J. W. (1995). *Lies my teacher told me.* New York: Simon & Schuster.

Magaña, Lisa. (2005). *Mexican Americans and the politics of diversity*: Querer es poder! Tucson: University of Arizona Press.

Mantsios, G. (2001). Class in America: Myths and realities. In P. S. Rothenberg (Ed.), *Race, class, and gender in the United States: An integrated study* (5th ed., pp. 168–182). New York: Worth.

Martin, J. N., & Butler, R. L. W. (2001). Toward an ethic of intercultural communication research. In V. H. Milhouse, M. K. Asante, & P. O. Nwosu (Eds.), *Transcultural realities: Interdisciplinary perspectives on cross-cultural relations* (pp. 283–298). Thousand Oaks, CA: Sage.

McGreal, C. (2010, August 12). Ground Zero mosque plans "fuelling anti-Muslim protests across US." *guardian.co.uk.* Retrieved April 29, 2011, from www.guardian.co.uk/world/2010/aug/12/ground-zero-mosque-islamophobia?.

McLuhan, M. (1967). *The medium is the message.* New York: Bantam Books.

Muzrui, A. (2001). Historical struggles between Islamic and Christian worldviews: An interpretation. In V. H. Milhouse, M. K. Asante, & P. O. Nwosu (Eds.), *Transcultural realities: Interdisciplinary perspectives on cross-cultural relations* (pp. 109–120). Thousand Oaks, CA: Sage.

Now a nation of more immigrants than ever. (2002, February 7). *Christian Science Monitor,* p. 1.

Paige, R. M., & Martin, J. N. (1996). Ethics in intercultural training. In D. Landis & R. Bhagat (Eds.), *Handbook of intercultural training* (pp. 35–60). Newbury Park, CA: Sage.

Passel, J. S., & Cohn, D. V. (2008, February 11). *U.S. populations projections: 2005–2050.* Washington, DC: Pew Research Center.

Rachman, G. (2011). Welcome to a zero-sum world. *The Economist: A 25 year Special Edition*, pp. 85–86.

Richtell, M. (2011, January 29). Egypt halts most Internet and cell service, and scale of shutdown surprises experts. *The New York Times*, Late Edition, Foreign Desk, p. 13A.

Rideout, V. J., Foehr, U. G., & Roberts, D. F. (2010). *Generation M2: Media in the lives of 8- to 18-year-olds* (A Kaiser Family Foundation Study). Menlo Park, CA: Henry J. Kaiser Family Foundation.

Roediger, D. (1991). *The wages of whiteness: Race and the making of the American working class.* New York: Verso.

Rojas, V., Straubhaar, J., Roychowdhury, D., & Okur, O. (2004). Communities, cultural capital, and the digital divide. In E. P. Bucy & J. E. Newhagen (Eds.), *Media access: Social and psychological dimensions of new technology use* (pp. 107–130). Mahwah, NJ: Lawrence Erlbaum.

Scheer, R. (2005, September 6). The real costs of a culture of greed. *Los Angeles Times*, p. B11.

Schmitt, E. (2001, April 3). Analysis of census finds segregation along with diversity, www.nytimes .com/2001/04/04/national/04CENS.html?ex= 987410510&ei=1&en=a2cf77e31f7952.

Scommegna, P. (2003). U.S. growing bigger, older and more diverse. Population Reference Bureau Web site. www.prb.org/Template.cfm? Section=PRB&template=/ContentManagement/ ContentDisplay.cfm&ContentID=10201.

Shepard, B. (2005, April 7). International numbers grow. *Chattanooga Times Free Press*, p. D6.

Slackman, M. (2006, August 6). Iranian 101: A lesson for Americans; the fine art of hiding what you mean to say. *The New York Times online.* Retrieved May 24, 2011, from http://query.nytimes.com/gst/fullpage.htm l?res=9A04E1DD1E3FF935A3575BC0A9609C8B63.

Smith, A. (2010, August 11). *Home broadband 2010.* Pew Internet & American Life Project. Retrieved April 29, 2011, from www.pewinternet.org/~/ media//Files/Reports/2010/Home%20broad- band%202010.pdf.

Smith, A. (2010, September 17). *Commentary: Tech- nology trends among people of color.* Pew Internet & American Life Project. Retrieved April 29, 2011, from www.pewinternet.org/Commentary/2010/ September/Technology-Trends-Among-People-of- Color.aspx#.

Smith, C. (2011, March 14). Twitter user statistics show stunning growth. *huffingtonpost.com*. Retrieved May 6, 2011, from www.huffingtonpost.com/2011/03/14/ twitter-user-statistics_n_835581.html.

Snyder, B. (2003, May). Teams that span time zones face new work rules. Stanford Graduate School of Business website: www.gsb.stanford.edu/news/ bmag/sbsm0305/feature_virtual_teams.shtml.

Spread the Wealth (2011, February 12-18), *The Econo- mist*, 398(8720), p. 12.

Takaki, R. (1989). *Strangers from a different shore.* New York: Penguin Books.

The world in figures: Industries, *The Economist: A 25 year Special Edition*, p. 125.

Tinsley, A. M. (2011, April 11). Texas lawmakers considering Sharia law ban. *The Miami Herald.* Retrieved April 29, 2011, from www.miamiherald .com/2011/04/11/2161529/texas-lawmakers- considering-sharia.html.

Tompkins, P. K. (2009). *Who is my neighbor? Commu- nicating and organizing to end homelessness.* Boulder, CO: Paradigm Publishers.

Turkle, S. (1995). *Life on the screen: Identity in the age of the Internet.* New York: Simon & Schuster.

Turkle, S. (2008). Always-on/Always on you: The tethered self. In J. E. Katz (Ed.), *Handbook of com- munication studies* (pp. 121–137). Cambridge, MA: MIT Press.

Undergraduate diversity: More minorities, more women (2010, September 24). *Chronicle of Higher Education, 57*(5), B45–B46.

U.S. Religious Landscape Survey. (2008). *Pew Forum on Religion and Public Life.* Retrieved May 13, 2008, from http://religions.pewforum.org/pdf/report- religious-landscape-study-full.pdf.

van Dijk, J. (2004). Divides in succession: Possession, skills, and use of new media for societal participa- tion. In E. P. Bucy & J. E. Newhagen (Eds.), *Media access: Social and psychological dimensions of new technology use* (pp. 233–254). Mahwah, NJ: Lawrence Erlbaum.

Varner, I., & Beamer, L. (2010). *Intercultural communication in the global workplace.* 5th ed. Boston: McGraw-Hill.

Walsh, M. F., Winterich, K. P., & Mittal, V. (2010). Do logo redesigns help or hurt your brand? The role of brand commitment. *Journal of Product & Brand Management, 19*(2), 76–84.

West, C. (1993). *Race matters.* Boston: Beacon Press.

Yen, H. (2010, September 28). Census finds record gap between rich and poor. *Salon.com.* Retrieved April 23, 2011, from www.salon.com/news/feature/ 2010/09/28/us_census_recession_s_impact_1.

THE HISTORY
OF THE STUDY
OF INTERCULTURAL
COMMUNICATION

CHAPTER OBJECTIVES

After reading this chapter, you should be able to:

1. Identify four early foci in the development of intercultural communication.
2. Describe three approaches to the study of intercultural communication.
3. Identify the methods used within each of the three approaches.
4. Explain the strengths and weaknesses of each approach.
5. Identify three characteristics of the dialectical approach.
6. Explain the strengths of a dialectical approach.
7. Identify six intercultural communication dialectics.

Now that we've described a rationale for studying intercultural communication, we turn to ways in which the study of intercultural communication is conducted. To understand the contemporary approaches to this discipline, it's important to examine its historical and philosophical foundations. Why should you study how the field of intercultural communication got started? Before answering this question, let us pose a few others: Whom do you think should be regarded as an expert in intercultural communication? Someone who has actually lived in a variety of cultures? Or someone who has conducted scientific studies on how cultural groups differ in values and attitudes? Or someone who analyzes what popular culture (movies, television, magazines, and so on) has to say about a particular group of people?

Consider a related question: What is the best way to study intercultural communication behavior? By observing how people communicate in various cultures? By asking people to describe their own communication patterns? By distributing questionnaires to various cultural groups? Or by analyzing books, videos, movies, and other cultural performances of various groups?

The answers to these questions help determine what kind of material goes into a textbook on intercultural communication. And intercultural communication scholars do not agree on what are the "right" answers to these questions. Thus, these questions and answers have implications for what you will be exposed to in this book and this course. By choosing some types of research (questionnaire, observation data), we may neglect other types (interviews, travel journal, media analysis).

To help you understand why we chose to include the material we did, we describe the origins of the discipline in the United States and the philosophical worldviews that inform the current study and practices of intercultural communication. We then outline three contemporary perspectives that recognize contributions from other disciplines. Finally, we outline our dialectical approach, which integrates the strengths from all three contemporary perspectives.

THE EARLY DEVELOPMENT OF THE DISCIPLINE

worldview Underlying assumptions about the nature of reality and human behavior.

The current study of intercultural communication is influenced in part by how it developed in the United States and in part by the **worldviews,** or research philosophies, of the scholars who pursue it. The roots of the study of intercultural communication can be traced to the post–World War II era, when the United States increasingly came to dominate the world stage. However, government and business personnel working overseas often found that they were ill equipped to work among people from different cultures. The language training they received, for example, did little to prepare them for the complex challenges of working abroad.

In response, the U.S. government in 1946 passed the Foreign Service Act and established the Foreign Service Institute (FSI). The FSI, in turn, hired Edward T. Hall and other prominent anthropologists and linguists (including Ray Birdwhistell and George Trager) to develop "predeparture" courses for overseas workers. Because intercultural training materials were scarce, they developed their own. In so doing, FSI theorists formed new ways of looking at culture and communication. Thus, the field of intercultural communication was born (Martin, Nakayama, & Carbaugh, 2012).

Nonverbal Communication

The FSI emphasized the importance of nonverbal communication and applied linguistic frameworks to investigate nonverbal aspects of communication. These researchers concluded that, just like language, nonverbal communication varies from culture to culture. E. T. Hall pioneered this systematic study of culture and communication with *The Silent Language* (1959) and *The Hidden Dimension* (1966), which influenced the new discipline. In *The Silent Language*, for example, Hall introduced the notion of **proxemics,** the study of how people use personal space to communicate. In *The Hidden Dimension*, in elaborating on the concept of proxemics, he identified four **distance zones**—intimate, personal, social, and public—at which people interact and suggested that people know which distance to use depending on the situation. He noted that each cultural group has its own set of rules for personal space and that respecting these cultural differences is critical to smooth communication.

proxemics The study of how people use personal space.

distance zones The area, defined by physical space, within which people interact, according to Edward Hall's theory of proxemics. The four distance zones for individuals are intimate, personal, social, and public. (See also **proxemics.**)

Application of Theory

The staff at the FSI found that government workers were not interested in theories of culture and communication; rather, they wanted specific guidelines for getting along in the countries they were visiting. Hall's initial strategy in developing materials for these predeparture training sessions was to observe variations in cultural behavior. At the FSI, he was surrounded by people who spoke many languages and who were from many cultures, so it was a great place to observe and test his theories about cultural differences. For example, he might have observed that Italians tend to stand close to each other when conversing, or that Greeks use lots of hand gestures when interacting, or that Chinese use few hand gestures in conversations. He could then have confirmed his observations by consulting members of different cultural groups. Today, most textbooks in the discipline retain this focus on practical guidelines and barriers to communication.

This emphasis on the application of theory spawned a parallel "discipline" of **cross-cultural training,** which began with the FSI staff and was expanded in the 1960s to include training for students and business personnel. More recently, it has come to include **diversity training,** which facilitates intercultural communication among members of various gender, ethnic, and racial groups, mostly in the corporate or government workplace (Landis, Bennett, and Bennett, 2004).

cross-cultural training Training people to become familiar with other cultural norms and to improve their interactions with people of different domestic and international cultures.

diversity training The training meant to facilitate intercultural communication among various gender, ethnic, and racial groups in the United States.

An Emphasis on International Settings

Early scholars and trainers in intercultural communication defined *culture* narrowly, primarily in terms of "nationality." Usually, scholars mistakenly compared middle-class U.S. citizens with all residents of other nations, and trainers tended to focus on helping middle-class professionals become successful overseas.

One might ask why so few scholars focused on domestic contexts, particularly in the 1960s and 1970s when the United States was fraught with civil unrest. One reason may be the early emphasis of the FSI on helping overseas personnel. Another reason may be that most scholars who studied intercultural communication gained their intercultural experience in international contexts such as the Peace Corps, the military, or the transnational corporation.

An Interdisciplinary Focus

The scholars at the FSI came from various disciplines, including linguistics, anthropology, and psychology. Not surprisingly, in their work related to communication, they drew from theories pertinent to their specific disciplines. Contributions from these fields of study blended to form an integrated approach that remains useful to this day.

Linguists help us understand the importance of language and its role in intercultural interaction. They describe how languages vary in "surface" structure and are similar in "deep" structure. They also shed light on the relationship between language and reality. For example, the **Sapir-Whorf hypothesis,** developed by linguists Edward Sapir and Benjamin Whorf, explores phenomena such as the use of formal and informal pronouns. French and Spanish, for instance, have both formal and informal forms of the pronoun *you.* (In French, the formal is *vous* and the informal is *tu;* in Spanish, the formal is *usted* and the informal is *tu.*) In contrast, English makes no distinction between formal and informal usage; one word, *you,* suffices in both situations. Such language distinctions affect our culture's notion of formality. In Chapter 6, we'll look at some more recent studies that problematize this hypothesis. Linguists also point out that learning a second or third language can enhance our **intercultural competence** by providing insights into other cultures and expanding our communication repertoire.

Anthropologists help us understand the role that culture plays in our lives and the importance of nonverbal communication. Anthropologist Renate Rosaldo (1989) encouraged scholars to consider the appropriateness of cultural study methods, and other anthropologists have followed Rosaldo's lead. They point out that many U.S. and European studies reveal more about the researchers than about their subjects. Further, many anthropological studies of the past, particularly of non-Europeans, concluded that the people studied were inferior. To understand this phenomenon, science writer Stephen Jay Gould (1993) argues that "we must first recognize the cultural milieu of a society whose leaders and intellectuals did not doubt the propriety of racial thinking, with Indians below whites, and blacks below everyone else" (p. 85).

The so-called scientific study of other peoples is never entirely separate from the culture in which the researchers are immersed. In his study of the Victorian era, for example, Patrick Brantlinger (1986) notes that "evolutionary anthropology often suggested that Africans, if not nonhuman or a different

Sapir-Whorf hypothesis The assumption that language shapes our ideas and guides our view of social reality. This hypothesis was proposed by Edward Sapir, a linguist, and his student, Benjamin Whorf, and represents the relativist view of language and perception.

intercultural competence The ability to behave effectively and appropriately in interacting across cultures.

species, were such an inferior 'breed' that they might be impervious to 'higher influences" (p. 201). Consider this famous case, which dates back to the early 19th century:

> The young African woman was lured to Europe with false promises of fame and fortune. She was paraded naked before jeering mobs. She was exhibited in a metal cage and sold to an animal trainer. When she died in Paris in 1816, she was penniless and friendless among people who derided her as a circus freak.
>
> White scientists intent on proving the inferiority of blacks dissected her body, bottled her brain and genitals, wired her skeleton and displayed them in a French museum. That might have been the end of Saartjie Baartman, the young African woman derisively labeled the "Hottentot Venus."
>
> [However,] 192 years after she last looked on these rugged cliffs and roaring sea [of South Africa], her remains returned to the land of her birth. In an agreement negotiated after years of wrangling between South Africa and France, her remains were finally removed from the Musée de l'Homme in Paris and flown back home. (Swarns, 2002, p. A28)

This return of Baartman's remains is part of a larger movement away from a scientific "era when indigenous people were deemed worthy of scientific study, but unworthy of the consideration commonly accorded to whites" (Swarns, 2002, p. A28). Indeed, the conclusions from such studies reveal more about the cultural attitudes of the researchers (e.g., ethnocentrism, racism, sexism) than they do about the people studied. An **interdisciplinary** focus can help us acquire and interpret information in a more comprehensive manner—in ways relevant to bettering the intercultural communication process, as well as producing knowledge.

Psychologists such as Gordon Allport help us understand notions of stereotyping and the ways in which prejudice functions in our lives and in intercultural interaction. In his classic study *The Nature of Prejudice* (1979), he describes how prejudice can develop from "normal" human cognitive activities such as categorization and generalization. Other psychologists, such as Richard Brislin (1999) and Dan Landis (Landis & Wasilewski, 1999), reveal how variables like nationality, ethnicity, personality, and gender influence our communication.

Whereas the early study of intercultural communication was characterized as interdisciplinary, over time, it became increasingly centered in the discipline of communication. Nevertheless, the field continues to be influenced by interdisciplinary contributions, including ideas from cultural studies, critical theory, and the more traditional disciplines of psychology and anthropology (Martin, Nakayama, & Carbaugh, 2012).

In her historical overview of the ways that "culture" has been viewed in intercultural communication, communication scholar Dreama Moon (2010) noted that how culture is defined determines how it is studied. She also argues for expanding the notion of culture to include the idea of a struggle over power. So while intercultural communication is more firmly rooted in the communication field, the definition of "culture" has expanded to make intercultural communication more interdisciplinary.

interdisciplinary
Integrating knowledge from different disciplines in conducting research and constructing theory.

As a child, I did not consciously think of myself as a German or as a Norwegian. Since I never viewed myself in terms of my culture, cultural heritage was something with which I never used to identify others. When I communicated with others, the cultural background of the person I was talking with never crossed my mind. To someone who constantly sees racism and prejudice, this situation may seem ideal, but ignoring a person's culture can cause as much harm as judging someone based upon that culture. Knowledge of someone's historical background is necessary when communicating on anything other than a superficial level.
        —Andrew

I grew up in northern Minnesota and we were very aware that we were Norwegian and not Swedish. We ate lutefisk and lefse, but we also ate American food. I really don't like lutefisk. My dad belonged to the Sons of Norway, but I think he was more interested in socializing with his friends than insisting that we learned about Norwegian culture. I don't speak Norwegian, but we always knew we were Norwegian.
I guess that I mostly feel like an American, and most of the time people probably see me as white.
        —Juliann

PERCEPTION AND WORLDVIEW OF THE RESEARCHER

paradigm A framework that serves as the worldview of researchers. Different paradigms assume different interpretations of reality, human behavior, culture, and communication.

A second influence on the current study of intercultural communication is the research **paradigm,** or worldview, of the scholars involved. People understand and learn about the world through filtering lenses; they select, evaluate, and organize information (stimuli) from the external environment through **perception.** As Marshal Singer (1987) explains:

> *We experience everything in the world not "as it is"—because there is no way that we can know the world "as it is"—but only as the world comes to us through our sensory receptors. From there, these stimuli go instantly into the "data-storage banks" of our brains, where they have to pass through the filters of our censor screen, our decoding mechanism, and the collectivity of everything we have learned from the day we were born. (p. 9)*

perception The process by which individuals select, organize, and interpret external and internal stimuli to create their view of the world.

In this sense, all of the information we have already stored in our brains (learning) affects how we interpret new information. Some of our learning and perception is group related. That is, we see the world in particular ways because of the cultural groups (based on ethnicity, age, gender, and so on) to which we belong. These group-related perceptions (worldviews or value orientations) are so fundamental that we rarely question them (Singer, 1998). They involve our assumptions about human nature, the physical and spiritual world, and the ways in which humans should relate to one another. For example, most U.S. Americans perceive human beings as separate from nature and believe that there is a fundamental difference between, say, a human and a rock. However, other cultural groups (Japanese, Chinese, traditional Native Americans) see humans and human reality as part of a larger physical reality. For them, the difference between a human and a rock is not so pronounced.

The key point here is that academic research is also cultural behavior because research traditions require particular worldviews about the nature of reality and knowledge and particular beliefs about how research should be conducted. For example, researchers studying communication often reflect their own cultural assumptions in their research projects. Asian scholars say that U.S. communication scholars often emphasize individuality and rationality—two strong cultural beliefs held by many U.S. Americans—and ignore human interdependence and feeling in human encounters, important beliefs for many people around the world (Miike, 2007a, 2007b; Gordon, 2007; Satoshi, 2007). And these research paradigms are often held as strongly as cultural or spiritual beliefs (Burrell & Morgan, 1988; Kuhn, 1970). There are even examples of intercultural conflicts in which scholars strongly disagree. For example, Galileo was excommunicated from the Catholic Church in the 17th century because he took issue with theologians' belief that the earth was the center of the universe.

More recent examples of the relation between academic research and cultural behavior can be seen in the social sciences. Some communication scholars believe there is an external reality that can be measured and studied, whereas others believe that reality can be understood only as lived and experienced by individuals (Casmir, 1994). In short, beliefs and assumptions about reality influence research methods and findings, and so also influence what we currently know about intercultural communication.

At present, we can identify three broad approaches, or worldviews, that characterize the study of culture and communication (Gudykunst, 2005; Hall, 1992). All three approaches involve a blend of disciplines and reflect different worldviews and assumptions about reality, human behavior, and ways to study culture and communication. As you read about each of these approaches, think about what kinds of assumptions concerning "culture" are used in each approach. How we think about "culture" influences how it is studied.

THREE APPROACHES TO STUDYING INTERCULTURAL COMMUNICATION

Three contemporary approaches to studying intercultural communication are (1) the social science (or functionalist) approach, (2) the interpretive approach, and (3) the critical approach. (See Tables 2-1 and 2-2.) These approaches are based on different fundamental assumptions about human nature, human behavior, and the nature of knowledge (Burrell & Morgan, 1988). Each one contributes in a unique way to our understanding of the relationship between culture and communication, but each also has limitations. These approaches vary in their assumptions about human behavior, their research goals, their conceptualization of culture and communication, and their preferred methodologies. As a student of intercultural communication, you may not see yourself doing research on

	Social Science (or Functionalist)	Interpretive	Critical
TABLE 2-1 THREE APPROACHES TO INTERCULTURAL COMMUNICATION			
Discipline on which approach is founded	Psychology	Anthropology, sociolinguistics	Various
Research goal	Describe and predict behavior	Describe behavior	Change behavior
Assumption of reality	External and describable	Subjective	Subjective and material
Assumptions of human behavior	Predictable	Creative and voluntary	Changeable
Method of study	Survey, observation	Participant observation, field study	Textual analysis of media
Relationship of culture and communication	Communication influenced by culture	Culture created and maintained through communication	Culture a site of power struggles
Contribution of the approach	Identifies cultural variations; recognizes cultural differences in many aspects of communication but often does not consider context	Emphasizes that communication and culture and cultural differences should be studied in context	Recognizes the economic and political forces in culture and communication; asserts that all intercultural interactions are characterized by power

intercultural communication issues; however, it is important to understand the assumptions behind the scholarship that is being undertaken. Think about the strengths and weaknesses of each assumption and what each approach reveals (and also hides) about other cultures and their communication patterns.

To examine these three approaches, let us start with a situation that illustrates a communication dilemma. You may remember when you first heard about Hurricane Katrina in August 2005: how it hit Florida, strengthened over the Gulf of Mexico, and then hit Louisiana, Mississippi, and Alabama. Shortly after, another hurricane, Rita, followed, bringing devastation and human suffering to millions on the Gulf Coast. One of the hardest hit communities was New Orleans, where, in addition to the devastation of the hurricanes, there was massive flooding due to the collapse of levees built to protect the below-sea-level areas (see Figure 2-1).

The events after the hurricanes that affected the city of New Orleans provide good examples of intercultural communication interaction and offer useful insights into how we might think about intercultural communication and

TABLE 2-2 THE SIGNIFICANCE OF RESEARCH APPROACHES	
Social scientific	This research style emphasizes statistical measures. Understanding quantitative approaches is critical to analyzing data and statistics. These are skills important in any walk of life.
Interpretive	Interpretive approaches emphasize using language to describe human behavior. Understanding interpretive approaches is important to understanding how news is reported, how information is transferred, and how most people make decisions.
Critical	Critical methodologies analyze the large power structures that guide everyday life. Understanding this approach helps students to grasp the invisible forces that alter our lives.

the ways that different cultural groups understood what happened and why. In analyzing these events, we will also outline the characteristics of the three approaches to studying intercultural communication—both contributions and limitations.

So what has happened to the people of New Orleans since Katrina? Where are they now? What has happened to the ones who stayed? What happened to the ones who left? And what can we learn about intercultural communication from their experiences and the events after Katrina?

The political, economic, environmental, and social impacts of Hurricanes Katrina and Rita and the subsequent floods cannot be underestimated. First, nearly a million people were displaced from Mississippi and Louisiana (Krupa, 2009). Those who could afford to left voluntarily before Katrina hit. Those who couldn't leave were shipped to shelters, pulled from rooftops in the Lower Ninth Ward and eastern New Orleans. Many went to states nearby (Texas, Oklahoma), and others went to states far away (Utah and Connecticut) to unfamiliar cultural settings—where everything was new, thus having the added burden of being separated from the financial and social support of friends and families. About half the residents never returned. In Chapter 8, we discuss this special group of migrants and some of the factors that helped and hindered their cultural adaptation to these new cultural contexts.

For those who stayed, New Orleans is now a different place. As one journalist describes it, there is cause for both pessimism and optimism. On the one hand, there are signs that something awful happened here rather recently: "empty lots overgrown by weeds, ramshackle, leaning houses, derelict public buildings still awaiting restoration." On the other hand, there is still a spirit of optimism—some good things happened: "institutions like police and school and government administration, some corrupt, have been overhauled" (Chins up, hopes high, 2010, p. 24). The population changed somewhat; some of the poor and black left and were replaced by middle-class whites (see Point of View on p. 58), and there are still dramatic social and economic disparities. As of 2008, black and Hispanic households in the metro area earn incomes that are 45% and 25%, respectively, lower than whites (New Orleans Index at 5, 2010).

FIGURE 2-1 It may be difficult to understand the various meanings of the aftermath of Hurricane Katrina. In this photo, people are trying to make their way to safety while the National Guard comes into New Orleans. How would you study the meanings of Katrina? What kinds of questions can you ask from each paradigm? What kinds of questions can't be asked from each paradigm? (© AP Photo/Bill Haber)

social science approach See **functionalist approach.**

functionalist approach A study of intercultural communication, also called the *social science approach,* based on the assumptions that (1) there is a describable, external reality, (2) human behaviors are predictable, and (3) culture is a variable that can be measured. This approach aims to identify and explain cultural variations in communication and to predict future communication. (Compare with **critical approach** and **interpretive approach.**)

quantitative methods Research methods that use numerical indicators to capture and ascertain the relationships among variables. These methods use survey and observation.

Let's take a look at how intercultural communication researchers, from three very different approaches, might try to understand the experiences and interactions of diverse groups of people involved in the aftermath of this natural and human disaster.

The Social Science Approach

The **social science approach** (also called the **functionalist approach**), popular in the 1980s, is based on research in psychology and sociology. This approach assumes a describable external reality. It also assumes that human behavior is predictable and that the researcher's goal is to describe and predict behavior. Researchers who take this approach often use **quantitative methods,** gathering data by administering questionnaires or observing subjects firsthand.

Social science researchers assume that culture is a **variable** that can be measured. This suggests that culture influences communication in much the same way that personality traits do. The goal of this research, then, is to predict specifically how culture influences communication.

Applications   How might social science researchers understand the communication issues of those involved in Katrina's aftermath? They might measure differences in perception among various cultural groups to try to understand how different cultures experienced Katrina and what they view as appropriate and inappropriate responses by the government. In this type of study, social scientists would be using culture as a variable to measure these differences while focusing on the perceptions that are widely held in a particular culture. For example, they might try to measure how African Americans and whites viewed the government response. One such study hypothesized that blacks would hold the government more responsible for the human tragedy that followed Hurricane Katrina than whites. And that blacks would hold the residents of New Orleans less responsible than whites. These researchers conducted an experimental study with a representative sample of the adult U.S. population in which they polled 250 black and 250 white respondents; they found their hypotheses were confirmed (Ben-Porath & Shaker, 2010). Based on these differences, social scientists might then try to predict how these different views may influence future differences in political views and conflicts between these groups.

Or social scientists might study what kinds of communication media people used after the hurricane and how they used them. One study found that "television, and cable news channels in particular, are the main sources of news for most Americans during a crisis, and that was again the case for Hurricane Katrina" (Kohut et al., 2005, p. 7). CNN was most cited as the main source of their news at 31%, whereas newspapers, radio, and the Internet all fell in the ratings compared to their use in more normal circumstances. Two-thirds gave favorable ratings of the media coverage that "is considerably more favorable than the public's ratings a year ago for press coverage of the presidential election campaign" (p. 7). This kind of study tries to see trends in communication usage and can then predict that people will again turn to cable television, particularly CNN, for news when a similar crisis situation emerges.

Other contemporary research programs illustrate the social science approach. One such program was headed by William Gudykunst, a leading communication researcher. Gudykunst was interested in whether people from different cultures varied in their strategies for reducing uncertainty on first encounter. He found that strategies varied depending on whether people were from **individualistic** or **collectivistic** cultures (Gudykunst, 1985, 1988). For example, many people in the United States, which has an individualistic orientation, ask direct questions when interacting with acquaintances. In cultures with a more collectivistic orientation, such as Japan and China, people are more likely to use an indirect approach.

Social scientists are interested in predicting human behavior, and each of these theories tries to predict intercultural communication interaction by emphasizing different aspects of the process, as well as different points in the process. In focusing on initial encounters with others, Gudykunst (1998, 2005b)

variable A concept that varies by existing in different types or different amounts and that can be operationalized and measured.

individualistic The tendency to emphasize individual identities, beliefs, needs, goals, and views rather than those of the group. (Compare with **collectivistic.**)

collectivistic The tendency to focus on the goals, needs, and views of the ingroup rather than individuals' own goals, needs, and views. (Compare with **individualistic.**)

anxiety uncertainty management theory The view that the reduction of anxiety and uncertainty plays an important role in successful intercultural communication, particularly when experiencing new cultures.

face negotiation theory The view that cultural groups vary in preferences for conflict styles and face-saving strategies.

later extended his theory to include the element of anxiety and mindfulness in the **anxiety uncertainty management** (AUM) **theory,** which explains the role of anxiety and uncertainty in individuals' communicating with host culture members when they enter a new culture. The theory suggests certain optimal levels of uncertainty and anxiety motivate individuals to engage in successful interaction. This theory is explained further in Chapter 8.

A related social science program is Stella Ting-Toomey's (1985, 2005) **face negotiation theory.** *Face* is the sense of favorable self-worth, and in all cultures people are concerned about saving face. Ting-Toomey suggests that conflict is a face negotiation process in which people often have their face threatened or questioned. She and her colleagues have conducted a number of studies in which they try to identify how cultures differ in conflict style and face concerns. For example, they found that members of individualistic societies like the United States are concerned with saving their own face in conflict situations and so use more dominating conflict resolution styles. In contrast, members of collectivistic cultures, like China, South Korea, and Taiwan, are more concerned with saving the other person's face in conflict situations and use more avoiding, obliging, or integrating conflict resolution styles (Ting-Toomey et al., 1991; Ting-Toomey, 2005). Some recent research shows that Latino and Asian Americans in the United States use more avoiding and third-party conflict styles than African Americans and more than do European Americans (Ting-Toomey, Yee-Jung, Shapiro, Garcia, Wright, & Oetzel, 2000).

conversational constraints theory The view that cultural groups vary in their fundamental concerns regarding how conversational messages should be constructed.

Another social science research program focuses on cultural differences in conversational strategies. In contrast to AUM, **conversational constraints theory,** developed by Min-Sun Kim (2005), attempts to explain how and why people make particular conversational choices. It suggests five universal conversational constraints, or concerns: (1) clarity, (2) minimizing imposition, (3) consideration for the other's feelings, (4) risking negative evaluation by the hearer, and (5) effectiveness. Kim and her colleagues have discovered that people from individualistic and collectivistic cultures place varying importance on these various conversational concerns. Individualists seem to be most concerned with clarity; collectivists, with concerns about hurting the other's feelings and minimizing imposition. Concerns for effectiveness and avoidance of negative evaluation by others seem to be universally important (Kim, 1994, 2005).

communication accommodation theory The view that individuals adjust their verbal communication to facilitate understanding.

The **communication accommodation theory** is the result of another social science program in which researchers attempted to identify how and when individuals accommodate their speech and nonverbal behavior to others during an interaction. Unlike AUM and conversational constraints theory, communication accommodation theory focuses on adaptation during intercultural interaction. The researchers posited that in some situations individuals change their communication patterns to accommodate others (Gallois, Ogay, & Giles, 2005). Specifically, individuals are likely to adapt during low-threat interactions or situations in which they see little difference between themselves and others. The underlying assumption is that we accommodate when we feel positive toward the other person. For example, when we talk to international students, we may speak more slowly, enunciate more clearly, use less jargon, and mirror their communication. We also may adapt to regional speech. For example, when Tom talks with someone from the South, he sometimes starts to drawl and use words like "y'all." Of course, it is possible to overaccommodate. For example, if a white American speaks black English to an African American, this may be perceived as overaccommodation.

The **diffusion of innovations theory**, developed by communication scholar Everett Rogers (2003), explains how cultural practices can be changed—largely due to communication. This theory explains why some innovations, like computer technology or the Internet, or certain behaviors, like "safe sex," are accepted by some people and rejected by others. The theory posits that in order for people to accept a new technology, they have to see the usefulness of it and it has to be compatible with their values and lifestyle. Communication also plays a key role; usually people first learn of innovations through impersonal channels—like mass media—but only decide to adopt an innovation later, after asking the opinion or observing the behavior of someone who is known, trusted, or considered an expert—an "opinion leader." If people important to the individual (e.g., peers for adolescents) adopt the innovation first, then the individual is more likely to adopt it. Opinion leaders can also be responsible for innovations *not* diffusing, if they ignore or speak out against an innovation. There seems to be a predictable, over-time pattern for the spread of an innovation, first to early adopters and then to many more individuals (Singhal & Dearing, 2006).

> **diffusion of innovations theory** The view that communication and relationships play important roles in how new ideas are adopted (or not) by individuals and groups.

Many social science studies explain how communication styles vary from culture to culture. Dean Barnlund (Barnlund & Yoshioka, 1990), a well-known intercultural communication scholar, compared Japanese and U.S. communication styles. He identified many differences, including how members of the two groups give compliments and offer apologies. Although people in both countries seem to prefer a simple apology, U.S. Americans tend to apologize (and compliment) more often; further, Japanese prefer to *do* something, whereas Americans tend to *explain* as a way to apologize.

Another group of social science studies investigated how travelers adapted overseas. In trying to predict which travelers would be the most successful, the researchers found that a variety of factors—including age, gender, language, preparation level, and personality characteristics—played a role (Kim, 2001).

Strengths and Limitations   Many of these social science studies have been useful in identifying variations in communication from group to group and specifying psychological and sociological variables in the communication process. However, this approach is limited. Many scholars now realize that human communication is often more creative than predictable and that reality is not just external but also internally constructed. We cannot identify all of the variables that affect our communication. Nor can we predict exactly why one intercultural interaction seems to succeed and another does not.

Scholars also recognize that some methods in this approach are not culturally sensitive and that researchers may be too distant from the phenomena or

POINT *of* VIEW

THE DISNEYFICATION OF NEW ORLEANS

In an article published several years after Katrina, journalist Ann Hartnell describes one important negative consequence of the New Orleans rebuilding program. As you read the account, think about the implications for intercultural communications between poor and middle class, whites and blacks in New Orleans.

In her article, Ms. Hartnell acknowledges that the city leaders have made great strides in bringing back important tourist dollars to New Orleans and continue to make strides to revitalize and rebound from the devastating economic and social impact of Katrina. She goes on to say that while many of the white evacuees have returned to their homes in New Orleans, many of the black residents have yet to return, and may never do so.

She suggests that the reason for this is because many have no homes to return to and probably never will—thanks to the combined efforts of developers and city administrators—who have sacrificed affordable housing in favor of new tourist facilities and venues:

> The authorities are quietly doing away with the city's remaining stocks of affordable housing in moves that the UN has recently claimed constitute human rights violations. The fact that these demolitions will overwhelmingly affect black people has led some to call this ethnic cleansing.

To make it worse, she says, they are also phasing out some parts of the public transportation system and public health facilities that have supported the existence of low-income residents in New Orleans for decades.

Hartnell claims that race and class stereotypes have paved the way for New Orleans' so-called revitalization and attributes the lack of concern to the negative portrayal of the poor African American victims by media and politicians, during and after the crisis:

people they are researching. In other words, researchers may not really understand the cultural groups they are studying. For example, suppose we conducted a study that compared self-disclosure in the United States and Algeria using the social science perspective. We might distribute Jourard's self-disclosure measure (a common instrument used in U.S. research) to students in both countries. However, we might not realize that the concept of self-disclosure does not translate exactly between the United States and Algeria, and that Algerians and U.S. Americans have different notions of this concept.

To overcome these kinds of problems, social scientists have developed strategies for achieving equivalence of measures. A leading cross-cultural psychologist, Richard Brislin (1999), has written extensively on guidelines for cross-cultural researchers. He has identified several types of equivalencies that researchers should establish, including **translation equivalence** and **conceptual equivalence**. For example, in cross-cultural studies, literal

translation equivalence
The linguistic sameness that is gained after translating and back-translating research materials several times using different translators. (See also **conceptual equivalence**.)

conceptual equivalence
The similarity of linguistic terms and meanings across cultures. (See also **translation equivalence**.)

58

News reports did focus on the government's apparent abandonment of its own people, but a hysterical and arguably racist undercurrent was almost compulsively drawn to rumors of rape and murder—nearly all of which turned out to be untrue.

And politicians were clear about how they wanted to see the future of New Orleans:

"We finally cleaned up public housing in New Orleans," declared Republican congressman Richard Baker soon after the storm. "We couldn't do it. But God did." Alphonso Jackson, the then US secretary of housing and urban development, made the racial implications of the gentrification process perfectly clear when he predicted that the reconstructed New Orleans would be a whiter city.

"We don't need soap opera-watchers right now," claimed the city council president, Oliver Thomas—perpetuating the view that New Orleans' high unemployment rate can be tracked to individual laziness as opposed to the systemic discrimination affecting most of America's inner cities. At the same time, those same forces that demonize poor and particularly black families—for their apparent "dysfunction"—are actively preventing the regrouping of some of the most close-knit black communities in the US.

Hartnell describes how some of these displaced residents, both black and white, are calling for the "right of return"—a grassroots organized protest against the city's controversial reconstruction program, and concludes:

What's certain is that the longer the world looks away, the more likely it is that a Disneyfied "new" New Orleans will mean the loss of a city that boasts one of the most complex cultural heritages in the world.

Source: A. Hartnell, "The Disneyfication of New Orleans," *guardian.co.uk*, August 28, 2008. Retrieved May 7, 2011, from www.guardian.co.uk/commentisfree/2008/aug/28/usa.hurricanekatrina.

translations are inadequate. To establish translation equivalence, research materials should be translated several times, using different translators. Materials that proceed smoothly through these multiple steps are considered translation equivalent.

In Chapter 6, we explore issues of translation in more detail; however, the advances in machine translation have been impressive. While computer translation cannot yet match human translators, machine translation has vastly improved. The European Union has been a major force behind these improvements, as well as in the goals of machine translation:

Machine translation has been an elusive goal since the earliest days of computer science. The Pentagon poured millions of dollars into efforts to get computers to translate Russian sentences into English. But disillusionment set in in the 1960s when it became clear that producing results indistinguishable from a human

interpretive approach An approach to intercultural communication that aims to understand and describe human behavior within specific cultural groups based on the assumptions that (1) human experience is subjective, (2) human behavior is creative rather than determined or easily predicted, and (3) culture is created and maintained through communication. (Compare with **critical approach** and **functionalist approach.**)

ethnography A discipline that examines the patterned interactions and significant symbols of specific cultural groups to identify the cultural norms that guide their behaviors, usually based on field studies.

qualitative methods Research methods that attempt to capture people's own meanings for their everyday behavior in specific contexts. These methods use participant observation and field studies.

participant observation A research method where investigators interact extensively with the cultural group being studied.

rhetorical approach A research method, dating back to ancient Greece, in which scholars try to interpret the meanings or persuasion used in texts or oral discourses in the contexts in which they occur.

translator wasn't going to happen soon, if ever. The major obstacles were not computational but linguistic. The missing ingredient was a fuller understanding of language itself.

That is still true. But computational linguists are nowadays making greater strides by being less ambitious. (Mark my words, 2007)

Machine translation can be enormously helpful for common phrases and rough drafts, but these translations cannot yet do away with humans. Advances are being made rapidly and, as the databases increase, the computer-generated translations will improve.

Researchers can establish conceptual equivalence by ensuring that the notions they are investigating are similar at various levels. For example, problem solving is one aspect of intelligence that may be conceptually equivalent in many cultures. Once this equivalence is established, researchers can identify culture-specific ways in which problem solving is achieved. In the United States and western Europe, good problem solving might mean quick cognitive reasoning; in other cultures, it might involve slow and careful thought (Serpell, 1982). Establishing these equivalencies allows researchers to isolate and describe what distinguishes one culture from another.

The Interpretive Approach

The **interpretive approach** gained prominence in the late 1980s among communication scholars. One interpretive approach, rooted in sociolinguistics, is the **ethnography** of communication (Hymes, 1974). Ethnographers of communication are devoted to descriptive studies of communication patterns within specific cultural groups. Interpretive researchers assume not only that reality is external to humans but also that humans construct reality. They believe that human experience, including communication, is subjective and human behavior is neither predetermined nor easily predicted.

The goal of interpretive research is to understand and describe human behavior. (Predicting behavior is not a goal.) Whereas the social scientist tends to see communication as influenced by culture, the interpretivist sees culture as created and maintained through communication (Carbaugh, 1996). This type of research uses **qualitative methods** derived from anthropology and linguistics such as field studies, observations, and participant observations. An example is shown in Figure 2-2. (A researcher engaging in **participant observation** contributes actively to the communication processes being observed and studied. The researcher thus is intimately involved in the research and may become good friends with members of the communities he or she is studying.)

Another example of interpretive research is the **rhetorical approach**, perhaps the oldest communication scholarship, dating back to the ancient Greeks. Rhetoricians typically examine and analyze texts or public speeches in the contexts in which they occur.

Cross-cultural psychologists use the terms **etic** and **emic** to distinguish the social science and interpretive approaches (Berry, 1997). These terms were

FIGURE 2-2 One way to study and learn about cultural patterns is to interview other people, which is this woman's approach. What are the strengths and weaknesses of interviewing as a research strategy? (© *Digital Vision/Alamy*)

borrowed from linguistics—*etic* from *phonetic* and *emic* from *phonemic*. Social science research usually searches for universal generalizations and studies cultures objectively, with an "outsider's" view; in this way, it is "etic." In contrast, interpretive research usually focuses on understanding phenomena subjectively, from within a particular cultural community or context; in this way, it is "emic." These researchers try to describe patterns or rules that individuals follow in specific contexts. They tend to be more interested in describing cultural behavior in one community than in making cross-cultural comparisons.

Applications How might an interpretive researcher investigate the various meanings given to the hurricane events? One possible approach would be to interview people who were in the Gulf Coast and experienced the hurricane, as well as those people who watched the media coverage but did not live in the affected areas. From these interviews, as well as conversations with others, the researcher might gain insight into a variety of potential responses. For example, in the weeks after Katrina, many of the people from the Gulf Coast were evacuated across the nation. An interpretive researcher might interview them about their experiences and their adaptation to their new environment. One reporter noted, "'The people are so nice, but this place is really strange to me,' said Desiree Thompson, who arrived in Albuquerque last Sunday with six of her children and two grandchildren, along with about 100 other evacuees. 'The air is different. My

etic A term stemming from *phonetic*. The etic inquiry searches for universal generalizations across cultures from a distance. (Compare with **emic.**)

emic A term stemming from *phonemic*. The emic way of inquiry focuses on understanding communication patterns from inside a particular cultural community or context. (Compare with **etic.**)

I think that, as Americans, we should always try to help others, such as those suffering from natural disasters. If we don't, who will? Some might ask, "Why should we help other countries if they haven't helped us in any way?" This sort of questioning is wrong—we always need to do the right thing. If one day we are in a dire situation, hopefully these countries will do what they can to help us.
      —Arielle

I was surprised that more people didn't leave New Orleans before the hurricane. After all, they know that their city is below sea level. I know that some of them are poor, but I don't think it's fair to blame FEMA for the hurricane. If you choose to live in a city like that, you have to be prepared for Mother Nature.
      —Debra

Hurricane Katrina shows how much poverty still exists in the richest country in the world. While we see rich people on television all the time, we can overlook the poverty and the racism in this country. I hope that we do not forget that there are many poor African Americans in the United States and our responsibilities to all of our citizens.
      —Brent

nose feels all dry. The only thing I've seen that looks familiar is the McDonald's'" (Egan, 2005, pp. A1, A32). Many had to decide if they wished to stay or move on, but the adaptation issues they face could be explored by an interpretive researcher to see how they make sense of their new environments, environmental differences as well as demographic differences.

Other interpretive researchers may want to focus on the rich oral culture of Louisiana and interview many who experienced Hurricane Katrina and/or Rita. One reporter after talking to survivors writes, "The disaster was incremental rather than cataclysmic. Instead of a crystalline moment of memory, there are infinite numbers, each with its own marker: a long journey, a recurring noise, the last words of a dear relative. Depending on where people were, what decisions they made in the blur of the crisis and how the authorities responded, every portrait of the storm is different, like a jigsaw puzzle in which no two pieces are alike" (Johnson, 2005, p. A25).

One interesting study analyzed the rhetorical style of New Orleans Mayor Ray Nagin in the aftermath of Hurricane Katrina. What do you think public leaders would need to communicate to their citizens after horrific natural or human disasters? Communication scholars Griffin-Padgett and Allison (2010) answer this question with "restorative rhetoric." They suggest that the communication of any leader, faced with situations of natural disaster, or even acts of terrorism, needs to focus on the substantive issues of repair, recovery, rebuilding, and helping victims to make sense of what has occurred and to envision a new reality (p. 377). Through their rhetorical analysis, they show how Nagin's speeches successfully followed the five steps in restorative rhetoric:

1. The initial reaction must include a *definition* of the situation, an *assertion* of a level of control over the damage, and a sincere *expression* of sorrow. Nagin included a mixture of frustration at the slow response of the federal government and even bragged that his administration was in control of the situation.

2. The second phase, *assessment* of the *crisis*, needs to include an assessment of damage, and a statement of the immediate needs and other resources to fuel the management of the situation. Nagin did this when he reported the evacuation plan and spoke favorably of the relocations efforts of the thousands of effected residents.

3. The third element deals with *issues of blame, accountability, and responsibility*. Also included here are historical factors that may have contributed to the disaster. Nagin noted that the president and governor took some responsibility for the failed response, but placed blame squarely on the national and state governments—he said his failure was that he "didn't scream a little bit earlier" (p. 387). He also noted that issues of race and social class played a role.

4. After blame is established, the fourth category is where leaders must *show the way toward healing and forgiveness*. The problem for Nagin was that many of the victims lacked any trust in their leaders after their failed responses. Nagin admitted this in public appearances and tried to encourage the residents of New Orleans, assuring them that together they would "get through this okay" (p. 388).

5. The fifth and final element is *rebuilding*, but not just showing a plan for physical structures; it involves establishing a rhetorical vision for a new state of existence. Nagin did this by telling residents that he was optimistic about the "rebirth" of New Orleans and focused on specific building plans—a plan to change housing codes to improve overall home designs and economic development plans, including a casino district downtown financed by tax incentives.

Some interpretive studies investigate the language patterns in many different groups—from the Burundi in Africa, to the Athabascan in northern Canada, to various groups within the United States, such as urban blacks or Cajuns. Other interpretive studies investigate the different communication patterns of one cultural group. For example, communication scholar Gerry Philipsen (1990) studied communication patterns in a white working-class neighborhood of Chicago called Teamsterville. Philipsen discovered that men in this community consider speaking to be important only in some situations. For example, Teamsterville men speak when expressing male solidarity but not when asserting power and influence in interpersonal situations. That is, they are more likely to talk when they are with their equals—their buddies—than when they are with their children or with authority figures. With superiors or subordinates, other forms of communication are appropriate. With children, for example, they are more likely to use gestures or disciplinary action than speech. When they

Communication scholar Ross Louis, a resident of New Orleans, recently described, in an autoethnography, his own (and many other residents') experiences in the aftermath of Katrina as they sought to reestablished their "citizenship" identities. Can you think of other ways that people can resist and recover from damaging language used against them?

Louis begins his essay describing the damaging effect of the labels and terms used to talk about the victims of Katrina and the effect these labels had on the residents' identities. One label that was resisted and rejected by many victims was "refugee." They felt that the term questioned their very citizenship and conjured up images of foreign people fleeing to other countries. As Louis describes it:

> *The media construction was painful enough ("the dirty, poor, inarticulate, faceless population too stupid to heed the dictates of the powerful"), but to describe New Orleanians as refugees implied a deficit of citizenship, both national and local. (p. 283)*

He then goes on to describe the various "performances" of residents in their attempt to reestablish, reclaim, and prove their citizenship—some humorous, some poignant, some in-your-face. For example, there were those who danced and sang in the Superdome in the middle of the horror; there were others who performed tongue-in cheek demonstrations in the next Mardi Gras parade. Louis himself marched with his family, "pushing a stolen grocery cart refashioned as a brown United Postal Service truck that mocked FEMA's Michael Brown. It read, 'United Bullshit Service: What Did Brown Do For You?'" (p. 285). His children wore brown UPS uniforms and handed out Lil' Debbie brownie snack cakes.

The final performance Louis described took place during the first post-Katrina game played in the Superdome, a fitting site, as this was the place where the Katrina "refugees" were symbolically stripped of their citizenship while waiting for the 828 evacuation buses September 1–3, 2005. Louis describes the excitement at the Superdome before the game even started—everyone in his section

> *standing, waiting it seemed for some sort of signal, but what would it bring? Reclamation? Reinstatement? Renaming? Already the crowd noise made it too loud to be heard without screaming, and so we met those around us by yelling back and forth, in several cases sharing Katrina stories. (p. 290)*

Source: R. Louis, "Reclaiming a Citizenship Site: Performing New Orleans in the Superdome," *Text and Performance Quarterly*, 29(3) (2009), pp. 279–295.

are with someone of higher status, such as a school principal, they may seek out a mediator (e.g., the neighborhood priest) rather than speak directly to the principal.

In more recent ethnography of communication studies, Donal Carbaugh (1999) describes the important role of silence and listening in Blackfeet (American Indian) communication; Carbaugh and Berry (2001) describe the tendency of

Finns to be rather reserved in communication. More importantly, they show how these communication patterns are inextricably tied to cultural identities in these communities (Carbaugh, 1996).

A number of interpretive scholars have emphasized that descriptions of the communication rules of a given people must be grounded in their beliefs and values. Most scholarly studies of communication are rooted in a European American perspective, and this frame of references is not necessarily applicable to communication of all cultural groups. For example, Molefi Asante (1987, 2001) developed the framework of **Afrocentricity** to apply to studies about African or African American communication. He identifies five cultural themes shared by peoples of African descent:

Afrocentricity An orientation toward African or African American cultural standards, including beliefs and values, as the criteria for interpreting behaviors and attitudes.

- A common origin and experience of struggle
- An element of resistance to European legal procedures, medical practices, and political processes
- Traditional values of humaneness and harmony with nature
- A fundamentally African way of knowing and interpreting the world
- An orientation toward communalism

Communication scholars have used this framework to understand various aspects of contemporary African American communication. For example, Thurmon Garner (1994) stresses the strong oral tradition of African Americans and identifies rhetorical patterns such as indirection, improvisation and inventiveness, and playfully toned behavior. These patterns underlay communication in many African American contexts, including rapping, playing the dozens (an aggressive verbal contest, often involving obscene language), and signifying (the verbal art of insult, in which a speaker jokingly talks about, needles, and puts down the listener).

Similarly, Asian scholars have developed Asiacentric frameworks to study communication of people from Asian cultures. Communication scholar Yoshitaka Miike (2003, 2004) has identified five Asiacentric themes (circularity, harmony, other-directedness, reciprocity, and relationality). Based on these themes, he developed five propositions on human communication. Communication is a process in which

- We remind ourselves of the interdependence and interrelatedness of the universe.
- We reduce our selfishness and egocentrism.
- We feel the joy and suffering of all beings.
- We receive and return our debts to all beings.
- We moralize and harmonize the universe.

From this Asiacentric framework, other scholars are developing specific communication theories, for example, a Chinese model of human relationship development (Chen, 1998) and a Buddhist consciousness-only model of intrapersonal communication (Ishii, 2004).

It is important to remember that scholars like Asante and Miike are not suggesting that these culture-specific frameworks are superior or should replace the traditional Eurocentric models, only that that they are not inferior.

Another important interpretive theory, a communication theory of identity, was developed by Michael Hecht (1993). He argues that communication is a communicative process and our identities emerge in relationships with others and are expressed in core symbols, meaning, and labels. He also contends there are four identity frames: personal, enacted, relational, and communal. These frames help us interpret reality and understand the social world. We discuss this theory further in Chapter 5.

Several scholars have used this framework to understand the identities of various cultural groups. For example, Mark Orbe (2004) conducted a recent study investigating how first-generation college students negotiated this identity—using the four frames in Hecht's identity theory. Through interviewing the students, he discovered that their identities as first-generation college students clearly emerged as personal (in the pressure to succeed and in the economic hardships they experienced), enacted, and relational (in their experiences with friends and families, who often give them special attention). However, they did not seem to develop a communal identity—they did not really know or interact with other groups of first-generation college students.

In a related study, Saskia Witteborn (2004) used this theory to understand how some Arab women changed the expression of their identity after 9/11. Through extensive interviews, she found that before September 11, the women referred to themselves mainly with their communal identities as Arab, Palestinian, or Arab American. And one of the core symbols related to this communal label was family. After September 11, the women emphasized their national identities, and the core symbol of family was expanded to include social relationships in a community organization.

Strengths and Limitations   The utility of the interpretivist approach is that it provides an in-depth understanding of communication patterns in particular communities because it emphasizes investigating communication in context. Thus, for example, we learn more about African American communication in religious contexts and more about popular U.S. communication in talk show contexts than we would by distributing questionnaires with general questions on African American or European American communication.

The main limitation of this approach is that there are few interpretivist studies of *intercultural* communication. Interpretive scholars typically have not studied what happens when two groups come in contact with each other. However, there are some comparative studies, including Charles Braithwaite's (1990), which compares rules for silence in 15 different communities, and Hammer and Rogan's (2002) study comparing how Latino and Indochinese view and negotiate conflict with law enforcement officers.

A second limitation is that the researchers often are outsiders to the communities under investigation, which means they may not represent accurately the communication patterns of members of that community. For example, Fred Jandt and Dolores Tanno (2001) recount the dilemma of many marginalized cultural groups who have been studied by outsiders who characterize the group rather erroneously and negatively. A number of scholars, members of these groups, are now trying to rewrite these cultural descriptions. One of these is Tuhiwai Smith (1999), a Maori scholar, who lists the words used to describe her people in anthropological accounts: not civilized, not literate, incapable of inventing, creating, or imagining, and not fully human. After analyzing the impact of these negative labels, she makes arguments for insider research and develops an indigenous research agenda and process—part of a movement by peoples throughout the world who have too long been explained by outsiders and have been offered no opportunity to explain themselves. One of her contributions is a Maori-based code of conduct for ethnographic researchers:

- A respect for people
- Presenting yourself face-to-face
- Look, listen . . . speak
- Share and host people, be generous
- Do not flaunt your knowledge

Jandt and Tanno conclude that this ethical code should apply to all those who study groups of people who traditionally have been the object of study rather than participants in research.

The Critical Approach

A third approach to the study of intercultural communication includes many assumptions of the interpretive approach. For instance, researchers who use the **critical approach** believe in subjective (as opposed to objective) and material reality. They also emphasize the importance of studying the context in which communication occurs—that is, the situation, background, or environment. However, critical researchers usually focus on **macrocontexts,** such as the political and social structures that influence communication. Critical scholars, unlike most social scientists and interpretivists, are interested in the historical context of communication (Delgado, 2002; Putnam & Pacanowsky, 1983). (See Figure 2-3.)

Critical scholars are interested in the power relations in communication. For them, identifying cultural differences in communication is important only in relation to power differentials. In this perspective, culture is, in essence, a battleground—a plan where multiple interpretations come together but a dominant force always prevails. The goal of critical researchers is not only to understand human behavior but also to change the lives of everyday communicators. Researchers assume that by examining and reporting how power functions in cultural situations, they can help the average person learn how to resist forces of power and oppression.

critical approach A metatheoretical approach that includes many assumptions of the interpretive approach but that focuses more on macrocontexts, such as the political and social structures that influence communication. (Compare with **interpretive approach** and **functionalist approach.**)

macrocontexts The political, social, and historical situations, backgrounds, and environments that influence communication.

FIGURE 2-3   This photo of Louisiana Governor Kathleen Blanco (left) and FEMA director Michael Brown (right) highlights the importance of communication in helping to shape our understanding of the response to Hurricane Katrina. How might each of the paradigms study these communication messages and their influence in shaping the response to Hurricane Katrina? (© *Jocelyn Augustino/epa/Corbis*)

textual analysis Examination of cultural texts such as media—television, movies, journalistic essays, and so on.

The methods preferred by critical scholars are usually **textual analyses,** which sometimes occur within the economic contexts of the culture industries that produce these texts. That is, the scholars generally analyze cultural "products," such as media (television, movies, journals, and so on), as powerful voices in shaping contemporary culture, rather than observing or participating in face-to-face interactions or conducting surveys.

Applications   In analyzing the aftermath of the hurricanes that swept the Gulf Coast, a critical scholar might try to situate the attacks within a larger cultural struggle that has a much longer history than simply the hurricanes that roared through the Gulf. A critical scholar would want to understand the larger political cultural and economic contexts of the disaster that created such havoc. The victims had no part in creating the horrible storm nor the failure of the levees, but what is interesting to intercultural communication scholars is that the effects and aftermath of the storms were experienced differently depending on race and socioeconomic status.

As you remember, most of the people who had the means (money and private transportation) left New Orleans ahead of the storm. "By the time Katrina struck, almost all the extreme poverty neighborhoods in New Orleans were predominantly black and these racially and economically segregated areas bore the brunt of the disaster" (Fussell, Sastry, & VanLandingham, 2010, p. 22). To be

more specific, about half of the city's white residents experienced serious flooding compared with three quarters of black residents (Brazile, 2006). Because
blacks tended to live in areas that experienced more flooding, they experienced
more housing damage, which delayed their return to the city. How do you think
these experiences of the different social and economic groups would affect their
perceptions of each other and their interactions with each other in the months
and years after the disaster?

Thrust on to the world stage, the international image of the United States
was up for discussion. The British Broadcasting Corporation wondered why, in
this time of need, did the food donations from Britain, France, Germany, Russia,
and Spain get turned down because of U.S. legalities ("Why Was UK's Katrina
Aid Rejected by the US?," 2005).

At the same time, however, *The New York Times* offered a different view from
Paris: "The French news media were captivated by Hurricane Katrina, pointing
out how the American government's faltering response brought into plain view
the sad lot of black Americans. But this time the French, who have long criticized
America's racism, could not overlook the parallels at home" (Tagliabue, 2005,
p. A4). In light of the riots that broke out in the fall of 2005, a *The New York Times*
writer noted: "Just two months ago, the French watched in horrified fascination
at the anarchy of New Orleans, where members of America's underclass were
seen looting stores and defying the police in the wake of Hurricane Katrina.
Last week, as rioters torched cars and trashed businesses in the immigrant-
concentrated suburbs of Paris, the images of wild gangs of young men silhou-
etted against the yellow flames of burning cars came as an unwelcome reminder
for France that it has its own growing underclass" (C. S. Smith, 2005, sec. 4, p. 3).
Thus, the struggle over the image of each nation is, in part, fought out in the
press.

A critical scholar might also look at the struggle over the maintenance
of Creole culture that has lost its geographical base: "The Creoles have been
more distinctly connected to a place—New Orleans—than perhaps any other
American ethnic group but their rural Louisiana neighbors, the Cajuns. But
unlike the Cajuns, who settled in Louisiana after being expelled from Canada by
the British, the Creoles lived in the birthplace of their culture" (Saulny, 2005).
Some people fear the loss of this cultural identity after the hurricane dispersed
them across the nation. Others predict that this dispersal will make them stronger. By watching how they rebuild their cultural community, what communication media they use, and what resources and barriers they encounter, a critical
scholar can situate the rebirth of this cultural community within the larger
social structure of the United States. A critical scholar might ask if the pressure
from other U.S. Americans and institutions to assimilate will overwhelm their
attempts to hang on to their unique culture.

Similarly, a critical scholar might focus on how different cultural groups are
responding to Hurricanes Katrina and Rita by looking at the ways that different media are covering Katrina. The anger in the African American news is very
clear in the editorial pages. For example, *Amsterdam News,* an African American newspaper in New York City, wrote, "We will be told again that this has

> *I think 9/11 is an intercultural issue because what happens in Jerusalem (Palestine) is actually the real definition of terrorism. But people from the West (i.e., the U.S., Canada) don't admit that, and the citizens of those countries don't know what's going on in the outside world. They claim that all Arabs are terrorists, but they don't take a minute to discover the truth. Also, in the news, you don't see what actually is going on in the Middle East, and this is just not fair to the Arab communities around the world.*
> —Mohammad

nothing to do with race or economic circumstance, but by an accident of history. Black Americans, white Americans who have a vision about what America is to become, should not allow this big lie to sit there like a 'Raisin in the Sun.' Black people know that there is little regard for them and for their lives here in America" (Tatum, 2005).

Asian Week, an Asian American newspaper, focused on the "tens of thousands [of Vietnamese Americans who] lived along the Louisiana and Mississippi coasts. Most of them worked in shrimping, shipbuilding and operating convenience stores" (Tang, 2005). This newspaper focused on the stories of these Asian Americans and their plans to rebuild.

Likewise, *The Advocate*, a gay and lesbian newsmagazine, noted, "Thousands of other gay men and lesbians say they owe it to the city to return. It's not an easy choice. Many New Orleans residents, especially those in lower income brackets, will likely never come back. [. . .] For more than a century this has been their town. Since the early 1800s New Orleans welcomes those with same-sex attractions into a sea of fabulous architecture, boozy decadent affairs, outrageous parades, fabulous costumes, and gender-bending" (Hernandez, 2005, p. 43). The emphasis on returning and rebuilding is emphasized in this report because of the importance of New Orleans' gay history, its community, and the commitment of the people.

Critical communication scholars were also interested in how New Orleans citizens, particularly the minority and poor populations, were viewed and described by politicians and news media. One study by communication scholar Hemant Shah (2009) analyzed conservative commentary from the highest-circulation daily newspapers and leading commentators to see how they talked about the black and poor victims of Katrina. Based on this analysis, Shah concludes that the overall theme in the description of these victims was of "irrationality" with three specific themes: (1) Black residents were described as a *different breed*, with the commentary usually accompanied by visual illustrations of actual violence and looting. One journalist wrote, "these loathsome creatures have filled industrial-size garbage bags with clothes and jewels and floated them down the street." Another lamented that these people "chose the law of the jungle over the rule of law" (p. 9). According to Shah, this language, typically reserved for animals, conjures up images of blacks as genetically inferior, the "savage negro," and implies black inferiority as an eternal and permanent condition (p. 9).

(2) The victims in the conservative commentaries are also portrayed as *socially flawed* (stupid, immoral, irresponsible, with a tendency toward violence). The descriptions invite comparisons of the supposedly irrational blacks with the rational established (white) community. As one commentator described the situation after Katrina, "hundreds of young men who should have taken charge in helping the aged, the sick and the women with babies . . . took to the streets to shoot, loot and rape" (p. 10).

(3) Finally, according to Shah (2009), those stuck in the floodwaters were also portrayed by conservative commentators as *unworthy victims*—unworthy of sympathy because they were not rational enough to leave town. One commentator said that, in fact, some didn't want to be rescued "because they were looting anything and everything they could carry" (p. 11). These descriptions would lead some readers to wonder why white America should help. Shah then shows how the description of poor blacks as irrational has a long history in American discourse and popular culture and that this irrationality is seen as related to violence, sexual aggression, and immorality—a threat to society at large. He concludes that these views also have real consequences—that it was these attitudes that contributed to the failure of government to respond and for the society at large to soon turn away from the problems and needs of the Katrina survivors.

Another ethnographic study, which shows the impact of the media portrayal of Katrina victims, reports a discussion about race relations that took place in an intercultural communication classroom. According to the author, communication professor Jennifer Simpson, her students were discussing the events of Katrina and the broken levees and one of the white students stated, "I'm not sure why so many people had to steal stuff." An African American student responded, "What you call looting, I call surviving. People took water, shoes, and food because that's what they needed." The discussion continues with various opinions ("Yeah, but the media showed pictures of people taking televisions and stereos, you can't eat TVs," and the response "You can sell them, and buy food with the money.") The discussion continues and a white student then asks, "What do they think of us, white people?" and a black student responds, "We think of you as white devils" and elaborates on some of the resentments held by blacks toward whites in the United States.

Simpson uses this exchange as the foundation for an examination of how race operates among individuals and institutions and how individuals like these students can "see" and acknowledge each other as individuals in discussions of race in U.S. classrooms. She notes that the students managed to get through the discussion and even seemed surprised that they could have such an intense, honest discussion and survive. She wonders how we can have productive discussions about race and asks: What happens when caring about ideas and caring about ourselves and each other come together? She explores the notion that there was "misrecognition" on both sides—*neither* seeing or understanding what the other saw—and that this misrecognition is always problematic; when related to race, however, it is clearly bound up with politics and power. She also suggests that the mainstream media's misnaming of African Americans as "looters" probably influenced the students' efforts to delegitimize the victims' actions, to see them as criminals rather than victims.

Taken together, these various viewpoints emphasize how different cultural groups are dealing with Hurricane Katrina, what different experiences they had, and how they look to the future. A critical perspective would emphasize the economic, political, and cultural differences among these groups, in understanding what happens to these cultural groups in the rebuilding phase, and how they do or do not recover.

postcolonialism An intellectual, political, and cultural movement that calls for the independence of colonialized states and also liberation from colonialist ways of thinking.

An important recent critical perspective is **postcolonialism,** an intellectual, political, and cultural movement that calls for the independence of colonized states and liberation from colonialist *mentalité,* or ways of thinking. The legacy of this cultural invasion often lasts much longer than the political relationship. "It theorizes not just colonial conditions but why those conditions are what they are, and how they can be undone and redone" (Shome & Hegde, 2002, p. 250).

Postcolonialism is not simply the study of colonialism but the study of how we might deal with that past and its aftermath, which may include the ongoing use of the colonial language, culture, and religion. For example, a study by Marwan Kraidy (2005) explores how youth in Lebanon negotiate their postcolonial identity though their media consumption. Lebanon was colonized at various times by Arabs, Ottomans, and the French, and partly because of this colonial past, Lebanese have access to a wide range of television channels (all Arab satellite channels, some Indian, and the major U.S. and European cable and satellite channels). Kraidy shows how the young people pick and choose specific shows to watch, and then he analyzes how they interpret those shows. He concludes that, because of their colonialist legacy, they gravitate toward Western shows in addition to the Arabic shows, and this media consumption ultimately contributes to their having a **hybrid identity**—an identity comprised of both Western and Arabic elements.

hybrid identity An identity that is consciously a mixture of different cultural identities and cultural traditions.

Hybrid identities form around the world where people mix and meld aspects of their cultural life from more than one culture. While Kraidy looked at the case in Lebanon, hybrid identities are emerging around the world. In his study of the use of Kiswahili as a regional language in East Africa, linguistics professor Benson Oduor Ojwang (in press) points to the colonial past of this part of Africa as a foundation for unification. Kenya, Uganda, and Tanzania, formerly British colonies, are looking for greater cooperation, as they were earlier closer under British colonial rule. Known as East African Cooperation, the former colonies have a colonial past that they are using to forge a new postcolonial entity. Kiswahili is emerging as the language on which this new integration might occur, rather than English.

Another example of a critical study is Davin Grindstaff and Kevin DeLuca's (2004) analysis of the media coverage of the kidnapping and execution of Daniel

Pearl, a journalist for *The Wall Street Journal* who was pursuing terrorism leads in Pakistan and was later captured and decapitated, which was videotaped. This videotape becomes a contested site where it "takes on starkly different meanings in the construction of both claims to 'terrorism' and to national identities in both Pakistan and the United States" (p. 306). The struggle between these readings must be contextualized within the larger power relations between Pakistan and the United States.

Grindstaff and DeLuca note that the same week Daniel Pearl was murdered, two Pakistani children were murdered in the United States. The outcry over Pearl and the deafening silence over these children's murders underscores the way that bodies represent national identities and "exacerbates Pakistani anti-Americanism and complicates Pakistani national identity" (2004, p. 316). In contrast, U.S. American discourses about Pearl's murder focus on Pearl as both a hero in the "war on terrorism" *and* an innocent victim. This paradox points to the way that multiple ideological needs are serviced and empowered by this video and its meanings.

A final example of a critical study is Dreama Moon's (1999) investigation of gender and social class communication. In her study, Moon analyzed interviews of white women from working-class backgrounds. She discovered that social class is a "marked feature" in the communication practices in academia that restricts upward mobility. Subtle communication practices that reinforce social class differences are not so invisible to women from working-class backgrounds. Moon shows how culture, social class, and communication work together to reproduce the contemporary social structure. She also identifies some strategies used by these women to resist this process of **social reproduction.**

social reproduction
The process of perpetuating cultural patterns.

Strengths and Limitations   The critical approach emphasizes the power relations in intercultural interactions and the importance of social and historical contexts. However, one limitation is that most critical studies do not focus on face-to-face intercultural interaction. Rather, they focus on popular media forms of communication—TV shows, music videos, magazine advertisements, and so on. Such studies, with their lack of attention to face-to-face interactions, may yield less practical results. Thus, for example, although understanding different discourses about racism may give us insights into U.S. race relations, it may not provide individuals with specific guidelines on how to communicate better across racial lines. However, one exception is co-cultural theory, presented in Chapter 6, which is used to understand how people's location in a social hierarchy influences their perceptions of reality regarding, among other things, relational issues or problems (Orbe, 1998).

Also, this approach does not allow for much empirical data. For example, Davin Grindstaff and Kevin DeLuca did not measure Pakistani or U.S. American reactions to the decapitation of Daniel Pearl; instead, their essay analyzed the media discourses. Grindstaff and DeLuca's argument rests on the discussions about the videotape of the murder, how it was used, and its influence on these international audiences.

Here are three different student perspectives on the various approaches to studying intercultural communication.

I am an engineer, so I think that hypotheses and research are very important in order to describe and predict a subject. On the other hand, it is important to understand the individual more like a person and not like a number.

　　—Liliana

I like the interpretive approach. I think that it is important to understand and to actually get involved hands-on to understand something so important and complicated as intercultural communication. Even though outsiders may never fully be considered an insider, they are better off than neither an insider nor an outsider.

　　—Matt

Having three different paradigms allows me to view intercultural communication from three different perspectives. I can then incorporate all three into how I interpret other cultures. I personally like the critical view the most because I agree that often cultural groups are in a power struggle against one another, and that's just human nature.

　　—Andrew

A DIALECTICAL APPROACH TO UNDERSTANDING CULTURE AND COMMUNICATION

Combining the Three Traditional Paradigms: The Dialectical Approach

dialectical approach An approach to intercultural communication that integrates three approaches—functionalist (or social science), interpretive, and critical—in understanding culture and communication. It recognizes and accepts that the three approaches are interconnected and sometimes contradictory.

processual Refers to how interaction happens rather than to the outcome.

As you can see from our discussion and the list of theories in Table 2-3, there are many different ways to approach the study of intercultural communication. The social science, interpretive, and critical approaches operate in interconnected and sometimes contradictory ways. Rather than advocating any one approach, we propose a **dialectical approach** to intercultural communication research and practice (see also Martin, Nakayama, & Flores, 2002). The dialectical approach emphasizes the processual, relational, and contradictory nature of intercultural communication, which encompasses many different kinds of intercultural knowledge.

First, with regard to the **processual** nature of intercultural communication, it is important to remember that cultures change, as do individuals. For example, the many cultures that constituted New Orleans and the Gulf Coast included Cajuns, Creoles, African Americans, white Americans, Vietnamese Americans, Chinese Americans, gay and lesbian Americans, and many other cultural groups. Intercultural communication studies provide a static but fleeting picture of these cultural groups. It is important to remember that the adaptation,

TABLE 2-3   SUMMARY OF THEORETICAL NOTIONS IN THREE RESEARCH APPROACHES

Social Science	Interpretive	Critical
Anxiety Uncertainty Management (AUM)	Ethnography of Communication	Postcolonial
Face Negotiation	Afrocentrism	Identity Hybridity
Conversational Constraints	Asiacentrism	Social Reproduction
Communication Accommodation Theory	Communication Theory of Identity	
Diffusion of Innovations	Interpretive Theory of Identity	

communication, and other patterns identified are dynamic and ever changing, even if the research studies only provide a snapshot in time.

Second, a dialectical perspective emphasizes the relational aspect of intercultural communication study. It highlights the relationship among various aspects of intercultural communication and the importance of viewing these holistically rather than in isolation. The key question becomes, Can we really understand culture without understanding communication, and vice versa? Specifically, can we understand the ways that different cultural groups responded to the hurricanes and how they survived without looking at the values, beliefs, and histories of the various cultural groups there, the cultural institutions that different groups had in place, the relative wealth available to different cultural groups, and so on?

A third characteristic of the dialectical perspective involves holding contradictory ideas simultaneously. This notion may be difficult to comprehend because it goes against most formal education in the United States, which emphasizes dichotomous thinking. Dichotomies such as "good and evil," "arteries and veins," and "air and water" form the core of our philosophical and scientific beliefs. The fact that dichotomies such as "far and near," "high and low," and "long and short" sound complete, as if the two parts belong together, reveals our tendency to form dichotomies (Stewart & Bennett, 1991). One such dichotomy that emerged after Hurricane Katrina was that government officials were callous and uncaring and many victims of the hurricane were further victimized by the nonresponse of these officials. However, a dialectical approach requires that we transcend dichotomous thinking in studying and practicing intercultural communication.

Certainly, we can learn something from each of the three traditional approaches, and our understanding of intercultural communication has been enriched by all three. One of our students described how the three perspectives can be useful in everyday communication:

The three paradigms help me understand intercultural communication by giving me insight into how we can work with people. Understanding how to predict communication behavior will make it easier for us to deal with those of other cultures—the social science approach. By changing unfair notions we have [about people from other cultures], we can gain more equality, as in the critical approach. We try to change things. Finally, the interpretive perspective is important so we can see face-to-face how our culture is.

Combining these approaches, as our discussion of the aftermath of Hurricane Katrina shows, provides us with extensive insight into the problems and challenges of this and other intercultural ventures. Clearly, if we limit ourselves to a specific research orientation, we may fail to see the complexities of contemporary intercultural interaction in contexts. Although this kind of paradoxical thinking is rather foreign to Western minds, it is quite accepted in many Asian cultures. For example, people doing business in China are advised to recognize this dialectical thinking: "It is not possible to overstate the importance of 'and' versus 'or' thinking. It recurs, in various forms, throughout business in China and the Orient as a whole" (Ambler & Witzel, 2000, p. 197).

In fact, research findings can make a difference in the everyday world. From the social science perspective, we can see how specific communication and cultural differences might create differing worldviews, which can help us to predict intercultural conflicts. An interpretive investigation gives us an opportunity to confirm what we predicted in a hypothetical social science study. In the case of Hurricane Katrina, a social science study might show large differences in responses among various cultural groups affected by this storm. An interpretive study might show how these different cultural groups interpreted these experiences and why they believe they had different experiences. These interpretations may help explain different responses and why some cultural groups feel differently from others and how some cultural groups adapted to new environments. The critical approach might focus on the different access to financial, political, and material resources among the cultural groups, such as the state of poverty before and after the storm, which groups were and were not relocated, and how these power differentials influenced their intercultural experiences.

Employing these different perspectives is similar to photographing something from different angles. No single angle or snapshot gives us the truth, but taking pictures from various angles gives a more comprehensive view of the subject. The content of the photos, of course, to some extent depends on the interests of the photographer. And the photos may contradict one another, especially if they are taken at different times. But the knowledge we gain from any of these "angles" or approaches is enhanced by the knowledge gained from the others.

However, a dialectical approach requires that we move beyond simply acknowledging the contributions of the three perspectives and accept simultaneously the assumptions of all three. That is, we need to imagine that reality can be at once external *and* internal, that human behavior is predictable *and* creative *and* changeable. These assumptions may seem contradictory, but that's the point. Thinking dialectically forces us to move beyond our familiar categories and opens us up to new possibilities for studying and understanding intercultural communication.

Six Dialectics of Intercultural Communication

We have identified six **dialectics** that characterize intercultural communication and have woven them throughout this book. Perhaps you can think of other dialectics as you learn more about intercultural communication.

Cultural–Individual Dialectic Intercultural communication is both cultural and individual, or idiosyncratic. That communication is *cultural* means we share communication patterns with members of the groups to which we belong. For example, Sandra, a fifth-generation Italian American, tends to be expressive, like other members of her family. However, some of her communication patterns—such as the way she gestures when she talks—are completely idiosyncratic (that is, particular to her and no one else). Consider another example, that of Angela, who tends to be relationally oriented. Although her role as a woman and the relationships she cultivates in that role are important, being a woman does not completely define her behaviors. In this book, we often describe communication patterns that seem to be related to membership in particular cultural groups. However, it is important to remember that communication for all of us is both cultural and individual. We need to keep this dialectic in mind as we try to understand and develop relationships across cultural differences.

Personal–Contextual Dialectic This dialectic involves the role of context in intercultural relationships and focuses simultaneously on the person and the context. Although we communicate as individuals on a personal level, the context of this communication is important as well. In some contexts, we enact specific social roles that give meaning to our messages. For example, when Tom was teaching at a Belgian university, he often spoke from the social role of professor. But this role did not correspond exactly to the same role in the United States because Belgian students accord their professors far more respect and distance than do U.S. students. In Belgium, this social role was more important than his communication with the students. In contrast, his communication with students in the United States is more informal.

Differences–Similarities Dialectic Intercultural communication is characterized by both similarities and differences, in that people are simultaneously similar to and different from each other. In this book, we identify and describe real and important differences between groups of people—differences in values, language, nonverbal behavior, conflict resolution, and so on. For example, Japanese and U.S. Americans communicate differently, just as do men and women. However, there also are many similarities in human experiences and ways of communicating. Emphasizing only differences can lead to stereotyping and prejudice (e.g., that women are emotional or that men are rational); emphasizing only similarities can lead us to ignore the important cultural variations that exist. Therefore, we try to emphasize both similarities and differences and ask you to keep this dialectic in mind.

dialectic (1) A method of logic based on the principle that an idea generates its opposite, leading to a reconciliation of the opposites; (2) the complex and paradoxical relationship between two opposite qualities or entities, each of which may also be referred to as a *dialectic*.

When I was working in the Philippines there was a privilege–disadvantage dialectic with the general population. My trip got extended for an extra week. I had to go out and buy clothes at a department store in Manila. I did not speak any Filipino so this was a very interesting experience. Knowing that the Filipino people can speak English and Spanish somewhat I knew I would be able to get by. While the prices on the clothes were clearly marked the lady at the register had inflated the price by 1000 pesos ($20). Knowing what the price should be I had to try to explain the situation to get the price down to the correct level. Americans are envied in the Philippines for what we have. After spending a good amount of time trying to explain my situation the Filipino lady appeared not to understand anything I was saying. I ended up not getting the clothes from her.
 —Bob

In the past African Americans have dealt with a lot of prejudice and discrimination against them. There used to be separate water fountains, bathrooms, seats on a bus, etc. . . . the list could go on. So today when any African Americans come to dine at the restaurant I work at, we try to avoid seating them at the back of the restaurant. Since there has been a complaint, we don't want them to feel as if we are discriminating against them by putting them in a place where they are tucked away. The discrimination that African Americans once felt should not translate over to the present since our society has come so far. Some might say we are giving them special treatment to make African Americans feel equal but I don't see it like that. I see it as a sign of respect and a way of showing the African American culture that the discrimination they once felt should not exist anymore and they are just as equal as anyone else.
 —Jodi

Static–Dynamic Dialectic This dialectic suggests that intercultural communication tends to be at once static and dynamic. Some cultural and communication patterns remain relatively constant, whereas other aspects of cultures (or personal traits of individuals) shift over time—that is, they are dynamic. For example, as we learned in Chapter 1, anti-immigrant sentiment traditionally has been a cultural constant in the United States, although the groups and conditions of discrimination have changed. Thus, the antagonism against Irish and Italian immigrants that existed at the turn of the 20th century has largely disappeared but may linger in the minds of some people. To understand interethnic communication in the United States today, we must recognize both the static and dynamic aspects of these relations.

History/Past–Present/Future Dialectic Another dialectic emphasizes the need to focus simultaneously on the past and the present in understanding intercultural communication. On the one hand, we need to be aware of contemporary forces and realities that shape interactions of people from different cultural groups. On the other hand, we need to realize that history has a significant impact on contemporary events. One of our students described how this dialectic was illustrated in a televised panel discussion on race relations:

> *The panelists frequently referred to and talked about the history of different cultural groups in the United States and the present. They also touched on racial conflicts of the past and future possible improvement for certain groups. They were, therefore, communicating in a history/past–present/future dialectical manner. The discussions of past and present were critical to the overall goal of understanding current cultural identity. Without understanding the history of, for example, the slave trade or the Jim Crow laws, can we truly comprehend the African American experience in the United States today? The history of each cultural group plays a major role in the present role of that group.*

Privilege–Disadvantage Dialectic   A dialectical perspective recognizes that people may be simultaneously privileged and disadvantaged, or privileged in some contexts and disadvantaged in others. For example, many tourists are in the position of economic privilege because they can afford to travel, but in their travels, they also may be disadvantaged if they do not speak the local language. We can also be simultaneously privileged and disadvantaged because of gender, age, race, socioeconomic status, and other identities. One of our Asian American colleagues relates how he is simultaneously privileged because he is educated, middle class, and male and disadvantaged because he experiences subtle and overt mistreatment based on his race and accent (Collier, Hegde, Lee, Nakayama, & Yep, 2002, p. 247).

Keeping a Dialectical Perspective

We ask that you keep a dialectical perspective in mind as you read the rest of this book. The dialectics relate in various ways to the topics discussed in the following chapters and are interwoven throughout the text. Keep in mind, though, that the dialectical approach is not a specific theory to apply to all aspects of intercultural communication. Rather, it is a lens through which to view the complexities of the topic. Instead of offering easy answers to dilemmas, we ask you to look at the issues and ideas from various angles, sometimes holding contradictory notions, but always seeing things in processual, relational, and holistic ways.

The dialectical approach that we take in this book combines the three traditional approaches (social science, interpretive, and critical) and suggests four components to consider in understanding intercultural communication: culture, communication, context, and power. Culture and communication are the foreground, and context and power are the backdrop against which we can understand intercultural communication. We discuss these four components in the next chapter.

INTERNET RESOURCES

http://katrina.louisiana.gov/
Even though Hurricane Katrina came through the Gulf Coast in 2005, the effects are still being felt today. This website is maintained by the state government of Louisiana in an attempt to prevent reoccurrences of the terrible events of 2005. The website contains useful information about current weather and flood/hurricane conditions and predictions, with links to the Emergency Preparedness Office and information about current flooding conditions and disaster emergency assistance.

www.state.gov/m/fsi/
This is the State Department's website for the Foreign Service Institute. The FSI is the primary mechanism the federal government uses for training individuals to go overseas to serve, in some capacity, as representatives of the U.S. government. Check out the "Youth and Education" link, which has useful information about studying and working abroad and information about how to be a "smart traveler" (preparing travel documents, what to do in emergency situation when traveling abroad, etc.).

www.peacecorps.gov/
This is the home page for the Peace Corps. Volunteering in the Peace Corps is a way that many young people travel overseas and experience different cultures. It is worth considering how traveling abroad is portrayed differently by the Peace Corps and the State Department.

www.aliveintruth.org
Alive in Truth is a group of New Orleans residents who got together to collect oral histories of those who survived Hurricane Katrina. Go to their web page and read some of these oral histories. Think about how this might help you better understand their experiences from an interpretivist perspective. Note the interviewing guidelines they suggest, and keep in mind the larger context for these interviews. How is this information different from what a social scientist or critical theorist might find?

SUMMARY

- The field of intercultural communication in the United States began with the establishment of the Foreign Service Institute in 1946.
- This new field was interdisciplinary and pragmatic. It emphasized non-verbal communication in international contexts.
- The perceptions and worldviews of scholars have an impact on the study of intercultural communication and have led to three contemporary approaches: the social science, interpretive, and critical approaches.

- This textbook advocates a dialectical approach that combines these three approaches.
- A dialectical approach emphasizes a processual, relational, and holistic view of intercultural communication, and it requires a balance of contradictory views.
- Intercultural communication is both cultural *and* individual, personal *and* contextual, characterized by differences *and* similarities, static *and* dynamic, oriented to both the present *and* the past, and characterized by both privilege *and* disadvantage.

DISCUSSION QUESTIONS

1. How have the origins of the study of intercultural communication in the United States affected its present focus?
2. How did business and political interests influence what early intercultural communication researchers studied and learned?
3. How have the worldviews of researchers influenced how they studied intercultural communication?
4. How have other fields contributed to the study of intercultural communication?
5. What are the advantages of a dialectical approach to intercultural communication?

 Go to the self-quizzes on the Online Learning Center at www.mhhe.com/martinnakayama6 to further test your knowledge.

ACTIVITIES

1. *Becoming Culturally Conscious.* One way to understand your cultural position within the United States and your own cultural values, norms, and beliefs is to examine your upbringing. Answer the following questions:

   a. What values did your parents or guardians attempt to instill in you?
   b. Why were these values considered important?
   c. What were you expected to do when you grew up?
   d. How were you expected to contribute to family life?
   e. What do you know about your ethnic background?
   f. What was your neighborhood like?

   Discuss your answers with classmates. Analyze how your own cultural position is unique and how it is similar to that of others.

2. *Analyzing Cultural Patterns.* Find a text or speech that discusses some intercultural or cultural issues, and analyze the cultural patterns present in the text. Consider, for example, the "I Have a Dream" speech by Martin Luther King, Jr. (Andrews & Zarefsky, 1992), or Chief Seattle's 1854 speech (Low, 1995).

3. *Analyzing a Video.* View a feature film or video (e.g., *Crash* or *Brokeback Mountain*) and assume the position of a researcher. Analyze the cultural meanings in the film from each of the three perspectives: social science, interpretive, and critical. What cultural patterns (related to nationality, ethnicity, gender, and class) do you see? What does each perspective reveal? What does each one fail to reveal?

KEY WORDS

Afrocentricity (65)
anxiety uncertainty
    management
    theory (56)
collectivistic (55)
communication
    accommodation
    theory (56)
conceptual
    equivalence (59)
conversational
    contraints theory (56)
critical approach (67)
cross-cultural
    training (47)
dialectic (77)
dialectical approach (74)
diffusion of innovations
    theory (58)

distance zones (47)
diversity training (47)
emic (60)
ethnography (60)
etic (60)
face negotiation
    theory (56)
functionalist
    approach (54)
hybrid identity (72)
individualistic (55)
intercultural
    competence (48)
interdisciplinary (49)
interpretive approach (60)
macrocontexts (67)
paradigm (50)
participant
    observation (60)

perception (50)
postcolonialism (72)
processual (74)
proxemics (47)
qualitative
    methods (60)
quantitative
    methods (54)
rhetorical approach (60)
Sapir-Whorf
    hypothesis (48)
social reproduction (73)
social science
    approach (54)
textual analyses (68)
translation
    equivalence (59)
variable (82)
worldview (46)

 The Online Learning Center at www.mhhe.com/martinnakayama6 features flashcards and crossword puzzles based on these terms and concepts.

REFERENCES

9/11 and 8/29. (2005, September 11). *Los Angeles Times*, p. M4.
Allport, G. W. (1979). *The nature of prejudice.* Reading, MA: Addison-Wesley.
Ambler, T., & Witzel, M. (2000). *Doing business in China.* New York: Routledge.

Andrews, J. R., & Zarefsky, D. (1992). *Contemporary American voices: Significant speeches in American history, 1945–present* (pp. 78–81). New York: Longman.
Après Katrina, l'Amérique s'interroge sur les failles de son modèle. (2005, September 7). *Le Monde.*

www.lemonde.fr/web/imprimer_element/
0,40-0@2-3222,50-686407,0.html.

Asante, M. K. (1987). *The Afrocentric idea.* Philadelphia: Temple University Press.

Asante, M. K. (2001). Transcultural realities and different ways of knowing. In V. H. Milhouse, M. K. Asante, & P. O. Nwosu (Eds.), *Transcultural realities: Interdisciplinary perspectives on cross cultural relations* (pp. 71–82). Thousand Oaks, CA: Sage.

Barnlund, D. C., & Yoshioka, M. (1990). Apologies: Japanese and American styles. *International Journal of Intercultural Relations, 14,* 193–205.

Ben-Porath, E. N., & Shaker, L. K. (2010). News images, race, and attribution in the wake of Hurrican Katrina. *Journal of Communication, 60,* 466–490.

Berry, J. W. (1997). Preface. In P. R. Dasen, T. S. Saraswathi, & J. W. Berry (Eds.), *Handbook of cross cultural psychology: Vol. 2. Basic processes and human development* (pp. xi–xvi). Boston: Allyn & Bacon.

Bowman, M. S., & Bowman, R. L. (2010). Telling Katrina stories: Problems and opportunities in engaging disaster. *Quarterly Journal of Speech, 96*(4), 455–461.

Braithwaite, C. (1990). Communicative silence: A cross cultural study of Basso's hypothesis. In D. Carbaugh (Ed.), *Cultural communication and intercultural contact* (pp. 321–328). Hillsdale, NJ: Lawrence Erlbaum.

Brantlinger, P. (1986). Victorians and Africans: The genealogy of the myth of the dark continent. In H. L. Gates, Jr. (Ed.), *"Race," writing and difference* (pp. 185–222). Chicago: University of Chicago Press. (Original work published 1985)

Brazile, D. L. (2006). New Orleans: Next steps on the road to recovery. In *The State of Black America 2006* (pp. 233–237). Washington, DC: National Urban League.

Brislin, R. (1999). *Understanding culture's infuence on behavior* (2nd ed.). Belmont, CA: Wadsworth.

Burrell, G., & Morgan, G. (1988). *Sociological paradigms and organizational analysis.* Portsmouth, NH: Heinemann.

Carbaugh, D. (1996). *Situating selves: The communication of social identities in American scenes.* Albany: State University of New York Press.

Carbaugh, D. (1999). "Just listen": "Listening" and landscape among the Blackfeet. *Western Journal of Communication, 63,* 250–270.

Carbaugh, D., & Berry, M. (2001). Communicating history, Finnish and American discourses: An ethnographic contribution to intercultural communication inquiry. *Communication Theory, 11,* 352–366.

Casmir, F. L. (1994). The role of theory and theory building. In F. L. Casmir (Ed.), *Building communication theories* (pp. 7–41). Hillsdale, NJ: Lawrence Erlbaum.

Chen, G.-M. (1998). A Chinese model of human relationship development. In B. L. Hoffer & J. H. Koo (Eds.), *Cross-cultural communication: East and West in the 90's* (pp. 45–53). San Antonio, TX: Institute for Cross-Cultural Research, Trinity University.

Chins up, hopes high. (2010, August 28), *The Economist, 396*(8697), 24–26.

Chomsky, N. (2001). *9–11.* New York: Seven Stories Press.

Collier, M. J., Hegde, R. S., Lee, W., Nakayama, T. K., & Yep, G. A. (2002). Dialogue on the edges: Ferment in communication and culture. In M. J. Collier (Ed.), *Transforming communication about culture* (*International and Intercultural Communication Annual,* Vol. 24, pp. 219–280). Thousand Oaks, CA: Sage.

Delgado, F. (2002). Mass-mediated communication and intercultural confict. In J. N. Martin, T. K. Nakayama, & L. A. Flores (Eds.), *Readings in intercultural communication: Experiences and contexts* (2nd ed., pp. 351–359). Boston: McGraw-Hill.

Egan, T. (2005, September 11). Uprooted and scattered far from the familiar. *The New York Times,* pp. A1, A32.

Eggler, B. (2007). N.O. a beacon for young people. *NOLA.com.* Retrieved May 7, 2011, from http://blog.nola.com/times-picayune//print.html.

Fussell, E., Sastry, N., & VanLandingham, M. (2010). Race, socioeconomic status, and return migration to New Orleans after Hurricane Katrina, *Population and Environment, 31,* 20–42.

Gallois, C., Ogay, T., & Giles, H. (2005). Communication accommodation theory. In W. B. Gudykunst (Ed.), *Theorizing about intercultural communication* (pp. 121–148). Thousand Oaks, CA: Sage.

Garner, T. (1994). Oral rhetorical practice in African American culture. In A. González, M. Houston, & V. Chen (Eds.), *Our voices: Essays in culture, ethnicity and communication* (pp. 81–91). Los Angeles: Roxbury.

Gordon, R. D. Beyond the failures of Western communication theory. *Journal of Multicultural Discourses, 2*(2), 89–107.

Gould, S. J. (1993). American polygeny and craniometry before Darwin: Blacks and Indians as separate, inferior species. In S. Harding (Ed.), *The "racial" economy of science: Toward a democratic future* (pp. 84–115). Bloomington: Indiana University Press. (Original work published 1981)

Griffin-Padgett, D. R., & Allison, D. (2010). Making a case for Restorative Rhetoric: Mayor Rudolph Giuliani's & Mayor Ray Nagin's response to disaster. *Communication Monographs, 7*(3), 376–392.

Grindstaff, D. A., & DeLuca, K. M. (2004). The corpus of Daniel Pearl. *Critical Studies in Media Communication, 21,* 305–324.

Gudykunst, W. B. (1985). A model of uncertainty reduction in intergroup encounters. *Journal of Language and Social Psychology, 4,* 79–98.

Gudykunst, W. B. (1998). Individualistic and collectivistic perspectives on communication: An introduction. *International Journal of Intercultural Relations, 22,* 107–134.

Gudykunst, W. B. (Ed.), (2005a). *Theorizing about intercultural communication.* Thousand Oaks, CA: Sage.

Gudykunst, W. B. (2005b). An anxiety/uncertainty management (AUM) theory of effective communication: Making the mesh of the net finer. In W. B. Gudykunst (Ed.), *Theorizing about intercultural communication* (pp. 281–323). Thousand Oaks, CA: Sage.

Hall, B. J. (1992). Theories of culture and communication. *Communication Theory, 1,* 50–70.

Hall, E. T. (1959). *The silent language.* Garden City, NY: Doubleday.

Hall, E. T. (1966). *The hidden dimension.* Garden City, NY: Doubleday.

Hamilton, R. (2010, August 30). Five years later, Houstonians conflicted about Katrina. *The Texas Tribune online.* Retrieved May 7, 2011, from www.texastribune.org/texas-politics/texas-political-news/five-years-houstonians-conflicted-about-katrina/.

Hammer, M. R., & Rogan, R. G. (2002). Latino and Indochinese interpretive frames in negotiating conflict with law enforcement: A focus group analysis. *International Journal of Intercultural Relations, 26,* 551–576.

Hartnell, A. (2008, August 28). The Disneyfication of New Orleans, *guardian.co.uk.* Retrieved May 7, 2011, from www.guardian.co.uk/commentisfree/2008/aug/28/usa.hurricanekatrina.

Hecht, M. L. (1993). A research odyssey: Towards the development of a communication theory of identity. *Communication Monographs, 60,* 76–82.

Hernandez, G. (2005, October 11). Rebuilding our city. *The Advocate,* pp. 42–44, 49–50, 52.

Hymes, D. (1974). *Foundations in sociolinguistics: An ethnographic approach.* Philadelphia: University of Pennsylvania Press.

Ishii, S. (2004). Proposing a Buddhist consciousness-only epistemological model for intrapersonal communication research. *Journal of Intercultural Communication Research, 33,* 63–76.

Jandt, F. E., & Tanno, D. V. (2001). Decoding domination, encoding self-determination: Intercultural communication research processes. *Howard Journal of Communications, 12,* 119–135.

Johnson, K. (2005, September 11). For storm survivors, a mosaic of impressions rather than a crystalline moment. *The New York Times,* pp. A25, A32.

Kim, M.-S. (1994). Cross-cultural comparisons of the perceived importance of conversational constraints. *Human Communication Research, 21,* 128–151.

Kim, M.-S. (2005). Culture-based conversational constraints theory: Individual and culture-level analyses. In W. B. Gudykunst (Ed.), *Theorizing about intercultural communication* (pp. 93–117). Thousand Oaks, CA: Sage.

Kim, Y. Y. (2001). *Becoming intercultural: An integrative theory of communication and cross-cultural adaptation.* Thousand Oaks, CA: Sage.

Kohut, A., Allen, J., Keeter, S., Doherty, C., Dimock, M., Funk, C., et al. (2005). *Two-in-three critical of Bush's relief efforts: Huge racial divide over Katrina and its consequences.* The Pew Center for the People & the Press. Available at http://people-press.org/reports/pdf/255.pdf. Accessed November 1, 2005.

Kraidy, M. M. (2005). *Hybridity, or the cultural logic of globalization.* Philadelphia: Temple University Press.

Krupa, M. (2009, July 25). Katrina's displaced worry about census count. *NOLA.com.* Retrieved May 7, 2011, from www.nola.com/news/index.ssf/2009/07/katrinas_displaced_worry_about.html.

Kuhn, T. (1970). *The structure of scientific revolutions* (Rev. ed.). Chicago: University of Chicago Press.

Landis, D., Bennett, J. M., & Bennett, M. J. (Eds.) (2004). *Handbook of intercultural training.* 3rd ed. (pp. 309–336). Thousand Oaks, CA: Sage.

Landis, D., & Wasilewski, J. H. (1999). Reflections on 22 years of the *International Journal of Intercultural Relations* and 23 years in other areas of intercultural practice. *International Journal of Intercultural Relations, 23,* 535–574.

Louis, R. (2009). Reclaiming a citizenship site: Performing New Orleans in the Superdome. *Text and Performance Quarterly, 29*(3), 279–295.

Low, D. (1995). Contemporary reinvention of Chief Seattle's 1854 speech. *American Indian Quarterly, 19*(3), 407.

Mark my words. (2007, February 16). *The Economist.* Retrieved May 13, 2008 from www.economist.com/science/displaystory.cfm?story_id=E1_RSNTRJD.

Martin, J. N., Nakayama, T. K., & Carbaugh, D. (In press). The history and development of the study of intercultural communication and applied linguistics. In J. Jackson (Ed.), *The Routledge handbook of intercultural communication.* New York: Routledge.

Martin, J. N., Nakayama, T. K., & Flores, L. A. (2002). A dialectical approach to intercultural communication. In J. N. Martin, T. K. Nakayama, & L. A. Flores (Eds.), *Readings in intercultural communication:*

Experiences and contexts (2nd ed., pp. 3–13). Boston: McGraw-Hill.

Miike, Y. (2004). Rethinking humanity, culture and communication: Asiacentric critiques and contributions. *Human Communication, 7*, 69–82.

Miike, Y. (2003). Beyond Eurocentrism in the intercultural field: Searching for an Asiacentric paradigm. In W. J. Storosta & G. M. Chen (Eds.), *Ferment in the intercultural field* (*International and Intercultural Communication Annual*, Vol. 26). Thousand Oaks, CA: Sage.

Miike, Y. (2007a). An Asiacentric reflection on Eurocentric bias in communication theory. *Communication Monographs, 74*(2), 272–278.

Miike, Y. (2007b). Asian contributions to communication theory: An introduction. *China Media Research, 3*(4), 1–6.

Moon, D. (1999). White enculturation and bourgeois ideology: The discursive production of 'good (white) girls'. In T. K. Nakayama & J. N. Martin (Eds.), *Whiteness: The communication of social identity* (pp. 177–197). Thousand Oaks, CA: Sage.

Moon, D. (2010). Critical reflections on culture and critical intercultural communication. In T. K. Nakayama & R. K. Halualani (Eds)., *The handbook of critical intercultural communication* (pp. 34–58). Malden, MA: Wiley-Blackwell.

New Orleans Index at 5 (2010, August). Greater New Orleans Community Data Center, Brookings Institute. Retrieved May 8, 2011, from https://gnocdc.s3.amazonaws.com/NOIat5/MeasuringProgress.pdf.

Ojwang, B. O. (2008). Prospects of Kishwahili as a regional language in a socioculturally heterogeneous East Africa. *Journal of International and Intercultural Communication, 1*(4), 327–347.

Orbe, M. (1998). *Constructing co-cultural theory: An explication of culture, power and communication.* Thousand Oaks, CA: Sage.

Orbe, M. P. (2004). Negotiating multiple identities with multiple frames: An analysis of first-generation college students. *Communication Education, 53*, 131–149.

Philipsen, G. (1990). Speaking "like a man" in Teamsterville. In D. Carbaugh (Ed.), *Cultural communication and intercultural contact* (pp. 11–20). Hillsdale, NJ: Lawrence Erlbaum.

Putnam, L., & Pacanowsky, M. (Eds.). (1983). *Communication and organizations: An interpretive approach.* Newbury Park, CA: Sage.

Rogers, E. M. (2003). *Diffusion of innovations.* 5th ed. New York: Free Press.

Rosaldo, R. (1989). *Culture and truth: The remaking of social analysis.* Boston: Beacon Press.

Satoshi, I. (2007). A Western contention of Asia-centred communication scholarship paradigms:

A commentary on Gordon's paper. *Journal of Multicultural Discourses, 2*(2), 108–114.

Saulny, S. (2005, October 11). Cast from their ancestral home, Creoles worry about culture's future. *The New York Times*, p. A13.

Serpell, R. (1982). Measures of perception, skills and intelligence: The growth of a new perspective on children in a third world country. In W. Hartrup (Ed.), *Review of child development research* (Vol. 6). Chicago: University of Chicago Press.

Shah, H. (2009). Legitimizing neglect: Race and rationality in conservative news commentary about Hurricane Katrina. *The Howard Journal of Communications, 20*, 1–17.

Shome, R., & Hegde, R. (2002). Postcolonial approaches to communication: Charting the terrain, engaging the intersections. *Communication Theory, 12*, 249–270.

Simpson, J. S (2008). "What do they think of us?": The pedagogical practices of cross-cultural communication, misrecognition, and hope. *Journal of International and Intercultural Communication, 1*(3), 181–201.

Singer, M. R. (1987). *Intercultural communication: A perceptual approach.* Englewood Cliffs, NJ: Prentice-Hall.

Singer, M. R. (1998). Culture: A perceptual approach. In M. J. Bennett (Ed.), *Basic concepts of intercultural communication* (pp. 97–110). Yarmouth, ME: Intercultural Press.

Singhal, A., & Dearing, J. W. (Eds.). (2006). *Communication of innovations: A journey with Ev Rogers.* Thousand Oaks, CA: Sage.

Smith, C. S. (2005, November 6). France has an underclass, but its roots are still shallow. *The New York Times*, sec D3. 4, p. 3.

Smith, L. T. (1999). *Decolonizing methodologies: Research and indigenous peoples.* New York: St. Martin's Press.

Stewart, E. C., & Bennett, M. J. (1991). *American cultural patterns: A cross-cultural perspective* (Rev. ed.). Yarmouth, ME: Intercultural Press.

Swarns, R. (2002, May 5). France returns old remains to homeland. *The Arizona Republic*, p. A28.

Tagliabue, J. (2005, September 21). A French lesson: Taunts about race can boomerang. *The New York Times*, p. A4.

Tang, I. (2005, September 16). Hurricane Katrina victims recover from 'tragic shock.' *Asian Week*. http://news.asianweek.com/news/view_article.html?article_id=736da18d1e494642b993e854400c7f30.

Tatum, W. A. (2005, September 21). Proof positive of a racist president, misleading a racist America. *Amsterdam News.* www.amsterdamnews.org/News/search/Article_Search.asp?NewsID=61723&sID=16.

Ting-Toomey, S. (1985). Toward a theory of conflict and culture. In W. Gudykunst, L. Stewart, & S. Ting-Toomey (Eds.), *Communication, culture and organizational processes* (pp. 71–86). Beverly Hills, CA: Sage.

Ting-Toomey, S. (2005). The matrix of face: An updated face-negotiation theory. In W. B. Gudykunst (Ed.), *Theorizing about intercultural communication* (pp. 71–92). Thousand Oaks, CA: Sage.

Ting-Toomey, S., Gao, G., Trubisky, P., Yang, Z., Kim, H. S., Lin, S.-L., et al. (1991). Culture, face maintenance, and styles of handling interpersonal conflict: A study in five cultures. *International Journal of Conflict Management, 2,* 275–296.

Ting-Toomey, S., Yee-Jung, K. K., Shapiro, R. B., Garcia, W., Wright, T. J., & Oetzel, J. G. (2000). Ethnic/cultural identity salience and conflict styles in four US ethnic groups. *International Journal of Intercultural Relations, 24,* 47–81.

Witteborn, S. (2004). Of being an Arab woman before and after September 11: The enactment of communal identities in talk. *Howard Journal of Communications, 15,* 83–98.

Why was UK's Katrina aid rejected by US? (2005, September 18). *British Broadcasting Corporation News.* http://news.bbc.co.uk/1/hi/magazine/4349916.stm.

CULTURE, COMMUNICATION, CONTEXT, AND POWER

CHAPTER OBJECTIVES

*After you read this chapter, you should be
able to:*

1. Identify three approaches
    to culture.
2. Define communication.
3. Identify and describe nine cultural
    value orientations.
4. Describe how cultural values
    influence communication.
5. Understand how cultural values
    influence conflict behavior.
6. Describe how communication can
    reinforce cultural beliefs
    and behavior.
7. Explain how culture can function as
    resistance to dominant value
    systems.
8. Explain the relationship between
    communication and context.
9. Describe the characteristics
    of power.
10. Describe the relationship between
    communication and power.

In Chapter 2, we touched on the history of intercultural communication studies, examined three theoretical approaches, and outlined an integrated dialectical approach to intercultural communication. In this chapter, we continue our discussion of the dialectical approach and identify four interrelated components or building blocks in understanding intercultural communication: culture, communication, context, and power. As noted previously, culture and communication are the foreground and context and power form the backdrop against which we can understand intercultural communication. First, we define and describe culture and communication. Then we examine how these two components interact with issues of context and power to enhance our understanding of intercultural communication.

WHAT IS CULTURE?

Culture is often considered the core concept in intercultural communication. Intercultural communication studies often focus on how cultural groups differ from one another: Muslims differ from Christians; Japanese differ from U.S. Americans; men differ from women; environmentalists differ from conservationists; pro-lifers differ from pro-choicers; old differ from young, and on and on (Gudykunst, 2002).

Perhaps it is more helpful here to think of the similarities–differences dialectic in trying to understand intercultural communication. That is, we are all similar to *and* different from each other simultaneously. Humans, regardless of cultural backgrounds, engage in many of the same daily activities and have many of the same wants and desires. We all eat, sleep, love, pursue friendships and romantic relationships and want to be respected and loved by those who are important to us.

And yet some real differences exist between cultural groups. How we pursue these activities varies from culture to culture. Men and women often do not see the world in the same way. Old and young have different goals and dreams. Muslims and Christians have different beliefs, and the old adage "When in Rome do as the Romans do" implies that it is easy simply to adapt to different ways of thinking and behaving, yet anyone who has struggled to adapt to a new cultural situation knows that only the Romans are Romans and only they know how to be truly Romans. The challenge is to negotiate these differences and similarities with insight and skill. First, we need to examine what we mean by the term *culture*.

Culture Learned patterns of behavior and attitudes shared by a group of people.

Culture has been defined in many ways—from a pattern of perceptions that influence communication to a site of contestation and conflict. Because there are many acceptable definitions of culture, and because it is a complex concept, it is important to reflect on the centrality of culture in our own interactions. The late British writer Raymond Williams (1983) wrote that culture "is one of the two or three most complicated words in the English language" (p. 89). And this very complexity indicates the many ways in which it influences intercultural communication (Williams, 1981). Culture is more than merely one aspect of the practice of intercultural communication. How we think about culture frames our ideas

In this essay, communication scholar Wen Shu Lee identifies different common uses of the term *culture* and then describes how each definition serves particular interests. She also defends her preferred choice, the sixth definition.

1. Culture = unique human efforts (as different from nature and biology). For example, "*Culture* is the bulwark against the ravages of nature."

2. Culture = refinement, mannerism (as different from things that are crude, vulgar, and unrefined). For example, "Look at the way in which he chows down his food. He has no *culture* at all."

3. Culture = civilization (as different from backward barbaric people). For example, "In countries where darkness reigns and people are wanting in *culture*, it is our mandate to civilize and Christianize those poor souls."

4. Culture = shared language, beliefs, values (as different from language beliefs and values that are not shared; dissenting voices; and voices of the "other"). For example, "We come from the same *culture*, we speak the same language, and we share the same tradition."

5. Culture = dominant or hegemonic culture (as different from marginal cultures). For example, "It is the *culture* of the ruling class that determines what is moral and what is deviant." [This definition is a more charged version of definitions 2, 3, and 4 through the addition of power consciousness.]

6. Culture = the shifting tensions between the shared and the unshared (as different from shared or unshared things). For example, "American *culture* has changed from master/slave, to white only/black only, to antiwar and black power, to affirmative action/multiculturalism and political correctness, to transnational capital and anti-sweatshop campaigns."

Each of these definitions privileges certain interests. Definition 2 privileges high culture and leaves out popular culture. . . . Definition 3 privileges nations that are/were imperialistic, colonizing. . . . Definition 4 privileges a "universal and representative" view of a society, but such a view often represents only a specific powerful group and silences other groups that do not readily share this view. Definition 5 privileges the interaction of the culture authorized by the dominant group/sector/nation—more politically explicit than definitions 2, 3, and 4. Definition 6 is the one I like the most. It is more of a meta view of cultures. It focuses on the "links" between "the shared" and the "little shared." But the sharedness, *the* unsharedness, *and their* links *remain not only situated but also unstable, shifting, and contested.*

Source: From Collier, Hegde, Lee, Nakayama, and Yep, "Dialogue on the Edges: Ferment in Communication and Culture." In M. J. Collier et al. (Eds.), *Transforming Communication About Culture* (Thousand Oaks, CA: Sage, 2002), pp. 229–230.

TABLE 3-1 THREE PERSPECTIVES ON DEFINING CULTURE		
Social Science	**Interpretive**	**Critical**
Culture is:		
Learned and shared	Learned and shared	Heterogeneous, dynamic
Patterns of perception	Contextual symbolic meanings	Site of contested meanings
	Involves emotion	
The relationship between culture and communication:		
Culture influences communication.	Culture influences communication.	Communication reshapes culture.
	Communication reinforces culture.	

Source: Adapted from J. N. Martin and T. K. Nakayama, "Thinking Dialectically About Culture and Communication," *Communication Theory, 9* (1999): 5.

and perceptions. For example, if we think that culture is defined by nation-states, then communication between a Japanese and an Italian would be intercultural communication because Japan and Italy are different nation-states. However, according to this definition, an encounter between an Asian American from North Carolina and an African American from California would not be intercultural because North Carolina and California are not different nation-states.

We do not advocate a singular definition of culture because any one definition is too restrictive (Baldwin & Lindsley, 1994). A dialectical approach suggests that different definitions offer more flexibility in approaching the topic. We believe that the best approach to understanding the complexities of intercultural communication is to view the concept of culture from different perspectives (see Table 3-1).

By and large, social science researchers focus not on culture per se but on the *influence* of culture on communication. In other words, such researchers concern themselves with communication differences that result from culture. They pay little attention to how we conceptualize culture or how we see its functions. In contrast, interpretive researchers focus more on how cultural contexts influence communication. Critical researchers, for their part, often view communication—and the power to communicate—as instrumental in reshaping culture. They see culture as the way that people participate in or resist society's structure.

Although research studies help us understand different aspects of intercultural communication, it is important to investigate how we think about culture, not simply as researchers but as practitioners as well. We therefore broaden our scope to consider different views of culture, especially in terms of how they influence intercultural communication.

Social Science Definitions: Culture as Learned, Group-Related Perceptions

Communication scholars from the social science paradigm, influenced by research in psychology, view culture as a set of learned, group-related perceptions (B. Hall, 1992). Geert Hofstede (1984), a noted social psychologist, defines culture as "the programming of the mind" and explains his notion of culture in terms of a computer program:

Every person carries within him or herself patterns of thinking, feeling, and potential acting which were learned throughout [his or her] lifetime. Much of [these patterns are] acquired in early childhood, because at that time a person is most susceptible to learning and assimilating. (p. 4)

Hofstede goes on to describe how these patterns are developed through interactions in the social environment and with various groups of individuals—first in the family and neighborhood, then at school and in youth groups, then at college, and so on. Culture becomes a collective experience because it is shared with people who live in and experience the same social environments.

To understand this notion of the collective programming of the mind, Hofstede and other scholars studied organizational behavior at various locations of a multinational corporation; this study is discussed in detail later in the chapter. Social scientists also have emphasized the role of perception in cultural patterns. They contend that cultural patterns of thought and meaning influence our perceptual processes, which, in turn, influence our behavior:

Culture is defined as a pattern of learned, group-related perception—including both verbal and nonverbal language attitudes, values, belief systems disbelief systems, and behavior. (Singer, 1987, p. 34)

Interpretive Definitions: Culture as Contextual Symbolic Patterns of Meaning, Involving Emotions

Interpretive scholars, influenced by anthropological studies, also view culture as shared and learned; however, they tend to focus on contextual patterns of communication behavior, rather than on group-related perceptions. Many interpretive scholars borrow anthropologist Clifford Geertz's definition of culture. According to Geertz (1973), culture denotes

an historically transmitted pattern of meaning embodied in symbols, a system of inherited conceptions expressed in symbolic forms by means of which men [sic] communicate, perpetuate and develop their knowledge about and attitudes toward life. (p. 89)

One of the most common examples of interpretive scholarship is **ethnography of communication**; these scholars look for symbolic meaning of verbal and nonverbal activities in an attempt to understand patterns and rules of communication. This area of study defines cultural groups rather broadly—for example, as talk show participants or Vietnam War veterans.

ethnography of communication A specialized area of study within communication. Taking an interpretive perspective, scholars analyze verbal and nonverbal activities that have symbolic significance for the members of cultural groups to understand the rules and patterns followed by the groups. (See **interpretive approach** on page 60.)

Ethnography of communication scholar Donal Carbaugh (2007) suggests that it is best to reserve the concept of culture for patterns of symbolic action and meaning that are deeply felt, commonly intelligible, and widely accessible. Patterns that are deeply felt are sensed collectively by members of the cultural group. Gathering around the coffee machine at work every morning, for example, could be a cultural pattern, but only if the activity holds **symbolic significance** or evokes feelings that extend beyond itself. Then the activity more completely exemplifies a cultural pattern. Suppose that gathering around the coffee machine each morning symbolizes teamwork or the desire to interact with colleagues. To qualify as a cultural pattern, the activity must have the same symbolic significance for all members of the group; they must all find the activity meaningful in more or less the same way. Further, all participants must have access to the pattern of action. This does not mean that they must all use the pattern; it only means the pattern is available to them.

symbolic significance
The importance or meaning that most members of a cultural group attach to a communication activity.

Communication theorist Gerry Philipsen extends Carbaugh's notion of culture by emphasizing that these patterns must endure over time, passed along from person to person. Philipsen (1992) writes,

> *Culture . . . refers to a socially constructed and historically transmitted pattern of symbols, meaning, premises, and rules. . . . A cultural code of speaking, then, consists of a socially constructed and historically transmitted system of symbols and meanings pertaining to communication—for instance, symbols "Lithuanian" or "communication" and their attendant definitions; beliefs about spoken actions (that a man who uses speech to discipline boys is not a real man); and rules for using speech (that a father should not interrupt his daughter at the dinner table). (pp. 7–8)*

These definitions of culture suggested by Philipsen are influenced by communication ethnographer Dell Hymes's (1972) framework for studying naturally occurring speech in depth and in context. The framework comprises eight elements: scene, participant, end, act sequence, key, instrumentality, norm, and genre. In this sequence, the terms form the acronym *SPEAKING*. The *S*cene is the setting of the communication event. The *P*articipants are the people who perform or enact the event. The *E*nd is the goal of the participants in conversation. The *A*ct sequence is the order of phrases during the enactment. The *K*ey is the tone of the conversation. The channel of communication is the *I*nstrumentality. The *N*orms, as you know, are the rules that people follow. And *G*enre is the type or category of talk. By analyzing speech using this descriptive framework, we can gain a comprehensive understanding of the rules and patterns followed in any given speech community. Later in this chapter, we'll provide an example of how the framework can be used to explore cultural communication in context.

Culture is not only experienced as perceptions and values, and contextual, but the concept of culture also involves emotions. When we are in our own cultural surroundings we *feel* a sense of familiarity and a certain level of comfort in the space, behavior, and actions of others. We might characterize this feeling as a kind of **embodied ethnocentrism,** which is normal (Bennett & Castiglioni, 2004). (Later on we'll discuss the negative side of ethnocentrism.) This aspect of culture has implications for understanding adaptation to other cultural norms

embodied ethnocentrism
Feeling comfortable and familiar in the spaces, behaviors, and actions of others in our own cultural surroundings.

B̲ob Marley, the well-known singer-songwriter and musician, was born in a rural area of Jamaica to a young, black, Jamaican woman and a white British officer during a time in Jamaica when society divided strictly along racial lines. Marley came to terms with his own racial identity at an early age and resisted being categorized as white or black:

> In the video biography, "Time Will Tell," Marley was asked whether he was prejudiced against white people. He replied, "I don't have prejudice against myself. My father was a white and my mother was black. Them call me half-caste or whatever. Me don't dip on nobody's side. Me don't dip on the black man's side nor the white man's side. Me dip on God's side, the one who create me and cause me to come from black and white." Perhaps it was his biracial background that led Marley to write songs with a universal message. One of his most profound songs addressing unification, "War," took the words of a speech by Emperor Haile Selassie I of Ethiopia and put them to music, "Until the philosophy which holds one race superior and another inferior is finally discredited and abandoned÷WAR!"

Source: http://jahworks.org/bob-marley/.

and spaces. That is, the stronger your identification with a particular space/cultural situation, the more difficult it might be to change spaces without experiencing a lot of discomfort—actual psychological and physiological changes. For example, students studying in France described their feelings in coping with the French language. Their self-esteem dropped and they became very self-conscious. Their whole bodies were entrenched in this effort of trying to communicate in French; it was a laborious and involved process that was connected to all aspects of themselves—a feeling of being out of their cultural comfort zone (Kristjánsdóttir, 2009). We should not underestimate the importance of culture in providing us a feeling of familiarity and comfort.

Although the notion of culture as shared, learned group patterns of perception or symbolic behavior has long been the standard in a variety of disciplines, more and more people are beginning to question its utility. They question how much of "culture" is truly shared. For example, one colleague reports that in a class discussion about the definition of culture in which most students were giving the usual definitions, "one student almost indignantly jumped into our discussion and said, 'Do we really have a common culture?'" She then followed with the question "Whose version of a shared and common culture are we talking about?" (Collier, Hegde, Lee, Nakayama, & Yep, 2002, p. 269). Indeed, these are important questions, and so the next section describes an alternative approach to defining culture. (For a challenge to common notions of a "shared" U.S. culture, take the "Test of U.S. Cultural Knowledge" on pages 98–99.)

Critical Definitions: Culture as Heterogeneous, Dynamic, and a Contested Zone

A more recent approach to culture, influenced by cultural studies scholarship, emphasizes the heterogeneity of cultural groups and the often conflictual nature of cultural boundaries. For example, what is the "U.S. American culture"? Is there *an* American culture? How many perceptions, attitudes, and beliefs and behaviors are actually shared among the many diverse people living in the United States? Critical scholars suggest that in emphasizing only the shared aspects of culture, we gloss over the many interesting differences among U.S. Americans. Further, they emphasize that cultural boundaries are often contested and not easily agreed upon. For example, increasing numbers of people have multicultural identities, growing up to negotiate *multiple* cultural realities. Perhaps the best known is President Barack Obama, whose father was an exchange student from Kenya and his mother a U.S. American student. Others include news anchor Soledad O'Brien, whose parents are Irish-Australian and Cuban; American singer Mariah Carey, who is black, Irish, and Venezuelan; and Jamaican singer Bob Marley. They often resist the many efforts by some to pigeonhole their race/ethnicity, as shown in the Point of View box on p. 93.

This notion of culture as heterogeneous and often conflictual originated with British cultural studies scholars in the 1960s. Cultural studies scholars were fiercely interdisciplinary and dedicated to understanding the richness, complexity, and relevance of cultural phenomena in the lives of ordinary people. This desire to make academic work relevant to everyday life resonated in other fields. Most people, in fact, want to find the connections between what they learn in the classroom and what is occurring in contemporary society. In any case, this movement led to the reconfiguration of the role of the university in society. Cultural studies soon spread from Britain to Australia, Latin America, and other parts of the world. Because of differing cultural and political situations, the specific construction of cultural studies differs from place to place. In the United States, for instance, cultural studies developed mainly within departments of communication (Grossberg, 1993).

You may sense that the concept of culture that emerged from this area of inquiry differs markedly from the concept expressed in social science or even interpretive research. However, it is in agreement with concepts found in recent work in anthropology. Many anthropologists have criticized research that categorizes people and characterizes cultural patterns as set, unchanging, and unconnected to issues of gender, class, and history (Keesing, 1994). Recent anthropological research sees cultural processes as dynamic and fluid "organizations of diversity" that extend across national and regional borders within contexts of history and power (Hannerz, 1996). Communication scholars who embrace the critical notions encourage us to

> *move beyond hegemonic definition of culture as "shared and transmitted from generation to generation" that assumes that we all experience a "common culture" and . . . is passed down from one generation to the next in a linear and seemingly static fashion. . . . [T]his is a dangerous myth . . . that works in invisible yet*

A recent news report from Phoenix, Arizona, illustrates the cultural struggles concerning who gets to be included as a U.S. American. Which of the three approaches to intercultural communication does this story typify?

On this Arizona State University graduation day, Angelica Hernández should be reflecting on her accomplishments and her future career prospects. Instead, she worries about being deported and not being able to get a job. She has no citizenship papers. "There's my degree but I can't use it as much as I want to get a job, as much as I want to help somewhere or do research, I can't. It's just very unfortunate."

Hernández' mom moved her and her sister to Arizona when Hernández was 9 years old, to be with their dad. "She knew that just having my dad there while growing up was worth the risk of crossing," recalls Hernández. Now she's the "outstanding distinguished senior" in mechanical engineering at ASU—which is what a valedictorian is to other universities. She wears a "Dream Act" button proudly.

"I'm just kind of hoping for the Dream Act to pass and to have those kinds of opportunities," she says. "There is really no place for me to go. They say go back home you don't belong here, but I do belong here, this is home for me."

It's a hot issue. Some sympathize with Angelica, while others think the concept is unfair. . . .

Samantha Kozuch is a recent graduate from the University of Arizona. She and her family immigrated from Australia 10 years ago, and she is now a U.S. citizen. . . . She thinks people shouldn't come into the country illegally, but after watching Angelica's story, Kozuch has sympathy for these dreamers. . . .

Jaime Molera, president of the Arizona School Board and former state superintendent, is a Republican, but on this issue he breaks with some of his colleagues.

"I think its a no brainer. She's an American citizen. She came here not of her own volition, but she was raised through our system, she did what she needed to do, she's been a good citizen, she's been a good student," says Molera. "These are kids that are going to end up at Intel or Microsoft, they're going to end up doing great things, they're going to be great contributors to our tax base . . . they'll be great assets to any community they live in. Their only crime is their parents came here illegally and they were babies."

Source: http://latino.foxnews.com/latino/news/2011/05/13/arizona-state-university-valedictorian-undocumented-immigrant/.

extremely powerful ways to suppress and erase marginalized voices and experiences. (Gust Yep, in Collier et al., 2002, p. 231)

Viewing culture as a contested site or zone helps us understand the struggles of various groups—Native Americans, Asian Americans, Pacific Islanders, African Americans, Latinos/as, women, gays and lesbians, working-class people, and so on—as they attempt to negotiate their relationships and promote their well-being within U.S. society. By studying the communication that springs from these ongoing struggles, we can better understand several intercultural concerns. Consider, for example, Proposition 227 in California, passed by voters in 1998, which eliminated public funding for bilingual education, or the debates surrounding the DREAM Act (Development, Relief, and Education for Alien Minors Act). The DREAM Act would allow some undocumented immigrant students who have grown up in the United States to apply for U.S. citizenship if they attend college or serve in the U.S. military (www.nilc.org/immlawpolicy/dream/index.htm). The controversies surrounding these and other propositions illustrate the concerns of many different cultural groups. (See Point of View, p. 95.)

Viewing culture as a contested site opens up new ways of thinking about intercultural communication. After all, the individuals in a given culture are not identical, which suggests that any culture is replete with cultural struggles. Thus, when we use terms like *Chinese culture* and *French culture*, we gloss over the heterogeneity, the diversity, that resides in that culture. Yet the ways in which various cultures are heterogeneous are not the same elsewhere as in the United States, which means it would be a mistake to map our structure of differences onto other cultures. How sexuality, ethnicity, gender, and class function in other cultures is not necessarily the same as, or even similar to, their function in the United States. By viewing any culture as a contested zone or site of struggle, we can understand the complexities of that culture; we can become more sensitive to how people in that culture live.

Our dialectical approach, though, enables us to accept and see the interrelatedness of these different views. Culture is at once a shared and a learned pattern of beliefs and perceptions that are mutually intelligible and widely accessible. It is also a site of struggle for contested meanings. A dialectic perspective can help facilitate discussions on conflicting cultural notions (e.g., how to reconcile U.S. patriotism and instances of anti-Americanism). Our task in taking a dialectical approach is not to say whose views are right or wrong, but to recognize "the truth in all sides of the conflict and understanding the ways in which multiple realities constitute the whole of the cultural quandary" (Cargile, 2005, p. 117).

WHAT IS COMMUNICATION?

communication A symbolic process whereby reality is produced, maintained, repaired, and transformed.

The second component, **communication,** is as complex as culture and can be defined in many different ways. The defining characteristic of communication is meaning, and we could say that communication occurs whenever someone attributes meaning to another person's words or actions. Communication may be understood as a "symbolic process whereby reality is produced, maintained, repaired and transformed" (Carey, 1989, p. 23). The three perspectives emphasize different aspects of this communication process.

For example, the social science perspective emphasizes the various components of communication: There is a sender/receiver, message, channel, and context. This perspective also emphasizes that communication tends to be patterned and therefore can be predicted. This tradition also focuses on the variables, or influences on the communication, like gender, or the nature of a relationship. For example, people in long-term relationships will communicate in a different way from individuals who have recently met, or men and women will tend to communicate in different ways.

The interpretive perspective emphasizes the symbolic, processual nature of communication; the symbolic nature of communication means that the words we speak or the gestures we make have no inherent meaning. Rather, they gain their significance from an agreed-upon meaning. When we use symbols to communicate, we assume that the other person shares our symbol system. Also, these symbolic meanings are conveyed both verbally and nonverbally. Thousands of nonverbal behaviors (gestures, postures, eye contact, facial expressions, and so on) involve shared meaning.

To make things more complicated, each message has more than one meaning; often, there are many layers of meaning. For example, the message *I love you* may mean, "I'd like to have a good time with you tonight," "I feel guilty about what I did last night without you," "I need you to do me a favor," "I have a good time when I'm with you," or "I want to spend the rest of my life (or at least the next few hours) with you." When we communicate, we assume that the other person takes the meaning that we intend. It is more likely, when individuals come from different cultural backgrounds and experiences, that this assumption may be faulty.

The interpretive perspective also emphasizes that the *process* by which we negotiate meaning is dynamic. Communication is not a singular event but is ongoing. It relies on other communication events to make sense. When we enter into communication with another person, we simultaneously take in messages through all of our senses. The messages are not discreet and linear but simultaneous, with blurry boundaries of beginning and end. When we negotiate meaning, we are creating, maintaining, repairing, or transforming reality. This implies that people are actively involved in the communication process. One person cannot communicate alone.

The critical perspective emphasizes the importance of societal forces in the communication process. That is, that all voices and symbols are not equal, but are arranged in a social hierarchy in which some individual characteristics are more highly valued than others; for example, people are more likely to listen carefully to a police officer than to a young child. In addition, powerful social symbols—for example, flags, national anthems, and Disney logos—also communicate meaning nonverbally. Many of these symbols are material as well; that is, they have material consequences in the world. For example, when schoolchildren in the United States bring guns to school and kill schoolmates, the symbolism of these acts communicates something, and the acts themselves are material.

THE RELATIONSHIP BETWEEN CULTURE AND COMMUNICATION

The relationship between culture and communication is complex. A dialectical perspective assumes that culture and communication are interrelated and reciprocal. That is, culture influences communication, and vice versa. Thus, cultural groups

TEST OF U.S. CULTURAL KNOWLEDGE

This test examines your knowledge of many of the cultures that comprise the contemporary United States.

1. *Lagniappe* is a term used in southern Louisiana for:
   a. Hurricanes
   b. Something free or sometimes a small gift given by a store owner to a customer after a purchase
   c. Inviting someone over for a meal
   d. Helping a friend with home remodeling or yard work

2. What is the name of the dish that features black-eyed peas and rice (although sometimes collards, ham hocks, stewed tomatoes, or other items) and is served in the South, especially on New Year's Day?
   a. Chitlings
   b. Jowls
   c. Hoppin' John
   d. Red rice

3. A very sweet pie made from molasses that originated with the Pennsylvania Dutch:
   a. Mincemeat pie
   b. Sugar pie
   c. Shoofly pie
   d. Lancaster pie

4. Which of the following is *not* the name of a Native American tribe?
   a. Seminole
   b. Apache
   c. Arapaho
   d. Illini

5. The month of Ramadan, a month of fasting for Muslims, ends with which holiday?
   a. Eid ul-Fitr
   b. Allahu Akbar
   c. Takbir
   d. Abu Bakr

6. On June 12 every year, some U.S. Americans celebrate "Loving Day" to commemorate:
   a. Your legal right to love someone of another race
   b. Your legal right to love someone of the same sex
   c. Your legal right to be a single parent
   d. Your legal right to get a divorce

7. The celebration of Buddha's birthday is not held on Christmas, but instead on:

   a. Fourth of July
   b. July 14
   c. Asian Lunar New Year's Day
   d. Hanamatsuri

8. Sometimes viewed as a Scandinavian tortilla, these potato flatcakes are often sold in areas with high Scandinavian American populations:

   a. Lefse
   b. Lutefisk
   c. Aquavit
   d. Fiskepudding

9. This traditional Mexican soup is made mostly from tripe, hominy, and chili:

   a. Tortilla soup
   b. Tomatillo
   c. Chorizo soup
   d. Menudo

10. Like a coconut pudding, this food comes from Hawaii:

    a. Lomi lomi
    b. Poke
    c. Haupia
    d. Kalua

Answers can be found on page 121.

influence the process by which the perception of reality is created and maintained: "All communities in all places at all times manifest their own view of reality in what they do. The entire culture reflects the contemporary model of reality" (Burke, 1985, p. 11). However, we might also say that communication helps create the cultural reality of a community. Let's see how these reciprocal relationships work.

How Culture Influences Communication

Intercultural communication scholars use broad frameworks from anthropology and psychology to identify and study cultural differences in communication. Two of the most relevant were developed by anthropologists Kluckhohn and Strodtbeck (1961) and by social psychologist Hofstede (1984).

Kluckhohn and Strodtbeck Value Orientations Researchers Florence Kluckhohn and Fred Strodtbeck studied contemporary Diné (Navaho) and descendants of Spanish colonists and European Americans in the Southwest in

International students describe the different cultural and communication patterns they encounter in the United States.

A graduate student from India noted the U.S. patterns of greeting. In her native culture people only say hello to those they know. Initially, she was surprised by the frequency with which Americans greet each other; she later became disillusioned:

> I thought, they are really interested in how I am. Then . . . "I'm fine and how about you?" Then I realized that people are really not interested in the answer. It is just a way of acknowledging you.

A British student commented on how openly Americans share their religious affiliation.

> At first, I felt like a bit separated because I didn't quite fit into any. . . . They didn't know quite how to respond to me. I thought, Oh, am I supposed to be religious? Am I going to fit in here?

A graduate student from Iran noted how Americans are taught to "sell themselves":

> The job search is another thing in this country that is culturally quite different. . . . In my society, mostly, they ask the professors in the university about efficient people or good students—there is not, you know, no selling yourself. And for the first couple of months I wasn't very successful because I didn't have the experience in selling myself.

Source: From L. A. Erbert, F. G. Perez, and E. Gareis (2003). Turning points and dialectical interpretations of immigrant experiences in the United States. *Western Journal of Communication*, 67, 113–137.

cultural values The worldview of a cultural group and its set of deeply held beliefs.

the 1950s. They emphasized the centrality of **cultural values** in understanding cultural groups. Values are the most deeply felt beliefs shared by a cultural group (see Figure 3-1); they reflect a shared perception of what ought to be, and not what is. Equality, for example, is a value shared by many people in the United States. It refers to the belief that all humans are created equal, even though we must acknowledge that, in reality, there are many disparities, such as in talent, intelligence, or access to material goods.

Intercultural conflicts are often caused by differences in value orientations. For example, some people feel strongly that it is important to consider how things were done in the past. For them, history and tradition help provide guidance. Values often conflict among participants in international assistance projects in which future-oriented individuals show a lack of respect for traditional ways of doing things. And conflicts may be exacerbated by power differentials, with some values privileged over others. Organizational communication scholars have pointed out that many U.S. workplaces reward extremely individualistic relationships and "doing" behaviors at the expense of more collaborative (and equally

---

TABLE 3-2 KLUCKHOHN AND STRODTBECK VALUE ORIENTATIONS

	Range of Values		
Human nature	Basically good	Mixture of good and evil	Basically evil
Relationship between humans and nature	Humans dominate	Harmony exists between the two	Nature dominates
Relationships between humans	Individual	Group oriented	Collateral
Preferred personality	"Doing": stress on action	"Growing": stress on spiritual growth	"Being": stress on who you are
Time orientation	Future oriented	Present oriented	Past oriented

Source: Adapted from F. Kluckhohn and F. Strodtbeck, *Variations in Value Orientation* (Chicago: Row, Peterson, 1961).

[handwritten annotations in margin: "-dia de los muertos", "define yourself as who you are (family, teacher, daughter)", "define yourself by what you do"]

productive) work (Buzzanell, 1994). Kluckhohn and Strodtbeck suggested that members of all cultural groups must answer the following important questions:

- What is human nature?
- What is the relationship between humans and nature?
- What is the relationship between humans?
- What is the preferred personality?
- What is the orientation toward time?

According to Kluckhohn and Strodtbeck, there are three possible responses to each question as they relate to shared values. (See Table 3-2.) Kluckhohn and Strodtbeck believed that, although all responses are possible in all societies, each society has one, or possibly two, preferred responses to each question that reflect the predominant values of that society. Religious beliefs, for example, may reinforce certain cultural values. The questions and their responses become a framework for understanding broad differences in values among various cultural groups. Although the framework was applied originally to ethnic groups, we can extend it to cultural groups based on gender, class, nationality, and so on.

The Nature of Human Nature As the table shows, there are three possible responses, or solutions, to basic questions about human nature. One solution is a belief in the fundamental goodness of human nature. Legal practices in a society that holds this orientation would emphasize rehabilitating violators of the law; jails and prisons would be seen as places to train violators to rejoin society as contributing citizens. Religions such as Buddhism and Confucianism tend toward this orientation, focusing on improving the natural goodness of humans.

A second solution reflects a perception of a combination of goodness and evil in human nature. Many groups within the United States hold this value

Values are complex, and in this post, Sang Won describes the negative and positive aspects of the *high power distance* value common in South Korea:

In South Korea, teachers get a lot of respect. Students must come to school on their best behavior. It is one of the commitments that they make before they come to school. Also, they do not eat or talk during class to show respect to their teachers. However, there is a negative aspect of being so respectful to their teachers. Sometimes, students do not speak up and say their opinion out of respect for the teacher. Consequently, teachers have to teach them how to speak up for their opinions.
—Sang Won

orientation, although there has been a shift in views for many U.S. Americans in the past 50 years. With regard to religious beliefs, there is less emphasis on the fundamental evil of humanity, which many European settlers of the Puritan tradition believed (Kohls, 1996). However, the current emphasis is on incarceration and punishment for violators of the law. For example, consider the increase in "three strikes" legislation and the lack of interest in rehabilitation and reform. Given this orientation, not surprisingly, the United States currently has a higher proportion of citizens incarcerated than any other industrialized country.

According to the third orientation, human nature is essentially evil. Societies that hold this belief would be less interested in rehabilitation of criminals than in punishment. We often have trouble understanding torture or the practice of cutting off hands and other limbs—practices prevalent in many societies in the past—without understanding their orientation to human nature. While he lived in Belgium, Tom was particularly struck by the display of punishments and tortures in the Counts of Flanders Castle in Ghent. Perhaps the key to understanding these cultural practices is an understanding of the Christian view of humans as essentially evil and born in sin.

Relationship Between Humans and Nature In most of U.S. society, humans dominate nature. For instance, scientists seed clouds when we need rain, and engineers reroute rivers and build dams to meet the needs for water, recreation, and power. We control births with drugs and medical devices, and we make snow and ice for the recreational pastimes of skiing and skating. Certainly, not everyone in the United States agrees that humans should always dominate nature. Conflicts between environmentalists and land developers often center on disagreements over this value orientation. And, of course, there are variations in how these values play out in different societies. For example, a country like Canada, which generally espouses a "humans over nature" orientation, still seems more concerned with environmental issues than does the United States. As described by a student,

Canada is very concerned about protecting their environment, and this is very clear even if you are just traveling through. They are concerned about clean water,

J ohn Engle, a professor of Anglo-American literature and civilization, teaches a course, "French and North African Cultural Patterns," to American students studying in France. In a recent article, he describes how difficult it is for many Americans to accept the notion of cultural difference—a problem that he attributes to their own cultural value of individualism. He says he starts his course with important distinctions between stereotypes and generalizations— pointing out that stereotypes are limiting and dangerous while generalizations can be useful, allowing for individual exceptions while permitting categorization, which is necessary for intelligent analysis. He describes how students resist his way of thinking:

"You can't say that," a student will object when you suggest that, say, the ritualized sit-down dinner or the five-week vacation might tell us something broadly significant about the French attitude toward the present moment. "I know people back home who eat long meals. Everyone is different. You can't generalize like that."

The irony is that in essentially refusing to discuss culture, my students are actually obeying powerful cultural imperatives. For what better manifestation of American mythic individualism is there than the conviction that the basic unit of human society is the autonomous self?

Even as a group of students eventually begins to adopt the language of cultural analysis and grudgingly admits an acceptance—at least in theory— of forms of social conditioning, that conviction remains stubbornly close to the surface. Suggest that universal health insurance sends an important cultural message about a European sense of community, and you'll hear that "my home state" of Massachusetts has just instituted similar health protection. Bring up the widespread visiting of French cemeteries on All Saints' Day as a communal sign of respect for the past, and frowns will appear. "Our family," someone will tell you, "visits my grandmother's grave every year."

One clear reason for that resistance to cultural generalization is an American social and economic individualism pounded home endlessly during the first 20 years of a student's life. Students see no reason to discard that outlook when they go abroad, as many of the foreign countries they visit have come to resemble the United States superficially. . . . Come on, aren't they really just like us? . . .

Coming from America—sometimes called a melting pot, sometimes a salad bowl—my students have received mixed, even confused, messages about culture. On their home campuses, they hear about the wonderful world of diversity. But off campus, they are likely to hear very little about the huge cultural differences that exist. Far too few Americans have much knowledge about, or real interest in, the values, social concerns, or politics of other countries. Abroad, the mixed messages limit my students' ability to analyze clean air and not doing too much logging of their trees, keeping streams free of pollution, etc.

In societies that believe mainly in the domination of nature over humans, decisions are made differently. Families may be more accepting of the number of children that are born naturally. There is less intervention in the processes of nature, and there are fewer attempts to control what people see as the natural order.

Many Native Americans and Japanese believe in the value of humans living in harmony with nature, rather than one force dominating the other. In this value orientation, nature is respected and plays an integral part in the spiritual and religious life of the community. Some societies—for example, many Arab groups—emphasize aspects of both harmony with and domination of nature. This reminds us that values are played out in very complex ways in any cultural group.

Relationships Between Humans Some cultural groups value individualism, whereas others are more group oriented. The cultural differences pertaining to these values distinguish two types of societies. Individualism, often cited as a value held by European Americans, places importance on individuals rather than on families, work teams, or other groups (Bellah, Madsen, Sullivan, Swidler, & Tipton, 2007). This characteristic is often cited as the most important European American cultural value. As you can see in the Point of View (p. 103), this value is so ingrained in many U.S. Americans that it rarely rises to a conscious level. In contrast, people from more collectivistic societies, like those in Central and South America, Asia, and many Arab societies, place a great deal of importance on extended families and group loyalty. In the United States, this is the case in Amish communities and in some Latino/a and Native American communities. A visitor to Mexico described one example of collectivism in that culture:

I remember that in public that children always seem to be accompanied by someone older, usually a family member. People went around in family groups—children with older siblings, grandparents, aunts—not nearly so age-segregated as it is here in the U.S.

FIGURE 3-1 Holidays are significant ways of enacting and transmitting culture and cultural values across the generations. For example, Kwanzaa is an important holiday for many African Americans. It was established in 1966 by Ron Karenga and lasts seven days—December 26 to January 1—to mark seven important cultural values: unity, self-determination, collective work and responsibility, cooperative economics, purpose, creativity, and faith. What holidays does your family celebrate? What cultural values are being transmitted in those celebrations? (© *Lawrence Migdale/Getty Images*)

The collateral orientation emphasizes the collectivist connection to other individuals (mostly family members) even after death. This orientation is found in cultures in which ancestors are seen as a part of the family and are influential in decisions even though they are not alive. Examples of this include the Asian practice of maintaining a table in the house to honor their ancestors or the Mexican "Day of the Dead" practice of having a picnic near the graves of the family members and leaving food for them.

Values may also be related to economic status or rural–urban distinctions. In the United States, for example, working-class people tend to be more collectivistic than middle- or upper-class people. (Working-class people reportedly donate a higher percentage of their time and money to help others.) Historian Roxanne A. Dunbar (1997), who grew up poor in Oklahoma, describes an encounter she had with middle-class individualism while on an extended car trip with her new husband, Jimmy. They passed several stranded motorists, the women sitting in the shade while the men worked on the cars. She was surprised when her husband didn't stop to help:

"Why don't we stop?" I asked. No one in my family would ever have passed up a stranded motorist. . . .

> *"They're hustlers, rob you blind, highway bandits," Jimmy said.*
> *"How do you know?"*
> *"I just know, they use the kids and old people for bait to get you to stop, then rob you, they're transients, fruit pickers, white trash."*
> *I stared at the sad faces as we passed by and tried to see the con artists and criminals behind the masks. But they merely looked familiar, like my own relatives. (p. 83)*

These cultural values may influence patterns of communication. For example, people who value individualism *tend* also to favor direct forms of communication and to support overt forms of conflict resolution. People in collectivistic societies *may* employ less direct communication and more avoidance-style conflict resolution. Of course, sometimes people belong to cultural groups that hold contradictory values. For example, most U.S. work contexts require highly individualistic communication, which may conflict with the collectivistic family or ethnic backgrounds of some workers. Workers may find it hard to reconcile and live with these competing values. Consider the experience of Lucia, a Native American college student. When one of her uncles passed away during the first week of school, she was expected to participate in family activities. She traveled out of state with her family to his home, helped cook and feed other family members, and attended the wake and the funeral. Then her mother became ill, and she had to care for her. Thus, she missed the first two weeks of school. Some of her professors were sympathetic; others were not. As Lucia describes it, she feels almost constantly torn between the demands of her collectivistic family and the demands of the individualistic professors and administration.

Preferred Forms of Activity The most common "activity value" in the United States is the "doing" orientation, which emphasizes productivity. (Remember the expression "Idle hands are the devil's workshop"?) Employment reward systems reflect this value in that workers often must document their progress (e.g., in numbers of sales made or numbers of clients seen). In general, the highest status is conferred on those who "do" (sports figures, physicians, lawyers), rather than on those who "think" (philosophers, professors, priests) (Stewart & Bennett, 1991).

The "growing" orientation emphasizes spiritual aspects of life. This orientation seems to be less prevalent than the other two, perhaps practiced only in Zen Buddhism and as a cultural motif in the United States in the 1960s (Stewart & Bennett, 1991). Some societies, as in Japan, combine both "doing" and "growing" orientations, emphasizing action and spiritual growth. The third solution is to emphasize "being," a kind of self-actualization in which the individual is fused with the experience. Some societies in Central and South America, as well as in Greece and Spain, exhibit this orientation.

Orientation to Time Most U.S. cultural communities—particularly European American and middle class—seem to emphasize the future. Consider the practices of depositing money in retirement accounts or keeping appointment books that reach years into the future. Other societies—for example, in Spain or Greece— seem to emphasize the importance of the present, a recognition of the value of

In an interview that appears in *Le Nouvel Observateur*, François Mas was asked to explain the popularity of the medication Viagra (a remedy for sexual impotence) in the United States. He relates the popularity to the "can do" value of the U.S. American people.

> *Probably the most revealing is the "can do" attitude. This attitude, inherited from the pioneers, is how American society, in general, deals with existing problems. Centered on the concrete and practical applications, and often seen as naive in the view of older cultures, this approach has the advantage of deploying a kind of energy and rejecting opposition to progress.*

(Le plus révélateur étant le "can do." . . . Cette attitude, héritée de pionniers, est celle de la société américaine en général face aux problèmes de l'existence. Centrée sur le réel et les applications pratiques, souvent naïve dans son expression aux yeux de cultures plus anciennes, cette approach a l'avantage de déployer une certaine énergie et de refuser l'immobilisme.)

Source: F. Mas, "Vers un Renouveau Sexuel," *Le Nouvel Observateur*, May 1998, pp. 21–27.

living fully in and realizing the potential of the present moment. One of our friends described her impression of this value difference after a visit to Mexico:

> *I had a wonderful experience in Mexico. I liked the energy—there was ALWAYS so much going on in the streets, and in the* zocalo, *all hours of the day and night. And when I returned to the U.S., the streets seemed so dead—everyone individually alone in their own little houses here. I felt suddenly so sensory-deprived!! I guess I also liked it partly because it is so different, culturally, from the way I grew up. The emphasis of expressing and focusing on life in the present. I don't want to imply that life is a constant thoughtless fiesta in Mexico, because it's not. But there was a kind of joie de vivre and enjoyment of life NOW that certainly was not present in my family's very constrained, restrained, serious lifestyle! And so Mexico seemed a great contrast!*

Many European and Asian societies strongly emphasize the past, believing that knowledge and awareness of history has something to contribute to an understanding of contemporary life. For example, the Leaning Tower of Pisa was closed for 10 years while Italian workers repaired structural damage to this historic building.

Hofstede Value Orientations   Social psychologist Geert Hofstede (1984) extended the work of Kluckhohn and Strodtbeck, based on extensive cross-cultural study of personnel working in IBM subsidiaries in 53 countries. Whereas Kluckhohn and Strodtbeck (1961) based their framework on cultural patterns of ethnic communities within the United States, Hofstede and colleagues examined value differences among national societies. Hofstede identified five areas of common problems. One problem type, individualism versus collectivism, appeared in the Kluckhohn and Strodtbeck framework. Although the problems were shared by different cultural groups, solutions varied from culture to culture (Hofstede & Hofstede, 2004). As shown in Table 3-3, the problem types are identified as follows:

- Power distance: social inequality, including the relationship with authority
- Femininity versus masculinity: the social implications of having been born male or female
- Ways of dealing with uncertainty, controlling aggression, and expressing emotions
- Long-term versus short-term orientation to life

Hofstede then investigated how these various cultural values influenced corporate behavior in various countries. Let's examine the other problem types more closely. (See Table 3-3.)

TABLE 3-3 HOFSTEDE VALUE ORIENTATIONS	
Power Distance	
Low power distance	**High power distance**
Less hierarchy better	More hierarchy better
e.g., Denmark, Israel, New Zealand	e.g., Mexico, India
Femininity/Masculinity	
Femininity	**Masculinity**
Fewer gender-specific roles	More gender-specific roles
Value quality of life, support for unfortunate	Achievement, ambition, acquisition of material goods
e.g., Denmark, Norway, Sweden	e.g., Japan, Austria, Mexico
Uncertainty Avoidance	
Low uncertainty avoidance	**High uncertainty avoidance**
Dislike rules, accept dissent	More extensive rules, limit dissent
Less formality	More formality
e.g., Great Britain, Sweden, Hong Kong	e.g., Greece, Portugal, Japan
Long-term/Short-term Orientation	
Short-term orientation	**Long-term orientation**
Universal guidelines for good and evil	Definition of good and evil depends on circumstances
Prefer quick results	Value perseverance and tenacity
e.g., Western Religions Judaism, Christianity, Islam	e.g., Confucianism, Hinduism, Buddhism

Source: Adapted from G. Hofstede and G. J. Hofstede, *Cultures and Organizations: Software of the Mind,* 2nd ed. (Boston: McGraw-Hill, 2004), p. 232.

Power distance refers to the extent to which less powerful members of institutions and organizations within a country expect and accept the unequal distribution of power. Denmark, Israel, and New Zealand, for example, value small power distance. Most people there believe that less hierarchy is better and that power should be used only for legitimate purposes. Therefore, the best corporate leaders in those countries are those who minimize power differences. In societies that value high power distance—for example, Mexico, the Philippines, and India—the decision-making process and the relationships between managers and subordinates are more formalized. In addition, people may be uncomfortable in settings in which hierarchy is unclear or ambiguous.

The **masculinity–femininity value** is two-dimensional (Hofstede, 1984). It refers to (1) the degree to which gender-specific roles are valued and (2) the degree to which cultural groups value so-called masculine values (achievement, ambition, acquisition of material goods) or so-called feminine values (quality of life, service to others, nurturance, support for the unfortunate). IBM employees in Japan, Austria, and Mexico scored high on the masculine values orientation, expressing a general preference for gender-specific roles, with some roles (e.g., main wage earner) better filled by men and other roles (e.g., homemaker, teacher) by women. In contrast, employees in northern Europe (Denmark, Norway, Sweden, and the Netherlands) tended to rank higher in feminine values orientation, reflecting more gender equality and a stronger belief in the importance of quality of life for all.

Uncertainty avoidance concerns the degree to which people who feel threatened by ambiguous situations respond by avoiding them or trying to establish more structure to compensate for the uncertainty. Societies that have a low uncertainty avoidance orientation (Great Britain, Sweden, Hong Kong, and the United States) prefer to limit rules, accept dissent, and take risks. In contrast, those with a high uncertainty avoidance orientation (Greece, Portugal, and Japan) usually prefer more extensive rules and regulations in organizational settings and seek consensus about goals.

Hofstede's original framework contained only four problem types and was criticized for its predominantly western European bias. In response, a group of Chinese researchers developed and administered a similar, but more Asian-oriented, questionnaire to people in 22 countries around the world (Chinese Culture Connection, 1987). Their questionnaire included ideas related to Confucian-based thinking. In comparing their framework to Hofstede's, they concluded that there was, in fact, a great deal of overlap. Indeed, the three dimensions of individualism—collectivism, power distance, and masculinity–femininity—seem to be universal. However, uncertainty avoidance seems to be more relevant to Western societies. A fifth dimension that emerged from the Asian study and that seems to apply to both Eastern and Western societies is the **long-term versus short-term orientation,** which reflects a society's search for virtue or truth.

Those with a short-term orientation are concerned with possessing the truth (reflected in the Western religions of Judaism, Christianity, and Islam), focus on quick results in endeavors, and recognize social pressure to conform. Those

power distance A cultural variability dimension that concerns the extent to which people accept an unequal distribution of power.

masculinity–femininity value A cultural variability dimension that concerns the degree of being feminine—valuing fluid gender roles, quality of life, service, relationships, and interdependence—and the degree of being masculine—emphasizing distinctive gender roles, ambition, materialism, and independence.

uncertainty avoidance A cultural variability dimension that concerns the extent to which uncertainty, ambiguity, and deviant ideas and behaviors are avoided.

time

long-term versus short-term orientation A cultural variability dimension that reflects a cultural-group orientation toward virtue or truth. The long-term orientation emphasizes virtue, whereas the short-term orientation emphasizes truth.

I recently spent two weeks in Mexico City. It was an amazing experience. The contrast between Phoenix and Mexico City totally blew me away, especially the architecture. I mean, just walking down the street you see buildings all around you that are hundreds of years old. We went to the Basilica of the Virgin of Guadalupe, and our guide showed us the exact hill where Juan Diego supposedly saw the Virgin and brought back roses to prove to the priests that he saw her. The priests then built a church exactly right there because that was what the Virgin told Juan to tell the priests to do. Juan Diego is like a national hero in Mexico, and this place where they built these churches is totally sacred. People come from all over Mexico to this exact place, and it is just so hugely important to them.

We also went to Teotihuacán and Templo Mayor. Both are ancient ruins from the Aztecs. These places were really, really amazing. Our guide pointed out for us places where the Spanish built buildings right on top of the ancient structures. It was their way of winning over the natives, of making the Spanish ways take over the ways of the native people. I realized that this change in architecture conveyed a whole history of different cultures and conquest. I was amazed that as I stood there at Templo Mayor, right in the heart of this huge city, I could literally see hundreds of years of history. And the domination also hit me. The Spanish had to build over the temples and other sacred sites of the Aztecs in order to win the hearts of the people. And they needed to make Juan Diego a national hero and make sacred the spot that he is said to have seen the Virgin of Guadalupe. And in order to make all that real to the people, they had to put it all in the architecture.

—Samantha

with a long-term orientation tend to respect the demands of virtue (reflected in Eastern religions such as Confucianism, Hinduism, Buddhism, and Shintoism); to focus more on thrift, perseverance, and tenacity in whatever they attempt; and to be willing to subordinate themselves to a larger purpose.

Limitations of Value Frameworks   Identifying cultural values helps us understand broad cultural differences, but it is important to remember that not everyone in a given society holds the dominant value (Kirkman, Lone, & Gibson, 2006). We shouldn't reduce individuals to mere stereotypes based on these value orientations. After all, not all Amish or Japanese are group oriented, and not all Americans and Australians are individualistic. Remember that cultures are dynamic and heterogeneous. Although people in small rural communities may be more collectively oriented, or more willing to help their neighbors, we cannot say that people in big cities ignore those around them.

Value heterogeneity may be particularly noticeable in a society that is undergoing rapid change. South Korea, for example has transformed itself in the past 50 years from a poor, agrarian country into a global economic and technological powerhouse; it is now the 10th largest economy, the world's #1 leader in broadband penetration, and has the most techno-savvy young people in the world. Influenced by Western capitalism and individualism, many young Koreans are now embracing more individualistic values, making their own decisions regarding marriage and career, rather than following their family's wishes—a practice unheard of 50 years ago (Shim, Kim, & Martin, 2008).

Another limitation of value frameworks is that they tend to "essentialize" people. In other words, people tend to assume that a particular group characteristic is the essential characteristic of a given member at all times and in all contexts. However, a recent study found that all Korean women interviewed expressed *both* a strong family orientation *and* a "relational" concept of self as well as a concept of the autonomous or independent self (Shim, Kim, & Martin, 2008). Similarly, researchers who have spent many years in China also observe that the contemporary Chinese "are not either individualist or collective but both at the same time" (Ambler & Witzel, 2000). It is useful to keep these tensions in mind when thinking about cultural groups—that they often reflect a set of dynamic contrasts, rather than a static set of specific characteristics or traits.

The cultural–individual dialectic reminds us that these value orientations exist on a continuum and are all present, to a greater or lesser extent, in all societies. For example, we could characterize the debate about health care in the United States as a struggle between "masculine" and "feminine" value orientations. Those with a "masculine" orientation believe that each person should take care of him- or herself and be free to achieve and to acquire as many material goods as possible. Others, representing a "feminine" position, believe that everyone should sacrifice a little for the good of the whole and that everyone should be assured access to health care and hospitalization.

The differences–similarities dialectic reminds us that although people may differ with respect to specific value orientations, they also may hold other value orientations in common. For example, people may have different views on the importance of individual or group loyalty but share a belief in the essential goodness of human nature and find similarity in religious faith and practice. Finally, a static–dynamic dialectic reminds us that although group-related values tend to be relatively consistent, people are dynamic, and their behavior varies contextually. Thus, they may be more or less individualistic or group oriented depending on the context.

How Communication Reinforces Culture

Culture not only influences communication but also is enacted through, and so is influenced by, communication. Scholars of cultural communication describe how various aspects of culture are enacted in speech communities in situ, that is, in contexts. They seek to understand communication patterns that are situated socially and give voice to cultural identity. Specifically, they examine how the cultural forms and frames (terms, rituals, myths, and social dramas) are enacted through structuring norms of conversation and interaction. The patterns are not connected in a deterministic way to any cultural group (Philipsen, 2002).

communication ritual
A set form of systematic interactions that take place on a regular basis.

Researcher Tamar Katriel (1990) examines "griping," a **communication ritual** that takes place among middle-class Israelis. Using the SPEAKING framework (scene, participant, end, act sequence, key, instrumentality, norm, and genre), Katriel analyzes the ritual in the following way: The griping topic must be one related to the domain of public life, and the purpose of the griping is not to solve the problem but to vent pent-up tensions and to affirm the shared reality of being Israeli. The ritual is a deeply felt, widely held, accessible behavioral pattern that affirms the cultural identity of Israelis. Although individuals belonging to other cultural groups may gripe, the activity may not be performed in this systematic cultural way and may not fill the same function.

The instrumentality (or channel) in griping is face-to-face, and the scene (or setting) usually is a Friday night gathering in a private home. Participants may be friends or acquaintances, or even strangers, but not real outsiders. (Katriel describes an embarrassing incident when a couple of gripers discovered that one of the group was merely a visiting Jew and not a native Israeli.) The key (or tone) of this ritual is one of plaintiveness and frustration. The act sequence comprises an initiation phase, when someone voices a complaint; this is followed by the acknowledgment phase, when others comment on the opener, and then a progression of subthemes. Finally, during the termination phase, everyone intellectually sighs and agrees that it is a problem: "It's no joke, things are getting worse all the time," the participants might say.

It is possible to compare different ways in which cultural norms and forms such as griping enact aspects of the culture and construct cultural identity. For example, although Katriel is not interested in making cross-cultural comparisons, she does allude to the difference between the Israeli griping ritual and a similar communication ritual that many white, middle-class U.S. residents engage in (Katriel & Philipsen, 1990). The communication ritual is a form of close, supportive, and flexible speech aimed at solving personal problems and affirming participants' identities. It is initiated when people sit down together, acknowledge the problem, and negotiate a solution. Katriel identifies similarities in these two rituals: Each fills the function of dramatizing major cultural problems, provides a preferred social context for the venting of problems and frustration, and promotes a sense of community identity (Katriel, 1990).

A related approach from cultural communication studies sees culture as **performative.** If we accept this metaphor, then we are not studying any external (cultural) reality. Rather, we are examining how persons enact and represent their culture's worldviews. (See Figure 3-2.) Several Latino/a communication scholars have described, in **autoethnographies** (writing about their own experiences), how they each perform their ethnic identity in various contexts, and they emphasize that being Latino is never just one thing; there are multiple, contingent, and overlapping ways to experience and articulate Latina/o identity (Delgado, 2009). They show us that individuals in the same cultural category (Latino/a) may share some similarities but also view and perform their identities in very different ways.

performative Acting or presenting oneself in a specific way so as to accomplish some goal.

autoethnography
Research method where writers examine their own life experiences to discover broader cultural insights.

For example, Hector Amaya (2007) describes how he has "rewritten" himself and performed this identity change through the process of acculturating to upper-middle-class academic life—after coming to the United States as an adult,

FIGURE 3-2 This photo of tourists watching Aztec dancers in Mexico City reflects an earlier context in which Aztec culture was dominant in Mexico. What role does Aztec culture play in Mexican life today? What does this communicate about the continued vitality of Aztec culture in today's Mexico? (*Courtesy Jackie Martinez, Arizona State University*)

learning English, and acquiring graduate degrees. He says that every immigrant must answer the question, "What kind of personal characteristics ought I have to be treated ethically by others?" (p. 195). He describes how he deliberately worked very hard to "learn to perform what others (white majority) value as evidence of moral worth" (p. 200), acquiring the necessary mannerisms, and tastes in clothing, food, and art. It is not easy; he says his "brownness" is still often seen as threatening to whites, and he feels he has to dress much better than most white middle-class people in order to get the same treatment they enjoy even when they are dressed in grubbies. He feels he has to pay more attention to clothing brand, to style, and to newness; things he never considered in Mexico.

Karma Chavez, daughter of a Mexican father and a white U.S. mother, describes growing up in rural Nebraska—in contrast to most Latina/os, who mostly live in urban U.S. areas on the two coasts—and what it means to be brown in the beet-growing heartland of the United States. She describes what happened when a meat-packing plant was opened and the *new* brown (Mexican migrant) workers moved into her town in the 1980s. Many whites were not welcoming to this new group—some even moved away. She tried to distance herself from this marginalized group and stressed her (fictionalized) Spanish heritage to her white friends. "Their Brown bodies reflected my family's history. Their Brown bodies, like a spotlight, highlighted our brownness to the Whites we had learned to relate to in ways that concealed our otherness from them. I learned to hide our food, our traditions, and my father. Those parts of me now seemed vulnerably naked in front of everyone's eyes" (Chavez, 2009, p. 170).

As she grew up, she became more conscious of the discrimination and prejudice against Latinos in her rural hometown and, as a scholar, committed to understanding and changing the marginalized position of many Latinas/os. She could never understand why her parents and grandparents never talked about their negative experiences. As a communication scholar now, she studied the situation and describes how the particular rural context, the distances between farms, and the relatively small Latino/a population affected her family's relationships and identity. In contrast to urban areas with large Latino/a populations, rural living—where Latino/as are few and far between—means you probably have to assimilate in order to survive. She concludes: "Latinas/os in rural spaces often lack Latina/o community, and thus lack the resources to resist discrimination or to reshape Brown-White relationships" (p. 173). Like Amaya, she sees that trying to assimilate to whiteness can be an invaluable resource for those who are capable of performing it. She also notes the high price of the assimilation and what it means to lack resources to resist—that her grandparents rarely speak of the discrimination and even violence they experienced in Nebraska. It is simply too painful.

Finally, Fernando Delgado views his performance as a Latino a little differently from Amaya and Chavez. He describes how he tactically and strategically performs his roles as a Latino teacher, scholar, and administrator in higher education, saying that one is more intentional and deliberate when one's presence is challenged institutionally. He recounts instances of being marginalized as the only Latino in his white Iowan graduate program and describes times where he deliberately seeks separation (not acculturation)—maybe in order to be accepted by Mexican Americans as well as the majority Anglos. He recounts instances of being marginalized by other minority faculty (an African American professor questioned his being listed as a "Faculty of Color," saying that Spanish aristocrats should not be counted toward diversity). He acknowledges he is committed to Latina/o politics, straddling *both* majority and minority worlds and that "Uncertainty, reflection, and self-critique often drive the contingent actions that I take because while on the one hand I may risk losing a job, on the other I may risk losing my self" (Delgado, 2009, p. 163).

Each of these three scholars interrogates their own performances of identity and identifies some constraints to those performances; what are some contextual constraints that might inhibit anyone's performances of identity?

These interpretive studies sometimes use cultural values as a way to explain cultural patterns. Kristine Fitch (1994) conducted a cross-cultural study comparing how people in Bogotá, Colombia, and Boulder, Colorado, got others to do what they wanted, a sociolinguistic form known as a *directive*. Fitch found that directives were seen as a problem in both societies, but as different kinds of problems that reflected and reinforced different value orientations. Individuals in Boulder seemed to think that telling someone what to do should be approached carefully so as not to infringe on that person's autonomy—reflecting a value of individualism. In Bogotá, where collectivistic values reign, directives must be negotiated within relationships; there must be enough *confianza* (respect) or authority that one person is required by the social hierarchy to do the other's bidding. As you can see, cultural values can be used to show how culture influences communication or to explain how communication reinforces cultural values.

Communication as Resistance to the Dominant Cultural System

Resistance is the metaphor used in cultural studies to conceptualize the relationship between culture and communication. Borrowing this metaphor, we can try to discover how individuals use their own space to resist the dominant cultural system. For example, in the fall of 2005, and again in 2007, nonwhite French youth rioted for days in the suburbs of Paris to communicate their resistance to the ways the French social system works. They felt that their efforts to integrate into mainstream French society were being thwarted by systematic racial discrimination. Similarly, workers can find ways to resist the authority structure of management and extreme competition in many ways, some subtle (e.g., work slowdowns, extending their autonomy) and some more obvious (e.g., whistle-blowing) (Mumby, 2005). Working-class clients involved in social services organizations resist the dominant authority structure and try to make relationships and contexts more equitable by breaking some of the rules, or reframing client–social worker relationships (refusing to be treated in demeaning ways) (Tretheway, 1997). Or students may sign their advisors' names on course registration forms, thereby circumventing the university bureaucracy. In all these ways of resisting the dominant cultural systems, people find ways to meet their needs and struggle to make relationships and contexts more equitable.

THE RELATIONSHIP BETWEEN COMMUNICATION AND CONTEXT

Context typically is created by the physical or social aspects of the situation in which communication occurs. For example, communication may occur in a classroom, a bar, or a church; in each case, the physical characteristics of the setting influence the communication. People communicate differently depending on the context. Context is neither static nor objective, and it can be multilayered. Context may consist of the social, political, and historical structures in which the communication occurs.

Not surprisingly, the social context is determined on the societal level. Consider, for example, the controversy over the Calvin Klein underwear ads in the early 1990s that used young adolescents as models: Many critics viewed the ads as equivalent to pedophilia. The controversy took place in a social context in which pedophilia was seen as perverse or immoral. This meant that any communication that encouraged or fed that behavior or perspective, including advertising, was deemed wrong by the majority of observers. However, pedophilia has not been considered wrong in all societies in all periods of history. To interpret the ads adequately, we would have to know something about the current feelings toward and meanings attached to pedophilia wherever the ads were displayed.

The political context in which communication occurs includes those forces that attempt to change or retain existing social structures and relations. For example, to understand the acts of protesters who throw blood or red paint on people who wear fur coats, we must consider the political context. In this case, the political context would be the ongoing informal debates about animal rights and cruelty to animals farmed for their pelts. In other locales or other eras, the protesters' communicative acts would not make sense or would be interpreted in other ways.

We also need to examine the historical context of communication. For example, the meaning of a college degree depends in part on the particular school's reputation. Why does a degree from Harvard communicate a different meaning than a degree from an obscure state university? Harvard's reputation relies on history—the large endowments given over the years, the important persons who have attended and graduated, and so forth.

THE RELATIONSHIP BETWEEN COMMUNICATION AND POWER

Power is pervasive in communication interactions, although it is not always evident or obvious how power influences communication or what kinds of meaning are constructed. We often think of communication between individuals as being between equals, but this is rarely the case (Allen, 2004). As communication scholar Mark Orbe (1998) describes it,

> In every society a social hierarchy exists that privileges some groups over others. Those groups that function at the top of the social hierarchy determine to a great extent the communication system of the entire society. (p. 8)

Orbe goes on to describe how those people in power, consciously or unconsciously, create and maintain communication systems that reflect, reinforce, and promote their own ways of thinking and communicating. There are two levels of group-related power: (1) the primary dimensions—age, ethnicity, gender, physical abilities, race, and sexual orientation—which are more permanent in nature and (2) the secondary dimensions—educational background, geographic location, marital status, and socioeconomic status—which are more changeable (Loden & Rosener, 1991). The point is that the dominant communication systems ultimately impede those who do not share the systems. The communication style most valued in college classrooms, for example, emphasizes public speaking and competition (because the first person who raises his or her hand gets to speak). Not all students are comfortable with this style, but those who take to it naturally are more likely to succeed.

Power also comes from social institutions and the roles individuals occupy in those institutions. For example, in the classroom, there is temporary inequality, with instructors having more power. After all, they set the course requirements, give grades, determine who speaks, and so on. In this case, the power rests not with the individual instructor but with the role that he or she is enacting.

Rose Weitz, a communication scholar, describes the importance of hair for women in U.S. society in attracting men. Although some writers say that women who use strategies like the "hair flip" in attracting men do so unconsciously and are just blindly obeying cultural rules, her interviews with women reveal that many are acutely aware of the cultural rules and the power of the "flip." Those who cannot participate feel marginalized.

A young white woman:

I have very long hair and use the hair flip, both consciously and unconsciously. When I do it [consciously], I check the room to see if anyone is looking in my direction but never catch a guy's eye first. I just do it in his line of vision. [I] bend over slightly, pretending to get something from a bag or pick something up) so that some of my hair falls in front of my shoulder. Then I lean back and flip my hair out and then shake my head so my hair sways a little.

A young Latino woman:

In Hispanic culture hair is very important for a woman. It defines our beauty and gives us power over men. Now that I cut my hair short, I miss the feeling of moving my hair around and the power it gave me. . . .

The hair flip is especially aggravating for those black women whose hair will not grow long. As one black graduate student explains,

As an African American woman, I am very aware of non–African American women "flipping" their hair. . . . I will speak only for myself here (but I think it's a pretty global feeling for many African American women), but I often look at women who can flip their hair with envy, wishfulness, perhaps regret?, . . . with my "natural" hair, if I run my fingers through it, it's going to be a mess [and won't] gracefully fall back into place.

Source: R. Weitz, *Rapunzel's Daughters: What Women's Hair Tells Us About Women's Lives* (New York: Farrar, Straus and Giroux, 2004).

Power is dynamic. It is not a simple one-way proposition. For example, students may leave a classroom at any time during a class period, or they may carry on a conversation while the professor is speaking—thus weakening the professor's power over them. They may also refuse to accept a grade and file a grievance with the university administration to have the grade changed. Further, the typical power relationship between instructor and student often is not perpetuated beyond the classroom. However, some issues of power play out in a broader social context (Johnson, 2006). For example, in contemporary society, cosmetic companies have a vested interest in a particular image of female beauty that involves purchasing and using makeup. Advertisements encourage women to feel compelled to participate in this cultural definition. Resistance can be expressed by a refusal to go along with the dominant cultural standards of beauty. Angela, a student from rural Michigan, describes how she resisted the "beauty culture" of her metropolitan university:

Just out of college, I went to Japan and lived with a family for a few months. I vividly remember the sense of shock upon realizing the gap between my Japanese homestay family's perception of my status, power, and role compared to my own view of the situation. I had seen the experience as a chance for them to show and teach me various facets of Japanese home life and, reciprocally, as a time for me to study my language books and appreciate them. And I tried to learn as much as I could from Ken, their son, whom I considered a role model. One day, however, after what I suppose was a lengthy period of frustration on her part, my Japanese mother took me aside and said, "You seem to look for learnings behind each of Ken's actions, Douglas-san, but remember that since you are older it is you who must teach and be the responsible one."

—Douglas

I came to school, and when I looked around I felt like I was inadequate. I had one of two choices: to conform to what the girls look like here, or to stay the same. I chose to stay true to my "Michigan" self. I felt more confident this way. I still remember looking at all of the blond girls with their fake boobs and black pants, strutting down campus. Four years later, I have a more mature attitude and realized that this culture wasn't for me.

What happens when someone like Angela decides not to buy into this definition? Regardless of the woman's individual reason for not participating, other people are likely to interpret her behavior in ways that may not match her own reasons. What her unadorned face communicates is understood against a backdrop of society's definitions—that is, the backdrop developed by the cosmetics industry.

Dominant cultural groups attempt to perpetuate their positions of privilege in many ways. However, subordinate groups can resist this domination in many ways too. Cultural groups can use political and legal means to maintain or resist domination, but these are not the only means of invoking power relations. Groups can negotiate their various relations to culture through economic boycotts, strikes, and sit-ins. Individuals can subscribe (or not subscribe) to specific magazines or newspapers, change TV channels, write letters to government officials, or take action in other ways to change the influence of power.

The disempowered can negotiate power in varied and subtle ways. Tracy's (2000) ethnographic study of organizational communication on cruise ships analyzes the complex, subtle power dynamics between the ship's staff and management. The staff found it very stressful to follow management's mandate to "never say no [to the customers]" and "smile, we are on stage"; they demonstrated their resistance to management by making fun of the guidelines. Similarly, students might text each other during class or leave the classroom during a lecture as a way of negotiating the power relations between professor and students.

Many of the Thai managers I spoke with while doing research on American companies in Thailand stressed to me that when working with Thais one needed to be very aware of relationships and the hierarchy in which they exist. A Thai woman I spoke with, who was the secretary to the company's American president, provided this example of the need for attention to the details of relationships:

> *I believe in the United States it is common for a boss to ask the secretary to request some materials from another person or to call people and tell them the boss wants to see them. In the United States, you all look at each other as equals. It is not so important what someone's title is, their age, or time with the company. In Thailand, those things are very important. For example, my boss, who is an American, was always asking me to go call so-and-so and request a meeting or go talk to so-and-so and get some reports from them. By having me do this, the Thais were wondering several things: Why should we deal with her; she is just a secretary, and have I done something wrong that the boss does not want to talk with me? Finally, I got my boss to understand that when he had a request for someone—especially someone who was high-ranking in the company, someone who was much older than me or had been with the company longer than me—I would write a short note to that person, he would sign it, then I would pass the note along. That way, everyone's face was saved, their positions were recognized, and the boss came across as show-ing that he cared about his personal relationships with everyone. Mind you, I can run over and ask others of my same rank, age, or time with the company for any information or a meeting, but it is important to show respect toward those in high positions.*

—Chris

Power is complex, especially in relation to institutions or the social struc-ture. Some inequities, such as in gender, class, or race, are more rigid than those created by temporary roles such as student or teacher. The power rela-tions between student and teacher, for example, are more complex if the teacher is a female challenged by male students. We really can't understand intercultural communication without considering the power dynamics in the interaction.

A dialectical perspective looks at the dynamic and interrelated ways in which culture, communication, context, and power intersect in intercultural communication interactions. Consider this example: When Tom first arrived in Brussels in January 1998, he asked for a national train schedule from the information office at one of the train stations. Because he does not speak Dutch, he talked to the agent behind the counter in French. The agent gave Tom a copy of the national train schedule in Dutch. When Tom asked if it was available in French, the man politely apologized, saying that it was the end of the season and there were no more available in French. It was clear to

Tom that, although both parties followed *la forme de la politesse*, the agent did not want to give him the train schedule in French. Indeed, it was not near the end of the season because the 1997–1998 train schedule ran from June 1 to May 23.

From a communication perspective, it might not be at all clear that an intercultural struggle had taken place. None of the traditional signals of conflict were manifested: no raised voices, no harsh words, no curtness. Indeed, the exchange seemed polite and courteous.

From a cultural perspective, however, with various contexts and power differentials in mind, a different view of this intercultural interaction emerges. Belgium is a nation largely divided by two cultures, Flemish and Walloon, although there is a small German-speaking minority in the far eastern part of the country. Belgium is officially trilingual (Dutch, French, German); that is, each language is the official language in its territory. Dutch is the official language in Flanders, and French is the official language in Wallonia, except in the eastern part, where German is the official language. The only part of Belgium that is officially bilingual is the "Brussels-Capital Region."

There are many historical contexts to consider here. For example, Brussels is historically a Flemish city, located in Flanders (but near the border with Wallonia). Also, the French language dominated in Belgium from the time it gained independence from the Netherlands in 1830 until the early 20th century when Flemish gained parity.

There are social and economic contexts to consider as well. Since the 1960s, Flanders has been more economically powerful than Wallonia. The Brussels-Capital Region, despite being in Flanders, has become increasingly French speaking; some estimates place the current percentage of francophones at 85% to 90%. And nearly 30% of Brussels' residents are foreigners, most of whom are francophones. The increasing migration of city dwellers to the suburbs has also caused tensions because a number of communes located in Flanders now have a francophone majority.

So, although the Brussels-Capital Region is officially bilingual, this is the site of a number of struggles between French and Dutch. Indeed, as many Walloons told Tom, one does not get a sense of the conflict in Wallonia, but it is evident in Brussels. In the context of the various tensions that existed at the time of Tom's arrival in Belgium, the intercultural conflict at the train station is merely a playing out of much larger issues in Belgian society. Tom's entry into that society, as another francophone foreigner, situated his communication interactions in largely prefigured ways.

Although he later secured a French train schedule, he continued to use the Dutch one so he could learn the Dutch names of many Belgian cities as well. In any case, Tom's experience involved various dialectical tensions: (1) being a francophone foreigner versus a traditional Flemish resident, (2) being in an officially bilingual region versus an increasingly francophone one, (3) recognizing the importance of formality and politeness in French versus the nature of this ancient conflict, (4) having abundant opportunities to learn French versus the

ANSWERS TO THE TEST OF U.S. CULTURAL KNOWLEDGE

1. The correct answer is B. Lagniappe refers to small freebies or some-times small gifts given by stores when you purchase something. It is used mostly in southern Louisiana and Mississippi but also along the Gulf Coast.

2. The correct answer is C. Hoppin' John is a New Year's tradition across the South. Normally it is simply rice and black-eyed peas, but it can include other items.

3. The correct answer is C. Shoofly pie, traditionally made from molasses, is a very sweet pie.

4. The correct answer is D. The Illini are a nonexistent tribe used as the mas-cot of the University of Illinois at Urbana-Champaign.

5. The correct answer is A. Also sometimes just called Eid, this is a three-day joyous festival that celebrates family, friendship, community, and the Cre-ator. It is a time of reconciliation.

6. The correct answer is A. It marks the anniversary of the Supreme Court ruling in *Loving v. Virginia* that overturned legal barriers to interracial marriage.

7. The correct answer is D. Hanamatsuri (or flower festival) is in the spring and marks a time of renewal and the birthday of Buddha.

8. The correct answer is A. Lefse is made primarily from potatoes.

9. The correct answer is D. Menudo is traditionally served on New Year's Day.

10. The correct answer is C. Haupia is made from coconut milk.

lack of opportunities to study Dutch in the United States, and (5) illustrating the economic power of the Flemish in Belgium versus that of the francophones in Brussels. From these dialectical tensions and others, Tom attempted to under-stand and contextualize his intercultural interaction.

There are no simple lists of behaviors that are key to successful inter-cultural interaction. Instead, we encourage you to understand the contexts and dialectical tensions that arise in your intercultural communication expe-riences. In this way, you will better understand the constraints you face in your interactions. You will also come to a better understanding of the culture you are in and the culture you are from. Although the dialectical perspective makes the investigation of culture and communication far more complex, it also makes it far more exciting and interesting and leads to a much richer understanding.

INTERNET RESOURCES

www.geert-hofstede.com/index.shtml
This Geert Hofstede Cultural Dimensions website provides a description of Hofstede's cultural values dimensions and the specific value scores for a variety of countries and regions of the world. For those of you who may be studying, working, or traveling abroad, you may find it useful to compare the values scores of your home culture and host culture to better understand how the two cultures are similar and different according to Hofstede's cultural dimensions.

www.powerofculture.nl/en
The Power of Culture website provides a review of art and cultural expressions, along with information on human rights, education, the environment, emancipation, and democratization. The website provides links to themes, such as cultural exchange and culture, conflict and culture, and ethics, with news stories and articles related to the subject matter.

http://www.unesco.org/new/en/culture/
This UNESCO Culture Sector website provides links to relevant news and events along with general background information about the changing realm of culture, both regionally and globally. The website also provides links that describe the culture and people from different regions worldwide, such as the Arab states, Latin America, the Caribbean, Europe, and North America.

www.globalvoicesonline.org/
The Global Voices Online website is sponsored by Harvard's Berkman Center for Internet and Society. The site provides blogs, podcasts, photo-sharing sites, and videoblogs from around the world. There is a site search available along with an index of countries and topics. You can select a topic, such as racism or politics, and select the country you wish to read and learn more about in terms of that topic.

SUMMARY

- There are four building blocks to understanding intercultural communication: culture, communication, context, and power.
- Culture can be viewed as
  - Learned patterns of group-related perceptions
  - Contextual symbolic patterns of meaning, involving emotions
  - Heterogeneous, dynamic, and a site of contestation
- Communication is a symbolic process whereby reality is produced, maintained, repaired, and transformed.

- Communication can be viewed as
  - Components of speaker, sender, receiver, message and channel, and variables
  - Symbolic and processual
  - Involving power dynamics
- The relationship between culture and communication is complex:
  - Culture influences communication and is enacted and reinforced through communication.
  - Communication also may be a way of contesting and resisting the dominant culture.
- The context also influences communication: It is the physical and social setting in which communication occurs or the larger political, social, and historical environment.
- Power is pervasive and plays an enormous, although often hidden, role in intercultural interactions.

DISCUSSION QUESTIONS

1. How do definitions of culture influence people's perspectives on intercultural communication?
2. How do the values of a cultural group influence communication with members of other cultural groups?
3. What techniques do people use to assert power in communication interactions?
4. How is culture a contested site?

 Go to the self-quizzes on the Online Learning Center at www.mhhe.com/martinnakayama6 to further test your knowledge.

ACTIVITIES

1. *Cultural Values.* Look for advertisements in newspapers and popular magazines. Analyze the ads to see if you can identify the social values to which they appeal.
2. *Culture: Deeply Felt or Contested Zone?* Analyze the lyrics of songs you listen to and try to identify patterns in the songs. Then think about your own cultural position and discuss which framework—the one proposed by cultural ethnographies (culture as deeply felt) or the one proposed by cultural studies (culture as a contested zone)—more adequately articulates the connection between culture and communication.

KEY WORDS

autoethnography (112)
communication (96)
communication
    ritual (112)
cultural values (100)
culture (88)
embodied
    ethnocentrism (92)

ethnography of
    communication (91)
long-term versus
    short-term
    orientation (109)
masculinity–femininity
    value (109)
performative (112)

power distance (109)
symbolic significance
    (92)
uncertainty
    avoidance (109)

The Online Learning Center at www.mhhe.com/martinnakayama6 features
flashcards and crossword puzzles based on these terms and concepts.

REFERENCES

Allen, B. (2004). *Difference matters: Communicating social identity*. Long Grove, IL: Waveland Press.

Amaya, H. (2007). Performing acculturation: Rewriting the Latino/a immigrant self. *Text and Performance Quarterly, 27*(3), 194–212.

Ambler, T., & Witzel, M. (2000). *Doing business in China*. New York: Routledge.

Baldwin, J. R., & Lindsley, S. L. (1994). *Conceptualizations of culture*. Tempe: Arizona State University Urban Studies Center.

Bellah, R. N., Madsen, R., Sullivan, W. M., Swidler, A., & Tipton, S. M. (2007). *Habits of the heart: Individualism and commitment in American life*. Berkeley: University of California Press.

Bennett, M. J., & Castiglioni, I. (2004). Embodied ethnocentrism and the feeling of culture. In D. Landis, J. M. Bennett, & M. J. Bennett (Eds.), *Handbook of intercultural training* (3rd ed., pp. 249–265). Thousand Oaks, CA: Sage.

Berger, Y. (1998, January 7). A bout portant. *Le Soir*, p. 2.

Burke, J. (1985). *The day the universe changed*. Boston: Little, Brown.

Buzzanell, P. M. (1994). Gaining a voice: Feminist organizational communication theorizing. *Management Communication Quarterly, 7*, 339–383.

Carbaugh, D. (2007). Cultural discourse analysis: Communication practices and intercultural encounters. *Journal of Intercultural Communication Research, 36*(3), 167–182

Carey, J. W. (1989). *Communication as culture: Essays on media and society*. Boston: Unwin Hyman.

Cargile, A. (2005). Describing culture dialectically. In W. J. Starosta & G.-M. Chen (Eds.), *Taking stock in intercultural communication: Where to now?* (pp. 99–123). Washington, DC: National Communication Association.

Chavez, K. (2009). Remapping *Latinidad*: A performance cartography of Latino/a in rural Nebraska. *Text and Performance Quarterly, 29*(2), 165–182.

Chinese Culture Connection. (1987). Chinese values and the search for culture-free dimensions of culture. *Journal of Cross-Cultural Psychology, 18*, 143–164.

Collier, M. J., Hegde, R. S., Lee, W., Nakayama, T. K., & Yep, G. A. (2002). Dialogue on the edges: Ferment in communication and culture. In M. J. Collier (Ed.), *Transforming communication about culture (International and Intercultural Communication Annual*, vol. 24, pp. 219–280). Thousand Oaks, CA: Sage.

Delgado, F. (2009). Reflections on being/performing Latino identity in the academy. *Text and Performance Quarterly, 29*(2), 149–164.

Dunbar, R. A. (1997). Bloody footprints: Reflections on growing up poor white. In M. Wray & A. Newitz (Eds.), *White trash: Race and class in America* (pp. 73–86). New York: Routledge.

Fitch, K. L. (1994). A cross-cultural study of directive sequences and some implications for compliance-gaining research. *Communication Monographs, 61*, 185–209.

Geertz, C. (1973). *The interpretation of culture*. New York: Basic Books.

Grossberg, L. (1993). Can cultural studies find true happiness in communication? *Journal of Communication, 43*(4), 89–97.

Gudykunst, W. B. (2002). Issues in cross-cultural communication research. In W. B. Gudykunst & B. Mody (Eds.), *Handbook of international and intercultural communication* (2nd ed., pp. 165–177). Thousand Oaks, CA: Sage.

Hall, B. (1992). Theories of culture and communication. *Communication Theory, 1*, 50–70.

Hall, S. (1992). Cultural studies and its theoretical legacies. In L. Grossberg, C. Nelson, &

P. Treichler (Eds.), *Cultural studies* (pp. 277–294). New York: Routledge.

Hannerz, U. (1996). *Transnational connections.* London: Routledge.

Hofstede, G. (1984). *Culture's consequences.* Beverly Hills, CA: Sage.

Hofstede, G., & Hofstede, G. J. (2004). *Cultures and organizations: Software of the mind* (2nd ed.). Boston: McGraw-Hill.

Hymes, D. (1972). Models of the interaction of language and social life. In J. Gumperz & D. Hymes (Eds.), *Directions in sociolinguistics: The ethnography of speaking* (pp. 35–71). New York: Holt, Rinehart & Winston.

Johnson, A. G. (2006). *Privilege, power, and difference.* 2nd ed. Boston: McGraw-Hill.

Katriel, T. (1990). "Griping" as a verbal ritual in some Israeli discourse. In D. Carbaugh (Ed.), *Cultural communication and intercultural contact* (pp. 99–112). Hillsdale, NJ: Lawrence Erlbaum.

Katriel, T., & Philipsen, G. (1990). What we need is communication: "Communication" as a cultural category in some American speech. In D. Carbaugh (Ed.), *Cultural communication and intercultural contact* (pp. 77–94). Hillsdale, NJ: Lawrence Erlbaum.

Keesing, R. M. (1994). Theories of culture revisited. In R. Brofsky (Ed.), *Assessing cultural anthropology.* New York: McGraw-Hill.

Kirkman, B. L., Lowe, K. B., & Gibson, C. B. (2006). A quarter century of culture's consequences: A review of empirical research incorporating Hofstede's cultural values framework. *Journal of International Business Studies, 37,* 285–320.

Kluckhohn, F., & Strodtbeck, F. (1961). *Variations in value orientations.* Chicago: Row, Peterson.

Kohls, L. R. (1996). *Survival kit for overseas living.* Yarmouth, ME: Intercultural Press.

Kristjánsdóttir, E. S. (2009). Invisibility dreaded and desired: Phenomenological inquiry of sojourners' cross-cultural adaptation. *Howard Journal of Communications, 20*(2), 129–146.

Loden, M., & Rosener, J. B. (1991). *Workforce American! Managing employee diversity as a vital resource.* Homewood, IL: Business One Irwin.

Martin, J. N., & Nakayama, T. K. (1999). Thinking dialectically about culture and communication. *Communication Theory, 9,* 1–25.

Orbe, M. O. (1998). *Constructing co-cultural theory: An explication of culture, power, and communication.* Thousand Oaks, CA: Sage.

Philipsen, G. (1992). *Speaking culturally: Explorations in social communication.* Albany: State University of New York Press.

Philipsen, G. (2002). Cultural communication. In W. B. Gudykunst & B. Mody (Eds.), *Handbook of international and intercultural communication* (2nd ed., pp. 51–67). Thousand Oaks, CA: Sage.

Shim, Y-j., Kim, M-S, & Martin, J. N. (2008). *Changing Korea: Understanding culture and communication.* New York: Peter Lang.

Singer, M. R. (1987). *Intercultural communication: A perceptual approach.* Englewood Cliffs, NJ: Prentice-Hall.

Stewart, E. C., & Bennett, M. J. (1991). *American cultural patterns: A cross-cultural perspective.* Yarmouth, ME: Intercultural Press.

Tracy, S. J. (2000). Becoming a character for commerce: Emotion labor, self-subordination, and discursive construction of identity in a total institution. *Management Communication Quarterly, 14*(1), 90–128.

Trethewey, A. (1997). Resistance, identity, and empowerment: A postmodern feminist analysis of clients in a human service organization. *Communication Monographs, 64,* 281–301.

Williams, R. (1981). The analysis of culture. In T. Bennett, G. Martin, C. Mercer, & J. Woollacott (Eds.), *Culture, ideology and social process: A reader* (pp. 43–52). London: Open University Press.

Williams, R. (1983). *Keywords: A vocabulary of culture and society* (Rev. ed). New York: Oxford University Press.

CHAPTER 4

HISTORY AND INTERCULTURAL COMMUNICATION

Frances Fitzgerald (1972), a journalist who has written about the U.S. involvement in the Vietnam War, analyzes the U.S. cultural orientation to the future rather than the past:

> *Americans ignore history, for to them everything has always seemed new under the sun. The national myth is that of creativity and progress, of a steady climbing upward into power and prosperity, both for the individual and for the country as a whole. Americans see history as a straight line and themselves standing at the cutting edge of it as representatives for all mankind. They believe in the future as if it were a religion; they believe that there is nothing they cannot accomplish, that solutions wait somewhere for all problems.*

This difference in orientation to the past framed the Vietnam conflict in a very narrow way for the United States. This contrasts greatly with the Vietnamese view of history, especially in the context of their struggles against outside aggression over thousands of years.

You may think it odd to find a chapter about history in a book on intercultural communication. After all, what does the past have to do with intercultural interaction? In this chapter, we discuss how the past is a very important facet of intercultural communication.

The history that we know and our views of that history are very much influenced by our culture. When people of different cultural backgrounds encounter one another, the differences among them can become hidden barriers to communication. However, people often overlook such dynamics in intercultural communication. We typically think of "history" as something contained in history books. We may view history as those events and people, mostly military and political, that played significant roles in shaping the world of today. This chapter examines some of the ways in which history is important in understanding intercultural interaction. Many intercultural interactions involve a dialectical interplay between past and present.

We have found, in the classes we teach, that European American students often want to deemphasize history. "Why do we have to dwell on the past? Can't we all move on?" they ask. In contrast, some other students argue that without history it is impossible to understand who they are. How do these different viewpoints affect the communication among such students? What is the possibility for meaningful communication interactions among them?

On a larger scale, we can see how history influences intercultural interaction in many different contexts. For example, the ongoing conflict between the Israelis and the Palestinians makes little sense without an understanding of the historical relations among the different groups that reside in the area. Historical antagonisms help explain the present-day animosity felt by many Pakistanis toward Indians. Disputes over the Kashmir region, Indian participation in the struggle for independence of Bangladesh, and conflicts over the Himalayas underscore deep-rooted bases for strife.

How we think about the past very much influences how we think about ourselves and others even here in the United States. Judith went to college in southern Virginia after growing up in Delaware and Pennsylvania. She was shocked to encounter the antipathy that her dormitory suitemates expressed toward northerners. The suitemates stated emphatically that they had no desire to visit the North; they felt certain that "Yankees" were unfriendly and unpleasant people.

For Judith, the Civil War was a paragraph in a history book; for her suitemates, that historical event held a more important meaning. It took a while for friendships to develop between Judith and her suitemates. In this way, their interactions demonstrated the present–past dialectic. Indeed, this exemplifies the central focus of this chapter: that various histories contextualize intercultural communication. Taking a dialectical perspective enables us to understand how history positions people in different places from which they can communicate and understand other people's messages.

Early in this book, we set forth six dialectical tensions that we believe drive much intercultural interaction. In this chapter, we focus on the history/past–present/future dialectic. As you will see, culture and cultural identities are intimately tied to history because they have no meaning without history. Yet there is no single version of history; the past has been written in many different ways. For example, your own family has its version of family history that must be placed in dialectical tension with all of the other narratives about the past. Is it important to you to feel positive about who your forebears were and where they came from? We often feel a strong need to identify in positive ways with our past even if we are not interested in history. The stories of the past, whether accurate or not, help us understand why our families live where they do, why they own or lost land there, and so on. We experience this dialectical tension between the past, the present, and the future every day. It helps us understand who we are and why we live and communicate in the ways we do.

In this chapter, we first discuss the various histories that provide the contexts in which we communicate: political, intellectual, social, family, national, and cultural-group histories. We then describe how these histories are intertwined with our various identities, based on gender, sexual orientation, ethnicity, race, and so on. We introduce two identities that have strong historical bases: diasporic and colonial. We pay particular attention to the role of narrating our personal histories. As you read this chapter, think about the importance of history in constructing your own identity and the ways in which the past–present dialectic helps us understand different identities for others in various cultural groups. Finally, we explore how history influences intercultural communication.

FROM HISTORY TO HISTORIES

Many different kinds of history influence our understanding of who we are—as individuals, as family members, as members of cultural groups, and as citizens of a nation. To understand the dialectics in everyday interaction, we need to think about the many histories that help form our different identities. These histories necessarily overlap and influence each other. For example, when Fidel Castro came to power over half a century ago, many Cubans fled to the United States.

FIGURE 4-1   In the United States, the history of racially segregated facilities extends well beyond drinking fountains. Drinking fountains were not segregated by sexual orientation, gender, or some other cultural difference but by race alone. What are some other facilities that were once racially segregated? How does that history help us understand race relations today? Do you know how your family experienced racial privilege and discrimination in the United States? (© *Corbis/Bettmann*)

The families that departed have histories about that experience which help them understand their cultural identity. Political histories tell the story of that exodus but not necessarily the story of every family, even though many families' histories were very much influenced by that event. Identifying the various forms of historical contexts is the first step in understanding how history affects communication. (See Figure 4-1.)

Political, Intellectual, and Social Histories

Some people restrict their notion of history to documented events. Although we cannot read every book written, we do have greater access to written history. When these types of history focus on political events, we call them **political histories**. Written histories that focus on the development of ideas are often called **intellectual histories**. Some writers seek to understand the everyday life experiences of various groups in the past; what they document are called **social histories**.

Although these types of history seem more manageable than the broad notion of history as "everything that has happened before now," we must also remember that many historical events never make it into books. For example, the

political histories Written histories that focus on political events.

intellectual histories Written histories that focus on the development of ideas.

social histories Written histories that focus on everyday life experiences of various groups in the past.

absent history Any part of history that was not recorded or that is missing. Not everything that happened in the past is accessible to us today because only some voices were documented and only some perspectives were recorded.

strict laws that forbade teaching slaves in the United States to read kept many of their stories from being documented. **Absent history,** of course, does not mean the people did not exist, their experiences do not matter, or their history has no bearing on us today. To consider such absent histories requires that we think in more complex ways about the past and the ways it influences the present and the future.

Absent history is also the result of concealing the past. One important way that this happens is when governments forbid access to documents that would give us better insight into the past. Recently, the U.S. government has been reclassifying documents so that they are not publicly available. Historian Matthew Aid (2006) of the National Security Archive at George Washington University notes:

> Beginning in the fall of 1999, and continuing unabated for the past seven years, at least six government agencies, including the Central Intelligence Agency (CIA), the Defense Intelligence Agency (DIA), the Defense Department, the military services, and the Department of Justice, have been secretly engaged in a wide-ranging historical document reclassification program at the principal National Archives and Records Administration (NARA) research facility at College Park, Maryland, as well as at the Presidential Libraries run by NARA. [. . .]
>
> The results of the multi-agency reclassification effort since it began have been dramatic and disturbing. According to figures released by NARA, since 2001 security personnel from the agencies involved have "surveyed" 43.4 million pages of documents held by NARA (i.e., NARA records boxes were sampled to determine if a page-by-page security review of these records was required); 6.1 million pages of NARA documents have been reviewed on a page-by-page basis (the NARA term of art for this process is "audited"); and that as a result of these reviews, since 2001 9,500 documents totaling 55,500 pages have been reclassified and withdrawn from public circulation. Most of the documents removed to date contained either military or intelligence-related information, in some cases dating back to World War II.

If documents are not available, then we cannot know this history—even if others have experienced that history, remember that history, and have written about it. Absent history, then, is not always caused by distant historical decisions; it can result from ongoing and contemporary decisions to deliberately withhold material from the public.

Family Histories

family histories Histories of individual families that are typically passed down through oral stories.

Family histories occur at the same time as other histories but on a more personal level. They often are not written down but are passed along orally from one generation to the next. Some people do not know which countries or cities their families emigrated from or what tribes they belonged to or where they lived in the United States. Other people place great emphasis on knowing that their ancestors fought in the Revolutionary War, survived the Holocaust, or traveled the Trail of Tears when the Cherokees were forcibly relocated from the

Southeast to present-day Oklahoma. Many of these family histories are deeply intertwined with ethnic-group histories, but the family histories identify each family's participation in these events.

Sometimes, family histories shed some light on well-known figures. In his autobiography, *Dreams From My Father*, Barak Obama recounts his family's history from his mother's family in Kansas and their migration to Hawaii to his father's Kenyan family and his connection to them. Although he did not have much contact with his father's family until after his father passed away, his visit to Kenya thrust him back into that part of his family history. More recently, on a visit to Ireland, Obama went to the town where his forebearer, Falmouth Kearney, a shoemaker, lived before immigrating to the United States in 1850 (Mason & Halpin, 2011). His family history is one of immigration and migration that is one part of U.S. history.

Michelle Obama's family reflects a very different family history that is entwined in another part of the nation's story: slavery. *The New York Times* traced her family history and found: "the more complete map of Mrs. Obama's ancestors—including the slave mother, white father and their biracial son, Dolphus T. Shields—for the first time fully connects the first African-American first lady to the history of slavery, tracing their five-generation journey from bondage to a front-row seat to the presidency" (Swarns & Kantor, 2009). Think about how these family histories inform us and the Obamas about their past, as well as their place in the United States and in the world.

You might talk to members of your own family to discover how they feel about your family's history. Find out, for example, how family history influences their perceptions of who they are. Do they wish they knew more about their family? What things has your family continued to do that your forebears probably also did? Do you eat some of the same foods? Practice the same religion? Celebrate birthdays or weddings in the same way? The continuity between past and present often is taken for granted.

National Histories

The history of any nation is important to the people of that nation. We typically learn **national history** in school. In the United States, we learn about the founding fathers—George Washington, Benjamin Franklin, John Jay, Alexander Hamilton, and so on—and our national history typically begins with the arrival of Europeans in North America in the 16th century.

national history
A body of knowledge based on past events that influenced a country's development.

U.S. citizens are expected to recognize the great events and the so-called great people (mostly men of European ancestry) who were influential in the development of the nation. In history classes, students learn about the Revolutionary War, Thomas Paine, the War of 1812, the Civil War, Abraham Lincoln, the Great Depression, Franklin D. Roosevelt, and so on. They are told stories, verging on myths, that give life to these events and figures. For example, students learn about Patrick Henry's "give me liberty or give me death" speech even though the text of the speech was collected by a biographer who "pieced together twelve hundred words from scattered fragments that ear witnesses remembered

COLONIAS

The relationship between the North American Free Trade Agreement (NAFTA) and the growth and development of colonias along the Texas–Mexico border is one example of nonmainstream or hidden history that impacts the population of the United States:

> These shantytowns, called colonias, are home to 1 of every 5 residents of the 14 Texas counties along the U.S.-Mexico border—counties whose population has surged by almost one-third since 1990. The persistent growth of colonias, coming at a time when free trade was supposed to be alleviating poverty in Mexico and along the border, is drawing increasing scrutiny by Texas lawmaker—and raising questions about a possible hemisphere-wide free-trade zone. "Our countries are becoming increasingly interrelated. And with all of its warts, the border area . . . is where things are being tested and proven," says Kermit Black of the Center for Housing and Urban Development at Texas A&M University in College Station. Indeed, since the 1994 North American Free Trade Agreement (NAFTA), economic progress along the border has been accompanied by problems—ones that could impede further success if not taken care of soon, experts say. The Texas State Legislature is taking greater notice. After years of faltering efforts, lawmakers in Austin are now pushing more than a dozen bills related to colonias—far more than past years—in an effort to improve health and safety, as well as to stop the colonias' growth.

Source: K. Axtman, "In Texas, free trade puts border colonias in spotlight." *The Christian Science Monitor*, May 10, 2001, p. 3.

from twenty years before" (Thonssen, Baird, & Braden, 1970, p. 335). Students also learn about George Washington having chopped down a cherry tree and confessing his guilt ("I cannot tell a lie"), although there's no evidence of this story's truth.

National history gives us a shared notion of who we are and solidifies our sense of nationhood. Although we may not fit into the national narrative, we are expected to be familiar with this particular telling of U.S. history so we can understand the many references used in communication. It is one way of constructing cultural discourses. Yet U.S. students seldom learn much about the histories of other nations and cultures unless they study the languages of those countries. As any student of another language knows, it is part of the curriculum to study not only the grammar and vocabulary of the language but also the culture and history of the people who speak that language.

Judith and Tom both studied French. Because we learned a great deal about French history, we understand references to the *ancien régime* (the political system prior to the French Revolution in 1789), *les Pieds-noirs* (colonial

French who returned to France during the struggle for Algerian independence in the mid-20th century), *la Bastille* (the notorious prison), and other commonly used terms. The French have their own national history, centering on the development of France as a nation. For example, French people know that they live in the *Vème République* (or Fifth Republic), and they know what that means within the grand narrative of French history.

When Judith lived in Algeria, her French friends spoke of *les Événements* (the events), but her Algerian friends spoke of *la Libération*—both referring to the war between France and Algeria that led to Algerian independence. When Tom lived in France, he also heard the expression *la Libération*, but here it referred to the end of the German occupation in France during World War II. Historical contexts shape language, which means we must search for salient historical features in communicating across cultural differences.

Cultural-Group Histories

Although people may share a single national history, each cultural group within the nation may have its own history. The history may be obscure (hidden), but it is still related to the national history. **Cultural-group histories** help us understand the identities of various groups.

Consider, for example, the expulsion of many Acadians from eastern Canada and their migration to and settlement in Louisiana. These historical events are central to understanding the cultural traits of the Cajuns. Their neighbors, the Creoles, have been displaced by a more recent historical event, Hurricane Katrina. It remains unclear how the hurricane will shape Creole culture. "With their geographic underpinnings swept away, many New Orleanians of Creole descent are trying to figure out how best to preserve a community separated from both its birthplace and home base" (Saulny, 2005, p. A13). The forced removal in 1838 of the Cherokees from Georgia to settlements in what eventually became the state of Oklahoma resulted in a 22% loss of the Cherokee population. This event, known as the Trail of Tears, explains much about the Cherokee Nation. The migration in 1846 of 12,000 Latter Day Saints from Nauvoo, Illinois, to the Great Basin region in the western United States was prompted by anti-Mormon attacks. These events explain much about the character of Utah. The northward migration of African Americans in the early part of the 20th century helps us understand the settlement patterns and working conditions in northern cities such as Cleveland, Detroit, Chicago, and New York. These cultural histories are not typically included in our national history, but they are important in the development of group identity, family histories, and contemporary lives of individual members of these co-cultures.

We prefer to view history as the many stories we tell about the past, rather than one story on a single time continuum. Certainly, the events of families, cultural groups, and nations are related. Even world events are related. Ignorance of the histories of other groups makes intercultural communication more difficult and more susceptible to misunderstandings.

cultural-group histories The history of each cultural group within a nation that includes, for example, the history of where the group originated, why the people migrated, and how they came to develop and maintain their cultural traits.

I am the fourth generation of females raised in Philadelphia. My great-grandmother raised me until she died, when I was 13. Her mother was a slave who had 19 children. Charlotte, North Carolina, was the place my great-grandmother said she was born. I care because my grandmother had personal information about why blacks should be glad slavery is over. She encouraged my family to make use of all of the benefits of freedom. She always said, "Get an education so you can own something, because we couldn't own anything. We couldn't even go to school." So that is why she moved to the city of Philadelphia. She made getting an education a reward instead of a joke.
—Marlene

I was born and raised in Pakistan, and lived there until I was 7 years old. I remember growing up there very well, but I also remember very well when we moved out of Pakistan. I am basically the first generation in my family to grow up outside of Pakistan. Today most of the immigrants that live in the United States moved here a very long time ago. They have ancestors that came to the United States a long time ago. That is not the case with my family. In addition the immigration to the United States for my family was different in the fact that at first we moved to Canada and then we moved to the United States.
—Waleed

My family immigrated to the United States for a better life. I didn't realize that my family history had so much involvement with the history I learned in class. For instance, my great-grandfather was an orphan who rode the orphan train west from New York until a family chose him and his brother to work on their farm. I also had a member of my family die during WWII, some lived in Chicago during the Chicago Fire, and my great grandpa was a rural mail carrier who used a horse and buggy to deliver the mail. Something I didn't know before was my grandpa, who now works for Burlington Northern, started out as an apprentice telegraph operator. . . . He has come quite far from that!
—William

HISTORY, POWER, AND INTERCULTURAL COMMUNICATION

Power is a central dynamic in the writing of history. It influences the content of the history we know and the way it is delivered. Power dictates what is taught and what is silenced, what is available and what is erased. Let's look at what this means.

The Power of Texts

History is extremely important in understanding identity. Think about all of the stories about the past that you have been taught. Yet, as literature professor Fredric Jameson (1981) notes, although history is not a narrative at all, it

FIGURE 4-2   These young boys are looking through the barbed wire fence at Manzanar, a U.S. internment camp for those of Japanese ancestry, which operated during World War II on the West Coast. Note the guard tower in the back. (© AP Photo/National Park Service)

is accessible to us only in textual, narrative form. However, people do not have equal access to the writing and production of these texts.

Political texts reflect the disparities of access to political participation in various countries at various times in history. Some languages have been forbidden, making the writing of texts difficult if not impossible. For example, U.S. government Indian schools did not permit Native American children to speak their native languages, which makes it more difficult for people today to understand what this experience was about.

With regard to the language we use to understand history, think about the difference between the terms *internment camp* and *concentration camp*. In 1942, at the height of World War II, after President Franklin Roosevelt signed Executive Order 9066, anyone of Japanese ancestry—whether they were U.S. citizens or not—was rounded up from a restricted zone, including parts of Arizona, Oregon, and Washington and all of California, and placed mostly into 10 camps. (See Figure 4-2.) The U.S. federal government used both terms in the 1940s, but the historical weight of the German concentration camps of the same era, in which millions of Jews perished, often casts a shadow over our understanding of the U.S. concentration camps. Denotatively, the use of the term *concentration camp* is correct, but connotatively, it invokes quite different responses. You may wish

POINT *of* **VIEW**

> The internment, or mass imprisonment, of Japanese Americans by the U.S. government in the 1940s has led to much discussion about the right term for these camps. What difference does it make if we call them "concentration camps" or "relocation centers"? This entry from the *Encyclopedia of Japanese American History* provides food for thought.
>
> > **Concentration camps.** *Euphemistically called "relocation centers" by the War Relocation Authority (WRA), the concentration camps were hastily constructed facilities for housing Japanese Americans forcibly removed from their homes and businesses on the West Coast during World War II. Located in isolated areas of the United States on either desert or swampland, the camps were usually surrounded by barbed wire and guarded by armed sentries. Although these sentries were presumably in place to protect the inmates from hostile outsiders, their guns usually pointed into the camps instead of away from them. Most inmates were transported to their camp by train from an assembly center between April and September 1942. In all, over 120,000 Japanese Americans served time in these camps.*
>
> Source: From B. Niiya (Ed.), *Encyclopedia of Japanese American History: An A-to-Z Reference from 1868 to the Present* (New York: Checkmark Books, 2001), p. 142.

to keep this in mind as you read Chapter 6, which discusses the importance of language and discourse in intercultural communication.

When U.S. Americans are taught history, they also learn a particular way of looking at the world from their history textbooks. This worldview, as James Loewen (1995) tells us, reinforces a very positive white American identity. In his analysis of history textbooks, he notes, "History is furious debate informed by evidence and reason. Textbooks encourage students to believe that history is facts to be learned" (p. 16). Yet these "facts" are often wrong or portray the past in ways that serve the white American identity. For example, he analyzes the way in which Native Americans are depicted in history texts:

> *Even if no Natives remained among us, however, it would still be important for us to understand the alternatives forgone, to remember the wars, and to learn the unvarnished truths about white–Indian relations. Indian history is the antidote to the pious ethnocentrism of American exceptionalism, the notion that European Americans are God's chosen people. Indian history reveals that the United States and its predecessor British colonies have wrought great harm in the world. We must not forget this—not to wallow in our wrongdoing, but to understand and to learn, that we might not wreak harm again. (p. 136)*

But the prevailing value of teaching history lies not in serving the future but in reinforcing a positive cultural identity for white Americans. How does power function in determining which stories are told and how they are told?

The relative availability of political texts and the ways that they reflect power-ful inequities are reinscribed in the process of writing history. History writing requires documentation and texts and, of course, is limited by what is available. In writing history, we often ask ourselves, "What was important?" without asking, "Important to whom? For what purposes?" Once texts are written, they are avail-able for teaching and learning about the past. But the seeming unity of the past, the linear nature of history, is merely the reflection of a **modernist identity,** grounded in the Western tradition.

The Power of Other Histories

We live in an era of rapid change, which causes us to rethink cultural struggles and identities. It may be difficult for you to envision, but at one time a unified story of humankind—the **grand narrative**—dominated how people thought of the past, present, and future. The grand narrative refers to the overarching, all-encompassing story of a nation or humankind in general. Because of the way it is built, this grand narrative organizes history into an understandable story that leads to some "truths" over other possible conclusions. In the story of human-kind, the grand narrative was one of progress and an underlying assumption that developments in science, medicine, and education would lead to progress and better lives. This is no longer the case. French philosopher Jean-François Lyotard (1984) writes:

> *In contemporary society and culture—postindustrial society, postmodern culture—the grand narrative has lost its credibility, regardless of what mode of unification it uses, regardless of whether it is a speculative narrative or a narrative of emancipation. (p. 37)*

More recently, communication scholar Dave Tell (2008) has analyzed how a grand narrative about the murder of Emmett Till arose. Tell argues that an arti-cle in *Look* magazine about the murder is key to establishing the narrative of Till's murder, which played an important role in the rise of the civil rights movement.

In the wake of continuous wars and global conflicts, global warming, failed promises of liberation, new diseases such as human immunodeficiency virus (HIV) and bird flu, and other events that challenge what we know and what has changed, the master narrative no longer seems as believable to many. In its place are many other narratives that tell different stories. In the context of intercul-tural communication, the master narratives of many cultures and nations are also undergoing reconsideration, and many new narratives are emerging.

In her work on the constructions of white identity in South Africa, com-munication scholar Melissa Steyn (2001) notes how the grand narrative in South Africa served white interests and led to the establishment of **apartheid.** Although racially restrictive laws existed in South Africa for many years, the South African government instituted a rigid framework for regulating race in 1948. This system, apartheid, lasted until it was dismantled from 1990 to 1994, but only after a long struggle against it. Under this apartheid system, every-one was required to register their race in one of four categories: black, white,

modernist identity
The identity that is grounded in the West-ern tradition of scientific and political beliefs and assumptions—for exam-ple, the belief in external reality, democratic repre-sentation, liberation, and independent subjects.

grand narrative
A unified history and view of humankind.

apartheid A policy that segregated people racially in South Africa.

Since the ending of apartheid in South Africa, there has been a rewriting of the nation's history textbooks in an attempt to forge a new national identity and a different understanding of the past. However, there are strongly contested and very different views about the South African past. Compare, for example, the apartheid view and the post-apartheid view of the establishment of separate areas for whites and blacks during the 1950s and 1960s. Think about how any understanding of history is important in creating cultural identity.

> *Apartheid View: The Group Areas Act is passed, dividing the country by race. Apartheid is an absolute necessity, because all nationalisms are mutually exclusive, and it is in the best interest of both races to live separately from one another. Hence black people must be relocated to "some of the best parts of the country."*
>
> *Post-Apartheid View: Tens of thousands of black people are violently removed from their homes, entire neighborhoods are bulldozed, and dispossessed residents are forced to move to some of the least fertile and most remote regions of the country, where employment opportunities are scarce, if not non-existent. Meanwhile, the white minority secures control of the best land and its mineral wealth.*

Source: From Sasha Polakow-Suransky, "Reviving South African History," *The Chronicle of Higher Education*, June 14, 2002, p. A37.

Indian, and coloured. These categories were used to restrict where people could live (e.g., blacks were permitted to live on only 13% of the land, although they constituted 60% of the population), employment, access to public facilities (e.g., hospitals, ambulances, educational institutions), and other aspects of public life. Although they were numerically a minority, whites dominated this social system and accrued most of the benefits of it. To do so, they needed to tell a master narrative in which this system seemed to make sense. It was only under tremendous domestic and international pressure that the system was dismantled (Bureau of African Affairs, 2005; Guelke, 2005; Thompson, 2001). The popular film *Cry Freedom* (Attenborough, 1987), starring Denzel Washington as Steven Biko, a black leader, highlights the struggle and consequences of apartheid. Steyn writes:

> *In drawing on the master narrative, interpreting it and adapting it to the particular circumstances in which they found themselves in the country, whites were able to maintain their advantage as the dominating group that controlled the political, material, and symbolic resources of the country for three centuries. (p. 43)*

By telling and retelling one view of the past, white South Africans were able to create a society in which a white minority dominated.

In place of the grand narrative are revised and restored histories that previously were suppressed, hidden, or erased. The cultural movements making this shift possible are empowering to the cultural identities involved. Recovering various histories is necessary to rethinking what some cultural identities mean. It also helps us rethink the dominant cultural identity.

For example, on June 30, 1960, at the signing of the treaty granting independence to the former Belgian colony of the Congo (formerly Zaire), the king of the Belgians, Baudouin, constructed one way of thinking about the past:

> All of our thoughts should be turned toward those who founded the African emancipation and after them, those who made the Congo into what it is today. They merit at the same time our admiration and your recognition since it was they who consecrated all of their efforts and even their lives for a grand ideal, bringing you peace and enriching your homeland materially and morally. They must never be forgotten, not by Belgium, not by the Congo. (Quoted in Gérard-Libois & Heinen, 1989, p. 143)

In response, Patrice Lumumba, who would become prime minister, offered a different view of Belgian colonialism:

> After eighty years of colonial rule, our wounds are still too fresh and too deep to be chased from our memory. . . . We have known the ironies, the insults, the beatings to which we had to submit morning, noon, and night because we were negroes. Who will forget that they spoke to Blacks with "tu" certainly not because of friendship, but because the honorary "vous" was reserved only for speaking to whites. (p. 147)

Lumumba's words created a different sense of history. These differences were clear to the people of the time and remain clear today. In this way, the grand narrative of Belgian colonialism has been reconfigured and no longer stands as the only story of the Belgian Congo.

Power in Intercultural Interactions

Power is also the legacy, the remnants of the history that leaves cultural groups in particular positions. We are not equal in our intercultural encounters, nor can we ever be equal. Long histories of imperialism, colonialism, exploitation, wars, genocide, and more leave cultural groups out of balance when they communicate. Regardless of whether we choose to recognize the foundations for many of our differences, these inequalities influence how we think about others and how we interact with them. They also influence how we think about ourselves—our identities. These are important aspects of intercultural communication. It may seem daunting to confront the history of power struggles. Nevertheless, the more you know, the better you will be positioned to engage in successful intercultural interactions.

HISTORY AND IDENTITY

The development of cultural identity is influenced largely by history. In this next section, we look at some of the ways that cultural identities are constructed through understanding the past. Note how different cultural-group identities are tied to history.

The Native American Indian history at Harvard is not widely known and was ignored for approximately 300 years. How might the United States be different, if Harvard had kept its focus on and developed its Indian College from 1675 onward?

Every graduate has a story. Tiffany Smalley's just happens to be 346 years old. . . . They are all Wampanoag Indians, these three. They are accomplished people. They all left Martha's Vineyard to prosper over four years at Harvard. There is, however, a key distinction: Caleb Cheeshateaumuck and Joel Iacommes hark from the 1600s, while Tiffany, sipping a Frappuccino and rushing off to an internship, is every bit of the modern world. [At commencement] she will stride across the stage to accept a diploma and become the first Wampanoag to graduate from Harvard College since Caleb received his degree in 1665. . . . Harvard officials plan to announce today that the university is granting a posthumous degree to Joel Iacommes, Caleb's classmate who was killed in a shipwreck while he visited his family on Martha's Vineyard just before graduation. . . . The awarding of the degree will have various meanings to different people. For the record keepers, it will be, almost certainly, the oldest posthumous diploma ever given in the United States. For Harvard, it marks a new front in rediscovering and highlighting its heritage as a university chartered to educate Indians alongside Puritans. For the Wampanoags from Aquinnah and Mashpee, it is a triumphant dose of hard-earned recognition. . . . [Smalley] was among the many students who have embarked on an archaeological dig for the last several years in the area of Harvard Yard where the Indian College once stood. . . . Those Indian origins run true and deep, though not consistently. The school stipulated in its 1650 charter that the goal was "the Education of the English and Indian youth of the Country" . . . Despite the early success, the mission—and missionary work—came to an abrupt halt in 1675, with King Philip's War. The Indian College was torn down by 1698. Harvard basically pushed aside the Indian tenets in its charter, until the 1970s, when recruiting began anew.

Source: B. McGrory, "Centuries of Interruption and a History Rejoined." *The Boston Globe*, May 11, 2011, pp. A1, A9.

Histories as Stories

Faced with these many levels or types of history, you might wonder how we make sense of them in our everyday lives. Although it might be tempting to ignore them all and merely pretend to be "ourselves," this belies the substantial influence that history has on our own identities.

According to communication scholar Walter Fisher (1984, 1985), storytelling is fundamental to the human experience. Instead of referring to humans as *Homo sapiens*, Fisher prefers to call them *Homo narrans* because it underscores the importance of narratives in our lives. Histories are stories that we use to make sense of who we are and who we think others are.

It is important to recognize that a strong element in our cultural attitudes encourages us to forget history at times. French writer Jean Baudrillard (1988) observes:

> *America was created in the hope of escaping from history, of building a utopia sheltered from history. . . . [It] has in part succeeded in that project, a project it is still pursuing today. The concept of history as the transcending of a social and political rationality, as a dialectical, conflictual vision of societies, is not theirs, just as modernity, conceived precisely as an original break with certain history, will never be ours [France's]. (p. 80)*

The desire to escape history is significant in what it tells us about how our culture negotiates its relation to the past, as well as how we view the relations of other nations and cultures to their pasts. By ignoring history, we sometimes come to wrongheaded conclusions about others that only perpetuate and reinforce stereotypes. For example, the notion that Jewish people are obsessed with money and are disproportionately represented in the world of finance belies the history of anti-Semitism, whereby Jews were excluded from many professions. The paradox is that we cannot escape history even if we fail to recognize it or try to suppress it.

Nonmainstream Histories

People from nonmainstream cultural groups often struggle to retain their histories. Theirs are not the histories that everyone learns about in school, yet these histories are vital to understanding how others perceive them and why. These nonmainstream histories are important to the people in these cultural groups, as they may play a significant role in their cultural identities.

Nonmainstream histories sometimes stand alongside the grand narrative, but sometimes they challenge the grand narrative. As we saw earlier, some nonmainstream histories are absent histories, as these histories have been lost or are not recoverable. Sometimes these nonmainstream histories are **hidden histories,** as they offer different views on the grand narrative and, therefore, have been suppressed or marginalized in our understanding of the past. Let's look at some of these nonmainstream histories and how these views of the past help us better understand different cultural groups.

hidden histories The histories that are hidden from or forgotten by the mainstream representations of past events.

Racial and Ethnic Histories Mainstream history has neither the time nor the space nor the inclination to include all **ethnic histories** and **racial histories.** This is especially true given that the histories of cultural groups sometimes seem to question, and even undermine, the celebratory nature of the mainstream national history.

ethnic histories The histories of ethnic groups.

racial histories The histories of nonmainstream racial groups.

When Tom's parents meet other Japanese Americans of their generation, they are often asked, "What camp were you in?" This question makes little sense outside of its historical context. Indeed, this question is embedded in understanding a particular moment in history, a moment that is not widely understood.

This letter from the president of the United States was sent to all of the surviving Japanese American internees who were in U.S. concentration camps during World War II. In recognizing that there is no way to change mistakes made in the past, what does this letter do? If you were to compose this letter, what would you write? How should we deal with the past to construct better intercultural relations in the future?

THE WHITE HOUSE
WASHINGTON

A monetary sum and words alone cannot restore lost years or erase painful memories; neither can they fully convey our Nation's resolve to rectify injustice and to uphold the rights of individuals. We can never fully right the wrongs of the past. But we can take a clear stand for justice and recognize that serious injustices were done to Japanese Americans during World War II.

In enacting a law calling for restitution and offering a sincere apology, your fellow Americans have, in a very real sense, renewed their traditional commitment to the ideals of freedom, equality, and justice. You and your family have our best wishes for the future.

Sincerely,

GEORGE BUSH
PRESIDENT OF THE UNITED STATES

OCTOBER 1990

Most Japanese Americans were interned in concentration camps during World War II. In the aftermath of the experience, the use of that history as a marker has been important in maintaining cultural identity.

The injustices done by any nation are often swept under the carpet. In an attempt to bring attention to and promote renewed understanding of the internment of Japanese Americans during World War II, academician John Tateishi (1984) collected the stories of some of the internees. He notes at the outset that

> *this book makes no attempt to be a definitive academic history of Japanese American internment. Rather it tries to present for the first time in human and personal terms the experience of the only group of American citizens ever to be confined in concentration camps in the United States. (p. vii)*

Although not an academic history, this collection of oral histories provides insight into the experiences of many Japanese Americans. Because this historical event demonstrates the fragility of our constitutional system and its guarantees in the face of prejudice and ignorance, it is not often discussed as significant in U.S. history. For Japanese Americans, however, it represents a defining moment in the development of their community.

While Pearl Harbor may feel like a distant historical event, the internment of Japanese Americans has drawn important parallels to the treatment of Muslims after 9/11. Because of the fears that arose after these events, "In recent years, many scholars have drawn parallels and contrasts between the internment of Japanese-Americans after the attack on Pearl Harbor, and the treatment of hundreds of Muslim noncitizens who were swept up in the weeks after the 2001 terror attacks, then held for months before they were cleared of links to terrorism and deported" (Bernstein, 2007). "When a federal judge in Brooklyn ruled last June that the government had wide latitude to detain noncitizens indefinitely on the basis of race, religion or national origin" (Bernstein, 2007), a number of Japanese Americans spoke out against the broad ruling and the parallels it had to their cultural group's historical experience.

Similarly, for Jewish people, remembering the Holocaust is crucial to their identity. A Jewish colleague recalls growing up in New York City in the 1950s and 1960s and hearing stories of Nazi atrocities. Survivors warned that such atrocities could happen again, that being victimized was always a possibility. Recent attempts by revisionists to deny that the Holocaust even happened have met with fierce opposition and a renewed effort to document that tragedy in unmistakable detail. The Holocaust Museum in Washington, D.C., is a memorial to that history for all of us.

Ethnic and racial histories are never isolated; rather, they crisscross other cultural trajectories. We may feel as if we have been placed in the position of victim or victimizer by distant historical events, and we may even seem to occupy both of these positions simultaneously. Consider, for example, the position of German American Mennonites during World War II. They were punished as pacifists and yet also were seen as aggressors by U.S. Jews. To further complicate matters, U.S. citizens of German ancestry were not interned in concentration camps, as were U.S. citizens of Japanese ancestry. How we think about being victims and victimizers is quite complex.

French writer Maurice Blanchot, in confronting the horrors of the Holocaust, the devastation of the atom bomb, and other human disasters, redefines the notion of responsibility, separating it from fault. In *The Writing of the Disaster*, Blanchot (1986) asserts,

The history of my race will never be forgotten. I am German and fit the typical blond hair, blue-eyed description. My mother and grandmother both were German so I do have German influences such as the food I eat and some German customs that have been passed down to me. I was always mistaken as a "skinhead," which was quite embarrassing for me. Kids would walk by me and throw up their arm doing the Heil Hitler salute, which was quite offensive to me. "I did not live in that time period, so don't affiliate me with the ignorance of thousands of Germans," is the way I used to handle the people that would insult me.
　—Steve

I was in Germany for a few hours in April. My boyfriend is Jewish, so lately I have been thinking about how the Holocaust has affected his family. I found myself angry at every German in the airport. I knew that I was placing a ridiculous stereotype on the German people.
　—Angela

My responsibility is anterior to my birth just as it is exterior to my consent, to my liberty. I am born thanks to a favor which turns out to be a predestination—born unto the grief of the other, which is the grief of all. (p. 22)

This perspective can help us face and deal with the different positions that history finds for us.

The displacement of various populations is embedded in the history of every migrating or colonizing people. Whether caused by natural disasters such as the drought in the Midwest during the Great Depression of the 1930s or determined by choice, migrations influence how we live today. Native peoples throughout most of the United States were exterminated or removed to settlements in other regions. The state of Iowa, for example, has few Native Americans and only one reservation. The current residents of Iowa had nothing to do with the events in their state's history, but they are the beneficiaries through the ownership of farms and other land. So, although contemporary Iowans are not in a position of fault or blame, they are, through these benefits, in a position of responsibility. Like all of us, their lives are entangled in the web of history from which there is no escape, only denial and silence.

Gender Histories　Feminist scholars have long insisted that much of the history of women has been obliterated, marginalized, or erased. Historian Mei Nakano (1990) notes:

The history of women, told by women, is a recent phenomenon. It has called for a fundamental reevaluation of assumptions and principles that govern traditional history. It challenges us to have a more inclusive view of history, not merely the chronicling of events of the past, not dominated by the record of men marching forward through time, their paths strewn with the detritus of war and politics and industry and labor. (p. xiii)

Although there is much interest in women's history among contemporary scholars, documenting such **gender histories** is difficult because of the traditional restrictions on women's access to public forums, public documents, and public records. Even so, the return to the past to unearth and recover identities that can be adapted for survival is a key theme of writer Gloria Anzaldúa (1987). She presents *la Llorona* (the crying woman) as a cultural and historical image that gives her the power to resist cultural and gender domination. *La Llorona* is well known in northern Mexico and the U.S. Southwest. This legend tells the story of a woman who killed her children and who now wanders around looking for them and weeping for them. Her story has been retold in various ways, and Anzaldúa rewrites the tale to highlight the power that resides in her relentless crying. This mythical image gives her the power to resist cultural and gender domination:

> *My Chicana identity is grounded in the Indian woman's history of resistance. The Aztec female rites of mourning were rites of defiance protesting the cultural changes which disrupted the equality and balance between female and male, and protesting their demotion to a lesser status, their denigration. Like* la Llorana, *the Indian woman's only means of protest was wailing. (p. 21)*

Anzaldúa's history may seem distant to us, but it is intimately tied to what her Chicana identity means to her.

Sexual Orientation Histories   In recounting his experiences as a young man whom the police registered as "homosexual," Pierre Seel (1994) recounts how police lists were used by the Nazis to round up homosexuals for internment. The incarceration and extermination of gays, as members of one of the groups deemed "undesirable" by Nazi Germany, is often overlooked by World War II historians. Seel recalls one event in his **sexual orientation history:**

> *One day at a meeting in the SOS Racisme [an antiracism organization] room, I finished by getting up and recounting my experience of Nazism, my deportation for homosexuality. I remarked as well the ingratitude of history which erases that which is not officially convenient for it. (p. 162)*
>
> *(Un jour de réunion, dans la salle de SOS Racisme, je finis par me lever et par raconter mon expérience du nazisme, ma déportation pour homosexualité. Je fis également remarquer l'ingratitude de l'histoire qui gomme ce qui ne lui convient pas officiellement.)*

This suppression of history reflects attempts to construct specific understandings of the past. If we do not or cannot listen to the voices of others, we miss the significance of historical lessons. For example, a legislative attempt to force gays and lesbians to register with the police in the state of Montana ultimately was vetoed by the governor after he learned of the law's similarities to laws in Nazi Germany.

gender histories The histories of how cultural conventions of men and women are created, maintained, and/or altered.

sexual orientation histories The historical experiences of gays and lesbians.

D
NA testing has helped uncover the hidden histories of families. For Hispanics in the Southwest, DNA testing has helped many realize that they are likely descendants of Marranos (Sephardic Jews) who fled the Inquisition over 400 years ago. Some of these descendants reclaim their Jewish heritage; others do not.

> *When she was growing up in a small town in southern Colorado, an area where her ancestors settled centuries ago, when it was on the fringes of the northern frontier of New Spain, Bernadette Gonzalez always thought some of the stories about her family were unusual, if not bizarre.*
>
> *Her grandmother, for instance, refused to travel on Saturday and would use a specific porcelain basin to drain blood out of meat before she cooked it. . . .*
>
> *Ms. Gonzalez started researching her family history and concluded that her ancestors were Marranos, or Sephardic Jews, who had fled the Inquisition in Spain and in Mexico more than four centuries ago. Though raised in the Roman Catholic faith, Ms. Gonzalez felt a need to reconnect to her Jewish roots, so she converted to Judaism three years ago. . . .*
>
> *Modern science may now be shedding new light on the history of the crypto-Jews after molecular anthropologists recently developed a DNA test of the male or Y chromosome that can indicate an ancestral connection to the Cohanim, a priestly class of Jews that traces its origin back more then 3,000 years to Aaron, the older brother of Moses. . . .*
>
> *Not everyone who discovers Jewish ancestry, either through genealogical research or DNA testing, has decided to convert to Judaism, but some Hispanics who have found links still feel drawn to incorporate Jewish customs into their life.*

Source: Simon Romero, "Hispanics Uncovering Roots as Inquisition's 'Hidden' Jews," *The New York Times*, October 29, 2005, p. A17.

The late Guy Hocquenghem (Hocquenghem & Blasius, 1980), a gay French philosopher, lamented the letting go of the past because doing so left little to sustain and nurture his community:

> *I am struck by the ignorance among gay people about the past—no, more even than ignorance: the "will to forget" the German gay holocaust. . . . But we aren't even the only ones who remember, we don't remember! So we find ourselves beginning at zero in each generation. (p. 40)*

How we think about the past and what we know about it help us to build and maintain communities and cultural identities. And our relationships with the past are intimately tied to issues of power. To illustrate, the book *The Pink Swastika: Homosexuality in the Nazi Party* attempts to blame the Holocaust on German gays and lesbians ("Under Surveillance," 1995). This book, in depicting gays and lesbians as perpetrators, rather than victims, of Nazi atrocities, presents the gay identity in a markedly negative light. However, stories of the horrendous treatment of gays and lesbians during World War II serve to promote a common history and influence intercultural communication among gays and lesbians in France, Germany, the Netherlands, and other nations. Today, a monument in Amsterdam serves to mark that history, to help ensure that we remember that gays and lesbians were victims of the Nazi Holocaust as well.

In the United States, Bayard Rustin is often forgotten, despite his enormous contributions to the civil rights movement. "His obscurity stemmed not only from amnesia but also from conscious suppression" (Kennedy, 2003), despite his major role in U.S. history. *The Nation* (2003) observed: "Rustin helped found the Congress of Racial Equality (CORE) and the Southern Christian Leadership Conference (SCLC). He advised Martin Luther King Jr., organized the 1963 March on Washington and wrote several essays that continue to repay close study. Throughout these pursuits, Rustin expressed a gay sexuality for which he was stigmatized as a sexual criminal, a smear that crippled his ability to lead the movements to which he passionately contributed ideas and inspiration."

Abraham Lincoln's sexual history has also been a major point of contention over a number of years (see Table 4-1). Psychologist C. A. Tripp's book *The Intimate World of Abraham Lincoln* once again raised the possibility that the former president's sexual history included men. While we may never know whatever really happened, the concern over this history underscores the way it may influence our national history. The Lincoln case points to the difficulty in understanding this type of history. The words, *homosexual*, *heterosexual*, and *bisexual* did not exist during Lincoln's era; therefore, those words would not be used to describe his private life. Among other examples, Tripp points to a member of Lincoln's bodyguard, Captain David V. Derickson, who would come over to the White House and sleep in the same bed with Lincoln. Is this evidence for how we might understand this sexual history? On the one hand, it seems odd for Captain Derickson to come to the White House and sleep in the same bed with Lincoln; however, "as many historians have noted, same-sex bed sharing was common at the time and hardly proof of homosexual activities or feelings" (Greenberg, 2005). There is no general agreement about Lincoln's sexual history, but more importantly, the debate over how we should think about Lincoln points to the power of these histories in understanding our national identity.

This concern about national identity is reflected in the way that the president of Iran insisted that there are no gay people in Iran. At a speech at Columbia University in 2007, President Mahmoud Ahmadinejad was booed for saying, "In Iran, we don't have homosexuals, like in your country. We don't have that in our country. In Iran, we do not have this phenomenon. I don't know who's told you that we have it" (quoted in Goldman, 2007). This claim was met with a lot of laughing and jeering from the audience. Interestingly, these comments were "cut out of official Farsi transcripts" (Ahmadinejad's comments, 2007), which influences the writing of history, although a different version is today evident on YouTube.com and other websites. It may seem unclear how these sexual histories influence national identity and cultural identity, but the controversies that arise over them highlight the need to view the past in particular ways.

TABLE 4-1 HISTORICAL CONTROVERSY: ABRAHAM LINCOLN'S SEXUALITY

Year	Event	Reaction	Outcome
1924	Carl Sandburg alludes to Lincoln's homosexual tendencies using euphemisms of the day like "streak of lavender."	This claim was not central to Sandburg's work and was widely dismissed.	Lingering questions over Lincoln's sexual history (Nobile, 2005).
1999	Prominent gay activist Larry Kramer claims to have acquired a journal of one of Lincoln's lovers.	Many historians and commentators rail against Kramer and his claim to have found the journal.	Kramer has kept the journal private, but the controversy has lived on (Lloyd, 1999).
2004	C. A. Tripp makes the definitive claim that Lincoln was gay in his 2004 biography.	Controversy erupts over Tripp's objectivity, his research, and the topic.	Most historians continue to claim that Lincoln was heterosexual, while some question this claim (Brookhiser, 2005).
2008	Charles E. Morris publishes an account of Lincoln's sexual history and an analysis of reactions to the topic (Morris, 2008).		

Sources: Philip Nobile, "Broken Promises, Plagiarism, Misused Evidence and the New Gay Lincoln Book Published by the Free Press," *The History News Network,* January 10, 2005. Retrieved from http://hnn.us/articles/9514.html; Carol Lloyd, "Was Lincoln Gay?" *Salon.com,* May 3, 1999. Retrieved from http://www.salon.com/books/it/1999/04/30/lincoln/index.html; Richard Brookhiser, "Was Lincoln Gay?" *The New York Times,* January 9, 2005. Retrieved from http://query.nytimes.com/gst/fullpage.html?res=9F05E5D61439F93AA35752C0A9639C8B63; Charles E. Morris III, "Profile," 2008. Retrieved from http://www.bc.edu/schools/cas/communication/faculty/fulltime/morris.html.

Diasporic Histories   The international relationships that many racial and ethnic groups have with others who share their heritage and history are often overlooked in intercultural communication. These international ties may have been created by transnational migrations, slavery, religious crusades, or other historical forces. Because most people do not think about the diverse connections people have to other nations and cultures, we consider these histories to be hidden. In his book *The Black Atlantic,* scholar Paul Gilroy (1993) emphasizes that to understand the identities, cultures, and experiences of African descendants living in Britain and the United States, we must examine the connections between Africa, Europe, and North America.

A massive migration, often caused by war or famine or persecution, that results in the dispersal of a unified group is called a **diaspora.** The chronicles of these events are **diasporic histories.** A cultural group (or even an individual) that flees its homeland is likely to bring some customs and practices to the new homeland. In fact, diasporic migrations often cause people to cling more strongly to symbols and practices that reflect their group's identity. Over the years, though, people become acculturated to some degree in their new homelands. Consider, for example, the dispersal of eastern European Jews who migrated during or after World War II to the United States, Australia, South America, Israel, and other parts of the world. They brought their Jewish culture and eastern European culture with them, but they also adopted new cultural patterns as they became New Yorkers, Australians, Argentinians, Israelis, and so on. Imagine the communication differences among these people over time. Imagine the differences between these groups and members of the dominant culture of their new homelands.

History helps us understand the cultural connections among people affected by diasporas and other transnational migrations. Indeed, it is important that we recognize these relationships. But we must also be careful to distinguish between the ways in which these connections are helpful or hurtful to intercultural communication. For example, some cultures tend to regard negatively those who left their homeland. Thus, many Japanese tend to look down on Japanese Canadians, Japanese Americans, Japanese Brazilians, Japanese Mexicans, and Japanese Peruvians. In contrast, the Irish tend not to look down on Irish Americans or Irish Canadians. Of course, we must remember, too, that many other intervening factors can influence diasporic relationships on an interpersonal level.

Colonial Histories   As you probably know, throughout history, societies and nations have ventured beyond their borders. Because of overpopulation, limited resources, notions of grandeur, or other factors, people have left their homelands to colonize other territories. It is important to recognize these **colonial histories** so we can better understand the dynamics of intercultural communication today.

Let's look at the significance of colonialism in determining language. Historically, three of the most important colonizers were Britain, France, and Spain. As a result of colonialism, English is spoken in Canada, Australia, New Zealand, Belize, Nigeria, South Africa, India, Pakistan, Bangladesh, Zimbabwe, Hong Kong, Singapore, and the United States, among many places in the world. French is spoken in Canada, Senegal, Tahiti, Haiti, Benin, Côte d'Ivoire, Niger, Rwanda, Mali, Chad, and the Central African Republic, among other places. And Spanish is spoken in most of the Western Hemisphere, from Mexico to Chile and Argentina, and including Cuba, Venezuela, Colombia, and Panama.

Many foreign language textbooks proudly display maps that show the many places around the world where that language is commonly spoken. Certainly, it's nice to know that one can speak Spanish or French in so many places. But the maps don't reveal *why* those languages are widely spoken in those

diaspora A massive migration often caused by war, famine, or persecution that results in the dispersal of a unified group.

diasporic histories The histories of the ways in which international cultural groups were created through transnational migrations, slavery, religious crusades, or other historical forces.

colonial histories The histories that legitimate international invasions and annexations.

In May 2011, Queen Elizabeth II made her first visit to Ireland. Given the long history between Britain and Ireland, there were tensions and protests during her visit. In her state dinner speech at Dublin Castle, the queen reflected back upon that tumultuous history. What role can such speeches play in helping to build peace and work toward reconciliation? How significant is it that she began her speech with a greeting in Irish?

"A hUachtarain agus a chairde [president and friends].

"Prince Philip and I are delighted to be here, and to experience at first hand Ireland's world famous hospitality.

"Together we have much to celebrate: the ties between our people, the shared values, and the economic, business and cultural links that make us so much more than neighbours, that make us firm friends and equal partners.

"Madame President, speaking here in Dublin Castle it is impossible to ignore the weight of history, as it was yesterday when you and I laid wreaths at the Garden of Remembrance.

"Indeed so much of this visit reminds us of the complexity of our history, its many layers and traditions, but also the importance of forbearance and conciliation, of being able to bow to the past but not be bound by it.

"Of course the relationship has not always been straightforward; nor has the record over the centuries been entirely benign.

"It is a sad and regrettable reality that through history our islands have experienced more than their fair share of heartache, turbulence and loss.

"These events have touched us all, many of us personally, and are a painful legacy. We can never forget those who have died or been injured or their families.

"To all those who have suffered as a consequence of our troubled past I extend my sincere thoughts and deep sympathy.

"With the benefit of historical hindsight we can all see things which we would wish had been done differently or not at all.

"But it is also true that no one who looked to the future over the past centuries could have imagined the strength of the bonds that are now in place between the governments and the people of our two nations, the spirit of partnership that we now enjoy, and the lasting rapport between us."

Source: "In full: Queen's Ireland state banquet speech." *BBC News*. Retrieved June 4, 2011, from www.bbc.co.uk/news/world-europe-13450099.

regions, and they don't reveal the legacies of colonialism in those regions. For example, the United Kingdom maintains close relations with many of its former colonies, and the queen of England is also the queen of Canada, Australia, New Zealand, and the Bahamas. But some colonial relationships are not close, such as the relationship with Ireland (see Figure 4-3 on page 156).

Other languages have been spread through colonialism as well, including Portuguese in Brazil, Macao, and Angola; Dutch in Angola, Suriname, and

Mozambique; and a related Dutch language, Afrikaans, in South Africa. Russian is spoken in the former Soviet republics of Kazakhstan, Azerbaijan, and Tajikistan. In addition, many nations have reclaimed their own languages in an effort to resist the influences of colonialism. For example, today Arabic is spoken in Algeria and Vietnamese is spoken in Vietnam; at one time, French was widely spoken in both countries. And in the recently independent Latvia, the ability to speak Latvian is a requirement for citizenship.

The primary languages that we speak are not freely chosen by us. Rather, we must learn the languages of the societies into which we are born. Judith and Tom, for example, both speak English, although their ancestors came to the United States from non-English-speaking countries. We did not choose to learn English among all of the languages of the world. Although we don't resent our native language, we recognize why many individuals might resent a language imposed on them. Think about the historical forces that led you to speak some language(s) and not others. Understanding history is crucial to understanding the linguistic worlds we inhabit, and vestiges of colonialism are often part of these histories.

Postcolonialism is useful in helping us understand the relationship between history and the present. In struggling with a colonial past, people have devised many ways of confronting that. As explained in Chapter 2, postcolonialism is not simply the study of colonialism, but the study of how we might deal with that past and its aftermath, which may include the *ongoing* use of the colonial language, culture, and religion. For example, many companies are locating parts of their businesses in India because of the widespread use of English in this former British colony. How should people in India deal with the ongoing dominance of English, the colonizer's language, but also the language of business?

For example, Hispanics or Latinos/as share a common history of colonization by Spain, whether their families trace their origins to Mexico, Puerto Rico, Cuba, and so on. Although Spain is no longer in political control of these lands, how do those who live in the legacy of this history deal with that history? In what ways does it remain important, as a part of this cultural identity, to embrace the colonizer's language (Spanish)? The colonizer's religion (Catholicism)? And are there other aspects of Spanish culture that continue to be reproduced over and over again? Postcolonialism is not simply a call to make a clean break from that colonial past, but "to examine the violent actions and erasures of colonialism" (Shome & Hegde, 2002, p. 250). In this case, that interrogation might even mean reconsidering the category "Hispanic" that incorporates a wide range of groups that share a Spanish colonial history but do not share other histories that constitute their cultures. The legacy of this cultural invasion often lasts much longer than the political relationship.

Socioeconomic Class Histories   Although we often overlook the importance of socioeconomic class as a factor in history, the fact is that economic and class issues prompted many people to emigrate to the United States. The poverty in Ireland in the 19th century, for example, did much to fuel the flight to the United States; in fact, today, there are more Irish Americans than Irish.

Yet it is not always the socioeconomically disadvantaged who emigrate. After the Russian Revolution in 1917, many affluent Russians moved to Paris. Likewise, many affluent Cubans left the country after Castro seized power in 1959. Today, Canada offers business immigration status to investors who own their own businesses and "who have a net worth, accumulated by their own endeavors, of at least CAD [Canadian dollars] $500,000" ("Immigrant Investor Program Redesign," 1998). Although the program varies somewhat from province to province, the policy ensures that socioeconomic class continues to influence some migrations.

The key point here is that socioeconomic class distinctions are often overlooked in examining the migrations and acculturation of groups around the world. Historically, the kinds of employment that immigrants supplied and the regions they settled were often marked by the kinds of capital—cultural and financial—that they were or were not able to bring with them. These factors also influence the interactions and politics of different groups; for example, Mexican Americans and Cuban Americans, as groups, frequently are at odds with the political mainstream.

Religious Histories   In the past, as well as today, religion is an important historical force that has shaped our planet. Religious conflicts have led to wars, such as the Christian Crusades nearly a thousand years ago. Religious persecution has also led to migration of various religious groups to new places. In the United States, one example of this movement are the Mormons, who left New York, settled in Illinois, and then left to go to Utah. Many French Huguenots (Protestants), persecuted by French Catholics, left France to settle primarily in North America, South Africa, and elsewhere in Europe.

Because many of these religious histories remain controversial, they are viewed differently, depending on with which side one identifies. Even recent historical events, and how they are interpreted, can create religious conflict. In August 2010, a New York City commission approved the construction of a mosque near "Ground Zero," the site of the former World Trade Center. This created a national controversy over the proposed mosque and the role of Islam in the attacks on 9/11. For many Muslims, the 9/11 attackers were extremists, much like the extremists in many other religions. For many non-Muslims, the 9/11 attackers were acting as Muslims. In a speech made a White House dinner, President Obama stated:

> *Now, that's not to say that religion is without controversy. Recently, attention has been focused on the construction of mosques in certain communities—particularly New York. Now, we must all recognize and respect the sensitivities surrounding the development of Lower Manhattan. The 9/11 attacks were a deeply traumatic event for our country. And the pain and the experience of suffering by those who lost loved ones is just unimaginable. So I understand the emotions that this issue engenders. And Ground Zero is, indeed, hallowed ground. But let me be clear. As a citizen, and as President, I believe that Muslims have the same right to practice their religion as everyone else in this country. (Applause.) And that includes the*

right to build a place of worship and a community center on private property in Lower Manhattan, in accordance with local laws and ordinances. This is America. And our commitment to religious freedom must be unshakeable. The principle that people of all faiths are welcome in this country and that they will not be treated differently by their government is essential to who we are.

In this example, we can see that different views about the role of religion in the past can create contemporary controversies. Although religious freedom is an important American cultural value, as noted by President Obama, that cultural value can be in tension with other views on what happened and why on 9/11.

INTERCULTURAL COMMUNICATION AND HISTORY

One way to understand specific relationships between communication and history is to examine the attitudes and notions that individuals bring to an interaction; these are the antecedents of contact. A second way is to look at the specific conditions of the interaction and the role that history plays in these contexts. Finally, we can examine how various histories are negotiated in intercultural interaction, applying a dialectical perspective to these different histories.

Antecedents of Contact

We may be able to negotiate some aspects of history in interaction, but it is important to recognize that we bring our personal histories to each intercultural interaction. These personal histories involve our prior experience and our attitudes. Social psychologist Richard Brislin (1981) has identified four elements of personal histories that influence interaction.

First, people bring childhood experiences to interactions. For example, both Judith and Tom grew up hearing negative comments about Catholics. As a result, our first interactions with adherents to this faith were tinged with some suspicion. This personal history did not affect initial interactions with people of other religions.

Second, people may bring historical myths to interactions. These are myths with which many people are familiar. The Jewish conspiracy myth—that Jewish people are secretly in control of U.S. government and business—is one example.

Third, the languages that people speak influence their interactions. Language can be an attraction or a repellent in intercultural interactions. For example, many people from the United States enjoy traveling in Britain because English is spoken there. However, these same people may have little desire, or even be afraid, to visit Russia, simply because it is not an English-speaking country.

Finally, people tend to be affected by recent, vivid events. For example, after the bombing of the World Trade Center in New York, interactions between Arab Americans and other U.S. residents were strained, characterized by suspicion, fear, and distrust. The media's treatment of such catastrophic events often creates barriers and reinforces stereotypes by blurring distinctions between

The complexities of dealing with racial history is reflected in the many actions taken in Florida. History, although it is past, continues to shape contemporary cultural experiences.

Mar. 30—It's not just sound bites that stir the melting pot.

Last week in Florida's Legislature, lawmakers approved a resolution expressing "profound regret" for slavery. At the same time, they are considering a bill that establishes a Confederate license plate. There's also a bill that would retire the state song—a tune known as "Swanee River" that is loved by some and considered a racist throwback by others.

Another bill prohibits hanging nooses to intimidate.

All of this is going on in a state capitol that flew the Confederate flag until seven years ago, when former Gov. Jeb Bush quietly removed it and put it in a history museum a few blocks away.

And in Hillsborough County, the county commission declared 2007 the year of Robert E. Lee—on the same day it honored local civil rights activist James A. Hammond. In another twist, the same body last year refused to acknowledge Confederate Memorial Day, a Florida holiday since 1895.

Whether Floridians see any of these measures as race-biased, their existence at the same time in the same place illustrates how complex the issue of race still is today.

"If people think race relations are solved, they're not living in our world," said Tony Morejon, Hillsborough County's liaison with Hispanic residents.

It's not just lawmakers who are dealing with the conflicts.

Twenty thousand people went to tiny Jena, La., last year to protest charges against six black teenagers arrested in the beating of a white classmate. Race was at the center of the Duke lacrosse rape case fiasco, which made national news when white players were accused of raping a black woman.

Here, a Seminole Heights resident found a noose hanging in her neighborhood last month, prompting questions about who would hang it and why.

Five months ago, 700 protesters marched in Tallahassee after boot camp guards were acquitted in the death of a black teen. They wore T-shirts and carried signs that recalled the killing of Emmett Till, a 14-year-old black boy who was killed in 1955 in Mississippi for whistling at a white woman.

They sang "We Shall Overcome."

Source: Gretchen Parker, "Dealing with Issues of Race in America," *Tampa Tribune*, March 30, 2008, http://www2.tbo.com/content/2008/mar/30/dealing-issues-race-america/.

Arabs, Persians, Muslims, and Palestinians. Perhaps recent histories, such as the racially motivated riots in Los Angeles in the mid-1990s, are more influential in our interactions than the hidden or past histories, such as the massacre in 1890 of some 260 Sioux Indians at Wounded Knee in South Dakota or the women's suffrage movement around the turn of the 20th century.

On May 2, 2011, Osama bin Laden was killed by U.S. military forces at his residence in Pakistan. In the course of the military action, the U.S. Defense Department chose the name "Geronimo" as the code word for Osama bin Laden or the operation itself. The use of Geronimo in this context created a controversy that highlights the ways the use of history can create conflict between cultural groups. Many Native Americans took great offense at the use of Geronimo's name. It's very important to think about how we use history for present needs, as heroes in one culture might be villains in another (and vice versa). Harlyn Geronimo, a great-grandson of Geronimo submitted a statement to the U.S. Senate Commission on Indian Affairs, which reads, in part:

> *Whether it was intended only to name the military operation to kill or capture Osama Bin Laden or to give Osama Bin Laden himself the code name Geronimo, either was an outrageous insult and mistake. And it is clear from the military records released that the name Geronimo was used at times by military personnel involved for both the military operation and for Osama Bin Laden himself.*
>
> *Obviously to equate Geronimo with Osama Bin Laden is an unpardonable slander of Native America and its most famous leader in history.*
>
> *And to call the operation to kill or capture Osama Bin Laden by the name Geronimo is such a subversion of history that it also defames a great human spirit and Native American leader. For Geronimo himself was the focus of precisely such an operation by the U.S. military, an operation that assured Geronimo a lasting place in American and human history.*

Source: "Indian Country Responds to Geronimo, bin Laden Connection," *Indian Country Today Media Network*, May 4, 2011. Retrieved June 11, 2011, from http://indiancountrytoday medianetwork.com/2011/05/indian-country-responds-to-geronimo-bin-laden-connection/.

The Contact Hypothesis

The **contact hypothesis** is the notion that better communication between groups of people is facilitated simply by bringing them together and allowing them to interact. Although history does not seem to support this notion, many public policies and programs in the United States and abroad are based on this hypothesis. Examples include desegregation rulings; the prevalence of master-planned communities like Reston, Virginia; and many international student exchange programs. All of these programs are based on the assumption that simply giving people from different groups opportunities to interact will result in more positive intergroup attitudes and reduced prejudice.

Gordon Allport (1979) and Yehudi Amir (1969), two noted psychologists, have tried to identify the conditions under which the contact hypothesis does and does not hold true. The histories of various groups figure prominently in their studies. Based on these and subsequent studies, psychologists have outlined at least eight

contact hypothesis
The notion that better communication between groups is facilitated simply by putting people together in the same place and allowing them to interact.

FIGURE 4-3   Irish dissident Republicans hold a protest close to Dublin Castle as Britain's Queen Elizabeth II made a historic address in Irish toward the end of her second day of her State Visit to Dublin, Ireland, May 18, 2011. The Queen began her speech in Irish by addressing "A hUachtarain agus a chairde." The Queen said it was impossible to ignore the weight of history, as so much of the visit reminds people of the complexity of the history between both countries. She said the relationship had not always been straightforward and that the islands had experienced more than their fair share of heartache, turbulence, and loss. (© *Enda Doran/epa/Corbis*)

conditions that must be met (more or less) to improve attitudes and facilitate intergroup communication (Schwarzwald & Amir, 1996; Stephan & Stephan, 1996). These are particularly relevant in light of increasing diversity in U.S. society in general and the workforce in particular. The eight conditions are as follows:

1. Group members should be of equal status, both within and outside the contact situation. Communication will occur more easily if there is no disparity between individuals in status characteristics (education, socioeconomic status, and so on). This condition does not include temporary inequality, such as in student–teacher or patient–doctor roles. Consider the implications of this condition for relations among various ethnic groups in the United States. How are we likely to think of individuals from specific ethnic groups if our interactions are characterized by inequality? A good example is the interaction between longtime residents and recent immigrants in the Southwest, where Mexican Americans often provide housecleaning, gardening, and similar services for whites. It is easy to see how the history of these two groups in the United States contributes to the lack of equality in interaction, leads to stereotyping, and inhibits effective

intercultural communication. But the history of relations between Mexican Americans and whites varies within this region. For example, families of Spanish descent have lived in New Mexico longer than other European-descent families, whereas Arizona has a higher concentration of recent immigrants from Mexico. Intergroup interactions in New Mexico are characterized less by inequality (Stephan & Stephan, 1989).

2. Strong normative and institutional support for the contact should be provided. This suggests that when individuals from different groups come together, positive outcomes do not happen by accident. Rather, institutional encouragement is necessary. Examples include university support for contact between U.S. and international students, or for contact among different cultural groups within the university, and local community support for integrating elementary and high schools. Numerous studies have shown the importance of commitment by top management to policies that facilitate intercultural interaction in the workplace (Brinkman, 1997). Finally, institutional support may also mean government and legal support, expressed through court action.

3. Contact between the groups should be voluntary. This may seem to contradict the previous condition, but it doesn't. Although support must exist beyond the individual, individuals need to feel that they have a choice in making contact. If they believe that they are being forced to interact, as with some diversity programs or affirmative action programs, the intercultural interaction is unlikely to have positive outcomes. For example, an air traffic controller was so incensed by a required diversity program exercise on gender differences that he sued the Department of Transportation for $300,000 (Erbe & Hart, 1994). A better program design would be to involve all participants from the beginning. This can be done by showing the benefits of an inclusive diversity policy—one that values all kinds of diversity, and not merely that based on gender, for example. Equally important is the mounting evidence of bottom-line benefits of diverse personnel who work well together (Harris, 1997).

4. The contact should have the potential to extend beyond the immediate situation and occur in a variety of contexts with a variety of individuals from all groups. This suggests that superficial contact between members of different groups is not likely to have much impact on attitudes (stereotypes, prejudice) or result in productive communication. For instance, simply sitting beside someone from another culture in a class or sampling food from different countries is not likely to result in genuine understanding of that perszon or appreciation for his or her cultural background (Stephan & Stephan, 1992). Thus, international students who live with host families are much more likely to have positive impressions of the host country and to develop better intercultural communication skills than those who go on "island programs," in which students interact mostly with other foreigners in the host country.

5. Programs should maximize cooperation within groups and minimize competition. For example, bringing a diverse group of students together should

not involve pitting the African Americans against the European Americans on separate sports teams. Instead, it might involve creating diversity within teams to emphasize cooperation. Especially important is having a superordinate goal, a goal that everyone can agree on. This helps diverse groups develop a common identity (Gaertner, Dovidio, & Bachman, 1996). For instance, there is a successful summer camp in Maine for Arab and Jewish youths; the camp brings together members of these historically conflicting groups for a summer of cooperation, discussion, and relationship building.

6. Programs should equalize numbers of group members. Positive outcomes and successful communication will be more likely if members are represented in numerical equality. Research studies have shown that being in the numerical minority can cause stress and that the "solo" minority, particularly in beginning a new job, is subject to exaggerated expectations (either very high or very low) and extreme evaluations (either very good or very bad) (Pettigrew & Martin, 1989).

7. Group members should have similar beliefs and values. A large body of research supports the idea that people are attracted to those whom they perceive to be similar to themselves. This means that, in bringing diverse groups of people together, we should look for common ground—similarities based on religion, interests, competencies, and so on. For example, an international group of mothers is working for peace in the Middle East. Although members represent different ethnic groups, they come together with a shared goal—to protect their children from military action between the warring factions in the region.

8. Programs should promote individuation of group members. This means that they should downplay the characteristics that mark the different groups (such as language, physical abilities, or racial characteristics). Instead, group members might focus on the characteristics that express individual personalities.

This list of conditions can help us understand how domestic and international contexts vary (Gudykunst, 1979). It is easy to see how the history within a nation-state may lead to conditions and attitudes that are more difficult to facilitate. For example, historical conditions between African Americans and white Americans may make it impossible to meet these conditions; interracial interactions in the United States cannot be characterized by equality.

Note that this list of conditions is incomplete. Moreover, meeting all of the conditions does not guarantee positive outcomes when diverse groups of people interact. However, the list is a starting place, and it is important to be able to identify which conditions are affected by historical factors that may be difficult to change and which can be more easily facilitated by communication professionals.

Negotiating Histories Dialectically in Interaction

How can a dialectical perspective help us negotiate interactions, given individual attitudes and personal and cultural histories? How can we balance past and present in our everyday intercultural interactions?

The question of how we deal with the past is never far away, particularly when the past is not really past. We are always working on our relationships with the past, as the past shapes our present and future. In Egypt, protests led to the downfall and resignation of former President Hosni Mubarak in February 2011. In the aftermath of nearly 30 years of his rule, Egyptians are working to renegotiate their relationship with this part of their history. In April 2011, a court ruled that images and the names of the Mubarak family be removed "from all squares, streets, schools, associations, libraries and all entities in Egypt" (El-Nasser, 2011). Although many people had already begun this process, this is an enormous task: "according to the Ministry of Education, there are 388 'Hosni Mubarak' schools, 160 named after his wife Suzanne—and one named after his son (and former president-to-be) Gamal Mubarak. There's a Mubarak portrait in every government building, and in virtually every single classroom, public or private" (El Dahshan, 2011). There are subway stations, streets, and much more to be renamed.

The question with how we deal with the past (even if it isn't very distant) means that we must make decisions about we will remember this period. Is the erasure of Mubarak the first step in the healing of the Egyptian people? Is it key to helping the nation move forward? Does erasing Mubarak really erase this period in Egyptian history? Does this erasure lead people to forget Mubarak? Or does it create the possibility of another Mubarak? Sarah Bond (2011), a lecturer in history writes: "Perhaps it is best that the people of Egypt be spared this forced amnesia and be allowed to retain some memories of their former president. Erasing the crimes of the past doesn't help us avoid them in the future."

Sources: S. E. Bond, "Erasing the face of history." *The New York Times*, May 4, 2011. Retrieved June 11, 2011, from www.nytimes.com/2011/05/15/opinion/15bond.html?scp=2&sq=history&st=Search; M. El Dahshan, "The 'demubarakization' of Egypt." *The New York Times*, March 1, 2011. Retrieved June 11, 2011, from http://opinionator.blogs.nytimes.com/2011/03/01/the-demubarakization-of-egypt/; M. El-Nassar, "Egypt to end the ubiquity of Mubarak." *The New York Times*, April 21, 2011. Retrieved June 11, 2011, from www.nytimes.com/2011/04/22/world/middleeast/22egypt.html.

First, it is important to recognize that we all bring our own histories (some known, some hidden) to interactions. We can try to evaluate the role that history plays for those with whom we interact.

Second, we should understand the role that histories play in our identities, in what we bring to the interaction. Communication scholar Marsha Houston (1997) says there are three things that white people who want to be her friends should never say: "I don't notice you're black," "You're not like the others," and "I know how you feel." In her opinion, each of these denies or rejects a part of her identity that is deeply rooted in history.

Sometimes it is unwise to ask people where they are "really from." Such questions assume that they cannot be from where they said they were from, due to racial characteristics or other apparent features. Recognizing a person's history and its link to her or his identity in communication is a first step in establishing intercultural relationships. It is also important to be aware of your own historical blinders and assumptions.

Sometimes the past–present dialectic operates along with the disadvantage–privilege dialectic. The Hungarian philosopher György Lukács wrote a book titled *History and Class Consciousness* (1971), in which he argues that we need to think dialectically about history and social class. Our own recognition of how class differences have influenced our families is very much affected by the past and by the conditions members experienced that might explain whom they married, why they lived where they did, what languages they do and do not speak, and what culture they identify with.

Two dialectical tensions emerge here: (1) between privilege and disadvantage and (2) between the personal and the social. Both of these dialectics affect our view of the past, present, and future. As we attempt to understand ourselves and our situations (as well as those of others), we must recognize that we arrived at universities for a variety of reasons. Embedded in our backgrounds are dialectical tensions between privilege and disadvantage and the ways in which those factors were established in the past and the present. Then there is the dialectical tension between seeing ourselves as unique persons and as members of particular social classes. These factors affect both the present and the future. In each case, we must also negotiate the dialectical tensions between the past and the present, and between the present and the future. Who we think we are today is very much influenced by how we view the past, how we live, and what culture we believe to be our own.

INTERNET RESOURCES

http://americanradioworks.publicradio.org/features/remembering/
The American Radio Works has compiled information and documents relating to segregation in the United States and posted them online. Students can listen to accounts of segregation and retrospective analyses as well as read many detailed accounts. There is also a section that outlines key laws of the Jim Crow era.

www.archives.gov/midatlantic/public/family-history.html
The National Archives in Philadelphia has this guide for exploring family history. There are other branches of the National Archives in many other cities in the United States. You can see what kinds of records they hold, if you decide to research your own family history.

www.discovernikkei.org/wiki/Japanese-American_and_Arab_American_Parallels
This site is part of a larger resource on Japanese migrants. The entire Website is worth exploring; however, this specific page is of special interest. It hosts a number of articles and essays linking the experiences of Japanese Americans

with the experiences of Arab Americans, which provides insight into the ways that America has changed and the ways it has stayed the same regarding race relations and national security.

www.monticello.org/site/plantation-and-slavery/thomas-jefferson-and-sally-hemings-brief-account
This website provides an accounting of the relationship between Thomas Jefferson and his slave Sally Hemmings. This controversial issue is explored through original documentation, narrative accounts, and links to other resources.

www.rumormillnews.com/jefferson.htm
This article is a response to the type of allegations put forth in the link listed above. A direct descendent of Thomas Jefferson responds to the proposed relationship between Hemmings and Jefferson. This site also contains links to primary documents and other accounts. Together, these websites are indicative of the controversies that can stem from contested intercultural history.

www.ushmm.org/museum/

www.ushmm.org/research/center/

www.ushmm.org/wlc/article.php?lang=en&ModuleId=10007058
The first web address is for the United States Holocaust Museum. The museum website offers many exhibits related to the Holocaust that are viewable online. The second web address is specifically designed for university students. This section includes a searchable database for tracing Holocaust survivors and archiving information. The third web address is an article/exhibit hosted by the museum on a forged document used to justify the persecution of Jews. This article is an especially powerful example of how rewriting intercultural history can have profound effects.

SUMMARY

- Multiple histories are important for empowering different cultural identities.
- Multiple histories include:
  - Political histories
  - Intellectual histories
  - Social histories
  - Family histories
  - National histories
  - Cultural-group histories
- Histories are constructed through narrative.
- Hidden histories are those typically not conveyed in a widespread manner and are based on race/ethnicity, gender, sexual orientation, diaspora, colonialism, socioeconomic class, and religion.

- People bring four elements of personal history to intercultural interactions:
  - Childhood experience
  - Historical myths
  - Language competence
  - Memories of recent political events
- Contact hypothesis suggests that simply bringing people from diverse groups together will only work if certain conditions are met:
  - Group members must be of equal status and relatively equal numbers.
  - Contact must be voluntary, extend beyond the superficial, have institutional support, and promote similarity and individuation of group members.
  - There should be maximum cooperation among participants.
- A dialectical perspective helps negotiate histories in intercultural interaction.

DISCUSSION QUESTIONS

1. What are some examples of hidden histories, and why are they hidden?
2. How do the various histories of the United States influence our communication with people from other countries?
3. How do you benefit or have been disenfranchised in the telling of certain histories? How do you take responsibility for the histories from which you benefit?
4. What factors in your experience have led to the development of positive feelings about your own cultural heritage and background? What factors have led to negative feelings, if any?
5. When can contact between members of two cultures improve their attitudes toward each other and facilitate communication between them?
6. How do histories influence the process of identity formation?
7. What is the significance of the shift from history to histories? How does this shift help us understand intercultural communication?
8. Why do some people in the United States prefer not to talk about history? What views of social reality and intercultural communication does this attitude encourage?

 Go to the self-quizzes on the Online Learning Center at www.mhhe.com/martinnakayama6 to further test your knowledge.

ACTIVITIES

1. *Cultural-Group History.* This exercise can be done by individual students or in groups. Choose a cultural group in the United States that is unfamiliar to you. Study the history of this group, and identify and describe significant events in its history. Answer the following questions:

a. What is the historical relationship between this group and other groups (particularly the dominant cultural groups)?

b. Are there any historical incidents of discrimination? If so, describe them.

c. What are common stereotypes about the group? How did these stereotypes originate?

d. Who are important leaders and heroes of the group?

e. What are notable achievements of the group?

f. How has the history of this group influenced the identity of group members today?

2. *Family Histories.* Write a brief personal narrative that tells the story of your family history. This may require additional research or conversations with family members. You may want to focus more on one parent's side, depending on how much information you can find or which story has more meaning to you. Try and trace this story back to its furthest beginning.

a. How did your family come to live where they currently live?

b. Were there any great historical events that affected them and the decisions they made (e.g., slavery, the Holocaust)?

c. How does this history have meaning for you?

KEY WORDS

absent history (130)
apartheid (137)
colonial histories (149)
concentration camps (136)
contact hypothesis (155)
cultural-group
   histories (133)
diaspora (149)

diasporic histories (149)
ethnic histories (141)
family histories (130)
gender histories (145)
grand narrative (137)
hidden histories (141)
intellectual histories
   (129)

modernist identity
   (137)
national history (131)
political histories (129)
racial histories (141)
sexual orientation
   histories (145)
social histories (129)

The Online Learning Center at www.mhhe.com/martinnakayama6 features flash-cards and crossword puzzles based on these terms and concepts.

REFERENCES

Ahmadinejad's comments on homosexuality cut out of transcripts on state-run Farsi Web sites. (2007, September 26). *San Diego Union-Tribune.* www.signonsandiego.com/news/world/20070926-1422-iran-ahmadinejad.htmlv. Retrieved May 8, 2008.

Aid, M. M. (2006, February 21). Declassification in reverse. The National Security Archive. www.gwu.edu/~nsarchiv/NSAEBB/NSAEBB179/#doc1. Retrieved May 9, 2008.

Allport, G. (1979). *The nature of prejudice.* New York: Addison-Wesley.

Amir, Y. (1969). Contact hypothesis in ethnic relations. *Psychological Bulletin, 71,* 319–343.

Anzaldúa, G. (1987). *Borderlands/La frontera: The new mestiza.* San Francisco: Spinsters/Aunt Lute.

Attenborough, R. (Director). (1987). *Cry Freedom* [Motion picture]. United States: Universal Studios.

Axtman, K. (2001, May 10). In Texas, free trade puts border colonias in spotlight. *The Christian Science Monitor*, p. 3.

Baudrillard, J. (1988). *America* (C. Turner, Trans.). New York: Verso.

Bernstein, N. (2007, April 3). Relatives of interned Japanese-Americans side with Muslims. *The New York Times*. www.nytimes.com/2007/04/03/ nyregion/03detain.html?pagewanted=1&sq=muslim &scp=153. Retrieved May 8, 2008.

Blanchot, M. (1986). *The writing of the disaster* (A. Smock, Trans.). Lincoln: University of Nebraska Press.

Bond, S. E. (2011, May 14). Erasing the face of history. *The New York Times*. Retrieved June 11, 2011, from www.nytimes.com/2011/05/15/opinion/15bond .html?scp=2&sq=history&st=Search.

Brinkman, H. (1997). Managing diversity: A review of recommendations for success. In C. D. Brown, C. Snedeker, & B. Sykes (Eds.), *Conflict and diversity* (pp. 35–50). Cresskill, NJ: Hampton Press.

Brislin, R. W. (1981). *Cross cultural encounters: Face to face interaction*. New York: Pergamon.

Bureau of African Affairs. (2005, September). Background note: South Africa. United States Department of State. www.state.gov/r/pa/ei/ bgn/2898. htm#history. Accessed October 30, 2005.

El Dahshan, M. (2011, March 1). The "demubarakiza-tion" of Egypt. *The New York Times*. Retrieved June 11, 2011, from opinionator.blogs.nytimes. com/2011/03/01/the-demubarakization-of-egypt/.

El-Nassar, M. (2011, April 21). Egypt to end the ubiquity of Mubarak. *The New York Times*. Retrieved June 11, 2011, from www.nytimes. com/2011/04/22/world/middleeast/22egypt.html.

Erbe, B., & Hart, B. (1994, September 16). Employer goes overboard on "gender sensitivity" issue. *The Evansville Courier*, p. A13.

Fisher, W. (1984). Narration as a human communica-tion paradigm: The case of public moral argument. *Communication Monographs, 51*, 1–22.

Fisher, W. (1985). The narrative paradigm: An elabo-ration. *Communication Monographs, 52*, 347–367.

Fitzgerald, F. (1972). *Fire in the lake: Vietnamese and Americans in Vietnam*. New York: Vintage Books.

Fleischer, A. (2001, September 18). Press briefing by Ari Fleischer. *The White House*. www.whitehouse .gov/news/releases/2001/09/20010918-5 .html. Retrieved May 8, 2008.

Gaertner, S. L., Dovidio, J. F., & Bachman, B. A. (1996). Revisiting the contact hypothesis: The induction of a common ingroup identity. *International Journal of Intercultural Relations, 20*, 271–290.

Gérard-Libois, J., & Heinen, J. (1989). *Belgique-Congo, 1960*. Brussels: Politique et Histoire.

Gilroy, P. (1993). *The Black Atlantic: Modernity and double consciousness*. New York: Verso.

Goldman, R. (2007, September 24). Ahmadinejad: No gays, No oppression of women in Iran. *ABC News*. a.abcnews.com/US/story?id=3642673&page=1. Retrieved May 8, 2008.

Greenberg, D. (2005, January 14). The gay emancipa-tor? Slate. www.slate.com/id/2112313/. Retrieved May 8, 2008.

Gudykunst, W. B. (1979). Intercultural contact and attitude change: A review of literature and sugges-tions for future research. *International and Intercul-tural Communication Annual, 4*, 1–16.

Guelke, A. (2005). *Rethinking the rise and fall of apart-heid: South Africa and world politics*. New York: Pal-grave Macmillan.

Harris, T. E. (1997). Diversity: Importance, ironies, and pathways. In C. D. Brown, C. Snedeker, & B. Sykes (Eds.), *Conflict and diversity* (pp. 17–34). Cresskill, NJ: Hampton Press.

Hocquenghem, G., & Blasius, M. (1980, April). Inter-view. *Christopher Street, 8*(4), 36–45.

Houston, M. (1997). When Black women talk with White women: Why dialogues are difficult. In A. González, M. Houston, & V. Chen (Eds.), *Our voices: Essays in ethnicity, culture, and communication* (2nd ed., pp. 187–194). Los Angeles: Roxbury.

Immigrant Investor Program Redesign. (1998, December). Guide for applying for permanent residence in Canada: Business applicants. cicnet. ci.gc.ca/press/ 98/9865-pre.html.

In full: Queen's Ireland state banquet speech. (2011, May 18). *BBC News*. Retrieved June 4, 2011, from www.bbc.co.uk/news/world-europe-13450099.

Indian Country responds to Geronimo, bin Laden connection. (2011, May 4). *Indian Country Today Media Network*. Retrieved June 11, 2011, from: http://indiancountrytodaymedianetwork. com/2011/05/indian-country-responds-to-geronimo-bin-laden-connection/.

Jameson, F. (1981). *The political unconscious: Narrative as a socially symbolic act*. Ithaca, NY: Cornell Univer-sity Press.

Kennedy, R. (2003, September 11). From protest to patronage. *The Nation*. www.thenation.com/ doc/20030929/kennedy. Retrieved May 8, 2008.

Kothari, G. (1995). Where are you from? In G. Hongo (Ed.), *Under Western eyes: Personal essays from Asian America* (pp. 151–173). New York: Anchor Books/ Doubleday.

Loewen, J. W. (1995). *Lies my teacher told me: Every-thing your American history textbook got wrong*. New York: Touchstone.

Lukács, György. (1971). *History and class consciousness: Studies in Marxist dialectics* (R. Livingstone, Trans.). Cambridge, MA: MIT Press.

Lyotard, J.-F. (1984). *The postmodern condition: A report on knowledge* (G. Bennington & B. Massumi, Trans.). Minneapolis: University of Minnesota Press.

Mason, J., & Halpin, P. (2011, May 23). Obama visits family roots in Ireland. *Reuters*. Retrieved May 30, 2011, from www.reuters.com/article/2011/05/23/us-obama-ireland-idUSTRE74M09F20110523.

McGrory, B. (2011, May 11). Centuries of interruption and a history rejoined. *The Boston Globe*, pp. A1, A9.

Nakano, M. (1990). *Japanese American women: Three generations, 1890–1990*. Berkeley and San Francisco: Mina Press/National Japanese American Historical Society.

Obama, B. H. (2010, August 13). Remarks by the President at Iftar Dinner. Office of the Press Secretary, White House. Retrieved June 11, 2011, from www.whitehouse.gov/the-press-office/2010/08/13/remarks-president-iftar-dinner-0.

Pettigrew, T. F., & Martin, J. (1989). Organizational inclusion of minority groups: A social psychological analysis. In J. P. VanOudenhoven & T. M. Willemsen (Eds.), *Ethnic minorities: Social psychological perspectives* (pp. 169–200). Amsterdam/Lisse: Swets & Zeitlinger.

Saulny, S. (2005, October 11). Cast from their ancestral home, Creoles worry about culture's future. *The New York Times*, p. A13.

Schwarzwald, J., & Amir, Y. (1996). Guest editor's introduction: Special issue on prejudice, discrimination and conflict. *International Journal of Intercultural Relations, 20*, 265–270.

Seel, P., with Bitoux, J. (1994). *Moi, Pierre Seel, déporté homosexual*. Paris: Calmann-Lévy.

Shaffer, M. (2002, June 9). Navajos protest national status for Old Spanish Trail. *The Arizona Republic*, pp. B1, B8.

Shome, R., & Hegde, R. (2002). Postcolonial approaches to communication: Charting the terrain, engaging the intersections. *Communication Theory, 12*, 249–270.

Stephan, C. W., & Stephan, W. G. (1989). Antecedents of intergroup anxiety in Asian Americans and Hispanic Americans. *International Journal of Intercultural Relations, 13*, 203–216.

Stephan, C. W., & Stephan, W. G. (1992). Reducing intercultural anxiety through intercultural contact. *International Journal of Intercultural Relations, 16*, 89–106.

Stephan, W. G., & Stephan, C. W. (1996). *Intergroup relations*. Boulder, CO: Westview Press.

Steyn, M. (2001). *"Whiteness just isn't what it used to be": White identity in a changing South Africa*. Albany: State University of New York Press.

Swarns, R. L. & Kantor, J. (2009, October 7). In First Lady's roots, a complex path from slavery. *The New York Times*. Retrieved May 30, 2011, from www.nytimes.com/2009/10/08/us/politics/08-genealogy.html?_r=3.

Tateishi, J. (1984). *And justice for all: An oral history of the Japanese American detention camps*. New York: Random House.

Tell, D. (2008). The "shocking story" of Emmett Till and the politics of public confession. *Quarterly Journal of Speech, 94*, 156–178.

Thompson, L. (2001). *A history of South Africa* (3rd ed.). New Haven: Yale University Press.

Thonssen, L., Baird, A. C., & Braden, W. W. (1970). *Speech criticism* (2nd ed.). New York: Ronald Press.

Tripp, C. A. (2004). *The intimate world of Abraham Lincoln*. New York: Free Press.

Under surveillance. (1995, December 26). *The Advocate*, p. 14.

PART II

Intercultural Communication Processes

IDENTITY AND INTERCULTURAL COMMUNICATION

CHAPTER OBJECTIVES

After reading this chapter, you should be able to:

1. Identify three communication approaches to identity.
2. Define identity.
3. Describe phases of minority identity development.
4. Describe phases of majority identity development.
5. Identify and describe nine social and cultural identities.
6. Identify characteristics of whiteness.
7. Describe phases of multicultural identity development.
8. Explain the relationship among identity, stereotyping, and prejudice.
9. Explain the relationship between identity and communication.

Now that we have examined some sociohistorical contexts that shape culture and communication, let us turn to a discussion of identity and its role in intercultural communication. Identity serves as a bridge between culture and communication. It is important because we communicate our identity to others, and we learn who we are through communication. It is through communication—with our family, friends, and others—that we come to understand ourselves and form our identity. Issues of identity are particularly important in intercultural interactions.

Conflicts can arise, however, when there are sharp differences between who we think we are and who others think we are. For example, a female college student living with a family in Mexico on a homestay may be treated protectively and chaperoned when she socializes, which may conflict with her view of herself as an independent person. In this case, the person's identity is not confirmed but is questioned or challenged in the interaction.

In this chapter, we describe a dialectical approach to understanding identity, one that encompasses three communication approaches: social science, interpretive, and critical. We then explore the important role language plays in understanding identity and how minority and majority identities develop. We then turn to the development of specific aspects of our social and cultural identity including those related to gender, race or ethnicity, class, religion, and nationality. We describe how these identities are often related to problematic communication—stereotypes, prejudice, and discrimination. We also examine an increasingly important identity—that of multicultural individuals. Finally, we discuss the relationship between identity and communication.

THINKING DIALECTICALLY ABOUT IDENTITY

identity The concept of who we are. Characteristics of identity may be understood differently depending on the perspectives that people take—for example, social science, interpretive, or critical perspectives.

impression management theory The ways by which individuals attempt to control the impressions others have of them.

Identity is a core issue for most people. It is about who we are and who others think we are. How do we come to understand who we are? And how do we communicate our identity to others? A useful theory is that of **impression management**—how people present themselves and how they guide the impression others form of them (Goffman, 1959). Some scholars suggest that individuals are constantly performing "spin control" campaigns to highlight their strengths and virtues while also attempting "damage control" by minimizing deficiencies (Tedeschi, Lindskold, & Rosenfeld, 1985; Rosenfeld and Giaclone, 1991). As we will see, individuals cannot control others' impressions completely, as those we interact with also play an important role in how our identities develop and are expressed.

What are the characteristics of identity? In this section we use both the static–dynamic and the personal–contextual dialectics in answering this question.

There are three contemporary communication perspectives on identity (see Table 5-1). The social science perspective, based largely on research in psychology, views the self in a relatively static fashion in relation to the various cultural communities to which a person belongs: nationality, race, ethnicity, religion,

TABLE 5-1 THREE PERSPECTIVES ON IDENTITY AND COMMUNICATION		
Social Science	**Interpretive**	**Critical**
Identity created by self (by relating to groups)	Identity formed through communication with others	Identity shaped through social, historical forces
Emphasizes individualized, familial, and spiritual self (cross-cultural perspective)	Emphasizes avowal and ascribed dimensions	Emphasizes contexts and resisting ascribed identity

gender, and so on. The interpretive perspective is more dynamic and recognizes the important role of interaction with others as a factor in the development of the self. Finally, the critical perspective views identity even more dynamically—as a result of contexts quite distant from the individual. As you read this chapter, keep in mind that the relationship between identity and intercultural interaction involves both static and dynamic elements and both personal and contextual elements.

The Social Science Perspective

The social science perspective emphasizes that identity is created in part by the self and in part in relation to group membership. According to this perspective, the self is composed of multiple identities, and these notions of identity are culture bound. How, then, do we come to understand who we are? That depends very much on our cultural background. According to Western psychologists like Erik Erikson, our identities are self-created, formed through identity conflicts and crises, through identity diffusion and confusion (Erikson, 1950, 1968). Occasionally, we may need a moratorium, a time-out, in the process. Our identities are created not in one smooth, orderly process but in spurts, with some events providing insights into who we are and long periods intervening during which we may not think much about ourselves or our identities.

Cross-Cultural Perspectives   In the United States, young people are often encouraged to develop a strong sense of identity, to "know who they are," to be independent and self-reliant, which reflects an emphasis on the cultural value of individualism. However, this was not always the case, and even today in many countries there is a very different, more collectivist notion of self. Min-Sun Kim (2002), a communication scholar, traces the evolution of the individualistic self. Before 1500, people in Europe as well as in most other civilizations lived in small cohesive communities, with a worldview characterized by the interdependence of spiritual and material phenomena. With the beginning of the industrial revolution in the 1600s came the notion of the world as a machine; this mechanistic view extended to living organisms and has had a profound effect on Western

Communication scholar Ge Gao contrasts the Western idea of the independent self with the Chinese notion of the interdependent self.

In the Western world, an "individual" signifies an independent entity with free will, emotions and personality. An individual, however, is not conceptualized in this way in the Chinese culture. . . . The incomplete nature of the self is supported by both Taoism and Confucianism even though they differ in many fundamental ways. Taoism defines self as part of nature. Self and nature together complete a harmonious relationship. Self in the Confucian sense is defined by a person's surrounding relations, which often are derived from kinship networks and supported by cultural values such as filial piety, loyalty, dignity, and integrity. . . .

The other-orientation thus is key to an interdependent self. Congruous with the notion of an interdependent self, the Chinese self also needs to be recognized, defined, and completed by others. The self's orientation to others' needs, wishes, and expectations is essential to the development of the Chinese self.

Source: Ge Gao, "Self and Other: A Chinese Perspective on Interpersonal Relationships." In W. G. Gudykunst et al. (Eds.), *Communication in Personal Relationships Across Cultures* (Thousand Oaks, CA: Sage, 1996), pp. 83–84.

thought. It taught people to think of themselves as isolated egos—unconnected to the natural world and society in general. Thus, according to Kim, a person in the West came to be understood as "an individual entity with a separate existence independent of place in society" (Kim, 2002, p. 12). In contrast, people in many other regions of the world have retained the more interdependent notion of the self.

Cross-cultural psychologist Alan Roland (1988) has identified three universal aspects of identity present in all individuals: (1) an individualized identity, (2) a familial identity, and (3) a spiritual identity. Cultural groups usually emphasize one or two of these dimensions and downplay the other(s). Let's see how this works. The **individualized identity** is the sense of an independent "I," with sharp distinctions between the self and others. This identity is emphasized by most groups in the United States, where young people are encouraged to be independent and self-reliant at a fairly early age—by adolescence.

In contrast, the **familial identity,** evident in many collectivistic cultures, stresses the importance of emotional connectedness to and interdependence with others. For example, in many African and Asian societies, and in some cultural groups in the United States, children are encouraged and expected to form strong, interdependent bonds, first with the family and later with other groups. As one of our students explains,

> *to be Mexican American is to unconditionally love one's family and all it stands for. Mexican-Americans are an incredibly close-knit group of people, especially when it comes to family. We are probably the only culture that can actually recite*

individualized identity The sense of self as independent and self-reliant.

familial identity The sense of self as always connected to family and others.

the names of our fourth cousins by heart. In this respect our families are like clans, they go much further than the immediate family and very deep into extended families. We even have a celebration, Dia de los Muertos *(Day of the Dead), that honors our ancestors.*

In these societies, educational, occupational, and even marital choices are made by individuals with extensive family guidance. The goal of the developed identity is not to become independent from others but rather to gain an understanding of and cultivate one's place in the complex web of interdependence with others. Communication scholar Ge Gao (1996) describes the Chinese sense of self:

> *The other-orientation thus is key to an interdependent self. Congruous with the notion of an interdependent self, the Chinese self also needs to be recognized, defined, and completed by others. The self's orientation to others' needs, wishes, and expectations is essential to the development of the Chinese self. (p. 84)*

In addition, the understanding of the familial self may be more connected to others and situation bound. According to studies comparing North Americans' and East Asians' senses of identity, when asked to describe themselves, the North Americans give more abstract, situation-free descriptions ("I am kind," "I am outgoing," "I am quiet in the morning"), whereas East Asians tend to describe their memberships and relationships to others rather than themselves ("I am a mother," "I am the youngest child in my family," "I am a member of a tennis club") (Cross, 2000).

The third dimension is the **spiritual identity,** the inner spiritual reality that is realized and experienced to varying extents by people through a number of outlets. For example, the spiritual self in India is expressed through a structure of gods and goddesses and through rituals and meditation. In Japan, the realization of the spiritual self tends more toward aesthetic modes, such as the tea ceremony and flower arranging (Roland, 1988).

spiritual identity Identification with feelings of connectedness to others and higher meanings in life.

Clearly, identity development does not occur in the same way in every society. The notion of identity in India, Japan, and some Latino/a and Asian American groups emphasizes the integration of the familial and the spiritual self but very little of the more individualized self.

This is not to say there is not considerable individuality among people in these groups. However, the general identity contrasts dramatically with the predominant mode in most U.S. cultural groups, in which the individualized self is emphasized and there is little attention to the familial self. However, there may be some development of the spiritual self among devout Catholic, Protestant, Jewish, or Muslim individuals.

Groups play an important part in the development of all these dimensions of self. As we are growing up, we identify with many groups, based on gender, race, ethnicity, class, sexual orientation, religion, and nationality (Tajfel, 1981, 1982). And depending on our cultural background, we may develop tight or looser bonds with these groups (Kim, 2002). By comparing ourselves and others with members of these groups, we come to understand who we are. Because we belong to various groups, we develop multiple identities that come into play at different times, depending on the context. For example, in going to church or temple, we may highlight our religious identity. In going to clubs or bars, we may highlight our sexual orientation identity. Women who join social groups exclusive to women (or men who attend social functions just for men) are highlighting their gender identity.

identity negotiation theory A theory that emphasizes the process of communicating one's own desired identities while reinforcing or resisting others' identities as the core of intercultural communication.

Communication scholar Ting-Toomey (1993, 2005) argues in her **identity negotiation theory** that cultural variability influences our sense of self and ultimately influences how successful we are in intercultural interactions. Her argument goes like this: Individuals define themselves in relation to groups they belong to due to the basic human need for security and inclusion. At the same time, humans also need differentiation from these same groups. Managing relationships to these various groups involves boundary regulation and working through the tension between inclusion and differentiation and can make us feel secure or vulnerable. How we manage this tension influences the coherent sense of self (identity)—individuals who are more secure are more open to interacting with members of other cultures. When people feel good about themselves and the groups to which they belong, they are more successful in intercultural interactions. However, as we will see in the next section, identities are formed not just by the individual but also through interactions with others.

The Interpretive Perspective

The interpretive perspective builds on the notions of identity formation discussed previously but takes a more dynamic turn. That is, it emphasizes that identities are negotiated, co-created, reinforced, and challenged though communication with others; they emerge when messages are exchanged between persons (Hecht, Warren, Jung, & Krieger, 2005; Ting-Toomey, 2005). This means that presenting our identities is not a simple process. Does everyone see you as you see yourself? Probably not. To understand how these images may conflict, the concepts of avowal and ascription are useful.

avowal The process by which an individual portrays himself or herself.

ascription The process by which others attribute identities to an individual.

Avowal is the process by which individuals portray themselves, whereas **ascription** is the process by which others attribute identities to them. Sometimes these processes are congruent. For example, we (Judith and Tom) see ourselves as professors and hope that students also see us as professors. We also see ourselves as young, but many students do not concur, ascribing an "old person" identity to us. This ascribed identity challenges our avowed identity. And these conflicting views influence the communication between us and our students.

Different identities are emphasized depending on the individuals we are communicating with and the topics of conversation. For example, in a social conversation with someone we are attracted to, our gender or sexual orientation identity is probably more important to us than other identities (ethnicity, nationality). And our communication is probably most successful when the person we are talking with confirms the identity we think is most important at the moment. In this sense, competent intercultural communication affirms the identity that is most salient in any conversation (Collier & Thomas, 1988).

For example, if you are talking with a professor about a research project, the conversation will be most competent if the interaction confirms the salient identities (professor and student) rather than other identities (e.g., those based on gender, religion, or ethnicity).

How do you feel when someone does not recognize the identity you believe is most salient? For example, suppose your parents treat you as a child (their ascription) and not as an independent adult (your avowal). How might this affect communication? One of our students describes how he reacts when people ascribe a different identity than the one he avows:

> *Pretty much my entire life I was seen not as American but as half Mexican. In reality I am 50% Mexican and 50% Dutch. So technically I am half Mexican and half Dutch American. I always say it like that but it was obvious that not everybody saw it like that. I was asked if I was Hawaiian, Persian, and even Italian, but I was able to politely tell them about myself.*

Central to the interpretive perspective is the idea that our identities are expressed communicatively—in core symbols, labels, and norms. **Core symbols** (or cultural values) tell us about the fundamental beliefs and the central concepts that define a particular identity. Communication scholar Michael Hecht and his colleagues (Hecht, 1998; Hecht, Jackson, & Ribeau, 2003) have identified the contrasting core symbols associated with various ethnic identities. For example, core symbols of African American identity may be positivity, sharing, uniqueness, realism, and assertiveness. Individualism is often cited as a core symbol of European American identity. Core symbols are not only expressed but also created and shaped through communication. Labels are a category of core symbols; they are the terms we use to refer to particular aspects of our own and others' identities—for example, *African American, Latino, white,* or *European American.*

core symbols The fundamental beliefs that are shared by the members of a cultural group. *Labels,* a category of core symbols, are names or markers used to classify individual, social, or cultural groups.

Finally, some norms of behavior are associated with particular identities. For example, women may express their gender identity by being more concerned about safety than men. They may take more precautions when they go out at night, such as walking in groups. People might express their religious identity by participating in activities such as going to church or Bible study meetings.

The Critical Perspective

Like the interpretive perspective, the critical perspective emphasizes the dynamic nature of identities, but in addition, it emphasizes the contextual and often conflictual elements of identity development. This perspective pays particular attention to the societal structures and institutions that constrain identities and are often the root of injustice and oppression (Collier, 2005).

Contextual Identity Formation   The driving force behind a critical approach is the attempt to understand identity formation within the contexts of history, economics, politics, and discourse. To grasp this notion, ask yourself, How and why do people identify with particular groups and not others? What choices are available to them?

FIGURE 5-1 We have many different identities—including gender, ethnicity, age, religion, and sexuality—that we express in different ways at different times. Celebrations are one way to highlight identity. Here, Sikhs in the northern Indian city of Chandigarh light candles in a temple to celebrate Diwali. Diwali marks the age-old culture of India and celebrates knowledge and the vanquishing of ignorance. (© AP Photo/Aman Sharma)

We are all subject to being pigeonholed into identity categories, or contexts, even before we are born. (See Figure 5-1.) Many parents ponder a name for their unborn child, who is already part of society through his or her relationship to the parents. Some children have a good start at being, say, Jewish or Chicana before they are even born. We cannot ignore the ethnic, socioeconomic, or racial positions from which we start our identity journeys.

The identities that others may ascribe to us are socially and politically determined. They are not constructed by the self alone. We must ask ourselves what drives the construction of particular kinds of identities. For example, the label "heterosexual" is a relatively recent one, created less than a hundred years ago (Katz, 1995). Today, people do not hesitate to identify themselves as "heterosexuals." A critical perspective insists on the constructive nature of this process and attempts to identify the social forces and needs that give rise to these identities.

These contextual constraints on identity are also reflected in the experience of a Palestinian woman who describes her feelings of not having a national "identity" as represented by a passport—because of political circumstances far beyond her control:

> *I am Palestinian but I don't have either a Palestinian passport or an Israeli passport. . . . If I take the Palestinian passport, the Israeli government would*

prevent me from entering Jerusalem and Jerusalem is a part of my soul. I just can't NOT enter it. And of course I'm not taking an Israeli passport, so . . . I get frustrated when I talk to people WITH identity, especially Palestinians with Israeli identity. I just get like kind of offended because I think they're more comfortable than me. (Collier, 2005, p. 243)

Resisting Ascribed Identities   When we invoke such discourses about identity, we are pulled into the social forces that feed the discourse. We might resist the position they put us in, and we might try to ascribe other identities to ourselves. Nevertheless, we must begin from that position in carving out a new identity.

French philosopher Louis Althusser (1971) uses the term **interpellation** to refer to this process. He notes that we are pushed into this system of social forces

> *by that very precise operation which I have called interpellation or hailing, and which can be imagined along the lines of the most commonplace everyday police (or other) hailing: "Hey you there!" . . . Experience shows that the practical tele- communication of hailings is such that they hardly ever miss their man: verbal call or whistle, the one hailed always recognizes that it is really him who is being hailed. And yet it is a strange phenomenon, and one which cannot be explained solely by "guilt feelings." (p. 163)*

This hailing process that Althusser describes operates in intercultural communication interactions. It establishes the foundation from which the interaction occurs. For example, occasionally someone will ask Tom if he is Japanese, a question that puts him in an awkward position. He does not hold Japanese citizenship, nor has he ever lived in Japan. Yet the question probably doesn't mean to address these issues. Rather, the person is asking what it means to be "Japanese." How can Tom reconfigure his position in relation to this question?

The Dynamic Nature of Identities   The social forces that give rise to particular identities are never stable but are always changing. Therefore, the critical perspective insists on the dynamic nature of identities. For example, the emergence of the European Union has given new meaning to the notion of being "European" as an identity. Similarly, the terrorist attacks of September 11, 2001, have caused many Americans to reconsider what it means to be "American." And the various and sometimes contradictory notions of what it means to be an American highlights the fluidity and dynamic nature of identities. For some, being "American" now means having a renewed patriotism, as described by one of our students:

> *To be an American is to be proud. After September 11, a sense of patriotism swept through this country that I have never felt before. Growing up I heard about how patriotic the United States was during WW I and WW II, but I had never experienced it personally. After that day, it was as if racial, religious, and democratic differences had stopped. Even if that tension only stopped temporarily, the point is that it did stop. Our country came together to help, pray, and donate. The feeling of being an American is a sense of feeling and strength and pride.*

interpellation The communication process by which one is pulled into the social forces that place people into a specific identity.

Writer Philippe Wamba describes how his multicultural identity developed across several continents and languages. His father (from the Republic of the Congo, formerly Zaire) and mother (an African American midwesterner) met and married while attending college in Michigan. His father's career took the family first to Boston (where Philippe was one of only a few blacks in his school), then to Dar es Salaam, Tanzania, where he learned flawless Swahili and added a third heritage to his cultural background: "half American, half Zairean, and half Tanzanian." Now an adult, he describes his answer to the question "Where are you from?"

> *I used to try to find succinct ways of responding to the question "Where are you from"—simple one-word answers that would satisfy the curious. I envied my friends their ability to state one place confidently and simply say "New York" or "Kenya." . . . For a period, I even referred to myself as a "a citizen of the world," a high-minded moniker, bred of my own boredom and frustration, that used to annoy people. . . . Now I have decided that the succinct answer is always inadequate and that the story of origin is always a complex saga. . . . I have come to reject the idea of a simple, dualized family heritage and the simple bicultural understanding of self I internalized as a child. . . . For a time I lived as a sophisticated cultural chameleon, attempting to blend with my shifting surroundings by assuming the appearance and habits of those around me. . . . In the end I am both African and African American and therefore neither. I envy others their hometowns and unconflicted patriotism, but no longer would I exchange them for my freedom to seek multiple homes and nations and to forge my own.*

Source: P. Wamba, "A Middle Passage." In C. C. O'Hearn (Ed.), *Half and Half: Writers on Growing up Biracial + Bicultural* (New York: Pantheon Books, 1998), pp. 168–169.

For others, the events of 9/11 led to more ambivalence about being "American":

> *The media showed negative responses that other countries displayed toward Americans. This makes me ponder what I've done, as a white mutt American, to make people feel this way. I know it is not necessarily my fault but actually American beliefs as a whole. . . . The "cop in the head" feeling occurs in me whenever I see a group of people gathered around speaking a foreign language and staring at me. Maybe it is an insecurity issue within me, aided by rumors I've heard, that initiates this uneasy feeling. I really hope Americans, as a whole, become more accepting of each other so that other countries will see that we can work together with such diversity.*

For another example, look at the way that identity labels have changed from "colored" to "Negro" to "black" to "Afro-American" to "African American." Although the labels seem to refer to the same group of people, the political and cultural identities of those so labeled are different. The term "Negro" was replaced by "Black" during the civil rights movement in the 1960s because it stood for racial pride, power, and rejection of the status quo. "Black is beautiful" and "Black power" became slogans during this time. In the late 1980s, Black leaders proposed that "Black" be replaced with "African American," saying that this label would provide African Americans a cultural identification with their heritage and ancestral homeland. The changes in these labels have worked to strengthen group identity and facilitate the struggle for racial equality (Smith, 1992). Currently, both terms are used—depending on people's preference—and "Black" is preferred by some because it shows commonality with people of African descent who are not U.S. American (e.g., Caribbean Islanders) (Sigelman, Tuch, & Martin, 2005; Why Black . . . , 2008).

IDENTITY DEVELOPMENT ISSUES

People can identify with a multitude of groups: gender, age, religion, nationality, to name only a few. How do we come to develop a sense of identities? As we noted earlier, our identities develop over a period of time and always through interaction with others. How an individual's identity develops depends partly on the relative position or location of the identity within the societal hierarchy. Some identities have a higher position on the social hierarchy. For example, a heterosexual identity has a more privileged position than a homosexual identity; a Christian religious identity is generally more privileged than a Jewish or Muslim religious identity in the United States. To distinguish among the various positions, we label the more privileged identities "majority identities" and label the less privileged "minority identities." This terminology refers to the relative dominance or power of the identity position, not the numerical quantity.

Social science researchers have identified various models that describe how minority and majority identities develop. (See Table 5-2.) Although the models center on racial and ethnic identities, they may also apply to other identities, such as class, gender, or sexual orientation (Ponterotto & Pedersen, 1993). It is also important to remember that, as with any model, these represent the experience of many people, but the stages are not set in stone. Identity development is a complex process; not everyone experiences these phases in exactly the same way. Some people spend more time in one phase than do others; individuals may experience the phases in different ways, and not everyone reaches the final phase.

Minority Identity Development

In general, minority identities tend to develop earlier than majority identities. For example, straight people tend to not think about their sexual orientation identity often, whereas gay people are often acutely aware of their sexual orientation identity being different from the majority and develop a sense of sexual orientation identity earlier than people who are straight. Similarly, while whites may develop a strong ethnic identity, they often do not think about their racial identity, whereas members of racial minority groups are aware of their racial identities at an early age (Ferguson, 1990).

TABLE 5-2 MAJORITY, MINORITY, AND BIRACIAL IDENTITY DEVELOPMENT STAGES

Minority	Majority	Biracial
1. Unexamined Identity • Lack of exploration of ethnicity • Acceptance of majority group values • Positive attitudes toward the majority group • Lack of interest in issues of ethnicity	1. Unexamined Identity • Lack of exploration of ethnicity • Acceptance of majority group values • Positive attitudes toward the majority group • Lack of interest in issues of ethnicity	1. May cycle through 3 stages of identity development • Awareness of differences and resulting dissonance • Awareness that they are different from other children • Sense that they don't fit in anywhere
2. Conformity • Internalization of dominant group norms; desire for assimilation into this group • Negative attitudes toward themselves and their groups until an experience causes them to question the dominant culture attitudes	2. Acceptance • Internalization of a racist ideology (passive or active acceptance) • The key point is that individuals are not aware that they have been programmed to accept this worldview.	2. Struggle for acceptance • May feel that they need to choose one race or another
3. Resistance and Separatism • Growing awareness that not all dominant values are beneficial to minorities • Often triggered by negative events • Blanket endorsement of one's group's values and attitudes • Rejection of dominant group values and norms	3. Resistance • Moving from blaming minority members for their situations and beginning to blame their own dominant group	3. Self-acceptance and self–assertion
4. Integration • Ideal outcome of identity development—achieved identity • Strong sense of their own group identity and an appreciation for other cultural groups	4. Redefinition • Nonacceptance of society's definition of white • Able to see positive aspects of being white • Becoming comfortable with being in dominant group	
	5. Integration • Ideal outcome of identity development—achieved identity • Strong sense of their own group identity and an appreciation for other cultural groups	

Minority identity often develops in the following stages (as shown in Table 5-2):

minority identity
A sense of belonging to a nondominant group.

Stage 1: Unexamined Identity   This stage is characterized by the lack of exploration of identity, be it racial, ethnic, sexual orientation, gender, or whatever. At this stage, individuals may simply lack interest in the identity issue. As one African American woman put it, "Why do I need to learn about who was the first black woman to do this or that? I'm just not too interested." Or minority group members may initially accept the values and attitudes of the majority culture, expressing positive attitudes toward the dominant group and negative views of their own group. Gay young people may try very hard to act "straight" and may even participate in "gay bashing."

Stage 2: Conformity   This stage is characterized by the internalization of the values and norms of the dominant group and a strong desire to assimilate into the dominant culture. Individuals in this phase may have negative, self-deprecating attitudes toward both themselves and their group. As one young Jewish woman said, "I tried very hard in high school to not let anyone know I was Jewish. I'd talk about Christmas shopping and Christmas parties with my friends even though my parents didn't allow me to participate at all in any Christmas celebration."

Individuals who criticize members of their own ethnic or racial group may be given negative labels such as "Uncle Tom" or "oreo" for African Americans, "banana" for Asian Americans, "apple" for Native Americans, and "Tio Taco" for Chicanos. Such labels condemn attitudes and behaviors that support the dominant white culture. This stage often continues until they encounter a situation that causes them to question prodominant culture attitudes, which initiates the movement to the next stage.

Stage 3: Resistance and Separatism   Many kinds of events can trigger the move to the third stage, including negative ones such as encountering discrimination or name-calling. A period of dissonance, or a growing awareness that not all dominant group values are beneficial to minorities, may also precede this stage.

International students sometimes develop their national identity as a minority identity when they study overseas. Dewi, an Indonesian student, reported that when she first arrived in the United States, she thought little of her national identity (because this was a majority identity in *her* country). She told everyone she thought the United States was the greatest place and really tried hard to use American slang, dress American, and fit in. After several experiences with discrimination, she moved to a more separate stage where she only socialized with other Indonesian or other international students for a time. For writer Ruben Martinez (1998), a defining moment was when he was rather cruelly rejected by a white girl whom he had asked to dance at a high school prom:

> *I looked around me at the dance floor with new eyes: Mexicans danced with Mexicans, blacks with blacks, whites with whites. Who the hell did I think I was? Still, it would take a while for the gringo-hater in me to bust out. It was only*

I believe that one of the most important identities to me is the minority identity, especially now. Ever since my arrival at college, I have felt more and more like a real minority. My hometown was over 90% Hispanic, and I really wasn't a minority. Here, there really aren't that many Hispanics. Every day, I feel a bit uncomfortable because I hear so many stereotypes about Hispanics, specifically Mexican-American. I feel as though I really can't speak up simply because this university is dominated by Anglo-Americans and it would be overwhelming. In one of my classes, we were talking about Mexican illegal immigration and a lot of people were cracking jokes. It made me feel quite uncomfortable, so I left. The only thing that I guess can improve this misunderstanding is to better communicate with one another and not base our judgments on stereotypes.
—Adrian

a matter of time before I turned away from my whiteness and became the ethnic rebel. It seemed like it happened overnight, but it was the result of years of pent-up rage in me. (p. 256)

Sometimes the move to this phase happens because individuals who have been denying their identity meet someone from that group who exhibits a strong identity. This encounter may result in a concern to clarify their own identity. So the young woman who was ashamed of being Jewish and tried hard to act "Christian" met a dynamic young man who was active in his synagogue and had a strong Jewish faith. Through their relationship she gained an appreciation of her own religious background, including the Jewish struggle for survival throughout the centuries. As often happens in this stage, she wholeheartedly endorsed the values and attitude attributed to the minority (Jewish) group and rejected the values and norms associated with the dominant group—she dropped most of her Christian friends and socialized primarily with her Jewish friends.

This stage may be characterized by a blanket endorsement of one's group and all the values and attitudes attributed to the group. At the same time, the person may reject the values and norms associated with the dominant group.

Stage 4: Integration According to this model, the ideal outcome of the identity development process is the final stage—an achieved identity. Individuals who have reached this stage have a strong sense of their own group identity (based on gender, race, ethnicity, sexual orientation, and so on) and an appreciation of other cultural groups. In this stage, they come to realize that racism and other forms of oppression occur, but they try to redirect any anger from the previous stage in more positive ways. The end result is individuals with a confident and secure identity characterized by a desire to eliminate all forms of injustice, and not merely oppression aimed at their own group.

Brenda: I had a hard time accepting my "old age identity." And for a while, I didn't even want to be around younger people. However, now

I realize there will always be some discrimination against older women. We're really just invisible. I walk into a store and if there is anyone younger and more attractive, salespeople will often look right though me. However, I accept that this is the way our society is. And I can enjoy being around younger people now—I love their energy and their optimism. And I know that there are positive things about being older. Like, many things I just don't worry about anymore.

Ryan: Because my name is Irish, people generally assume I'm Catholic, but my family has always been Protestant. I knew from an early age that we were different from other Irish. I didn't really understand anything about the history of Ireland, and I always thought of myself as just an American. Now that I know more about this history and my family's history, I feel comfortable being a Protestant and Irish American. I'm happy to be both and different from other Irish Americans.

Majority Identity Development

Rita Hardiman (1994, 2003), educator and pioneer in antiracism training, presents a model of **majority identity** development that has similarities to the model for minority group members. Although she intended the model to represent how white people develop a sense of healthy racial identity, it can also be helpful in describing how other majority identities develop—straight sexual orientation, Christian religious identity, male gender identity, middle-class identity, and so on. Again, remember that majority identity, like minority identity, develops through a complex process. And this model—unlike some other identity development models—is prescriptive. In other words, it outlines the way some scholars think a majority identity *should* develop, from accepting societal hierarchies that favor some identities and diminish others to resisting these inequities.

majority identity A sense of belonging to a dominant group.

Hardiman (1993, 2004) outlines five stages:

Stage 1: Unexamined Identity This first stage is the same as for minority identities. In this case, individuals may be aware of some physical and cultural differences, but they do not fear the other or think much about their own identity. There is no understanding of the social meaning and value of gender, sexual orientation, religion, and so on. Although young boys may develop a sense of what it means to be a male by watching their fathers or other males, they are not aware of the social consequences of being born male over female. Those with majority identities, unlike those with minority identities, may stay in this stage for a long time.

Stage 2: Acceptance The second stage represents the internalization, conscious or unconscious, of a racist (or otherwise biased) ideology. This may involve passive or active acceptance. The key point is that individuals are not aware that they have been programmed to accept this worldview.

In the passive acceptance stage, individuals have no conscious identification with being white, straight, male, and so forth. However, they may hold some assumptions based on an acceptance of inequities in the larger society. In general, the social hierarchy is experienced as "normal" for the dominant group, and they may view minority groups as being unduly sensitive and assume that if the minority members really wanted to change their lot in life they could. Here are some possible assumptions.

Being male in this stage may involve the following (sometime unconscious) assumptions:

- Men and women may be different, but they are basically equal. Kyle, a student, tells us, "I never heard so much whining from 'feminists' until I came to college. Frankly, it is a little much. Although women may have faced barriers in the past, that's in the past. Women can pretty much do whatever they want in society today. If they want to be doctors, lawyers, police officers, firefighters, or anything else, they just need to set their minds to it and do it."
- If women really want to make it professionally, they can work as hard as men work and they will succeed.

Being straight may involve these assumptions:

- Gay people choose to be gay.
- Gay people whine a lot, unfairly, about discrimination. There is no recognition of the many privileges given to those who are straight.
- Gay people put their gayness in straight people's faces. At this stage there is no recognition of the vast societal emphasis on heterosexuality.

Being white may involve these assumptions:

- Minority groups are culturally deprived and need help to assimilate.
- Affirmative action is reverse discrimination because people of color are being given opportunities that whites don't have.
- White culture—music, art, and literature—is "classical"; works of art by people of color are folk art or "crafts."
- People of color are culturally different, whereas whites have no group identity or culture or shared experience of racial privilege.

Individuals in this stage usually take one of two positions with respect to interactions with minorities: (1) They avoid contact somewhat with minority group members or (2) they adopt a patronizing stance toward them. Both positions are possible at the same time.

In contrast, those in the active acceptance stage are conscious of their privileged position and may express their feelings of superiority collectively (e.g., join male-only clubs). Some people never move beyond this phase—whether it is characterized by passive or active acceptance. And if they do, it is usually a result of a number of cumulative events. For example, Judith gradually came to realize that her two nieces, who are sisters—one of whom is African American and one of whom is white—had very different experiences growing up. Both girls lived in middle-class neighborhoods, both were honor students in high school, and both went to Ivy League colleges. However, they often had very different experiences. On more than one occasion, the African American girl was followed by security while shopping; she also was stopped several times by police while driving her mother's sports car. Her white sister never had these experiences. Eventually, awareness of this reality prodded Judith to the next stage.

This model recognizes that it is very difficult to escape the societal hierarchy that influences both minority and majority identity development because of its pervasive, systemic, and interlocking nature. The hierarch is a by-product of living within and being impacted by the institutional and cultural systems that surround us.

Stage 3: Resistance   The next stage represents a major paradigm shift. It involves a move from blaming minority members for their condition to naming and blaming their own dominant group as a source of problems. This resistance may take the form of passive resistance, with little behavioral change, or active resistance—trying to reduce, eliminate, or challenge the institutional hierarchies that oppress. In reference to one's own identity, this stage is often characterized by embarrassment about one's own privileged position, guilt, shame, and a need to distance oneself from the dominant group.

> *Our student, Kayla, says: I was raised as a Christian, so I was never taught to question our beliefs. Since I've left home, I have met gay and lesbian students and I no longer understand why my church has such a problem with homosexuality. I get angry and sometimes I speak out when I'm at home and my parents get upset, but I don't want to stand around and let bigots take over my church. I have begun to question my Christian values, as I no longer know if they are compatible with my sense of right and wrong.*

Stage 4: Redefinition   In the fourth stage, people begin to refocus or redirect their energy toward redefining their identity in a way that recognizes their privilege and works to eliminate oppression and inequities. They realize that they don't have to accept uncritically the definitions of being white, straight, male, Christian, U.S. American that society has instilled in them. For example, Nick tells us, "As a straight white guy, I often find myself in social situations in which people feel free to make offhand remarks or jokes that are somewhat racist, heterosexist, or sexist. They assume that I would agree with them, since I'm not a minority, gay, or a woman, but I don't. I am happy to be who I am, but this doesn't mean that being a straight white man means I need to be racist, sexist, or homophobic. I am proud to be who I am, but I don't think that means I have to put down others."

Stage 5: Integration   As in the final stage of minority identity development, majority group individuals now are able to internalize their increased consciousness and integrate their majority identities into all other facets of their identity. They not only recognize their identity as white but also appreciate other groups. This integration affects other aspects of social and personal identity, including religion and gender.

Hardiman (2003) acknowledges that this model is rather simplistic in explaining the diverse experiences of people. It does not acknowledge the impact of diverse environments and socialization processes that influence how people experience their dominant identities or the realities of interlocking identities.

Systems of privilege are complicated; this is one reason why people can belong to a privileged category and not feel privileged. You may have several identities that are more privileged and several that are less privileged. So, for example, a middle-class white lesbian, benefiting from and yet unaware of the privileges of race or class, may think that her experience of sexual orientation and gender inequality enables her to understand what she needs to know about other forms of privilege and oppression. Or a straight working-class white man may be annoyed at the idea that his sexual orientation, whiteness, and maleness somehow gives him access to privilege. As a member of the working class, he may feel insecure in his job, afraid of being outsourced, downsized, and not at all privileged (Johnson, 2001).

To make it more complicated, our multiple identities exist all at once in relation to one another. People never see us solely in terms of race or gender or nationality—they see us as a complex of identities. So it makes no sense to talk about the experience of one identity—being white, for example—without looking at other identities. A dialectical perspective helps here in avoiding falling into the trap of thinking we are or are not privileged. Most of us are both.

SOCIAL AND CULTURAL IDENTITIES

People can identify with a multitude of groups. This section describes some of the major types of groups.

Gender Identity

gender identity The identification with the cultural notions of masculinity and femininity and what it means to be a man or a woman.

We often begin life with gender identities. When newborns arrive in our culture, they may be greeted with clothes and blankets in either blue for boys or pink for girls. To establish a **gender identity** for the newborn, visitors may ask if the baby is a boy or a girl. But gender is not the same as biological sex or sexual identity. This distinction is important in understanding how our views on biological sex influence gender identities.

What it means to be a man or a woman in our society is heavily influenced by cultural notions. For example, some activities are considered more masculine or more feminine. Thus, whether people hunt or sew or fight or read poetry can transform the ways that others view them. Similarly, the programs that people watch on television—soap operas, football games, and so on—affect how they socialize with others, contributing to gendered contexts.

As culture changes, so does the notion of what we idealize as masculine or feminine. Cultural historian Gail Bederman (1995) observes,

> *Even the popular imagery of a perfect male body changed. In the 1860s, the middle class had seen the ideal male body as lean and wiry. By the 1890s, however, an ideal male body required physical bulk and well-defined muscles. (p. 15)*

In this sense, the male body, as well as the female body, can be understood not in its "natural" state but in relation to idealized notions of masculinity and femininity. To know that this man or that woman is particularly good-looking requires an understanding of the gendered notions of attractiveness in a culture.

Our notions of masculinity and femininity change continually, driven by commercial interests and other cultural forces. For example, there is a major push now to market cosmetics to men. However, advertisers acknowledge that this requires sensitivity to men's ideas about makeup:

> *Unlike women, most men don't want to talk about makeup, don't want to go out in public to shop for makeup and don't know how to use makeup. The first barrier is getting men to department stores or specialty shops to buy products. (Yamanouchi, 2002, p. D1)*

Our expression of gender not only communicates who we think we are but also constructs a sense of who we want to be. Initially, we learn what masculinity and femininity mean in our culture. Communication scholar Julia T. Wood (2005) has identified feminine and masculine themes in U.S. society. These are the femininity themes: appearance still counts; be sensitive and caring; accept negative treatment by others; and be a superwoman. The masculinity themes are don't be female; be successful; be aggressive; be sexual; and be self-reliant. Masculinity themes are often the opposite of what it means to be a woman or a gay man. According to Wood, U.S. American men are socialized first and foremost that, being a man is about *not* being a woman. Then, through various media, we monitor how these notions shift and negotiate to communicate our gendered selves to others.

Consider, for example, the contemporary trend in the United States for women to have very full lips. If one's lips are not naturally full, there is always the option of getting collagen injections or having other body fat surgically inserted into the lips. In contrast, our Japanese students tell us that full lips are not considered at all attractive in Japan. The dynamic character of gender reflects its close connection to culture. Society has many images of masculinity and femininity; we do not all seek to look and act according to a single ideal. At the same time, we *do* seek to communicate our gendered identities as part of who we are.

Gender identity is also demonstrated by communication style. For example, women's communication style is often described as supportive, egalitarian, personal, and disclosive, whereas men's is characterized as competitive and assertive (Wood, 2005). However, these differences may be more perception than fact. Results of recent research suggest that women's and men's communication styles are more similar than they are different (Canary & Hause, 1993; Pennebaker, Mehl, & Niederhoffer, 2003). And yet these stereotypes of gender differences persist, maybe partly because of the stereotypical depictions of men and women in magazines, on television, and in movies.

However, what it means to be feminine and masculine are not stable, clear-cut identity categories. Rather, these notions are created, reinforced, and reconstructed by society through communication and overlap with our other identities.

In the United States, the fixed gender identity categories of male and female do not account for the fluid and changing reality of gender identities, especially as they are realized and lived by people with transgender identities. The absence of societal recognition of transgendered people can result in discrimination and violence against them, as in the following example of the beating of a 22-year-old on April 18, 2011, in Maryland:

> *A transgender woman beaten at a Baltimore County McDonald's spoke out on Saturday, saying that the attack was "definitely a hate crime" and that she's been afraid to go out in public ever since. "They said, 'That's a dude, that's a dude and she's in the female bathroom,'" said Chrissy Lee Polis, 22, who said she stopped at the Rosedale restaurant to use the restroom. "They spit in my face." A worker at the restaurant taped Monday's attack and created a graphic video that went viral last week. After the video garnered hundreds of thousands of views on websites, McDonald's issued a statement condemning the incident, and on Saturday the worker who taped the incident was fired. The video shows two females—one of them a 14-year-old girl—repeatedly kicking and punching Polis in the head as an employee and a patron try to intervene. Others can be heard laughing, and men are seen standing idly by.*
>
> *Toward the end of the video, one of the suspects lands a punishing blow to the victim's head, and Polis appears to have a seizure. A man's voice tells the women to run because police are coming. "I knew they were taping me; I told the guy to stop," said Polis, a resident of Baltimore. "They didn't help me. They didn't do nothing for me."*

Source: J. Rosen, "Victim of McDonald's beating speaks out; transgender woman says attack was a 'hate crime,'" *The Baltimore Sun*, April 24, 2011. Retrieved May 31, 2011, from http://articles.baltimoresun.com/2011-04-24/news/bs-md-mcdonalds-beating-20110423_1_transgender-woman-mcdonalds-county-police.

Sexual Identity

sexual identity One's identification with various categories of sexuality.

Sexual identity refers to one's identification with various categories of sexuality. You are probably most familiar with heterosexual, gay or lesbian, and perhaps bisexual categories; however, sexual identity categories vary from culture to culture and have been variously viewed throughout history (Foucault, 1988). These sexual identities are connected to notions of what was and was not permissible or desirable, for example, Iranian President Mahmoud Ahmadinejad sparked controversy when he denied there were gay people in Iran when he said in a public speech at Columbia University, "In Iran, we don't have homosexuals, like in your country" (Ahmadinejad speaks, 2007). Also, views on sexual identities differ in various historical contexts. Same-sex activities were not always looked down upon, pedophilia was accepted in some eras and cultures, and on the occasions when children were born with both male and female sexual organs, they were not necessarily operated on or forced to be male or female (Foucault, 1988).

Our sexual identities influence our consumption, which television shows we watch, which magazines we read, which Internet sites we visit. Some assume a certain level of public knowledge about sexual identities or stereotypes; for example, *Glee, Modern Family*, and *Grey's Anatomy* assumed viewers were familiar with stereotypes of gays. What are some cultural products that assume knowledge of heterosexual culture?

Official recognition of gay, lesbian, and transgender people varies around the world. **Transgender** refers to identification with a gender that differs from the biologically assigned gender. Some countries recognize transgender people; others do not. Some allow gay marriage; others do not. We discuss this in more detail in chapter 10. In terms of a nation's demographic profile, many use a census to get a picture of their population. Recently, "Nepal's Central Bureau of Statistics is giving official recognition to gay and transgender people" (Shrestha, 2011). In the 2011 census, India is also giving respondents the choice of a third gender in answering census questions about gender, which has roots in Indian culture: "The transgender community, which has long hoped for more social acceptance, is being given an 'other' option under gender apart from 'male' and 'female.' The results will give India a firm count for its 'third-gender' hijra community—the origins of which go back millennia to a time when transsexuals, eunuchs and gays held a special place in society backed by Hindu myths of their power to grant fertility" (Daigle, 2011).

> **transgender** identification with a gender that does not match one's biological gender

The notion of a third sex is not new: "The 'third sex' is far from a recent concept in many parts of the world, having existed for thousands of years. References to a third sex (*triteeyaprakrti* in Sanskrit) appeared at least as early as the 2nd century BC. In Pakistan in 2009, the Supreme Court ordered that eunuchs be given national identification cards identifying their special gender status" (Haub & Sharma, 2011). The long history of thinking about gender and sexuality in different ways, in different cultures, can be reflected in how gender and sexuality are recognized.

In contrast, the 2010 U.S. census gave two gender choices—male or female—and there is no national recognition of a third gender. The census also does not collect data on the population characteristics of gays, lesbians, or transgender people in the United States. Hostility toward those who are different can arise. (See Point of View on page 188.)

Age Identity

As we age, we also play into cultural notions of how individuals our age should act, look, and behave; that is, we develop an **age identity.** As we grow older, we sometimes look at the clothes displayed in store windows or advertised in newspapers and magazines and feel that we are either too old or too young for that "look." These feelings stem from an understanding of what age means and how we identify with people that age.

> **age identity** The identification with the cultural conventions of how we should act, look, and behave according to our age.

Some people feel old at 30; others feel young at 40 or 50. Nothing inherent in age tells us we are young or old. Rather, our notions of age and youth are all based on cultural conventions. The United States is an age-conscious society.

One of the first things we teach children is to tell their age. And children will proudly tell their age, until about the mid-20s on, when people rarely mention their age. In contrast, people older than 70 often brag about their age. Certain ages have special significance in some cultures. Latino families sometimes celebrate a daughter's 15th birthday with a *quinceañera* party—marking the girl's entry into womanhood. Some Jewish families celebrate with a bat mitzvah ceremony for daughters and a bar mitzvah for sons on their 13th birthday (Allen, 2004). These same cultural conventions also suggest that it is inappropriate to engage in a romantic relationship with someone who is too old or too young.

Our notions of age often change as we grow older ourselves. When we are quite young, someone in college seems old; when we are in college, we do not feel so old. Yet the relative nature of age is only one part of the identity process. Social constructions of age also play a role. Different generations often have different philosophies, values, and ways of speaking. For example, recent data show that today's college freshmen are more liberal politically and more interested in volunteer work and civic responsibility than were Gen Xers. Scholars who view generations as "cultural groups" say that these characteristics make them similar to the World War I generation—politically curious and assertive and devoted to a sense of personal responsibility (Sax, Lindholm, Astin, Korn, & Mahoney, 2001).

Different generations often have different philosophies, values, and ways of speaking (Strauss & Howe, 1997). For example, recent data show that the millennium generation (or Gen Y, those born between 1982–2001) are more diverse and globally oriented and more knowledgeable about computers and technology than any preceding generation. They are also more optimistic, more committed to contributing to society and more interested in life balance between work and play than the previous, Gen X, group (those born between 1961–1981) (Strauss & Howe, 2006). This also is reflected in the way they learn and work (multitasking, use of multimedia, etc.).

Sometimes these generational differences can lead to conflict in the workplace. For example, young people who entered the job market during the "dot .com" years have little corporate loyalty and think nothing of changing jobs when a better opportunity comes along. This can irritate baby boomer workers, who emphasize the importance of demonstrating corporate loyalty, of "paying one's dues" to the establishment while gradually working one's way "up the corporate ladder" (Howe & Strauss, 2007). Although not all people in any generation are alike, the attempt to find trends across generations reflects our interest in understanding age identity.

Racial and Ethnic Identities

Racial Identity   Race consciousness, or **racial identity,** is largely a modern phenomenon. In the United States today, the issue of race is both controversial and pervasive. It is the topic of many public discussions, from television talk shows to talk radio. Yet many people feel uncomfortable talking about it or think it should not be an issue in daily life. Perhaps we can better understand the contemporary issues if we look at how the notion of race developed historically in the United States.

Current debates about race have their roots in the 15th and 16th centuries, when European explorers encountered people who looked different from themselves. The debates centered on religious questions of whether there was "one family of man." If so, what rights were to be accorded to those who were different? Debates about which groups were "human" and which were "animal" pervaded popular and legal discourse and provided a rationale for slavery. Later, in the 18th and 19th centuries, the scientific community tried to establish a classification system of race based on genetics and cranial capacity. However, these efforts were largely unsuccessful.

Most scientists have abandoned a strict biological basis for classifying racial groups, especially in light of recent genetic research. To date, researchers have found only 55 genes out of almost 3 million that differentiate various groups. Their conclusions about the implications of their research: "All in all, the school of thought which holds that humans, for all their outward variety, are a pretty homogenous species received a boost" ("Human races or human race," 2008, p. 86). Rather than adhere to the rather outdated notion of a biological basis for racial categorization, most scholars hold a social science viewpoint—agreeing that racial categories like white and black are constructed in social and historical contexts.

Several arguments refute the physiological basis for race. First, racial categories vary widely throughout the world. In general, distinctions between white and black are fairly rigid in the United States, and many people become uneasy when they are unable to categorize individuals. In contrast, Brazil recognizes a wide variety of intermediate racial categories in addition to white and black. These variations indicate a cultural, rather than a biological, basis for racial classification (Omi & Winant, 2001). Terms like *mulatto* and *Black Irish* demonstrate cultural classifications; terms like *Caucasoid* and *Australoid* are examples of biological classification.

Second, U.S. law uses a variety of definitions to determine racial categories. A 1982 case in Louisiana reopened debates about race as socially created rather than biologically determined. Susie Phipps applied for a passport and discovered that under Louisiana law she was black because she was $1/32$ African (her great-grandmother had been a slave). She then sued to be reclassified as white. Not only did she consider herself white, inasmuch as she grew up among whites, but she also was married to a white man. And because her children were only $1/64$ African, they were legally white. Although she lost her lawsuit, the ensuing political and popular discussions persuaded Louisiana lawmakers to change the way the state classified people racially. It is important that the law was changed, but this legal situation does not obscure the fact that social definitions of race continue to exist (Hasian & Nakayama, 1999).

racial identity Identifying with a particular racial group. Although in the past racial groups were classified on the basis of biological characteristics, most scientists now recognize that race is constructed in fluid social and historical contexts.

A third example of how racial categories are socially constructed is illustrated by their fluid nature. As more and more southern Europeans immigrated to the United States in the 19th century, the established Anglo and German society tried to classify these newcomers (Irish and Jewish, as well as southern European) as nonwhite. However, this attempt was not successful because, based on the narrower definition, whites might have become demographically disempowered. Instead, the racial line was drawn to include all Europeans, and people from outside of Europe (e.g., immigrants from China) were designated as nonwhite (Roediger, 2005). We intentionally use the term *nonwhite* here to highlight the central role of *whiteness* in defining racial identity in the United States.

Racial categories, then, are based to some extent on physical characteristics, but they are also constructed in fluid social contexts. It probably makes more sense to talk about racial *formation* than racial *categories*, thereby casting race as a complex of social meanings rather than as a fixed and objective concept. How people construct these meanings and think about race influences the ways in which they communicate.

ethnic identity (1) A set of ideas about one's own ethnic group membership; (2) a sense of belonging to a particular group and knowing something about the shared experience of the group.

Ethnic Identity   In contrast to racial identity, **ethnic identity** may be seen as a set of ideas about one's own ethnic group membership. It typically includes several dimensions: (1) self-identification, (2) knowledge about the ethnic culture (traditions, customs, values, and behaviors), and (3) feelings about belonging to a particular ethnic group. Ethnic identity often involves a shared sense of origin and history, which may link ethnic groups to distant cultures in Asia, Europe, Latin America, or other locations.

Having an ethnic identity means experiencing a sense of belonging to a particular group and knowing something about the shared experience of group members. For instance, Judith grew up in an ethnic community. She heard her parents and relatives speak German, and her grandparents made several trips back to Germany and talked about their German roots. This experience contributed to her ethnic identity.

For some U.S. residents, ethnicity is a specific and relevant concept. They see themselves as connected to an origin outside the United States—as Mexican American, Japanese American, Welsh American, and so on—or to some region prior to its being absorbed into the United States—Navajo, Hopi, and so on. As one African American student told us, "I have always known my history and the history of my people in this country. I will always be first African American and then American. Who I am is based on my heritage." For others, ethnicity is a vague concept. They see themselves as "American" and reject the notion of **hyphenated Americans.** One of our students explains:

hyphenated Americans U.S. Americans who identify not only with being U.S. citizens but also as being members of ethnic groups.

I am American. I am not German American or Irish American or Native American. I have never set foot on German or Irish land. I went to Scotland a couple years ago and found a Scottish plaid that was my family crest. I still didn't even feel a real connection to it and bought it as more of a joke, to say, "Look! I'm Scottish!" even though in my heart I know I'm not.

We discuss the issues of ethnicity for white people later.

What, then, does *American* mean? Who defines it? Is there only one meaning, or are there many different meanings? It is important to determine what definition is being used by those who insist that we should all simply be "Americans." If one's identity is "just American," how is this identity formed, and how does it influence communication with others who see themselves as hyphenated Americans (Alba, 1985, 1990; Carbaugh, 1989)?

Racial Versus Ethnic Identity   Scholars dispute whether racial and ethnic identity are similar or different. Some suggest that ethnic identity is constructed by both selves and others but that racial identity is constructed solely by others. They stress as well that race overrides ethnicity in the way people classify others (Cornell & Hartmann, 1998). The American Anthropological Association has suggested that the U.S. government phase out use of the term *race* in the collection of federal data because the concept has no scientific validity or utility.

On the one hand, discussions about ethnicity tend to assume a "melting pot" perspective on U.S. society. On the other hand, discussions about race as shaped by U.S. history allow us to talk about racism. If we never talk about race, but only about ethnicity, can we consider the effects and influences of racism?

Bounded Versus Dominant Identities   One way to sort out the relationship between ethnicity and race is to differentiate between bounded and dominant (or normative) identities (Frankenburg, 1993; Trinh, 1986/1987). Bounded cultures are characterized by groups that are specific but not dominant. For most white people, it is easy to comprehend the sense of belonging in a bounded group (e.g., an ethnic group). Clearly, for example, being Amish means following the *ordnung* (community rules). Growing up in a German American home, Judith's identity included a clear emphasis on seriousness and very little on communicative expressiveness. This identity differed from that of her Italian American friends at college, who seemed much more expressive.

However, what it means to belong to the dominant, or normative, culture is more elusive. *Normative* means "setting the norm for a society." In the United States, whites clearly are the normative group in that they set the standards for appropriate and effective behavior. Although it can be difficult for white people to define what a normative white identity is, this does not deny its existence or importance. It is often not easy to see what the cultural practices are that link white people together. For example, we seldom think of Thanksgiving or Valentine's Day as white holidays.

Our sense of racial or ethnic identity develops over time, in stages, and through communication with others. These stages seem to reflect our growing understanding of who we are and depend to some extent on the groups we belong to. Many ethnic or racial groups share the experience of oppression. In response, they may generate attitudes and behaviors consistent with a natural internal struggle to develop a strong sense of group identity and self-identity. For many cultural groups, these strong identities ensure their survival.

Characteristics of Whiteness

What does it mean to be white in the United States? What are the characteristics of a white identity? Is there a unique set of characteristics that define whiteness, just as other racial identities have been described?

It may be difficult for most white people to describe exactly what cultural patterns are uniquely white, but scholars have tried to do so. For example, scholar Ruth Frankenburg (1993) says that whiteness may be defined not only in terms of race or ethnicity but also as a set of linked dimensions. These dimensions include (1) normative race privilege; (2) a standpoint from which white people look at themselves, others, and society; and (3) a set of cultural practices (often unnoticed and unnamed).

Normative Race Privilege   Historically, whites have been the normative (dominant) group in the United States and, as such, have benefited from privileges that go along with belonging to the dominant group (see Point of View on page 195). However, not all whites have power, and not all have equal access to power. In fact, at times during U.S. history, some white communities were not privileged and were viewed as separate, or different, if not inferior. Examples include the Irish and Italians in the early 20th century and German Americans during World War II. And as scholars point out, the memory of marginality outlasts the marginality. For example, memories of discrimination may persist in the minds of some Italian Americans although little discrimination exists today. There also are many white people in the United States who are poor and so lack economic power.

There is an emerging perception that being white no longer means automatic privilege, particularly as demographics change in the United States and as some whites perceive themselves to be in the minority. This has led some whites to feel threatened and "out of place." A Chicago college professor tells the story of how her white students thought that 65% of the population near their university was African American; they perceived themselves to be in the minority and based their estimate on their observations and anecdotes. When she corrected them, they were stunned. In fact, according to the 2000 U.S. Census, the percentage of blacks in Chicago was only 37% (Myers, 2003, p. 130). Students' perceptions affected their sense of identity, which, in turn, can affect intercultural communication.

Some white young people today are very aware of their whiteness (Frankenburg, 2001). Further, they believe that being white is a liability, that they are sometimes prejudged as racist and blamed for social conditions they personally did not cause, and that they are denied opportunities that are unfairly given to minority students. One of our white students describes this feeling:

> *When I was trying to get into college I had to fight for every inch. I didn't have a lot of money to go to school with, so to get a scholarship was of great importance to me. So I went out and bought a book titled* The Big Book of Scholarships. *Ninety percent of the scholarships that this book contained didn't apply to me. They applied to the so-called minorities. . . . I think this country has gone on so long with the notion that white equals wealth or with things like affirmative action, that it has lost sight of the fact that this country is not that way any longer.*

THE INVISIBLE KNAPSACK

Scholar Peggy McIntosh compares the everyday privileges of being white in the United States to an invisible, weightless "knapsack" she carries, full of unearned assets, like road maps, codes, and blank checks that she is not supposed to notice, but that she can count on every day nevertheless. She compiled a list of these privileges that "as far as I can tell, my African American coworkers, friends, and acquaintances with whom I come into daily or frequent contact in this particular time, place and time of work cannot count on most of the [time]." Although she initially compiled this list about 25 years ago, which do you think are still applicable today?

As a White person

- *I can if I wish arrange to be in the company of people of my race most of the time.*
- *When I am told about our national heritage or about "civilization," I am shown that people of my color made it what it is.*
- *Whether I use checks, credit cards or cash, I can count on my skin color not to work against the appearance of financial reliability.*
- *I can swear, or dress in second hand clothes, or not answer letters, without having people attribute these choices to the bad morals, the poverty or the illiteracy of my race.*
- *I can do well in a challenging situation without being called a credit to my race.*
- *I am never asked to speak for all the people of my racial group.*
- *I can be pretty sure that if I ask to talk to the "person in charge," I will be facing a person of my race.*
- *I can go home from most meetings of organizations I belong to feeling somewhat tied in, rather than isolated, out-of-place, outnumbered, unheard, held at a distance or feared.*
- *I can be late to a meeting without having the lateness reflect on my race.*
- *I can easily find academic courses and institutions which give attention only to people of my race.*
- *I will feel welcomed and "normal" in the usual walks of public life, institutional and social.*

Source: Adapted from Working Paper 189, "White Privilege and Male Privilege: A Personal Account of Coming to See Correspondences through Work in Women's Studies" (1988), The Wellesley College Center for Research on Women, Wellesley, MA 02181.

In addition, because of corporate downsizing and the movement of jobs overseas in recent decades, increasing numbers of middle-aged white men have not achieved the degree of economic or professional success they had anticipated. They sometimes blame their lack of success on immigrants who will work for less or on the increasing numbers of women and minorities in the workplace. In these cases, whiteness is not invisible; it is a salient feature of the white individuals' identities.

The point is not whether these perceptions are accurate. Rather, the point is that identities are negotiated and challenged through communication. People act on their perceptions, not on some external reality. As the nation becomes increasingly diverse and whites no longer form a majority in some regions, there will be increasing challenges for all of us as we negotiate our cultural identities.

How can whites in the United States incorporate the reality of not belonging to a majority group? Will whites find inclusive and productive ways to manage this identity change? Or will they react in defensive and exclusionary ways?

One reaction to feeling outnumbered and being a "new member" of an ethnic minority group is to strengthen one's own ethnic identity. For example, white people may tend to have stronger white identities in those U.S. states that have a higher percentage of nonwhites (e.g., Mississippi, South Carolina, Alabama). In these states, the white population traditionally has struggled to protect its racial privilege in various ways. As other states become increasingly less white, we are beginning to see various moves to protect whiteness.

For example, is the Birther Movement questioning President Obama's birthplace a contemporary expression of whiteness? The recent election of President Obama, coupled with an economic recession, has created the opportunity to explore some of these issues. Charles Gallagher, a sociologist who studies white identity, notes: "We went from being a privileged group to all of a sudden becoming whites, the new victims . . . You have this perception out there that whites are no longer in control or the majority. Whites are the new minority group" (quoted in Blake, 2011). Although they are not numerically a minority group, their experiences may be shaping what white identity means. Tim Wise, a writer, says: "For the first time since the Great Depression, white Americans have been confronted with a level of economic insecurity that we're not used to. It's not so new for black and brown folks, but for white folks, this is something we haven't seen since the Depression" (quoted in Blake, 2011). Fears about the loss of white America drive much of this discussion. Yet, as a Vassar College professor prefers to see it: "This moment was not the end of white America; it was not the end of anything. It was a bridge, and we crossed it" (Hsu, 2009).

A Standpoint from Which to View Society Opinion polls reveal significant differences in how whites and blacks view many issues, including President Obama. For example, a Pew Research Center study conducted one year after President Obama's election found that blacks were more likely to view President Obama as black (55%) rather than mixed race (34%). For whites, the responses were reversed: 53% of whites saw President Obama as mixed race and 24% as black. When asked if opposition to Obama's policies is racially motivated, 52% of blacks thought so, whereas only 17% of whites felt that way. And since the election of President Obama, blacks and whites feel that blacks are better off than five years ago (see Figure 5-2), but a 10 percentage point difference remains ("Blacks upbeat about black progress, prospects," 2010).

A Set of Cultural Practices Is there a specific, unique "white" way of viewing the world? As noted previously, some views held consistently by whites are not

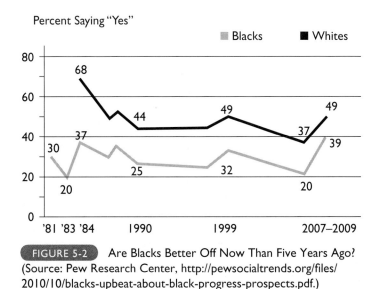

FIGURE 5-2 Are Blacks Better Off Now Than Five Years Ago? (Source: Pew Research Center, http://pewsocialtrends.org/files/ 2010/10/blacks-upbeat-about-black-progress-prospects.pdf.)

necessarily shared by other groups. And some cultural practices and core symbols (e.g., individualism) are expressed primarily by whites and significantly less by members of minority groups. We need to note here that not everyone who is white shares all cultural practices. (See Figure 5-3.) For example, recent immigrants who are white, but not born in the United States, may share in the privilege accorded all white people in the United States; however, they might not necessarily share in the viewpoints or the set of cultural practices of whites whose families have been in the United States for many generations. It is important to remember that some whites may identify fairly strongly with their European roots, especially if their families are more recent immigrants and they still have family members in Europe; other whites may not feel any connection to Europe and feel completely "American." These cultural practices are most clearly visible to those who are not white, to those groups who are excluded (Bahk & Jandt, 2004). For example, in the fairy tale of Snow White, the celebration of her beauty—emphasizing her beautiful, pure white skin—is often seen as problematic by people who are not white.

Religious Identity

Religious identity can be an important dimension of many people's identities, as well as an important site of intercultural conflict. Religious identity often is conflated with racial or ethnic identity, which makes it difficult to view religious identity simply in terms of belonging to a particular religion. For example, when someone says, "I am Jewish," does it mean that he practices Judaism? That he views Jewish identity as an ethnic identity? Or when someone says, "She has a Jewish last name," is it a statement that recognizes religious identity? With a historical view, we can see Jews as a racial group, an ethnic group, and a religious group.

Drawing distinctions among various identities—racial, ethnic, class, national, and regional—can be problematic. For example, Italians and Irish are often viewed

religious identity
A sense of belonging to a religious group.

FIGURE 5-3   White culture is difficult to define. White people do not often think of some of their activities as white cultural practices, such as sunbathing, a common leisure activity among many white people. Not all cultural groups place a high value on suntans. In this photo, a Chinese man holds an umbrella to shield his wife from the sun as she takes a photo of her parents at Tiananmen Square. In this culture, darker skin, particularly on a woman, is seen as more negative than light skin. Gender and racial identities function together to place a low cultural value on suntanning.
(© Andrew Wong/Reuters/Corbis)

as Catholics, and Episcopalians are frequently seen as belonging to the upper classes. Issues of religion and ethnicity have come to the forefront in the war against Al-Qaeda and other militant groups. Although those who carried out the attacks against the Pentagon and the World Trade Center were Muslims and Arabs, it is hardly true that all Muslims are Arabs or that all Arabs are Muslims (Feghali, 1997).

Religious differences have been at the root of contemporary conflicts from the Middle East to Northern Ireland, and from India and Pakistan to Bosnia-Herzegovina. In the United States, religious conflicts caused the Mormons to flee the Midwest for Utah in the mid-19th century. More recently, religious conflicts have become very real for some Arab Americans as the U.S. government presses the war against terrorism, with many of those people subject to suspicion if not persecution. And militant Muslims in the Middle East and elsewhere see their struggle against the United States as a very serious endeavor and are willing to die for their religious beliefs.

In the United States, we often believe that people should be free to practice whatever religion they wish. Conflicts arise, however, when the religious beliefs of some individuals are imposed on others who may not share those beliefs. For example, some Jews see the predominance of Christmas trees and Christian

FIGURE 5-4   You might not know someone's religious identity, except for certain religious observances, like Ash Wednesday for some Christians. (© *Sean Gardner/Getty Images*)

crosses as an affront to their religious beliefs. The influence of religious identities on Americans' attitudes was evidenced in 2007 during Mitt Romney's (a Mormon politician) presidential campaign. A research study found that bias against Mormons was significantly more intense than bias against either African Americans or women and that bias against Mormons was even more pronounced among conservative Evangelicals (Luo, 2007; "New Vanderbilt . . . ," 2007).

People in some religions communicate and mark their religious differences by their clothing. For example, Hassidic Jews wear traditional, somber clothing, and Muslim women are often veiled according to the Muslim guideline of female modesty. Of course, most religions are not identified by clothing. For example, you may not know if someone is Buddhist, Catholic, Lutheran, or atheist based upon the way he or she dresses. (See Figure 5-4.) Because religious identities are less salient, everyday interactions may not invoke religious identity.

Class Identity

We don't often think about socioeconomic class as an important part of our identity. Yet scholars have shown that class often plays an important role in shaping our reactions to and interpretations of culture. For example, French sociologist Pierre Bourdieu (1987) studied the various responses to art, sports, and other cultural activities of people in different French social classes. According to Bourdieu, working-class people prefer to watch soccer, whereas upper-class individuals like tennis, and middle-class people prefer photographic art, whereas upper-class individuals favor less representational art. As these findings reveal, class distinctions are real and can be linked to actual behavioral practices and preferences.

class identity A sense of belonging to a group that shares similar economic, occupational, or social status.

English professor Paul Fussell (1992) shows how similar signs of **class identity** operate in U.S. society. According to Fussell, the magazines we read, the foods we eat, and the words we use often reflect our social class position. At some level, we recognize these class distinctions, but we consider it impolite to ask directly about a person's class background. Therefore, we may use communication strategies to place others in a class hierarchy. Unfortunately, these strategies don't always yield accurate information. For example, people may try to guess your class background by the foods you eat. Some foods are seen as "rich folk's food"—for instance, lamb, white asparagus, brie, artichokes, goose, and caviar. Do you feel as if you are revealing your class background if you admit that these foods are unfamiliar to you? Perhaps not admitting your unfamiliarity is a form of "passing," of representing yourself as belonging to a group you really don't belong to. Another strategy that people may use to guess a person's class background is to ask where that person did her or his undergraduate work.

Most people in the United States recognize class associations even as they may deny that such class divisions exist. What does this apparent contradiction indicate? Most importantly, it reveals the complexities of class issues, particularly in the United States. We often don't really know the criteria for inclusion in a given social class. Is membership determined by financial assets? By educational level? By profession? By family background? These factors may or may not be indicators of class.

Another reason for this apparent contradiction is that people in the majority or normative class (the middle class) tend not to think about class, whereas those in the working class are often reminded that their communication styles and lifestyle choices are not the norm. David Engen (2004), a communication scholar, describes his own experience of entering college from a working-class background and feeling like he had entered a new culture. For one thing, the working-class communication style he was accustomed to was very different from the proper English required in his classes. "I vividly recall coming to college saying things such as 'I seen that,' 'I ain't worried about that' and 'that don't mean nothing to me.' I am glad my professors and friends helped me acquire a language that allowed me to succeed in mainstream American society" (p. 253). And the philosophical conversations expected in class were a challenge. As he describes it, working-class communication is about getting things done, very different from the abstract conversations he was expected to participate in—designed to broaden perspective rather than to accomplish any particular task. In this respect, class is like race. For example, terms like *trailer trash* and *white trash* show the negative connotations associated with people who are not middle class (Moon & Rolison, 1998).

A central assumption of the American dream is that, with hard work and persistence, individuals can improve their class standing, even in the face of overwhelming evidence to the contrary. And the American dream seems alive and well. An estimated 94% of Americans still think that "people who work full time should be able to earn enough to keep their families out of poverty" (Allen, 2004, p. 105).

In this article, the author argues that the best colleges are for those from elite backgrounds. Aside from how this affects you personally, how does this practice affect our nation and its ability to move forward collectively? How much mobility really exists in U.S. society?

> *For all of the other ways that top colleges had become diverse, their student bodies remained shockingly affluent. At the University of Michigan, more entering freshmen in 2003 came from families earning at least $200,000 a year than came from the entire bottom half of the income distribution. At some private colleges, the numbers were even more extreme. . . . The truth is that many of the most capable low- and middle-income students attend community colleges or less selective four-year colleges close to their home. Doing so makes them less likely to graduate from college at all, research has shown. . . . The United States no longer leads the world in educational attainment, partly because so few low-income students—and surprisingly few middle-income students—graduate from four-year colleges. Getting more of these students into the best colleges would make a difference.*

Source: D. Leonhardt, "Top colleges, largely for the elite," *The New York Times*, May 24, 2011. Retrieved June 1, 2011, from www.nytimes.com/2011/05/25/business/economy/25leonhardt.html?pagewanted=1&ref=education.

The mobility myth, like the American dream, is just that, a myth, as discussed in Chapter 1. The United States has the most unequally distributed wealth and income in the world.

However, holding on to the mobility myth has consequences. According to Allen (2004), the ideology underlying the myth persuades us that poor people are the ones to blame for being poor, that "poor people collectively exhibit traits that keep them down. . . . [It] blames the poor for their plight and ignores the fact that many wealthy people have inherited their wealth and resources or that they were better positioned to attain the American dream. This does not acknowledge that economic, cultural and social capital can tilt the playing field in favor of those who have accumulated wealth, knowledge, and/or connections" (p. 105). And the media often reinforce these notions. As Leonardo DiCaprio's character in the movie *Titanic* shows us, upward mobility is easy enough—merely a matter of being opportunistic, charming, and a little bit lucky.

Working-class individuals who aren't upwardly mobile are often portrayed in TV sitcoms and movies as unintelligent, criminal, or unwilling to do what they have to do to better their lot in life. (Consider, for example, the TV shows "Teen Mom" and "Shameless.") Members of the real working class, as frequent guests on television talk shows like *Jerry Springer* and on court shows like *Judge Judy* and *Judge Joe Brown*, are urged to be verbally contentious and even physically aggressive with each other.

The point is that although class identity is not as readily apparent as, say, gender identity, it still influences our perceptions of and communication with others. Race, class, and sometimes gender identity are interrelated. For example, statistically speaking, being born African American, poor, and female increases one's chances of remaining in poverty (Mishel, Bernstein, & Allegretto, 2006). But, of course, race and class are not synonymous. There are many poor whites, and there are increasing numbers of wealthy African Americans. In this sense, these multiple identities are interrelated but not identical.

National Identity

national identity
National citizenship.

Among many identities, we also have a **national identity,** which should not be confused with racial or ethnic identity. Nationality, unlike racial or ethnic identity, refers to one's legal status in relation to a nation. Many U.S. citizens can trace their ethnicity to Latin America, Asia, Europe, or Africa, but their nationality, or citizenship, is with the United States.

Although national identity may seem to be a clear-cut issue, this is not the case when the nation's status is unclear. For example, bloody conflicts erupted over the attempted secession in the mid-1800s of the Confederate States of America from the United States. Similar conflicts erupted in more recent times when Eritrea tried to separate from Ethiopia, and Chechnya from Russia. Less bloody conflicts that involved nationhood led, in the former Czechoslovakia, to the separation of Slovakia and the Czech Republic. The former Yugoslavia was broken up into a number of smaller countries, but the terrible conflicts ensued. (See Point of View on Novak Djokovic.)

More recently, nationhood discussions look promising for Scotland to become independent of the United Kingdom, but there is less interest in seeking independence for Quebec from Canada. Tensions remain high between Flanders and Wallonia as the political conflict means that they have been unable to seat a national government. Will this lead to the dissolution of Belgium? Sometimes nations disappear from the political map but persist in the social imagination and eventually reemerge, such as Poland, Ukraine, Latvia, Lithuania, and Estonia. Other times, national identity may shift in significant ways, as in the United States after the attacks of September 11, 2001, when ideas about national identity seemed to incorporate increased expressions of patriotism. One of our Japanese graduate students explains how her feeling of national identity is much different from what she sees in the United States:

> *I have seen so many "God bless America," "Proud to be American" messages EVERYWHERE as I have lived here as a Japanese sojourner. . . . Coming from Japan, I don't think I have the same notion of "I am proud about my country." I love my culture, the beauty, the meanings, the spirituality that surround it. But I feel that I have been consciously or subconsciously taught that being proud of your country can be dangerous, misleading, blinding. Look at what happened before 1945—how many people in my country thought about their country and framed the "cause" which led to a disaster (WW II). In fact, I have talked to my Japanese friends about this sentiment and mixed emotion I feel about the concept of "patriotism," and almost all of them agreed with me—we were not taught to be proud of*

After the breakup of the former Yugoslavia, Serbia gained a negative image in relation to its former Yugoslavian neighbors, Bosnia & Herzegovina, Slovenia, Croatia, Macedonia, and Kosovo. What role can sports play in creating a more positive, external image of Serbian national identity? How do sports influence your image of other national identities? Let's look at the case of tennis player Novak Djokovic.

For years, the Balkan nation has been a pariah because of its role in the bloody 1992–95 Bosnian war, the conflict that added "ethnic cleansing" to the political lexicon. The Serbian government on May 31 made a great leap forward in rehabilitating itself by extraditing Ratko Mladic, the Bosnian Serb general accused of the biggest European atrocity since World War II, the massacre of 8,000 Muslim men and boys in the town of Srebrenica, Bosnia-Herzegovina. . . .

"We do not want the world to remember us for our war commanders, but as the country of tennis star Novak Djokovic," Serbia's deputy war crimes prosecutor, Bruno Vekaric, said upon Mladic's arrest May 26. . . .

At the 2009 Australian Open, dozens of spectators of Serbian and Croatian descent were evicted from the tournament grounds after hurling abuse—and chairs—at each other after Djokovic's win against a Bosnia-born American player. A woman was knocked unconscious.

At this year's Australian Open, in January, Djokovic was the voice of tolerance, appealing for calm before his match against Croatian player Ivan Dodig.

"We are very good friends, actually, off the court, all of us Serb and Croatian players. There's no reason to create any kind of bad feeling about our countries," said Djokovic, who went on to win his second Grand Slam title. . . .

Now Djokovic and Serbia want their moment in the sun, as little by little they seek to banish the shadows that hang over their past.

Source: H. Chu, "Tennis star may bring shine back to Serbia's tarnished reputation," *Los Angeles Times*, June 5, 2011. Retrieved June 9, 2011, from www.latimes.com/news/nationworld/world/la-fg-serbia-tennis-djokovic-20110605,0,6643304.story.

our country in the post–WW II era. Of course, each country has a different history, political situation, so what I am saying here doesn't necessarily translate to other people in other cultures.

It may sound funny, but one thing I would say I am proud of about my country is that I don't have to say I am proud of my country. I am proud that I can see both beautiful and ugly sides of my country's history. I feel free there, for not being pressured by anyone to say that I am proud of my country.

In contrast, the devastating earthquake and tsunami that hit northern Japan in March 2011 was a pivotal moment in Japanese national identity. Media coverage included the astonishing civility and patience that the Japanese displayed in the aftermath. In a report on the disaster response, it was noted that: "in the aftermath of the disaster, the Japanese people demonstrated remarkable resilience and discipline with no reports of rioting or large-scale disruptions" (Carafano, 2011, p. 4). For the Japanese, this has meant a turning point in their national identity:

> *Oddly enough, the Japanese are proud to be Japanese now. . . . Prior to the quake, Japan was a timid nation worrying about its eventual decline. . . . But maybe the Japanese people could use the experience of this catastrophe to rebuild a society bound together with a renewed trust. While many will revert to their indecisive selves, the experience of discovering our own public-minded, patriotic selves that had been paralyzed within a pernicious cynicism is not likely to fade away. . . . I hear that the foreign media has been reporting with amazement the calmness and moral behavior of the Japanese faced with the disaster. But actually this was a surprise to the Japanese themselves. "Yeah, we can do it if we put our minds to it." "We aren't so bad as a whole nation after all." (Azuma, 2011)*

In the wake of the fourth largest earthquake in recorded history, perhaps Japanese national identity is undergoing its own shift.

In sum, people have various ways of thinking about nationality, and they sometimes confuse nationality and ethnicity. Thus, we have overheard students asking minority students, "What is your nationality?" when they actually meant, "What is your ethnicity?" This confusion can lead to—and perhaps reflects—a lack of understanding about differences between, say, Asian Americans (ethnic group) and Asians (nationality groups). It can also tend to alienate Asian Americans and others who have been in the United States for several generations but are still perceived as foreigners.

Regional Identity

regional identity
Identification with a specific geographic region of a nation.

Closely related to nationality is the notion of **regional identity.** Many regions of the world have separate, but vital and important, cultural identities. The Scottish Highlands is a region of northern Scotland that is distinctly different from the Lowlands, and regional identity remains strong in the Highlands.

Here in the United States, regional identities remain important, but perhaps less so as the nation moves toward homogeneity. Southerners, for example, often view themselves, and are viewed by others, as a distinct cultural group. Similarly, Texas advertises itself as "A Whole Other Country," promoting its regional identity. Although some regional identities can fuel national independence movements, they more often reflect cultural identities that affirm distinctive cuisines, dress, manners, and language. These identities may become important in intercultural communication situations. For example, suppose you meet someone who is Chinese. Whether the person is from Beijing, Hong Kong, or elsewhere in China may raise important communication issues. After all, Mandarin is not understood by Cantonese speakers, although both are dialects of the Chinese language. Indeed, there are many dialects in China, and they certainly are not understood by all other Chinese speakers.

One fairly recent variation in regional identities has to do with the degree of diversity within certain parts of the United States. Data from the 2000 census reveal that the South and the West are the most diverse, along with the coastal Northeast. The Midwest, in contrast, with a few exceptions, remains relatively homogenous (Brewer & Suchan, 2001, pp. 22–23). In addition, the overwhelming majority of multiracial individuals (67%) live in the South and the West (pp. 87–89). What are the implications for identity and intercultural communication? It could mean that people in these areas have more opportunities for understanding and practicing intercultural communication and so benefit from the diversity. Or they may withdraw into their own groups and protect their racial and ethnic "borders."

PERSONAL IDENTITY

Many issues of identity are closely tied to our notions of self. Each of us has a **personal identity,** which is the sum of all our identities, but it may not be unified or coherent. A dialectical perspective allows us to see identity in a more complex way. We are who we think we are; at the same time, however, contextual and external forces constrain and influence our self-perceptions. We have many identities, and these can conflict. For example, according to communication scholar Victoria Chen (1992), some Chinese American women feel caught between the traditional values of their parents' culture and their own desire to be Americanized. From the parents' point of view, the daughters are never Chinese enough. From the perspective of many people within the dominant culture, though, it is difficult to relate to these Chinese American women simply as "American women, born and reared in this society" (p. 231). The dialectical tension related to issues of identity for these women reveals the strain between feeling obligated to behave in traditional ways at home and yet holding a Western notion of gender equality. A dialectical perspective sees these contradictions as real and presenting challenges in communication and everyday life.

> **personal identity** Who we think we are and who others think we are.

Our personal identities are important to us, and we try to communicate them to others. We are more or less successful depending on how others respond to us. We use the various ways that identity is constructed to portray ourselves as we want others to see us.

MULTICULTURAL PEOPLE

Multicultural people, a group currently dramatically increasing in number, are those who live "on the borders" of two or more cultures. They often struggle to reconcile two very different sets of values, norms, worldviews, and lifestyles. Some are multicultural as a result of being born to parents from different racial, ethnic, religious, or national cultures or they were adopted into families that are racially different from their own family of origin. Others are multicultural because their parents lived overseas and they grew up in cultures different from their own, or because they spent extended time in another culture as an adult, or married someone from another cultural background. Let's start with those who are born into biracial or multiracial families. Some contemporary examples of multiracial individuals include Barack Obama, Carmelo Anthony, Derek Jeter, Freddie Prinze Jr., Jordin Sparks, Mariah Carey, Norah Jones, Tiger Woods, and Vanessa Williams (multiracial celebrities).

According to the 2010 census, the United States has almost 9 million multiracial people—that is, people whose ancestry includes two or more races (Saulny, 2011). This number has increased about 32% from the 2000 census, which was the first time people were given the option of selecting several categories to indicate their racial identities. This rapidly growing segment of our population must be understood in its historical context. The United States has a long history of forbidding miscegenation (the mixing of two races). The law sought not to prevent *any* interracial marriage but to protect "whiteness"; interracial marriage between people of color was rarely prohibited or regulated (Root, 2001). Thus, in 1957, the state of Virginia ruled the marriage of Mildred Jeter (African American and Native American heritage) and Peter Loving (white) illegal. The couple fought to have their marriage legalized for almost 10 years. Finally, in 1967, the Supreme Court ruled in their favor, in *Loving v. Virginia*, overturning 200 years of antimiscegenation legislation.

As shown earlier in Table 5-2, the development of racial identity for the children of parents like the Lovings is a fluid process of complex transactions between the child and the broader social environment (Nance & Foeman, 2002). Whereas majority and minority identities seem to develop in a fairly linear fashion, biracial children may cycle through three stages: (1) awareness of differentness and resulting dissonance, (2) struggle for acceptance, and (3) self-acceptance and self-assertion. And as they mature, they may experience the same three phases with greater intensity and awareness.

In the first stage, multiracial children realize that they are different from other children—they may feel that they don't fit in anywhere. Tiffany, whose mother is white and father is black, describes her experience:

> *Growing up I had kids make fun of me because they said I did not know what color I was. That really hurt me as a kid because even at a young age, I started questioning my own race.*

At the next stage, struggle for acceptance, multiracial adolescents may feel that they have to choose one race or the other—and indeed this was Tiffany's experience:

> *During my teenage years I still was a little confused about my race because I would only choose one side. When people asked me what color I was I would tell them I was black because I was embarrassed about being mixed. I was afraid of not being accepted by the black community if I said I was mixed. . . . I would go around telling people that I am black and would get mad if someone said I was white. I never thought about being mixed with both black and white.*

After being torn between the two (or more) races, multiracial individuals may reach the third stage, of self-acceptance and self-assertion. Tiffany describes how this happened for her:

I can recall a time when I had to spend Christmas with my mother's side of the family. This was the first time I met her side of the family and I felt myself being scared. Honestly, I have never been around a lot of white people, and when I was there I realized that I am mixed and this is who I am and I cannot hide it anymore. . . . From then on I claimed both sides.

And she goes on to demonstrate her self-acceptance and self-assertion:

Being mixed is wonderful, and most importantly, being mixed taught me many things especially growing up. It taught me how to be strong, not to worry about what other people think and to just be myself. It also taught me not to like only one color and that all colors are beautiful. My race made me who I am today. I am strong and I know my race. I no longer have to deny what my race is or who I am.

As you might imagine, many positive aspects are associated with having a biracial identity. In one recent study, the majority of biracial respondents "did not express feelings of marginality as suggested by traditional theories of bicultural identity. Instead, these youth exhibited a clear understanding and affiliation with both groups' cultures and values" (Miller, Watling, Staggs, & Rotheram-Borus, 2003, p. 139). Later in the chapter we discuss further the important role that multicultural people can play in intercultural relations.

In addition to multicultural identities based on race and ethnicity, there are multicultural identities based on religion, sexual orientation, or other identities. For example, children growing up with a Jewish and a Christian parent may feel torn between the two and follow some of the same identity development phases as biracial children—where they feel different, forced to choose between one or the other. Teresa says, "My father is Mexican American and my mother is white, so I have a Latino last name. When I was younger, some kids would tease me with racial slurs about Mexicans. My mother totally didn't understand and just said that I should ignore them, but my father understood much better. He faced the same taunting as a child in Indiana." A straight child of gay parents may have similar feelings of needing to negotiate between straight and gay worldviews.

Individuals develop multicultural identities for other reasons. For example, **global nomads** (or **third-culture kids**—TCKs) grow up in many different cultural contexts because their parents move around a lot (e.g., missionaries, international business employees, and military families). According to a recent study, these children have unique challenges and unique opportunities. They move an average of about eight times, experience cultural rules that may be constraining (e.g., in cultures where children have less freedom), and endure periods of family separation. At the same time, they have opportunities not provided to most people—extensive travel, living in new and different places around the world. As adults they settle down and often feel the need to reconnect with other global nomads (easier now through technologies such as the Internet) (Ender, 2002).

global nomads (third-culture kids) People who grow up in many different cultural contexts because their parents relocated.

President Barack Obama is a good example of a global nomad—his father was an African exchange student and his mother a U.S. American college student. He spent his childhood first in Hawaii and then in Indonesia when his mother and his Indonesian stepfather moved there. Like many TCKs, he was separated from his family during high school when he returned to Hawaii to live with his grandparents. His stepsister credits his ability to understand people from many different backgrounds to his many intercultural experiences as a child and adolescent—like many global nomads, these experiences "gave him the ability to . . . understand people from a wide array of backgrounds. People see themselves in him . . . because he himself contains multitudes" ("Obama's sister talks about his childhood," 2008).

Children of foreign-born immigrants may also develop multicultural identities. Foreign-born immigrants in the United States represent one of the fastest-growing segments—almost a third of the current foreign-born population arrived in the United States since 1990. These include refugees from war zones like Kosovo and the Balkans and migrants who come to the United States to escape dire economic conditions. They often struggle to negotiate their identities, torn between family expectations and their new American culture. Khoa, a first-generation Vietnamese American, describes how important his family's values are:

> *What does it mean to be "Asian" then? Being Asian is being proud of my heritage, my family, and the values that they have passed down to you. I am proud of my parents' discipline upon me. . . . I learned very early in life the differences between right and wrong. . . . I am proud that my parents taught me to respect my elders. I value the time I spend with my grandparents. I love the time I spend with my uncles and aunts, and my cousins. Having a deep love and honest respect for my family, both immediate and extended, is what being "Asian" means to me.*

Then he recounts the struggle to reconcile being both Vietnamese and American:

> *There are a few things, though, that my parents believe in that I do not agree with. I think it is important that you know where you came from and to have pride in your nationality. However, I do not think that just because I am Vietnamese I am obligated to marry a Vietnamese girl. A Vietnamese girl is not any better or worse than any other girl of another nationality.*

Like Khoa, multicultural adolescents often feel pulled in different directions as they develop their own identities.

A final category of multicultural people includes those who have intense intercultural experiences as adults—for example, people who maintain long-term romantic relationships with members of another ethnic or racial group or who spend extensive time living in other cultures. Miguel tells us, "My father is an American, but my mother is from Chile. Because they divorced when I was young and my father returned to the United States, I spent a lot of time traveling back and forth and learning to adapt to two different cultures and languages. I don't feel completely Chilean or American, but I feel like I am both. I have family and friends in both places and I feel connected in different ways."

We discuss these multicultural identities more in Chapter 8, "Understanding Intercultural Transitions." All multicultural people may feel as if they live in cultural margins, struggling with two sets of cultural realities: not completely part of the dominant culture but not an outsider, either.

Social psychologist Peter Adler (1974) describes the multicultural person as someone who comes to grips with a multiplicity of realities. This individual's identity is not defined by a sense of belonging; rather, it is a new psychocultural form of consciousness. Milton Bennett (1993) describes how individuals can develop an "ethnorelative" perspective based on their attitudes toward cultural difference. The first, and most ethnocentric, stage involves the denial or ignoring of difference. The next stage occurs when people recognize difference but attach negative meaning to it. A third stage occurs when people minimize the effects of difference—for example, with statements like "We're really all the same under the skin" and "After all, we're all God's children." Bennett recognizes that minority and majority individuals may experience these phases differently. In addition, minority individuals usually skip the first phase. They don't have the option to deny difference; they are often reminded by others that they are different.

The remainder of the stages represent a major shift in thinking—a paradigm shift—because positive meanings are associated with difference. In the fourth phase (acceptance), people accept the notion of cultural difference; in the fifth phase (adaptation), they may change their own behavior to adapt to others. The final phase (integration) is similar to Peter Adler's (1974) notion of a "multicultural person."

According to Adler, multicultural individuals may become **culture brokers**— people who facilitate cross-cultural interaction and reduce conflict, which we'll discuss in more detail in Chapter 12. For example, third-culture kids/global nomads often develop resilience, tolerance, and worldliness, characteristics essential for successful living in an increasingly diverse and global social and economic world (Ender, 1996). And, indeed, there are many challenges and opportunities today for multicultural people, who can reach a level of insight and cultural functioning not experienced by others. One of our students, who is Dutch (ethnicity) and Mexican (nationality), describes this:

culture brokers
Individuals who act as bridges between cultures, facilitating cross-cultural interaction and conflict.

> *Being the makeup I am to me means I come from two extremely proud cultures. The Dutch in me gives me a sense of tradition and loyalty. The Mexican side gives me a rich sense of family as well as closeness with not only my immediate family, with my aunts, uncles, and cousins as well. My unique mix makes me very proud of my identity. To me it means that I am proof that two parts of the world can unite in a world that still believes otherwise.*

However, Adler (1974) also identifies potential stresses and tensions associated with multicultural individuals:

They may confuse the profound with the insignificant, not sure what is really important.

They may feel multiphrenic, fragmented.

They may suffer a loss of their own authenticity and feel reduced to a variety of roles.

They may retreat into existential absurdity. (p. 35)

Communication scholar Janet Bennett (1993) provides insight into how being multicultural can be at once rewarding *and* challenging. She describes two types of multicultural individuals: (1) *encapsulated marginals*, who become trapped by their own marginality and (2) *constructive marginals*, who thrive in their marginality.

Encapsulated marginals have difficulty making decisions, are troubled by ambiguity, and feel pressure from both groups. They try to assimilate but never feel comfortable, never feel "at home." In contrast, constructive marginal people thrive in their marginal existence and, *at the same time*, they recognize the tremendous challenges. They see themselves (rather than others) as choice makers. They recognize the significance of being "in between," and they are able to make commitments within the relativistic framework. Even so, this identity is constantly being negotiated and explored; it is never easy, given society's penchant for superficial categories. Writer Ruben Martinez (1998) describes the experience of a constructive marginal:

> *And so I can celebrate what I feel to be my cultural success. I've taken the far-flung pieces of myself and fashioned an identity beyond that ridiculous, fraying old border between the United States and Mexico. But my "success" is still marked by anxiety, a white noise that disturbs whatever raceless utopia I might imagine. I feel an uneasy tension between all the colors, hating and loving them all, perceiving and speaking from one and many perspectives simultaneously. The key word here is "tension": nothing, as yet, has been resolved. My body is both real and unreal, its color both confining and liberating. (p. 260)*

IDENTITY, STEREOTYPES, AND PREJUDICE

stereotypes Widely held beliefs about a group of people.

model minority A stereotype that characterizes all Asians and Asian Americans as hardworking and serious and so a "good" minority.

The identity characteristics described previously sometimes form the basis for stereotypes, prejudice, and racism. We will see in the next chapter that these can be communicated verbally, nonverbally, or both. The origins of these have both individual and contextual elements. To make sense out of the overwhelming amount of information we receive, we necessarily categorize and generalize, sometimes relying on **stereotypes**—widely held beliefs about some group. Stereotypes help us know what to expect from others. They may be positive or negative. For example, Asian Americans have often been subjected to the positive **model minority** stereotype, which characterizes all Asians and Asian Americans as hardworking and serious. This stereotype became particularly prevalent in the United States during the civil rights movement of the 1960s and 1970s. At that time, Asian Americans were seen as the "good" minority—in contrast to African Americans, who were often confrontative and even militant in their fight for equality.

Even positive stereotypes can be damaging in that they create unrealistic expectations for individuals. Simply because someone is Asian American (or pretty, or smart) does not mean that he or she will excel in school or be outgoing and charming. Stereotypes become particularly detrimental when they are negative and are held rigidly. Research has shown that, once adopted, stereotypes are difficult to discard. In fact, people tend to remember information that supports a stereotype but may not retain information that contradicts it (Hamilton, Sherman, & Ruvolo, 1990).

We pick up stereotypes in many ways, including from the media. In TV shows and movies, older people often are portrayed as needing help, and Asian Americans, African Americans, or Latinos/as rarely play leading, assertive roles. Current research also shows that although obvious negative stereotypes of Native American Indians are less common in the media, they are still commonly represented in print media as degraded outsiders, often "corrupt, alcoholic and doomed objects of pity" (Miller & Ross, 2004, p. 255) or as either the "good" or "bad" Indians. Communication scholar Bishetta D. Merritt (2000) analyzes portrayals of African American women on television shows and decries the lack of multi-dimensional roles. She identifies the kinds of roles that perpetuate stereotypes:

> Portrayals that receive little or no attention today are the background characters that merely serve as scenery on television programs. These characters include the homeless person on the street, the hotel lobby prostitute, or the drug user making a buy from her dealer. They may not be named in the credits or have recurring roles, but their mere appearance can have an impact on the consciousness of the viewer and, as a result, an impact on the imagery of the African American women. (p. 52)

We may learn stereotypes from our families and peers. One student described how she learned stereotyping and prejudice from her classmates:

> One of my earliest experiences with a person ethnically diverse from me was when I was in kindergarten. A little girl in my class named Adelia was from Pakistan. I noticed that Adelia was a different color from me, but I didn't think it was a bad thing. I got along with her very well. We played the same games, watched the same cartoons, and enjoyed each other's company. Soon I discovered that my other friends didn't like Adelia as much as I did. They didn't want to hold hands with her, and they claimed that she was different from us. When I told them that Adelia was my friend, they didn't want to hold hands with me either. They started to poke fun at me and excluded me from their games. This hurt me so much that I stopped playing with Adelia, and I joined my friends in avoiding her. As a result, Adelia began to resent me and labeled me prejudiced.

Stereotypes can also develop out of negative experiences. If we have unpleasant encounters with people, we may generalize that unpleasantness to include all members of that group, whatever group characteristic we focus on (e.g., race, gender, or sexual orientation). This was demonstrated repeatedly after the attacks of September 11, 2001. Many people of Middle Eastern descent became victims of stereotyping, particularly when traveling. For example, one Arab American software developer from Dallas who was waiting for his flight

I fell in love with a first-generation Mexican American. It took many arguments and lots of time before he was accepted into my family. Once everyone saw what an incredible person Gabe is, I think they favored him more than me. . . . He and I had been together for a year and a half and the time had come for me to meet his family. I was extremely nervous because his parents spoke only Spanish and I only spoke English. How was I going to communicate with my boyfriend's family? To my surprise, this was the least of my worries. When we were introduced, I thought his parents were going to faint. I am "white." I am not the same race as this family, and they resented my having a relationship with their son. I must be very naive, but I never thought prejudices would be directed toward me. This was quite an eye-opener for me. . . .

Unfortunately, Gabriel's sisters spoke English. They made quite a point to be rude and neglect me in every conversation they had. I felt terrible. Before I knew it, Gabe's sister, Amelia, pulled me into her room. She began explaining to me how I would never be part of their family. Because I was not of Hispanic descent, I was not worthy to be with her brother. She went on to tell me that her parents hated me. . . . This was really difficult for me to swallow. This family hated me because of something I have absolutely no control over, my race.

I sat there, not sure of what to say or do. I was so hurt and upset, I stood up and yelled. I told her that this is the problem with society. Why, when we have a chance to change what we hate, do we resist? How can we consciously continue doing these things? Basically, the same countless arguments I had with my parents, I had with Gabe's sister. Whatever happened in that room was the most rewarding experience. We continued discussing the problem. By the end of the conversation, we were such good friends. Shortly after that, Gabe's family felt like my family.

The slight taste of prejudice I felt has to be minimal compared to other people's experiences. I am thankful I was fortunate enough to have such an experience early in my life. I honestly have to admit, Amelia changed me for the better.

—Jennifer

home from Seattle to leave the gate was told by a flight attendant to take his belongings and get off the plane. Apparently, the pilot had been suspicious of his looks. He was questioned for more than an hour by authorities before being allowed to proceed.

Because stereotypes often operate at an unconscious level and so are persistent, people have to work consciously to reject them. First, they must recognize the stereotype, and then they must obtain information to counteract it. This is not easy because, as noted previously, we tend to "see" behavior that fits our stereotypes and to ignore that which doesn't. For example, if you think that most women are bad drivers, you will tend to notice when a female motorist makes a mistake but to ignore bad male driving. To undo this stereotype, you have to be very vigilant and do something that isn't "natural"—to be very conscious of how you "see" and categorize bad driving and to note bad driving by both males and females.

Prejudice is a negative attitude toward a cultural group based on little or no experience. It is a prejudgment of sorts. Whereas stereotypes tell us what a group is like, prejudice tells us how we are likely to feel about that group (Newberg, 1994). Scholars disagree somewhat on the origins of prejudice and its relationship to stereotyping. Prejudice may arise from personal needs to feel positive about our own groups and negative about others, or it may arise from perceived or real threats (Hecht, 1998). Researchers Walter Stephan and Cookie Stephan (1996) have shown that tension between cultural groups and negative previous contact, along with status inequalities and perceived threats, can lead to prejudice.

prejudice An attitude (usually negative) toward a cultural group based on little or no evidence.

Why do people hold prejudices? Psychologist Richard Brislin (1999) suggests that just as stereotyping arises from normal cognitive functioning, holding prejudices may serve understandable functions. These functions may not excuse prejudice, but they do help us understand why prejudice is so widespread. He identifies four such functions:

1. The utilitarian function. People hold certain prejudices because they can lead to rewards. For example, if your friends or family hold prejudices toward certain groups, it will be easier for you simply to share those attitudes, rather than risk rejection by contradicting their attitudes.

2. The ego-defensive function. People hold certain prejudices because they don't want to believe unpleasant things about themselves. For example, if either of us (Judith or Tom) is not a very good teacher, it will be useful for us to hold negative stereotypes about students, such as that they are lazy and don't work hard. In this way, we can avoid confronting the real problem— our lack of teaching skills. The same kind of thing happens in the workplace: It is easier for people to stereotype women and minorities as unfit for jobs than to confront their own lack of skill or qualifications for a job.

3. The value-expressive function. People hold certain prejudices because they serve to reinforce aspects of life that are highly valued. Religious attitudes often function in this way. Some people are prejudiced against certain religious groups because they see themselves as holding beliefs in the one true God, and part of their doctrine is the belief that others are wrong. For instance, Judith's Mennonite family held prejudices against Catholics, who were viewed as misguided and wrong. This may also be operating today as some U.S. Americans search for validation of prejudices again Muslims. A more extreme example involves the atrocities committed against groups of people by others who want to retain the supposed values of a pure racial stock (e.g., "ethnic cleansing" by Serbs against Muslims in the former Yugoslavia).

4. The knowledge function. People hold certain prejudices because such attitudes allow them to organize and structure their world in a way that makes sense to them—in the same way that stereotypes help us organize

our world. For example, if you believe that members of a certain group are flaky and irresponsible, then you don't have to think very much when meeting someone from that group in a work situation. You already know what they're like and so can react to them more automatically.

Prejudices can serve several of these functions over the life span. Thus, children may develop a certain prejudice to please their parents (utilitarian) and continue to hold the prejudice because it helps define who they are (value-expressive). Brislin (1999) points out that many remedial programs addressing the problem of prejudice fail because of a lack of recognition of the important functions that prejudice fulfills in our lives. Presenting people with factual information about groups addresses only one function (knowledge) and ignores the more complex reasons that we hold prejudices. Prejudice and stereotypes can also lead to *acts* of discrimination, which will be discussed in Chapter 7.

IDENTITY AND COMMUNICATION

Identity has a profound influence on intercultural communication processes. We can employ some of the dialectics identified in earlier chapters to illuminate this relationship. First, we can use the individual–cultural dynamic to examine the issues that arise when we encounter people whose identities we don't know. In intercultural communication interactions, mistaken identities are often exacerbated and can create communication problems.

Sometimes we assume knowledge about another person's identity based on his or her membership in a particular cultural group. When we do so, we are ignoring the individual aspect. Taking a dialectical perspective can help us recognize and balance both the individual and the cultural aspects of another's identity. This perspective can guide the ways that we communicate with that person (and conceivably with others). "The question here is one of identity: Who am I perceived to be when I communicate with others? . . . My identity is very much tied to the ways in which others speak to me and the ways in which society represents my interests" (Nakayama, 2000, p. 14).

Think about the assumptions you might make about others based on their physical appearance. What do you "know" about people if you know only that they are from, say, the South, or Australia, or Pakistan? Perhaps it is easier to think about the times that people have made erroneous assumptions about you based on limited information—assumptions that you became aware of in the process of communication. Focusing solely on someone's nationality, place of origin, education, religion, and the like, can lead to mistaken conclusions about the person's identity.

Another way to understand how we communicate our identities comes from the study of performance. Although we can look at someone's individual performance of identity to better understand how they understand who they think they are, we can also look at cultural performance to understand cultural identities.

One part of U.S. history often hidden is the horrific practice of lynching. Yet we must acknowledge that lynching was a widespread and common practice

I would have to say that the most important identity to me is being Pakistani and being a Muslim. My religion and culture are both very important to me. I have not really had too many experiences in which I thought that my identity was not being affirmed. However, there have been some minor experiences that I have faced. We all know that after that incident, Muslims really got a bad name. People used to associate all Muslims with being terrorists. During that time, that seemed to be the subject of discussion in every single class.

I remember in one of my classes, a guy said that all Muslims are terrorists. That really hurt me and I took offense to that. I spoke up and said that if you are not a Muslim then you have no right to say that. I said that if you are not a Muslim, then you really do not know what it means to be one, and you do not know the true values and beliefs of the religion. I am a practicing Muslim, and I know my religion very well, and I know that the religion of Islam does not teach anything but to love one another. I did not care if someone did not believe me because everyone is entitled to their own opinion, but my main purpose was to say that it was wrong for the guy to say something that big about a whole group of people. It would be best if people could keep comments like that to themselves. If the guy just kept that comment to himself, it would not have hurt him and it would have not hurt me for sure. That was one time, that I thought that my identity was not being affirmed. But other than that, most people that I have come across and most people who I tell that I am a Muslim do not react with any sort of hostility. That makes me feel really good and accepted in a society in which most people are not Muslims.

—Shazim

in U.S. culture, and we can often be confused when we see many of the perpetrators smiling in these photos because it seems incomprehensible that they were not horrified by this event.

Performance studies scholar Kirk Fuoss (1999) suggests that a performance perspective can help us better understand how people can participate in these atrocities and the purpose of these lynchings for the perpetrators. For example, Fuoss argues that lynching in the United States functioned as a cultural performance that served to reinforce a particular kind of racial order for those who participated in or heard about the lynching. Lynchings took place outside of the legal system, and therefore a belief in the evilness of the victim substituted for a proof or evidence of guilt. This inversion of right and wrong served to relieve the group identity of the lynchers from their own evil behavior. These murders reflect aspects of our culture that have deep historical roots. By examining these performative acts, we can begin to see what they communicate to others and the kinds of social order they encourage. Thus, lynchings are a public act that serve to communicate the positions of various cultural groups in society.

It is important to remember that performances not only are artistic and interesting but can also be horrific. In both cases, performances of identity can offer insights into our culture.

Now let's turn to the static–dynamic dialectic. The problem of erroneous assumptions has increased during the information age, due to the torrent of information about the world and the dynamic nature of the world in which we live. We are bombarded daily with information from around the globe about places and people. This glut of information and intercultural contacts has heightened the importance of developing a more complex view of identity.

Given the many identities that we all negotiate for ourselves in our everyday interactions, it becomes clear how our identities and those of others make intercultural communication problematic. We need to think of these identities as both static and dynamic. We live in an era of information overload, and the wide array of communication media only serves to increase the identities we must negotiate. Consider the relationships that develop via e-mail, for example. Some people even create new identities as a result of online interactions. We change who we are depending on the people we communicate with and the manner of our communication. Yet we also expect some static characteristics from the people with whom we communicate. We expect others to express certain fixed qualities; these help account for why we tend to like or dislike them and how we can establish particular communication patterns with them. The tensions that we feel as we change identities from e-mail to telephone to mail to fax and other communication media demonstrate the dynamic and static characters of identities.

Finally, we can focus on the personal–contextual dialectic of identity and communication. Although some dimensions of our identities are personal and remain fairly consistent, we cannot overlook the contextual constraints on our identity.

INTERNET RESOURCES

www.racialicious.com
This blog was developed to provide perspectives on race and racism in popular culture. It comments on news stories of celebrities dealing with race and media representations of race. Links to other podcasts and blogs, such as "Race in the Workplace," are also available. An archive of former postings is also provided.

http://pewforum.org/
The Pew Forum on Religion and Public Life website provides research, news, and discussions regarding topics related to religious identity, for example, college students' beliefs about religion, the role of religion in debates on gay marriage, science education, politics, and so forth. The site also provides religious demographic profiles for different countries.

www.pbs.org/race/001_WhatIsRace/001_00-home.htm
This website provided by PBS is a comprehensive exploration of myths and constructions of race. It has some interesting interactive links, such as "Sorting

People," which allows a person to categorize pictures of people based on contemporary U.S. racial categories and then see how the government would classify the pictures. It also provides a "race timeline"—how the notion of race developed through history.

www.intermix.org.uk/word_up/index.asp
This British web page was developed to benefit mixed-race families and multiracial individuals. It contains news stories about Mariah Carey, Halle Berry, Craig David, and other multiracial celebrities.

SUMMARY

There are three approaches to identity: social science, interpretive, and critical.

- A dialectical view of identity emphasizes that identities are both static (as described by the social science perspective) and dynamic (described by the interpretive and critical perspectives), as well as personal and contextual.
- Identities also develop in relation to minority and majority group membership.
- Identities are multiple and reflect gender, sexuality, age, race, ethnicity, religion, class, nationality, regionality, and other aspects of our lives.
- Increasing numbers of multicultural people live "on the borders" between two or more cultures—based on race, ethnicity, religion, and nationality.
- Identity characteristics sometimes form the basis for stereotypes and prejudice.
- Communication plays an important role in identity—identities are formed and expressed through communication.

DISCUSSION QUESTIONS

1. How do our perceptions of our own cultural identity influence our communication with others?
2. What are some ways in which we express our identities?
3. How does being white affect one's experience in the United States?
4. What are the roles of avowal and ascription in the process of identity formation?
5. What are some of the ways in which members of minority cultures and members of majority cultures develop their cultural identities?

 Go to the self-quizzes on the Online Learning Center at www.mhhe.com/ martinnakayama6 to further test your knowledge.

ACTIVITIES

1. *Stereotypes in Your Life.* List some of the stereotypes you have heard about U.S. Americans. Then answer the following questions:

   a. How do you think these stereotypes developed?

   b. How do they influence communication between U.S. Americans and people from other countries?

2. *Stereotypes in Prime-Time TV.* Watch four hours of television during the next week, preferably during evening hours when there are more commercials. Record the number of representatives of different identity groups (ethnic, racial, gender, age, class, and so on) that appear in the commercials; also record the role that each person plays. Answer the following questions:

   a. How many different groups were represented?

   b. What groups were most represented? Why do you think this is so?

   c. What groups were least represented? Why do you think this is so?

   d. What differences (if any) were there in the roles that members of the various groups played? Did one group play more sophisticated or more glamorous roles than others?

   e. In how many cases were people depicted in stereotypical roles—for example, African Americans as athletes, or women as homemakers?

   f. What stereotypes were reinforced in the commercials?

   g. What do your findings suggest about the power of the media and their effect on identity formation and intercultural communication? (Think about avowal, ascription, and interpellation.)

3. *Communication of White Identity.* Go to the website http://stuffwhitepeople-like.com/. This website parodies the stereotypes of white people, and by extension, the stereotyping of other groups. Read through a number of these entries, and then be ready to discuss how whiteness, racism, stereotyping, and identity function in society.

KEY WORDS

religious identity (197)   spiritual identity (173)   third-culture kids (207)
sexual identity (188)   stereotypes (210)   transgender (189)

 The Online Learning Center at www.mhhe.com/martinnakayama6 features
flashcards and crossword puzzles based on these terms and concepts.

REFERENCES

Adler, P. (1974). Beyond cultural identity: Reflections on cultural and multicultural man. *Topics in culture learning* (vol. 2, pp. 23–40). Honolulu: East-West Center.

Ahmadinejad speaks; outrage and controversy follow. (24 September, 2007). *CNN.com.* Retrieved February 7, 2008, from www.cnn.com/2007/US/09/24/us.iran/index.html.

Alba, R. D. (1985). The twilight of ethnicity among Americans of European ancestry: The case of Italians. *Ethnic and Racial Studies, 8,* 134–158.

Alba, R. D. (1990). *Ethnic identity: The transformation of white America.* New Haven, CT: Yale University Press.

Allen, B. (2004). *Difference matters: Communicating social identity.* Waveland Press.

Althusser, L. (1971). Ideology and ideological state apparatuses (notes toward an investigation). In B. Brewster (Trans.), *Lenin and philosophy and other essays* (pp. 134–165). London: NLB.

Azuma, H. (2011, March 16). For a change, proud to be Japanese. *The New York Times.* Retrieved June 9, 2011, from.nytimes.com/2011/03/17/opinion/17azuma.html.

Bahk, C. M., & Jandt, F. E. (2004). Being white in America: Development of a scale. *The Howard Journal of Communications, 15,* 57–68.

Bederman, G. (1995). *Manliness and civilization: A cultural history of gender and race in the United States, 1880–1917.* Chicago: University of Chicago Press.

Bennett, J. M. (1993). Cultural marginality: Identity issues in intercultural training. In R. M. Paige (Ed.), *Education for the intercultural experience* (pp. 109–136). Yarmouth, ME: Intercultural Press.

Bennett, M. J. (1993). Towards ethnorelativism: A developmental model of intercultural sensitivity. In R. M. Paige (Ed.), *Education for the intercultural experience* (pp. 21–72). Yarmouth, ME: Intercultural Press.

Bernstein, J., & Mishel, L. (2007, September 3). *Economy's gains fail to reach most workers' paychecks.* Economic Policy Institute Briefing Paper #195. Retrieved February 18, 2008, from www.epi.org/content.cfm/bp195.

Blacks upbeat about black progress, prospect: A year after Obama's election. (2010, January 12). Pew Research Center. Retrieved June 9, 2011, from http://pewsocialtrends.org/files/2010/10/blacks-upbeat-about-black-progress-prospects.pdf.

Bourdieu, P. (1987). *Distinction: A social critique of the judgment of taste* (R. Nice, Trans.). Cambridge, MA: Harvard University Press.

Blake, J. (2011, March 4). Are whites racially oppressed? *CNN.* Retrieved June 9, 2011, from www.cnn.com/2010/US/12/21/white.persecution/index.html?hpt=T2.

Brewer, C. A., & Suchan, T. A. (2001). *Mapping Census 2000: The geography of U.S. diversity* (U.S. Census Bureau, Census Special Reports, Series CENSR/01-1). Washington, DC: U.S. Government Printing Office.

Brislin, R. (1999). *Understanding culture's influence on behavior* (2nd ed.). Belmont, CA: Wadsworth.

Canary, D. J., & Hause, K. S. (1993). Is there any reason to research sex difference in communication? *Communication Quarterly, 41,* 129–144.

Carafano, J. J. (2011, May 25). The great Eastern Japan earthquake: Assessing disaster response and lessons for the *U.S. Heritage Special Report* 94. Retrieved June 9, 2011, from http://thf_media.s3.amazonaws.com/2011/pdf/sr0094.pdf.

Carbaugh, D. (1989). *Talking American: Cultural discourse on* Donahue. Norwood, NJ: Ablex.

Chen, V. (1992). The construction of Chinese American women's identity. In L. F. Rakow (Ed.), *Women making meaning* (pp. 225–243). New York: Routledge.

Collier, M. J. (2005). Theorizing cultural identification: Critical updates and continuing evolution. In W. B. Gudykunst (Ed.), *Theorizing about intercultural communication* (pp. 235–256). Thousand Oaks, CA: Sage.

Collier, M. J., & Thomas, M. (1988). Cultural identity: An interpretive perspective. In Y. Y. Kim & W. B. Gudykunst (Eds.), *Theories in intercultural communication* (pp. 99–122). Newbury Park, CA: Sage.

Cornell, S., & Hartmann, D. (1998). *Ethnicity and race: Making identities in a changing world.* Thousand Oaks, CA: Pine Forge Press.

Cross, S. E. (2000). What does it mean to "know thyself" in the United States and Japan?: The cultural construction of the self. In T. J. Owens (Ed.), *Self and identity through the life course in cross-cultural perspective* (pp. 159–180). Stamford, CT: JAI Press.

Daigle, K. (2011, February 12). India census counts "third gender." *Edge Boston*. Retrieved May 31, 2011, from www.edgeboston.com/index.php?ch=news&sc=&sc2=news&sc3=&id=116206.

Ehrenreich, B. (2001). *Nickel and dimed: On (not) getting by in America.* New York: Metropolitan Books.

Ehrenreich, B. (2005). *Bait and switch: The (futile) pursuit of the American Dream.* New York: Metropolitan Books.

Ender, M.D. (1996). Recognizing healthy conflict: The postmodern self. *Global Nomad Perspectives Newletter, 4*(1), 12–14.

Ender, M. G. (2002). Beyond adolescence: The experiences of adult children of military parents. In M. G. Ender (Ed.), *Military brats and other global nomads* (pp. 83–100). Westport, CT: Praeger.

Engen, D. (2004). Invisible identities: Notes on class and race. In A. Gonzalez, M. Houston, & V. Chen (Eds.), *Our voices: Essays in culture, ethnicity and communication* (pp. 250–255). Los Angeles: Roxbury.

Erikson, E. (1950). *Childhood and society.* New York: Norton.

Erikson, E. (1968). *Identity: Youth and crisis.* New York: Norton.

Feghali, E. (1997). Arab cultural communication patterns. *International Journal of Intercultural Relations, 21*, 345–378.

Ferguson, R. (1990). Introduction: Invisible center. In R. Ferguson, M. Gever, T. M. Trinh, & C. West (Eds.), *Out there: Marginalization and contemporary cultures* (pp. 9–14). New York and Cambridge: New Museum of Contemporary Art/MIT Press.

Foucault, M. (1988). *History of sexuality* (R. Hurley, Trans.). New York: Vintage Books.

Frankenburg, R. (1993). *White women, race matters: The social construction of whiteness.* Minneapolis: University of Minnesota Press.

Frankenberg, R. (2001). The mirage of an unmarked whiteness. In B. B. Rasmussen, E. Klineberg, I. J. Nexica, & M. Wray (Eds.), *The making and unmaking of whiteness* (pp. 72–96). Durham, NC: Duke University Press.

Fuoss, K. W. (1999). Lynching performances, theaters of violence. *Text and Performance Quarterly, 19*, 1–37.

Fussell, P. (1992). *Class: A guide through the American status system.* New York: Touchstone Books. (Original work published 1979)

Gallager, C. A. (1994). White construction in the university. *Socialist Review, 1/2*, 167–187.

Gao, G. (1996). Self and other: A Chinese perspective on interpersonal relationships. In W. G. Gudykunst, S. Ting-Toomey, & T. Nishida (Eds.), *Communication in personal relationships across cultures* (pp. 81–101). Thousand Oaks, CA: Sage.

Goffman, E. (1959). *The presentation of self in everyday life.* Garden City, New York: Doubleday.

Hall, S. (1985). Signification, representation, ideology: Althusser and the poststructuralist debates. *Critical Studies in Mass Communication, 2*, 91–114.

Hamilton, D. L., Sherman, S. J., & Ruvolo, C. M. (1990). Stereotype-based expectancies: Effects on information processing and social behavior. *Journal of Social Issues, 46*, 35–60.

Hardiman, R. (1994). White racial identity development in the United States. In E. P. Salett & D. R. Koslow (Eds.), *Race, ethnicity and self: Identity in multicultural perspective* (pp. 117–142). Washington, DC: National MultiCultural Institute.

Hardiman, R. (2003). White racial identity development in the United States. In E. P. Salett & D. R. Koslow (Eds.), *Race, ethnicity and self* (2nd ed., pp. 117–136). Washington, DC: National MultiCultural Institute.

Hargittai, E. (2007). Whose space? Differences among users and non-users of social network sites. *Journal of Computer-Mediated Communication, 13*(1), article 14. Retrieved February 18, 2008, from http://jcmc.indiana.edu/vol13/issue1/hargittai.html.

Hasian, M., Jr., & Nakayama, T. K. (1999). Racial fictions and cultural identity. In J. Sloop & J. McDaniels (Eds.), *Treading judgment.* Boulder, CO: Westview Press.

Hecht, M. L. (1998). Introduction. In M. L. Hecht (Ed.), *Communicating prejudice* (pp. 3–23). Thousand Oaks, CA: Sage.

Haub, C., & Sharma, O. P. (2011, January 21). A first for census taking: The third sex. *Population Reference Bureau.* Retrieved May 31, 2011, from http://prbblog.org/index.php/2011/01/21/india-census-third-sex/.

Hecht, M. L., Jackson, R. L. III, & Ribeau, S. A. (2003). *African American communication: Exploring identity and culture* (2nd ed.). Mahwah, NJ: Lawrence Erlbaum.

Hecht, M. L., Warren, J. R., Jung, E., & Krieger, J. L. (2005). A communication theory of identity: Development, theoretical perspective and future directions. In W. B. Gudykunst (Ed.), *Theorizing about intercultural communication* (pp. 257–278). Thousand Oaks, CA: Sage.

Howe, N., & Strauss, W. (2007). The next 20 years: How customer and workforce attitudes will evolve. *Harvard Business Review, 85*(7–8), 41.

Hsu, H. (2009, January/February). The end of white America? *The Atlantic.* Retrieved June 9, 2011, from www.theatlantic.com/magazine/archive/2009/01/the-end-of-white-america/7208/.

Human races or human race? *The Economist, 386*(8566), 86.

Katz, J. (1995). *The invention of heterosexuality.* New York: Dutton.

Kim, M.-S. (2002). *Non-western perspectives on human communication.* Thousand Oaks, CA: Sage.

Leonard, M. F. (2004). Struggling for identity: Multiethnic and biracial individuals in America. In A. Gonzalez, M. Houston, & V. Chen (Eds.), *Our voices* (pp. 228–239). Los Angeles: Roxbury.

Leonhardt, D. (2011, May 24). Top colleges, largely for the elite. *The New York Times.* Retrieved June 9, 2011, from www.nytimes.com/2011/05/25/business/economy/25leonhardt.html?_r=1.

Luo, M. (2007, December 6). Crucial test for Romney in speech on his religion. *The New York Times.* Retrieved February 4, 2008, from www.nytimes.com.

Martinez, R. (1998). Technicolor. In C. C. O'Hearn (Ed.), *Half and half: Writers on growing up biracial + bicultural* (pp. 245–264). New York: Pantheon Books.

Mehl, M. R., & Pennebaker, J. W. (2003). The sounds of social life: A psychometric analysis of students' daily social environments and natural conversations. *Journal of Personality and Social Psychology, 84,* 857–870.

Merritt, B. D. (2000). Illusive reflections: African American women on primetime television. In A. Gonzalez, M. Houston, & V. Chen (Eds.), *Our voices: Essays in culture, ethnicity and communication* (3rd ed., pp. 47–53). Los Angeles: Roxbury.

Miller, A., & Ross, S. D. (2004). They are not us: Framing of American Indians by the *Boston Globe. Howard Journal of Communications, 15,* 245–259.

Miller, R. L., Watling, J. R., Staggs, S. L., & Rotheram-Borus, M. J. (2003). Growing up biracial in the United States. In E. P. Salett & D. R. Koslow (Eds.), *Race, ethnicity and self* (2nd ed., pp. 139–168). Washington, DC: National MultiCultural Institute.

Mishel, L., Bernstein, J., & Allegretto, S. (2006). *The state of working America 2006/2007.* An Economic Policy Institute Book. Ithaca, NY: ILR Press, an imprint of Cornell University Press.

Moon, D. G., & Rolison, G. L. (1998). Communication of classism. In M. L. Hecht (Ed.), *Communicating prejudice* (pp. 122–135). Thousand Oaks, CA: Sage.

Morin, R. (2001, July 11). Misperceptions cloud whites' view of blacks. *The Washington Post,* p. A01.

Multiracial celebrities. (n.d.). *Blackfix.com.* Retrieved May 24, 2011, from www.blackflix.com/articles/multiracial.html.

Myers, K. (2003). White fright: Reproducing white supremacy through casual discourse. In A. W. Doane & E. Bonilla-Silva (Eds.), *White out: The continuing significance of racism* (pp. 129–144). New York: Routledge.

Nakayama, T. K. (2000). Dis/orienting identities: Asian Americans, history, and intercultural communication. In A. González, M. Houston, & V. Chen (Eds.), *Our voices: Essays in ethnicity, culture, and communication* (3rd ed., pp. 13–20). Los Angeles: Roxbury.

Nance, T. A., & Foeman, A. K. (2002). On being biracial in the United States. In J. N. Martin, T. K. Nakayama, & L. A. Flores (Eds.), *Readings in intercultural communication: Experiences and contexts* (pp. 53–62). Boston: McGraw-Hill.

Newberg, S. L. (1994). Expectancy-confirmation processes in stereotype-tinged social encounters: The moderation of social goals. In M. P. Zanna & J. M. Olson (Eds.), *Ontario symposium on personality and social psychology: Vol 7. The psychology of prejudice* (pp. 103–130). Hillsdale, NJ: Lawrence Erlbaum.

New Vanderbilt scientific poll reveals intense bias against Mormons (2007, December 4). Retrieved February 18, 2008 from www.vanderbilt.edu/news/releases?.

Obama's sister talks about his childhood. (2008, February 14). *CBSNews.com.* Retrieved May 1, 2008 from www.cbsnews.com/stories/2008/02/14/politics/main3831108.shtml.

Omi, M., & Winant, H. (1998). Racial formation. In P. S. Rothenberg (Ed.), *Race, class and gender in the United States* (pp. 26–35). New York: St. Martin's Press.

Omi, M., & Winant, H. (2001). Racial formation. In P. S. Rothenberg (Ed.), *Race, class and gender in the United States* (pp. 11–21). New York: Worth.

Pennebaker, J. W., Mehl, M. R., & Niederhoffer, K. G. (2003). Psychological aspects of natural language use: Our words, our selves. *Annual Review of Psychology, 54,* 547–577.

Pew Research Center for the People & the Press. (2005, September 8). Huge racial divide over Katrina and its consequences. News release. Available from http://people-press.org/reports/pdf/255.pdf.

Pew Research Center for the People & the Press. (2007 May). Muslim Americans: Middleclass and mostly mainstream. Report available at http://pewresearch.org/assets/pdf/muslim-americans.pdf.

Phinney, J. S. (1993). A three-stage model of ethnic identity development in adolescence. In M. E. Bernal & G. Knight (Eds.), *Ethnic identity* (pp. 61–79). Albany: State University of New York Press.

Ponterotto, J. G., & Pedersen, P. B. (1993). *Preventing prejudice* (Chaps. 4 & 5). Newbury Park, CA: Sage.

Roediger, D. R. (2005). *Working toward whiteness: How America's immigrants became white.* New York: Basic Books.

Roland, A. (1988). *In search of self in India and Japan: Towards a cross-cultural psychology.* Princeton, NJ: Princeton University Press.

Root, M. P. P. (2001). *Love's revolution: Interracial marriage.* Philadelphia, PA: Temple University Press.

Rosefeld, P., & Giaclone, R. A. (1991). From extreme to the mainstream: Applied impression management in organization. In R. A. Giaclone & P. Rosenfeld (Eds.), *Applied impression management: How image making affects managerial decision making.* Newbury Park, CA: Sage.

Rosen, J. (2011, April 24). Victim of McDonald's beating speaks out; transgender woman says attack was a 'hate crime.' *The Baltimore Sun.* Retrieved May 31, 2011 from http://articles.baltimoresun.com/2011-04-24/news/bs-md-mcdonalds-beating-20110423_1_transgender-woman-mcdonalds-county-police.

Saulny, S. (2011, March 24). Census data presents rise in multiracial population of youths. *The New York Times.* Retrieved May 24, 2011, from.nytimes.com/2011/03/25/us/25race.html.

Shrestha, M. (2011, May 31). Nepal census recognizes "third gender." *CNN.* Retrieved May 31, 2011, from www.cnn.com/2011/WORLD/asiapcf/05/31/nepal.census.gender/index.html.

Sigelman, L., Tuch, S. A., & Martin, J. K. (2005). What's in a name? Preference for "Black" versus "African-American" among Americans of African descent. *Public Opinion Quarterly, 69,* 429–438.

Smith, T.W. (1992). Changing racial labels: From "Colored" to "Negro" to "Black" to "African American." *Public Opinion Quarterly, 56*(4), 496–514.

Stephan, W., & Stephan, C. (1996). Predicting prejudice: The role of threat. *International Journal of Intercultural Relations, 20,* 409–426.

Strauss, W., & Howe, N. (1997). *The fourth turning: American Prophecy.* New York: Broadway Books.

Strauss, W., & Howe, N. (2006). *Millennials and the pop culture.* Great Falls, VA: LifeCourse Associates.

Tajfel, H. (1978). Social categorization, social identity and social comparison. In H. Tajfel (Ed.), *Differentiation between social groups* (pp. 61–76). London: Academic Press.

Tajfel, H. (1981). *Human categories and social groups.* Cambridge: Cambridge University Press.

Tajfel, H. (1982). *Social identity and intergroup relations.* Cambridge: Cambridge University Press.

Tanno, D. (2000). Names, narratives, and the evolution of ethnic identity. In A. González, M. Houston, & V. Chen (Eds.), *Our voices: Essays in ethnicity, culture, and communication* (3rd ed., pp. 25–28). Los Angeles: Roxbury.

Tedeschi, J. T., Lindskold, S., & Rosenfeld, P. (1985). *Introduction to social psychology.* St. Paul, MN: West.

Ting-Toomey, S. (1993). Communication resourcefulness: An identity negotiation perspective. In R. Wiseman & J. Koester (Eds.), *Intercultural communication.* Newbury Park, CA: Sage.

Ting-Toomey, S. (2005). Identity negotiation theory: Crossing cultural boundaries. In W. B. Gudykunst (Ed.), *Theorizing about intercultural communication* (pp. 211–233). Thousand Oaks, CA: Sage.

Trinh, T. M. (1986/1987). Difference: A special third world women issue. *Discourse,* 8.

Why Black and not African American? (20 April 2007). Retrieved February 16, 2008 from http://theangryblackwoman.wordpress.com/2007/04/20/why-black-and-not-african-american/.

Witteborn, S. (2004). Of being an Arab woman before and after September 11: The enactment of communal identities in talk. *Howard Journal of Communications, 15,* 83–98.

Wood, J. T. (2005). *Gendered lives: Communication, gender and culture* (6th ed.). Belmont, CA: Wadsworth.

Yamanouchi, K. (2002, May 19). Cosmetic companies market products aimed at men, *Arizona Republic,* p. D1.

LANGUAGE AND INTERCULTURAL COMMUNICATION

CHAPTER OBJECTIVES

After reading this chapter, you should be able to:

1. Discuss the four components of language.
2. Explain the nominalist, relativist, and qualified relativist positions on language and perception.
3. Describe the role of metaphor in understanding intercultural communication.
4. Identify cultural variations in communication style.
5. Give examples of variations in contextual rules.
6. Explain the power of labels.
7. Understand the challenges of multilingualism.
8. Explain the difference between translation and interpretation.
9. Understand the phenomenon of code switching and interlanguage.
10. Discuss the complexities of language policies.

When I first came to Sor Juana, *I wasn't doing well in biology and . . . my mom talked to my teacher about it. My mother has a very thick [Spanish] accent. When she asked my teacher what was wrong, he replied that . . . my junior high probably didn't prepare me as well as others for this course. When my mom said that I went to a prestigious school and had a 4.0, he was stupefied. . . . "Oh, oh, oh. Laurie's your daughter. I'm so sorry, I thought you were someone else's mother," my teacher replied. It was pitiful. My teacher made an obviously racist assumption that because my mother was Hispanic I went to an inferior junior high and that was the reason for my problems in Biology. . . .*

Mendoza-Denton, p. 50

Language use plays an important role in intercultural communication and is often the first barrier encountered in intercultural interactions. After all, people who don't speak the same language have great difficulty communicating. However, communication is much more than language. In the story above, Laurie's mother and the teacher could communicate easily in English. However the interaction here is about much more than just the language spoken; in this case, *the way* English was spoken (Laurie's mother's accent) played an enormous role in how the encounter unfolded—resulting in (false) assumptions about Laurie's academic preparation, her social class, her place in society—and these assumptions influenced the whole communication encounter.

Language is closely tied with our and others' identities, as we saw in the chapter on identity, and it is also related to the groups we belong to and our social place in society. It is a central element in the intercultural communication process. In this chapter, we focus on language-related barriers in verbal communication processes; the next chapter focuses on the nonverbal elements.

The social science approach generally focuses on individual aspects of language in relation to intercultural communication, the interpretive approach focuses on contextual uses of language practices, and the critical approach emphasizes the relations between discourse and power. This chapter uses a dialectical perspective to explore how language works dynamically in intercultural contexts. With the personal–contextual dialectic, we can consider not only how language use operates on an individual level but also how it is influenced by context. We also use the static–dynamic dialectic to distinguish between language and discourse, to identify the components of language, and to explore the relationship among language, meaning, and perception. Although it may seem that the components of language are static, the *use* of language is a dynamic process.

In this chapter, we also explore cultural variations of language and some of the barriers presented by these variations. Then we discuss the relationship between language and power, and between language and identity, and examine issues of multilingualism, translation, and interpretation. Finally, we look at language and identity, language policies and politics, and globalization.

SOCIAL SCIENCE PERSPECTIVE ON LANGUAGE

The social science perspective focuses on the individual aspects of language use: the components of language, language perception and thought, the way cultural groups use language in different ways, and the barriers presented by these variations. The study of linguistics is just one of many ways to think about language, and this study provides us with a useful foundation for our exploration of language in intercultural communication. As shown Table 6-1, linguists generally divide the study of language into four parts: semantics, syntactics, phonetics, and pragmatics.

Pragmatics is probably the most useful for students of intercultural communication because it focuses on actual language use—what people do with language—the focus of this chapter. People around the world speak many different languages and some scholars think that the particular language we speak influences how we see the world. Before we address the question of how to reduce language barriers in intercultural communication, we need to ask the following questions: Do speakers of Japanese, Chinese, Arabic, and other languages actually perceive the world differently, depending on the particular language they speak? Or do we all experience the world in the same way but have different ways of expressing our experiences? We tackle these questions in the next section.

TABLE 6-1 THE COMPONENTS OF LANGUAGE

Component	Definition	Example
Semantics	The study of meaning—how individual words communicate the meanings we intend.	Think about the word *chair*. Do we define *chair* by its shape? By its function? Does a throne count as a chair? How about a table we sit on? Is this a chair?
Syntactics	The study of the structure, or grammar—the rules for combining words into meaningful sentences. Order of words is important.	"The red car smashed into the blue car" has different meaning than "The blue car smashed into the red car."
Pragmatics	The study of how meaning is constructed in relation to receivers, how language is actually used in particular contexts in language communities.	Saying "that's an awesome outfit" has different meanings depending on the context. It could be mocking, flirting, or just descriptive.
Phonetics	The study of the sound system of language—how words are pronounced, which units of sounds (phonemes) are meaningful for a specific language and which sounds are universal. (See Figure 6-1.)	French has no equivalent sound of English *th*; Japanese has a sound which is between *r* and *l*.

MODERN LANGUAGES PROBABLY ORIGINATED IN AFRICA

As described here, recent research suggests that all modern human languages may have originated in Africa. Isn't it interesting that as humans, our languages connect us all on the one hand and, on the other, is often what divides us and prevents us from communicating and understanding each other?

After studying the phonemes (sounds) in languages around the world, Dr. Quentin D. Atkinson, an evolutionary psychologist from New Zealand concluded that all modern languages originate from the same place—Southern Africa. He discovered that a language area uses fewer phonemes the farther that early humans had to travel from Africa to reach it. That is, as early humans began to migrate from southern Africa, it affected the number of distinct sounds that got used. Using mathematical modeling he found that the greater the distance from Africa, the fewer number of phonemes were detected in the languages spoken. So, for example, while some African languages have more than 100 sounds, English has about 45. Hawaiian, even farther from Africa, has only 13.

He concludes that this linguistic origin diversity parallels genetic origin diversity—as scientists have also suggested that human species originated in Southern Africa.

Sources: Q. D. Atkinson, "Phonemic diversity supports a serial founder effect model of language expansion in Africa," *Science*, 332 (April 15, 2011), 346–349; www.neatorama.com/tag/quentin-d-atkinson/.

Language and Perception

The question of how much of our perception is shaped by the particular language we speak is at the heart of the "political correctness" debate. We can address these questions from two points of view: the nominalist and the relativist.

nominalist position The view that perception is not shaped by the particular language one speaks. (Compare with **relativist position** and **qualified relativist position**.)

relativist position The view that the particular language individuals speak, especially the structure of the language, shapes their perception of reality and cultural patterns. (Compare with **nominalist position** and **qualified relativist position**.)

226

The Nominalist Position According to the **nominalist position,** perception is not shaped by the particular language we speak. Language is simply an arbitrary "outer form of thought." Thus, we all have the same range of thoughts, which we express in different ways with different languages. This means that any thought can be expressed in any language, although some may take more or fewer words. The existence of different languages does not mean that people have different thought processes or inhabit different perceptual worlds. After all, a tree may be an *arbre* in French and an *arbol* in Spanish, but we all perceive the tree in the same way.

The Relativist Position According to the **relativist position,** the particular language we speak, especially the structure of that language, determines our thought patterns, our perceptions of reality, and, ultimately, important cultural components (see Figure 6-1). This position is best represented by the Sapir-Whorf hypothesis. As you may recall from Chapter 2, this hypothesis was proposed by

My co-worker, Nam, who moved to the US from Vietnam with his parents when he was a child, talked with me about his difficulties with learning English. He indicated that he learned English about 10 years ago and that the first difficulty he encountered while learning English was the way we structure our words while forming sentences. He indicated to me that in English we have more "continuous tense" sentences compared to Vietnamese or Chinese. For example, the straight translation of Vietnamese to English without the reordering of words would turn "The phone rang while I was taking a bath" into "I had a bath when the phone rang."
—Jason

Edward Sapir (1921), a linguist, and his student, Benjamin Whorf (1956), based on linguistic research they conducted in the 1930s and 1940s on Native American languages. According to the Sapir-Whorf hypothesis, language defines our experience. For example, there are no possessives (*his/her/our/your*) in the Diné (Navajo) language; we might conclude, therefore, that the Diné think in a particular way about the concept of possession. Another example is the variation in verb forms in English, Spanish, and French. In English and Spanish, the present continuous verb form is frequently used; thus, a student might say, "I am studying" or *"Estoy estudiando."* A French speaker, in contrast, would use the simple present form, *"J'étudie."* The Sapir-Whorf hypothesis suggests that, based on this variation in verb form, French, English, and Spanish speakers may think differently about movement or action. Variations in formal and informal forms raises similar issues. Consider that English speakers do not distinguish between a formal and an informal you (as in German, with *du* and *Sie*, or in Spanish, with *tu* and *usted*). In Japanese, formality is not simply noted by you; it is part of the entire language system. Nouns take the honorific "o" before them, and verbs take more formal and polite forms. Thus, *"Doitsu-go ga dekimasen"* [I—or you, he, she, we, they—don't speak German] is more polite and formal than *"Doitsu-go ga dekinai."* Does this mean that English, German, and Spanish speakers think about formality and informality differently?

Another frequently cited example involves variation in color vocabulary. The Diné use one word for blue and green, two words for two different colors of black, and one word for red; these four words form the vocabulary for primary colors in Diné culture. The Sapir-Whorf hypothesis suggests that English and Diné speakers perceive colors differently. Other examples of variations in syntax and semantics reflect differences in perception.

As a final example, note that some languages are gendered and others are not. Thus, in English you could tell your friend, "I had dinner with a neighbor last night," and the friend would not know if the neighbor was male or female. However, if you were speaking French, you would have to indicate the gender of your neighbor: *voisine* (female) or *voisin* (male). The same is true for the many other "gendered" languages, including Spanish, German, and Russian. In these languages, not only

FIGURE 6-1   Language is an important aspect of intercultural communication. The particular symbols used in any language are arbitrary and have no meaning in and of themselves, as these multilanguage optometrist charts illustrate. Language symbols communicate meaning only when used in particular contexts. (© *David Rubinger/Corbis*)

are people gendered, but also inanimate objects—the clock, the bridge, the chair, and so forth—are all either masculine or feminine. And while speakers of gendered languages obviously know that inanimate objects do not really have biological sex, the Sapir-Whorf hypothesis would suggest that using gendered language can shape the feelings and associations speakers have concerning objects around them. For example, when French and Spanish speakers were asked to assign human voices to some cartoon objects (e.g., a fork) in a recent study, the French thought the fork *(la forchette)* should speak in a male voice; the Spanish thought it should be a man's because fork in Spanish is masculine *(el tenedor)* (Deutscher, 2010).

The Sapir-Whorf hypothesis has had tremendous influence on scholarly thinking about language and its impact on everyday communication. It questions the basic assumption that we all inhabit the same perceptual world, the same social reality.

However, the Sapir-Whorf hypothesis position has been critiqued by a number of studies that challenge the connection between language and how we think (Deutscher, 2010). The most recent position, the **qualified relativist position,** takes a more moderate view of the relationship between language and perception. Steven Pinker (2007), a renowned cognitive scientist, for example, cautions against assuming a simplistic connection between language and thought and rejects the Sapir-Whorf assumption that the particular language we speak compels us to perceive the world in a particular way or prevents us from thinking in different ways. At the same time, he also rejects the extreme nominalist position. He, and most other contemporary language experts, advocate a middle ground, suggesting that while not a "prison," the language habits that our culture has instilled in us from the time we first learn to speak probably does shape our orientation to the world and the people and objects we encounter (Deutscher, 2010). This view allows for more freedom than the Sapir-Whorf hypothesis. As you read the research findings that follow, you may see the wisdom of the qualified relativist position.

qualified relativist position The view that the particular language we speak *influences* our perception but does not *completely* determine our perception.

Recent Research Findings

There are three areas of research that investigate the Sapir-Whorf hypothesis: (1) children's **language acquisition,** (2) cross-cultural differences in language, and (3) cognitive development of children who are deaf. As you will see, most of the research in these areas does not support a strict interpretation of the Sapir-Whorf hypothesis.

language acquisition The process of learning language.

Language Acquisition in Children If language structures thought, then language must precede, and only subsequently influence, thought. This raises the question of whether it is possible to think without language. B. F. Skinner, Jean Piaget, Lev Vygotsky, and other psychologists have long wrestled with this question. As their works indicate, they seem to conclude that language and thought are so closely related that it is difficult to speak of one as initiating influence over the other. Their works thus do not provide evidence for a strong relativist position.

Cross-Cultural Differences in Language Do groups with different language labels perceive the world in different ways? Consider a familiar example. Many men in the United States might identify someone's shirt as "red," whereas women viewing the same shirt might call it "cranberry" or "cherry" or "scarlet." Both the men and the women recognize the color distinctions, but men tend to use fewer words than women to distinguish colors.

The consensus has been that different ways to label color probably does not affect the perception of color in any systematic way. But very recent research shows that language might affect how quickly perceptions of color are categorized. While English speakers have one word for blue, Russian speakers have two words and distinguish between lighter blues (*goluboy*) and darker blues (*siniy*).

In one study, Russian and English speakers were asked to look at three blocks of color and say which two were the same. If the Russians were shown three blue squares with two *goluboy* and one *siniy* or the other way around, they picked the two matching colors faster than if all three squares were shades from one blue group.

Other examples of cross-cultural research involves language and spatial reasoning. Can people who speak a language that has few words to describe spatial relationships (like right angles, parallel lines, triangles, etc.) recognize geometric relationships? The results of many recent studies say yes (Li & Gleitman, 2002). For example, one recent study focused on the Munduruku people, who live in isolated villages in Brazil, with no formal schooling. Their language has few words describing geometrical, or spatial, concepts and they had no rulers, compasses, or maps. Researchers showed the Munduruku subjects a diagram of three containers arranged in a triangle with one container identified as holding a hidden object. They were also shown three actual containers on the ground arranged in the same way. The subjects were then asked to identify which of three containers on the ground hid an object. The results showed that the Munduruku were able to relate the geometrical information on the map to the geometrical relationships on the ground at a rate of 71%, about the same as American subjects. They understood parallelism and right angles and can use distance, angles, and other relationships in maps to locate hidden objects. The finding suggests, contrary to the Sapir-Whorf hypothesis, that language is not required to think about or perceive the world in a particular way (Dehaene, Izard, Pica, & Spelke, 2006).

Another example of cross-cultural research involves variations in verb forms. The Chinese language has no counterfactual verb form (illustrated by "If I had known, I *would have gone*, but I did not"). Researchers constructed stories using the counterfactual form and found that the Chinese respondents understood the concept of counterfactual and could answer questions appropriately even though this structure is not present in Chinese (Au, 1983, 1984, 1985; Bloom, 1981, 1984). No evidence indicates that Chinese speakers are unable to think in terms of counterfactuals; rather, they simply do not normally express thoughts using such constructions. Although these research examples do not support the nominalist position, they do not provide strong evidence for the relativist position either.

Cognition of Children Who Are Deaf Researchers have also tried to determine if children who are deaf or who have limited language use have diminished ability in perception or logical thinking. In one study, children with disabilities had the same categorizing competence, the same level of cognitive skill, as those children who could hear. The children were deficient in purely linguistic skills and short-term memory storage. The researchers concluded that children who are deaf do not seem to have a different worldview (Rhodda & Grove, 1987).

However, recent research comparing hearing children and home-signers (those who have hearing parents but hadn't learned sign language) found that children who knew spatial terms (e.g., middle, top, bottom) could locate a card in a box more quickly than those who did not. All the children were shown a box with cards; one card had a special star on the back. The children were asked to map the position of the target card in the first box to the same position in the

Because we live in a more global world, think about the impact of language differences in hospital emergency rooms, as well as other everyday needs, such as fire departments, police departments, and so on. How can we ensure adequate services for everyone?

When a Spanish-speaking hospital receptionist refused to interpret during her lunch hour, doctors at St. Vincent's Staten Island Hospital turned to a 7-year-old child to tell their patient, an injured construction worker, that he needed an emergency amputation.

In some cases, the monitors themselves witnessed the medical consequences of communication failures. Ana Maria Archila, executive director of the Latin American Integration Center, an immigrant rights and social service agency, said she and two others overheard doctors at St. Vincent's telling a construction worker, through his 7-year-old cousin, that the worker needed an amputation.

"The child said, 'I'm not sure if they said foot or said toe,'" Ms. Archila recalled. "This worker, he was about to cry."

The monitors later learned that it was the man's third trip to the emergency room after a construction accident that had crushed his toe weeks earlier. Unable to explain his symptoms in English, he reported, he had been handled dismissively until he returned with his big toe blackened by gangrene.

Later, after the toe was amputated, Ms. Archila added, he had to rely on a patient in the next bed to translate the doctors' instructions for post-operative care.

With no one to bridge the language gap for another patient, a newly pregnant immigrant from Mexico with life-threatening complications, doctors pressed her to sign a consent form in English for emergency surgery. Understanding that the surgery was needed "to save the baby," the young married woman awoke to learn that the operation had instead left her childless and sterile. . . .

Source: N. Bernstein, "Language Barrier Called Health Hazard in E.R.," *The New York Times*, April 21, 2005, p. B1.

second—similar to the activity in the study of the Munduruku. The researchers in this case found that those hearing children who knew words for spatial relationships had less trouble finding the special card in the second box than those without words for spatial relationship, whether young hearing children or home-signers. This may show that words can help us focus our thoughts . . . helps us carve up the world in specific ways (Kenneally, 2008).

Language and Thought: Metaphor

One way of thinking about the relationship between language and thought is to look at metaphors. A *metaphor* is an expression where a word (or words) is used outside of its normal conventional meaning to express a *similar* concept (Lakoff, 1992). For example, "you are my sunshine." Although an individual cannot literally *be* sunshine, comparing someone to sunshine expresses a particular positive meaning. Experts used to think that metaphors are about language, or literary writing, not useful for understanding everyday speech. A famous cognitive scientist and linguist, George Lakoff, disagrees and proposes that metaphors are part of thinking, one way we organize our thoughts, in everyday living; in fact, metaphors are "a major and indispensable part of our ordinary conventional way of conceptualizing the world, and that our everyday behavior reflects our metaphorical understanding of experience" (p. 203).

Understanding a culture's metaphors, then, helps us understand something about the culture itself. Consider the English metaphor of likening love to a journey: *Our relationship has hit a dead-end street. Look how far we've come. It's been a long, bumpy road. We can't turn back now. We're at a crossroads. We may have to go our separate ways. The relationship isn't going anywhere. We're spinning our wheels. Our relationship is off the track.* These are ordinary, everyday English expressions. They are not poetic, nor are they necessarily used for special rhetorical effect, but for *reasoning about* our relationships (Lakoff, p. 205).

Metaphors can also be a useful way to understand other cultures. Some metaphors are universal, like the metaphor of an angry person as a pressurized container, for example (Kövecses, 2005). Consider these English phrases: "His pent-up anger *welled up* inside him. Billy's just *blowing off* steam. He was *bursting* with anger. When I told him *he just exploded.*" Other languages have similar expressions. The universality of the metaphor may rest in the universal human physiology—since physical bodily changes actually occur when we are angry (blood pressure rises, pulse rate increases, temperature rises). Metaphors may focus on different parts of the body; the Japanese, for example, have a number of metaphors that refer to the belly—where emotions are thought to rest. In contrast, U.S. Americans and Chinese tend to refer to the heart as the source of emotions (My heart is breaking; his heart swelled with pride).

In English, metaphors for happiness seem to center on a feeling of being up, light, fluid in a container (She was floating on air, bursting with happiness). However, the Chinese have a metaphor that does not exist in English—that happiness is flowers in the heart. Experts suggest that metaphors reflect cultural beliefs and values; in this case, the metaphor reflects the more restrained Chinese communication style, while the English metaphor of "happiness is being off the ground" reflects the relatively expressive English communication style (Kövecses, p. 71).

Cultural Variations in Communication Style

communication style The metamessage that contexualizes how listeners are expected to accept and interpret verbal messages.

metamessage The meaning of a message that tells others how they should respond to the content of our communication based on our relationship to them.

What else do we need to understand in order to reduce the language and verbal barriers in intercultural communication? In addition to cultural differences in metaphor use, social science scholars also identify differences in the way people use language in everyday conversations. By this, we mean that even if people are speaking the same language, there can be misunderstandings due to differences in communication style.

Communication style combines both language and nonverbal communication. It is the **metamessage** that contextualizes how listeners are expected to receive and interpret verbal messages. A primary way in which cultural groups differ in communication style is in a preference for high- versus low-context communication. A **high-context communication** style is one in which "most of the information is either in the physical context or internalized in the person, while very little is in the coded, explicit, transmitted part of the message" (Hall, 1976, p. 79). This style of communication emphasizes understanding messages without direct verbal communication. People in long-term relationships often communicate in this style. For example, one person may send a meaningful glance across the room at a party, and his or her partner will know from the nonverbal clue that it is time to go home.

In contrast, in **low-context communication,** the majority of meaning and information is in the verbal code. This style of communication, which emphasizes explicit verbal messages, is highly valued in many settings in the United States. Interpersonal communication textbooks often stress that we should not rely on nonverbal, contextual information. It is better, they say, to be explicit and to the point, and not to leave things ambiguous. However, many cultural groups around the world value high-context communication. They encourage children and adolescents to pay close attention to contextual cues (body language, environmental cues), and not simply the words spoken in a conversation (Gudykunst & Matsumoto, 1996).

William Gudykunst and Stella Ting-Toomey (2003) identify two major dimensions of communication styles: direct versus indirect and elaborate versus understated.

Direct Versus Indirect Styles This dimension refers to the extent to which speakers reveal their intentions through explicit verbal communication and emphasizes low-context communication. A direct communication style is one in which verbal messages reveal the speaker's true intentions, needs, wants, and desires. An indirect style is one in which the verbal message is often designed to camouflage the speaker's true intentions, needs, wants, and desires (Gudykunst, Ting-Toomey, & Chua, 1988). Most of the time, individuals and groups are more or less direct depending on the context.

Many English speakers in the United States favor the direct speech style as the most appropriate in most contexts. This is revealed in statements like "Don't beat around the bush," "Get to the point," and "What exactly are you trying to say?" Although "white lies" may be permitted in some contexts, the direct style emphasizes honesty, openness, forthrightness, and individualism.

However, some cultural groups prefer a more indirect style, with the emphasis on high-context communication. Preserving the harmony of relationships has a higher priority than being totally honest. Thus, a speaker might look for a "soft" way to communicate that there is a problem in the relationship, perhaps by providing contextual cues (Ueda, 1974). Some languages have many words and gestures that convey the idea of "maybe." For example, three Indonesians studying in the United States were invited by their advisor to participate in a cross-cultural training workshop. They did not want to participate, nor did they have the time. But neither did they want to offend their professor, whom they held in high regard. Therefore, rather than tell him they couldn't attend, they simply didn't return his calls and didn't show up at the workshop.

high-context communication A style of communication in which much of the information is contained in the contexts and nonverbal cues rather than expressed explicitly in words. (Compare with **low-context communication.**)

low-context communication A style of communication in which much of the information is conveyed in words rather than in nonverbal cues and contexts. (Compare with **high-context communication.**)

An international student from Tunisia told Judith and Tom that he had been in the United States for several months before he realized that if someone was asked for directions and didn't know the location of the place, that person should tell the truth instead of making up a response. He explained that he had been taught that it was better to engage in conversation, to give *some* response, than to disappoint the person by revealing he didn't know.

Different communication styles are responsible for many problems that arise between men and women and between persons from different ethnic groups. These problems may be caused by different priorities for truth, honesty, harmony, and conflict avoidance in relationships.

Elaborate Versus Understated Styles   This dimension of communication styles refers to the degree to which talk is used. The elaborate style involves the use of rich, expressive language in everyday talk. For example, the Arabic language has many metaphorical expressions used in everyday speech. In this style, a simple assertive statement means little; the listener will believe the opposite.

In contrast, the understated style values succinct, simple assertions, and silence. Amish people often use this style of communication. A common refrain is, "If you don't have anything nice to say, don't say anything at all." Free self-expression is not encouraged. Silence is especially appropriate in ambiguous situations; if one is unsure of what is going on, it is better to remain silent.

The exact style falls between the elaborate and the understated, as expressed in the maxim "Verbal contributions should be no more or less information than is required" (Grice, 1975). The exact style emphasizes cooperative communication and sincerity as a basis for interaction.

In international negotiations, visible differences in style can contribute to misperceptions and misunderstandings. For example, if we look at two speeches concerning the Libyan conflict in the spring of 2011, we can see striking differences in the styles used by President Barack Obama and Libyan leader Muammar Gaddafi. In February 2011, there was an uprising of many Libyan people against Gaddafi (see Figure 6-2). Gaddafi responded by severe reprisals against the protestors. Obama made the decision to send U.S. troops along with other NATO forces to stop Gaddafi's forces, and on March 28, 2011, Obama explained U.S. plans in a speech to the American people in a direct and dispassionate manner:

> *We knew that if we waited one more day, Benghazi—a city nearly the size of Charlotte—could suffer a massacre that would have reverberated across the region and stained the conscience of the world.*
>
> *It was not in our national interest to let that happen. I refused to let that happen. And so nine days ago, after consulting the bipartisan leadership of Congress, I authorized military action to stop the killing and enforce UN Security Council Resolution 1973. We struck regime forces approaching Benghazi to save that city and the people within it. We hit Gaddafi's troops in neighboring Ajdabiya, allowing the opposition to drive them out. We hit his air defenses, which paved the way for a No Fly Zone. We targeted tanks and military assets that had been choking off towns and cities and we cut off much of their source of supply. And tonight,*

I can report that we have stopped Gaddafi's deadly advance. (www.newstatesman. com/north-america/2011/03/gaddafi-libyan-military-united)

Gaddafi addressed his people in a long, 75-minute speech, full of metaphors, and in a more indirect and elaborated style:

I am bigger than any Rank, I am a Revolutionary, I am the Bedouin from oasis that brought victory to enjoy it from generation to generation. Libya will remain at the top and will lead Africa and South America. We cannot hinder the process of this revolution from these greasy rats and cats. I am paying the price for staying here and my grandfather, Abdus Salam Bomanyar, who fell a martyr in 1911. I will not leave the country and I will die as a martyr in the end. The remains of my father, grandfather and my uncle Sheikh Saadi in the cemetery of Neder is the proof. I will not leave these righteous remains. Saddam says that freedom cannot enjoy the shadow of these trees unless we planted these trees and we watered it with our blood. I am talking to you from the house which was bombarded by a hundred and seventy planes by America and Britain. They left all houses and were aiming for Muammar's houses. Is it because he is president of the country? They could have treated him like other presidents, but Muammar Qaddafi is history, resistance, freedom, victory, revolution. This is a testimony from the highest authority that Muammar Qaddafi is not the president, he is not a normal person. You cannot poison him or lead demonstrations against him. When bombs were falling on my house and killing my children, where were you, you rats? Where were you,

FIGURE 6-2   Libyans in the capital city of Tripoli celebrate their new-found independence after toppling their government in summer 2011. (© *Ivan LaBianca/ Demotix/Corbis*)

*those with big beards? Where were you? You were in America. You were applaud-
ing your master, the Americans. One hundred and seventy planes, left all palaces
and leaders and kings and came to the great house of Muammar Qaddafi. This
is a victory that should not be relinquished by anybody, any country or people in
Africa or any nation. Fighting back the tyranny of America, we did not give in,
we were resilient. (www.beyondthefirstworld.com/?p=17866)*

While some analysts were quick to point out that Gaddafi is prone to
extreme language and not held in high regard by many Arab leaders, other
experts point to the particular challenges of the Arab language as it is spoken
today. The classical form of the Arabic language (that based on the Qur'an),
while rich and poetic, is actually nobody's mother tongue. Each Arab country/
region has its own local dialect, making communication within the Arab world
a distinct challenge. A former British ambassador to Libya notes that Gaddafi's
personal speaking style is often unintelligible to anyone who doesn't speak the
Libyan dialect and clearly reflects his Bedouin background—where elaborated
speech is commonplace, people talk for hours at a time, and Gaddafi's speeches
regularly go on for three or four hours at a stretch (Miles, 2011).

Slang and Humor in Language Use

Another cultural variation in language use that can present barriers is slang.
According to language expert Tom Dalzell (2005), slang is generally wittier
and cleverer than standard language. It's inventive and creative and serves an
important function—it establishes a sense of community identity among its
users, often in opposition to standard language users. Slang, then, can be perceived as a barrier to those outside the language group. Dalzell suggests that
the cultural groups most likely to produce slang in a society are the young, the
powerless, sports participants, and criminals. Slang is particularly important for
youth cultures; it's almost imperative to invent slang that belongs to each generation and is unintelligible to parents and other adults. For example, black slang
of hip-hop culture and rap music has dominated the language use of all social
classes of youth and even adults (Dalzell, 2005).

International students struggle to learn slang (see Point of View, p. 237), as
well as parents and grandparents who are mystified by the language of their children. What makes it particularly challenging is the fact that slang is dynamic and
can be fleeting: here today, gone tomorrow, sometimes passing from group to
group, and often co-opted by mainstream media and then passing into common
usage. A blogger described the transformation of one American English slang
term: *junk mail to spam to spim:* "You do not hear about junk mail as much anymore though. Then you heard about spam, or junk email. Spam was the dread of
everyone. Now, a new word has come into play: Spim, or spam through instant
message. For teens, this shows how much their communication has changed.
Penpal letters turned to email chains, which turned to IM" (Van Petten, 2009).

Communication accommodation theory suggests that there is an optimum
use of slang by an outsider accommodating to the slang of a particular culture.

Knowing another language isn't necessarily enough to communicate well. Consider all the slang used by speakers in every language. Here's a list given to international students studying U.S. English. Do you know what these mean?

In hot water

Put your money where your mouth is

That takes the cake

Not playing with a full deck

Put a lid on it

Paint the town red

Or more recent ones (and these are just the A's and B's of the alphabet!):

Awesome

Baby Mama

Booty

Bling

Bogus

To be broke

Bubbly

Some education experts in England say that young people are using so much slang that they are unable to know what is appropriate or inappropriate, making them ill-equipped to deal with the wider world. Paul Kerswill, professor of sociolinguistics at Lancaster University says that a new dialect, "multicultural English," is emerging among the young there and replacing the traditional cockney—a mixture of cockney, West Indian, East African Bangladeshi, and Kuwaiti. Here's a list of common words:

Nang/nanging: excellent

What's good: hello

I'm ghost: goodbye

Chung, peng: attractive

Bare: lots of, very

Sik: cool

Sources: "American Slang," retrieved June 2, 2011, from www.schandlbooks.com/AmericanSlangIdiom.html; "Cool American English," retrieved June 2, 2011, from www.coolamericanenglish.com/american-english-slang.php; V. Barford, "Mind Your Slanguage," *BBC News* (December 9, 2010), retrieved June 2, 2011, from http://news.bbc.co.uk/2/hi/uk_news/magazine/8388545.stm.

Using too much slang, or using it in inappropriate contexts, can sound awkward to the "native" listener, like when your parents try to use your slang or foreign students use lots of slang, but make mistakes in grammar and pronunciation.

Humor can be another cultural language variation that presents challenges, even when two cultural groups speak the same language. For example, some say that British humor is nuanced and subtle and often relies on irony, while American humor tends to be more obvious and straightforward—much like U.S. Americans themselves. However, these differences don't seem to present much of a barrier—comedy TV sitcoms have been adapted between the two countries for many years (e.g., *The Office*) (Emma, 2009).

Trying to use humor in a foreign language can be really challenging because the basis of humor is so often linked to particular cultural experiences (or history). For example, understanding Chinese sarcasm requires a thorough understanding of Chinese history and politics; sarcasm is often used in a very subtle way to criticize someone (often politicians) without losing face. So one way to mock present politicians is by criticizing an ancient Chinese emperor who was evil because he killed scholars and oppressed the peasants. A foreigner might not get the true humor (sarcasm) at all, but Chinese listeners would understand (www.quora.com/How-is-Chinese-sarcasm-different-from-Western-sarcasm). The best advice to cultural outsiders or language learners is to use humor and slang fairly sparingly, if at all.

Another type of humor that presents a barrier in intercultural communication is humor at the expense of another. For example, individuals sometimes mock another's accent or language use—a situation encountered by one of our students, Alejandro:

> *I am extremely proud of my Mexican heritage, and I usually feel offended when my identity is not respected. I have a slight accent and occasionally when I go out and mispronounce something people crack jokes. They think that it is all in good humor but it can be offensive.*

As he goes on to say, it's especially hurtful because the humor usually reflects (and perpetuates) negative stereotypes:

> *People connect too many stereotypes to Hispanics; society must learn to stop stereotyping minorities. When this happens then everyone can truly be united and respected, without preconceived notions based off a person's race.*

These different uses of language communicate different things to their culturally disparate audiences. As they also demonstrate, it is not easy to interpret language use from other people's perspectives.

Taking a dialectical perspective, though, should help us avoid stereotyping specific groups (such as Arabic or English speakers) in terms of communication style. We should not expect any group to use a particular communication style all the time. Instead, we might recognize that style operates dynamically and is related to context, historical forces, and so on. Furthermore, we might consider how tolerant we are when we encounter others who communicate in very different ways and how willing or able we are to alter our own style to communicate better.

INTERPRETIVE PERSPECTIVE ON LANGUAGE

The interpretive perspective focuses on an in-depth understanding of communication use in context and how communication practices may vary from one cultural context to another.

Variations in Contextual Rules

A dialectical perspective reminds us that the particular communication style we use may vary from context to context. Think of the many contexts in which you communicate during the day—classroom, family, work, and so on—and about how you alter your communication to suit these contexts. You may be more direct with your family and less direct in classroom settings. Similarly, you may use high-context informal communication in interaction with friends and more low-context formal with your professors. These same cultural variations can apply to written communication. You probably write in more formal language when communicating with professors by e-mail than when texting to your friends.

Many research studies have examined the rules for the use of socially situated language in specific contexts. They attempt to identify contexts and then "discover" the rules that apply in these contexts for a given speech community. For example, several studies examined gender differences in the interpersonal communication "rules" of text messaging for men and women in India. In a first study, researchers discovered that in contrast to men, women tended to send and receive text messages mostly when they were alone (Shuter & Chattopadhyay, 2010). In a second study, through in-depth interviews, Indian women reported receiving negative reactions from parents, extended family members, husbands, and male friends when sending or reading text messages in their presence. In addition, they reported being subjected to "Eve Teasing," a form of interpersonal harassment by males who observed them text messaging. The study also revealed the creative strategies used by Indian women to deal with these limitations placed on them by others: storing phone numbers of male friends under female names, erasing all text messages daily, communicating through social networking sites (SNSs) rather than texting. The study concludes that these differential "textiquettes" (text messaging rules) for women and men in India reflect the unequal power relations between men and women in India, and that women texting represents a threat to male patriarchy (Shuter, 2012).

A related study examined the communication patterns involved in the common practice of "nagging" in U.S. American family contexts (Boxer, 2002). Nagging (repeated requests by one family member to another) usually concerns household chores and is often a source of conflict. More importantly, the communication practice seems to be related to issues of gender, power, and control. To be more specific, men are rarely perceived as the naggers; in this study, only six of the seventy sequences involved men nagging women. The researcher suggests that this is because they are perceived as having more power and, therefore, able to successfully request and gain compliance from another family member without resorting to nagging. This also means that children can have power (if they refuse to comply with a request despite lacking status), and parents can lack power despite having status. If our styles constrain how we request and respond to requests, then by nagging we lose power. Without power we are forced into nagging, and so it seems a vicious cycle.

Another study examines communication patterns in the Australian elementary school classroom, specifically "teacher talk" and how teachers dominate through their questioning of students, which makes up a large part of the student-teacher interaction (Gale & Cosgrove, 2004). These researchers, through analysis of very specific teacher-student exchanges, explore the power dynamics revealed in this questioning, as the teacher maintains her position of power as she gives the student a series of questions to which (she) already knows the answers. In this particular instance, the focus of the questions is concerned with eliciting responses from the student that the teacher then examines for their grammatical and pronunciation accuracy in a rather demeaning way. The researchers find that this particular type of "teacher talk" devalues and disempowers the students because of the focus on the "wrong" words they say, rather than values and empowers because of what they do know—taking away their confidence as speakers. In summary, they show how, in a classroom, many things teachers say—by virtue of their position—would be deemed completely "out of line" if said by students, by virtue of their position. This might never be stated explicitly, but is learned through what is commonly referred to as schooling's "hidden curriculum" (Gale & Cosgrove, 2004). These studies show, through in-depth contextual analysis, that what we do with words affects many of our important relationships.

Other studies compare communication styles used by two different speech communities. For example, researchers have examined how communication style varies from generation to generation. They suggest that millennials (those born between 1982 and 2001) tend to be polite, prefer electronic communication, are not as skilled at face-to-face communication because they are more used to technical ways of communicate, like visual pictures in language, and prefer action-oriented communication. Gen Xers, a little older, are comfortable with more direct and informal communication and like immediate communication and results. In comparison, the oldest generation, traditionalists, prefer good grammar and manners, more formal language and use of titles, and a focus on words rather than body language (www .camex.org/Portals/CAMEX/uploaded_docs/handouts/2-12_HO.pdf).

People communicate differently in different speech communities. Thus, the context in which the communication occurs is a significant part of the meaning. Although we might communicate in one way in one speech community, we might change our communication style in another. Understanding the dynamics of various speech communities helps us see the range of communication styles.

CRITICAL PERSPECTIVE ON LANGUAGE

A critical perspective on language suggests that, in order to use language effectively in intercultural encounters, we need to understand the role of power and of power differentials in these encounters. Recall that discourse refers to language in use. This means that all discourse is social. The language used—the words and the meanings that are communicated—depends not only on the context but also on the social relations that are part of that interaction. For example, bosses and workers may use the same words, but the meanings communicated are not always the same. A boss and a worker may both refer to the company personnel as a "family." To the boss, this may mean "one big happy family," whereas to a disgruntled employee, it may mean a "dysfunctional family." To some extent, the disparity is related to the inequality between boss and worker, to the power differential.

In Chapter 2, we introduced communication accommodation theory. There are different ways that people accommodate or resist accommodating, depending on the situation. One such theory that encompasses various approaches is co-cultural communication, which we examine next.

Co-Cultural Communication

The co-cultural communication theory, proposed by communication scholar Mark Orbe (1998), describes how language works between dominant and non-dominant groups—or **co-cultural groups.** Groups that have the most power (whites, men, heterosexuals) consciously or unconsciously formulate a communication system that supports their perception of the world. This means that co-cultural group members (ethnic minorities, women, gays) must function in communication systems that often do not represent their experiences. Nondominant groups thus find themselves in dialectical struggles: Do they try to adapt to the dominant communication style, or do they maintain their own styles? Women in large male-dominated corporations often struggle with these issues. Do they adapt a male corporate style of speaking, or do they assert their own style?

There seem to be three general answers to the question of how co-cultural groups can relate to the more powerful (dominant) groups: They can communicate nonassertively, assertively, or aggressively. Within each of these communication postures, co-cultural individuals may emphasize assimilation—trying to become like the dominant group—or they can try to accommodate and adapt to the dominant group. They can also try to remain separate from the dominant groups as much as possible. These three sets of orientations result in nine types of communication strategies (Table 6-2). The strategy chosen depends on many things, including preferred outcome, perceived costs and rewards, and context.

The point here is that there are both costs and benefits for co-cultural members when they choose which of these strategies to use. Because language is structured in ways that do not reflect their experiences, they must adopt some strategy for dealing with the linguistic framework. For example, if Mark wants to refer to his relationship with Kevin, does he use the word *boyfriend, friend, roommate, husband, partner,* or some other word? If Mark and Kevin were married where it is legal (e.g., Massachusetts, Canada, Belgium), should they refer to their "husband" when they are in places that explicitly say they do not

co-cultural groups
Nondominant cultural groups that exist in a national culture, such as African American or Chinese American.

TABLE 6-2 CO-CULTURAL COMMUNICATION ORIENTATIONS			
	Separation	**Accommodation**	**Assimilation**
Nonassertive	Avoiding	Increasing visibility	Emphasizing commonalities
	Maintaining interpersonal barriers	Dispelling stereotypes	Developing positive face
			Censoring self
			Averting controversy
Assertive	Communicating self	Communicating self	Extensive preparation
			Overcompensating
	Intragroup networking	Intragroup networking	Manipulating stereotypes
			Bargaining
	Exemplifying strengths	Using liaisons	
		Educating others	
	Embracing stereotypes		
Aggressive	Attacking	Confronting	Dissociating
	Sabotaging others	Gaining advantage	Mirroring
			Strategic distancing
			Ridiculing self

Source: M. Orbe, *Constructing Co-Cultural Theory: An Explication of Culture, Power, and Communication* (Thousand Oaks, CA: Sage, 1998), p. 110.

recognize same-sex marriages from elsewhere (e.g., Arizona, Michigan, Texas, or Colorado)? What about work? Thanksgiving dinner with the family? Let's look at how these strategies might work, and the costs and the benefits of them.

Assimilation Strategies   The three assimilation strategies are nonassertive, assertive, and aggressive. Some co-cultural individuals tend to use nonassertive assimilation strategies. These strategies emphasize trying to fit and be accepted by the dominant group. Such strategies might emphasize commonalities ("I'm not that different"), be self-monitoring ("I'd better be careful about what I say in this organization to make sure I don't offend those in power"), and, above all, avoid controversy. There are potential costs to this approach, because these co-cultural individuals may feel they cannot be honest about themselves and may also feel uncomfortable reinforcing the dominant group's worldview and power.

The second assimilation strategy is assertive assimilation. Co-cultural individuals taking this strategy may downplay co-cultural differences and try to fit into the existing structures. Unlike the nonassertive assimilation strategy, this individual will try to fit in but also let people know how she or he feels from time to time. However, this strategy can promote an us-versus-them mentality, and some people find it difficult to maintain this strategy for very long.

Aggressive assimilation strategies emphasize fitting in, and co-cultural members who take this approach can go to great lengths to prove they are like members of the dominant group. Sometimes this means distancing themselves from other members of their co-culture, mirroring (dressing and behaving like the dominant group), or self-ridiculing. The benefit of this strategy is that the co-cultural member is not seen as "typical" of members of that co-culture. The cost may entail ridicule from members of that co-culture who may accuse this individual of acting white, thinking like a man, or "straight." Thus, these individuals may find themselves constantly negotiating their position with the dominant group while being isolated from their own co-cultural group.

Accommodation Strategies   Nonassertive accommodation strategies emphasize blending into the dominant culture but tactfully challenging the dominant structure to recognize co-cultural practices. For example, a Jewish co-worker may want to put up a menorah near the company's Christmas tree as a way of challenging the dominant culture. By gently educating the organization about other religious holidays, the co-cultural member may be able to change their presumptions about everyone celebrating Christmas. Using this strategy, the co-cultural individual may be able to influence group decision making while still showing loyalty to the larger organization's goals. The cost of this strategy may be that others feel that she or he is not pushing hard enough to change larger structural issues in the organization. Also, this strategy does not really promote major changes in organizations to make them more inclusive and reflective of the larger society.

Assertive accommodation strategies try to strike a balance between the concerns of co-cultural and dominant group members. These strategies involve communicating self, doing intragroup networking, using liaisons, and educating others. For example, Asian American co-workers may share information about themselves with their co-workers, but they also share information about words that are offensive, such as *Oriental* and *slope*.

Aggressive accommodation strategies involve moving into the dominant structures and then working from within to promote significant changes—no matter how high the personal cost. Although it may seem as if co-cultural workers who use these strategies are confrontational or self-promoting, they also reflect a genuine desire to work with and not against dominant group workers. For example, a disabled co-worker may consistently remind others that facilities need to be more accessible, such as door handles, bathrooms that can accommodate wheelchairs, and so on. Co-cultural members with this orientation may periodically use assertive as well as aggressive accommodation strategies and so may be perceived as genuinely committed to the larger group's good. In this way, they reap the benefits of being perceived positively by the dominant group and also have an impact on the organization. However, co-cultural members who consistently use aggressive accommodating strategies may find themselves alienated from both other co-cultural members and from dominant group colleagues for being too confrontational.

Separation Strategies   Nonassertive separation strategies are often used by those who assume that some segregation is part of everyday life in the United States. Generally, people live, work, learn, socialize, and pray with those who resemble them. This is generally easier for the dominant group than for co-cultural members. Some co-cultural individuals regard segregation as a natural phenomenon but also use subtle communication practices to maintain separation from the dominant group. Perhaps the most common strategy is simply avoiding interactions with dominant group members whenever possible. Thus, gay people using this orientation may spend their social time with other gay people. Or women may prefer to use professional women's services (having a female doctor, dentist, and attorney) and socialize with other women. The benefit of this approach is that co-cultural members do not have to deal with any negative feelings or stereotypes about their group, but the cost is that they cannot network and make connections with those in power positions.

Assertive separation strategies reflect a conscious choice to maintain space between dominant and co-cultural group members. Typical strategies my include stressing strengths and embracing stereotypes, as well as intragroup networking. One of the benefits of this approach, like the nonassertive separation strategy, is that it promotes co-cultural unity and self-determination. The cost, however, is that co-cultural group members must try to survive without having access to resources controlled by the dominant group.

Aggressive separation strategies are used by those for whom co-cultural segregation is an important priority. These strategies can include criticizing, attacking, and sabotaging others. The benefit of this approach for co-cultural members is that it enables them to confront pervasive, everyday, assumed discriminatory practices and structures. The cost may be that the dominant group retaliates against this open exposure of the presumed way of doing things.

Again, when confronted with various situations, dominant and co-cultural group members need to think carefully about how they wish to respond. There are benefits and costs to all of the decisions made. Although dominant group members are likely to be less harmed than co-cultural group members, everyone may suffer in the end. If Miguel is "cut out of the loop" at work and not told about an important meeting that affects his job, how should he handle this situation? He could pursue an assertive accommodation strategy and remind his co-workers that he needs to be included by pointing out when he is excluded. This could work and produce a more inclusive work environment, or the exclusion may continue because he is ignored. Or he could adopt a more aggressive accommodation strategy and meet with the manager and insist he be included. What are the costs and benefits of this approach? There are no easy answers, but it is important to consider what verbal communication strategy you may want to use when interacting in intercultural communication situations.

Discourse and Social Structure

Just as organizations have particular structures and specific positions within them, societies are structured so that individuals occupy social positions. Differences in **social positions** are central to understanding intercultural communication. For one thing, not all positions within the structure are equivalent; everyone is not the same. When men whistle at an attractive woman walking by, it has a different force and meaning than if women were to whistle at a man walking by.

Power is a central element, by extension, of this focus on social position. For instance, when a judge in court says what he or she thinks *freedom of speech* means, it carries much greater force than when a neighbor or a classmate gives an opinion about what the phrase means. When we communicate, we tend to note (however unconsciously) the group membership and positions of communication participants. To illustrate, consider the previous example. We understand how communication functions, based on the group membership of the judge (as a member of the judicial system) and of the neighbors and classmates; we need know nothing about their individual identities.

Groups also hold different positions of power in the social structure. Because intercultural contact occurs between members of different groups, the positions of the groups affect communication. Group differences lend meaning to intercultural communication because, as noted previously, the concept of differences is key to language and the semiotic process.

social positions The places from which people speak that are socially constructed and thus embedded with assumptions about gender, race, class, age, social roles, sexuality, and so on.

The "Power" Effects of Labels

We often use labels to refer to other people and to ourselves. Labels, as signifiers, acknowledge particular aspects of our social identity. For example, we might label ourselves or others as "male" or "female," indicating sexual identity. Or we might say we are "Canadian" or a "New Englander," indicating a national or regional identity. The context in which a label is used may determine how strongly we feel about the label. On St. Patrick's Day, for example, someone may feel more strongly about being an Irish American than about being a woman or a student or a Texan.

Sometimes people feel trapped or misrepresented by labels. They might complain, "Why do we have to have labels? Why can't I just be me?" These complaints belie the reality of the function of discourse. It would be nearly impossible to communicate without labels. People rarely have trouble when labeled with terms they agree with—for example, "man," "student," "Minnesotan," or "Australian." Trouble arises, however, from the use of labels that they don't like or that they feel describe them inaccurately. Think about how you feel when someone describes you using terms you do not like.

Labels communicate many levels of meaning and establish particular kinds of relationships between speaker and listener. Sometimes people use labels to communicate closeness and affection for others. Labels like "friend," "lover," and "partner" communicate equality. Sometimes people intentionally invoke labels to establish a hostile relationship. Labels like "white trash" and "redneck"

Growing up in Pakistan, my first languages were Urdu and Gujarati and learning English was a struggle when I came to the U. S. Grammar was especially difficult for me and I would often say things like "I ranned there" or "I supposed" (I was supposed to). One of the things one can do when trying to speak with someone who does not speak English fluently is be sensitive and not treat them like they're dumb. When I first came to America people would talk to me very loudly as if I were completely incapable of understanding.
—Amir

My native language is Spanish. Since I was a little kid, I've been learning English so I already knew the language when I moved to the U.S. However, even to this day, I have trouble understanding slang. I feel uncomfortable when situations arise where I don't understand what is being said because of slang. . . . I think that when speaking with someone from another culture, specifically with someone who speaks (American) English as a second language, one must be more considerate toward that person's needs; e.g., speaking slower, repeating oneself if necessary, explaining and/or avoiding slang terms.
—Sergio

intentionally communicate inequality. Sometimes people use labels that are unintentionally offensive to others.

Many times, these labels are spoken without any knowledge or understanding of their meanings, origin, or even current implications and can demonstrate prejudicial feelings (Cruz-Jansen, 2002). For example, many descendents of Spanish-speaking people living in the United States reject the term "Hispanic" since it was a census term created by the U.S. government in 1970 to identify a group of people; it was never used by people to describe themselves. Similarly, "Oriental" is a term rejected by many Asians and Asian Americans, and "homosexual" communicates negative characteristics about the speaker and establishes distance between the speaker and listener. Similarly, many indigenous people reject the term "Native American"—saying that it is only used by white people—preferring their more specific tribal name or the terms "American Indian" or "Indian." Many prefer "First Nations" people—to underscore the fact that tribes are in fact nations, recognized by the U.S. government (Yellow Bird, 1999). And you can probably think of many other labels ("bitch," "ho," "faggot," etc.) that are sometimes casually uttered that could be considered offensive by the targeted group.

Discourse is tied closely to social structure, so the messages communicated through the use of labels depend greatly on the social position of the speaker. If the speaker and listener are close friends, then the use of particular labels may not lead to distancing in the relationship or be offensive. But if the speaker and listener are strangers, then these same labels might invoke anger or close the lines of communication. Cultures change over time, as do languages. It is important that you stay aware of these changes as much as possible so you do not unintentionally offend

I know three languages: Spanish, Serbian, and English. However, I am not satisfied with this. With an expanding world, Americans have to be more aggressive in their pursuit of cultural knowledge. I feel that learning a fourth language, specifically Chinese, would greatly benefit me in my job aspects as well as in my ability to communicate with more of the world. What many people must keep in mind is that in other parts of the world, a second and third language aside from their native language is required, not suggested.
—Katarina

others. Regardless of the intentions of the speaker, negative labels can work in small but powerful ways: Each utterance works like a grain of sand in sedimentary rock or like one roll of snowball going down a hill—small in itself but said over and over serves to reproduce systems of sexism, racism, homophobia, and the like.

Furthermore, if the speaker is in a position of power, then he or she has potentially an even greater impact. For example, when politicians use discourse that invokes racist, anti-Semitic, or other ideologies of intolerance, many people become concerned because of the influence they may have. These concerns were raised in the 2002 presidential elections in France over candidate Jean-Marie Le Pen, whose comments over the years have raised concerns about anti-immigrant, anti-Semitic discourse. Similar concerns have arisen over the political discourse of Austria's Joerg Haider and Louisiana's David Duke. Of course, political office is not the only powerful position from which to speak. Fundamentalist Christian leaders have caused concern with their antigay discourse, and celebrities like actor Mel Gibson and designer John Galliano have been criticized for racist, sexist, and anti-Semitic discourse.

Judith and Tom collaborated on a study about reactions to labeling. We asked white students which of the following they preferred to be called: white, Caucasian, white American, Euro-American, European American, Anglo, or WASP. They did not favor such specific labels as "WASP" or "European American" but seemed to prefer a more general label like "white." We concluded that they probably had never thought about what labels they preferred to be called. As we noted in Chapter 5, the more powerful aspects of identity seem to go unnoticed; for many people, whiteness just "is," and the preferred label is a general one that does not specify origin or history. Individuals from powerful groups generally do the labeling of others; they themselves do not get labeled (Martin, Krizek, Nakayama, & Bradford, 1996). For example, when men are asked to describe their identities, they often forget to specify gender as part of their identity. Women, in contrast, often include gender as a key element in their identity. This may mean that men are the defining norm and that women exist in relation to this norm. We can see this in the labels we use for men and women and for people of color. We rarely refer to a "male physician" or a "white physician," but we do refer to a "female doctor" or a "black doctor."

MOVING BETWEEN LANGUAGES

Multilingualism

Why do some people choose to learn foreign languages and others do not? Given the choice, some people, particularly in the United States, do not feel the need to learn a second language. They assume that most people they encounter either at home or abroad will be able to speak English (see Figure 6-3). Or perhaps they feel they have been successful so far without learning another language, so why start now? If the need arises in a professional context, they can always hire an interpreter. In fact, a recent survey of Canadian and U.S. professionals concluded that a foreign language was not essential in doing business abroad and that language was *not* that crucial. However, international business experts pointed out that the conclusions of this study were probably premature; first, the professionals surveyed were monolingual and would probably not advocate for

FIGURE 6-3 French/English stop sign.
(*Courtesy T. K. Nakayama*)

fluency in a foreign language and also did not include anyone whose native language wasn't English. Further, they did not examine the implications of monolingualism in a competitive global environment (Varner & Beamer, 2011).

While the advantage of being an English speaker may make it easier for Americans to travel overseas, there may be some downsides. As shown in the Point of View on p. 264, one professor thinks that a being monolingual makes American less cosmopolitan and more provincial—compared to others we're competing against in the current global economy. The fact is that a person who only knows one language may be understood by others, if the language is commonly spoken (like English) as a foreign language, but that person can never understand what others are saying in their own languages and will always have to rely on translators and are more likely to misunderstand what others are saying. Perhaps more importantly, such people miss the opportunity to learn about a culture. As we have described it, language and culture are so inextricably intertwined that to learn a new language is to gain insight into another culture and another world. Language acquisition studies have shown that it is nearly impossible for individuals to learn the language of a group of people they dislike. For instance, Tom was talking to a student about meeting the program's foreign language requirement. The student said, "I can't take Spanish. I'm from California." When Tom said that he did not understand what she meant, she blurted that she hated Mexicans and wouldn't take Spanish under any circumstances. As her well-entrenched racism suggested, she would indeed never learn Spanish.

While some learn a foreign language in order to compete in global markets or to navigate the increasingly global village, more personal imperatives also drive people to become bilingual. Alice Kaplan (1993), a French professor at Duke University, noted, "Speaking a foreign language is, for me and my students, a chance for growth, for freedom, a liberation from the ugliness of our received ideas and mentalities" (p. 211). Many people use foreign languages to escape from a legacy of oppression in their own languages. Consider the case of Sam Sue (1992), a Chinese American born and raised in Mississippi, who explains his own need to alter his social reality—often riddled by stigmatizing stereotypes—by changing the way he speaks:

> *Northerners see a Southern accent as a signal that you're a racist, you're stupid, or you're a hick. Regardless of what your real situation is. So I reacted to that by adapting the way I speak. If you talked to my brother, you would definitely know he was from the South. But as for myself, I remember customers telling my dad, "Your son sounds like a Yankee." (p. 4)*

Among the variations in U.S. English, the southern accent unwittingly communicates many negative stereotypes. Escaping into another accent is, for some, the only way to escape the stereotypes.

People who speak two languages are often called **bilingual;** people who speak more than two languages are considered **multilingual.** Rarely do bilinguals speak both languages with the same level of fluency. More commonly, they prefer to use one language over another, depending on the context and the topic.

bilingual The ability to speak two languages fluently or at least competently.

multilingual The ability to speak more than two languages fluently or at least competently.

Sometimes entire nations are bilingual or multilingual. Belgium, for example, has three national languages (Dutch, German, and French), and Switzerland has four (French, German, Italian, and Romansh).

On either the individual or the national level, multilinguals must engage in language negotiation. That is, they need to work out, whether explicitly or implicitly, which language to use in a given situation. These decisions are sometimes clearly embedded in power relations. For example, French was the court language during the reign of Catherine the Great in 18th-century Russia. French was considered the language of culture, the language of the elite, whereas Russian was considered a vulgar language, the language of the uneducated and the unwashed. Special-interest groups in many U.S. states, especially Arizona and California, have attempted to pass laws declaring English the official language. These attempts reflect a power bid to determine which language will be privileged.

Sometimes a language is chosen as a courtesy to others. For example, Tom joined a small group going to see the fireworks display at the Eiffel Tower on Bastille Day one year. (Bastille Day is a French national holiday, celebrated on July 14, to commemorate the storming of the Bastille prison in 1789 and the beginning of the French Revolution.) One woman in the group asked, "*Alors, on parle français ou anglais?*" ["Are we speaking French or English?"]. Because one man felt quite weak at English, French was chosen as the language of the evening.

interlanguage A kind of communication that emerges when speakers of one language are speaking in another language. The native language's semantics, syntactics, pragmatics, phonetics, and language styles often overlap and create a third way of communicating.

An interesting linguistic phenomenon known as **interlanguage** has implications for the teaching and learning of other languages. Interlanguage refers to a kind of communication that emerges when speakers of one language are speaking in another language. The native language's semantics, syntactics, pragmatics, and phonetics often overlap into the second language and create a third way of communicating. For example, many English-speaking female students of German might say, "*Ich bin ein Amerikanerin,*" which is incorrect German but is structured on the English way of saying, "I am an American." The correct form is "*Ich bin Amerikanerin.*" The insertion of "*ein*" reveals the English language overlap.

In his work on moving between languages, Tom has noted that this creation of other ways of communicating can offer ways of resisting dominant cultures. He notes that "the powerful potential of translation for discovering new voices can violate and disrupt the systemic rules of both languages" (Nakayama, 1997, p. 240). He gives the example of "*shiros,*" which is used by some Japanese Americans to refer to whites. *Shiro* is the color white, and adding an *s* at the end is the English grammatical way to pluralize words. Tom explains,

> *Using the color for people highlights the overlay of the ideology of the English language onto Japanese and an odd mixing that probably would not make sense to people who speak only English or Japanese, or those who do not live in the spaces between them. (p. 242n)*

Different people react differently to the dialectical tensions of a multilingual world. Some work hard to learn other languages and other ways of communicating, even if they make numerous errors along the way. Others retreat into their familiar languages and ways of living. The dialectical tensions that arise over different languages and different systems of meaning are played out around the world. But these dialectical tensions never disappear; they are always posing new challenges for intercultural communicators.

Translation and Interpretation

Because no one can learn all of the languages in the world, we must rely on translation and interpretation—two distinct but important means of communicating across language differences. The European Union (EU), for example, has a strict policy of recognizing all of the languages of its constituent members. Hence, many translators and interpreters are hired by the EU to help bridge the linguistic gaps.

Translation generally refers to the process of producing a written text that refers to something said or written in another language. The original language text of a translation is called the **source text;** the text into which it is translated is the **target text.**

Interpretation refers to the process of verbally expressing what is said or written in another language. Interpretation can either be simultaneous, with the interpreter speaking at the same time as the original speaker, or consecutive, with the interpreter speaking only during the breaks provided by the original speaker.

As we know from language theories, languages are entire systems of meaning and consciousness that are not easily rendered into another language in a word-for-word equivalence. The ways in which different languages convey views of the world are not equivalent, as we noted previously. Consider the difficulty involved simply in translating names of colors. The English word *brown* might be translated as any of these French words, depending on how the word is used: *roux, brun, bistre, bis, marron, jaune,* and *gris* (Vinay & Darbelnet, 1977, p. 261).

Issues of Equivalency and Accuracy   Some languages have tremendous flexibility in expression; others have a limited range of words. The reverse may be true, however, for some topics. This slippage between languages is both aggravating and thrilling for translators and interpreters. Translation studies traditionally have tended to emphasize issues of **equivalency** and accuracy. That is, the focus, largely from linguistics, has been on comparing the translated meaning with the original meaning. However, for those interested in the intercultural communication process, the emphasis is not so much on equivalence as on the bridges that people construct to cross from one language to another.

Many U.S. police departments are now hiring officers who are bilingual, because they must work with a multilingual public. In Arizona, like many other states, Spanish is a particularly important language. Let's look at a specific case in which a police detective for the Scottsdale (Arizona) Police Department explained an unusual phrase:

> *Detective Ron Bayne has heard his share of Spanish phrases while on the job. But he recently stumped a roomful of Spanish-speaking police officers with an unusual expression.*
>
> *A suspect said, "Me llevaron a tocar el piano" [They took me to play the piano].*

translation The process of producing a written text that refers to something said or written in another language.

source text The original language text of a translation. (See also **target text.**)

target text The new language text into which the original language text is translated. (See also **source text.**)

interpretation The process of verbally expressing what is said or written in another language.

equivalency An issue in translation, the condition of being equal in meaning, value, quantity, and so on.

I would love to travel and experience all there is to experience. I think I would experience some culture shock because that is natural. I would want to learn some of the language that the country I would be going to speaks. I think that is extremely important because I should not expect everyone or anyone to speak my language. Seeing as how I am in their country, I should try to speak their language.
—Nate

I have learned some Spanish. I think that it is difficult to learn a new language when you are so set in your own language. I think it would be best to learn a second language when you are young.
—James

> *"I knew it couldn't mean that," said Bayne, a translator for the Scottsdale Police Department. "But I had no idea what it really meant." (Meléndez, 2002, p. B1)*

This slang term, popular with undocumented aliens, highlights the differences between "street" Spanish and classroom Spanish. It also points to the importance of context in understanding meaning. In this context, we know that the police did not take a suspect to play a piano. Instead, this suspect was saying that the police had fingerprinted him. The varieties of expression in Spanish reflect social class and other differences that are not always communicated through translation or interpretation.

Yet the context for interpreters and translators must also be recognized. The need for Spanish speakers in the U.S. Southwest represents only the tip of the "linguistic iceberg." The continuing "war on terror" has created another need for translators and interpreters who are fluent in Arabic, Farsi, Urdu, Punjabi, Pashto, and Dari. The changing context for intelligence work has changed the context for translators and interpreters as well, to say nothing of the languages that are highly valued. These issues, although beyond the scope of equivalency and accuracy, are an important part of the dynamic of intercultural communication.

The Role of the Translator or Interpreter   We often assume that translators and interpreters are "invisible," that they simply render into the target language whatever they hear or read. The roles that they play as intermediaries, however, often regulate how they render the original. Tom believes that it is not always appropriate to translate everything that one speaker is saying to another, in exactly the same way, because the potential for misunderstanding due to cultural differences might be too great. Translation is more than merely switching languages; it also involves negotiating cultures. Writer Elisabeth Marx (1999) explains,

> *It is not sufficient to be able to translate—you have to comprehend the subtleties and connotations of the language. Walter Hasselkus, the German chief executive of Rover, gave a good example of this when he remarked: "When*

Translation can create amusing and interesting intercultural barriers. Consider the following translation experiences.

1. A Canadian importer of Turkish shirts destined for Quebec used a dictionary to help him translate into French the label "Made in Turkey." His final translation: "Fabriqué en Dinde." True, "dinde" means "turkey." But it refers to the bird, not the country, which in French is Turquie.

2. An Otis Engineering Corp. display at a Moscow exhibition produced as many snickers among the Russians as it did praise. Company executives were not happy to learn that a translator had rendered in Russian a sign identifying "completion equipment" as "equipment for orgasms."

3. Japan's Olfa Corp. sold knives in the United States with the warning "Caution: Blade extremely sharp. Keep out of children."

4. In one country, the popular Frank Perdue Co. slogan, "It takes a tough man to make a tender chicken," read in local language something akin to "It takes a sexually excited man to make a chicken affectionate."

5. One company in Taiwan, trying to sell diet goods to expatriates living there, urged consumers to buy its product to add "roughage" to their systems. The instructions claimed that a person should consume enough roughage until "your tool floats." Someone dropped the "s" from "stool."

6. How about the Hong Kong dentist who advertised "Teeth extracted by the latest Methodists."

7. Or the hotel in notoriously polluted Mexico City that proclaimed: "The manager has personally passed all the water served here."

8. General Motors Corp.'s promotion in Belgium for its car that had a "body by Fisher" turned out to be, in the Flemish translation, "corpse by Fisher."

Source: From Laurel Delaney, "8 Global Marketing Gaffes," 2002, www.marketingprofs.com/2/delany2.asp.

the British say that they have a 'slight' problem, I know that it has to be taken seriously." There are numerous examples of misunderstandings between American English and British English, even though they are, at root, the same language. (p. 95)

It might be helpful to think of translators and interpreters as cultural brokers who must be highly sensitive to the contexts of intercultural communication.

We often assume that anyone who knows two languages can be a translator or an interpreter. Research has shown, however, that high levels of fluency in two languages do not necessarily make someone a good translator or interpreter. The task obviously requires the knowledge of two languages. But that's not enough.

Think about all of the people you know who are native English speakers. What might account for why some of them are better writers than others? Knowing English, for example, is a prerequisite for writing in English, but this knowledge does not necessarily make a person a good writer. Because of the complex relationships between people, particularly in intercultural situations, translation and interpretation involve far more than linguistic equivalence, which traditionally has been the focus.

The field of translation studies is rapidly becoming more central to academic inquiry as it moves from the fringes to an area of inquiry with far-reaching consequences for many disciplines. These developments will have a tremendous impact on how academics approach intercultural communication. Perhaps intercultural communication scholars will begin to play a larger role in the developments of translation studies.

LANGUAGE AND IDENTITY

In the previous chapter, we discussed cultural identity and its complexities. One part of our cultural identity is tied to the language(s) that we speak. As U.S. Americans, we are expected to speak English. If we travel to Nebraska, we assume the people there speak English. When we travel around the world, we expect Russians to speak Russian, Koreans to speak Korean, and Indonesians to speak Indonesian. But things get more involved, as we noted in Chapter 4, when we consider why Brazilians speak Portuguese, Congolese speak French, and Australians speak English. The relationship between language and culture becomes more complicated when we look at the complexity of cultural identities at home and abroad.

Language and Cultural Group Identity

When Tom was at the Arizona Book Festival recently, a white man held up a book written in Chinese and asked Tom what it was about. "I don't read Chinese," Tom replied. "Well, you should," he retorted and walked away. Two assumptions seem to be at work here: (1) Anyone who looks Asian must be Chinese and (2) Asian Americans should be able to speak their ancestral languages. This tension has raised important identity questions for Asian Americans. Writer Henry Moritsugu (1992), who was born and raised in Canada and who later immigrated to the United States, explains,

> *There is no way we could teach our children Japanese at home. We speak English. It wasn't a conscious effort that we did this. . . . It was more important to be accepted. . . . I wish I could speak the language better. I love Japanese food. I love going to Japanese restaurants. Sometimes I see Japanese groups enjoying themselves at karaoke bars . . . I feel definitely Western, more so than Asian. . . . But we look Asian, so you have to be aware of who you are. (p. 99)*

Languages develop in relation to their environments. Changes in the global climate are bringing vast changes to the environment of the Arctic regions. Note how the indigenous languages are working to adapt to these changes.

What are the words used by indigenous peoples in the Arctic for "hornet," "robin," "elk," "barn owl" or "salmon?"

If you don't know, you're not alone.

Many indigenous languages have no words for legions of new animals, insects and plants advancing north as global warming thaws the polar ice and lets forests creep over tundra.

"We can't even describe what we're seeing," said Sheila Watt-Cloutier, chair of the Inuit Circumpolar Conference, which says it represents 155,000 people in Canada, Alaska, Greenland and Russia.

In the Inuit language Inuktitut, robins are known just as the "bird with the red breast," she said. Inuit hunters in north Canada recently saw some ducks but have not figured out what species they were, in Inuktitut or any other language. . . .

In Arctic Europe, birch trees are gaining ground and Saami reindeer herders are seeing roe deer or even elk, a forest-dwelling cousin of moose, on former lichen pastures.

"I know about 1,200 words for reindeer—we classify them by age, sex, color, antlers," said Nils Isak Eira, who manages a herd of 2,000 reindeer in north Norway.

"I know just one word for elk—'sarvva'," said 50-year-old Eira. "But the animals are so unusual that many Saami use the Norwegian word 'elg.' When I was a child it was like a mythical creature."

Source: A. Doyle, "As Ice Melts, Arctic People at Loss for Words," *MSNBC*, November 24, 2004. Available at www.msnbc.msn.com/id/6530026.

The ability to speak another language can be important in how people view their group membership.

Many Chicana/os also have to negotiate a relationship to Spanish, whether or not they speak the language. Communication scholar Jacqueline Martinez (2000) explains,

> *It has taken a long time for me to come to see and feel my own body as an ethnic body. Absent the capacity to express myself in Spanish, I am left to reach for less tangible traces of an ethnic self that have been buried under layers of assimilation into Anglo culture and practice. . . . Yet still there is a profoundly important way in which, until this body of mine can speak in Spanish, gesture in a "Spanishly" way, and be immersed in Spanish-speaking communities, there will remain ambiguities about its ethnic identification. (p. 44)*

Although some people who migrate to the United States retain the languages of their homelands, many other U.S. American families no longer speak the language of their forebears. Historically, bilingualism was openly discouraged in the United States. Writer Gloria Anzaldúa (1987) recalls how she was discouraged from speaking Spanish:

> I remember being caught speaking Spanish at recess—that was good for three licks on the knuckles with a sharp ruler. I remember being sent to the corner of the classroom for "talking back" to the Anglo teacher when all I was trying to do was tell her how to pronounce my name. If you want to be American, speak "American." If you don't like it, go back to Mexico where you belong. (p. 53)

Even today we often hear arguments in favor of making English the official language of the nation. The interconnections between cultural identity and language are indeed strong.

Another intersection between identity and language occurred in 2006, when a controversy arose over the release by some Latino pop stars of a Spanish version of the U.S. national anthem ("Star Spangled Banner"), with somewhat different lyrics ("The time has come to break the chains"), called *Nuestro Himno* (Our Anthem). For the song's producer and singers, it was about trying to help engage immigrants, as a tribute to the United States. For others, the national anthem was a symbol of unity that should be sung only in English. Here we see the importance of contexts. What many people don't know is that the national anthem was translated into Spanish (and many other languages) by the Bureau of Education and has been available in those languages since 1919—with no controversy until the issue becomes related to the current immigration debate (Goldstein, 2006).

What about the challenges facing cultural groups whose languages are nearing extinction? Whereas millions of people speak Chinese, Japanese, and Spanish, some languages are spoken by only a handful of people. One Osage Indian laments,

> Even though I am painfully aware of what needs to be said and how to say it, my words usually fall upon noncomprehending ears, for only a handful of Osage Indians can speak or understand our tribal language. And, after each such occasion, I often silently lament that this may be the last time the Osage language is publicly spoken and that within a mere 10 years it might not ever be heard again. (quoted in Pratt & Buchanan, 2000, p. 155)

Many Native American tribes are currently working to save their tribal languages, but they face enormous challenges. Yet it is their culture and identity that are at risk.

The languages we speak and the languages others think we should speak can create barriers in intercultural communication. Why might some U.S. Americans assume that someone whose ancestors came from China continues to speak Chinese, while someone whose ancestors came from Germany or Denmark is assumed to no longer speak German or Danish? Here, again, we can see how identity, language, and history create tensions between who we think we are and who others think we are.

Code Switching

Code switching is a technical term in communication that refers to the phenomenon of changing languages, dialects, or even accents. People code switch for several reasons: (1) to accommodate the other speakers, (2) to avoid accommodating others, or (3) to express another aspect of their cultural identity.

Linguistics professor Jean-Louis Sauvage (2002) studied the complexity of code switching in Belgium, which involves not only dialects but languages as well. He explains the practical side of code switching:

> For example, my house was built by a contractor who sometimes resorted to Flemish subcontractors. One of these subcontractors was the electrician. I spoke Dutch to him but had to use French words when I referred to technical notions that I did not completely understand even in French. This was not a problem for the electrician, who knew these terms in Dutch as well as in French but would have been unable to explain them to me in French. (p. 159)

Given the complex language policies and politics in Belgium, code switching takes on particularly important political meaning. Who code switches and who does not is a frequent source of contestation.

In her work on code switching, communication scholar Karla Scott (2000) discusses how the use of different ways of communicating creates different cultural contexts and different relationships between the conversants. Based on a series of interviews with black women, she notes "the women's shared recognition that in markedly different cultural worlds their language use is connected to identity" (p. 246). She focuses on the use of the words *girl* and *look* as they relate to communicative practices in different contexts. She identifies three areas in which code switching occurs with *girl*: "(1) in discourse about differences between Black and White women's language use, (2) in discourse about being with other Black women, and (3) in uses of '*girl*' as a marker in discourse among participants during the interview" (p. 241). The use of *look* in code switching occurs in three contexts as well: "(1) in discussions and descriptions of talking like a Black woman versus White women's talk, (2) in the women's reports of interactions with Whites, both male and female, and (3) in the women's reports of interactions with Black men" (p. 243). *Girl* creates a sense of solidarity and shared identity among black women, whereas *look* is particularly important in white-dominated contexts because it asserts a different identity. Thus, code switching between these two words reflects different ways of communicating and different identities and relationships among those communicating.

There are similar examples of code switching between English and Spanish, as increasing numbers of U.S. Americans speak both languages—18 million now according to the U.S. census (Silverstein, 2007). Scholar Holly Cashman (2005) investigated how a group of bilingual women code switched during a game of *lotería* (Mexican bingo). She makes the point that code switching does not just demonstrate linguistic competence but, as in Scott's (2000) study, also communicates important information about ethnic identities and social position. Throughout the game, the women's choices to speak Spanish and/or English

code switching A technical term in communication that refers to the phenomenon of changing languages, dialects, or even accents.

Is it rude to code switch between languages when someone in the room only understands one of the languages?

Growing up in a household that predominately spoke Spanish was challenging when I brought friends over. Not everyone in my family spoke English and not all of my friends spoke Spanish. For as long as I can remember, my father expected me to translate everything that my friends and I said when family members were around us, even if they were not a part of the conversation. My father instilled the importance of respecting people around me by ensuring that everyone was included in the conversation, and to be sensitive to those around me who do not understand the language by giving them a general idea of what was being said.

As I have gotten older, I wonder when is it appropriate to switch languages when someone in the room does not understand the language being spoken. The first time that I really thought about this was when I attended a dinner at a friend's house. All of the people, excluding myself, were from Serbia. When one of the guests realized that I did not speak Serbian, she said, "Oh, so we will have to speak English all night?" My immediate reaction was that I did not think that everyone had to adjust to my needs. After all, this was their time to share food and conversations in their language.

However, I recently went Salsa dancing with a friend who did not speak Spanish. Knowing that most of the people around us were bilingual, I asked people if they could speak in English so that we did not exclude my friend. Most people would start speaking in English, but then break out into conversations in Spanish, which frustrated me. I ended up interpreting conversations for him and felt bad that he was excluded from the conversation. As I apologized to him, my friend said, "Don't feel bad. It is my fault that I do not speak Spanish."

Reflecting on these situations, I wondered when is it appropriate to code switch between languages when someone in the room only understands one of the languages? Why did I not think it was offensive in a situation where I was the one who did not understand and offensive when it was a friend of mine who did not?

—Liz

demonstrated various identifications and social places. When they preferred to speak Spanish, they were identifying inclusively with both English and Spanish speakers. In correcting other's language choices, they were also identifying as not just bilingual, but as arbiters of the spoken language. And in rejecting others' corrections of their language use, they were also asserting certain identifications, as when one woman in refusing another's correction of her Spanish "categorizes herself as 'Chicana,' bringing about a bilingual, oppositional social identity, and rejecting the social structures previously talked into being" (p. 313).

This discussion of code switching and language settings brings up the question of how does a bilingual person decide which language to speak in a setting where there are multiple languages spoken? Is it rude to switch between two languages when some people in the room only understand one language? As our student Liz describes (in the preceding Student Voices box), this is not always an easy question to answer. A helpful theory here is Communication Accommodation Theory (CAT), discussed in Chapter 2. As you might remember, this theory posits that in some situations individuals change their communication patterns to accommodate others—depending on the situation and the attitude of the speaker toward other people. So, for example, if the situation is a neutral one and the speaker feels positively toward others, they will more likely accommodate others. This seems to be the case in Liz's family. Her father instructed her to accommodate everyone in the situation. Liz's experience at a recent party was different. Here, the Serbian speakers did not want to accommodate Liz. At the Salsa party, she tried to accommodate everyone, but it was difficult and her friends did not follow her lead. What is important to remember is that the outcome of accommodation is usually a positive feeling. However, in some situations (like high threat) speakers may not want to accommodate, may even want to accentuate their linguistic differences, or perhaps, as in Liz's Salsa party experience, the effort of accommodating is too challenging.

LANGUAGE POLITICS AND POLICIES

Nations can enact laws recognizing an official language, such as French in France or Irish in Ireland (despite the fact that more Irish speak English than Irish). Some nations have multiple official languages. For instance, Canada has declared English and French to be the official languages. Here in the United States, there is no official national language, although English is the de facto national language. Yet the state of Hawai'i has two official languages, English and Hawaiian. Other U.S. entities have also declared official languages, such as Guam (Chamorro and English), New Mexico (English and Spanish), and Samoa (English and Samoan). Laws or customs that determine which language is spoken where and when are referred to as **language policies.** These policies often emerge from the politics of language use. As mentioned previously, the court of Catherine the Great of Russia used not Russian but French, which was closely tied to the politics of social and economic class. The history of colonialism also influences language policies. Thus, Portuguese is the official national language of Mozambique, and English and French are the official national languages of Cameroon. (See Figure 6-4.)

language policies Laws or customs that determine when and where which language will be spoken.

Language policies are embedded in the politics of class, culture, ethnicity, and economics. They do not develop as a result of any supposed quality of the language itself. There are different motivations behind the establishment of language policies that guide the status of different languages in a place. Sometimes nations decide on a national language as part of a process of driving people to assimilate into the national culture. If the state wishes to promote assimilation, language policies that encourage everyone to speak the official language and

conduct business in that language are promoted. One such group, U.S. English, Inc., has been advocating for the establishment of English as the official language of the United States.

Sometimes nations develop language policies as a way of protecting minority languages so these languages do not disappear. Welsh in Wales is one example, but Irish in Ireland and Frisian in Germany and the Netherlands are legally protected languages. Some language policies recognize the language rights of its citizens wherever they are in the nation. One example of this is Canada (English and French). Another is Kenya (Swahili and English). Government services are available in either language throughout the nation.

Other language policies are governed by location. In Belgium, Dutch (Flemish) is the official language in Flanders in the north part of the country. French is the official language in Wallonia in the South, and German is the official language in the Eastern Cantons bordering Germany. Thus, if you are boarding a train to go from Antwerp to Liège, you would need to look for "Luik" in the Antwerp train station. When you returned to the train station in Liège to go back, you would look for the train to "Anvers." The signs would not be posted in both languages, except in the Brussels-Capital region (the only bilingual part of the nation).

In Quebec, Canada, Law 101—passed in the early 1980s—required all Quebec students to attend French-speaking schools (unless their parents went to an English-speaking school in Quebec). So lots of immigrants from all over the

After interviewing many bilinguals, this author provides some general guidelines to help bilinguals know when to code switch.

CONVERSING IS NO SIMPLE MATTER FOR THE BILINGUAL

Cuban-born Maria Carreira, the co-author of two college Spanish textbooks, can glide easily between her native tongue and English. But in her daily life in Southern California, picking which language to speak can be very complicado. *Such as the time when she was at a taco stand where everyone seemed to be ordering and chatting in Spanish. Carreira started placing her order* en espanol, *but she quickly switched to English after she got a look at the young employee behind the counter. "He had the bluest eyes," Carreira said. . . . Although the counterman responded in English, it dawned on her that he had been capably handling orders in Spanish. Yet her flub reflects a language-etiquette question confronted daily by the nation's growing ranks of English-Spanish bilinguals: When to use singles and when to speak Spanish? . . . Carreira said, "it's a land mine." For example, switching to Spanish might seem rude if it suggests the other speaker is inept in English. Yet among Hispanics proud of their ethnic heritage, completely avoiding Spanish can come across as standoffish. Experts such as Carreira say the language decision among bilinguals is often made in a split second, based on cues such as age, clothing and apparent social status—along with skin, eye and hair color. Names can be giveaways—or traps. When University of California, Los Angeles student Maricruz Cecena introduced herself with a friendly* hola *to one of her freshman-year dormitory roommates, Laura Sanchez, and then tried to strike up a phone conversation in Spanish, all she got was an earful of English. . . .*

As with all etiquette, making the other person comfortable is key.

Although Carreira regrets the incident with the blue-eyed counterman, she has a finely honed sense of Spanish-English etiquette that leads her to use Spanish sparingly in public, unless she is approached in Spanish. . . . Say Carreira needs directions and bumps into somebody who appears Hispanic. She'll ask in English and stick with the language even if the other person speaks with a heavy accent. Switching quickly to Spanish, Carreira reasons, would be "sort of saying, 'Huh, I get it. You can't speak English.' " But by refusing to speak Spanish, "you also risk coming across as aloof or superior, more Americanized, or not one of them," she said. The solution? Carreira will continue an exchange in English to avoid insult but will toss in a well-pronounced gracias *or* por favor *as "a way of being gracious and showing solidarity."*

Source: S. Silverstein, "Conversing Is No Simple Matter for the Bilingual," *Los Angeles Times,* November 15, 2007.

world, few of whom spoke French, were required to attend French-speaking schools. Years later, these former students talked about this experience and how this law is changing Quebec. It's creating a more multicultural identity in contrast to previous years when most immigrants would choose English, leaving French to be spoken only by a small, relatively isolated group (Roy, 2007).

Sometimes language policies are developed with language parity, but the implementation is not equal. In Cameroon, for example, English and French are both official languages, although 247 indigenous languages are also spoken. Although Germany was the initial colonizer of Cameroon, Britain and France took over in 1916—with most of the territory going to France—and these "new colonial masters then sought to impose their languages in the newly acquired territory" (Echu, 2003, p. 34). At independence in 1960, French Cameroon established French as its official language and English became the official language in the former British Cameroon areas once they joined together to form Cameroon. Once united in 1961, Cameroon established both languages as official languages. Because French speakers are far more numerous than English speakers, "French has a de facto dominance over English in the areas of administration, education and the media. In fact, it is not an exaggeration to say that French influence as expressed in language, culture and political policy prevails in all domains" (p. 39). So although Cameroon is officially bilingual, French dominates in nearly all domains, because most of the people are French speakers. Thus, "what appears to be a language policy for the country is hardly clearly defined, in spite of the expressed desire to promote English-French bilingualism and protect the indigenous languages" (p. 44). European colonialism has left its mark in this African nation, and the language policy and language realities remain to be worked out.

We can view the development of language policies as reflecting the dialectical tensions between the nation's history and its future, between the various language communities, and between economic and political relations inside and outside the nation. Language policies can help resolve or exacerbate these tensions.

LANGUAGE AND GLOBALIZATION

In a world in which people, products, and ideas can move easily around the globe, rapid changes are being made in the languages spoken and learned. Globalization has sparked increased interest in some languages while leaving others to disappear. In addition, communication technologies, along with globalization, have tremendous impact on how languages are used (and misused). Let's look more closely now at these impacts.

Linguists estimate that half of the world's 6,000 languages of today will be gone within the next century. Some language loss, like species loss, is natural and predictable. No language exists forever. Languages are disappearing more quickly today for various reasons. Sometimes, small, unindustrialized communities are forced to choose between their language and participation in the larger world—due to global economic pressures. East Africans speak Swahili; many feel they need to speak English. On the other hand, disappearing languages can make a comeback. Cornish (a language spoken in southwestern England) disappeared in 1777 when the last speaker died. Recently, working from old written documents, descendents of Cornish speakers began to learn the language and speak it; now there are more than 2,000 Cornish speakers. Modern Hebrew is another example. For centuries, it was a religious and scholarly language; in the late 19th century, it was revived in Palestine and is now taught in the schools and is the common language of Israeli citizens (Ostler, 2000).

Media and communication technologies also have made a dramatic impact on language use. In small communities, children gain from them a knowledge of the world that doesn't come from their elders. Children are less interested in the traditional language. Consider how e-mail and text messaging have changed written language practices. Experts say that language is not just about meaning but has far-reaching social and political impact. First, it can present intergenerational communication challenges for parents and children. (Do your parents and grand-parents know the meanings of TTYL8R, ROTFL, TTFN, IMHO, CWYL?) Second, perhaps language limits what we can convey. In reducing everything to a very basic language, it doesn't leave much room for communication nuances. How might this influence our interpersonal encounters and relationships? A survey conducted in England found that 76% of Britons admitted to using abbreviations and text slang but hated receiving it (Ross, 2009). Third, some experts suggest that children who use text messages often could be stunting their literacy and language skills; however, it turns out, at least for adults, that although being exposed to numerous misspellings may cause some decrease in spelling ability, texting in general can actually have a positive effect (Powell & Dixon, 2011).

Global forces can sometimes produce other changes in language use, like producing a new dialect—the new *multicultural English*, which is emerging among the young in England and replacing the traditional cockney. (See Point of View, p. 239.)

The dream of a common international language has long marked Western ways of thinking. Ancient Greeks viewed the world as filled with Greek speakers or those who were *barbaroi* (barbarians). The Romans attempted to establish Latin and Greek, which led to the subsequent establishment of Latin as the learned language of Europe. Latin was eventually replaced by French, which became the **lingua franca** of Europe. More recently, English has become the lingua franca of international communication.

lingua franca A commonly shared language that is used as a medium of communication between people of different languages.

Many native English speakers are happy with the contemporary status of the language. They feel much more able to travel around the world, without the burden of having to learn other ways of communicating, given that many people around the world speak English. Having a common language also facilitates intercultural communication, but it can also create animosity among those who must learn the other's language. Dominique Noguez (1998) explains,

> *In these language affairs, as in many other moral or political affairs—tolerance, for example—is the major criteria for reciprocity. Between comparable languages and equal countries, this must be: I speak and learn your language and you speak and learn mine. Otherwise, it's sadomasochism and company—the sadist being*

Harumi Befu, emeritus professor at Stanford University, discusses the consequences of English domination for monolingual Americans.

Instead of language enslavement and intellectual imperialism, however, one more often is told of the benefit of learning a second language, such as English. For example, non-native English speakers can relativize their own language and appreciate each language on its own terms. It was Goethe who said that one who does not know a foreign language does not know his/her own language. . . .

Thanks to the global dominance of their country, American intellectuals have acquired the "habitus" (Bourdieu) of superiority, whereby they exercise the license of expressing their thoughts in English wherever they go instead of showing respect to locals through expending efforts to learn their language. This privileged position, however, spells poverty of the mind.

For their minds are imprisoned in a single language; they are unable to liberate their minds through relativizing English. In short, other things being equal, monolingual Americans (not all Americans are monolingual) are the most provincial and least cosmopolitan among those who traffic in the global interlinguistic community—a price they pay for the strength of the country backing them.

Source: H. Befu, "English Language Intellectual Imperialism and Its Consequences," *Newsletter: Intercultural Communication,* 37 (Intercultural Communication Institute, Kanda University of International Studies, Japan), June 2000, p. 1.

simply the one with the gall to say to another: "I am not speaking your language, therefore speak mine!" This is what Anglo-Saxons have been happily doing since at least 1918. (p. 234)

(En ces affaires de langue, comme en bien d'autres affaires morales ou politiques—la tolérance, par exemple—le critère majeur, c'est la réciprocité. Entre langues comparables et pays égaux, ce devrait être: je parle et enseigne votre langue et vous parlez et enseignez la mienne. Autrement, c'est sadomasochisme et compagnie—le sadique étant tout simplement celui qui l'aplomb de declarer à l'autre: "Je ne parle pas votre langue, parlez donc la mienne!" C'est ce que font, avec assez de bonheur, les Anglo-Saxons depuis au moins 1918.)

What is the relationship between our four touchstones and this contemporary linguistic situation? That is, how do culture, communication, power, and context play out in the domination of English? First, the intimate connections between language and culture mean that the diffusion of English is tied to the spread of U.S. American culture around the world. Is this a new form of colonialism? If we consider issues of power, what role does the United States play in the domination of English on the world scene? How does this marginalize or disempower those who are not fluent in English in intercultural communication?

Colonial histories have influenced how people communicate. In Brazil, colonialists developed their own language to communicate across the many indigenous communities they colonized. Although imposed by colonists, today this general language is used to resist domination by Portuguese. How does a language serve political ends? What are the politics of speaking English in the world today?

When the Portuguese arrived in Brazil five centuries ago, they encountered a fundamental problem: the indigenous peoples they conquered spoke more than 700 languages. Rising to the challenge, the Jesuit priests accompanying them concocted a mixture of Indian, Portuguese and African words they called "língua geral," or the "general language," and imposed it on their colonial subjects.

Elsewhere in Brazil, língua geral as a living, spoken tongue died off long ago. But in this remote and neglected corner of the Amazon where Brazil, Colombia and Venezuela meet, the language has not only managed to survive, it has made a remarkable comeback in recent years. . . .

Two years ago, in fact, Nheengatú, as the 30,000 or so speakers of língua geral call their language, reached a milestone. By vote of the local council, São Gabriel da Cachoeira became the only municipality in Brazil to recognize a language other than Portuguese as official, conferring that status on língua geral and two local Indian tongues.

As a result, Nheengatú, which is pronounced neen-gah-TOO and means "good talk," is now a language that is permitted to be taught in local schools, spoken in courts and used in government documents. People who can speak língua geral have seen their value on the job market rise and are now being hired as interpreters, teachers and public health aides. . . .

"Nheengatú came to us as the language of the conqueror," explained Renato da Silva Matos, a leader of the Federation of Indigenous Organizations of the Rio Negro. "It made the original languages die out" because priests and government officials punished those who spoke any language other than Portuguese or Nheengatú.

But in modern times, the language acquired a very different significance. As the dominion of Portuguese advanced and those who originally imposed the language instead sought its extinction, Nheengatú became "a mechanism of ethnic, cultural and linguistic resistance," said Persida Miki, a professor of education at the Federal University of Amazonas.

Source: L. Rohter, "Language Born of Colonialism Thrives Again in Amazon," *The New York Times*, August 28, 2005, p. A6.

What kinds of resentment might be fostered by forcing people to recognize their disempowerment?

In what intercultural contexts is it appropriate to assume that others speak English? For English speakers, this is a particularly unique context. Latvians, for example, cannot attend international meetings and assume that others will speak Latvian; and Albanians will have difficulty transacting international trade if they assume that others know their language.

This brings up the question of what languages U.S. Americans should be studying in order to communicate better with others in global contexts. For many years, the most studied languages in high schools and colleges in the United States were French, Spanish, and German. However, some suggest that, in order for the United States to remain a key player on the global stage, its citizens should be studying Chinese and Arabic. Experts estimate that by the year 2015 China will have overtaken the United States as the predominant actor in the major power system (Kissane, 2005).

In his study of the developing use of English in Switzerland, Christof Demont-Heinrich (2005) focused on Switzerland in global and local contexts, cultural and national identity issues, power, and communication. The nation recognizes four national languages—French, German, Italian, and Romansh. Three of these are recognized as official languages—German, French, and Italian—which means that all national government materials are available in the three official languages. Some of the power differences among these language communities are reflected in the demographics from the 2000 census in which "63.9% of respondents named German, 19.5% listed French, 6.6% claimed Italian, and 0.5% named Romansh as their first language" (p. 72). In this context, English has become more influential, not only among the banking and financial sectors but increasingly in "consumer and pop culture" (p. 74). Recently, at the initiation of the Zürich canton, a proposal was made to allow English to be the first foreign language taught in school (rather than one of the national languages), and eight other German-speaking cantons quickly aligned themselves with this idea. The Swiss Conference of Cantonal Ministers of Education decided that by 2012 all Swiss students must study two foreign languages, but only one must be a national language. Given the value of English in the global economy and the use of English to communicate with other Swiss, one can see why there would be support for the Zürich position. Given the importance of Swiss national identity and their multilingual identity that is shaped by the languages spoken by other Swiss, one can also see why some French-speaking politicians preferred a policy where one of the other national languages would be the first foreign language. Zürich and other cantons are now proposing a ballot initiative that would "require just one foreign language to be taught, ideally English, at the primary school level" (p. 76), which would leave the other national language to be taught in secondary school. Demont-Heinrich concludes by noting that Romansh is likely headed for linguistic extinction, but what will happen to Switzerland? Can Swiss national identity be maintained with English? And what about the world? "Can such a colossal human social order sustain the diverse forms of human linguistic expression" (p. 81), or must humanity reduce its linguistic expression to a few dominant languages that facilitate economic trade? In the era of globalization, where economic growth is driven by external relations and trade, should we be studying Chinese?

INTERNET RESOURCES

http://anthro.palomar.edu/language/default.htm
This web resource is an interactive guide to understanding the relationships between language and culture. The site contains very interesting information on a variety of language topics. It also includes audio files that highlight regional differences in pronunciation and dialect and flash cards to test your mastery of the material.

www.aber.ac.uk/media/Documents/S4B/semiotic.html
This is an excellent resource for students seeking additional information on semiotics. This semiotics guide is complete with charts, easy-to-understand text, and lists of other resources. For those of you looking to write a paper using semiotics, the last chapter listed is a "do-it yourself" guide to semiotics analysis!

www.us-english.org/
www.lsadc.org/
These two websites contain very different views on the "English-only" issue in the United States. The group US English is a strong advocate for English-only within the United States. Its website contains lots of information about the group's legislative activities and political agenda. The second website is the home page of the Linguistic Society of America. This group was not formed to counter English-only policies, but it is a strong advocate of a multilingual society. The group's statement on language rights can be found at www.smo.uhi.ac.uk/saoghal/mion-chanain/LSA_statement.txt.

http://babelfish.altavista.digital.com/translate.dyn
This website is an example of one of the ways that technology is changing translation. The "Babel" feature, which can be added to web content, translates from a great number of languages to a great number of languages. A similar feature is also available in the on-line community of Second Life. What opportunities and challenges does automated translation present for intercultural communication?

SUMMARY

- The social science approach focuses on individual aspects of language. The interpretive approach focuses on contextual aspects of language. The critical approach emphasizes the role of power in language use.
- There are different positions on the relationship between language and our perceptions. The nominalist position feels that our perception is not shaped by the language we speak. The relativist position argues that our perception is determined by the language we speak. The qualified relativist position argues that language influences how we perceive.
- Communication styles can be high context or low context, more direct or indirect, or more elaborate or understated.

- Slang and humor are two additional variations in language use.
- Co-cultural groups may use one of three orientations to dealing with dominant groups—assimilation, accommodation, or separation. Within each of these approaches are nonassertive, assertive, and aggressive strategies. Each of these strategies comes with benefits and costs to the co-cultural individual.
- We use language from our social positions, and the power of our language use and labels comes from that social position.
- People have various reasons for learning or not learning new languages.
- People can be bilingual or multilingual, and they may engage in code switching or changing languages in different situations, depending on the contexts.
- Translation refers to expressing what was said in another language in a written text. Interpretation is the same process but is oral rather than written.
- Language policies are instituted with different goals. Sometimes language policies are meant to encourage assimilation into a language and national identity. Sometimes language policies are meant to provide protection to minority languages. Sometimes language policies regulate language use in different parts of a nation.
- Globalization, along with technology, has affected how languages are used or not used. Globalization has meant that English has become more important worldwide but also has created other intercultural communication conflicts.

DISCUSSION QUESTIONS

1. Why is it important for intercultural communication scholars to study both language and discourse?
2. What is the relationship between our language and the way we perceive reality?
3. What are some cross-cultural variations in language use and communication style?
4. What aspects of context influence the choice of communication style?
5. What does a translator or an interpreter need to know to be effective?
6. Why is it important to know the social positions of individuals and groups involved in intercultural communication?
7. Why do some people say that we should not use labels to refer to people but should treat everybody as individuals? Do you agree?
8. Why do people have such strong reactions to language policies, as in the "English-only" movement?
9. In what ways is the increasing and widespread use of English around the world both a positive and a negative change for U.S. Americans?

 Go to the self-quizzes on the Online Learning Center at www.mhhe.com/ martinnakayama6 to further test your knowledge.

ACTIVITIES

1. *Regional Language Variations.* Meet in small groups with other class members and discuss variations in language use in different regions of the United States (accent, vocabulary, and so on). Identify perceptions that are associated with these variations.

2. *"Foreigner" Labels.* Meet in small groups with other class members and generate a list of labels used to refer to people from other countries who come to the United States—for example, "immigrants" and "aliens." For each label, identify a general connotation (positive, negative, mixed). Discuss how connotations of these words may influence our perceptions of people from other countries. Would it make a difference if we referred to them as "guests" or "visitors"?

3. *Values and Language.* Although computer-driven translations have improved dramatically over earlier attempts, translation is still intensely cultural. Communication always involves many layers of meaning, and when you move between languages, there are many more opportunities for misunderstanding. Try to express some important values that you have (e.g., freedom of the press) on this website, and see how they are retranslated in five different languages: www.tashian.com/multibabel/.

KEY WORDS

bilingual (249)
co-cultural groups (241)
code switching (257)
communication
    style (232)
equivalency (251)
high-context
    communication (233)
interlanguage (250)

interpretation (251)
language
    acquisition (229)
language policies (259)
lingua franca (263)
low-context
    communication (233)
metamessage (232)
multilingual (249)

nominalist position (226)
qualified relativist
    position (229)
relativist position (226)
social positions (245)
source text (251)
target text (251)
translation (251)

 The Online Learning Center at www.mhhe.com/martinnakayama6 features flashcards and crossword puzzles based on these terms and concepts.

REFERENCES

Anzaldúa, G. (1987). *Borderlands/la frontera: The new mestiza*. San Francisco: Spinsters/Aunt Lute.

Au, T. K. (1983). Chinese and English counterfactuals: The Sapir-Whorf hypothesis revisited. *Cognition, 15*, 155–187.

Au, T. K. (1984). Counterfactuals: In reply to Alfred Bloom. *Cognition, 17*, 239–302.

Au, T. K. (1985). Language and cognition. In L. L. Lloyd & R. L. Schiefelbusch (Eds.), *Language perspectives II*. Baltimore: University Park Press.

Barthes, R. (1980). *Elements of semiology* (A. Lavers & C. Smith, Trans.). New York: Hill & Wang. (Original work published 1968)

Befu, H. (2000, June). English language intellectual imperialism and its consequences. *Newsletter: Intercultural Communication, 37* (Intercultural Communication Institute, Kanda University of International Studies, Japan), p. 1.

Boxer, D. (2002). Nagging: The familial conflict arena. *Journal of Pragmatics, 34,* 49–61.

Cashman, H. (2005). Identities at play: Language preference and group membership in bilingual talk in interaction. *Journal of Pragmatics, 37,* 301–315.

Cruz-Janzen, M. (2002). Lives on the crossfire: The struggle of multiethnic and multiracial Latinos for identity in a dichotomous and racialized world. *Race, Gender & Class, 9*(2), 47–62.

Dazell, T. (2005). Sez who? The power of slang. *PBS.org.* Retrieved June 4, 2011, from www.pbs.org/speak/words/sezwho/slang/.

Dehaene, S., Izard, V., Pica, P., & Spelke, E. (2006). Core knowledge of geometry in an Amazonian indigene group. *Science, 311,* 381–384.

Demont-Heinrich, C. (2005). Language and national identity in the era of globalization: The case of English in Switzerland. *Journal of Communication Inquiry, 29,* 66–84.

Desnoes, E. (1985). The death system. In M. Blonsky (Ed.), *On signs* (pp. 39–42). Baltimore, MD: Johns Hopkins University Press.

Deutscher, G. (2010). *Through the language glass: Why the world looks different in other languages.* New York: Metropolitan Books.

Echu, G. (2003). Coping with multilingualism: Trends in the evolution of language policy in Cameroon. *PhiN, 25,* 31–46. Available at http://web.fuberlin.de/phin/phin25/p25t2.htm#ech99b.

Emma (2009, October). English humour vs. American humor—Is there a difference? *LEXOPHILES.com.* Retrieved June 4, 2011, from www.lexiophiles.com/english/english-humour-vs-american-humor-is-there-a-difference.

Gale, T., & Cosgrove, D. (2004). "We learnt that last week": Reading into the language practices of teachers. *Teachers and Teaching: Theory and Practice, 10*(2), 125–134.

Goldstein, D. (2006, May 6). National anthem in other languages? Heard this before. *Seattle Times.* Retrieved April 28, 2008, from http://seattletimes.nwsource.com/html/nationworld/2002975852_anthem06.html.

Grice, H. (1975). Logic and conversation. In P. Cole & J. Morgan (Eds.), *Syntax and semantics: Vol. 3. Speech acts.* New York: Academic Press.

Gudykunst, W. B., & Matsumoto, Y. (1996). Cross-cultural variability of communication in personal relationships. In W. B. Gudykunst, S. Ting-Toomey, & T. Nishida (Eds.), *Communication in personal relationships across cultures* (pp. 19–56). Thousand Oaks, CA: Sage.

Gudykunst, W. B., Ting-Toomey, S., with Chua, E. (1988). *Culture and interpersonal communication.* Newbury Park: Sage Publications.

Gudykunst, W. B., & Ting-Toomey, S. (2003). *Communicating with strangers: An approach to intercultural communication* (4th ed.). New York: McGraw-Hill.

Hall, E. T. (1976). *Beyond culture.* Garden City, NY: Doubleday.

Hill, P., & Van Zyl, S. (2002). English and multilingualism in the South African engineering workplace. *World Englishes, 21*(1), 23–35.

Jameson, F. (1972). *The prisonhouse of language.* Princeton, NJ: Princeton University Press.

Karlson, D. (2005, December 2). Swastika on sign unnerves residents. *The Cape Codder.* www.townonline.com/brewster/localRegional/view.bg?articleid=382002&format=&page=1.

Kenneally, C. (2008, April 22). When language can hold the answer. *The New York Times,* p. F1.

Kissane, D. (2005). 2015 and the rise of China: Power cycle analysis and the implications for Australia, *Security Challenges, 1*(1), 105–121.

Kövecses, Z. (2005). *Metaphor in culture: Universality and variation.* Cambridge: Cambridge University Press.

Lakoff, G. (1989). Some empirical results about the nature of concepts. *Mind & Language, 4,* 103–129.

Lakoff, G. (1992). The contemporary theory of metaphor. In Ortony, A. (Ed.), *Metaphor and thought* (2nd ed.) (pp. 202–251). New York: Cambridge University Press.

Li, P., & Gleitman, L. (2002). Turning the tables: Language and spatial reasoning. *Cognition,* 265–294.

Martin, J. N., Krizek, R. L., Nakayama, T. K., & Bradford, L. (1996). Exploring whiteness: A study of self-labels for White Americans. *Communication Quarterly, 44,* 125–144.

Martinez, J. (2000). *Phenomenology of Chicana experience and identity: Communication and transformation in praxis.* Lanham, MD: Rowan & Littlefield.

Marx, E. (1999). *Breaking through culture shock.* London: Nicholas Brealey.

Meléndez, M. (2002, April 7). Police try to connect, reach out in Spanish. *The Arizona Republic,* p. B1.

Mendoza-Denton, N. (1999). Fighting words: Latina girls, gangs and language attitudes. In D. G. Galindo & M. D. Gonzales (Eds.), *Speaking Chicana: Voice, power, and identity* (pp. 39–56). Tucson: University of Arizona Press.

Miles, O. (2011, February 24). How Gaddafi's words get lost in translation. *BBC News Africa*. Retrieved June 2, 2011, from www.bbc.co.uk/news/world-africa-12566277?print=true.

Moritsugu, H. (1992). To be more Japanese. In J. F. J. Lee (Ed.), *Asian Americans* (pp. 99–103). New York: New Press.

Nakayama, T. K. (1997). Les voix de l'autre. *Western Journal of Communication, 61*(2): 235–242.

Noguez, D. (1998). *La colonisation douce: Feu la langue française, carnets, 1968–1998*. Paris: Arléa.

Orbe, M. P. (1998). *Constructing co-cultural theory: An explication of culture, power, and communication*. Thousand Oaks, CA: Sage.

Ostler, R. (2000). Disappearing language of the 6000 languages still on earth, 90 percent could be gone by 2100. *BNET*. Retrieved June 3, 2011, from http://findarticles.com/p/articles/mi_m0GER/is_2000_Spring/ai_61426207/pg_2/?tag=mantle_skin;content.

Pinker, S. (2007). *The stuff of thought: Language as a window into human nature*. New York: Viking.

Powell, D. & Dixon, M. (2011). Does SMS text messaging help or harm adults' knowledge of standard spelling. *Journal of Computer Assisted Learning, 27*(1), 55–66.

Pratt, S. B., & Buchanan, M. C. (2000). Wa-zha-zhe-i-e: Notions on a dying ancestral language. In A. Gonzàley, M. Houston, & U. Chen (Eds.), *Essays in culture, ethnicity, and communication* (3rd ed., pp. 155–163). Los Angeles: Roxbury.

Rhodda, M., & Grove, C. (1987). *Language, cognition, and deafness*. Hillsdale, NJ: Lawrence Erlbaum.

Roy, J-H. (2007, September 15). *Les enfants de la loi 101* (Children of Law 101). *L'actualite, 32*(14), 34–50.

Ross, S. (2009, March 5). How txt spk is now a pain n d neck. *NEWS.scotsman.com*. Retrieved June 3, 2011, from http://news.scotsman.com/uk/How-txt-spk—is.5040192.jp.

Sapir, E. (Ed.). (1921). *Language: An introduction to the study of speech*. New York: Harcourt, Brace & World.

Saussure, F. de. (1966). *Course in general linguistics* (C. Bally & A. Sechehaye, Eds.; W. Baskin, Trans.). New York: McGraw-Hill.

Sauvage, J.-L. (2002). Code-switching: An everyday reality in Belgium. In J. N. Martin, T. K. Nakayama, & L. A. Flores (Eds.), *Readings in intercultural communication: Experiences and contexts* (2nd ed., pp. 156–161). New York: McGraw-Hill.

Scott, K. D. (2000). Crossing cultural borders: "Girl" and "look" as markers of identity in Black women's language use. *Discourse & Society, 11*(2): 237–248.

Shuter, R. When Indian women text message; culture, identity and emerging interpersonal norms of new media. In P. H. Cheong, J. N. Martin & L. P. Macfadyen (Eds.), *New media and intercultural communication*. New York: Peter Lang.

Shuter, R., & Chattopadhyay, S. (2010). Emerging interpersonal norms of text messaging in India and the United States. *Journal of Intercultural Communication Research, 39*(2), 121–145.

Silverstein, S. (2007, November 12). Biding their tongues. *Los Angeles Times*, p. A1.

Ueda, K. (1974). Sixteen ways to avoid saying "no" in Japan. In J. C. Condon & M. Saito (Eds.), *Intercultural encounters with Japan* (pp. 185–192). Tokyo: Simul Press.

Van Petten, V. (2009). Understanding generational differences through slang. *Talking about Generations.com*. Retrieved June 4, 2011, from www.talkingabout generations.com/index.php/2009/10/understanding-generational-differences-through-slang/.

Varner, I., & Beamer, L. (2010). *Intercultural communication in the global workplace*, 5th ed. Boston: McGraw-Hill.

Vinay, J. P., & Darbelnet, J. (1977). *Stylistique comparée du français et de l'anglais: Méthode de traduction*. Paris: Marcel Didier.

West, F. (1975). *The way of language: An introduction*. New York: Harcourt Brace Jovanovich.

Whorf, B. L. (1956). *Language, thought and reality*. Cambridge, MA: MIT Press.

Yellow Bird, M. (1999). What we want to be called. *American Indian Quarterly, 23*(2), 1–20.

CHAPTER

7

NONVERBAL CODES AND CULTURAL SPACE

Nonverbal elements of cultural communication are highly dynamic and play an important role in understanding intercultural communication. Consider misunderstandings based on expectations for one very routine daily activity—pedestrian behavior. U.S. Americans tend to glance, smile, and nod more often than Japanese pedestrians (Patterson et al., 2007). Or consider expected spatial distance. A colleague recently observed that walking on the sidewalks in England, she found herself frequently bumping into oncoming pedestrians—and figured out it was because people tend to walk on the same side of the pavement as they drive on the road. So walking in England, as they approached her and she steps to her left, they step to their right.

While the consequences for these encounters may be a bit awkward, in some other instances, understanding nonverbal communication can be a key to survival. A news story during the Iraq war described how nonverbal behaviors at military checkpoints in Baghdad played an important role in the safety and security of Iraqi civilians. Military investigators asked U.S. soldiers if they had shot at women and children in cars at checkpoints, and one soldier answered, "Yes." Asked why, he replied, "They didn't respond to the signs [we gave], the presence of troops or warning shots. Basically, we were at a checkpoint, we had two Arabic signs that said to turn around or be shot. Once [they passed] . . . the first sign, they fired a warning shot. If they passed the second sign, they shot the vehicle. Sometimes it bothers me. What if they couldn't read the signs?" (Smith & Tyson, 2005).

You may never need to know the right nonverbal behavior to pass through a military checkpoint (see Figure 7-1), but you certainly will find yourself in many intercultural communication situations and cultural spaces. Your own nonverbal communication may create additional problems and, if the behaviors are inappropriate for the particular cultural space, may exacerbate existing tensions. In other cases, your use of nonverbals might reduce tension and confusion.

The first part of this chapter focuses on the importance of understanding nonverbal aspects of intercultural communication. We can examine nonverbal communication in terms of the personal–contextual and the static–dynamic dialectics. Although nonverbal communication can be highly dynamic, personal space, gestures, and facial expressions are fairly static patterns of specific nonverbal communication codes. These patterns are the focus of the second part of this chapter. Finally, we investigate the concept of cultural space and the ways in which cultural identity is shaped and negotiated by the cultural spaces (home, neighborhood, and so on) that people occupy.

There are no guidebooks for reading everyday nonverbal behaviors, and nonverbal communication norms vary from culture to culture; therefore, we believe it is useless to list nonverbals to memorize. Instead, it will be more beneficial for you to learn the framework of nonverbal communication and cultural spaces so you can tap into the nonverbal systems of whatever cultural groups become relevant to your life. Understanding communication is a matter of understanding how to think dialectically about *systems* of meaning, and not discrete elements. Nonverbal intercultural communication is no exception.

FIGURE 7-1   Nonverbal behaviors at military checkpoints in Iraq play an important role in the safety and security of Iraqi civilians. (© *Wathiq Khuzaie/Getty Images*)

THINKING DIALECTICALLY ABOUT NONVERBAL COMMUNICATION: DEFINING NONVERBAL COMMUNICATION

In this chapter, we discuss two forms of communication beyond speech. The first includes facial expression, personal space, gestures, eye contact, paralanguage, use of time, and conversational silence. (What is not said is often as important as what is spoken.) The second includes the cultural spaces that we occupy and negotiate. **Cultural spaces** are the social and cultural contexts in which our identity forms—where we grow up and where we live (not necessarily the physical homes and neighborhoods, but the cultural meanings created in these places).

In thinking dialectically, we need to consider the relationship between the nonverbal behavior and the cultural spaces in which the behavior occurs, and between the nonverbal behavior and the verbal message. Although there are patterns to nonverbal behaviors, they are not always culturally appropriate in all cultural spaces. Remember, too, that some nonverbal behaviors are cultural, whereas others are idiosyncratic, that is, peculiar to individuals.

cultural space The particular configuration of the communication that constructs meanings of various places.

Comparing Verbal and Nonverbal Communication

Recognizing Nonverbal Behavior   Both verbal and nonverbal communication are symbolic, communicate meaning, and are patterned—that is, they are governed by contextually determined rules. Societies have different nonverbal languages, just as they have different spoken languages. However, some differences between nonverbal and verbal communication codes have important implications for intercultural interaction.

Let's look at some examples of these differences. The following incident occurred to Judith when she was new to Algeria, where she lived for a while. One day she stood at her balcony and waved to one of the young Algerian teachers, who was walking across the school yard. Several minutes later, the young teacher knocked on the door, looking expectantly at Judith, as if summoned. Because Judith knew that it was uncommon in Algeria for men to visit women they didn't know well, she was confused. Why had he come to her door? Was it because she was foreign? After a few awkward moments, he left. A few weeks later, Judith figured it out. In Algeria (as in many other places), the U.S. "wave" is the nonverbal signal for "come here." The young teacher had assumed that Judith had summoned him to her apartment. As this example illustrates, rules for nonverbal communication vary among cultures and contexts (see Point of View, p. 284).

Let's consider another example. Two U.S. students attending school in France were hitchhiking to the university in Grenoble for the first day of classes. A French motorist picked them up and immediately started speaking English to them. They wondered how he knew they spoke English. Later, when they took a train to Germany, the conductor walked into their compartment and berated them in English for putting their feet on the opposite seat. Again, they wondered how he had known that they spoke English. As these examples suggest, nonverbal communication entails more than gestures—even our appearance can communicate loudly. The students' appearance alone probably was a sufficient clue to their national identity. One of our students explains,

> When I studied abroad in Europe, London more specifically, our clothing as a nonverbal expression was a dead giveaway that we were from America. We dressed much more casual, wore more colors, and had words written on our T-shirts and sweatshirts. This alone said enough; we didn't even have to speak to reveal that we were Americans.

As these examples also show, nonverbal behavior operates at a subconscious level. We rarely think about how we stand, what gestures we use, and so on. Occasionally, someone points out such behaviors, which brings them to the conscious level. Consider one more example, from our student Suzanne:

> I was in Macedonia and I was traveling in a car, so I immediately put on my seat belt. My host family was very offended by this because buckling my seat belt meant I didn't trust the driver. After that I rode without a seat belt.

When misunderstandings arise, we are more likely to question our verbal communication than our nonverbal communication. We can search for different ways to explain verbally what we mean. We can also look up words in a dictionary or ask someone to explain unfamiliar words. In contrast, it is more difficult to identify nonverbal miscommunications or misperceptions.

I have a couple of good friends who are deaf, and it is evident that body language, eye contact, and visual communication are far more important in our conversations than between two hearing people. I found that both of my friends, who lived very close to me, would much rather stop by my house than call me on the relay. I can see the cultural implications of space and distance. We keep in touch mostly by using e-mail. It's funny because the e-mails that I get from those guys have more commonly used slang words than most of my hearing friends use. The question is: Do my friends understand the slang, make it a part of their language, and create a sign for it, or do they know the words through somewhat of a verbal exchange with the hearing?
—Andrea

Learning Nonverbal Behavior Whereas we learn rules and meanings for language behavior in grammar and language arts lessons, we learn nonverbal meanings and behaviors by more implicit socialization. No one explains, "When you talk with someone you like, lean forward, smile, and touch the person frequently, because that will communicate that you really care about him or her." In many contexts in the United States, such behaviors communicate immediacy and positive meanings (Ray & Floyd, 2006). But how is it interpreted if someone does not display these behaviors?

Sometimes, though, we learn strategies for nonverbal communication. Have you ever been told to shake hands firmly when you meet someone? You may have learned that a limp handshake indicates a weak person. Likewise, many young women learn to cross their legs at the ankles and to keep their legs together when they sit. These strategies combine socialization and the teaching of nonverbal codes.

Coordinating Nonverbal and Verbal Behaviors Generally our nonverbal behaviors reinforce our verbal behaviors. For example, when we shake our heads and say "no," we are reinforcing verbal behavior, and not surprisingly, consistency between verbal and nonverbal behaviors usually translates into perceptions of credibility and positive first impressions (Weisbuch, Ambady, Clark, Achor, & Weele, 2010). However, nonverbal behaviors can also contradict our verbal communication. If we tell a friend, "I can't wait to see you," and then don't show up at the friend's house, our nonverbal behavior is contradicting the verbal message. Because nonverbal communication operates at a less conscious level, we tend to think that people have less control over their nonverbal behavior. Therefore, we often think of nonverbal behaviors as conveying the "real" messages.

What Nonverbal Behavior Communicates

relational messages
Messages (verbal and nonverbal) that communicate how we feel about others.

Although language is an effective and efficient means of communicating explicit information or content, every communication also conveys **relational messages**—information on how the talker wants to be understood and viewed by the listener.

These messages are communicated not by words, but through nonverbal behavior, including facial expressions, eye gaze, posture, and even our tone of voice (Watzlawick, Beavin, & Jackson, 1967). Nonverbal behavior also communicates **status** and power. For example, a supervisor may be able to touch subordinates, but it is usually unacceptable for subordinates to touch a supervisor. Broad, expansive gestures are associated with high status; conversely, holding the body in a tight, closed position communicates low status.

status The relative position an individual holds in social or organizational settings.

In addition, nonverbal behavior communicates **deception.** Early researchers believed that some nonverbal behaviors (e.g., avoiding eye contact or touching or rubbing the face) indicated lying. However, as more recent research has shown, deception is communicated by fairly idiosyncratic behaviors and seems to be revealed more by inconsistency in nonverbal communication than by specific nonverbal behaviors (Henningsen, Cruz, & Morr, 2000; Vrij, 2004). In addition, cultural groups have different ways of communicating deception (Vrij, Granhag, & Mann, 2010). For example, one study showed that Jordanian students agreed with U.S. American students about some behaviors signaling deception (shifting posture, hesitations, and speech rates). However, they identified additional behaviors (e.g., blinking, touching body, gestures, blushing) (Al-Simadi, 2000).

deception The act of making someone believe what is not true.

Most nonverbal communication about affect, status, and deception happens at an unconscious level. For this reason, it plays an important role in intercultural interactions. Both pervasive and unconscious, it communicates how we feel about each other and about our cultural groups.

A useful theory in understanding nonverbal communication across cultures is **expectancy violations theory.** This theory suggests that we have expectations (mostly subconscious) about how others should behave nonverbally in particular situations. When these expectations are violated (e.g., when someone stands too close to us), we will respond in specific ways. If an act is unexpected and interpreted negatively, for example, when someone stands too close to us at a religious service, we tend to regard the person and the relationship rather negatively. However, if the act is unexpected and interpreted positively (e.g., an attractive person stands close at a party), we will probably regard the relationship rather favorably; in fact, more favorably than if someone stands the exact "expected" distance from us at a religious service or party. Because nonverbal communication occurs at a subconscious level, our negative or positive feelings toward someone may be due to the fact that they violated our expectations—without our realizing it (Burgoon, 1995; Floyd, Ramirez, & Burgoon, 2008).

expectancy violations theory The view that when someone's nonverbal behavior violates our expectations, these violations will be perceived positively or negatively depending on the specific context and behavior.

THE UNIVERSALITY OF NONVERBAL BEHAVIOR

Most traditional research in intercultural communication focuses on identifying cross-cultural differences in nonverbal behavior. How do culture, ethnicity, and gender influence nonverbal communication patterns? How universal is most nonverbal communication? Research traditionally has sought to answer these questions.

As we have observed in previous chapters, it is neither beneficial nor accurate to try to reduce individuals to one element of their identity (gender, ethnicity, nationality, and so on). Attempts to place people in discrete categories tend to reduce their complexities and to lead to major misunderstandings. However, we often classify people according to various categories to help us find universalities. For example, although we may know that not all Germans are alike, we may seek information about Germans in general to help us communicate better with individual Germans. In this section, we explore the extent to which nonverbal communication codes are universally shared. We also look for possible cultural variations in these codes that may serve as tentative guidelines to help us communicate better with others.

Recent Research Findings

Research investigating the universality of nonverbal communication has focused on four areas: (1) the relationship of human behavior to that of primates (particularly chimpanzees), (2) nonverbal communication of sensory-deprived children who are blind or deaf, (3) facial expressions, and (4) universal functions of nonverbal social behavior.

Chimpanzees and humans share many nonverbal behaviors. For example, both exhibit the eyebrow flash—a slight raising of the eyebrow that communicates recognition—one of the most primitive and universal animal behaviors. Primates and humans also share some facial expressions, and very recent research reveals another gesture shared by chimps and humans—the upturned palm, meaning "gimme." Chimps have been observed using it in the wild and in captivity, to ask other chimps to share food, for help in a fight, or to request a grooming session (Pollick, Jeneson, & de Waal, 2008). Some nonhuman primates also communicate status through nonverbal means. Chimps display their rank in the social hierarchy by a "pant-grunt" greeting along with a crouching or bobbing motion. Baboons display status by a "wahoo" sound (Weisbuch & Ambady, 2008). There do seem to be compelling parallels between specific facial expressions and gestures displayed by human and nonhuman primates, universally interpreted to hold similar meanings. However, it still remains true that communication among nonhuman primates, like chimps and monkeys, appears to be less complex than among humans (Preuschoft, 2000)

Recent studies compared the facial expressions of children who were blind with those of sighted children and found many similarities. Even though the children who were blind couldn't see the facial expressions of others to mimic them, they still made the same expressions. This suggests some innate, genetic basis for these behaviors (Galati, Sini, Schmidt, & Tinti, 2003).

Indeed, many cross-cultural studies support the notion of some universality in nonverbal communication, particularly in **facial expressions.** Several facial gestures seem to be universal, including the eyebrow flash just described, the nose wrinkle (indicating slight social distancing), and the "disgust face" (a strong sign of social repulsion). It is also possible that grooming behavior is universal (as it is in animals), although it seems to be somewhat suppressed in Western

facial expressions
Facial gestures that convey emotions and attitudes.

societies (Schiefenhovel, 1997). Recent findings indicate that at least six basic emotions—including happiness, sadness, disgust, fear, anger, and surprise—are communicated by similar facial expressions in most societies. Expressions for these emotions are recognized by most cultural groups as having the same meaning for the same intensity (Ekman, 2003; Matsumoto 2006).

Recent research on the universality of nonverbal behavior has also focused on how some nonverbal behavior fills universal human social needs for promoting social affiliation or bonding. For example, according to this research, laughter is not just a message about the positive feeling of the sender but an attempt to influence others, to make them feel more positive toward the sender. Similarly, the social purpose of mimicry—when interaction partners adopt similar postures, gestures, and mannerisms—is to create an affective or social bond with others. Researchers point out that people in all cultures use these nonverbal behaviors to influence others, and over time, these behaviors that contributed to positive relationships were favored and eventually became automatic and nonconscious (Montepare, 2003; Patterson, 2003).

Although research may indicate universalities in nonverbal communication, some variations exist. The evoking stimuli (i.e., what causes the nonverbal behavior) may vary from one culture to another. Smiling, for example, is universal, but what prompts a person to smile may be culture-specific. Similarly, there are variations in the rules for nonverbal behavior and the contexts in which nonverbal communication takes place. For example, people kiss in most cultures, but there is variation in who kisses whom and in what contexts. When French friends greet each other, they often kiss on both cheeks but never on the mouth. Friends in the United States usually kiss on greeting only after long absence, with the kiss usually accompanied by a hug. The rules for kissing also vary along gender lines.

Finally, it is important to look for larger cultural patterns in the nonverbal behavior, rather than trying simply to identify all of the cultural differences. Researcher David Matsumoto (2006) suggests that although cultural differences in nonverbal patterns are interesting, noting these differences is not sufficient. Studying and cataloging every variation in every aspect of nonverbal behavior would be an overwhelming task. Instead, he recommends studying nonverbal communication patterns that vary with other cultural patterns, such as values.

For example, Matsumoto links cultural patterns in facial expressions with cultural values of power distance and individualism versus collectivism. He found that cultural groups that emphasize status differences will tend to express emotions that preserve these status differences.

Nonverbal Codes

Physical Appearance　Physical appearance is an important nonverbal code. It includes physical characteristics like height, weight, and body shape, as well as personal grooming (including body hair, clothing choices) and personal artifacts such jewelry, glasses, and backpacks/briefcases/purses.

Of course, physical attractiveness is dynamic and variable—beauty is in the eye of the beholder, to some extent (Swami, Furnham, Chamorro-Premuzic,

POINT *of* VIEW

In a recent essay, Steven M. Croucher, a communication scholar, identified reasons given by Muslim women for wearing the hijab (Islamic veil/headscarf). This information was based on interviews with 42 women living in France—following the passing of a 2004 law banning the hijab in French public schools. What do you think are some implications for intercultural communication in societies implementing bans against hijabs?

1. The hijab and Muslim heritage: The women explained that wearing the hijab helped integrate their multicultural identity. They identified as French and also with their country of origin (e.g., Algeria, Tunisia, Morocco) and as Muslim women. As one woman said—growing up hearing a hijab has taught her Islamic and Algerian values in France.

2. The hijab as security in public: The word for "to shield" in Arabic is "hijaba" and many of the women talked about how the hijab provides "a shroud of protection," that they could move easily and comfortably within it, shielded from staring at their bodies—and feeling that people then saw their "real" identity as a religious person.

3. Relationship with Muhammad and the community. Women also talked about how wearing the hijab made them feel closer to Muhammad—akin to a marriage relationship—similar to wearing a wedding ring. Also, that it represents a transformation from a women into a mother within their community. It "helps me show my virtue and be a good example for my community" (p. 207).

4. Protest against the French government: In response to the French ban, many women wear the hijab as a silent protest and an expression of unity with other Muslim women. In fact, some said that before the ban, they only saw themselves as French and Muslim, and now have a stronger feeling of being Muslim and more respect for the hijab.

Source: S. M. Croucher, "French-Muslims and the Hijab: An Analysis of Identity and the Islamic Veil in France," *Journal of Intercultural Communication Research*, 37(3), (2008), 199–213.

Akbar, Gordon, Harris, Finch, & Tovée, 2010). However, are there any universal measures of attractiveness? Do different cultures have different standards for beauty? It turns out that two aspects of beauty seems to be present in many cultures: (1) There is more emphasis on female attractiveness than male and (2) men consistently express stronger preferences for attractive mates than women (Gottschall, 2008).

Research shows that the notion of female attractiveness varies from culture to culture: preferences for different body weights in Malaysia and Britain varied with socioeconomic status, and body shape played a relatively minor role. In a study comparing Britain and Japan, the Japanese participants found smaller-bodied women more attractive than the British participants, and in general, preferred small-headed and longer-legged women—the so-called *hattou shin* beauty (Swami, Caprario, & Tovée, 2006). Our Japanese students tell us that generally, Japanese find thinner lips more attractive than do U.S. Americans.

A study comparing notions of male physical attractiveness in Britain and Greece found that waist-to-chest ratio (WCR) was the most important indicator of male physical attractiveness to women in both countries; however, Greek women showed a preference for smaller men—a lower WCR and smaller overall body weight—than did the British women (Swami et al., 2007).

Some experts have argued that the importance of body shape to physical attractiveness may vary according to gender roles in particular cultural settings: Where traditional sex roles prevail, people prefer "traditional" body shapes (V-shaped for men, hour-glass for women). This seems to be true to some degree. In one study, the Portuguese (Portugal is more of a sex-role-stereotyped European country) were more likely to preferred traditional, "curvaceous" females and V-shaped male bodies when compared to the Danish (Denmark is a less sex-role-stereotyped European country). The Danes preferred thinner, angular shapes (with small hips) for both males and females (Swami et al., 2006).

How do clothing choices and artifacts like purses and backpacks figure in? We might argue that these can be individual choices that express elements of one's personality and affiliation with particular social groups—for example, goth clothing versus jock or preppie. Some clothing may reflect religious affiliation and expressions of religious identity, as we discussed in Chapter 5 (see Figure 7-2). For example, some orthodox Jewish women cover their heads at all times with scarves or hats; some of Judith's relatives wear prayer bonnets that cover the head and "cape" dresses (modest, shirtwaist dresses with an extra layer of material designed to deemphasize the female shape); Muslim women in many countries wear the Islamic hijab (headscarf) or burqa (sheet-like covering of the entire body with only eyes showing.) (See Point of View on p. 280.) As you might expect, women have various reasons for their clothing choices. Sometimes, these choices conflict with secular society. In 2010, the French parliament made it illegal for Muslim women to wear the full veil, a law supported by a majority of French citizens, and there are similar sentiments in Britain (Thompson, 2011). Bans have also been proposed in Italy, Netherlands, and Belgium. Most U.S. Americans are not in favor, and some suggest that values of tolerance and religious freedom should prevail—banning the burqa in very limited contexts (schools, courts) where faces need to be seen (Banning the burqa a bad idea, 2010). Some compare the ban to the French requiring Jews to wear a Star of David during World War II, emphasizing the underlying intolerance and prejudice (Zaretsky, 2010), which will be discussed later in this chapter.

Facial Expressions   As noted earlier, there have been many investigations of the universality of facial expressions. During the past 40 years, psychologist Paul Ekman and colleagues, through extensive and systematic research, have discovered that there seem to be six basic emotions expressed through universal facial expressions: happiness, sadness, disgust, surprise, anger, and fear.

They took many photographs, not always posed, of facial expressions of members from many different cultural groups; then they asked the subjects to identify the emotion conveyed by the facial expression. They showed these photographs to many different individuals in many different countries, including some without exposure to media. Their conclusion supports the notion of universality of facial expressions. Specifically, basic human emotions are expressed in a fairly finite number of facial expressions, and these expressions can be recognized and identified universally (Ekman, 2004; Elfenbein & Ambady, 2002; Matsumoto, Olide, Schug, Willingham, & Callan, 2009).

While a smile may signal a universally positive emotion, there are cultural variations in how much and how often people are expected to smile. Recent studies show that eastern Europeans tend to smile less than western Europeans, and North Americans tend to smile more often than any other cultural group. Communication experts suggest that these differences stem from deeply held cultural preferences involving friendliness and sincerity. America is a "culture of affirmation," where friendliness reigns and people should be happy, or at least appear to be happy. In comparison, French, German, and eastern European cultures place a strong emphasis on sincerity and presenting one's feelings "truthfully," so people are expected to smile only when they are truly feeling happy. In fact, someone who smiles a lot is seen as a bit loony or perhaps insincere; after all, who is truly happy all the time? In most cultures women tend to smile more than men, probably reflecting the social expectations that women are supposed to be more affiliative and communal, and smiling is a way to express these attributes (Szarota, 2010).

Proxemics Unlike facial expressions, the norms for personal space seem to vary considerably from culture to culture. As you may recall from Chapter 2, proxemics is the study of how people use various types of space in their everyday lives: fixed feature space, semifixed space, and informal space. Fixed feature space is characterized by set boundaries (divisions within an office building); semifixed feature space is defined by fixed boundaries such as furniture. Informal space, or personal space, is characterized by a personal zone or "bubble" that varies for individuals and circumstances. The use of each of these spatial relationships can facilitate or impede effective communication across cultures; the area that humans control and use most often is their informal space.

O. M. Watson (1970), a proxemics specialist, investigated nonverbal communication between Arab and U.S. students after hearing many complaints from each group about the other. The Arab students viewed the U.S. students as distant and rude; the U.S. students saw the Arab students as pushy, arrogant, and rude. As Watson showed, the two groups were operating with different rules concerning personal space. Watson's research supports Edward Hall's (1966) observations about the cultural variations in how much distance individuals place between themselves and others. Hall distinguished contact cultures from noncontact cultures. He described **contact cultures** as those societies in which people stand closer together while talking, engage in more direct eye contact, use face-to-face body orientations more often while talking, touch more frequently,

contact cultures
Cultural groups in which people tend to stand close together and touch frequently when they interact—for example, cultural groups in South America, the Middle East, and southern Europe. (See **noncontact cultures.**)

FIGURE 7-2   Muslim women in many countries wear the Islamic burqa as an expression of religious identity. (© *Royalty-Free/Corbis*)

and speak in louder voices. He suggested that societies in South America and southern Europe are contact cultures, whereas those in northern Europe, the United States, and the Far East are **noncontact cultures**—in which people tend to stand farther apart when conversing, maintain less eye contact, and touch less often. Subsequent research seems to confirm Hall's and Watson's early studies (Andersen, Hecht, Hoobler, & Smallwood, 2002).

Of course, many other factors besides regional culture determine how far we stand from someone. Gender, age, ethnicity, context, and topic all influence the use of personal space. In fact, some studies have shown that regional culture is perhaps the least important factor. For example, in many Arab and Muslim societies, gender may be the overriding factor, because unmarried men and women rarely stand close together, touch each other, or maintain direct eye contact. In contrast, male friends may stand very close together, kiss on the cheek, and even hold hands—reflecting loyalty, great friendship, and, most important, equality in status, with no sexual connotation (Fattah, 2005; Khuri, 2001).

Gestures   Gestures, perhaps even more so than personal space, vary greatly from culture to culture. (See Figure 7-3.) The consequences for this variation can be quite dramatic, as President G. W. Bush discovered when he gave the "hook 'em horns" greeting to the University of Texas Longhorn marching band during his inauguration. The photos of this greeting were met with confusion in Norway, where the gesture is considered a salute to Satan ("Norwegians Confused by Bush 'Horns' Salute," 2005).

noncontact cultures Cultural groups in which people tend to maintain more space and touch less often than people do in contact cultures. For instance, Great Britain and Japan tend to have noncontact cultures. (See **contact cultures.**)

POTENTIALLY EMBARRASSING GESTURAL MIXUPS

U.S. Gesture	Other Interpretations
Waving good-bye	Come here (Japan)
Good luck/ "thumbs up"/hitchhiking	Five (Japan)
	One (European countries)
	Screw you (Greece, Nigeria)
Screw you sign	I don't believe you (Uruguay)
AOK sign	Money (Japan)
	Zero (France, Belgium)
	Screw you (Brazil, Turkey)
	Sex (Mexico)
	Homosexual (Ethiopia, Greece)

Source: R. E. Axtell, *Essential Do's and Taboos: Complete Guide to International Business and Leisure Travel* (Hoboken, NJ: John Wiley & Sons, 2007).

Researcher Dane Archer (1997) describes his attempt to catalog the various gestures around the world on video. He began this video project with several hypotheses: first, that there would be great variation, and this he found to be true. However, more surprising, his assumption regarding the existence of some universal gestures or at least some universal *categories* of gestures (e.g., every culture must have an obscene gesture) was not confirmed.

He gathered his information by visiting English as a Second Language classes and asking international students to demonstrate gestures from their home cultures, resulting in the documentary *A World of Gestures: Culture and Nonverbal Communication.* He drew several conclusions from his study: first, that gestures and their meaning can be very subtle. His work "often elicited gasps of surprise, as ESL students from one culture discovered that what at first appeared to be a familiar gesture actually means something radically different in another society" (p. 87). For example, in Germany, and many other European cultures, the gesture for "stupid" is a finger on the forehead; the American gesture for "smart" is nearly identical, but the finger is held an inch to the side, at the temple. Similarly, the American raised thumb gesture of "way to go" is a vulgar gesture, meaning "sit on this" in Sardinia and "screw you" in Iran. (See the Point of View, above.) And of course, we've already mentioned the difference between the the "hook 'em horns" gesture and the salute to Satan.

Second, Archer emphasizes that gestures are different from many other nonverbal expressions in that they are accessible to conscious awareness—they can be explained, illustrated, and taught to outsiders. Finally, as noted earlier, he had assumed there would be some universal categories—a gesture for "very good," a gesture for "crazy," an obscene gesture. Not so. A number of societies (e.g., the Netherlands, Norway, Switzerland) have no such gesture. In the end, he concludes that through making the video, "We all acquired a deeply enhanced

FIGURE 7-3   In many Asian countries, the traditional greeting is a bow. The depth of the vow
signals the status relationship of the two individuals.
(© Andersen Ross/Blend Images LLC)

sense of the power, nuances, and unpredictability of cultural differences" (p. 87).
And the practical implication of the project was to urge travelers to practice
"gestural humility"—assuming that the familiar gestures of our home culture
will not mean the same things abroad and also "that we cannot infer or intuit the
meaning of any gestures we observe in other cultures" (p. 80).

Eye Contact   **Eye contact** often is included in proxemics because it regulates
interpersonal distance. Direct eye contact shortens the distance between two
people, whereas less eye contact increases the distance. Eye contact communicates meanings about respect and status and often regulates turn-taking.

eye contact A non-
verbal code, eye gaze, that
communicates meanings
about respect and status
and often regulates turn-
taking during interactions.

Patterns of eye contact vary from culture to culture. In many societies,
avoiding eye contact communicates respect and deference, although this may
vary from context to context. For many U.S. Americans, maintaining eye contact communicates that one is paying attention and showing respect.

When they speak with others, most U.S. Americans look away from their listeners most of the time, looking at their listeners perhaps every 10 to 15 seconds.

SHAKE HANDS? OR BOW?

Handshakes and bows are important nonverbal greetings around the world. In many Asian countries, the traditional greeting is a bow. It does not signal subservience, but rather humility and respect. The most important guideline here is to observe the other's bow carefully and try to bow to the same depth. The depth of the vow signals the status relationship of the two individuals. Too deep a bow will be seen as ingratiating, too shallow a bow will seem arrogant. In many countries now, particularly in a business context, people may combine the bow and handshake: A slight bow or nod accompanied with a handshake.

Handshakes can vary in frequency and firmness. Some Europeans shake hands at each encounter during the day and may spend as much as 30 minutes a day shaking hands. Here are some guidelines:

Germans:	Firm, brisk, and frequent
French:	Light, quick, and frequent
Latin American:	Firm and frequent
North America:	Firm and infrequent, compared to France and Latin America
Arabs:	Gentle, repeated and lingering (may place hand over heart after)
Koreans:	Moderately firm
Most other Asians:	Very gentle and infrequent

Sources: R. E. Axtell, *Essential Do's and Taboos: Complete Guide to International Business and Leisure Travel* (Hoboken, NJ: John Wiley & Sons, 2007), p. 20; T. Morrison & W. A. Conaway, *Kiss, Bow, Shake Hands* (Avon, MA: Adams Media, 2006).

When a speaker is finished taking a turn, he or she looks directly at the listener to signal completion. However, some cultural groups within the United States use even less eye contact while they speak. For example, some Native Americans tend to avert eye gaze during conversation.

paralinguistics The study of vocal behaviors include voice qualities and vocalization.

voice qualities The "music" of the human voice, including speed, pitch, rhythm, vocal range, and articulation.

Paralinguistics **Paralinguistics** refers to the study of paralanguage—vocal behaviors that indicate *how* something is said, including speaking rate, volume, pitch, and stress. Saying something very quickly in a loud tone of voice will be interpreted differently from the same words said in a quieter tone of voice at a slower rate. There are two types of vocal behavior—voice qualities and vocalizations (Alberts, Nakayama, & Martin, 2007).

Voice qualities—or the nontechnical term, tone of voice—means the same thing as vocal qualities. Voice qualities include speed, pitch, rhythm, vocal range, and articulation; these qualities make up the "music" of the human voice. There do appear to be some universal meanings for particular vocal qualities. A recent study found that vocalizations (e.g., screams, laughter, tone of voice showing disgust, fear) communicating the six basic emotions were recognized equally by two dramatically different cultural groups: European native English speakers and residents of remote, culturally isolated Namibian villages. The researchers conclude that some emotions are psychological universals, shared by all humans. Furthermore, these emotions can be communicated not only by facial expressions, but also by vocal signals that can be broadly interpreted across cultures that do not share language or culture (Sauter, Eisner, Ekman, & Scott, 2010). We all know people whose voice qualities are widely recognized. For example, the voice of actor Fran Drescher, who starred in the TV sitcom *The Nanny*, has been frequently remarked upon. Her trademark whiny chuckle and nasal voice allow her to be recognized no matter where she is. Speakers also vary in how they articulate sounds, that is, how distinctly they pronounce individual words and sounds. We tend not to notice these paralinguistic features unless someone articulates very precisely or very imprecisely. Paralinguistics often lead people to negatively evaluate speakers in intercultural communication contexts even when they don't understand the language. For example, Chinese speakers often sound rather musical and nasal to English speakers; English speakers sound rather harsh and guttural to French speakers.

Vocalizations are the sounds we utter that do not have the structure of language. Tarzan's yell is one famous example. Vocalizations include vocal cues such as laughing, crying, whining, and moaning as well as the intensity or volume of one's speech. They also include sounds that aren't actual words but that serve as fillers, such as "uh-huh," "uh," "ah," and "er." The paralinguistic aspects of speech serve a variety of communicative functions. They reveal mood and emotion; they also allow us to emphasize or stress a word or idea, create a distinctive identity, and (along with gestures) regulate conversation. Paralanguage can be a confusing factor in intercultural communication. For example, Europeans interpret the loudness of Americans as aggressive behavior, while Americans might think the British are secretive because they talk quietly. The amount of silence in conversations and also the speaking rate differ among cultures. For instance, the Finnish and Japanese are comfortable having pauses in their conversations, while most U.S. Americans are seen to talk rapidly and are pretty uncomfortable with silences.

vocalizations The sounds we utter that do not have the structure of language.

Chronemics **Chronemics** concerns concepts of time and the rules that govern its use. There are many cultural variations regarding how people understand and use time. Edward Hall (1966) distinguished between monochronic and polychronic time orientation. People who have a **monochronic** concept of time regard it as a commodity: time can be gained, lost, spent, wasted, or saved. In this orientation, time is linear, with one event happening at a time. In general, monochronic cultures value being punctual, completing tasks, and keeping to schedules. Most university staff and faculty in the United States maintain a monochronic orientation to time. Classes, meetings, and office

chronemics The concept of time and the rules that govern its use.

monochronic An orientation to time that assumes it is linear and is a commodity that can be lost or gained.

appointments start when scheduled; faculty members see one student at a time, hold one meeting at a time, and keep appointments except in the case of emergency. Family problems are considered poor reasons for not fulfilling academic obligations—for both faculty and students.

polychronic An orientation to time that sees it as circular and more holistic.

In contrast, in a **polychronic** orientation, time is more holistic, and perhaps more circular: Several events can happen at once. Many international business negotiations and technical assistance projects falter and even fail because of differences in time orientation. For example, U.S. businesspeople often complain that meetings in the Middle East do not start "on time," that people socialize during meetings, and that meetings may be canceled because of personal obligations. Tasks often are accomplished *because* of personal relationships, not in spite of them. International students and business personnel observe that U.S. Americans seem too tied to their schedules; they suggest that U.S. Americans do not care enough about relationships and often sacrifice time with friends and family to complete tasks and keep appointments.

Silence   Cultural groups may vary in the degree of emphasis placed on silence, which can be as meaningful as language (Acheson, 2007). One of our students recalls his childhood:

> *I always learned while growing up that silence was the worst punishment ever. For example, if the house chore stated clearly that I needed to take the garbage out, and I had not done so, then my mother would not say a word to me. And I would know right away that I had forgotten to do something.*

In most U.S. American contexts, silence is not highly valued. Particularly in developing relationships, silence communicates awkwardness and can make people feel uncomfortable. According to scholar William B. Gudykunst's (1985, 2005) uncertainty reduction theory, the main reason for communicating verbally in initial interactions is to reduce uncertainty. In U.S. American contexts, people employ active uncertainty reduction strategies, such as asking questions. However, in many other cultural contexts, people reduce uncertainty using more passive strategies—for example, remaining silent, observing, or perhaps asking a third party about someone's behavior.

In many communities silence is not simply associated with uncertainty. Silence also is associated with social situations in which a known and unequal distribution of power exists among participants (Braithwaite, 1990).

Recently, scholar Covarrubias (2007) points out that some of the early investigations of silence in American Indian communities did not fully value the communicative importance of silence in these and other cultures. She now encourages communication scholars to rethink the way they view silence, to see it not "as an absence, but, rather, as a fullness of opportunity for being and learning" (p. 270) and perhaps ask what American Indian perspectives can contribute to our knowledge of communication, "particularly to the much underengaged and much needed inquiry into the worlds humans create within silence?" (p. 271)

Recent research has found similar patterns in other cultures. For example, researchers have described the *Asaillinen* (matter-of-fact) verbal style among

> *Giving gifts seems to be a universal way to please someone, if the gift is appropriate. One colleague of mine, Nishehs, once tried to impress our boss, Joe. Nishehs brought a well-wrapped gift to Joe when they first met with each other in person. Joe was indeed pleased as he received the gift from Nishehs, but his smile faded away quickly right after he opened the gift. Joe questioned Nishehs angrily, "Why is it green?" Shocked and speechless, Nishehs murmured, "What's wrong with a green hat?"*
>
> *The miscommunication resulted from the cultural differences between them. Nishehs is an Indian, whereas Joe is Chinese. For the Chinese, a green hat means one's wife is having an extramarital affair.*
> —Chris

Finnish people that involves a distrust of talkativeness as "slickness" and a sign of unreliability (Carbaugh & Berry, 2001; Sajavaara & Lehtonen, 1997). Silence, for Finns, reflects thoughtfulness, appropriate consideration, and intelligence, particularly in public discourse or in educational settings like a classroom. In an ethnographic study investigating this communication pattern, Wilkins (2005) reports two excerpts from interviews that illustrate this pattern—one interview with a Finnish student and one with an American student:

Excerpt 1

Finnish Student: I have been to America.

Wilkins: Can you tell me what the experience was like?

Student: The people and the country were very nice.

Wilkins: Did you learn anything?

Student: No.

Wilkins: Why not?

Student: Americans just talk all the time.

Excerpt 2

Wilkins: Do you like Finland?

American Student: Oh yes, I like it a lot.

Wilkins: How about the people?

Student: Sure, Finns are very nice.

Wilkins: How long have you been at the university?

Student: About nine months already.

Wilkins: Oh, have you learned anything?

Student: No, not really.

Wilkins: Why not?

Student: Finns do not say anything in class.

In addition to a positive view of silence, nonverbal facial expressions in the *Asaillinen* style tend to be rather fixed—and expressionless. The American student, of course, did not have the cultural knowledge to understand what can be accomplished by thoughtful activity and silence.

Other scholars have reported similar distrust of talk in Japanese and Chinese cultures influenced by Confucianism and Taoism. Confucius rejected eloquent speaking and instead advocated hesitancy and humble talk in his philosophy of the ideal person (Chang, 1997; Kim, 2001). As one of our Taiwanese students told us, "In America, sometimes students talk about half the class time. Compared to my classes in Taiwan, if a student asked too many questions or expressed his/her opinions that much, we would say that he or she is a show-off."

In a recent review of scholarly research on silence, communication scholar Kris Acheson (2007) acknowledges that silence in the United States has often been associated with negative, unhealthy relationships, or with disempowerment, for example, when women and/or minorities feel their voices are not heard. However, she tells us that increasingly U.S. Americans recognize the positive and sometimes powerful uses of silences in certain contexts. For example, nurses and doctors are encouraged to honor silent patients and learn to employ silence in their ethical care; young people are advised to seek out silence in their lives for the sake of health and sanity, to even noiseproof their homes in an attempt to boost health. In business contexts, sometimes keeping quiet is the best strategy and talking too much can kill a business deal. In education, teachers can create a space for understanding rather than counterarguments by asking for silent reflection after comments or performances. Finally, she admits that in some contexts, like politics and law, silence is still seen as completely negative; for example, pleading the Fifth equates silence with guilt, and silence by politicians is often viewed as too much secrecy.

Stereotype, Prejudice, and Discrimination

As noted previously, one of the problems with identifying cultural variations in nonverbal codes is that it is tempting to overgeneralize these variations and stereotype people. For example, researchers in the early 1970s identified certain nonverbal behaviors associated with African Americans—"getting and giving skin," the ritualistic handshakes (Black Power handshake), the stance and strutting walk of pimps and "players," and the "Afro-style" hairdo (Cook, 1972; Kochman, 1972). Since then, these nonverbal behaviors have been used to stereotype all blacks—still seen in pop culture images on television and film. However, a recent study showed that black students acknowledged a few of the behaviors, not as described 40 years ago and always context-dependent. That is, there are still some ritualistic handshakes and touching [e.g., the "pound" or "brother-man hug" (gripping right hands and pulling other into half-embrace)]—but not carried out with intensity or high frequency. They acknowledged that they sometimes strutted (males) or "walked sexy" (females)—but the walks and posture were always context-dependent. Choice of grooming style was now not so much about showing a connection to Africa but more of an individual expression (Green & Stewart, 2011).

In any case, we would be wise to be careful about generalizations. Cultural variations are tentative guidelines that we can use in intercultural interaction. They should serve as examples, to help us understand that there is a great deal of variation in nonverbal behavior. Even if we can't anticipate how other people's behavior may differ from our own, we can be flexible when we do encounter differences in how close someone stands or how she or he uses eye contact or conceptualizes time.

While explicit racial slurs are less common today, a series of recent studies showed that bias (both negative and positive) is demonstrated through subtle facial expressions and body language in popular television programs. They also showed that the more viewers watched shows that had pro-white nonverbal bias, the more biased viewers became—even though they could not consciously identify the biased behaviors they had seen in the programs. Overall, the findings suggest that these "hidden" patterns of biased nonverbal behavior influence bias among viewers (Weisbuch, Pauker, & Ambady, 2009). These same researchers conducted similar studies regarding nonverbal biases toward slim women (see Point of View, p. 292).

Prejudice is often based on nonverbal aspects of behavior. That is, the negative prejudgment is triggered by physical appearance or behavior. For example, prejudice is sometimes expressed toward Muslim women who wear the hijab, or toward men from the Middle East or South Asia wearing turbans, or even toward people who appear to belong to a particular ethnic group. The following news report of violence toward two Mexican nationals, attacked because of their skin color, underscores the importance of physical appearance in prejudice. One victim, attacked by assailants yelling "white power," was

> *surrounded by five men who punched and kicked him in the face, putting boots to him, while he was being held down—to the point of unconsciousness. Another man who came to his aid was similarly attacked. (Burack, 2011)*

As in many instances of hate crimes, the victim's appearance was more significant than his specific cultural heritage. From these kinds of experiences with prejudice, victims can often spot prejudicial behavior and people with surprising accuracy. In an interesting study, blacks were able to detect prejudiced people (identified previously by objective survey measurement) after only 20 seconds of observation, with much higher accuracy than whites (Richeson & Shelton, 2005). Victims may also then develop imaginary "maps" that tell them where they belong and where they are likely to be rejected. They may even start to avoid places and situations in which they do not feel welcome (Marsiglia & Hecht, 1998). Can you identify places you've been where you or others were not welcome?

Stereotyping or prejudice can lead to overt nonverbal actions to exclude, avoid, or distance and are called **discrimination.** Discrimination may be based on race (racism), gender (sexism), or any of the other identities discussed in Chapter 5. It may range from subtle, nonverbal behavior such as lack of eye contact or exclusion from a conversation, to verbal insults and exclusion from

discrimination
Behaviors resulting from stereotypes or prejudice that cause some people to be denied equal participation or rights based on cultural-group membership, such as race.

POINT *of* VIEW

UNSPOKEN CULTURAL INFLUENCE: EXPOSURE TO AND INFLUENCE OF NONVERBAL BIAS

Researcher Max Weisbuch and his colleagues hypothesized that nonverbal behavior plays a subtle but powerful role in communicating and perpetuating positive and negative bias. One set of studies looked at positive nonverbal bias toward slim women.

STUDY 1

The first study examined nonverbal bias, especially toward slim women. They selected 18 popular national television programs, and took clips of interactions where there were a range of slim and heavy women. They eliminated the slim or heavy character in each clip and the audio—so all that could be seen were the nonverbal reactions of other characters to the "target" female character.

These clips were shown to judges (people who had not seen the show, so they wouldn't have preexisting knowledge of the characters). The judges then rated the degree to which other characters demonstrated positive nonverbal behaviors toward the unseen female characters.

Results: The results showed that slim female characters elicited more favorable nonverbal responses than did heavier female characters.

STUDY 2

The second study investigated whether exposure to nonverbal slimness bias *influenced* women's general attitudes about ideal body image and their own body ideals. The researchers created two sets of video clips from study 1 materials. One set had clips of female characters with pro-slim bias and the second set had pro-heavy nonverbal bias. But characters were equivalent on all other characteristics—average body size, ethnicity, intelligence, character kindness, sociability. Female participants then viewed one of these two sets of clips and later answered questions about their attitudes toward ideal body size and their own body size.

Results: Young women who viewed clips showing nonverbal pro-slim bias (favoring slim women) (a) judged slim female bodies as especially attractive and (b) desired a slimmer body size. These rather strong effects occurred despite the fact that the clips contained nonverbal bias that was inaccessible to conscious awareness.

STUDY 3

The third study examined the extent to which individual differences in media exposure to nonverbal bias could account for body-related attitudes, beliefs, and

jobs or other economic opportunities, to physical violence and systematic exclusion. To see how exclusion and avoidance can be subtle, consider all the communication choices people can make that affect whether other people feel welcome or valued or like outsiders who don't belong (Johnson, 2006):

- Whether we look at people when we talk with them

behavior. Researchers asked women to complete a survey asking about their favorite television shows and various attitudes.

Results: Women who saw more television shows with pro-slim nonverbal bias also (1) desired smaller body size, (2) demonstrated a prejudice against fat people, and (3) indicated a fear of becoming fat.

STUDY 4

The final study investigated whether exposure to nonverbal pro-slim bias influenced actual behavior—especially, dieting behavior. Here, the researchers compared the regional patterns in television viewing, determining the nonverbal bias of television shows in each region of the country. They also looked at the results of a national survey, distributed by the Centers for Disease Control (CDC), which asked questions about dieting behavior. They then compared these two sets of data to see if there was a relationship between watching pro-slim television shows and dieting behaviors.

Results: People in regions of the country with high pro-slim nonverbal bias in TV programming also tended to have higher unhealthy dieting behavior. They also controlled for overweight women, to make sure that relationships were not influenced by regional differences in body size.

SUMMARY

To summarize, these studies show

1. Millions of young women are regularly exposed to nonverbal bias.

2. This nonverbal bias can cause young women to have especially slim body ideals and to attribute such ideals to others.

3. Nonverbal bias can account for substantial variance in young women's body-related beliefs, attitudes, and behavior.

4. Widespread exposure to nonverbal bias can partially account for regional trends in unhealthy dieting behavior.

For these reasons, the researchers argue that nonverbal bias—at least with regard to one type of social characteristic—is likely to play an important role in the formation of culturally shared beliefs, attitudes, and behavior.

Source: M. Weisbuch & N. Ambady, "Unspoken Cultural Influence: Exposure to and Influence of Nonverbal Bias," *Journal of Personality and Social Psychology*, 96(6), (2009) 1104–1119.

- Whether we smile at people when they walk into the room or stare as if to say "What are you doing?" or stop the conversation with a hush they have to wade through to be included in the smallest way

- Whether we listen and respond to what people say, or drift away to someone or something else; whether we talk about things they know about, or stick to what's peculiar to the "in-group"

- Whether we acknowledge people's presence, or make them wait as if they weren't there; whether we avoid touching their skin when giving or taking something; how closely we watch them to see what they're up to
- Whether we avoid someone walking down the street, giving them a wide berth when we pass or even cross to the other side
- Whether we share with new colleagues the informal rules that you have to know to succeed, belong, or get along—or turn the conversation to something light and superficial when they're around
- Whether we invite people to our home or out for a drink and talk

Discrimination may be interpersonal, collective, or institutional. In recent years, interpersonal racism has become not only more subtle and indirect but also more persistent. Equally persistent is institutionalized or collective discrimination whereby individuals are systematically denied equal participation in society or equal access to rights in informal and formal ways (Maluso, 1995).

A study by the U.S. Justice Department found that black, Latino/a, and white motorists are equally likely to pulled over by police, but blacks and Latinos are much more likely to be searched, handcuffed, arrested, and subjected to force or the threat of it. Handcuffs were used on a higher percentage of black (6.4%) and Latino/a motorists (5.6%) than white (2%). Also, blacks (2.7%) and Latinos (2.4%) were far more likely than whites (0.8%) to report that police used force or the threat of force (Sniffen, 2005).

Semiotics and Nonverbal Communication

semiotics The analysis of the nature of and relationship between signs.

semiosis The process of producing meaning.

signs In semiotics, the meanings that emerge from the combination of the signifiers and signifieds.

signifiers In semiotics, the culturally constructed arbitrary words or symbols that people use to refer to something else.

signified In semiotics, anything that is expressed in arbitrary words or signifiers.

The study of **semiotics,** or semiology, offers a useful approach to examining how different signs communicate meaning. While semiotics is often used for analyzing language/discourse, we find it more useful in analyzing nonverbals and cultural spaces. A particularly useful framework comes from literary critic Roland Barthes (1980). In his system, **semiosis** is the production of meaning and is constructed through the interpretation of **signs**—the combination of signifiers and signified. **Signifiers** are the culturally constructed arbitrary words or symbols we use to refer to something else, the **signified.** For example, the word *man* is a signifier that refers to the signified, an adult male human being.

Obviously, *man* is a general signifier that does not refer to any particular man. The relationship between this signifier and the sign (the meaning) depends on how the signifier is used (for example, as in the sentence, "There is a man sitting in the first chair on the left.") or on our general sense of what *man* means. The difference between the signifier *man* and the sign rests on the difference between the word *man* and the meaning of that word. At its most basic level, *man* means an adult human male, but the semiotic process does not end there. *Man* carries many other layers of meaning. *Man* may or may not refer to any particular adult male, but it provides a concept that you can use to construct particular meanings based on the way the sign *man* functions. What does *man* mean when someone says, "Act like a real man!"

A close friend I used to have in high school was very intelligent. He took honors classes and did great in school. He was Hispanic and dressed more or less like a "cholo," with baggy pants and long shirts. When he went to speak with his counselor upon entering university, the counselor came to the conclusion that my friend was going to take easy classes rather than honors classes. His mother, who had accompanied him to the advising meeting, couldn't believe what the counselor was saying! My friend's appearance obviously caused the counselor to come to a conclusion about who and what type of person my friend was.
—Adriana

What do you have in mind when you think of the term *man?* How do you know when to use this signifier (and when not to use it) to communicate to others? Think of all of the adult males you know. How do they "fit" under this signifier? In what ways does the signifier reign over their behaviors, both verbal and nonverbal, to communicate particular ideas about them? We are not so much interested in the discrete, individual signifiers, but rather the ways that signifiers are combined and configured. The goal is to establish entire systems of semiosis and the ways that those systems create meaning. Semiotics allows us one way to "crack the codes" of another cultural framework.

The use of these semiotic systems relies on many codes taken from a variety of contexts and places: economic institutions, history, politics, religion, and so on. For example, when Nazi swastikas were spray-painted on Jewish graves in Lyon, France, in 1992, the message they communicated relied on semiotic systems from the past. The history of the Nazi persecution of Jews during World War II is well known: The power behind the signifier, the swastika, comes from that historical knowledge and the codes of anti-Semitism that it invokes to communicate its message. Relations from the past influence the construction and maintenance of intercultural relations in the present. Semiotics is a useful tool for examining the various ways that meaning is created in advertisements, clothing, tattoos, and other cultural artifacts. Semioticians have been attentive to the context in which the signifiers (words and symbols) are placed to understand which meanings are being communicated. For example, wearing certain kinds of clothes in specific cultural contexts may communicate unwanted messages, as shown in the Student Voices box. Or not wearing a particular artifact can also communicate meaning, as illustrated by the controversy over Senator Barack Obama's choosing not to wear a flag lapel pin (see Point of View, p. 297.) For example, in China, the color red symbolizes good luck and celebration; in India it denotes purity; however, in South Africa, red is the color of mourning. In Egypt, yellow is the color of mourning; and in Japan, yellow symbolizes courage (Kyrnin, 2008). In the United States, black clothing can hold various meanings depending on the context: In some high schools, black is considered to denote gang membership; an elegant black dress is suitable for a formal dinner event but probably has a different meaning if worn by a bride's mother at her wedding.

Yet cultural contexts are not fixed and rigid. Rather, they are dynamic and fleeting, as Marcel Proust (1981) noted in writing about Paris in *Remembrance of Things Past:*

> *The reality that I had known no longer existed. It sufficed that Mme Swann did not appear, in the same attire and at the same moment, for the whole avenue to be altered. The places we have known do not belong only to the world of space on which we map them for our own convenience. None of them was ever more than a thin slice, held between the contiguous impressions that composed our life at that time; the memory of a particular image is but regret for a particular moment; and houses, roads, avenues are as fugitive, alas, as the years. (p. 462)*

As this excerpt shows, there is no "real" Paris. The city has different meanings at different times for different people, and for different reasons. For example, executives of multinational corporations moving into Paris see the city quite differently from immigrants arriving in Paris for personal reasons. Remember the tremendous unrest in the suburbs of Paris in the fall of 2005? Therefore, to think about cultural contexts as dynamic means that we must often think about how they change and in whose interests they change.

DEFINING CULTURAL SPACE

At the beginning of this book, we provided some background information about where we grew up. Our individual histories are important in understanding our identities. As writer John Preston (1991) explains, "Where we come from is important to who we are" (p. xi). There is nothing in the rolling hills of Delaware and Pennsylvania or the red clay of Georgia that biologically determined who Judith and Tom are. However, our identities are constructed, in part, in relation to the cultural milieu of the Mid-Atlantic region or the South. Each region has its own histories and ways of life that help us understand who we are. Our decision to tell you where we come from was meant to communicate something about who we think we are. So, although we can identify precisely the borders that mark out these spaces and make them real, or material, the spaces also are cultural in the ways that we imagine them to be.

The discourses that construct the meanings of cultural spaces are dynamic and ever changing. For example, the Delaware that Judith left behind and the Georgia that Tom left behind are not characterized by the same discourses that construct those places now. In addition, the relationship between those cultural spaces and our identities is negotiated in complex ways. For example, both of us participated in other, overlapping cultural spaces that influenced how we think about who we are. Thus, just because someone is from, say, Rhode Island or Samoa or India does not mean that his or her identity and communication practices are reducible to the history of those cultural spaces.

What is the communicative (discursive) relationship between cultural spaces and intercultural communication? Recall that we define cultural space as

OBAMA'S LAPELS

In a television interview in fall 2007, presidential candidate Barack Obama was asked why he wasn't wearing an American flag lapel pin worn by many politicians. Some in the audience felt that wearing a flag pin is a sign of patriotism and shows visible support for the United States in a time of war—a prerequisite for being a viable candidate for the office of the president of the United States.

> *"The truth is that right after 9/11 I had a pin," Mr. Obama replied. "Shortly after 9/11, particularly because as we're talking about the Iraq war, that became a substitute for, I think, true patriotism, which is speaking out on issues that are of importance to our national security. I decided I won't wear that pin on my chest," he added. "Instead I'm gonna' try to tell the American people what I believe what will make this country great and hopefully that will be a testimony to my patriotism. . . . My attitude is that I'm less concerned about what you're wearing on your lapel than what's in your heart. And you show your patriotism by how you treat your fellow Americans, especially those who served."*

Source: J. Zeleny (2007, October 4), "Obama's Lapels," *The New York Times*. Retrieved March 21, 2008, from http://thecaucus.blogs.nytimes.com/2007/10/04/obamas-lapels/.

the particular configuration of the communication (discourse) that constructs meanings of various places. This may seem like an unwieldy definition, but it underscores the complexity of cultural spaces. A cultural space is not simply a particular location that has culturally constructed meanings. It can also be a metaphorical place from which we communicate. We can speak from a number of social locations, marked on the "map of society," that give added meaning to our communication. Thus, we may speak as parents, children, colleagues, siblings, customers, Nebraskans, and a myriad of other "places." All of these are cultural spaces.

Cultural Identity and Cultural Space

Home   Cultural spaces influence how we think about ourselves and others. One of the earliest cultural spaces we experience is our home. As noted previously, nonverbal communication often involves issues of status. The home is no exception. As English professor Paul Fussell (1983) notes, "Approaching any house, one is bombarded with class signals" (p. 82). Fussell highlights the semiotic system of social class in the American home—from the way the lawn is maintained, to the kind of furniture within the home, to the way the television is situated. These signs of social class are not always so obvious from all class positions, but we often recognize the signs.

Even if our home does not reflect the social class to which we aspire, it may be a place of identification. We often model our own lives on the patterns from our childhood homes. Although this is not always the case, the home can be a place of safety and security. African American writer bell hooks (1990) remembers:

> When I was a young girl the journey across town to my grandmother's house was one of the most intriguing experiences. . . . I remember this journey not just because of the stories I would hear. It was a movement away from the segregated blackness of our community into a poor white neighborhood [where] we would have to pass that terrifying whiteness—those white faces on porches staring down on us with hate. . . . Oh! that feeling of safety, of arrival, of homecoming when we finally reached the edges of her yard. (p. 41)

Home, of course, is not the same as the physical location it occupies or the building (the house) at that location. Home is variously defined in terms of specific addresses, cities, states, regions, and even nations. Although we might have historical ties to a particular place, not everyone has the same relationship between those places and their own identities. Indeed, the relationship between place and cultural identity varies. Writer Steven Saylor (1991) explains,

> Texas is a long way, on the map and otherwise, from San Francisco. "Steven," said my mother once, "you live in another country out there." She was right, and what I feel when I fly from California to Texas must be what an expatriate from any country feels returning to his childhood home. . . . Texas is home, but Texas is also a country whose citizenship I voluntarily renounced. (p. 119)

The discourses surrounding Texas and giving meaning to Texas no longer "fit" Saylor's sense of who he is or wants to be. We all negotiate various relationships to the cultural meanings attached to the particular places or spaces we inhabit. Consider writer Harlan Greene's (1991) relationship to his hometown in South Carolina:

> Now that I no longer live there, I often think longingly of my hometown of Charleston. My heart beats faster and color rushes to my cheek whenever I hear someone mentioning her; I lean over and listen, for even hearing the name casts a spell. Mirages rise up, and I am as overcome and drenched in images as a runner just come from running. I see the steeples, the streets, the lush setting. (p. 55)

Despite his attachment to Charleston, Greene does not believe that Charleston feels the same way toward him. He explains, "But I still think of Charleston; I return to her often and always will. I think of her warmly. I claim her now, even though I know she will never claim me" (p. 67).

The complex relationships we have between various places and our identities resist simplistic reduction. These three writers—hooks, Saylor, and Greene—have negotiated different sentiments toward "home." In doing so, each demonstrates the complex dialectical tensions that exist between identity and location.

Neighborhood   One significant type of cultural space that emerged in U.S. cities in the latter 19th and early 20th centuries was the ethnic or racial neighborhood. (See Figure 7-4.) Historical studies show, however, that the ethnic neighborhoods of the European immigrants were rarely inhabited by only

FIGURE 7-4 Many cities abound with multiple cultural spaces. In this photo, several different cultural contexts are adjacent and emphasize the increasing significance of multiculturalism. How would people in this urban place experience cultural spaces differently from people who live in less diverse cultural spaces? How might it influence their intercultural communication patterns? (© *Robert Brenner/PhotoEdit, Inc.*)

one ethnic group, despite memories to the contrary. According to labor historian D. R. Roediger (2005), even the heart of Little Italy in Chicago was 47% non-Italian, and "No single side of even one square block in the street between 1890 and 1930 was found to be 100 percent Italian. . . . The percentage of Russians, Czechs, Italians and Poles living in segregated neighborhoods ranged from 37 percent to 61 percent" (p. 164). However, this type of real segregation was reserved for the African Americans—where 93 percent of African Americans lived in ghettos. By law and custom, and under different political pressures, some cities developed segregated neighborhoods. Malcolm X (Malcolm X & Haley, 1964), in his autobiography, tells of the strict laws that governed where his family could live after their house burned down:

> *My father prevailed on some friends to clothe and house us temporarily; then he moved us into another house on the outskirts of East Lansing. In those days Negroes weren't allowed after dark in East Lansing proper. There's where Michigan State University is located; I related all of this to an audience of students when I spoke there in January, 1963. . . . I told them how East Lansing harassed us so much that we had to move again, this time two miles out of town, into the country. (pp. 3–4)*

The legacy of "white-only" areas pervades the history of the United States and the development of its cultural geography. The segregation of African

Americans was not accidental. Beginning in 1890 until the late 1960s (when fair-housing laws were passed) whites in America created thousands of whites-only towns, commonly known as "sundown towns," a reference to the signs often posted at their city limits that warned, as one did in Hawthorne, California, in the 1930s: "Nigger, Don't Let the Sun Set on YOU in Hawthorne." In fact, historian J. Loewen (2005) claims that, during that 70-year period, "probably a majority of all incorporated places [in the United States] kept out African Americans."

Neighborhoods exemplify how power influences intercultural contact. Thus, some cultural groups defined who got to live where and dictated the rules by which other groups lived. These rules were enforced through legal means and by harassment. For bell hooks and Malcolm X, the lines of segregation were clear and unmistakable.

In San Francisco, different racial politics constructed and isolated Chinatown. The boundaries that demarcated the acceptable place for Chinese and Chinese Americans to live were strictly enforced through violence:

> *The sense of being physically sealed within the boundaries of Chinatown was impressed on the few immigrants coming into the settlement by frequent stonings which occurred as they came up Washington or Clay Street from the piers. It was perpetuated by attacks of white toughs in the adjacent North Beach area and downtown around Union Square, who amused themselves by beating Chinese who came into these areas. "In those days, the boundaries were from Kearny to Powell, and from California to Broadway. If you ever passed them and went out there, the white kids would throw stones at you," Wei Bat Liu told us.* (Nee & Nee, 1974, p. 60)

In contrast to Malcolm X's exclusion from East Lansing, the Chinese of San Francisco were forced to live in a marked-off territory. Yet we must be careful not to confuse the experience of Chinese in San Francisco with the experiences of all Chinese in the United States. For example, a different system developed in Savannah, Georgia, around 1900:

> *Robert Chung Chan advised his kinsmen and the other newly arrived Chinese to live apart from each other. He understood the distrust of Chinatowns that Caucasians felt in San Francisco and New York. . . . Robert Chung Chan, probably more than anyone else, prevented a Chinatown from developing in Savannah.* (Pruden, 1990, p. 25)

Nor should we assume that vast migrations of Chinese necessarily led to the development of Chinatowns in other cities around the world. The settlement of Chinese immigrants in the 13th Arrondissement of Paris, for example, reflects a completely different intersection between cultures: "There is no American-style Chinatown [*Il n'y a pas de Chinatown à la américaine*]" in Paris (Costa-Lascoux & Yu-Sion, 1995, p. 197).

Within the context of different power relations and historical forces, settlement patterns of other cultural groups created various ethnic enclaves across the U.S. landscape. For example, many small towns in the Midwest were settled by particular European groups. Thus, in Iowa, Germans settled in Amana, Dutch in Pella, and Czechs and Slovaks in Cedar Rapids. Cities, too, have their

EIGHT MILE ROAD

Sometimes called Detroit's mini Berlin Wall, sometimes called the Wailing Wall, this seemingly innocent looking wall in Joe Louis Park does little to betray its shameful past.

After World War I, some black residents of Detroit moved into a then rural and vacant area near the intersection of Wyoming and Eight Mile. In 1940, a developer sought to build homes for middle income whites in a nearby area. However, the Federal Housing Administration's policies of that era precluded their approving loans in racially mixed areas. To secure FHA approval, this developer put up a wall six feet high, one foot in width and one half mile in length, to clearly demark the white and black areas. His wall led the FHA to approve loans for his project.

Built in 1940, this wall presaged the racial divisions that have come to be symbolized by Eight Mile Road. (© *Clayton Sharrard/PhotoEdit, Inc.*)

Source: http://detroityes.com/webisodes/2002/8mile/021106-04-8mile-berlin-wall.htm.

neighborhoods, based on settlement patterns. South Philadelphia is largely Italian American, South Boston is largely Irish American, and Overtown in Miami is largely African American. Although it is no longer legal to mandate that people live in particular districts or neighborhoods based on their racial or ethnic backgrounds, the continued existence of such neighborhoods underscores their historical development and ongoing functions. This is especially true in Detroit, Michigan—the most segregated metropolitan region in the country—where the 8-mile road was made famous by the title and the location of the film starring Detroit hip-hop artist Eminem. The eight-mile, eight-lane road separates one city that is 91% white from the other that is overwhelmingly African American (Chinni, 2002). (See the Point of View box on the preceding page.) Economics, family ties, social needs, and education are some factors in the perpetuation of these cultural spaces.

Similar spaces exist in other countries as well. Remember the days of rioting and car burning that took place in the Parisian suburbs in the fall of 2005? Guillaume Parmentier, the head of the French Institute, commented on the relationship between place and human relations: "We are the victims of our architecture," he said, referring to the sterile high-rise ghettos populated by France's Muslim immigrants. They are the French equivalent of ghettos or *zones de no-droit* (lawless areas) where police do not go as a matter of policy. Instead, there are checkpoints on the perimeter of these high-rise islands, and those who live there are left to fend for themselves (Hoagland, 2005).

The relationships among identity, power, and cultural space are quite complex. Power relations influence who (or what) gets to claim who (or what), and under what conditions. Some subcultures are accepted and promoted within a particular cultural space, others are tolerated, and still others may be unacceptable. Identifying with various cultural spaces is a negotiated process that is difficult (and sometimes impossible) to predict and control. The key to understanding the relationships among culture, power, people, and cultural spaces is to think dialectically.

Regionalism   Ongoing regional and religious conflict, as well as nationalism and ethnic revival, point to the continuing struggles over who gets to define whom. Such conflicts are not new, though. In fact, some cultural spaces (such as Jerusalem) have been sites of struggle for many centuries.

regionalism Loyalty to a particular region that holds significant cultural meaning for that person.

Although regions are not always clearly marked on maps of the world, many people identify quite strongly with particular regions. **Regionalism** can be expressed in many ways, from symbolic expressions of identification to armed conflict. Within the United States, people may identify themselves or others as southerners, New Englanders, and so on. In Canada, people from Montreal might identify more strongly with the province of Quebec than with their country. Similarly, some Corsicans might feel a need to negotiate their identity with France. Sometimes people fly regional flags, wear particular kinds of clothes, celebrate regional holidays, and participate in other cultural activities to communicate their regional identification. However, regional expressions are not always simply celebratory, as the conflicts in Kosovo, Chechnya, Eritrea, Tibet, and Northern Ireland indicate.

National borders may seem straightforward, but they often conceal conflicting regional identities. To understand how intercultural communication may be affected by national borders, we must consider how history, power, identity, culture, and context come into play. Only by understanding these issues can we approach the complex process of human communication.

Changing Cultural Space

Chapter 8 discusses in greater detail the intercultural experiences of those who traverse cultural spaces and attempt to negotiate change. In this chapter, however, we want to focus on some of the driving needs of those who change cultural spaces.

Travel   We often change cultural spaces when we travel. Traveling is frequently viewed as an unimportant leisure activity, but it is more than that. In terms of intercultural communication, traveling changes cultural spaces in ways that often transform the traveler. Changing cultural spaces means changing who you are and how you interact with others. Perhaps the old saying "When in Rome, do as the Romans do" holds true today as we cross cultural spaces more frequently than ever.

On a recent trip to Belgium, Tom flew nonstop on British Airways from Phoenix to London and then on to Brussels. Because the entire flight was conducted in English, Tom did not have a sense of any transition from English to French. Unlike flying the now defunct Sabena (Belgian National Airlines) from the United States to Belgium, flying British Airways provided no cultural transition space between Arizona and Belgium. Thus, when he got off the plane in Brussels, Tom experienced a more abrupt cultural and language transition, from an English environment to a Flemish/French environment.

Do you alter your communication style when you encounter travelers who are not in their traditional cultural space? Do you assume they should interact in the ways prescribed by your cultural space? These are some of the issues that travel raises.

Migration   People also change cultural spaces when they relocate. Moving, of course, involves a different kind of change in cultural spaces than traveling. In traveling, the change is fleeting, temporary, and usually desirable; it is something that travelers seek out. However, people who migrate do not always seek out this change. For example, in recent years, many people have been forced from their strife-torn homelands in Rwanda and in Bosnia and have settled elsewhere. Many immigrants leave their homelands simply so they can survive. But they often find it difficult to adjust to the change, especially if the language and customs of the new cultural space are unfamiliar.

Even within the United States, people may have trouble adapting to new surroundings when they move. Tom remembers that when northerners moved to the South they often were unfamiliar with the custom of banks closing early on Wednesday or with the traditional New Year's Day foods of black-eyed peas and collards. Ridiculing the customs of their new cultural space simply led to further intercultural communication problems.

Postmodern Cultural Spaces

Space has become increasingly important in the negotiation of cultural and social identities, and so to culture more generally. As Leah Vande Berg (1999) explains, scholars in many areas "have noted that identity and knowledge are

This student explains her difficulty in knowing when she is in Japan as she moves through the airport and onto the airplane. How are these cultural spaces different from national borders?

Whenever I am at LAX [Los Angeles International Airport] on the way back to Japan, my sense of space gets really confused. For example, I fly into LAX from Phoenix, and as I line up at the Korean Air check-in counter, I see so many Asian-looking people (mostly Japanese and Koreans). Then, as I proceed, getting past the stores (e.g., duty-free shops) and walk farther to the departure gate, I see a lot less Americans and, eventually and practically, NOBODY but Asian-looking people (except for a very limited number of non-Asian-looking passengers on the same flight). So, when I wait at the gate, hearing Japanese around me, I get confused—"Where am I? Am I still in the U.S.? Or am I already back in Japan?" This confusion gets further heightened when I go aboard and see Japanese food served for meals and watch a Japanese film or TV program on the screen. So, to me, arriving at the Narita International Airport is not the moment of arriving in Japan. It already starts while I am in the U.S. This is just one of the many examples of postmodern cultural spaces that I have experienced in my life.
—Sakura

postmodern cultural spaces Places that are defined by cultural practices—languages spoken, identities enacted, rituals performed—and that often change as new people move in and out of these spaces.

profoundly spatial (as well as temporal), and that this condition structures meaningful embodiment and experience" (p. 249). **Postmodern cultural spaces** are places that are defined by cultural practices—languages spoken, identities enacted, rituals performed—and they often change as new people move in and out of these spaces. Imagine being in a small restaurant when a large group of people arrives, all of whom are speaking another language. How has this space changed? Whose space is it? As different people move in and out of this space, how does the cultural character change?

In his study of listening among the Blackfeet, Donal Carbaugh (1999) reports that listening is intimately connected to place as a cultural space. It is both a physical location and a cultural phenomenon. Through his cultural informant, Two Bears, Carbaugh notes that

in his oral utterance to us about "listening," in this landscape, he is commenting about a non-oral act of listening to this landscape. This nonverbal act is itself a deeply cultural form of action in which the Blackfeet persona and the physical place become intimately linked, in a particularly Blackfeet way. (p. 257)

But these places are dynamic, and "listening" is not limited to fixed locations: "Some kinds of places are apparently more appropriate for this kind of Blackfeet 'listening' than are others, although—according to Two Bears—'just about anywhere' might do" (p. 257). Physical place, in this sense, can become a cultural space in that it is infused with cultural meanings. Think about how the same physical place might have a different meaning to someone from a different cultural group.

Another set of postmodern spaces that are quite familiar are those on new media. There are MMORPGs (massively multiplayer online role-playing games), virtual worlds like *Second Life* and *Entropia*, where people meet in real time and interact primarily for recreational purposes—assuming their own or another identity. There are other new media spaces like blogs and discussion boards where people meet for fun, to gain information, or as a place to experience a supportive community (e.g., an online blog for heart patients or a blog where gay, lesbian, and transgender people can offer support and exchange useful information).

Of course, almost everyone visits social networking sites (SNSs) like Facebook or MySpace. In fact, almost 50% of U.S. Americans say they use at least one social networking site (83% of young adults aged 18 to 33), and by some accounts, they spend more time on SNSs than any other online activity (Hampton, Goulet, Rainie, & Purcell, 2011). New media spaces now offer the possibility for constant connectivity to others, and scholars wonder how this constant connection affects our relationships. We'll explore cyber relationships further in Chapter 10.

Early researchers thought that people who spent a lot of time in online communication were less socially skilled, substituting online communication for "real" face-to-face communication. Actually, as it turns out, the average user of a social networking site has more close friends and is half as likely to feel socially isolated as the average person; in addition, people who use mobile phones and instant messaging also have, on average, more friends. Further, MySpace and Twitter users are more racially diverse than users of other mainstream SNSs (Hampton et al., 2011).

The fluid and fleeting nature of cultural space stands in sharp contrast to the 18th- and 19th-century notions of space, which promoted land ownership, surveys, borders, colonies, and territories. No passport is needed to travel in the postmodern cultural space, because there are no border guards. The dynamic nature of postmodern cultural spaces underscores its response to changing cultural needs. The space exists only as long as it is needed in its present form.

Postmodern cultural spaces are both tenuous and dynamic. They are created within existing places, without following any particular guide. There is no marking off of territory, no sense of permanence or official recognition. The postmodern cultural space exists only while it is used.

The ideology of fixed spaces and categories is currently being challenged by postmodernist notions of space and location. Phoenix, for example, which became a city relatively recently, has no Chinatown, or Japantown, or Koreatown, no Irish district, or Polish neighborhood, or Italian area. Instead, people of Polish descent, for example, might live anywhere in the metropolitan area but congregate for special occasions or for specific reasons. On Sundays, the Polish Catholic Mass draws many people from throughout Phoenix. When people want to buy Polish breads and pastries, they can go to the Polish bakery and also speak Polish there. Ethnic identity is only one of several identities that these people negotiate. When they desire recognition and interaction based on their Polish heritage, they can meet that wish. When they seek other forms of

TECHNOLOGY TRENDS AMONG PEOPLE OF COLOR

A recent report by the Pew Internet & American Life Project shows that although disparities in access have been greatly reduced, there are some differences between the way ethnic minorities and whites use cultural spaces of new media. Research specialist Aaron Smith outlines three trends:

1. *The Internet and broadband population have become more diverse over the last decade, although key disparities do remain.* Specifically, African Americans have made huge gains in Internet access during the past 10 years. English speaking Latinos and Whites are very similar in the ways they access and use the Internet—Spanish speakers are much less like to access the Internet.

2. *Access to the digital world is increasingly being untethered from the desktop, and this is especially true for people of color.* Minorities and Whites have parity when it comes to owning laptops and mp3 players, but Blacks and English-speaking Latinos are more likely than Whites to own a mobile phone and they use a much wider range of phone capabilities (text message, access social networking sites, record and watch videos, etc.).

3. *Minority Internet users don't just use the social web at higher rates, their attitudes toward these tools differ as well.* Minorities access social networking sites (SNSs) like Facebook, Twitter at higher rates than Whites. They also believe, more so than Whites, that government should use social media for making government more accessible, e.g., agencies should post information and alerts on social networking sites. They are also more likely to use social media to keep informed of community events and news.

Source: "Technology trends among people of color," Pew Research Center's Internet & American Life Project, September 17, 2010. Retrieved August 30, 2011, from www.pewinternet.org/Commentary/2010/September/Technology-Trends-Among-People-of-Color.aspx.

identification, they can go to places where they can be Phoenix Suns fans, or community volunteers, and so on. Ethnic identity is neither the sole factor nor necessarily the most important one at all times in their lives.

The markers of ethnic life in Phoenix are the urban sites where people congregate when they desire ethnic cultural contact. At other times, they may frequent different locations in expressing aspects of their identities. In this sense, the postmodern urban space is dynamic and allows people to participate in the communication of identity in new ways (Drzewiecka & Nakayama, 1998).

Cultural spaces can also be metaphorical, with historically defined places serving as sources of contemporary identity negotiation in new spaces. In her study of academia, Olga Idriss Davis (1999) turns to the historical role of the kitchen in African American women's lives and uses the kitchen legacy as a way to rethink the university. She notes that "the relationship between the kitchen and the Academy [university] informs African American women's experience and historically interconnects their struggles for identity" (p. 370). In this sense, the kitchen is a metaphorical cultural space that is invoked in an entirely new place, the university. Again, this postmodern cultural space is not material but metaphoric, and it allows people to negotiate their identities in new places.

INTERNET RESOURCES

http://nonverbal.ucsc.edu/
This website provided by the University of California–Santa Cruz allows students to explore and test their ability to read and interpret nonverbal communication. The site provides videos that examine nonverbal codes, including personal space and gestures, to better understand cross-cultural communication.

www.cba.uni.edu/buscomm/nonverbal/Culture.htm
This website provided by the University of Northern Iowa outlines how nonverbal communication varies across cultures in relation to Hofstede's value dimensions.

http://webdesign.about.com/od/color/a/bl_colorculture.htm
This web page is dedicated to providing information pertaining to the color symbolism that exists throughout different cultures. Its purpose is to allow web page designers to understand how their usage of color might be interpreted by different groups and world regions. The page also provides informative links on how gender, age, class, and current trends also play a factor in the meaning of color.

SUMMARY

- Nonverbal communication differs from verbal communication in two ways: It is more unconscious and learned implicitly.
- Nonverbal communication can reinforce, substitute for, or contradict verbal communication.
- Nonverbal communication communicates relational meaning, status, and deception.
- Research investigating the universality of nonverbal behaviors includes comparison of primate behavior, behavior of deaf/blind children, cross-cultural studies, and search for universal social needs filled by nonverbal behaviors.
- Nonverbal codes include physical appearance, facial expressions, eye contact, gestures, paralanguage, chronemics, and silence.
- Sometimes cultural differences in nonverbal behaviors can lead to stereotyping of others and overt discrimination.

- Cultural space influences cultural identity and includes homes, neighborhoods, regions, and nations.
- Two ways of changing cultural spaces are travel and migration.
- Postmodern cultural spaces, like cyberspace, are tenuous and dynamic.

DISCUSSION QUESTIONS

1. How does nonverbal communication differ from verbal communication?

2. What are some of the messages that we communicate through our nonverbal behaviors?

3. Which nonverbal behaviors, if any, are universal?

4. How do our cultural spaces affect our identities?

5. What role does power play in determining our cultural spaces?

6. What is the importance of cultural spaces to intercultural communication?

7. How do postmodern cultural spaces differ from modernist notions of cultural space?

 Go to the self-quizzes on the Online Learning Center at www.mhhe.com/martinnakayama6 to further test your knowledge.

ACTIVITIES

1. *Cultural Spaces.* Think about the different cultural spaces in which you participate (clubs, churches, concerts, and so on). Select one of these spaces and describe when and how you enter and leave it. As a group, discuss the answers to the following questions:

   a. Which cultural spaces do many students share? Which are not shared by many students?

   b. Which cultural spaces, if any, are denied to some people?

   c. What factors determine whether a person has access to a specific cultural space?

2. *Nonverbal Rules.* Choose a cultural space that you are interested in studying. Visit this space on four occasions to observe how people there interact. Focus on one aspect of nonverbal communication (e.g., eye contact or proximity). List some rules that seem to govern this aspect of nonverbal communication. For example, if you are focusing on proximity, you might describe, among other things, how far apart people tend to stand when conversing. Based on your observations, list some prescriptions about proper (expected) nonverbal behavior in this cultural space. Share your conclusions with the class. To what extent do other students share your conclusions? Can we generalize about nonverbal rules in cultural spaces? What factors influence whether an individual follows unspoken rules of behavior?

KEY WORDS

chronemics (287)

contact cultures (282)

cultural space (274)

deception (277)

discrimination (291)

eye contact (285)

expectancy violations
   theory (277)

facial expressions (278)

monochronic (287)

noncontact cultures
   (283)

paralinguistics (286)

polychronic (288)

postmodern cultural
   spaces (304)

regionalism (302)

relational messages (276)

semiosis (294)

semiotics (294)

signified (294)

signifiers (294)

signs (294)

status (277)

vocalizations (287)

voice qualities
   (286)

The Online Learning Center at www.mhhe.com/martinnakayama6 features
flashcards and crossword puzzles based on these terms and concepts.

REFERENCES

Acheson, C. (2007). Silence in dispute. In C. S. Beck
   (Ed.), *Communication Yearbook 31* (pp. 2–59),
   New York: Lawrence Erlbaum Associates.

Alberts, J. K., Nakayama, T. K., & Martin, J. N.
   (2007). *Human communication in society*. Boston:
   Allyn-Bacon.

Al-Simadi, F. A. (2000). Jordanian students' beliefs
   about nonverbal behaviors associated with deception in Jordan. *Social Behavior and Personality, 28*(5),
   437–442.

Andersen, P. A., Hecht, M. L., Hoobler, G. D., &
   Smallwood, M. (2002). Nonverbal communication
   across cultures. In W. B. Gudykunst & B. Mody
   (Eds.), *Handbook of international and intercultural
   communication* (2nd ed., pp. 89–106). Thousand
   Oaks, CA: Sage.

Archer, D. (1997). Unspoken diversity: Cultural differences in gestures. *Qualitative Sociology, 20*, 79–105.

Banning the burqa a bad idea . . . whose time may soon
   come in parts of Europe. (2010, May 15). *Economist,
   395*(8682), 16–18.

Boyd, D. (2007). Why youth (heart) social network
   sites: The role of networked publics in teenage
   social life. In D. Buckingham (Ed.), *Youth, identity,
   and digital media* (MacArthur Foundation Series on
   Digital Learning). Cambridge, MA: MIT Press.

Braithwaite, C. A. (1990). Communicative silence:
   A cross-cultural study of Basso's hypothesis. In
   D. Carbaugh (Ed.), *Cultural communication and
   intercultural contact* (pp. 321–327). Hillsdale, NJ:
   Lawrence Erlbaum.

Burack, A. (2011, March 18). District Attorney
   George Gascón says hate crimes on the rise in San

Francisco. *San Francisco Examiner online*. Retrieved
   August 30, 2011, from www.sfexaminer.com/local/
   crime/2011/03/district-attorney-gasc-n-says-hate-
   crimes-rise-san-francisco.

Burgoon, J. K. (1995). Cross-cultural and intercultural
   applications of expectancy violations theory. In
   R. L. Wiseman (Ed.), *Intercultural communication
   theory* (International and Intercultural
   Communication Annual, vol. 19, pp. 194–214).
   Thousand Oaks, CA: Sage.

Carbaugh, D. (1999). "Just listen": "Listening" and
   landscape among the Blackfeet. *Western Journal of
   Communication, 63*(3), 250–270.

Carbaugh, D., & Berry, M. (2001). Communicating
   history, Finnish and American discourses:
   An ethnographic contribution to intercultural
   communication inquiry. *Communication Theory, 11*,
   352–366.

Chang, H. (1997). Language and words:
   Communication in the analects of Confucius.
   Journal of Language and Social Psychology, 16,
   107–131.

Checkpoints: Baghdad's Russian Roulette. (2007,
   September 5). Institute for War and Peace
   Reporting. Retrieved March 17, 2008, from
   www.iwpr.net/?p=icr&s=f&o=337693&
   apc_state=henficr337691.

Chinni, D. (2002, November 15). Along Detroit's
   Eight Mile Road, a stark racial split. *Christian
   Science Monitor*. Accessed at www.csmonitor
   .com/2002/1115/p01s02-ussc.htm.

Cooke, B. (1972). Nonverbal communication
   among Afro-Americans: An initial classification.

In T. Kochman (Ed.), *Rappin' and stylin' out: Communication in urban Black America* (pp. 32–64). Urbana: University of Illinois Press.

Costa-Lascoux, J., & Yu-Sion, L. (1995). *Paris-XIIIe, lumières d'Asie*. Paris: Éditions Autrement.

Covarrubias, P. (2007). (Un)Biased in Western theory: Generative silence in American Indian communication. *Communication Monographs, 74*(2), 265–271.

Croucher, S. M. (2008). French-Muslims and the hijab: An analysis of identity and the Islamic veil in France. *Journal of Intercultural Communication Research, 37*(3), 199–213.

Davis, O. I. (1999). In the kitchen: Transforming the academy through safe spaces of resistance. *Western Journal of Communication, 63*(3), 364–381.

Drzewiecka, J. A., & Nakayama, T. K. (1998). City sites: Postmodern urban space and the communication of identity. *Southern Communication Journal, 64*, 20–31.

Ekman, P. (2003). *Emotions revealed: Recognizing faces and feelings to improve communication and emotional life*. New York: Times Books.

Ekman, P. (2004, October 2). Happy, sad, angry, disgusted: Secrets of the face. *New Scientist, 184*(2467), 4–5.

Ekman, P., & Friesen, W. V. (1987). Universals and cultural differences in the judgments of facial expressions of emotion. *Journal of Personality and Social Psychology, 53*, 712–717.

Elfenbein H. A. & Ambady, N. (2002) On the universality and cultural specificity of emotion recognition: A meta-analysis. *Psychological Bulletin, 128*, 203–235.

Fattah, H. M. (2005, May 1). Why Arab men hold hands. *The New York Times*, Week in Review, 2.

Fisher, M. L. & Voracek, M. (2006). The shape of beauty: Determinants of female physical attractiveness. *Journal of Cosmetic Dermatology, 5*(2), 190–194.

Floyd, K., Ramirez, A., & Burgoon, J. K. (2008). Expectancy violations theory. In L. K. Guerrero, J. A. DeVito, & M. L. Hecht (Eds.), *The nonverbal communication reader: Classic and contemporary readings* (3rd ed., pp. 503–510). Prospect Heights, IL: Waveland.

Fussell, P. (1983). *Class*. New York: Ballantine Books.

Galati, D., Sini, B., Schmidt, S., & Tinti, C. (2003). Spontaneous facial expressions in congenitally blind and sighted children aged 8–11. *Journal of Visual Impairment and Blindness, 97*, 418–428.

Gottschall, J. (2008). The "beauty myth" is no myth. *Human Nature, 19*(2), 174–188.

Greene, H. (1991). Charleston, South Carolina. In J. Preston (Ed.), *Hometowns: Gay men write about where they belong* (pp. 55–67). New York: Dutton.

Green, D. M., & Stewart, F. R. (2011). African American students' reactions to Benjamin Cooke's "Nonverbal communication among Afro-Americans: An initial classification." *Journal of Black Studies, 42*(3), 389–401.

Gudykunst, W. B. (1985). A model of uncertainty reduction in intergroup encounters. *Journal of Language and Social Psychology, 4*, 79–98.

Gudykunst, W. B. (2005). An anxiety/uncertainty management (AUM) theory of effective communication: Making the mesh of the net finer. In W. B. Gudykunst (Ed.), *Theorizing about intercultural communication* (pp. 281–323). Thousand Oaks, CA: Sage.

Hall, E. T. (1966). *The hidden dimension*. New York: Anchor Books.

Hampton, K. N., Goulet, L. S., Rainie, L. & Purcell, K. (2011). Social networking sites and our lives. Pew Internet & American Life Project. Retrieved July 22, 2011, from www.pewinternet.org/Reports/2011/Technology-and-social-networks.aspx.

Harper, M., & Jones, T. (2005, November 23). Blackface costumes spark Stetson diversity lesson. *Daytona Beach News-Journal* online. Accessed at www.news-journalonline.com/NewsJournalOnline/News/Headlines/03NewsHEAD04112305.htm.

Henningsen, D. D., Cruz, M. G., & Morr, M. C. (2000). Pattern violations and perceptions of deception. *Communication Reports, 13*, 1–9.

Hoagland, J. (2005, November 9). French lessons. *Washington Post*, p. A31. Accessed at www.washingtonpost.com/wp-dyn/content/article/2005/11/08/AR2005110801257

hooks, b. (1990). *Yearning: Race, gender, and cultural politics*. Boston: South End Press.

Johnson, A. (2006). *Privilege, power and difference*, (2nd ed.). New York: Academic Internet Publishers.

Kim, M.-S. (2001). *Non-Western perspectives on human communication*. Thousand Oaks, CA: Sage.

Khuri, F. I. (2001). *The body in Islamic culture*. London: Saqi Books.

Kochman, T. (Ed.). (1972). *Rappin' and stylin' out: Communication in urban Black America*. Urbana: University of Illinois Press.

Kyrnin, J. Color symbolism chart by culture. Retrieved March 3, 2008, from http://webdesign.about.com/od/color/a/bl_colorculture.htm.

Loewen, J. (2005). *Sundown towns: A hidden dimension of American racism*. New York: New Press.

Malcolm X, & Haley, A. (1964). *The autobiography of Malcolm X*. New York: Grove Press.

Maluso, D. (1995). Shaking hands with a clenched fist: Interpersonal racism. In B. Lott & D. Maluso (Eds.), *The social psychology of interpersonal discrimination* (pp. 50–79). New York: Guilford.

Marsiglia, F. F., & Hecht, M. L. (1998). Personal and interpersonal interventions. In M. L. Hecht (Ed.),

Communicating prejudice (pp. 287–301). Thousand Oaks, CA: Sage.

Matsumoto, D. (2006). Culture and nonverbal behavior. In V. Manusov & M. Patterson (Eds), *The Sage handbook of nonverbal communication* (pp. 219–235). Thousand Oaks, CA: Sage.

Matsumoto, D., Olide, A., Schug, J., Willingham, B., & Callan, M. (2009). Cross-cultural judgments of spontaneous facial expressions of emotions. *Journal of Nonverbal Behavior, 33*(4), 213–238.

Montepare, J. M. (2003). Evolution and nonverbal behavior: Adaptive social interaction strategies. *Journal of Nonverbal Behavior, 27*, 141–143.

Nee, V. G., & Nee, B. D. B. (1974). *Longtime Californ': A documentary study of an American Chinatown.* Boston: Houghton Mifflin.

Norwegians confused by Bush "homs" salute. (2005, December 1). *USAToday.* Accessed at www .usatoday.com/news/washington/2005-01-21-bush-norwegians_x.htm?csp=34& POE=click-refer.

Patterson, M. L. (2003). Commentary: Evolution and nonverbal behavior: Functions and mediating processes. *Journal of Nonverbal Behavior, 27*, 201–207.

Patterson, M., Iizuka, Y., Tubbs, M., Ansel, J., Tsutsumi, M., & Anson, J. (2007). Passing encounters East and West: Comparing Japanese and American pedestrian interactions. *Journal of Nonverbal Behavior, 31*(3), 155–166.

Pollick, A. S., Jeneson, A., & de Waal, F. B. M. (2008). Gestures and multimodal signaling in bonobos. In T. Furuichi & J. Thompson (Eds.), *Bonobos: Behaviour, ecology, and conservation.* New York: Springer.

Preston, J. (1991). Introduction. In J. Preston (Ed.), *Hometowns: Gay men write about where they belong* (pp. xi–xiv). New York: Dutton.

Preuschoft, S. (2000). Primate faces and facial expressions. *Social Research, 67*, 245–271.

Proust, M. (1981). *Swann in love: Remembrance of things past* (C. K. S. Moncrieff & T. Kilmartin, Trans.). New York: Vintage.

Pruden, G. B., Jr. (1990). History of the Chinese in Savannah, Georgia. In J. Goldstein (Ed.), *Georgia's East Asian connection: Into the twenty-first century: Vol. 27. West Georgia College studies in the social sciences* (pp. 17–34). Carrollton: West Georgia College.

Ray, G. B., & Floyd, K. (2006). Nonverbal expressions of liking and disliking in initial interaction: Encoding and decoding perspectives. *Southern Communication Journal, 71*(1), 45–65.

Richeson, J., & Shelton, J. N. (2005). Brief report: Thin slices of racial bias. *Journal of Nonverbal Behavior, 29*, 75–86.

Roediger, D. R. (2005). *Working toward whiteness: How America's immigrants became white.* New York: Basic Books, 2005.

Running for cover. (2010, May 15). *Economist, 395*(8682), 66–67.

Sajavaara, K., & Lehtonen, J. (1997). The silent Finn revisited. In A. Jaworski (Ed.), *Silence: Interdisciplinary perspectives* (pp. 263–283). New York: Mouton de Gruyter.

Sauter, D. A., Eisner, F., Ekman, P., & Scott, S. K. (2010). Cross-cultural recognition of basic emotions through nonverbal emotional vocalizations. *Proceedings of the National Academy of Sciences of the United States of America, 107*(6), 2408–2412.

Saylor, S. (1991). Amethyst, Texas. In J. Preston (Ed.), *Hometowns: Gay men write about where they belong* (pp. 119–135). New York: Dutton.

Schiefenhovel, W. (1997). Universals in interpersonal interactions. In U. Segerstråle & P. Molnár (Eds.), *Nonverbal communication: Where nature meets culture* (pp. 61–79). Mahwah, NJ: Lawrence Erlbaum.

Shannon, M. L., & Stark, C. P. (2003). The influence of physical appearance on personnel selection. *Social Behavior & Personality: An International Journal, 31*(6), 613–624.

Smith, R. J., & Tyson, A. S. (2005, March 7). Shootings by U.S. at Iraq checkpoints questioned page. *Washington Post*, p. A01. Retrieved March 17, 2008, from www.washingtonpost.com/wp-dyn/articles/A12507-2005Mar6.html.

Sniffen, M. J. (2005, August 24). Race disparity seen during traffic stops. The Associated Press News Service.

Sudip, M. (2004, January 26). A hairy situation. *Newsweek*, p. 12.

Suomi, S. J. (1988). Nonverbal communication in nonhuman primates: Implications for the emergence of culture. In U. Segerstråle & P. Molnár (Eds.), *Nonverbal communication: Where nature meets culture* (pp. 131–150). Mahwah, NJ: Lawrence Erlbaum.

Swami, V., Caprario, C., & Tovée, M. J. (2006). Female physical attractiveness in Britain and Japan: A cross-cultural study. *European Journal of Personality, 20*, 69–81.

Swami, V., Smith, J., Tsiokris, A., Georgiades, C., Sangareau, Y., Tovée, M. J., & Furnham, A. (2007). Male physical attractiveness in Britain and Greece: A cross-cultural study. *Journal of Social Psychology, 147*(1), 15–26.

Swami, V., Furnham, A., Chamorro-Premuzic, T., Akbar, K., Gordon, N., Harris, T., Finch, J., & Tovée, M. J. (2010). More than just skin deep? Personality information influences men's ratings of the attractiveness of women's body sizes. *Journal of Social Psychology, 150*(6), 628–647.

Szarota, P. (2010). The mystery of the European smile: A comparison based on individual photographs provided by Internet users. *Journal of Nonverbal Behavior, 34*(4), 249–256.

Teske, J. A. (2002). Cyberpsychology, human relationships and our virtual interiors. *Zygon, 37,* 677–700.

Thompson, H. (2011, April 4). Two thirds Brits want burqa ban. *Yougov.com.* Retrieved August 5, 2011, from http://today.yougov.co.uk/life/two-thirds-brits-want-burqa-ban.

Vande Berg, L. R. (1999). An introduction to the special issue on "spaces." *Western Journal of Communication, 63*(3), 249.

Vrij, A. (2004). Why professionals fail to catch liars and how they can improve. *Legal and Criminological Psychology, 9,* 159–181.

Vrij, A., Granhag, P. A., & Mann, S. (2010). Good liars. *Journal of Psychiatry & Law, 38*(1/2), 77–98.

Watson, O. M. (1970). *Proxemic behavior: A cross cultural study.* The Hague: Mouton.

Watzlawick, P., Beavin, J. H., & Jackson, D. D. (1967). *Pragmatics of human communication.* New York: W. W. Norton.

Weisbuch, M., Ambady, N., Clarke, A. L., Achor, S., & Weele, J. V-V. (2010). On being consistent: The role of verbal–nonverbal consistency in first impressions. *Basic & Applied Social Psychology, 32*(3), 261–268.

Weisbuch, M., & Ambady, N. (2009). Unspoken cultural influence: Exposure to and influence of nonverbal bias. *Journal of Personality and Social Psychology, 96*(6), 1104–1119.

Weisbuch, M., Pauker, K., & Ambady, N. (2009, December 18). The subtle transmission of race bias via televised nonverbal behavior. *Science, 326*(5960), 1711–1714.

Wilkins, R. (2005). The optimal form: Inadequacies and excessiveness within the *Asiallinen* [matter of fact] nonverbal style in public and civic settings in Finland. *Journal of Communication, 55,* 383–401.

Yang, P. (2010). Nonverbal gender differences: Examining gestures of university-educated Mandarin Chinese speakers. *Text & Talk, 30*(3), 333–357.

Zaretsky, R. (2010, September 17). Uncovering the French ban on veils. *Chronicle of Higher Education, 57*(4), B4–B5.

PART III

Intercultural Communication Applications

UNDERSTANDING INTERCULTURAL TRANSITIONS

CHAPTER

8

CHAPTER OBJECTIVES

After reading this chapter, you should be able to:

1. Describe a dialectical approach to cultural transitions.
2. Identify four types of migrant groups.
3. Define cultural adaptation.
4. Identify three approaches to understanding cultural adaptation.
5. Identify individual characteristics that may influence how people adapt.
6. List outcomes of the adaptation process.
7. Define and describe the occurrence of culture shock.
8. Describe the reentry process and how it differs from adaptation to a host culture.
9. Describe a phenomenological approach to understanding cultural adaptation.
10. Describe how the adaptation process is influenced by contextual elements.
11. Explain how different approaches to adaptation are related to cultural identity.
12. Discuss the effect on the identity of living on the border and making multiple returns.

In Chapter 7, we discussed how we define and move through various cultural spaces. In this chapter, we look more specifically at how we move between cultural contexts. People may travel for work, study, or adventure, or in response to political or other events. Consider the following migration stories:

My name is Valdimir. At first when I emigrate[d] to the United States . . . [from Mexico] I had many struggles . . . I did not know anybody here, did not have enough money for rent, a place to live, and pay for food; I did not understand and speak English. . . . After two weeks I got a job and my life changed; I started to earn money and rented a place to live. Then I saw that it is important to learn English, and two months later I started school. (From http://www.otan.us/webfarm/emailproject/grace.htm)

My name Ashkon, and I was raised in a semi-traditional Iranian family. My parents moved here and got married when they were only twenty years old, and I'm proud to say that they are still married today. I've been to Iran twice when I was seven and eleven years old and can remember Iran quite well. I can honestly say that there is vast difference in everything from life to culture between here and Iran; however, I feel that the culture is changing and that is something that I'm very excited about.

My name is Dashawn. I studied in Australia for six months. This was the most amazing and surreal experience I have had thus far in my twenty-one years of life. I would have to say that the people of Australia stand out to me the most . . . outrageously friendly. My experience taught me that there is so much more to our world than the U.S. Traveling is the best way to learn about oneself and others.

Throughout history people have traveled across cultural boundaries for many different reasons. According to experts, there have been three great waves of global migration. The first wave was motivated by a search for resources and military conquest and lasted into the 16th century. The second, illustrated by Tamara's great-grandparents' arrival in the United States, was dominated by the European migration into poorer "empty territories" of the new world and led to the colonization of Africa, Asia, and America; it lasted until the middle of the 20th century. Valdimir's story illustrates the third and most recent wave. This wave—reversing the European colonization from the poorer countries of Asia, Africa, and South America to the richer ones in the postwar period—is more complex and multidimensional (Tehranian, 2004, p. 20).

According to the International Organization for Migration (Facts and Figures), there are an estimated 214 million immigrants worldwide, and 1 out of every 33 people in the world is a migrant. People leave their countries for many reasons, including wars and famine (Iraq, Somalia, South Sudan). In addition, millions of global nomads are roaming around the world as transnational corporate or government employees, guest workers, refugees, tourists, or study-abroad students, like Dashawn (see Figure 8-1). According to the U.S. Census Bureau, in 2009 there were an estimated 38.5 million foreign-born residents of the United States, which accounts for 12.5% of the U.S. population (Grieco and Trevelyan, 2010). And there are internal migrations—where people move from one place to another within national boundaries—often for the same reasons: for better economic opportunities or because of war or famine.

FIGURE 8-1 People have always traveled from their homelands, but with the increasing technological ease of travel, people are moving much more than ever before. Sojourners, business travelers, tourists, immigrants, and refugees have very different reasons for traveling. These people are waiting for international arrivals at the Atlanta airport. How might reasons for traveling shape intercultural experiences? (© *Jeff Greenberg/PhotoEdit, Inc.*)

Perhaps you can look at your own family and think about your migration history. Perhaps your ancestors came to the United States in the second wave, from western Europe in the 1800s, or perhaps in the third wave, from Europe, Asia, or Latin or South America. Perhaps you've had a global nomad experience of studying abroad or living abroad as an exchange student.

THINKING DIALECTICALLY ABOUT INTERCULTURAL TRANSITIONS

Understanding the process of adaptation in intercultural transitions depends on several dialectical tensions. Unfortunately, there are no easy answers. Think about how the privilege–disadvantage dialectic structures some kinds of intercultural transitions. For example, businesspeople who live abroad while working for transnational corporations often are economically privileged: They receive additional pay, housing relocation money, and so on. They also meet many people through work and can afford to travel in their new host location. In contrast, refugees often lack financial resources in their new host location, which may have been chosen out of sheer necessity. They may have few opportunities

This article discusses the joys of being a foreigner and the peril as well. This discussion refers to voluntary foreigners. How might the experience of involuntary foreigners (e.g., refugees) be different from voluntary foreigners?

For the first time in history across much of the world, to be foreign is a perfectly normal condition. It is no more distinctive than being tall, fat, or left-handed. Nobody raises an eyebrow at a Frenchman in Berlin, a Zimbabwean in London, a Russian in Paris or a Chinese in New York. . . . And, yes, no doubt many people do feel most at ease with a home and a homeland. But what about the others, who find home oppressive and foreignness liberating? . . . Foreignness was a means of escape—physical, psychological and moral. In another country you could flee easy categorization by your education, your work, your class, your family, your accent, your politics. You could reinvent yourself, if only in your own mind. You were not caught up in the mundanities of the place you inhabited, any more than you wanted to be. You did not vote for the government, its problems were not your problems. . . . Perhaps foreigners are, by their nature, hard to satisfy. A foreigner is, after all, someone who didn't like their own country enough to stay there. Even so, the complaining foreigner poses something of a logical contradiction. He complains about the country in which he finds himself, yet he is there by choice. Why doesn't he go home?

The foreigner answers that question by thinking of himself as an exile—if not in a judicial sense then in a spiritual sense. . . . He becomes even a touch jealous of the real exile. Life abroad is an adventure. . . His enjoyment of life is intensified, not undermined by the absence of a homeland. And the homeland is a place to which he could return at any time. The funny thing is, with the passage of time, something does happen to long-term foreigners which makes them more like real exiles, and they do not like it at all. The homeland which they left behind changes. The culture, the politics, and their old friends all change, die, forget them. They come to feel that they are foreigners even when visiting "home."

Source: "The others," *The Economist*, December 19, 2009, pp. 107–110.

to meet other people, travel in their new homeland, or purchase basic necessities. In this way, they may not view their new environment in the same way as a more privileged migrant. These dialectical differences shape the intercultural migrant's identity and the changes that this identity undergoes.

We might also invoke the personal–contextual dialectic. Often, in adapting to new cultural contexts, people may find themselves challenged to be culturally competent by behaving in ways that may be contradictory to their personal identities. For example, a Muslim woman may feel that she can't wear her chador in certain U.S. contexts and thus can't express her religious identity. The dialectic calls for a balance between the individual and contextual demands.

What can we learn about cultural transitions from these particular intercultural experiences? Why are some transitions easy for some people and more

As China's economy continues to grow and it becomes a destination for new immigrants, how well will other countries compete for new workers? What will the new China look like?

In the past few decades, China has undergone enormous political, economic, and demographic changes that have transformed the realities of migration to and from the country. . . . The driving force behind the recent trend of immigration to China—the world's most populous nation—has been the country's rapid economic growth, compounded by its passage through a demographic transition. The growth of the Chinese labor force is slowing drastically at a time of mounting demand for labor, and this fact has increased pressure on wages and the country's aging population. . . .

As China develops economically and ages, perhaps the greatest consequence for migration and the West will be that China will contribute to an increasing competition for labor within the global system as it, too, must seek out workers for its labor market. China, with its vibrant economy, is now clearly a major participant in the global migration system and has become an emergent destination for migration.

Source: R. Skeldon, "China: An Emerging Destination for Economic Migration," *Migration Information Source*, May 2011. Retrieved June 3, 2011, from www.migrationinformation.org/Profiles/display.cfm?ID=838.

difficult for others? Why do some people choose to adapt and others resist adaptation? What can we learn about culture and communication from these experiences?

We begin this chapter by discussing four groups of travelers (migrants), and using a dialectical approach, we describe five ways in which migrants and hosts can relate. Then we turn our attention to the individual experience of dealing with cultural adaptation and describe three social science models of adaptation: the AUM model, the transition model, and the integrated theory of communication and cultural adaptation model. Interpretive approaches follow, which focus more on in-depth analysis and description of cultural adaptation, including culture shock and the reentry shock process. Finally, employing a critical lens, we describe the contextual elements (social institutions and political, historical, and economic structures) that influence cultural adaptation.

TYPES OF MIGRANT GROUPS

A dialectical perspective requires that we examine intercultural transitions on both a personal and a contextual level (Berry, 1992). On the personal level, we can look at individual experiences of adapting to new cultural contexts. But we also can examine the larger social, historical, economic, and political contexts

TABLE 8-1 FOUR TYPES OF MIGRANT GROUPS		
Motivation for Migration	**Short-Term Duration**	**Long-Term Duration**
Voluntary	Sojourners	Immigrant
Involuntary (Forced)	Short-term refugee	Long-term refugee

in which these personal transitions occur. To understand cultural transitions, we must simultaneously consider both the individual migrant groups and the contexts in which they travel.

Migration may be long term or short term and voluntary or involuntary. A **migrant** is an individual who leaves the primary cultural contexts in which he or she was raised and moves to a new cultural context for an extended period. For instance, exchange-students' sojourns are relatively short term and voluntary, and these transitions occur within a structured sociopolitical context. In contrast, the experience of being forced to relocate because of an unstable sociopolitical context would make the sojourn a long-term one. Cultural transitions may vary in length and in degree of voluntariness. We can identify four types of migrant groups based on these criteria. (See Table 8-1.)

Voluntary Migrants

There are two groups of voluntary travelers: sojourners and immigrants. **Sojourners** are those travelers who move into new cultural contexts for a limited time and a specific purpose. They are often people who have freedom and the means to travel. This includes international students who go abroad to study and technical assistance workers, corporate personnel, and missionaries who go abroad to work for a specific period. Some domestic sojourners move from one region to another within their own country for a limited time to attend school or work (e.g., Native Americans who leave their reservations).

Another type of voluntary traveler is the **immigrant,** first discussed in Chapter 1. Families who voluntarily leave one country to settle in another exemplify this type of migrant. Although many U.S. Americans believe that most immigrants come to the United States in search of freedom, the truth is that the primary reason people come to the United States is to join other family members; two other primary reasons are for employment and to escape from war, famine, or poverty. There is often a fluid and interdependent relationship between the countries that send and those that receive immigrants. Countries like the United States welcome working immigrants, even issuing special visas and developing programs (such as the *bracero* program of the 1940s between the United States and Mexico) during times of economic prosperity. Currently, only five major countries officially welcome international migrants as permanent residents: the United States, Canada, Australia, Israel, and New Zealand. Altogether, these countries accept 1.2 million immigrants a year, a small percentage of the estimated annual global immigration—and these countries can

migrant An individual who leaves the primary cultural context in which he or she was raised and moves to a new cultural context for an extended time. (See also **immigrant** and **sojourners.**)

sojourners People who move into new cultural contexts for a limited period of time and for a specific purpose, such as for study or business.

immigrants People who come to a new country, region, or environment to settle more or less permanently.

quickly restrict immigration during economic downturns (Martin & Zürcher, 2008). However, most migrants who move to another country are not accepted as official immigrants. And because of shifts in economic and political policy, family members of migrants may be trapped in the home country, unable to join the rest of the family in the new home country.

There are two kinds of migrant labor: cheap manual labor and highly skilled intellectual labor. Newly industrializing countries need trained labor for routine and repetitive tasks, and also newly rich countries and individuals are in need of domestic services. Increasing numbers of immigrant workers are women. Because they are often more reliable than men, they are increasingly doing manual work and employed as domestics. Ehrenreich and Hochschild (2003) label this recent pattern of female migration a "worldwide gender revolution" in their book *Global Woman*. They describe how millions of women from poor countries in the south (Philippines, Sri Lanka, and India) migrate to do the "women's work" of the north (North America, Europe, and the Middle East)— work that middle- and upper-class women are no longer able or willing to do. For example, Mexican and Latin American women are the domestics for U.S. women; Asian migrant women work in British homes; North African women work in French homes; Turkish women in German homes; Filipinas work in Spain, Italy, and Greece; and Filipino, Indian, and Sri Lankan women travel to Saudi Arabia to work. Ehrenreich and Hochschild raise many issues concerning this migration, one of which is who is taking care of the nanny's children. Most of these women leave their own children to care for the children of their employer.

More and more people are moving temporarily. Overseas study options are increasing, and today some 40% of Australia's skilled migrants are drawn from the overseas student cohort, with similar trends in Canada, the United States, and Europe. A core principle of the 27 countries who belong to the European Union (EU) is "freedom of movement," meaning that an EU national may travel to another EU member state and live, study, or work on an equal basis with native-born residents. For example, a French worker who applies for a job at Volkswagen in Germany must be treated just like a German applicant and can complain if a private employer discriminates in favor of local workers (Martin & Zürcher, 2008).

Involuntary Migrants

As shown in Table 8-1, two types of migrants move involuntarily: **long-term refugees** and **short-term refugees.** According to the United Nations High Commissioner for Refugees, there were an estimated 10.4 million refugees at the end of 2009. Of those refugees, 80%, or 8.3 million, were hosted by developing countries. Most refugees are from developing countries and flee to other nearby developing countries. For example, in 2009, the highest numbers of refugees came from Afghanistan and Iraq, and the countries who hosted the largest numbers of refugees were their neighboring countries, Pakistan and Iran. In Africa, conflict between the Muslim north and the Christian south of Sudan

long-term refugees
People who are forced to relocate permanently because of war, famine, and oppression.

short-term refugees
People who are forced for a short time to move from their region or country.

POINT *of* VIEW

U.S. HIKERS IN IRAQ/IRAN

In July 2009, three U.S. American hikers in Iraq—Shane Bauer, Josh Fattal, and Sarah Shourd—were arrested when they allegedly crossed the border into Iran. The three hikers claim that, if they crossed the border into Iran, it was a mistake. Sarah Shourd was released for humanitarian reasons in September 2010. In August 2011, Bauer and Fattal were convicted of espionage and illegally entering Iran. They were sentenced to eight years in prison. They were released on September 21, 2011.

What began as a "voluntary, short-term" sojourn turned into "involuntary, long-term." The conditions under which people travel are not always under their control. This hike must be put into the larger context of U.S. relations in the Middle East, especially with Iran.

The public has also weighed in by supporting the mothers who are trying to win the release of their sons. Their activities are coordinated on the web page: www.freethehikers.org. Others have questioned why they were hiking along the Iraq/Iran border. Were they spies? Naïve privileged Americans?

The point here is that travel can be very politicized. Public opinion about immigration, migration, and refugees—as well as these hikers—should be understood as a combination of an individual's experience in the larger global, political contexts.

Sources: H. Howard, "The hikers in Iran: One year later," *The New York Times*, July 26, 2010. Retrieved August 24, 2011, from http://kristof.blogs.nytimes.com/2010/07/28/the-hikers-in-iran-one-year-later/; N. Karimi, N. (2011, August 21). "Families hope Iran will release hikers," *San Francisco Chronicle*, August 21, 2011. Retrieved August 24, 2011, from www.sfgate.com/cgi-bin/article.cgi?f=/n/a/2011/08/20/international/i063525D08.DTL.

moved refugees to Chad, Kenya, and other neighboring countries. Similarly, in Somalia and the Democratic Republic of Congo, internal conflicts have sent refugees fleeing over the last decade.

At the end of the 2009, there were an estimated 43.3 million "internally displaced people" (IDP) worldwide—people who migrate involuntarily within their own country, usually because of civil war or famine—many from the Democratic Republic of the Congo, Pakistan, and Somalia (*UNHCR Statistical Yearbook 2009*).

Most refugees, whether they have migrated domestically or internationally, want to return home as soon as possible, and an unprecedented number have done just that in the last four years—an estimated 6 million. In 2004, almost a million Afghanis and 200,000 Iraqis returned to their homes (*UNHCR Statistical Yearbook 2006*).

One of our students, Naida, describes how her family fled Bosnia to become refugees and then immigrants in the United States:

> *During the year 1992, civil war erupted in my home country, Bosnia. Overnight my life shifted from a peaceful existence to fear, persecution, and anxiety. My family and I were forcefully taken to a concentration camp, where we witnessed the blind*

rage of mankind expressed through physical and mental abuses, humiliation, destruction, rapes, and killings. Six months later, we were among the 5,000 people released. We returned home to fight for simple survival. At the age of 16, I found myself spending my days planning ways for my family to escape. My family and I were again forced from our home and experienced three years of uncertainty, fear and anger. The life we knew and had taken for granted was abruptly changed by others' political agendas. Having our basic human rights violated was the experience that literally changed my life.

Her family was eventually rescued by the International Red Cross in 1995 and transported to Phoenix, Arizona.

There are also cases of domestic refugees who are forced, for short or indefinite periods, to move within a country. Examples include the Japanese Americans sent to internment camps during World War II; the Cherokees forcibly removed in 1838 from their own nation, New Echota, to Oklahoma (the devastating Trail of Tears); and the Mormons, who fled the East and eventually settled in Utah and elsewhere in the West. Populations also relocate temporarily because of natural disasters, such as hurricanes or floods. This mass migration of refugees presents complex issues for intercultural communication, pointing to the importance of the relationship between the migrants and their host cultures.

MIGRANT–HOST RELATIONSHIPS

The relationships between immigrants and their hosts are very complex, and understanding these relationships requires a dialectical approach. International migration is usually a carefully considered individual or family decision (see Figure 8-2). The major reasons to migrate can involve economic and/or noneconomic reasons and complex push–pull (dialectical) factors. An economic migrant may be encouraged to move by a host employer recruiter—pulling him or her to migrate, or a push factor might be lack of jobs in the home country. Migrants crossing borders for noneconomic reasons may be moving to escape persecution—a push factor. One of the most important noneconomic motivations for crossing national borders is family unification—a pull factor for family migration (Martin & Zürcher, 2008). Once in the host country, the migrant may face a range of reactions from people there. For example, in Arizona and many other states, business interests depend on cheap labor provided by Mexican immigrants; the general economy also depends on dollars spent by immigrants. At the same time, citizens may fear the consequences of rising illegal immigration and the pressure on the medical, social, and educational systems. The immigrants may be simultaneously accepted and rejected, privileged and disadvantaged, and relationships may be both static and dynamic. These relationships have implications for intercultural communication.

Migrant–host relationships exist in multiple tensions: The migrants want to cherish and retain their own culture as well as value their host culture. The host culture also may be motivated to accept or reject the new migrants. When migrants value the host culture more than their own, they assimilate. When migrants value

FIGURE 8-2   Voluntary international migration can be very challenging and is usually a carefully considered individual or family decision. (© *Reuters/Corbis*)

their heritage culture more than the host, they separate. When migrants value both the host and their heritage culture, they integrate. Of course, we must also consider the reception of the host culture toward the migrants. Scholars point out that many migrant experiences do not fit neatly into one of these types—migrants may shift from one to the other depending on the context—resulting in cultural hybridity (Rosenau, 2004). Let's examine each of these relationships more closely.

Assimilation

assimilation A type of cultural adaptation in which an individual gives up his or her own cultural heritage and adopts the mainstream cultural identity. (See **cultural adaptation**.)

In an **assimilation** mode, the individual does not want to maintain an isolated cultural identity but wants to maintain relationships with other groups in the new culture. The migrant is more or less welcomed by the new cultural hosts. When this course is freely chosen by everyone, it creates the archetypal "melting pot." The central focus in assimilation is not on retaining one's cultural heritage. Many immigrant groups, particularly those from Europe, follow this mode of adapting in North America. For them, assimilating may not require adjusting to new customs. The same religions dominate, eating practices (the use of forks, knives, and spoons) are the same, and many other cultural practices (clearly originated in Europe) are already familiar. However, when the dominant group forces assimilation, especially on immigrants whose customs are different from those of the host society, it creates a "pressure cooker." This mode of relating often entails giving up or losing many aspects of the original culture, including language. One of our students, Rick, describes the process:

> *I am Mexican American and I grew up in a household where we took part in cultural events, but we never discussed why we did them. I am always asked if I know how to speak Spanish. I guess people ascribe this to my appearance. My parents speak Spanish fluently, as well as English, but they never taught my siblings or myself because they did not want us to have any problems when we entered school, as they did.*

Some people question why immigrants need to give up so much to assimilate. As one of our students said, "Why must we lose our history to fit into the American way of life? I suppose that, because race is such a sensitive issue in our country, by not discussing culture and race we feel it makes the issue less volatile." A recent study of African Americans and Hispanic Americans showed the effects of society's pressure on groups to assimilate. According to the study, the more experiences people had with ethnic or racial discrimination (on the job, in public settings, in housing, and in dealings with police), the less importance they assigned to maintaining their own cultural heritage. This suggests that heavy doses of discrimination can discourage retention of immigrants' original cultural practices (Ruggiero, Taylor, & Lambert, 1996).

Separation

There are two forms of **separation**. The first is when migrants choose to retain their original culture and avoid interaction with other groups. This is the mode followed by groups like the Amish, who came to the United States from Europe in the 18th century. They maintain their own way of life and identity and avoid prolonged contact with other groups. Many strict religious groups actively resist the influence of the dominant society. The Amish, for example, do not participate in U.S. popular culture; they don't have televisions or radios, go to movies, or read mainstream newspapers or books. An important point here is that these groups choose separation, and the dominant society respects their choice.

More recently, the 2010 census shows increasing residential segregation. Despite the overall increasing diversity of the U.S. population, "The average non-Hispanic white person continues to live in a neighborhood that looks very different from neighborhoods where the average black, Hispanic and Asian live. Average whites in metropolitan America live in a neighborhood that's 74% white" (El Nasser, 2010). As laws barring various racial or ethnic groups from living in certain areas have been struck down, the desire to live in separate neighborhoods may explain this phenomenon. Not only might the minority cultural group choose to live separately, but the dominant cultural group might also choose to live mostly among others of their group. An important point here is that these groups *choose* separation, and the dominant society respects, or accepts, their choice.

separation A type of cultural adaptation in which an individual retains his or her original culture while interacting minimally with other groups. Separation may be initiated and enforced by the dominant society, in which case it becomes segregation.

FIGURE 8-3 Harvesters Picking Lettuce. Migrant farm workers picking lettuce crop in Central Valley, California. (© *Charles Smith/CORBIS*)

segregation The policy or practice of compelling groups to live apart from each other.

However, if such separation is initiated and enforced by the dominant society, the condition constitutes a second type of separation, **segregation** (see Figure 8-3). Many cities and states in the United States historically had quite restrictive codes that dictated where members of various racial and ethnic groups could and could not live. For example, Oregon passed legislation in 1849 excluding blacks from the state; it was not repealed until 1926 (Henderson, 1999, p. 74). You may recall the excerpt in Chapter 7 from Malcolm X's autobiography in which he notes that his family could not live in East Lansing, Michigan, because it was for whites only. An example of de facto segregation is the practice of redlining, in which banks refuse loans to members of particular ethnic groups. This practice perpetuates ethnic segregation.

Native American reservations are another example of segregation: These tribes were forced to give up their ancestral lands and live on a designated parcel of land away from the rest of U.S. society. Jewish ghettos in Europe also have a long history of segregation.

Segregation is not uniquely American. Under apartheid in South Africa, racial segregation was the established legal norm. Today in Israel we find that: "Segregation of Jews and Arabs in Israel of 2010 is almost absolute. For those of us who live here, it is something we take for granted. But visitors from abroad cannot believe their eyes: segregated education, segregated businesses, separate entertainment venues, different languages, separate political parties . . . and of course, segregated housing" (Sulitzeanu, 2010). The case of Israel highlights

Does this French paradox of assimilation (erasure of differences) versus nondiscrimination (respect for differences) function in other nations? How about the United States?

One of the interesting aspects of immigration in France is that it highlights the tension between integration and anti-discrimination. Like other countries, France has at times been in the business of soliciting immigrants, but not just any immigrants. Of course, as we saw with Australia, a country can't just pick and choose its immigrants, unless it has the will and the capacity to fiercely enforce its borders against irregular migration. And so France, in recognition of this reality and with its high degree of cultural self-regard, adopted an aggressive stance on integration. Patrick Simon, the head of France's National Institute for Demographic Studies, explained that by the 2005 "integration contract," would-be immigrants were checked on "integration skills" such as knowledge of French values and norms, and linguistic proficiency. Integration was thereby not just an abstract concept or a vague policy goal: it was a selection criterion. "The idea is to produce invisibility," said Mr Simon, "invisibility so equality will be reached."

But there is an implicit contradiction between integration, says Mr Simon, and the anti-discrimination provisions France has also adopted. Integration aims to try to change immigrants, to make them the same as other French people; anti-discrimination rules are meant to change the system, to accommodate people who aren't the same. This mixed message from the state has contributed to the tensions that are apparent over, for example, whether women should be allowed to wear the burqa in public. And homogeneity is harder for some groups to achieve than others. Mr Simon said that in his research, surveys had found that although most foreign-born French people say that they feel French, fully half of the racial minorities—people from Africa, the French Caribbean, and Arabs—said that they do not feel that other people see them as French.

Source: E. G. Austin, "Immigration: The French Paradox and the British Backlash," *The Economist*, May 24, 2011. Retrieved June 3, 2011, from www.economist.com/blogs/democracyinamerica/2011/05/immigration_1.

the complexity of these terms, because there is little effort and desire to integrate on both sides. Hence, both types of separation can work together in establishing how we live.

Some people, realizing they have been excluded from the immigrant advancement version of the melting pot by legal or informal discriminatory practices, in turn promote a separate mode of relating to the host culture. They may demand group rights and recognition but not assimilation.

Integration

Integration occurs when migrants have an interest both in maintaining their original culture and language and in having daily interactions with other groups. This differs from assimilation in that it involves a greater interest in maintaining one's own cultural identity. Immigrants can resist assimilation in many ways—for example, by insisting on speaking their own language in their home. One immigrant from Ghana, Meri, describes her home:

> *English was spoken only in the presence of people who could not communicate in any of our languages (Ga or Twi). It wasn't as if my parents forbade me to speak English, but if I addressed either of them in English, the response I got was always in Ga. . . . My mother still insists upon conversing with me in Ga. When it appeared as though I was losing fluency, she became adamant and uncompromising about this; in her mind, to forget one's mother tongue was to place the final sever in the umbilical cord. I do believe that she was right, but over the years I have praised and cursed her for this. (quoted in O'Hearn, 1998, p. 102)*

Meri also describes how her family participated in other aspects of American life, such as enjoying American music: "We listened to reggae, calypso, high life, jazz and sometimes R&B. We listened to country music—Kenny Rogers and Willie Nelson" (p. 103).

Other immigrants, like Asian Indians in the United States, maintain a strong sense of their ethnic identity by celebrating Indian holidays like Navarātrī, the Hindu festival that celebrates cosmic good over evil. Communication scholar Radha Hegde (2000) describes how these kinds of celebrations

> *provide a connection and sense of affirmation to immigrants, playing an important part in the process of redefining selfhood and establishing a sense of community in the new environment. . . . To immigrants like myself, these are opportunities to enjoy being Indian and to savor the colors, clothes, tastes, and sounds of a home left behind. (p. 129)*

Migrant communities can actively resist assimilation in many ways. They may refuse to consume popular culture products (TV, radio, movies) or the fashions of the host society, often for many generations. In any case, integration depends on the openness and willingness of those in the dominant society to accept and accommodate somewhat the cultures of others. For example, an interesting debate is occurring in the multicultural city of Liverpool, England. There are currently 122 ethnic support groups, from the Afro-Caribbean lunch club to a forum for Chinese diabetics, and local state-funded "faith schools" can select students according to their religious background. However, when the town was considering "women only" nights at the local swimming pools (in deference to the religious traditions of local Muslims), city officials published guidelines to restrict using public money on projects that "might unnecessarily keep people apart." The challenge for host and immigrant groups is to find the balance of "integration," somewhere between segregation and assimilation ("The search for social glue," 2008).

Cultural Hybridity

Migrants and their family often combine these different modes of relating to the host society—at times assimilating, other times integrating, and still other times separating, forming a cultural hybridity relationship with the host culture. They may desire economic assimilation (via employment), linguistic integration (bilingualism), and social separation (marrying someone from the same group and socializing only with members of their own group), producing not the "melting pot" society where everyone was supposed to try to become the same, but rather a "salad" society, where each group retains a distinctive flavor but blends together to make up one great society. Different societies are taking different approaches. (See Point of View on the French approach to integration, p. 327.)

Many people in today's world who consider themselves the product of many cultures, not easily fitting into any of the categories, are also cultural hybrids. Consider the case of Virginia:

> *I was born in Argentina, my entire family is Argentinean, and culturally I have been raised Argentinean. Yet at age four I moved out of Argentina and only returned on vacations. I grew up in Panama until I was thirteen and then moved to California. So where does that leave me? I speak perfect English and Spanish. Physically, I can pass as Californian, Panamanian, or Argentinean. I know many people who are in my same situation. In a sense, we identify with each other. We have created our own territory, imagined, but a territory nonetheless.*

In some families, individual members choose different paths of relating to the larger culture. This can cause tensions when children want to assimilate and parents prefer a more integrative mode.

One of the more difficult aspects of adaptation involves religion. How do immigrants pass on their religious beliefs to their children in a host country with very different religious traditions? Or should they? Aporva Dave, an honors student at Brown University, was curious about this question and conducted (along with another student) a study as an honors thesis. He interviewed members of South Asian Indian families that, like his own, had immigrated to the United States. He was curious about how strictly the parents followed the Hindu religion, how strongly they wanted their children to practice Hinduism in the future, and how the children felt about following the religious practices of their parents. In general, as expected, the children had a tendency to move away from the traditional practices of Hinduism, placing more emphasis on Hindu values than on Hindu practices (e.g., prayer). Although many of the parents themselves prayed daily, most were more concerned that their children adopt the morals and values of Hinduism. The parents seemed to understand that assimilation requires a move away from strict Hindu practices. Most viewed Hinduism as a progressing, "living" religion that would change but not be lost. And many spoke of Hinduism as becoming more attractive as a religion of the future generation.

TABLE 8-2	CONTRIBUTIONS OF THREE APPROACHES TO CULTURAL ADAPTATION	
Social Science	**Interpretive**	**Critical**
Role of individual migrant characteristics and background; theories of culture shock and reentry shock; outcomes of adaptations	In-depth analysis of adaptation experience	Importance of history, politics, and societal structures in migrant adaptation and identity

However, the study also revealed that children raised in the same house could have very different attitudes toward adaptation and religion. For example, two sisters who participated in the study were raised with "moderately" religious parents who worship weekly, read religious articles, and spend much time thinking about God. One sister followed the traditions of the parents: She prays every day, spends time reading religious scriptures, and is committed to marrying a Hindi. The other sister does not practice Hinduism and places emphasis on love in making a marriage decision. These kinds of differences can sometimes make communication difficult during the adaptation process.

As individuals encounter new cultural contexts, they have to adapt to some extent. This adaptation process occurs in context, varies with each individual, and is circumscribed by relations of dominance and power in so-called host cultures. Let's look more closely at this process.

CULTURAL ADAPTATION

cultural adaptation
A process by which individuals learn the rules and customs of new cultural contexts.

Cultural adaptation is the long-term process of adjusting to and finally feeling comfortable in a new environment (Y. Y. Kim, 2001, 2005). How one adapts depends to some extent on the host environment—whether it is welcoming or hostile. There are three communication approaches to studying cultural adaptation, and they vary in the degree to which they emphasize individual or contextual/environmental influences in the adaptation process. A dialectical perspective incorporates both the individual and the contextual. As shown in Table 8-2, the social science approach emphasizes the role of personal characteristics of the migrant; the interpretive focuses on the experience of the migrant in the adaptation context; the critical explores the role of larger contexts that influence cultural adaptation: social institutions and history, politics, and economic structures.

Social Science Approach

The social science approach focuses on the individual in the adaptation process, individual characteristics and background of the migrant, and the individual outcomes of adaptation. It includes three models: the anxiety and uncertainty management (AUM) model, the transition model, and the integrative model.

No one ever asks if I belong here. People are friendly. I am rarely regarded with suspicion. The only place I get funny looks is inside the International Student office. When I moved to the U.S. from Canada, where I grew up as a working class white kid watching American TV, I felt almost no culture shock. In fact, I was shocked by the similarities. Don't get me wrong; there are many differences. It's just that no one seems to notice them.

See, until I "out" myself as Canadian, most Americans assume they know a lot about me. They assume I am just like them. They don't know that I grew up watching Mr. Dressup, that I like eating poutine, or that I crave Tim Horton's coffee (every day). They don't understand my politics, or my government's structure, or my cultural idioms or heroes. They don't know the difference between my Canada and the one they poke fun at. They don't have to, because I am the one who is supposed to assimilate. I guess I have, though I never did so consciously.

People sometimes ask me about the differences between here and Canada. It saddens me when they can't understand that the differences are simultaneously subtler and more powerful than they imagine. In the end, it's the assumption of similarity that stings the most, even as it affords me many privileges. I am invisible because many Americans assume that I have no culture of my own. That makes me feel like an alien.

—Shauan

Individual Influences on Adaptation   Many individual characteristics—including age, gender, preparation level, and expectations—can influence how well migrants adapt (Ward, 1996). But there is contradictory evidence concerning the effects of age and adaptation. On the one hand, younger people may have an easier time adapting because they are less fixed in their ideas, beliefs, and identities. Because they adapt more completely, though, they may have more trouble when they return home. On the other hand, older people may have more trouble adapting because they are less flexible. However, for that very reason, they may not change as much and so have less trouble when they move back home (Kim, 2001).

Level of preparation for the experience may influence how migrants adapt, and this may be related to expectations. Many U.S. sojourners experience more culture shock in England than in other European countries because they expect little difference between life there and life here in the United States (Weissman & Furnham, 1987). In contrast, sojourners traveling to cultures that are very different expect to experience culture shock. The research seems to show that overly positive and overly negative expectations lead to more difficulty in adaptation; apparently, positive but realistic or slightly negative expectations prior to the sojourn are best (Martin, Bradford, & Rohrlich, 1995).

uncertainty reduction
The process of lessening
uncertainty in adapting to
a new culture by seeking
information.

predictive uncertainty
A sense of uncertainty that
stems from the inability to
predict what someone will
say or do.

**explanatory
uncertainty** In the
process of cultural adap-
tation, uncertainty that
stems from the inability
to explain why people
behave as they do. (See
cultural adaptation.)

Anxiety and Uncertainty Management Model   Communication theorist William
Gudykunst (1995, 1998, 2005) stresses that the primary characteristic of relationships in intercultural adaptation is ambiguity. The goal of effective intercultural
communication can be reached by reducing anxiety and seeking information, a
process known as **uncertainty reduction.** There are several kinds of uncertainty.
Predictive uncertainty is the inability to predict what someone will say or do.
We all know how important it is to be relatively sure how people will respond to
us. **Explanatory uncertainty** is the inability to explain why people behave as they
do. In any interaction, it is important not only to predict how someone will behave
but also to explain why the person behaves in a particular way. How do we do this?
Usually, we have prior knowledge about someone, or we gather more information
about the person. One of our students, Linda, describes her interactions with a
Swedish exchange student:

> *I remember feeling very uncomfortable and unsure about how to communicate with
> her. . . . I can remember asking simple questions about her hobbies, her family, and
> why she wanted to be a foreign exchange student. Basically, I was seeking to reduce my
> own uncertainty so that I could better predict her behavior. . . . The experience was a
> very positive one.*

Migrants also may need to reduce the anxiety that is present in intercultural
contexts. Some level of anxiety is optimal during an interaction. Too little anxiety
may convey that we don't care about the person, and too much causes us to focus
only on the anxiety and not on the interaction. One student recalls her anxiety
about communicating during a visit to Italy: "Once I decided to let go of my anxiety and uncertainty, I was much better at assessing behavior and attitudes [of Ital-
ians] and thereby increasing my understanding of aspects of the Italian culture."

This model assumes that to communicate effectively we will gather information to help us reduce uncertainty and anxiety. How do we do this? The theory is
complicated; however, some general suggestions for increasing effectiveness are
useful. The theory predicts that the most effective communicators (those who are
best able to manage anxiety and predict and explain others' behaviors) (1) have
a solid self-concept and self-esteem, (2) have flexible attitudes (a tolerance for
ambiguity, empathy) and behaviors, and (3) are complex and flexible in their categorization of others (e.g., able to identify similarities and differences and avoid
stereotypes). The situation in which communication occurs is important in this
model. The most conducive environments are informal, with support from and
equal representation of different groups. Finally, this model requires that people be
open to new information and recognize alternative ways to interpret information.

Of course, these principles may operate differently according to the cultural
context; the theory predicts cultural variability. For example, people with more
individualistic orientations may stress independence in self-concepts and communities; self-esteem may become more important in interactions. Individualists also may seek similarities more in categorizing. (See also Witte, 1993.)

The Transition Model   Culture shock and adaptation have been viewed as a
normal part of human experience, as a subcategory of transition shock. Janet

In this essay, Grant Pearse, a New Zealander of mixed ethnicity, writes about his experience as a student in the United States. Note his description of conflicting feelings: simultaneously missing his home, enjoying his life in his host country, and feeling uncomfortable with the emphasis on individuality.

AN INDIVIDUAL, BUT NOT TOTALLY

Whatever the reason people come to the United States, whether it is for escape from economic, political or social unrest, or for adventure or just to experience another country, we're all faced with one thing and that is that our home culture is different from the one we experience here. . . .

I think of when my mother died in New Zealand and I went back. While standing in line at the supermarket, my mother's best friend came up to me and we embraced for about 10 minutes, just standing there in line at the supermarket, hugging and weeping. Then this friend invited me to her home for a special New Zealand meal, so that I wouldn't forget that this was my home.

In the Maori traditions, the body lies in the house, just as my mother did, with a Tongan tapa cloth draped over our sturdy coffee table, and the casket on top. Then people come and visit, bring food and gifts of money. I miss the singing, the vehemence, the subtle harmonies so unrehearsed and yet so moving as to bring change into a soul. I miss the participation at the grave site, each of the family shoveling the earth onto the coffin in the final gesture of love.

Yet I love my new home here in the United States with its beauty and excitement, but am torn by its adoration of individuality and lack of community. I believe that I am an individual but not totally, as I can never separate myself from my relationship to a family, a community, the earth and God. What I do enhances these groups, and what I fail to do, fails these groups. I can't give up the Polynesian attitude that if everyone else can't rise with me, it is not worth rising at all.

Source: C. C. Ottesen, *L.A. Stories: The Voices of Cultural Diversity* (Yarmoutri, ME: Intercultural Press, 1993), p. 39.

Bennett (1998), a communication scholar, suggests that culture shock and adaptation are just like any other "adult transition." Adult transitions include going away to college for the first time, getting married, and moving from one part of the country to another. These experiences share common characteristics and provoke the same kinds of responses.

All transition experiences involve change, including some loss and some gain, for individuals. For example, when people marry, they may lose some independence, but they gain companionship and intimacy. When international students come to the United States to study, they leave their friends and customs behind but find new friends and new ways of doing things.

flight approach
A strategy to cope with a new situation, being hesitant or withdrawn from the new environment. (Compare with **fight approach.**)

Cultural adaptation depends in part on the individual. Each person has a preferred way of dealing with new situations. Psychologists have found that most individuals prefer either a "flight" or a "fight" approach to unfamiliar situations. Each of these approaches may be more or less productive depending on the context. Migrants who prefer a **flight approach** when faced with new situations tend to hang back, get the lay of the land, and see how things work before taking the plunge and joining in. Migrants who take this approach may hesitate to speak a language until they feel they can get it right, which is not necessarily a bad thing. Taking time out from the stresses of intercultural interaction (by speaking and reading in one's native language, socializing with friends of similar background, and so on) may be appropriate. Small periods of "flight" allow migrants some needed rest from the challenges of cultural adaptation. However, getting stuck in the "flight" mode can be unproductive. For example, some U.S. students abroad spend all of their time with other American students and have little opportunity for intercultural learning.

fight approach
A trial-and-error approach to coping with a new situation. (Compare with **flight approach.**)

A second method, the **fight approach,** involves jumping in and participating. Migrants who take this approach use the trial-and-error method. They try to speak the new language, don't mind if they make mistakes, jump on a bus even when they aren't sure it's the right one, and often make cultural gaffes. For example, Bill, a U.S. exchange teacher in France, took this approach. His French was terrible, but he would speak with anyone who would talk to him. When he and his wife first arrived in their town late at night, he went to the Hôtel de Ville (City Hall) and asked for a room! His wife, Jan, was more hesitant. She would speak French only when she knew she could get the grammar right, and she would study bus schedules for hours rather than risk getting on the wrong bus or asking a stranger. Getting stuck in the "fight" mode can also be unproductive. Migrants who take this approach to the extreme tend to act on their surroundings with little flexibility and are likely to criticize the way things are done in the new culture.

Neither of these preferences for dealing with new situations is inherently right or wrong. Individual preference is a result of family, social, and cultural influences. For example, some parents encourage their children to be assertive, and others encourage their children to wait and watch in new situations. Society may encourage individuals toward one preference or the other. A third alternative is the "flex" approach, in which migrants use a combination of productive "fight" or "flight" behaviors. The idea is to "go with the flow" while keeping in mind the contextual elements. Hostile contexts (such as racism or prejudice) may encourage extreme responses, but a supportive environment (tolerance) may encourage more productive responses.

The Integrative Model   The three approaches discussed so far concentrate on the psychological feelings of migrants, on how comfortable they feel. What role does communication play in the adaptation process? For an answer, we turn to a model of adaptation developed by communication scholar Young Yun Kim (2001, 2005). Kim suggests that adaptation is a process of stress, adjustment, and growth. As individuals experience the stress of not fitting in with the environment, the natural response is to seek to adjust. This process of adjustment represents a psychic breakdown of previously held attitudes and behaviors—ones that worked in original cultural contexts. This model fits very well with our dialectical approach in its emphasis on the interconnectedness of individual and context in the adaptation process.

Adaptation occurs through communication. That is, the migrant communicates with individuals in the new environment and gradually develops new ways of thinking and behaving. In the process, the migrant achieves a new level of functioning and acquires an intercultural identity. Of course, not everyone grows in the migrant experience. Some individuals have difficulty adapting to new ways. According to the cognitive dissonance theorists of the 1950s, individuals typically have three options when confronting ideas or behaviors that do not fit with previously held attitudes: They can (1) reject the new ideas, (2) try to fit them into their existing frameworks, or (3) change their frameworks (Festinger, 1957).

Communication may have a double edge in adaptation: Migrants who communicate frequently in their new culture adapt better but also experience more culture shock. Beulah Rohrlich and Judith Martin (1991) conducted a series of studies of U.S. American students living abroad in various places in Europe. They discovered that those students who communicated the most with host culture members experienced the most culture shock. These were students who spent lots of time with their host families and friends in many different communication situations (having meals together, working on projects together, socializing, and so on). However, these same students also adapted better and felt more satisfied with their overseas experience than the students who communicated less. Along the same lines, communication scholar Stephanie Zimmerman (1995) found that international students who interacted most often with U.S. American students were better adapted than those who interacted less.

Another dimension of communication is the important role of social support. When migrants leave their home countries they are deprived of important others who endorse their sense of self. When feelings of helplessness and inadequacy arise during the cultural adaptation, **social support** from friends can play an important role in helping the newcomer reduce stress, clarify uncertainty, and increase a sense of identity and self-esteem (Adelman, 1988). However, the social support system needs to include individuals both from the home culture and from the host culture. For example, studies show that international students' relationships with host culture members and also with other international students lead to better adjustment in general (Kashima & Loh, 2006).

Dan Kealey (1996), who worked for many years with the Canadian International Development Agency, conducted studies of overseas technical assistance workers in many different countries. Kealey and his colleagues tried to understand what characterized effective workers and less effective workers. They interviewed the Canadian workers, their spouses, and their host country co-workers. They discovered that the most important characteristics in adaptation were the interpersonal communication competencies of the workers.

social support Ties with other people that play a significant part in mediating psychological health over time.

In one study, Kealey (1989) found that those who communicated more in the host country experienced a greater degree of culture shock and had more initial difficulty in adapting to the new country. These people also were rated by their host country co-workers as more successful. As with the student sojourners, for these workers, communication and adaptation seem to be a case of "no pain, no gain." Intercultural interaction may be difficult and stressful but ultimately can be highly rewarding.

Outcomes of Adaptation   Much of the early research on cultural adaptation concentrated on a single dimension. More recent research emphasizes a multidimensional view of adaptation and applies best to voluntary transitions. There are at least three aspects, or dimensions, of adaptation: (1) psychological health, (2) functional fitness, and (3) intercultural identity (Kim, 2001). Again, we must note that these specific aspects are dialectically related to the contexts to which individuals adapt.

psychological health
The state of being emotionally comfortable in a cultural context.

Part of adapting involves feeling comfortable in new cultural contexts. **Psychological health** is the most common definition of adaptation, one that concentrates on the emotional state of the individual migrant (Berry, Kim, Minde, & Mok, 1987). Obviously, the newcomer's psychological well-being will depend somewhat on members of the host society. As mentioned previously, if migrants are made to feel welcome, they will feel more comfortable faster. But if the host society sends messages that migrants don't really belong, psychological adjustment becomes much more difficult.

functional fitness The ability to function in daily life in many different contexts.

Achieving psychological health generally occurs more quickly than the second outcome, **functional fitness,** which involves being able to function in daily life in many different contexts (Ward, 1996). Some psychologists see adaptation mainly as the process of learning new ways of living and behaving (Ward, Bochner, & Furnham, 2001). That is, they view the acquisition of skills as more important than psychological well-being. They have tried to identify areas of skills that are most important for newly arrived members of a society to acquire. Specifically, newcomers to a society should learn the local rules for politeness (e.g., honesty), the rules of verbal communication style (e.g., direct, elaborate), and typical use of nonverbal communication (e.g., proxemic behavior, gestures, eye gaze, facial expressions).

Obviously, this outcome of becoming functionally fit takes much longer and also depends on the cooperation of the host society. Newcomers will become functionally fit more quickly if host members are willing to communicate and interact with them. Even so, it takes most migrants a long time to function at an optimal level in the new society.

intercultural identity
Identity based on two or more cultural frames of reference.

Another potential outcome of adaptation is the development of an **intercultural identity,** a complex concept. Social psychologist Peter Adler (1975) writes that the multicultural individual is significantly different from the person who is more culturally restricted. One student describes her change in identity after living abroad for a year:

The year I studied abroad in France was crucial to developing my identity. Not only was I interacting among French people, but I also dealt with intercultural relations among other international students and American exchange students. I developed a new identity of myself and braved a complete transformation of self. All my intercultural experiences have helped me to become a more competent and understanding person.

The multicultural person is neither a part of nor apart from the host culture; rather, this person acts situationally. But the multicultural life is fraught with pitfalls and difficulty. Multicultural people run the risk of not knowing what to believe or how to develop ethics or values. They face life with little grounding and lack the basic personal, social, and cultural guidelines that cultural identities provide.

Interpretive Approach

The interpretive approach focuses on in-depth descriptions of the adaptation process, often employing a phenomenological approach (see Table 8-2). Scholars using this approach explore the essential structures of lived experience through careful and systematic analysis of interview data and participant observation. Whereas the social science approach tends to see the adaptation experience in terms of stable categories like phases and variables like age, gender, and so on, that affect adaptation, an interpretive approach emphasizes the complex and continuous nature of cultural adaptation. To understand this process, researchers generally employ qualitative research methods—like interviewing and focus groups. There are three such interpretive models: the U-curve model, W-curve model, and phenomenological model.

U-Curve Model   Many theories describe how people adapt to new cultural environments. The pattern of adaptation varies depending on the circumstances and the migrant, but some commonalities exist. The most common theory is the **U-curve theory** of adaptation. This theory is based on research conducted by a Norwegian sociologist, Sverre Lysgaard (1955), who interviewed Norwegian students studying in the United States. He was interested in understanding the experience of cultural adaptation. His results have been confirmed by many other subsequent studies and have been applied to many different migrant groups.

The main idea is that migrants go through fairly predictable phases in adapting to a new cultural situation. They first experience excitement and anticipation, followed by a period of shock and disorientation (the bottom of the U curve); then they gradually adapt to the new cultural context. Although this framework is simplistic and does not represent every migrant's experience, most migrants experience these general phases at one time or another.

Anticipation: The first phase is the anticipation or excitement phase. When a migrant first enters a new cultural context, he or she may be excited to be in the new situation and only a little apprehensive. This was the case for Helga María, who moved from Iceland to the United States so that her mother could attend graduate school in Florida. She describes the excitement of moving to the States:

> *The travel date finally arrived. My grandma cried as we walked toward our gate at the airport, but I still felt as if we were just going on a long, fun vacation. . . . I remember how huge the supermarket was, the first time we went*

U-curve theory
A theory of cultural adaptation positing that migrants go through fairly predictable phases—excitement/anticipation, shock/disorientation, adjustment—in adapting to a new cultural situation.

buying groceries. Every aisle had more and more food and I wanted to taste all the different types of candy and cakes. Even the bread was different, so soft and it felt like a pillow.

Although moving was mostly fun for Helga María, someone adapting to a new job in a new region of the country may experience more apprehension than excitement during the first part of the transition. The same would be true for, say, an international student from East Africa who experiences prejudice in the first months at a U.S. college, or for refugees who are forced to migrate into new cultural contexts.

Culture Shock: The second phase, culture shock, happens to almost everyone in intercultural transitions. Individuals face many challenges of transition in new cultural contexts. **Culture shock** is a relatively short-term feeling of disorientation, of discomfort due to the unfamiliarity of surroundings and the lack of familiar cues in the environment. Kalvero Oberg, the anthropologist who coined the term *culture shock*, suggests it is like a disease, complete with symptoms (excessive hand washing, irritability, and so on). If it is treated properly (that is, if the migrant learns the language, makes friends, and so on), the migrant can "recover," or adapt to the new cultural situation and feel at home (Oberg, 1960).

Although most individuals experience culture shock during the period of transition to a new culture, they are less likely to experience it if they maintain separateness because culture shock presumes cultural contact. For instance, military personnel who live abroad on U.S. bases and have very little contact with members of the host society often experience little culture shock. However, in more recent military operations (e.g., Iraq and Afghanistan), soldiers are having much more contact with civilians, experiencing strong culture shock and some negative outcomes—searching homes without the presence of a male head of household and males conducting body searches of females—very inappropriate behavior in these Muslim contexts. Almost all migrants who cross cultural boundaries, whether voluntarily or not, experience culture shock. Training before encountering a new culture can help with a smoother transition. For example, incidents of disrespect by American soldiers suggest a need for cultural training and better cultural understanding, since "issues of ethnocentrism and analytical bias can affect tactical, operations, and strategic success" (Chandler 2005, p. 21). High-ranking military personnel very recently emphasized that U.S. advisors need to understand the Iraqi perspective by being trained in "general knowledge of the history of the Middle East with a specific focus on the development of Islam and Arab history—which are not the same thing . . . they need to understand the overlapping and competing spheres of influence at play in this complex culture . . . to see the informal networks behind the formal bureaucracy . . . to more effectively comprehend and influence the behavior of the Iraqi counterparts. . . ." (Allardice & Head, 2008).

For many individuals, long-term adaptation is not easy. Some people actively resist assimilation in the short term. For example, many students from Muslim

culture shock A relatively short-term feeling of disorientation and discomfort due to the lack of familiar cues in the environment.

countries, especially females, often continue to wear traditional clothing while living in the United States, thus actively resisting participating in U.S. popular culture. Others resist assimilation in the long term, as is the case with some religious groups, like the Amish and the Hutterites. Some would like to assimilate but are not welcome in the new culture, as is the case with many immigrants to the United States from Latin America. And some people adapt to some aspects of the new culture but not to others.

For Helga María, culture shock happened pretty quickly:

After a few weeks, when my school started, the heat became rather tiring. I could hardly be outside for more than five minutes without looking like I just came out of the shower. . . . I walked around from class to class feeling almost invisible. Thankfully, I could understand some of what people were saying, but not communicate back to them.

For Helga María's mother, Erla, it was even harder:

The first semester in Pensacola was one of the hardest in our lives. . . . I missed my colleagues, my work, and my family at home. I felt so ignorant, unintelligent, and old when I first started. I walked from one building to another, between classes. I kept my mouth shut, and when I tried to speak, the southern instructors often didn't understand what I was trying to say. This was awful. . . . Maybe my friends were right after all; I was being crazy and selfish. But here we were, and not about to give up.

Not everyone experiences culture shock when they move to a new place. For example, migrants who remain isolated from the new cultural context may experience minimal culture shock. As noted previously, U.S. military personnel, as well as diplomatic personnel, often live in compounds overseas where they associate mainly with other U.S. Americans and have little contact with the indigenous cultures. Similarly, spouses of international students in the United States sometimes have little contact with U.S. Americans. In contrast, corporate spouses may experience more culture shock because they often have more contact with the host culture: placing children in schools, setting up a household, shopping, and so on.

During the culture shock phase, migrants like Helga María and her family may experience disorientation and a crisis of identity. Because identities are shaped and maintained by cultural contexts, experiences in new cultural contexts often raise questions about identities. For example, Judy, an exchange teacher in Morocco, thought of herself as a nice person. Being nice was part of her identity. But when she experienced a lot of discipline problems with her students, she began to question the authenticity of her identity. When change occurs to the cultural context of an identity, the conditions of that identity also change.

Adjustment: The third phase in Lysgaard's model is adjustment, in which migrants learn the rules and customs of the new cultural context. As Erla says, "After the first semester, we started adapting pretty well. My daughters made

STRATEGIES FOR FACILITATING GROWTH

Communication scholar Shelly Smith provides the following strategies to help sojourners gain maximum benefits from long-term living, working, or studying abroad:

1. *When your cultural assumptions are challenged, try to suspend judgment until you understand the reasons for your reaction. Reactions can be emotional and intense. When it is hardest to be rational, it is important to stop, take a deep breath and figure out why you feel as you do.*

2. *Try to remember that not all values are created equal. Many differences can be accepted, embraced and enjoyed over time but others remain inviolable. . . . Being able to engage in mindfulness allows you to understand it's a personal choice . . . and OK that others embrace behaviors you cannot.*

3. *Be willing to engage the culture. Genuine interest, curiosity, and a willingness to take risks involves the possibility of making mistakes and looking foolish . . . but it's inevitable and OK.*

4. *Keep a sense of humor. The mistakes one makes will make the best stories later and if you can laugh at yourself, adjustment becomes much easier.*

5. *Be patient. Adjusting to a new culture takes time and happens in increments.*

6. *It's OK to temporarily retreat and embrace your emotions. All sojourners experience moments of anger, frustration, confusion and occasionally even contempt. It's better to take a break than explode needlessly in front of your hosts.*

7. *Remember that successful adaptation involves identity change that will affect your reentry. Take account of how you changed and what you've learned and this will help you explain your experiences to others back home, making reentry a little easier.*

Source: Adapted from S. Smith, "The Cycle of Cross-Cultural Adaptation and Reentry." In J. Martin, T. K. Nakayama, and L. A. Flores (Eds.), *Readings in Intercultural Communication* (Boston: McGraw-Hill, 2002), pp. 253–255.

new friends and so did my husband and I. I got used to studying, and started looking at it as any other job. My daughters learned how to speak English very well." Like Helga María, Erla, and the rest of their family, many migrants learn a new language, and they figure out how much of themselves to change in response to the new context. Remember Naida, the immigrant from Bosnia? After several years here in the States, she, too, has adapted. But she also acknowledges that life here still has its challenges:

> *I need to be thankful that I have a stable and peaceful life, a roof over my head, and food to eat. Unlike in some other parts of the world, here I have the opportunity to educate myself, and to make things better, and I must take advantage of it and appreciate it. I should know. I also know that I am going to experience many*

setbacks, disappointments, and emotional crises in my life, but I want to look forward, beyond that and learn.

However, this phase may be experienced very differently if the sociopolitical context is not conducive to individual adaptation. This was the experience of Maria and her sister, who migrated from Greece to Germany:

Unfortunately, I am also the victim of discrimination at the moment. I am applying for a job here in Germany, and although I have finished the German university with an excellent grade and I have the permission to work here, I always get rejected because of my nationality! All the other students from my university have already found a job, only because they are German!! The same experience I had in the UK. And I was only looking for a temporary job!! . . . I think that a cultural adaptation will only take place if we all first learn to respect one another!!

Although the U curve seems to represent the experiences of many short-term sojourners, it may be too simplistic for other types of migrants (Berry, 1992). A more accurate model represents long-term adaptation as a series of U curves. Migrants alternate between feeling relatively adjusted and experiencing culture shock; over the long term, the sense of culture shock diminishes.

W-Curve Model   When migrants return home to their original cultural contexts, the same process of adaptation occurs and may again involve culture, or reentry, shock depicted by the W-curve model (Gullahorn & Gullahorn, 1963). Sometimes this adaptation is even more difficult because it is so unexpected. Coming home, we might think, should be easy. However, students who return home from college, businesspeople who return to corporate headquarters after working abroad, and Native Americans who return to their nations all notice the difficulty of readjusting (Martin & Harrell, 2004).

Scholars refer to this process as the **W-curve theory** of adaptation because sojourners seem to experience another U curve: the anticipation of returning home, culture shock in finding that it's not exactly as expected, and then gradual adaptation (Storti, 2001). Other terms for the process of readapting to one's home culture include: *reverse culture shock*, *reentry shock*, and *repatriation*. Recall Helga María, who migrated from Iceland to Florida with her family. She returned home to Iceland for a short visit and found it was not what she expected:

W-curve theory A theory of cultural adaptation that suggests that soujourners experience another U curve upon returning home. (See **U-curve theory** and **sojourners**.)

We were all pretty excited about going back and seeing our friends and family again. We kind of expected everything to be the same, but it wasn't. My sister and I still talked English to each other. Even when I talked my own language, people said I had an American accent. I never thought that could happen. Being there, I felt more like a visitor, instead of it being my home country.

There are two fundamental differences between the first and second U curves, related to issues of personal change and expectations (Martin, 1984). In the initial curve or phase, the sojourner is fundamentally unchanged and is experiencing new cultural contexts. In the reentry phase, the sojourner has changed

Corporate management often neglects to take advantage of the skills that many returning workers have acquired in overseas assignments. Cross-cultural specialist Craig Storti identifies specific skills that these returnees can offer the home organization.

WHAT RETURNEES OFFER THEIR ORGANIZATION

Anyone who has been posted abroad comes home with some old skills greatly enhanced and some skills that are new to the organization. Management should highlight these skills and take advantage of them.

1. The returnee may have invaluable knowledge of certain regions, countries, or markets with which the company or organization does business or competes.

2. The returnee brings a different, perhaps unique perspective to issues, discussions, and problem solving.

3. The returnee is likely to be more flexible in dealing with others and more open to new ideas, more likely to try something that hasn't been tried before.

4. The returnee has increased tolerance for different ideas, behaviors, and opinions and, hence, an increased ability to work with or manage a culturally or ethnically diverse workforce.

5. The returnee is more able to compromise, to be more humble and less rigid.

6. The returnee understands the home culture better, can step outside it and observe objectively how it influences decisions and other organizational behavior.

7. The returnee has more self-confidence, having survived and prospered in a challenging environment.

Source: Craig Storti, *The Art of Coming Home* (2nd ed.) (Yarmoutri, ME: Nicolas Brealey/ Intercultural Press, 2001), p. 92.

through the adaptation process and has become a different individual. The person who returns home is not the same person who left home. Helga María's mother, Erla, describes how much she had changed as a result of her sojourn in the United States and how these changes affected her reentry to Iceland:

Surprisingly, I felt like a stranger in my own country; everything seemed so small, the streets, houses, road signs, and I saw my home city in a completely new light. And when I tried to describe all these wonderful, dreadful, amazing, beautiful, and funny things that I had experienced, it seemed like my family and friends weren't interested. Whatever bliss I might have had was quickly blown away, and

I felt that I didn't fit into my own culture. I realized that I had changed and so had my previous friends. . . . This was quite a shock for me.

International students who return home also talk about how their friends and families expect them to be a little different (more educated) but basically the same as before they went off to school (Martin, 1986). This lack of interest on the part of friends and family can be especially detrimental for corporations that send employees overseas. The home corporation often does not take advantage of the knowledge and skills that returnees have acquired during their overseas assignments. Rather, employees in the home office often expect the returnees to fit back in, as if the overseas assignment had never happened (Black & Gregersen, 1999).

Like other sojourners and migrants, the reentry for military personnel can be very stressful, even more stressful than deployment. For example, the website for reservists and their families has extensive information to facilitate the homecoming, including the importance of communication, transitional health care benefits, reemployment rights, as well as emotional issues associated with a reunion. It also acknowledges the importance of recognizing changes undergone by soldiers and their families and the need to have realistic expectations (Army reserve family programs, 2008).

Returnees also need to recognize that the cultural context of reentry is different from being overseas. Depending on how long the person was away, political figures, popular culture, family, technology, and even language may have changed. For instance, when Tom's father went to Japan for the first time, a Japanese taxi driver said to him, "I don't know where you are from, but you have been away for a long, long time." Tom's father had never been to Japan before, so the taxi driver was responding to his use of Japanese. Many words in the Japanese language have changed from the 19th century when Tom's family immigrated to the United States, but many now archaic words and structures remain in use by Japanese speakers in the United States.

Sojourners who leave their countries during times of political upheaval and return when peace is reestablished may have to contend with the ambivalence many of those who stayed have toward those who left. In this excerpt, a Lebanese woman describes her feelings toward a friend who had left during the civil war but who has now returned:

When you tried to be one of us again, the dominant expression on your face was pity, for everyone who'd stayed here. As you moved you clasped people to you, then touched their faces, then held them again, as if you were saying, "I know what you're suffering." Why were you so sure that those who stayed were the only ones suffering? (Al-Shaykh, 1995, p. 8)

Phenomenological Model   Using a **phenomenological approach,** Chen (2000) interviewed Chinese international students and described in depth how they *experienced and made sense* of the adaptation process. She describes three phases: taking things for granted, making sense of new patterns, and coming to understand new information.

phenomenological approach A research approach that seeks in-depth explanations of human experiences.

In the first phase, migrants realize that their assumptions are wrong and need to be altered. Chen describes the experiences of one of the students she interviewed, Mr. An. He was arriving in the middle of the night at his new U.S. university, but he wasn't worried. In China, student housing is always arranged for by university officials. However, in conversations on the plane with a friendly seatmate named Alice, he began to realize that his expectations of having a place to stay were probably a mistake. He was grateful when Alice offered her home. Mr. An explained, "Alice said she could put me up for the night, that I could live in her house until I found a place. . . . I was surprised but also very grateful" (Chen, 2000, p. 221).

In the second stage, migrants slowly begin to make sense of new patterns, through communication experiences. The first step in making sense for Mr. An took place the next day when he went to the International Students Office. A clerk handed him a map and told him to find his own housing. Although he had heard that people in the United States were individualistic and independent, this cultural pattern was now a living experience for him. The dorms were full, but Mr. An learned how to seek alternatives. He explained how he began to make sense of the experience: "I started to better understand the meaning of independence. I felt I really understood America and was overjoyed [to find] there was a Chinese Student Association on campus. This meant that maybe I could get help from them" (p. 224).

As migrants begin to make sense of their experiences and interactions in new cultural contexts, they come to understand them in a more holistic way. This enables them to fit the new information into a pattern of cultural understanding. Again, this happens through communication with members of the host country and others who implicitly or explicitly explain the new cultural patterns. Mr. An stayed in touch with Alice for a while, but this changed over time. He explained,

> *One day I realized I had not called Alice in a long time, then it occurred to me that she rarely called me; I was the one who usually made the calls. . . . I just didn't get around to calling her again, but now I don't feel guilty about it. She didn't seem to mind one way or the other. I've learned that many Americans are ready to help others, but never see them again afterwards. (p. 226)*

At that point, Mr. An understood the U.S. cultural emphasis on helpful intervention, and he was able to make sense of his friendship with Alice—as a momentary helping relationship. As Chen notes, "Coming to a tentative understanding is the last stage in a cycle of sense-making. . . . In the long run, however, this new perspective will never be completely fulfilled by one's accumulation of knowledge" (p. 227). As Chen points out, there are always more sense-making cycles.

In a more recent study, Kristjánsdóttir (2009) explored the adaptation experience of a group of undergraduate chemistry majors who worked in French chemistry labs during their summer break. Using a phenomenological approach, she interviewed the students several times before they left, during their sojourn in France, and after they returned to the States. Her findings reflect the embodied,

> *When I first arrived in Belgium, I watched a lot of TV. I always liked to watch TV before I left the United States, so it was a good way for me to learn French. And it was certainly a lot easier and less painful than trying to talk with Belgians. I always hated that pained look they got on their faces when I would screw up the language in my halting speech.*
> —Jesse

visceral experience of their cultural adaptation—specifically in struggles with the language, their experience of their national and ethnic identity, and their acquired knowledge.

The students described vividly their struggles with the language, how the inability to speak French made their stay in France difficult and how their inability to "read" the social context added to the stress of being misunderstood. One student said, "I feel kind of stupid." Others talked about feeling alone and isolated because no one seemed to want to interact with them. As Kristjánsdóttir describes it, "Due to the language barrier, their embodied relation to the world became problematic. Their self-esteem dropped and they became very self-conscious about themselves. Their whole bodies were entrenched in this effort of trying [to communicate] in French. For the students, it was a laborious and involved process that was connected to all aspects of themselves, being, human sensibilities, and human existence."

The students' experience of their national and ethnic identity was also important in their adaptation process and is described as an experience of feeling invisibility and visibility. Specifically, the white students found that they were often disliked just because they were from the United States—adding stress in the adaptation process. They sometimes feared to talk, knowing their accent would reveal their nationality, and so they would often choose to remain "invisible." They described the experience as a "feeling of being suffocated" because of their Americanness and then a feeling of being extremely visible and standing out when they spoke. Because of their whiteness, they experienced both invisibility and visibility.

In contrast, the students of color did not have the option of experiencing invisibility, and they described their feeling of "standing out" and being extremely visible all the time. They felt their race/ethnicity was adding another layer of stress, of not fitting in the French cultural space. Their "differentness" was apparent even before they opened their mouths to speak, although their nationality might not be entirely obvious. One African American student said, "People are going to look at you . . . they might stare, if they see me looking, and all of a sudden they stare at you all the time." This caused him to feel very uneasy, especially when he was sharing a table with someone at a restaurant or at the university cafeteria. The other students of color described similar experiences.

Having lived through the experience of being rejected enabled the white students to understand a little how it feels to belong to a minority group in the United States. The students' bodily experience of not having a voice in society and the feeling of being invisible created a new embodied relation to their Americanness. Learning about the French value system aided them in erasing stereotypes they used to have about the French people being lazy. The students' intercultural experience of living in France was eye opening; they not only learned about a new culture but, more importantly, learned about themselves as persons and their home culture of the United States.

These interpretive phenomenological studies help flesh out the social science studies—helping us understand the visceral, embodied experience of cultural adaptation, as shown in Table 8-2.

Mass media also play a role in helping sojourners and immigrants adapt. Radio, television, movies, and so on, are powerful transmitters of cultural values and readily accessible as sources of socialization for newcomers. The mass media may play an especially important role in the beginning stages of adaptation. When sojourners or immigrants first arrive, they may have limited language ability and limited social networks. Listening to the radio or watching TV may be the primary source of contact at this stage, one that avoids negative consequences of not knowing the language (Nwanko & Onwumechili, 1991).

Critical Approach: Contextual Influences

The critical approach reminds us that cultural adaptation depends on the context. Some contexts are easier to adapt to than others, and some environments are more accepting. Young Yun Kim (2001) writes about the receptivity of the host environment and the degree to which the environment welcomes newcomers. She maintains that in a country like Japan, which emphasizes homogeneity, people may be less welcoming toward outsiders than in less homogeneous settings, as in many contexts in the United States. Communication scholar Satoshi Ishii (2001) explains the ambivalent feelings of contemporary Japanese toward foreigners and traces their historical roots: "Since ancient times the Japanese have consistently held not positive–negative dichotomous feelings but the conventional welcome–nonwelcome and inclusion–exclusion ambivalence in encountering and treating . . . strangers" (p. 152). Similarly, many Muslim societies tend to be fairly closed to outsiders. In these societies, the distinction between ingroup (family and close friends) and outgroup (everyone else) is very strong.

Institutional, Political, and Class Influences   Local institutions, like schools, religious institutions, and social service agencies, can facilitate or hinder immigrants' adaptation. For example, schools can help immigrant children to adapt by offering language classes to bring them up to speed. In the United States today, there are approximately 3.5 million schoolchildren with limited English ability, and most are concentrated in a small number of schools. Some regions offer language programs; however, many are cutting their bilingual programs as part of the English-only movement. In Arizona, for example, Proposition 203 banned bilingual education and required schools to use mostly English immersion to teach children with limited English proficiency (Gonzalez, 2005). Some schools are working hard to mainstream these students, reaching out

VEIL CONFLICT

On April 11, 2011, a ban in France on wearing full-face covering veils in public places went into effect. France is the first European country to impose such a law. According to Gavin Hewitt of the BBC, "The French government says the face-covering veil undermines the basic standards required for living in a shared society and also relegates its wearers to an inferior status incompatible with French notions of equality." However, this policy has specific and complex cultural implications, as Michael Saba of CNN observes: "There is no express mandate in the Quran for women to wear a veil, and there are a wide range of differing theological positions on the issue within contemporary Islamic thought. Still, many Muslims view wearing the veil as an integral expression of their faith." On the day the ban went into effect, Muslim women gathered at Notre Dame Cathedral in Paris wearing naqibs (a face-covering veil) in protest of what they felt to be a violation of their civil rights.

Sources: A. Chrisafis, "Muslim women protest on first day of France's face veil ban," *Guardian.co.uk*, April 11, 2011, retrieved May 6, 2011, from www.guardian.co.uk/world/2011/apr/11/france-bans-burqa-and-niqab; G. Hewitt, "Women in face veils detained as France enforces ban," *BBC.com*, April 11, 2011, retrieved May 6, 2011, from www.bbc.co.uk/news/world-europe-13031397; M. Saba, "France's Islamic veil ban spurs passionate reaction worldwide," *CNN U.S.*, April 25, 2011, retrieved May 6, 2011, from http://articles.cnn.com/2011-04-25/us/defining.islam.irpt_1_head-scarves-france-s-islamic-french-ban?_s=PM:IREPORT.

to parents and community leaders to ease the students' linguistic and social adaptation (Reid, 2005). Others are leading the fight to cut such programs. In Australia, children of undocumented parents have been removed from school and placed in detention (Sedgman, 2005). Similar situations occur in the United States (Garcia, 2005). More recently, Alabama passed a strict law that requires schools to check the immigration status of students. Many parents pulled their children from schools to avoid drawing attention to them ("Alabama," 2011).

Religious institutions can also play an important role in assisting immigrants. Many churches, synagogues, and mosques delivered aid to the victims of Hurricane Katrina. Muslims in the United States have a long tradition of assisting new immigrants financially and socially, through local mosques and civic organizations (Bahadur, 2005). Religious institutions, in turn, can be revitalized by immigrants. For example, a Baptist church in St. Paul, Minnesota, reached out to immigrants from Myanmar, providing them accommodations and airport pickups. People in the church bring donations of food and clothes. The downtown church, with dwindling membership, has been revitalized with the new immigrants (Pratik, 2005). Synagogues in South Florida have been revitalized by Russian immigrants who fled Russia and the religious oppression there (Collie, 2005). Today, religious organizations are working very closely with many governments to help refugees resettle in their new countries (Ralston, 2010).

But religious institutions do not always play facilitative roles in migrant transitions. Many Christian organizations in the United States, Canada, and

When I moved to Arizona from San Francisco to go to school, it was a big shock. I was used to seeing many different kinds of people—Asian Americans, African Americans. At my new university in Phoenix, almost everyone is white. And I was treated differently in Phoenix than I was at home. I often got passed by at the supermarket while the clerk waited on someone who was white. Some of the children who lived in my apartment complex followed me one day, yelling, "Chink, Chink, Chinaman."
    —Lois

Australia victimized indigenous children by requiring them to attend church schools far away from their homes in an attempt to "drum their native culture from their psyches," where they were often abused and maltreated. Fortunately, some churches are now seeking to redress these abuses (Duff-Brown, 2005).

The relative status and power of sojourners and host groups also influence adaptation. Several recent studies have found that Asian, African, and Latino students in the United States report experiences of discrimination and hostility based on their race/ethnicity while white international students report very few such experiences. These difficulties make it very difficult to adapt to a new country and range from being ignored to verbal insults, confrontation, and even physical assaults—in a variety of contexts, both in and outside the classroom, by peers, faculty, and members of the local community (Lee & Rice, 2007; Poyrazli & Lopez, 2007).

The authors of the studies point to the institutional accountability for international student satisfaction and, ultimately, for positive relations with potential future students in the internationals' home countries:

> *We recommend that members of the educational community be made aware of this issue and their responsibility in creating intellectual environments that foster cross-national acceptance and learning . . . [and] that guidelines concerning teaching and working with international students be articulated so that administrators and faculty are aware of their responsibility in providing a safe and welcoming environment for international students (Lee & Rice, p. 405.)*

Similarly, it can be difficult for women to adapt in many contexts because of their relatively lower status.

Class issues often enter into the picture. Sometimes immigrant workers are seen as necessary but are not really welcomed into the larger society because of their class (which is often fused with racial differences). And sometimes the discrimination and class issues result in conflict between recent migrants and emigrants from the same country who have been in the host country for a long time. For example, Mexicans have come in increasing numbers to work in the carpet plants in the Southeast and in the meatpacking plants in the Midwest. This has led to tension between those Latinos/as, who have worked hard to achieve harmony with whites and to attain middle-class status, and the newcomers, who are usually poor and have lower English proficiency. The older Latinos/as feel caught between the two—ridiculed by whites for not speaking English correctly and now by recently arrived Mexicans for mangling Spanish. This resentment between old and new immigrants has always been present in America—from the arrival of the first Europeans.

However, there is an upside to the arrival of these new immigrants. Journalist Arian Campo-Flores (2001), writing about the relationships between these two groups in one Midwest town, observes,

> *Cultural collisions can be as enriching as they are threatening. . . . Older Chicanos have learned to adjust, too. In fact many say that the fresh infusion of Hispanic culture brought by immigrants has revitalized their identity as Latinos. Their girls are cel-ebrating* quinceaneras, *the equivalent of "sweet 16" parties. They're singing to their departed relatives at the cemetery. They've resuscitated their language . . . both com-munities have recognized that their complexions will become only more richly hued. And Chicanos, who in a way are the arbiters between what the towns used to be and what they've become, are uniquely qualified to lead. (p. 51)*

The United States is not the only country grappling with an influx of new workers. When Germany needed low-cost laborers, the country brought in many Turkish guest workers, but these immigrants were not necessarily wel-comed into German society. Citizenship and other signs of entry into German society were not easily obtainable, and many immigrants (or those perceived to be immigrants) were victims of violent attacks. In fact, all over Europe, people of color seem to be facing increasing trends in racism that make life more difficult than it is for the average citizen in any of these countries (Akwani, 2006). Eco-nomic changes that resulted from the reuniting of East and West Germany have reduced the need for guest workers.

Which groups of migrants do you think have a positive image in the United States? Which groups do you think have a negative image? Which groups of international students do you think U.S. students would want to meet and socialize with? Which groups would students not want to meet? The stereo-types of various cultural groups should make it easy for you to sense which groups would face resistance from U.S. Americans in trying to adapt to U.S. culture.

Identity and Adaptation How individual migrants develop multicultural identities depends on three issues. One is the extent to which migrants want to maintain their own identity, language, and way of life compared to how much they want to become part of the larger new society. Recall that the immigrant–host culture relationship can be played out in several ways. Immigrants to the United States often are encouraged to "become American," which may entail relinquishing their former cultural identity. For example, Mario and his family emigrated from Mexico to Germany when Mario's father took a new job. Mario and his siblings have taken different paths with respect to their relationship to Mexican culture. Mario, the oldest child, has tried to keep some Mexican traditions. His brother, who was very young when the family migrated to Germany, did not learn to speak Spanish at home but is now trying to learn it in college.

The second issue that affects how migrants develop multicultural identities is the extent to which they have day-to-day interactions with others in the new society. Some migrants find it painful to deal with the everyday prejudices that they experience and so retreat to their own cultural groups.

The third issue that affects how migrants relate to their new society involves the ownership of political power. In some societies, the dominant group virtually dictates how nondominant groups may act; in other societies, nondominant groups are largely free to select their own course. For instance, Tom learned that when his mother first went to grammar school she had to pick an "American name" because her own name "was too hard to pronounce." As a first grader, she chose the name "Kathy" because she thought it sounded pretty. This kind of forced assimilation reflects the power of dominant groups over nondominant groups. In this case, *American* means "English" or "British," even though we are a nation of emigrants from all parts of the world. Looking at how migrants deal with these identity issues in host culture contexts can help us understand different patterns of contact (Berry, 1992).

Living on the Border   As international migration increases and more and more people travel back and forth among different cultures, the lines between adaptation and reentry become less clear (Onwumechilia, Nwosu, Jackson, & James-Huges, 2003). More and more people are living on the border physically, making frequent trips between countries, or living on the border psychologically between bicultural identities.

liminality The experience of being between two or more cultural positions.

The experience of living on the border was described by anthropologist Victor Turner (1969) as the experience of **liminality.** According to Turner, liminal people are "threshold people"; they are neither "here nor there," they are "betwixt and between various cultural positions . . . frequently likened to death, to being in the womb, to invisibility, to bisexuality" (p. 95). The trend calls for a new view of cultural boundaries and adaptation.

> *The emerging "interethnic identity" is a special kind of mindset that promises greater fitness in our increasingly interfaced world. It represents a continuous struggle of searching for the authenticity in self and others within and across ethnic groups. . . . A particular emphasis has been placed on the possibility of identity development from a monoethnic identity to a more interethnic identity, from a categorical identity to a more flexible and inclusive identity of individuated and universalized self-other orientation.* (Kim, 2006, pp. 292, 295)

transnationalism The activity of migrating across the borders of one or more nation-states.

multicultural identity A sense of in-betweenness that develops as a result of frequent or multiple cultural border crossings.

This **transnationalism** calls into question comforting notions like nation-states, national languages, and coherent cultural communities. People who move back and forth between cultural worlds often develop a **multicultural identity,** as discussed in Chapter 5. Denis, an international student from France, describes this transnational experience:

I have been living outside my home country for several years now, and it seems that the returns home are not as hard as they were in the past. . . . I have learned to just take things as they come and become nonjudgmental regarding people's actions and behaviors. . . . to be able to step back and also realize that in most interactions problems are rarely with the people who live in a country, but rather they are within your own framework of beliefs and behaviors that you have to mentally put aside in order to see the other culture or your own.

Communication scholar Radha Hegde (1998) uses the metaphor of swinging on a trapeze to describe the immigrant's experience of vacillating between the cultural patterns of the homeland and the new country. Writer Gloria Anzaldúa (1999) also stresses the fluidity and the active roles that individuals must take when living on the borders. She thinks that we need to resist being placed in set categories—like "Chicano/a" or "black" or "Asian American." She also insists that all our identities are in flux and interact with each other. Anzaldúa herself is Chicana, gay, and female. She describes how she has struggled to reconcile the indigenous with the Spanish, the male with the female, and her rather patriarchal Catholic upbringing with her spiritual and sexual identity. The result is the "mestiza"—a person who has actively confronted the negative aspects of identity, such as being silenced as a woman in a patriarchal Mexican-Catholic context, and then constructed a provisional identity:

The new mestiza copes by developing a tolerance for contradictions, a tolerance for ambiguity. She learns to be an Indian in Mexican culture, to be Mexican from an Anglo point of view. She learns to juggle cultures. She has a plural personality, she operates in a pluralist mode—nothing is thrust out, the good the bad and the ugly, nothing rejected, nothing abandoned. Not only does she sustain contradictions, she turns the ambivalence into something else. (p. 101)

This "something else" is the construction of her own historical legacy, a transformation that involves facing her fear of change. Once she accomplishes her personal inner journey, she comes to recognize her multiple identities. In her writing, she demonstrates the many facets of her many identities—writing in several languages (Spanish, English, and Nuhuatl), and in prose (the academic) and poetry (the artistic and spiritual):

I will no longer be made to feel ashamed of existing. I will have my voice: Indian, Spanish, white. I will have my serpent's tongue—my woman's voice, my sexual voice, my poet's voice. I will overcome the tradition of silence. (p. 81)

Technological developments have made global travel much easier, and we can change cultural contexts as never before. Yet the movement between cultures is never as simple as getting on a plane (Clifford, 1992). David Mura (1991), a Japanese American from the Midwest, went to live in Japan and wrote about his experiences there:

Japan helped me balance a conversation which had been taking place before I was born, a conversation in my grandparents' heads, in my parents' heads, which, by my generation, had become very one-sided, so that the Japanese side was virtually silenced.

My stay helped me realize that a balance, which probably never existed in the first place, could no longer be maintained. In the end, I did not speak the language well enough; I did not have enough attraction to the culture. In the end, the society felt to my American psyche too cramped, too well defined, too rule-oriented, too polite, too circumscribed. I could have lived there a few more years if I had had the money and the time, but eventually I would have left.

The entanglements of history, identity, language, nonverbal communication, and cultural spaces are all salient concerns for understanding these global movements.

INTERNET RESOURCES

www.state.gov/m/dghr/flo/c21995.htm
This web page provided by the U.S. Department of State provides information on third-culture kids. It provides resources, publications, and web links on the topic, including one for transition workshops designed for third-culture kids—children whose parents live/work internationally.

www.migrationinformation.org/index.cfm
This web page provided by Migration Information Source gives "Fresh thought, Authoritative Data, Global Reach" and provides information regarding immigration flows, what to expect when immigrating to certain countries, U.S. perspective, etc.

www.interchangeinstitute.org/html/about.htm
This website offers advice, information, and support for transitioning to the United States. It provides insights on the migration experience and also describes the types of support systems that are available for migrants and travelers.

www.arfp.org/skins/ARFP/home.aspx?AllowSSL=true
This Army Reserve Family Programs Online page provides various links that offer services for army personnel and their families. Among these links you will find the "Army Family Action Plan" and "Child and Youth Services." It provides extensive information and guidelines for both returning soldiers and their families to facilitate the often stressful time of homecoming and reunion.

SUMMARY

- A dialectical perspective on transitions reveals the tension between the individual and societal level of cultural adaptation.
- The four types of migrants are sojourners, immigrants, short-term refugees, and long-term refugees.

- There are four modes of migrant–host relationships: assimilation, separation, integration, and hybridity.
- A social science approach to adaptation emphasizes individual influences and outcomes and includes the AUM model, the transition model, and the integrative model.
- An interpretive approach emphasizes the lived experience and includes the U-curve theory, the W-curve theory, and phenomenological studies.
- A critical approach emphasizes the contextual influences on adaptation: social institutions, and political, historical, and economic structures.
- Cultural identity and adaptation are related in many ways.
- Those who live "on the borders" often develop multicultural identities.

DISCUSSION QUESTIONS

1. Why does culture shock occur to people who make cultural transitions?
2. Why are adaptations to cultures difficult for some people and easier for others?
3. What is the role of communication in the cultural adaptation process?
4. How do relations of power and dominance affect adaptation?
5. What factors affect migration patterns?
6. What dialectical tensions can you identify in the process of adapting to intercultural transitions?

 Go to the self-quizzes on the Online Learning Center at www.mhhe.com/martinnakayama6 to further test your knowledge.

ACTIVITIES

Culture Shock. Meet with other students in your class in small groups and explore your own experiences of cultural adaptation. Find out how many students experienced culture shock during the first year of college in terms of the three phases of the U-curve model. What did it feel like? How many experienced culture shock when traveling abroad? How about reentry shock? If there are differences in students' experience, explore why these differences exist. Are they related to differences in individual experience? In contexts?

KEY WORDS

assimilation (324)	fight approach (334)	intercultural
cultural adaptation (330)	flight approach (334)	identity (336)
culture shock (338)	functional fitness (336)	liminality (350)
explanatory	immigrants (320)	long-term refugees (321)
uncertainty (332)	integration (328)	migrant (320)

multicultural identity
(350)
phenomenological
approach (343)
predictive uncertainty
(332)
psychological health (336)

segregation (326)
separation (325)
short-term
refugees (321)
social support (335)
sojourners (320)

transnationalism
(350)
U-curve theory (337)
uncertainty
reduction (332)
W-curve theory (341)

 The Online Learning Center at www.mhhe.com/martinnakayama6 features flashcards and crossword puzzles based on these terms and concepts.

REFERENCES

Adelman, M. B. (1988). Cross-cultural adjustment: A theoretical perspective on social support. *International Journal of Intercultural Relations, 12*, 183–204.

Adler, P. (1975). The transition experience: An alternative view of culture shock. *Journal of Humanistic Psychology, 15*, 13–23.

Alabama. (2011, September 30). Many immigrants pull children from schools. *The New York Times.* Retrieved January 17, 2012 from: www.nytimes.com/2011/10/01/us/alabama-many-immigrants-pull-children-from-schools.html.

Allardice, R. R., & Head, K. (2007, Winter). The coalition Air Force Transition Team. *Air & Space Power Journal.* Retrieved April 2, 2008, from www.airpower.maxwell.af.mil/airchronicles/apj/apj07/win07/allardice.html.

Akwani, O. (2006, June 10). Racism against blacks is a growing trend in Europe. Global News Digest. Retrieved March 28, 2008, from http://imdcontentnew.searchease.com/villages/global/civil_human_equal_rights/RacismagainstBlacksinEurope.asp.

Al-Shaykh, H. (1995). *Beirut blues.* New York: Anchor Books.

Anzaldúa, G. (1999). *Borderlands/La frontera: The new mestiza* (2nd ed.). San Francisco: Aunt Lute Press.

Army reserve family programs (website). Retrieved April 2, 2008, from www.arfp.org/skins/ARFP/home.aspx?AllowSSL=true.

Bahadur, G. (2005, August 7). Muslims here balance between two cultures. *Philadelphia Inquirer*, p. B01.

Bennett, J. M. (1998). Transition shock: Putting culture shock in perspective. In M. J. Bennett (Ed.), *Basic concepts in intercultural communication: Selected readings* (pp. 215–224). First published in 1977, in N. C. Jain (Ed.), *International and Intercultural Communication Annual, 4*, 45–52.

Berry, J. W. (1992). Psychology of acculturation: Understanding individuals moving between two cultures. In R. W. Brislin (Ed.), *Applied cross cultural psychology* (pp. 232–253). Newbury Park, CA: Sage.

Berry, J. W., Kim, U., Minde, T., & Mok, D. (1987). Comparative studies of acculturative stress. *International Migration Review, 21*, 491–511.

Black, J. S., & Gregersen, H. B. (1999). *So you're coming home.* San Diego: Global Business.

Campo-Flores, A. (2001, September 18). Brown against brown. *Newsweek*, pp. 49–51.

Chandler, J. V. (2005). *Why culture matters: An empirically-based pre-deployment training program.* Masters Thesis, Naval Postgraduate School.

Chen, L. (2000). How we know what we know about Americans: How Chinese sojourners account for their experiences. In A. González, M. Houston, & V. Chen (Eds.), *Our voices: Essays in culture, ethnicity and communication* (3rd ed., pp. 220–227). Los Angeles: Roxbury.

Clifford, J. (1992). Traveling cultures. In L. Grossberg, C. Nelson, & P. Treichler (Eds.), *Cultural studies* (pp. 96–116). New York: Routledge.

Collie, T. (2005, October 30). Rediscovering Judaism: Synagogues, religious schools are booming as Russian Jews reclaim their culture. *South Florida Sun-Sentinel*, p. 3J.

Danquah, M. N.-A. (1998). Life as an alien. In C. C. O'Hearn (Ed.), *Half + half.* New York: Pantheon Books.

Doyle , M. W. (2004). The challenge of worldwide migration. *Journal of International Affairs, 57*(2), 1–5.

Duff-Brown, B. (2005, November 24). Canada, Aboriginals discuss redress plan. Associated Press News Service.

Ehrenreich, B., & Hochschild, A. R. (2003). Introduction. In B. Ehrenreich & A. R. Hochschild (Eds.), *Global woman: Nannies, maids, and sex workers* (pp. 1–14). New York: Metropolitan Books.

El Nasser, H. (2010, December 20). Census data show "surprising" segregation. *USA Today.* Retrieved

June 2, 2011, from www.usatoday.com/news/nation/census/2010–12–14-segregation_N.htm.

Facts and figures (n.d.). *International Organization for Migration*. Retrieved May 7, 2011, from www.iom.int/jahia/Jahia/pid/241.

Festinger, L. (1957). *A theory of cognitive dissonance.* Stanford, CA: Stanford University Press.

Gonzalez, D. (2005, October 12). Language gap grows. Studies: Schools face increased challenges. *Arizona Republic*, p. B1.

Gudykunst, W. B. (1995). Anxiety uncertainty management (AUM) theory: Current status. In R. L. Wiseman (Ed.), *Intercultural communication theory* (pp. 8–58). Newbury Park, CA: Sage.

Gudykunst, W. B. (1998). Applying anxiety/uncertainty management (AUM) theory to intercultural adjustment training. *International Journal of Intercultural Relations, 22*, 187–227.

Gudykunst, W. B. (2005). An anxiety/uncertainty management (AUM) theory of effective communication: Making the mesh of the net finer. In W. B. Gudykunst (Ed.), *Theorizing about intercultural communication* (pp. 281–323). Thousand Oaks, CA: Sage.

Gullahorn, J. T., & Gullahorn, J. E. (1963). An extension of the U-curve hypothesis. *Journal of Social Issues, 19*, 33–47.

Grieco, E. M., & Trevelyan, E. N. (2010). Place of birth of foreign-born population: 2009. *American Community Service Briefs*. Retrieved May 7, 2011, from www.census.gov/prod/2010pubs/acsbr09–15.pdf.

Hegde, R. S. (1998). Swinging the trapeze: The negotiation of identity among Asian Indian immigrant women in the United States. In D. V. Tanno & A. González (Eds.), *Communication of identity across cultures* (pp. 34–55). Thousand Oaks, CA: Sage.

Hegde, R. S. (2000). Hybrid revivals: Defining Asian Indian ethnicity through celebration. In A. González, M. Houston, & V. Chen (Eds.), *Our voices: Essays in culture, ethnicity and communication* (3rd ed., pp. 133–138). Los Angeles: Roxbury.

Henderson, M. (1999). *Forgiveness: Breaking the chain of hate.* Wilsonville, OR: Book-Partners.

Ishii, S. (2001). The Japanese welcome-nonwelcome ambivalence syndrome toward Marebito (Ijin) Gaijin strangers: Its implications for intercultural communication research. *Japan Review, 13*, 145–170.

Kashima, E. S., & Loh, E. (2006). International students' acculturation: Effects of international, conational, and local ties and need for closure. *International Journal of Intercultural Relations, 30*, 471–486.

Kealey, D. J. (1989). A study of cross-cultural effectiveness: Theoretical issues, practical applications. *International Journal of Intercultural Relations, 13*, 387–427.

Kealey, D. J. (1996). The challenge of international personnel selection. In D. Landis & R. S. Bhagat

(Eds.), *Handbook of intercultural training* (2nd ed., pp. 81–105). Thousand Oaks, CA: Sage.

Kim, M.-S. (2002). Models of acculturative communication competence: Who bears the burden of adaptation? In *Non-western perspectives on human communication* (pp. 141–154). Thousand Oaks, CA: Sage.

Kim, Y. Y. (2001). *Becoming intercultural: An integrative theory of communication and cross-cultural adaptation.* Thousand Oaks, CA: Sage.

Kim, Y. Y. (2005). Adapting to a new culture: An integrative communication theory. In W. B. Gudykunst (Ed.), *Theorizing about intercultural communication* (pp. 375–400). Thousand Oaks, CA: Sage.

Kim, Y. Y. (2006). From ethnic to interethnic: The case for identity adaptation and transformation. *Journal of Language and Social Psychology, 25*(3), 283–300.

Kim, Y. Y., & Gudykunst, W. B. (Eds.). (1988). *Cross cultural adaptation: Current approaches.* International and Intercultural Communication Annual 11. Newbury Park, CA: Sage.

Kristjánsdóttir, E. S. (2009). Invisibility dreaded and desired: Phenomenological inquiry of sojourners' cross-cultural adaptation. *Howard Journal of Communications, 20*(22).

Lee, J. J., & Rice, C. (2007). Welcome to America? International student perceptions of discrimination, *Higher Education, 53*, 381–409.

Lysgaard, S. (1955). Adjustment in a foreign society: Norwegian Fulbright grantees visiting the United States. *International Social Science Bulletin, 7*, 45–51.

Martin, J. N. (1984). The intercultural reentry: Conceptualizations and suggestions for future research. *International Journal of Intercultural Relations, 8*, 115–134.

Martin, J. N. (1986). Communication in the intercultural reentry: Student sojourners' perceptions of change in reentry relationships. *International Journal of Intercultural Relations, 10*, 1–22.

Martin, J. N., Bradford, L., & Rohrlich, B. (1995). Comparing predeparture expectations and post-sojourn reports: A longitudinal study of U.S. students abroad. *International Journal of Intercultural Relations, 19*, 87–110.

Martin, J. N., & Harrell, T. (2004). Intercultural reentry of students and professionals: Theory and practice. In D. Landis, J. M. Bennett, & M. J. Bennett (Eds.), *Handbook of intercultural training* (3rd ed., pp. 309–336). Thousand Oaks, CA: Sage.

Martin, P., & Zürcher, G. (2008) Managing migration: The global challenge. *Population Bulletin, 63*(1), 1–18.

Mather, M. (2007). Education and occupation separates two kinds of immigrants in the United States. Population Reference Bureau. Retrieved March 28, 2008, from www.prb.org/Articles/2007/Education AndOccupationSeparatesUSImmigrants.aspx.

Mead, J. C. (2003, September 28). In Island's wealthiest area, backlash against the poorest. *The New York Times*, Section 14LI, p. 1.

Mura, D. (1991). *Turning Japanese: Memoirs of a sansei.* New York: Anchor Books.

Numbers. (2008, February 4). *Time*, p. 18.

Nwanko, R. N., & Onwumechili, C. (1991). Communication and social values in cross-cultural adjustment. *Howard Journal of Communications, 3*, 99–111.

Oberg, K. (1960). Cultural shock: Adjustment to new cultural environments. *Practical Anthropology, 7*, 177–182.

O'Hearn, C. C. (ed). (1998). *Half and Half: Writers on growing up biracial and bicultural.* New York: Pantheon Books.

Omelaniuk, I., & Weiss. T. L. (2005). Introduction. In I. Omelaniuk (Ed.), *World migration 2005: Costs and benefits of international migration* (pp. 13–22). Geneva, Switzerland: International Organization for Migration.

Onwumechilia, C., Nwosu, P. O., Jackson, R. L., & James-Huges, J. (2003). In the deep valley with mountains to climb: Exploring identity and multiple reacculturation. *International Journal of Intercultural Relations, 27*, 41–62.

Poyrazli, S., & Lopez, M. D. (2007). An exploratory study of perceived discrimination and homesickness: A comparison of international students and American students. *Journal of Psychology, 141*(3), 263–280.

Pratik, J. (2005, May 15). Refugees renew church. *St. Paul Pioneer Press*, p. C1.

Ralston, J. (2010, July 28). Refugees and the role of religious groups. *Australian Broadcasting Corporation.* Retrieved January 17, 2012 from: www.abc.net.au/religion/articles/2010/07/28/2966921.htm.

Reid, B. (2005, November 10). Options are available for students, parents: Finding the right fit for English learners. *Arizona Republic*, p. B3.

Rohrlich, B., & Martin, J. N. (1991). Host country and reentry adjustment of student sojourners. *International Journal of Intercultural Relations, 15*, 163–182.

Rosenau, J. N. (2004). Emergent spaces, new places, and old faces: Proliferating identities in a globalizing world. In J. Friedman & S. Randeria (Eds.), *Worlds on the move: Globalization, migration and cultural security* (pp. 23–62). New York: I. B. Tauris.

Ruggiero, K. M., Taylor, D. M., & Lambert, W. E. (1996). A model of heritage culture maintenance. *International Journal of Intercultural Relations, 20*, 47–67.

Santos, B. (2004). Transnational third world. In J. Friedman & S. Randeria (Eds.), *Worlds on the move: Globalization, migration and cultural security* (pp. 293–318). New York: I. B. Tauris.

Search for social glue. (2008, February 23). *The Economist, 386*(8568), 74.

Sedgman, J. M. (2005, March 16). Children removed from schools by immigration officials. *The World Today, ABC Online.* Accessed at www.abc.net.au/cgi-bin/common/printfriendly.pl?www.abc.net.au/worldtoday/content/2005/s1324795.htm.

Storti, C. (2001). *The art of coming home* (2nd ed.). Yarmouth, ME: Nicholas Brealey/Intercultural Press.

Sullivan, K. (1997, December 6). "White" Australia in identity crisis: Many fear Asian immigrants are taking away jobs, culture. *Washington Post*, p. A1.

Sulitzeanu, A. B. (2010, November 1). Segregation of Jews and Arabs in 2010 is almost absolute. *Salem (OR), News.* Retrieved June 2, 2011, from http://salem-news.com/articles/november012010/israel-apartheid-abs.php.

Tehranian, M. (2004). Cultural security and global governance: International migration and negotiations of identity. In J. Friedman & S. Randeria (Eds.), *Worlds on the move: Globalization, migration and cultural security* (pp. 3–22). New York: I. B. Tauris.

Telles, E. E., & Ortiz, V. (2008). *Generations of exclusion: Mexican Americans, assimilation, and race.* New York: Russell Sage Foundation.

Turner, V. W. (1969). *The ritual process.* Chicago: Aldine.

UNHCR Statistical Yearbook 2009, United Nations High Commissioner for Refugees. Retrieved May 7, 2011, from www.unhcr.org/4ce532ff9.html.

Vanderpool, T. (2002, April 2). Lesson no. 1: Shed your Indian identity. *Christian Science Monitor*, p. 14.

Ward, C. (1996). Acculturation. In D. Landis & R. S. Bhagat (Eds.), *Handbook of intercultural training* (2nd ed., pp. 125–147). Thousand Oaks, CA: Sage.

Ward, C., Bochner, S., & Furnham, A. (2001). *The psychology of culture shock* (2nd ed.). East Sussex: Routledge. (Simultaneously published in the United States by Taylor & Francis, Philadelphia, PA.)

Weissman, D., & Furnham, A. (1987). The expectations and experiences of a sojourning temporary resident abroad: A preliminary study. *Human Relations, 40*, 313–326.

Witte, K. (1993). A theory of cognitive and negative affect: Extending Gudykunst and Hammer's theory of uncertainty and anxiety reduction. *International Journal of Intercultural Relations, 17*, 197–216.

Zimmerman, S. (1995). Perceptions of intercultural communication competence and international student adaptation to an American campus. *Communication Education, 44*, 321–335.

POPULAR CULTURE AND INTERCULTURAL COMMUNICATION

CHAPTER OBJECTIVES

After reading this chapter, you should be able to:

1. Differentiate between high and low culture.
2. Discuss the importance of popular culture as a public forum.
3. Identify the four characteristics of popular culture.
4. Identify some patterns of how people consume popular culture.
5. Identify some ways that people resist popular culture.
6. Describe some of the ways that popular culture influences how people understand another culture.
7. Explain the role of popular culture in stereotyping.
8. Explain how the global movement of popular culture influences people around the world.
9. Discuss the concerns of some governments about the influence of foreign media in their countries.

Originally broadcast in the Netherlands, *Big Brother* has expanded around the world from the United States and United Kingdom to Australia and Nigeria. The 2007 season of *Big Brother* Australia features a diverse cast of participants, all of whom are Australian. Yet, because not all of them are white, one of the contestants wanted them evicted:

> *"Aussies, I don't think there are enough Aussies in the house," big brother contestant, Andrew, said. The "Big Brother" contestant appeared to have analyzed the appearance of housemates in the house before declaring that maybe "Big Brother" should have a special eviction to non-appearing Australians in the house because according to him the "Aussies" seemed to be numbered by darker looking housemates. (Harris, 2007).*

Charges of racism and racist remarks in the Australian version have followed similar charges in the U.K. version. In discussing the racist comments made on the U.K. version of *Big Brother*, sociologist Steve Spencer observes: "Yes this is racism—the sort of everyday racism which is normally invisible—not overt, but in the private domain of the general population. Racist and xenophobic reactions like these 'private' conversations which are broadcast to a mass audience are a bizarre inversion of the everyday racism—the sneering comments, the cultural ignorance and intolerance which is commonplace in our society" (quoted in "Big Brother," 2007). In the United States, the Internet feed for *Big Brother* season 13 showed Jeff Schroeder, a contestant, making anti-gay comments. In a statement, CBS noted: "At times, the houseguests make comments, reveal prejudices and other beliefs that we do not condone" (quoted in Rice, 2011). This controversy is not new for Jeff: "Back in 2009 during the show's 11th season, Schroeder was caught on camera repeatedly calling housemates he was in fights with anti-gay slurs, including 'homos' and the f-word" (GLAAD, 2011). Do some reality shows create a climate of intolerance?

The popularity of *Big Brother* and reality television more generally opens up the private space of the home and interpersonal relationships to the public arena. The kinds of intercultural interaction and intercultural conflicts that take place in reality television are broadcast widely to a very large audience. These shows bring some of these cultural tensions into public discussion on various discussion boards, web pages, newspapers, and other outlets.

This chapter explores one type of culture that is often overlooked by intercultural communication scholars but that plays an important role in the construction, maintenance, and experience of culture, particularly in intercultural interactions. This type of culture is popular culture.

LEARNING ABOUT CULTURES WITHOUT PERSONAL EXPERIENCE

As discussed in Chapter 8, people can experience and learn about other cultures by traveling to and relocating and living in other regions. But there will always be many places around the world that we have not visited and where we have not lived. How do we know about places we have never been? Much of what we know probably comes from popular culture—the media experience of films, television, music, videos, books, and magazines that most of us know and share. How does this experience affect intercultural communication?

The Power of Popular Culture

Neither Tom nor Judith has ever been to Nigeria, India, Russia, or China. Yet both of us hold tremendous amounts of information about these places from the news, movies, TV shows, advertisements, and more. The kind and quality of information we all have about other places are influenced by popular culture. But the views that the media portray supplement the information we get from other sources. For example, audiences that see the movie *Jarhead* are likely to be familiar with the military mission in Iraq, even if they have not been in military service there. In this sense, popular culture is pervasive.

The complexity of popular culture is often overlooked. People express concern about the social effects of popular culture—for example, the influence of television violence on children, the role of certain kinds of music in causing violent behavior by some youths, and the relationship between heterosexual pornography and violence against women. Yet most people look down on the study of popular culture, as if this form of culture conveys nothing of lasting significance. So, on the one hand, we are concerned about the power of popular culture; on the other, we don't look on popular culture as a serious area of academic research. This inherent contradiction can make it difficult to investigate and discuss popular culture.

As U.S. Americans, we are in a unique position in relationship to popular culture. Products of U.S. popular culture are well known and circulate widely on the international market. The popularity of U.S. movies such as *Transformers 3* and *Captain America;* U.S. music stars such as Lady Gaga and Katy Perry; and U.S. television shows such as *True Blood, NCIS,* and *Desperate Housewives* create an uneven flow of texts between the United States and other nations. Scholars Elihu Katz and Tamar Liebes (1987) have noted the "apparent ease with which American television programs cross cultural and linguistic frontiers. Indeed, the phenomenon is so taken for granted that hardly any systematic research has been done to explain the reasons why these programs are so successful" (p. 419).

In contrast, U.S. Americans are rarely exposed to popular culture from outside the United States. Exceptions to this largely one-way movement of popular culture include pop music stars who sing in English, such as Wyclef Jean (Haitian), Shakira (Colombian), and Enrique Iglesias (Spanish). Consider how difficult it is to find foreign films or television programs throughout most of the United States. Even when foreign corporations market their products in the United States, they almost always use U.S. advertising agencies—collectively known as "Madison Avenue." The apparent imbalance of cultural texts globally not only renders U.S. Americans more dependent on U.S.-produced popular culture but also can lead to cultural imperialism, a topic we discuss later in this chapter.

I was on my way to Rome from Newark last summer. Since I took the Polish Airlines, I had to make a stopover there in Warsaw. During my first morning in Warsaw, I got up, took a shower, and turned on the TV, just out of curiosity to see what was showing. I guess I expected to hear Polish, some local news and dramas, etc.

The first thing that jumped at me from the TV screen was Ricky Martin! Then followed Destiny's Child! I was shocked! U.S. popular culture really is everywhere! And I thought I already knew that! But I didn't expect it, all the way in Poland.

—Mina

The study of popular culture has become increasingly important in the communication field. Although intercultural communication scholars traditionally have overlooked popular culture, we believe that it is a significant influence in intercultural interaction.

What Is Popular Culture?

The 19th-century essayist and poet Matthew Arnold, who expressed concern about protecting civilization, defined *culture* as "the best that has been thought and said in the world"—a definition that emphasizes quality. In this context, many Western societies distinguish "high culture" from "low culture."

High culture refers to those cultural activities that are often the domain of the elite or the well-to-do: ballet, symphony, opera, great literature, and fine art. These activities sometimes are framed as *international* because supposedly they can be appreciated by audiences in other places, from other cultures, in different time periods. Their cultural value is seen as transcendent and timeless. To protect these cultural treasures, social groups build museums, symphony halls, and theaters. In fact, universities devote courses, programs, and even entire departments to the study of aspects of high culture.

In opposition to high culture is low culture, which refers to the activities of the nonelite: music videos, game shows, professional wrestling, stock car racing, graffiti art, TV talk shows, and so on. Traditionally, low-culture activities have been seen as unworthy of serious study—and so of little interest to museums or universities. The cultural values embedded in these activities were considered neither transcendent nor timeless.

The elitism reflected in the distinction between high and low culture points to the tensions in Western social systems. In recent decades, however, this distinction has begun to break down. Rapid social changes propelled universities to alter their policies and also have affected how we study intercultural communication. For example, the turbulent 1960s brought to the university a powerful new interest in ethnic studies, including African American studies and women's and gay and lesbian issues. These areas of study did not rely on the earlier distinctions between high and low culture. Rather, they contributed to a new conceptual framework by arguing for the legitimacy of other cultural forms that traditionally would have been categorized as low culture but were now framed as **popular culture.** Because of this elitist view of culture, the distinction between "high culture" and "low culture" has led to low culture being reconceptualized as popular culture. Barry Brummett (1994), a contemporary rhetorician, offers the following definition: "Popular culture refers to those systems or artifacts that most people share and that most people know about" (p. 21). According to this definition, television, music videos, YouTube, Disney, advertising, soap operas, and popular magazines are systems of popular culture. In contrast, the symphony and the ballet do not qualify as popular culture because most people cannot identify much about them unless they have studied them.

So, popular culture often is seen as populist—including forms of contemporary culture that are made popular by and for the people. John Fiske (1989), professor of communication arts, explains,

> To be made into popular culture, a commodity must also bear the interests of the people. Popular culture is not consumption, it is culture—the active process of generating and circulating meanings and pleasures within a social system: culture, however industrialized, can never be adequately described in terms of the buying and selling of commodities. (p. 23)

In his study of popular Mexican American music in Los Angeles, ethnic studies professor George Lipsitz (1990) highlights the innovative, alternative ways that marginalized social groups are able to express themselves. In this study, he demonstrates how popular culture can arise by mixing and borrowing from other cultures: "The ability of musicians to learn from other cultures played a key role in their success as rock-and-roll artists" (p. 140). The popular speaks to—and resonates from—the people, but it does so through multiple cultural voices. Lipsitz continues,

> The marginality of Chicano rock-and-roll musicians has provided them with a constant source of inspiration and a constant spur toward innovation that gained them the attention of mainstream audiences. But this marginal sensibility amounts to more than novelty or personal eccentricity; it holds legitimacy and power as the product of a real historical community's struggle with oppression. . . . As Chicano musicians demonstrate in their comments about their work, their music reflects a quite conscious cultural politic that seeks inclusion in the American mainstream by transforming it. (p. 159)

Intercultural contact and intercultural communication play a central role in the creation and maintenance of popular culture. Yet, as Lipsitz points out, the popular is political and pleasurable, which further complicates how we think about popular culture.

There are four significant characteristics of popular culture: (1) It is produced by culture industries, (2) it differs from **folk culture,** (3) it is everywhere, and (4) it fills a social function. As Fiske (1989) points out, popular culture is nearly always produced within a capitalist system that sees the products of

popular culture A new name for *low culture,* referring to those cultural products that most people share and know about, including television, music, videos, and popular magazines.

folk culture Traditional and nonmainstream cultural activities that are not financially driven.

| | TABLE 9-1 | DISTINCTIONS AMONG HIGH CULTURE, FOLK CULTURE, AND POPULAR CULTURE | | |

Type	Definition	Who Knows It?	What Does It Look Like?
High culture	Elite aristocratic expressions of culture	Rich members of the political establishment	Opera, classic sculpture, symphony performances
Folk culture	Traditional and nonmainstream cultural activities that are not financially driven	Most cultural groups, but especially middle-class groups	Folk music
Popular culture	Ever-present cultural products designed for profitable consumption	Almost everyone in a social group	Mainstream music, movies, television, romance novels

culture industries
Industries that produce and sell popular culture as commodities.

popular culture as commodities that can be economically profitable (see Table 9-1.) They are produced by what are called **culture industries.** The Disney Corporation is a noteworthy example of a culture industry because it produces amusement parks, movies, cartoons, and a plethora of associated merchandise.

More recently, communication scholars Joshua Gunn and Barry Brummett (2004) have challenged the second point that there is an important difference between folk culture and popular culture. They suggest, "We write as if there is a fundamental difference between a mass-produced and mass-marketed culture and a more authentic 'folk' culture or subculture. Such a binary is dissolving into a globally marketed culture. A few remaining pockets of folk culture remain here and there: on the Sea Islands, in Amish country, in departments of English. The rest of folk culture is now 50% off at Wal-Mart" (p. 707). In the new context of globalization, whatever happened to folk traditions and artifacts? Have they been unable to escape being mass-produced and marketed around the globe? Where would you look for folk culture today? Whatever happened to traditional folk dancing, quilting bees, and other forms of folk culture?

Popular culture is ubiquitous. We are bombarded with it, every day and everywhere. On average, U.S. Americans watch more than 40 hours of television per week. Movie theaters beckon us with the latest multimillion-dollar extravaganzas, nearly all U.S. made. Radio stations and music TV programs blast us with the hottest music groups performing their latest hits. (See Figure 9-1.) And we are inundated with a staggering number of advertisements and commercials daily.

It is difficult to avoid popular culture. Not only is it ubiquitous but it also serves an important social function. How many times have you been asked by friends and family for your reaction to a recent movie or TV program? Academicians Horace Newcomb and Paul Hirsch (1987) suggest that television

FIGURE 9-1 Shakira is a multilingual Colombian singer whose songs have hit the charts in many countries, including Turkey and the United States. She exemplifies non-U.S. popular culture making an impact internationally. (© *Miriam Alster/epa/Corbis*)

serves as a cultural forum for discussing and working out our ideas on a variety of topics, including those that emerge from the programs themselves. Television, then, has a powerful social function—to serve as a forum for dealing with social issues.

In his study of the role of the local newspaper, *The Newsboy*, in restoring the image of Jasper, Texas, after the dragging murder of James Byrd, Jr., Jack Glascock (2004) found that the newspaper's editorials played an important role in guiding the community response to the hate crime. He notes that the "paper's involvement in community affairs at the outset allowed it to convey the agreed-upon objectives of the crisis discourse to the rest of the community. As the crisis played out the paper extended its leadership role by continuing, dropping or modifying its strategies. The paper's opinion pages also provided a forum for the community to participate, primarily by bolstering the town's image, both within the community [and] to outsiders" (p. 45). In this case, the paper is both a forum for public discussion and a leader in community restoration.

In a similar study, communication scholars Dreama Moon and Tom Nakayama (2005) analyzed newspaper accounts of the murder of Arthur "J. R." Warren in West Virginia. Although the small town where he was murdered did not have a local paper, they found that the media coverage did highlight significant differences in how African Americans, gays and lesbians, and white heterosexual residents experienced and perceived life there. Through the media, African Americans and gays and lesbians were able to offer an alternative view that differed from the dominant view of idealized small-town life. Again, newspapers served as a forum for discussion of this tragic event and related aspects of everyday life and community in this small West Virginia town.

In contrast, not all popular culture may serve as a forum for public deliberation. In his study of baseball tributes in ballparks after the attacks of September 11, 2001, Michael Butterworth (2005) found that these rituals tended to discourage expression of opinions that differed from a nationalistic patriotism at the expense of democratic deliberation. Butterworth describes these baseball tributes and notes, "If baseball can be understood as a representative institution of American democratic culture, then the ways in which it performs (or fails to perform) democratically merit scrutiny and criticism. In the aftermath of unprecedented tragedy (for Americans), baseball could have been a site not only for communal healing but also for productively engaging the pluralism that the game does or should represent" (p. 122). Baseball tributes, then, are a form of popular culture that does not serve a cultural forum for the democratic exchange of ideas.

The ways that people negotiate their relationships to popular culture are complex, and it is this complexity that makes understanding the role of popular culture in intercultural communication so difficult. Clearly, we are not passive recipients of this deluge of popular culture. We are, in fact, quite active in our consumption of or resistance to popular culture, a notion that we turn to next.

CONSUMING AND RESISTING POPULAR CULTURE

Consuming Popular Culture

cultural texts Popular culture messages whether television shows, movies, advertisements, or other widely disseminated messages.

Faced with this onslaught of **cultural texts,** people negotiate their ways through popular culture in quite different ways. Popular culture texts do not have to win over the majority of people to be "popular." People often seek out or avoid specific forms of popular culture. For example, romance novels are the best-selling form of literature, but many readers have no interest in such books. Likewise, whereas many people enjoy watching soap operas or professional wrestling, many others find no pleasure in those forms of popular culture.

encoding The process of creating a message for others to understand.

decoding The process of interpreting a message.

Stuart Hall's (1980) encoding/decoding model might be helpful here. Hall is careful to place "meaning" at several stages in the communication process, so that it is never fixed but is always being constructed within various contexts. Thus, in his model, he places **encoding**—or the construction of textual meaning by popular culture institutions—within specific social contexts. **Decoding**—the interpretation of the text's meaning by receivers—is performed by various audiences in different social contexts, whose members have different interests at stake. In this way, the meaning(s) of various popular culture texts can be seen as negotiated throughout the communication process. The "real meaning" of any popular culture text cannot simply be located in either the senders or the receivers. Although this model may seem to suggest tremendous unpredictability in popular culture, people do not create just any meaning out of these texts. We are always enmeshed in our social identities, which help guide our interpretations as decoders. Encoders, in turn, rely on these larger identity formations to help them fashion their texts to sell to particular markets. (See Figure 9-2.)

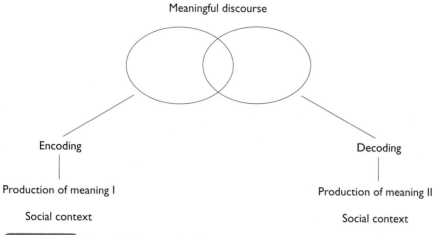

Meaningful discourse

Encoding

Decoding

Production of meaning I

Production of meaning II

Social context

Social context

FIGURE 9-2 Stuart Hall's encoding/decoding model. Try to use this model to discuss how different people might arrive at different interpretations of your favorite TV show.

For example, communication researcher Antonio La Pastina (2004) did an interpretive study of how people in a rural Brazilian community, Macambira in northeastern Brazil, decoded the meanings of the telenovela *The Cattle King*. This telenovela is set in urban Brazil and features many melodramatic stories about socioeconomic class, romance, and sexuality. In interviewing the people of this very rural and isolated community, he found that these viewers tended to interpret the telenovelas based on their own cultural values about gender, relationships, and sexuality. He also found that these telenovelas tended to shape how the viewers saw urban life in Brazil. Although the producers of this telenovela may not have encoded the shows with this audience in mind when they wrote and produced these narratives, the viewers in this community used their own cultural values to decode their own meanings of the shows.

There is some unpredictability in how people navigate popular culture. After all, not all men enjoy watching football, and not all women like to read romance novels. However, some profiles emerge. Advertising offices of popular magazines even make their **reader profiles** available to potential advertisers. These reader profiles portray what the magazine believes its readership "looks" like. Although reader profiles do not follow a set format, they generally detail the average age, gender, individual and household incomes, and so on, of their readership. The reader profile for *Vogue*, for example, will not look like the reader profile for *Esquire*.

reader profiles
Portrayals of readership demographics prepared by magazines.

Each magazine targets a particular readership and then sells this readership to advertisers. The diversity of the U.S. American population generates very different readerships among a range of magazines, in several ways. Let's explore some of the ways this diversity is played out in the magazine market.

How Magazines Respond to the Needs of Cultural Identities   A wide range of magazines respond to the different social and political needs of groups with different cultural identities. You may already be familiar with magazines geared toward a male or a female readership. But many other kinds of magazines serve important functions for other cultural groups. For example, *Ebony* is one of many magazines that cultivate an African American readership. Similar magazines exist for other cultural identities. *Hispanic Magazine*, published in Florida, targets a Latino/a audience; *The Advocate* claims to be the national newsmagazine for gays and lesbians. These magazines offer information and viewpoints that are generally unavailable in other magazines. They function as a discussion forum for concerns that mainstream magazines often overlook. They also tend to affirm, by their very existence, these other cultural identities, which sometimes are invisible or are silenced in the mainstream culture.

In addition, many non-English-language newspapers circulate among readers of specific ethnic groups, serving the same functions as the magazines just mentioned. However, because their production costs are low, they are better able to survive and reach their limited readerships. For instance, newspapers printed in Cantonese, Spanish, Vietnamese, Japanese, French, Korean, Arabic, Polish, Russian, and other languages reach non-English-speaking readers in the United States.

How Readers Negotiate Consumption   Readers actively negotiate their way through cultural texts such as magazines—consuming those that fulfill important cultural needs and resisting those that do not. Hence, it is possible to be a reader of magazines that reflect various cultural configurations; that is, someone might read several women's magazines and Spanish-language newspapers and magazines, as well as *Newsweek* and *Southern Living*.

Cultural Texts Versus Cultural Identities   We must be careful not to conflate the magazines with the cultural identities they are targeting. After all, many publications offer different points of view on any given topic. Thus, there is no single, unified "Asian American position" on immigration reform or any "Latino position" on affirmative action. Rather, there can be a preponderance of opinions on some issues. These often are played out through popular culture forums.

People come together through cultural magazines and newspapers to affirm and negotiate their relationships with their cultural identities. In this way, the texts resemble cultural spaces, which we discussed in Chapter 7. However, magazines are but one example of how popular culture can function. Not all popular culture texts are easily correlated to particular cultural groups. Think about the various TV programs, movies, mass-market paperbacks, and tabloids that flood our everyday lives. The reasons that people enjoy some over others cannot easily be determined. People negotiate their relationships to popular culture in complex ways.

Resisting Popular Culture

Sometimes people actively seek out particular popular culture texts to consume; other times they resist cultural texts. But resistance to popular culture is a complex process. Avoiding certain forms of popular culture is one kind of resistance, but resistance can occur in a variety of ways.

Let's look at the ongoing controversy over the use of the logo of the University of North Dakota's Fighting Sioux. In August 2005, the National Collegiate Athletic Association (NCAA) placed "a ban on Indian imagery that it considers 'hostile or abusive'" (Borzi, 2005, p. B15) in postseason play. In appealing the NCAA division, the University of North Dakota and the NCAA have settled this dispute. This settlement means that "the university will have three years to obtain approval of the mascot from the two Sioux tribes with a significant presence in the state" (U. of North Dakota, 2007). The university was unable to obtain permission to use the mascot and logo from both tribes, but this mascot controversy may come to a close soon. In March 2011, the North Dakota state legislature passed House Bill 1263, which prevents UND from changing its mascot. This bill was signed by Governor Dalrymple, which leaves UND "with the dilemma of having to either disobey the government that controls its purse-strings or to flout the rules of the NCAA, the entity that controls the arguably mightier purse-strings of college football" (Conlon, 2011). Given the current situation, then, "Within the coming months, North Dakota is going to have to make a decision. The reconvening of the Legislature in the fall gives hope to mascot critics that the state will reverse its initial decision to keep the mascot" (Bartholomew, 2011).

Let's look at how this logo creates strong feelings on both sides and how people are responding to the NCAA decision. There is mixed reaction to the meaning of the way the logo is used. Among American Indians as well there is disagreement about the use of the logo. It is important to recognize that all members of any cultural group have diverse reactions to popular images. For example, not all women are offended by the Hooters restaurant/bar chain that features scantily clad waitresses. Some women, however, do not like the way that women are represented at Hooters.

If we return to our touchstones to examine this controversy, we can see how communication, culture, power, and context play out in this example. American Indians are a relatively small segment of the population. At the University of North Dakota, there were 358 American Indian students out of 14,194 students in the 2010–2011 academic year (http://und.edu/university-relations/student-profile/). They are the largest minority group at the university, but only 2.52% of the total enrollment. To whom, then, is this logo communicating? Which groups have a dominant voice in how the logo is interpreted? Think about who is communicating with whom. What kind of power differential is at work here when primarily non–American Indians choose and circulate these images to mostly non–American Indians?

The context is important as well. As we noted earlier in this book, we need to consider the historical context as one important frame that helps us understand how meaning is created in intercultural contexts. The history of American Indian imagery is reflected in a distorted media image: "The Hollywood Indian is a mythological being who exists nowhere but within the fertile imaginations of its movie actors, producers, and directors" (Jojola, 1998, p. 12). How might these other distorting images influence the reading of this logo?

Because some of these stereotypes are negative, they have negative consequences for members of that social group. In his study of the controversy at the University of North Dakota over their mascot, the Fighting Sioux, communication scholar Raúl Tovares (2002) points to the climate at sporting events, which highlights the ways in which stereotypes, cultural values, and popular culture images can come together. (See Figure 9-3.) He explains,

> *Hockey and football games have become sites where offensive images of Native Americans are common. Students from NDSU [North Dakota State University] show up at athletic events with cartoonish images of bison forcing themselves sexually on Native Americans. At "sporting" events, it is not uncommon to hear phrases such as "kill the Sioux," "Sioux suck," "f———k the Sioux," and "rape Sioux women." Such phrases, many Native American students claim, are a direct result of the Fighting Sioux logo. (p. 91)*

Now a Division I school, NDSU (North Dakota State University) is not scheduled to play the University of North Dakota in football. North Dakota State does not currently host a men's hockey team. Think about the ways that this mascot might circulate on jackets, T-shirts, cartoons, and other popular culture forms. How does popular culture represent an important site for negotiating this cultural identity? Why do non–Native Americans have a dominant voice and more power in these representations?

Finally, an interpretivist who is studying the logo controversy might go to the University of North Dakota and speak to the people there. One professor highlights this aspect of the controversy: "'Unless you're here, you don't know what it's like and how nasty it can get,' said a psychology professor, Doug McDonald, who is Sioux. 'I've had students in my office in tears because of the harassment we get'" (quoted in Borzi, 2005, pp. B15–B16). The logo and associated meaning (e.g., the sale of "Sioux-per dogs") create an environment in which some students clearly see negative meanings.

Here we saw a clear example of a group's resistance to popular culture and popular images because they construct American Indian identity in undesirable ways. Indeed, people often resist particular forms of popular culture by refusing to engage in them. For example, some people feel the need to avoid television and even decide not to own televisions. Some people refuse to go to movies that contain violence or sexuality because they do not find pleasure in such films. In this case, these kinds of conscious decisions are often based on concerns about the ways that cultural products should be understood as political.

Resistance to popular culture can also be related to social roles. Likewise, some people have expressed concern about the supposedly homophobic or racist ideologies embedded in Disney films such as *Aladdin* (Boone, 1995). *Aladdin* plays into Western fears of homosexuality and the tradition of projecting those concerns on Arab culture. Resistance stems mainly from concerns about the representation of various social groups. Popular culture plays a powerful role in how we think about and understand other groups. The Disney film *Pocahontas* was criticized for its rewriting of the European encounters with Native Americans. According to communication scholars Derek Buescher and Kent Ono (1996),

FIGURE 9-3 Concern about sports mascots centers on issues of how they are interpreted and how they create barriers to intercultural communication. This woman's concern that Indian mascots reflect racism is not always understood by sports fans. Although many people know that these mascots are offensive to some, what might drive people to resist changing sports mascots? How does this conflict demonstrate the diversity that resides within U.S. culture? (© Steve Skjold/ PhotoEdit, Inc.)

this film "helps audiences unlearn the infamous history of mass slaughter by replacing it with a cute, cuddly one" (p. 128).

Sometimes resistance is targeted at the profits of popular culture corporations. For example, in Iraq, many Iraqis buy pirated DVDs of U.S. films. These pirated DVDs are sold on the black market and the U.S. film corporations do

POINT *of* VIEW

not earn profits from these sales. Milad Tareq, 21, who runs the Option CDs shop, explains that "The best-pirated movies come from Malaysia. Among the more popular movies in the Iraqi capital are those starring Robert DeNiro, Tom Hanks or Julia Roberts," (Sabah, 2006). While this kind of resistance may be oriented toward the store owner making a profit rather than undercutting the U.S. film corporations, these sales both spread U.S. popular culture, as well as hurt the potential profits of the filmmakers.

REPRESENTING CULTURAL GROUPS

As noted at the beginning of this chapter, people often are introduced to other cultures through the lens of popular culture. These introductions can be quite intimate, in ways that tourists may not experience. For example, movies may portray romance, familial conflict, or a death in the family; the audience experiences

A Belgian student describes his first impressions on arriving in the United States.

When I first landed at JFK Airport, I felt like I was going crazy. When I was younger, I only knew about America through television, radio, books, and movies. Even if people don't like America, it is still like a dream-land because it is a place where everything is big, where movies are made, especially police movies. American movies are very well made, with special effects, and so the first time I saw the real America, it was like in the movies. The police in the airport were like cowboys, wearing sunglasses, big mustaches, with badges everywhere and they were big and unafraid, like cowboys. You must respect the customs lines, and all the rules are very strict.

When we left the airport to go to Manhattan, we saw really poor neighborhoods near the airport. I wondered, is America really so poor with small houses? The houses look like they are made of wood and flimsy, unlike the brick ones in Belgium. Once you cross into Manhattan, however, you understand that in America you either have money or you don't. There are majestic cities and poverty; you can get lots of money or nothing. It is another way of living. In Belgium, you do not have to struggle so much for money. Once you have a job in Belgium, there are lots of job protections. In Belgium, if you want to live, you don't have to work.

—Christophe

the private lives of people they do not know, in ways that they never could simply as tourists.

Yet we must also think about how these cultural groups are portrayed through that lens of popular culture. Not everyone sees the portrayal in the same way. For example, you may not think that the TV shows *Modern Family* and *Two and a Half Men* represent quintessential U.S. American values and lifestyles. But some viewers may see it as their entree into how U.S. Americans (or perhaps European Americans) live.

In a social science study on television coverage of affirmative action and African Americans, communication researchers Alexis Tan, Yuki Fujioka, and Gerdean Tan (2000) found that more negative coverage increased negative stereotypes about African Americans. However, they also found that "positive TV portrayals did not lead to positive stereotypes, nor did they influence opinions" (p. 370). They conclude that "negative portrayals are remembered more than positive portrayals, are more arousing and therefore are more influential in the development of stereotypes" (p. 370). Given this dynamic, it is clear how TV news coverage can continue to marginalize and reinforce negative stereotypes, even if the reports also present positive information about minority groups.

In a more recent social science study, Mary Beth Oliver and her colleagues (2004) examined news readers' memories of racial facial features of people in the news. They presented one of four different kinds of news stories—nonstereotyped, stereotyped/noncrime, nonviolent crime, and violent crime—with the same photograph of the individual in the story. Participants were asked to recall this individual's facial features on a computer screen. They conclude, in part, that "[w]hen the stories pertained to crime, Afrocentric features were significantly more pronounced than the actual photograph depicted, whereas when the stories were unrelated to crime, the selected features did not differ significantly from the photograph actually seen" (p. 99). They suggest that certain topics might activate stereotypes and thus influence how these news stories are interpreted.

Migrants' Perceptions of Mainstream Culture

Ethnographers and other interpretive scholars have crossed international and cultural boundaries to examine the influence of popular culture. In an early study, Elihu Katz and Tamar Liebes (1987) set up focus groups to see how different cultural groups perceived the popular 1980s TV drama *Dallas*:

> *There were ten groups each of Israeli Arabs, new immigrants to Israel from Russia, first and second generation immigrants from Morocco, and kibbutz members. Taking these groups as a microcosm of the worldwide audience of* Dallas, *we are comparing their readings of the program with ten groups of matched Americans in Los Angeles. (p. 421)*

Katz and Liebes found that the U.S. Americans in Los Angeles were much less likely to perceive *Dallas* as portraying life in the United States. In contrast, the Israelis, Arabs, and immigrants were much more inclined to believe that this television show was indeed all about life in the United States. Katz and Liebes note, "What seems clear from the analysis, even at this stage, is that the non-Americans consider the story more real than the Americans. The non-Americans have little doubt that the story is about 'America'; the Americans are less sure" (p. 421). The results of this study are not surprising, but we should not overlook what they tell us about the intercultural communication process. We can see that these popular culture images are often more influential in constructing particular ways of understanding other cultural groups than our own. Notably, "Dallas" is being resurrected and a new version of the series is set to appear in 2012.

Another study (Lee & Cho, 1990) that focused on immigrants to the United States yielded similar results. The researchers asked female Korean immigrants why they preferred watching Korean TV shows (which they had to rent at the video store) instead of U.S. programs. The respondents stated that, because of the cultural differences, the Korean shows were more appealing. Yet, as one respondent noted,

> *I like to watch American programs. Actors and actresses are glamorous and the pictures are sleek. But the ideas are still American. How many Korean women are that independent? And how many men commit incest? I think American*

*programs are about American people. They are not the same as watching the
Korean programs. But I watch them for fun. And I learn the American way of
living by watching them. (p. 43)*

Here, both consumption of and resistance to U.S. television are evident. This
woman uses U.S. television to learn about the U.S. American "way of living," but
she prefers to watch Korean shows because they relate to her cultural identity.
As she says, "I like the Korean programs because I get the sense of what's going
on in my country" (p. 43).

The use of popular culture to learn about other cultures should not be surprising. After all, many teachers encourage their students to use popular culture
in this manner, not only to improve their language skills but also to learn many
of the nuances of another culture. When Tom was first studying French, his
French professor told the students that *Le dernier métro* (*The Last Metro*), a film
by director François Truffaut, was playing downtown. The point, of course, was
to hear French spoken by natives. But Tom remembers being amazed at the
subtle references to anti-Semitism, the treatment of lesbianism, and the film's
style, which contrasted sharply with that of Hollywood films.

Popular Culture and Stereotyping

In what ways does reliance on popular culture create and reinforce stereotypes
of different cultures? As we noted at the outset of this chapter, neither author
has had the opportunity to travel all over the world. Our knowledge about other
places, even places we have been, is largely influenced by popular culture. For
people who do not travel and who interact in relatively homogeneous social circles, the impact of popular culture may be even greater.

Film studies scholar Richard Dyer (1993) tells us that

*the effectiveness of stereotypes resides in the way they invoke a consensus. . . . The
stereotype is taken to express a general agreement about a social group, as if that
agreement arose before, and independently of, the stereotype. Yet for the most part
it is from stereotypes that we get our ideas about social groups. (p. 14)*

Dyer makes an important observation that stereotypes are connected to social
values and social judgments about other groups of people. These stereotypes are
powerful because they function to tell us how "we" value and judge these other
groups.

Many familiar stereotypes of ethnic groups are represented in the media.
Scholar Lisa Flores (2000) describes the portrayal of a diverse group of high
school students in the television show *Matt Waters*. Flores focuses her analysis
on Angela, a Puerto Rican student. According to Flores, there is a strong theme
of assimilation at work in this show. She notes,

*to follow the seeming logic of this assimilationist politics requires an initial belief in
the goal of a single, unified American culture expressed in a harmonious community such as that found within the* Matt Waters *community. The assimilationist*

I see plenty of ethnic groups on the television. Asians are portrayed as highly paid, intelligent, yet quiet individuals. Whites are portrayed mostly as middle to upper class individuals, also well paid. Most blacks and Hispanics are seen as criminal and poor, mostly on welfare. Arabs and other Middle Eastern peoples are seen as terrorists or in subservient roles, but almost always seen as outsiders. I think that urban blacks as well as Asians are portrayed in the most fair light. While their portrayal might still be stereotypical, I think that it sums up what I see on a daily basis pretty accurately.

The portrayals of race and socioeconomic status on television seriously affect intercultural communication between members of other groups in a negative way. People internalize the stereotypical portrayals of these groups and communicate based on them, in ways that affect the feelings of other groups.

—Michael

perspective also mandates an assumption that ethnic minorities cannot maintain cultural difference except in rejection of all of dominant or mainstream society. (pp. 37–38)

She turns to Chicana feminism to show how we can resist these popular culture representations.

African American women also traditionally have been portrayed stereotypically on TV, especially in the 1950s and 1960s, when the roles they held were secondary (e.g., as domestics). Scholar Bishetta Merritt (2000) also reminds us of the African American female characters who often appear as background scenery: the person buying drugs, the homeless person on the sidewalk, the hotel lobby prostitute. Merritt points out that these women still project images, even if they aren't the focus:

If the majority of black women the television audience is exposed to are homeless, drug-addicted, or maids, and if viewers have no contact with African American women other than through television, what choice do they have but to believe that all women of this ethnic background reflect this television image? . . . It is, therefore, important, as the twenty-first century approaches and the population of this country includes more and more people of color, that the television industry broaden the images of African American women to include their nuances and diversity. (p. 53)

In her more recent study of local news coverage of Freaknik, an annual African American spring break event in Atlanta that ended in 2000, communication scholar Marian Meyers (2004) studied the ways that the violence perpetrated by African American men on African American women was represented. She found that the media coverage brought together issues of race, class, and gender and therefore tended to identify the perpetrators as nonstudent local

HATE MUSIC

"Hate music groups" and "hate music" distribute and produce music with racist and anti-Semitic lyrics and are a global phenomenon. According to the Anti-Defamation League:

> *Resistance Records, the leading American hate rock record label and distributor, reportedly ships about 50 orders each day, with each order worth about $70. Owned by leading American neo-Nazi group the National Alliance, Resistance may gross more than $1 million this year. Hate rock concerts in the United States regularly draw many hundreds of attendees, and similar concerts in Germany have attracted more than 2,000 people.*

In a review of the VH1 documentary, "Inside Hate Rock," Julie Salamon of the *The New York Times* observes that while record sales of this genre of music are in the thousands and not the millions, the reach the Internet does provide extended reach. The Anti-Defamation League provides a list identifying 541 hate music groups at www.adl.org/extremism/bands/bands_country.asp.

Sources: "Bigots Who Rock: An ADL List of Hate Music Groups," *Anti-Defamation League*, 2011. Retrieved May 8, 2011, from www.adl.org/extremism/bands/default.asp; J. Salamon, "Television review; on the fringe of rock 'n' roll, music with a heart full of hatred," *The New York Times*, February 18, 2002. Retrieved May 8, 2011, from www.nytimes.com/2002/02/18/arts/television-review-on-the-fringe-of-rock-n-roll-music-with-a-heart-full-of-hatred.html.

troublemakers rather than as students. The news coverage also "minimizes the seriousness of the violence and portrays its victims primarily as stereotypic Jezebels who provoke male violence through their own behavior" (p. 96). The continued use of this sexualized stereotype for African American women displaces responsibility for what happened from the male perpetrators to the women who were attacked.

What about those ethnic groups that simply don't appear except as infrequent stereotypes—for example, Native Americans and Asian Americans? How do these stereotypes influence intercultural interaction? Do people behave any differently if they don't hold stereotypes about people with whom they are interacting? Two communication researchers, Valerie Manusov and Radha Hegde (1993), investigated these questions in a study in which they identified two groups of college students: those who had some preconceived ideas about India (which were fairly positive) and those who didn't. Manusov and Hegde asked all of the students to interact, one at a time, with an international student from India who was part of the study.

When the students with preconceptions talked with the Indian student, they interacted differently from those who had no expectations. Specifically, students from the former group relied less on small talk, covered more topics, and asked fewer questions within each topic. Overall, their conversations were more like

CAPTAIN AMERICA

When *Captain America: The First Avenger* was released in cinemas in 2011, it did quite well at the box office its opening weekend. Earning $65.8 million, this film bumped *Harry Potter and the Deathly Hollows Part 2* from its first place finish the previous weekend. The film is set during World War II, and Captain America's enemies are Nazis. Although the film is fiction and focuses on a superhero, any film has to be attentive to historical contexts and also take liberties to ensure the narrative is enticing. So, people in a film set in the 1950s should not be surfing the Internet or chatting on smart phones. In the case of Captain America, a discussion began about the liberties taken about social relations. As Robin Quivers notes: "A woman leads men in combat and even takes part in some of the fighting. Later, when Captain America puts together his own little group of commandos, the crew includes an African American and a Japanese American." These characters defy historical contexts for both gender and race. Indeed, there were no integrated fighting units in the U.S. military at that time. In what ways is this historical revision of the past a good or a bad influence on intercultural relations? Is it helpful to pretend that our past was more open to gender and racial difference than it really was? Or should we be concerned about historical revisionism in popular culture?

Sources: C. M. Blow, "My very own Captain America," *The New York Times*, July 29, 2011. Retrieved August 23, 2011, from www.nytimes.com/2011/07/30/opinion/blow-my-very-own-captain-america.html?scp=1&sq=captain%20america&st; S. Bowles, " 'Captain America' unseats 'Potter' at box office," *USA Today*, July 24, 2011. Retrieved August 23, 2011, from www.usatoday.com/life/movies/news/2011-07-24-captain-america_n.htm; C. DeVega, "Captain America: The first avenger's dishonest and cowardly racial politics," AlterNet, July 23, 2011. Retrieved August 23, 2011, from http://blogs.alternet.org/speakeasy/2011/07/23/captain-america-the-first-avengers-dishonest-and-cowardly-racial-politics/; R. Quivers, "Captain America's USA," *Huffington Post*, August 1, 2011. Retrieved August 23, 2011, from www.huffingtonpost.com/robin-quivers/captain-americas-usa_b_915142.html.

those between people who know each other. The students with the preconceptions also were more positive about the conversation.

What can we learn from this study? Having some information and positive expectations may lead to more in-depth conversations and positive outcomes than having no information. But what happens when negative stereotypes are present? It is possible that expectations are fulfilled in this case too.

For example, in several studies at Princeton University, whites interviewed both white and black "job applicants" who were actually part of the study and were trained to behave consistently, no matter how interviewers acted toward them. The interviews were videotaped. The interviewers clearly behaved differently toward blacks: Their speech deteriorated, they made more grammatical errors, they spent less time, and they showed fewer "immediacy" behaviors—that is, they were less friendly and less outgoing. In a second study, interviewers were trained to be either "immediate" or "nonimmediate" as they interviewed white job applicants. A panel of judges watched the videotapes and agreed that those applicants interviewed by the "nonimmediate" interviewer performed less well and were more nervous. This suggests that the African American applicants in the first study never had a chance: They were only reacting to the nonimmediate behavior of the interviewers. Mark Snyder (1998) summarizes: "Considered together, the two investigations suggest that in interracial encounters, racial stereotypes may constrain behavior in ways to cause both blacks and whites to behave in accordance with those stereotypes" (p. 455).

U.S. POPULAR CULTURE AND POWER

One of the dynamics of intercultural communication that we have highlighted throughout this text is power. In considering popular culture, we need to think about not only how people interpret and consume popular culture but also how these popular culture texts represent particular groups in specific ways. If people largely view other cultural groups through the lens of popular culture, then we need to think about the power relations that are embedded in these popular culture dynamics.

Global Circulation of Images and Commodities

As noted previously, much of the internationally circulated popular culture is U.S. popular culture. U.S.-made films, for example, are widely distributed by an industry that is backed by considerable financial resources. Some media scholars have noted that the U.S. film industry earns far more money outside the United States than from domestic box office receipts (Guback, 1969; Guback & Varis, 1982). This situation ensures that Hollywood will continue to seek overseas markets and that it will have the financial resources to do so. The film *Spider-Man* exemplifies this economic position of Hollywood. Although the producers and distributors certainly made a considerable amount of money from the domestic screenings, they earned significant amounts of money from non-U.S. showings as well. (See Figure 9-4.)

Many other U.S. media are widely available outside the United States, including television and newspapers. For example, MTV and CNN are broadcast internationally. And the *International Herald Tribune*, published jointly by the *The New York Times* and the *Washington Post*, is widely available in some parts of the world. The implications of the dominance by U.S. media and popular culture have yet to be determined, although you might imagine the consequences. India produces more films than the United States but makes less money in box office receipts. (See the Point of View box on page 382.)

Not all popular culture comes from the United States. For example, James Bond is a British phenomenon, but the famous character has been exported to the United States. In their study of the popularity of the Bond series, scholars Tony Bennett and Janet Woollacott (1987) note that in the Bond film *A License to Kill* "the threat to the dominance of white American male culture is removed not by a representative of that culture, and certainly not by a somewhat foppish English

FIGURE 9-4 James Dean remains a popular cultural icon in the United States and abroad. This 1996 photo shows that one of his films, *East of Eden,* continues to play in Tokyo. How does Dean's popularity in Japan contrast with the absence of a similarly popular Japanese male star in the United States? What might explain this disparity? Think about the issues of cultural imperialism raised in this chapter. (*Courtesy T. K. Nakayama*)

spy, but by the self-destruction of the forces ranged against it" (pp. 293–294). Here, a British character becomes a hero for U.S. and international audiences through the U.S. film industry. It is not always easy to know what is and what is not U.S. popular culture.

Recently, the Korean Wave (*Hallyu*) has demonstrated the profitability of South Korean popular culture. This popular culture phenomenon has "become a rallying cry within Korea for the perceived success of its cultural industries in Asia" (J. Kim, 2007, p. 48). *The Korea Times* reports that "according to the Ministry of Culture, Sports and Tourism, the nation exported about $1.4 billion worth of entertainment products last year" (S.-Y. Kim, 2008). While primarily popular in Asia, *Hallyu* has even made the city of Chuncheon a popular tourist destination, as the local drama "Winter Sonata" (2002) gained popularity abroad (S.-Y. Kim, 2008, see Figure 9-5).

Key to this South Korean phenomenon, however, is the global circulation of popular culture. Thus, "Hallyu is a term that can *only* be applied to a cultural product once it has been exposed to foreign audiences. In other words, not every Korean drama, film or pop song, no matter how popular in Korea, will be labeled Hallyu—only those that have been exported and done so successfully" (J. Kim, 2007, pp. 49–50). The focus of *Hallyu,* however, is on "Asian rather than global domination" (p. 55). In any case, the international circulation of Korean popular culture has important implications for the production of Asian standards of beauty and relationships, as well as international trade.

We are shaped by a variety of influences, and popular culture is among those influences. While it is difficult to know how much popular culture shapes our worldviews, some studies have been done on body image in different cultures. For example, "Asian men show less dissatisfaction with their bodies than males in the United States and Europe, according to a Harvard study. This may explain why anabolic steroid abuse is much less prevalent in places like Taiwan than in the United States, Europe, and Australia". Also, "Black and Asian women generally have a more positive body-image than Caucasian women" while "A study of Mexican immigrants in America found that those who had immigrated after the age of 17 were less affected by the prevailing super-thin ideal than those who were 16 or younger when they came to the US". A more recent study of body image found that European Americans generally have a more negative body image than Hispanic/Latina/Latinos with women having a more negative image than men. It is difficult to make a direct correlation to the influence of popular culture, but with the images of beauty (not necessarily evenly distributed across the racial/ethnic diversity of the population), are some groups affected more than others?

Sources: Ceballos, N. & Czyzewska, N. (2010). Body Image in Hispanic/Latino vs. European American Adolescents: Implications for Treatment and Prevention of Obesity in Underserved Populations. *Journal of Health Care for the Poor and Underserved*, 21(3): 823-838; Cromie, W. J. (2005, February 10). Male body image: East doesn't meet west. Harvard Gazette. Retrieved September 12, 2011 from: http://news.harvard.edu/gazette/2005/02.10/11-bodyimage.html; Fox, K. (1997). Mirror, mirror: A summary of research findings on body image. *Social Issues Research Centre*. Retrieved September 11, 2011 from: www.sirc.org/publik/mirror.html.

Much popular culture that is expressed in non-English languages has a difficult time on the global scene. Although Céline Dion, who sings in English, has been able to reach a worldwide audience, a fellow French Canadian, Garou, who sings in French, has not reached the same level of notoriety. Still, Garou (Pierre Garand) is extremely popular in the francophone world. Have you ever heard of Garou? To reach a worldwide audience, must he sing in English? Garou released his next CD, *Reviens*, in 2003 and decided that because of "the generosity of his French-speaking public . . . [the album] would be written and sung in French" (www.garouland.com/Reviens/english/bio_08.html). What does this tell us about popular culture? What does it tell us about the unequal power relations that are evident in popular culture? How does it influence how we think about the world?

Cultural Imperialism

It is difficult to measure the impact of the U.S. and Western media and popular culture on the rest of the world, but we know that we cannot ignore this dynamic. The U.S. government in the 1920s believed that having U.S. movies on foreign screens would boost the sales of U.S. products because the productions would be furnished with U.S. goods. The government thus worked closely with the Hays Office (officially, the Motion Picture Producers and Distributors of America) to break into foreign markets, most notably in the United Kingdom (Nakayama & Vachon, 1991).

Discussions about **media imperialism, electronic colonialism,** and **cultural imperialism,** which began in the 1920s, continue today. The interrelationships among economics, nationalism, and culture make it difficult to determine with much certainty how significant cultural imperialism might be. The issue of cultural imperialism is complex because the definition is complex. In his survey of the cultural imperialism debates, scholar John Tomlinson (1991) identifies five ways of thinking about cultural imperialism: (1) as cultural domination, (2) as media imperialism, (3) as nationalist discourse, (4) as a critique of global capitalism, and (5) as a critique of modernity (pp. 19–23). Tomlinson's analysis underscores the interrelatedness of issues of ethnicity, culture, and nationalism in the context of economics, technology, and capitalism—resources that are distributed unevenly throughout the world. To understand the concerns about cultural imperialism, therefore, it is necessary to consider the complexity of the impact of U.S. popular culture. (See Table 9-2.) There

media imperialism
Domination or control through media.

electronic colonialism
Domination or exploitation utilizing technological forms.

cultural imperialism
Domination through the spread of cultural products.

TABLE 9-2 U.S. INTERNATIONAL POP CULTURE INFLUENCE

Product	Destination	Impact
Avatar		Number 1 film of all time at the box office. It earned more than $760 million in the U.S., but almost $2.8 billion worldwide (boxofficemojo).
Captain America		This film did well overseas despite concerns that it was too patriotic about the U.S. Although the studio offered the alternative title, "The First Avenger," only three countries distributed it under that name: Russia, South Korea, and Ukraine (McClintock).
The film industry	Iran	Iran's fledgling film industry has been sheltered by a protective government unwilling to air many American films. There is broad concern that American films will "overwhelm" Iranian industry and "debase" the moral foundations of the nation. As a result, many popular international films are simply unavailable in Iran (Crothers, 2007).

Sources: "All time box office," retrieved September 24, 2011, from http://boxofficemojo.com/alltime/; P. McClintock, "Box Office Shocker: 'Captain America' Earns More Overseas than in U.S." *The Hollywood Reporter,* September 14, 2011, retrieved September 24, 2011, from www.hollywoodreporter.com/news/box-office-shocker-captain-america-235464; Lane Crothers, *Globalization and American Popular Culture.* Plymouth U.K.: Rowman & Littlefield Publishers, 2007.

FIGURE 9-5 South Korean actor Bae Yong Joon is shown arriving at the Tokyo airport with thousands of fans awaiting his arrival. He is a very popular television drama star who is part of the Korean Wave. The Korean Wave highlights how non-U.S. popular culture can circulate and become very marketable in other parts of the world. (© *AP Photo/Katsumi Kasahara*)

is no easy way to measure the impact of popular culture, but we should be sensitive to its influences on intercultural communication. Let's look at some examples.

Some governments have become concerned about the amount of popular culture coming into their countries. The French government, for example, has expressed dismay about the domination of the English-language broadcasting of CNN because it feels it projects a view of the world it does not share. In order to challenge this view, the French are launching their own international broadcasting network to present their views on the world. Although informally referred to as "CNN à la française," this new "channel would promote a vision of a 'multipolar' world that is not dominated by one superpower, such as the United States" (Louet, 2005). This new channel will not initially be available in the United States, but it hopes to expand from Europe, Africa, and the Middle East to Asia, South America, and the United States later. This will allow the French to compete with CNN, the BBC, and Al Jazeera as international broadcasting networks.

In a study on this tension between global networks and local networks, Jonathan Cohen (2005) examined the situation in Israel. He looked at Israel's 99 channels and identified six different ways that these channels function in

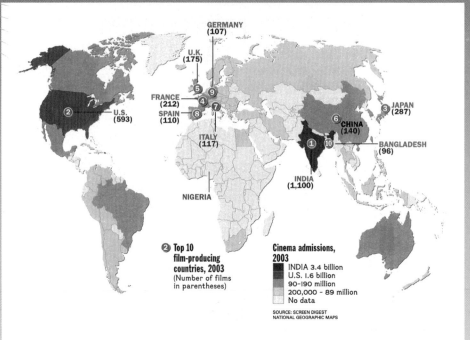

Top 10 film-producing countries, 2003 (Number of films in parentheses)

GERMANY (107)
U.K. (175)
FRANCE (212)
SPAIN (110)
U.S. (593)
ITALY (117)
NIGERIA
JAPAN (287)
CHINA (140)
BANGLADESH (96)
INDIA (1,100)

Cinema admissions, 2003
- INDIA 3.4 billion
- U.S. 1.6 billion
- 90–190 million
- 200,000 – 89 million
- No data

SOURCE: SCREEN DIGEST
NATIONAL GEOGRAPHIC MAPS

THE REEL WORLD

Nigerians don't go to the movies; the movies come to them. With few operating cinemas in Nigeria's largest city of Lagos, screenings often occur in local restaurants and private homes; videos are sold at market stands and sometimes hawked to motorists caught in traffic. This distribution of films from "Nollywood," as the country's ultralow-budget industry is known, may seem unusual, but it still satisfies the demand for movies—an obsession shared by people around the world.

In 2003, according to film industry source *Screen Digest*, some seven billion movie tickets were sold worldwide, earning an estimated $22 billion. The greatest share of these global box-office receipts—more than 43 percent—came from U.S. theaters. Japanese theaters charged the most for tickets: Reserved seats can

the global and local environment. He then noted, "Foreign television is often thought to be harmful because it separates people from their national communities" (p. 451), but he warned that we should not so easily view foreign television in this way. He doesn't think it is yet clear that watching U.S. television shows "like *Sex and the City* or *The Apprentice* weakens viewers' connections to Israeli culture or strengthens them by providing a stark contrast to viewers' lives" (p. 451). Think back to Stuart Hall's encoding and decoding model. Cohen is emphasizing that we cannot assume people who watch certain shows will decode them in any particular way. The influence of media is more complex than a simple imposition of meaning from abroad.

(© William Albert Allard/National Geographic Stock)

cost up to $25. Though India made more films than Hollywood, it made less money from them; the price of admission to an Indian theater averaged just 20 cents.

Many American blockbusters rake in more money internationally than at home. *Titanic*, the highest grossing film of all time, made two-thirds of its $1.8 billion take overseas. American movies have long been retooled for foreign sale. In the 1930s stars such as the comedy team Laurel and Hardy reshot their films in German and other languages—coached with phonetically spelled cue cards. Now native speakers are recorded over original actors' voices with varying success. In the French version of *Star Wars*, the villain's voice is considerably less menacing, and his name's been changed to Dark Vador.

American movies may be popular abroad, but foreign concession stands still cater to local tastes. Some European audiences wash their popcorn down with beer. In China the popcorn's sweetened. Other film snack favorites there—spicy cabbage, salted plums, dried squid shreds—have a flavor all their own.

Source: Scott Elder, "The Reel World," Geographica, *National Geographic*, March 2005.

Sometimes the Western images are imported and welcomed by the ruling interests in other countries. For example, the government of the Ivory Coast in West Africa has used foreign (mostly French) media to promote its image of a "new" Ivoirien cultural identity. The government purchased a satellite dish that permits 1,400 hours of French programming annually, which represents 77% of all programming. But it has been criticized by many for borrowing heavily from the Western media—for inviting cultural imperialism:

> *While television, as mirror, sometimes reflects multiple Ivoirien cultures, the latter are expected to acquiesce to a singular national culture in the image of the*

> ome people seek out foreign films; others avoid them. In choosing either response to foreign films, are you choosing films based on the narrative or the subtitles?

> *I do not like foreign films because I have a hard time understanding what is going on even with the subtitles. I can't understand a lot of the humor in foreign movies. I also don't think that all languages translate to English exactly, and it makes it hard to understand these movies.*
> —Elizabeth

> *Foreign films seem to paint a picture that rings more true to me than Hollywood films. In Hollywood films, there seems to be recurring themes: the strong man, the materialistic woman, heterosexuality, white stars with a token minority. They seldom get a role free of the most ridiculous stereotypes. The foreign independent films seem to have more diversity, more balance, a better depiction of the world.*
> —Sam

Party, which is also synonymous with a Western cultural image. . . . The cultural priority is openness for the sake of modernization in the quest of the Ivoirien national identity. (Land, 1992, p. 25)

In another take on globalization, communication scholar Radhika Parameswaran (2004) undertook a textual analysis of Indian newspaper and magazine coverage of India's six Miss Universe and Miss World titleholders. In the context of a global economy, these women are upheld as role models who are ordinary women who worked hard to become a beauty queen while maintaining their national identities. Noting that "the therapeutic vocabulary of the beauty queen as role model, a recent construct of liberal individualism in South Asia, induces amnesia and insulates middle class citizens from the contradictions that such individualized discourses of empowerment can conceal. . . . [G]lobalization's ideologies of prosperity in India offer no recourse for the vast majority of poor citizens to attain even the humble ordinariness of the middle class consumer who desires the status of the global beauty queen" (p. 367). By asking what social functions these narratives serve, this critical study argues that they serve the more elite segments of society in India.

In all of these examples, popular culture plays an enormous role in explaining relations around the globe. It is through popular culture that we try to understand the dynamics of other cultures and nations. Although these representations are problematic, we also rely on popular culture to understand many kinds of issues: the conflict in Kashmir between India and Pakistan, the sex abuse scandals in the Catholic Church, the conflict in the West Bank between Israelis and Palestinians, and global warming. For many of us, the world exists through popular culture.

INTERNET RESOURCES

http://culturalpolitics.net/popular_culture
This website has links to other materials, articles, and a bibliography of resources. It is run by a professor at Washington State University. It has sections on class, gender, sexuality, censorship, race/ethnicity, cultural imperialism, and popular culture.

www.npr.org/sections/pop-culture
National Public Radio hosts a web page devoted to identifying and commenting on popular culture trends. This resource is not specifically about intercultural issues, but these issues are covered. The website is a good mix of information and political commentary for students doing research on emerging popular culture issues.

www.uiowa.edu/~commstud/resources/POP-Culture.html
The well-respected communication department at the University of Iowa has compiled a wonderful resource for students doing popular culture research. This website lists and direct links to hundreds of communication-oriented articles on pop culture subjects ranging from Bazooka Joe to Madonna. The articles are categorized and easily accessible.

www.wsu.edu/~amerstu/pop/race.html#articles
Washington State University hosts this web resource. This website is a compilation of academic and popular press articles related to the intersection of popular culture and race. It contains direct links to articles, a directory of other websites, and a useful bibliography.

www.mediaed.org/cgi-bin/commerce.cgi?key=402&preadd=action
This is the Web resource for the bell hooks video on *Cultural Criticism and Transformation*, a 1997 edited interview with cultural critic bell hooks. The video is not available in its full form online (though sections are available on www.Youtube.com/), but this site does contain related articles and a section for comments.

SUMMARY

- We learn about other cultures through popular culture.
- Popular culture is popular because of its wide dissemination and easy access to many people.
- Popular culture is produced by culture industries, is not folk culture, is ubiquitous, and serves social functions.
- Popular culture can serve as a public forum.
- Cultural texts are not the same as cultural identities.
- People can seek out or resist popular culture.

- Cultural groups are often represented in ways that can play into stereotypes.
- Migrants can learn about other cultures through popular culture.
- The United States still dominates global production of popular culture, but other nations produce significant amounts that are important locally.
- Concerns about cultural imperialism need to be considered.

DISCUSSION QUESTIONS

1. Why do people select some popular culture forms over others?
2. How do the choices you make about what forms of popular culture to consume influence the formation of your cultural identity?
3. What factors influence culture industries to portray cultural groups as they do?
4. How does the portrayal of different cultural groups by the media influence intercultural interactions with those groups?
5. What stereotypes are perpetuated by U.S. popular culture and exported to other countries?
6. How do our social roles affect our consumption of popular culture?
7. What strategies can people apply to resist popular culture?

 Go to the self-quizzes on the Online Learning Center at www.mhhe.com/ martinnakayama6 to further test your knowledge.

ACTIVITIES

1. *Popular Culture.* Meet with other students in small groups and answer the following questions:
   a. Which popular culture texts (magazines, TV shows, and so on) do you watch or buy? Why?
   b. Which popular culture texts do you choose *not* to buy or watch? Which do you *not* like? Why?
   c. Think about and discuss why people like some products compared to others. (For example, do they support our worldview and assumptions?)
2. *Ethnic Representation in Popular Culture.* For a week, keep a log of the TV shows you watch. Record the following information for each show and discuss in small groups:
   a. How many different ethnic groups were portrayed in this show?
   b. What roles did these ethnic groups have in the show?
   c. What ethnic groups were represented in the major roles?
   d. What ethnic groups were represented in the minor roles?

e. What ethnic groups were represented in the good-guy roles?

f. What ethnic groups were represented in the bad-guy roles?

g. What types of roles did women have in the show?

h. What intercultural interaction occurred in the show?

i. What was the outcome of the interaction?

j. How do the roles and interactions support or refute common stereotypes of the ethnic groups involved?

KEY WORDS

cultural imperialism (380)
cultural texts (364)
culture industries (362)
decoding (364)

electronic colonialism (380)
encoding (364)
folk culture (361)

media imperialism (380)
popular culture (361)
reader profiles (365)

 The Online Learning Center at www.mhhe.com/martinnakayama6 features flashcards and crossword puzzles based on these terms and concepts.

REFERENCES

Arseneault, M. (2001, December 15). Il chante avec les loups. *L'actualité*, pp. 76–82.

Bartholomew, D. (2011, September 5). Sioux mascot controversy continues in North Dakota. *Iowa State Daily*. Retrieved September 12, 2011, from www .iowastatedaily.com/news/article_3c0e4ed0-d813-11e0-a3a4-001cc4c002e0.html.

Bennett, T., & Woollacott, J. (1987). *Bond and beyond: The political career of a popular culture hero.* New York: Methuen.

Big Brother has exposed "everyday racism." (2007, January 19). *Social Science News.* Sheffield Hallam University. Retrieved May 15, 2008, from www.shu.ac.uk/social/news2.html.

Boone, J. A. (1995). Rubbing Aladdin's lamp. In M. Dorenkamp & R. Henke (Eds.), *Negotiating lesbian and gay subjects* (pp. 149–177). New York: Routledge.

Borzi, P. (2005, November 26). A dispute of great spirit rages on: North Dakota fights to keep a logo, Indians consider its use profane. *The New York Times*, pp. B15–B16.

Brummett, B. (1994). *Rhetoric in popular culture.* New York: St. Martin's Press.

Buescher, D. T., & Ono, K. A. (1996). Civilized colonialism: *Pocahontas* as neocolonial rhetoric. *Women's Studies in Communication, 19*, 127–153.

Butterworth, M. (2005). Ritual in the "church of baseball": Suppressing the discourse of democracy after 9/11. *Communication & Critical/Cultural Studies, 2*, 107–129.

Cohen, J. (2005). Global and local viewing experiences in the age of multichannel television: The Israeli experience. *Communication Theory, 15*, 437–455.

Conlon, K. (2011, August 14). North Dakota, NCAA spar over mascot. *CNN*. Retrieved September 11, 2011, from http://articles.cnn.com/2011-08-14/us/north.dakota.mascot.fight_1_fighting-sioux-nickname-and-logo-nickname-controversy?_s=PM:US.

Dyer, R. (1993). *The matter of images: Essays on representations.* New York: Routledge.

Fiske, J. (1989). *Understanding popular culture.* New York: Routledge.

Flores, L. (2000). Challenging the myth of assimilation: A Chicana feminist perspective. In Mary Jane Collier (Ed.), *Constituting cultural difference through discourse* (pp. 26–46). International and Intercultural Communication Annual 12. Thousand Oaks, CA: Sage.

GLAAD. (2011, July 18). CBS "inadequate" response to "Big Brother" gay bashing. *Opposing Views.* Retrieved September 12, 2011, from www .opposingviews.com/i/entertainment/cbs-inadequate-response-big-brother-gay-bashing.

Glascock, J. (2004). The Jasper dragging death: Crisis communication and the community newspaper. *Communication Studies, 55*, 29–47.

Guback, T. (1969). *The international film industry: Western Europe and America since 1945.* Bloomington: Indiana University Press.

Guback, T., & Varis, T. (1982). *Transnational communication and cultural industries.* Paris: UNESCO.

Gunn, J., & Brummett, B. (2004). Popular culture after globalization. *Journal of Communication, 54,* 705–721.

Hall, S. (1980). Encoding/decoding. In S. Hall, D. Hobson, A. Lowe, & P. Willis (Eds.), *Culture, media, language.* London: Hutchinson.

Harris, A. (2007, June 19). Racism hits "Big Brother" Australia. *NewsBlaze.* Retrieved May 15, 2008, from http://newsblaze.com/story/20070619155951alih .nb/topstory.html.

Jojola, T. (1998). Absurd reality II: Hollywood goes to the Indians. In P. C. Rollins & J. E. O'Connor (Eds.), *Hollywood's Indian: The portrayal of the Native American in film* (pp. 12–26). Lexington: University Press of Kentucky.

Katz, E., & Liebes, T. (1987). Decoding *Dallas:* Notes from a cross-cultural study. In H. Newcomb (Ed.), *Television: The critical view* (4th ed., pp. 419–432). New York: Oxford University Press.

Kim, J. (2007). Why does Hallyu matter? The significance of the Korean Wave in South Korea. *Critical Studies in Television, 2,* 47–59.

Kim, S.-Y. (2008, May 5). Korean wave "Hallyu" abroad waning. *The Korea Times.* Retrieved May 15, 2008, from www.koreatimes.co.kr/www/news/ special/2008/05/180_23641.html.

La Pastina, A. C. (2004). Telenovela reception in rural Brazil: Gendered readings and sexual mores. *Critical Studies in Media Communication, 21,* 162–181.

Land, M. (1992). Ivoirien television, willing vector of cultural imperialism. *Howard Journal of Communications, 4,* 10–27.

Lee, M., & Cho, C. H. (1990, January). Women watching together: An ethnographic study of Korean soap opera fans in the U.S. *Cultural Studies, 4*(1), 30–44.

Lipsitz, G. (1990). *Time passages: Collective memory and American popular culture.* Minneapolis: University of Minnesota Press.

Louet, S. (2005, November 30). "French CNN" seen operational by end of 2006. Reuters Business Channel. Retrieved from December 3, 2005, from http://today.reuters.com/business/newsArticle .aspx?type=media&storyID=nL30762703.

Manusov, V., & Hegde, R. (1993). Communicative outcomes of stereotype-based expectancies: An observational study of cross-cultural dyads. *Communication Quarterly, 41,* 338–354.

Merritt, B. D. (2000). Illusive reflections: African American women on primetime television. In A. González, M. Houston, & V. Chen (Eds.), *Our voices* (3rd ed., pp. 47–53). Los Angeles: Roxbury.

Meyers, M. (2004). African American women and violence: Gender, race, and class in the news. *Critical Studies in Media Communication, 21,* 95–118.

Moon, D. G., & Nakayama, T. K. (2005). Strategic social identities and judgments: A murder in Appalachia. *Howard Journal of Communications, 16,* 1–22.

Nakayama, T. K., & Vachon, L. A. (1991). Imperialist victory in peacetime: State functions and the British cinema industry. *Current Research in Film, 5,* 161–174.

Newcomb, H., & Hirsch, P. M. (1987). Television as a cultural forum. In H. Newcomb (Ed.), *Television: The critical view* (4th ed., pp. 455–470). New York: Oxford University Press.

Oliver, M. B., Jackson, R. L., Moses, N. N., & Dangerfield, C. L. (2004). The face of crime: Viewers' memory of race-related facial features of individuals pictured in the news. *Journal of Communications, 54,* 88–104.

Parameswaran, R. (2004). Global queens, national celebrities: Tales of feminine triumph in post-liberalization India. *Critical Studies in Media Communication, 21,* 346–370.

Rice, L. (2011, July 13). CBS responds to homophobic comments made in "Big Brother" house. *Entertainment Weekly.* Retrieved September 11, 2011, from http://insidetv.ew.com/2011/07/13/ jeff-schroeder-big-brother/.

Sabah, Z. (2006, January 19). Pirated DVDs among hottest items on Iraqi shelves. *USA Today.* Retrieved May 15, 2008, from www.usatoday.com/news/ world/iraq/2006-01-19-iraq-dvds_x.htm#.

Snyder, M. (1998). Self-fulfilling stereotypes. In P. Rothenburg (Ed.), *Race, class and gender in the United States* (4th ed., pp. 452–457). New York: St. Martin's Press.

Tan, A., Fujioka, F., & Tan, G. (2000). Television use, stereotypes of African Americans and opinions on affirmative action: An affective model of policy reasoning. *Communication Monographs, 67*(4), 362–371.

Tomlinson, J. (1991). *Cultural imperialism.* Baltimore, MD: Johns Hopkins University Press.

Tovares, R. (2002). Mascot matters: Race, history, and the University of North Dakota's "Fighting Sioux" logo. *Journal of Communication Inquiry, 26*(1), 76–94.

U. of North Dakota and NCAA settle lawsuit over "Fighting Sioux" mascot. (2007, October 26). *The Chronicle of Higher Education.* Retrieved May 15, 2008, from http://chronicle.com/news/article/3317/ u-of-north-dakota-and-ncaa-settle-lawsuit-over- fighting-sioux-mascot.

CULTURE, COMMUNICATION, AND INTERCULTURAL RELATIONSHIPS

CHAPTER OBJECTIVES

After reading this chapter, you should be able to:

1. Identify three benefits and three challenges to intercultural relationships.
2. Describe six dialectics of intercultural relationships.
3. Identify three approaches to understanding intercultural relationships.
4. Describe some cultural differences in the notion of friendship.
5. Describe cultural differences in relational development.
6. Describe "turning points" in intercultural friendships.
7. Explain the frequency of intercultural dating today.
8. Identify challenges of intercultural marriages.
9. Identify four interaction styles in intercultural marriages.
10. Identify and describe characteristics of gay and lesbian friendships.
11. Describe how institutional, historical, or political contexts can facilitate or hinder intercultural relationships.

In 2004, Anthony John Makk and Bradford Wells were married in Massachusetts. Today, Wells is seriously ill, and Makk is his primary caretaker. They have lived together for 19 years. Wells is a U.S. citizen, but Makk is an Australian. They applied for permanent residency for Makk, but the U.S. Citizenship and Immigration Services denied their application in July 2011. Citing the Defense of Marriage Act, the agency only recognizes marriages of one man and one woman. Wells responded: "At this point, the government can come in and take my husband and deport him. It's infuriating. It's upsetting. I have no power, no right to keep my husband in this country. I love this country, I live here, I pay taxes and I have no right to share my home with the person I married" (quoted in Lochhead, 2011).

The situation of this same-sex international couple underscores the complexity of intercultural relationships, due to complex national laws, state laws, and what is recognized as "family." Had one of these men been a woman, the couple would have been eligible to stay together under an I-130 visa. Or had both men been U.S. citizens, they would be together.

We may not often think about how our personal relationships might be split by the deportation of one member, but we must recognize that not all relationships are equally valued in all cultures. The case of Mr. Makk and Mr. Wells is not unique. Many other same-sex, international couples are also facing similar challenges (see the Point of View box on p. 415). Some have chosen to leave the United States to remain a family, such as Michael Hefferon, who moved to Canada so he could live with his husband and their son (Jones, 2011). While there are many challenges to any relationship, intercultural and international relationships often face even more difficulties, but there are rewards from these relationships as well.

How do we develop relationships with people who differ from us in terms of age, ethnicity, religion, class, or sexual orientation? Think about friends who differ from you in any of these ways. How did you get to know them? Are these relationships any different from those that are characterized by similarity? Why do we develop relationships with some people and not with others? There seems to be some truth to *both* adages "Birds of a feather flock together" and "Opposites attract."

What is the role of communication in intercultural relationships? And how do contexts (social, historical, political) influence our relationships? In this chapter, we explore the benefits and challenges of intercultural relationships, examine how relationships develop over time, and identify some cultural differences in relational development and maintenance. Throughout the chapter, we emphasize a dialectical perspective on intercultural relationships—both friendship and romantic. Contextual issues exist along with individual relational issues, so for each of these topics we'll examine contextual issues.

There are increasing opportunities to meet people from other cultures through the Internet and increasing cultural diversity in many schools and workplaces, yet a survey shows that first-year college students have less interest in meeting people who are different from them (Farrell, 2005). In surveys, young people repeatedly say they are open to intercultural romantic relationships, yet for some groups, the rate of intercultural dating is exactly the same as it was 20 years ago (Clark-Ibanez & Felmlee, 2004).

Why do some people get involved in intercultural relationships and others not? Why do some intercultural relationships seem to flourish and others not? We think the answer lies in a dialectic: Although individual style and preference may play a large role, the contexts in which people meet and interact have much to contribute to the viability of intercultural friendships and romantic relationships. That is, social, religious, and educational contexts may promote *or* discourage intercultural relationships. Historical and political contexts also play a big role. For example, it was only 50 years ago that it was illegal for whites and African Americans to marry (Root, 2001). This, no doubt, is part of the reason that rates of interracial dating and marriage are the lowest among these two groups when compared to rates for other ethnic and racial groups (Martin, Bradford, Drzewiecka, & Chitgopekar, 2003). Who we choose to befriend is determined both by our individual preferences *and* by social, religious, and political contexts.

In this chapter, we first examine the benefits and challenges of intercultural relationships. Then we describe six dialectics as a way of thinking about intercultural friendships and intercultural romantic relationships. Then we present the contributions of three communication perspectives on intercultural relationships—starting with the social science approach that emphasizes cross-cultural comparisons of relational notions. We then move to the interpretive perspective that has contributed in-depth information about various types of intercultural relationships, and finally we discuss the critical approach that emphasizes the role of context in determining who we form relationships with and how these relationships develop.

BENEFITS AND CHALLENGES OF INTERCULTURAL RELATIONSHIPS

Benefits

Most people have a variety of **intercultural relationships** that may feature differences in age, physical ability, gender, ethnicity, class, religion, race, or nationality. The potential rewards and opportunities in these relationships are tremendous. The key to these relationships often involves maintaining a balance between differences and similarities. One example is the relationship between Judith and a Chicana colleague. When they first met, they thought they had little in common, coming as they did from very different ethnic and cultural backgrounds. But once they found commonality in their academic work, they discovered that they actually had a great deal in common. For instance, both come from large religious families, both have parents who contributed a great deal to their communities, and both are close to their older sisters and their nieces. Through the relationship, they also have learned a lot about each other's different worlds.

The benefits of such relationships include (1) acquiring knowledge about the world, (2) breaking stereotypes, and (3) acquiring new skills. You can probably think of a lot more. In intercultural relationships, we often learn specific

intercultural relationships Relationships that are formed between individuals from different cultures.

information about unfamiliar cultural patterns and languages. Nancy, an undergraduate student, describes how she learned about culture and religion through her relationship with her boyfriend:

> *My family and I are Buddhists; however, we are not very religious. We still celebrate the holidays and traditions, but we do not attend the temple often. Anyway, my boyfriend, being Catholic, asked me to go to his church for an Easter celebration one year. I decided to go because I am an open person and not restricted to believing in just one religion. Anyhow, I went to his church, and I must say it was a good learning experience and a fun one, too. I was glad that I went to see what "Catholics" do to celebrate Easter.*

A romance or a close intercultural friendship may be the vehicle through which we learn something about history. Jennifer, a student in one of our classes, told us how she learned more about the Holocaust from her Jewish friends and about the Middle Passage from her African American friends. These are examples of **relational learning**—learning that comes from a particular relationship but generalizes to other contexts. Relational learning is often much more compelling than knowledge gained from books, classes, and so on. And once we develop one close intercultural relationship, it becomes much easier to form others. (See Figure 10-1.)

relational learning
Learning that comes from a particular relationship but generalizes to other contexts.

Intercultural relationships also can help break stereotypes. Andy, a student at Arizona State University, told us about how he used to view Mexicans as lazy. This opinion was formed from media images, discussions with friends, and political speeches about immigration in the Southwest. However, when he met and made friends with emigrants from rural Mexico, his opinion changed. He saw that in everyday life his friends were anything but indolent. They had family responsibilities and sometimes worked two jobs to make ends meet. Later, we'll discuss how breaking stereotypes actually works in relationships.

We often learn how to do new things in intercultural relationships. Through her friendships with students in the United States and abroad, Judith has learned to make paella (a Spanish dish) and *nopalitos con puerca* (a cactus-and-pork stew), to play bridge in French, and to downhill ski. Through intercultural relationships, newcomers to a society can acquire important skills. Andy's immigrant friends often ask him for help with new tasks and activities, such as buying car insurance or shopping for food. When Tom first moved to France, his new French friends helped him navigate the university cafeteria. All of these potential benefits can lead to a sense of interconnectedness with others and can establish a lifelong pattern of communication across differences. We also hope that it helps us become better intercultural communicators.

Challenges

Intercultural relationships are unique in several ways, and as such present particular challenges. By definition, they are characterized by cultural differences in communication style, values, and perceptions. The dissimilarities probably are most prominent in the early stages of relational development when people

College students often benefit from the experience of forming intercultural relationships. Through these relationships, we can learn about other
cultural groups, as well as gain additional insight into our own cultural backgrounds.
How often do you come into contact with people who are different from you? How
often do you seek out intercultural friendships? (© *Chuck Savage/Corbis*)

tend to exchange less personal information. However, if some commonality is
established and the relationship develops beyond the initial stages, these cultural differences may have less of an impact because all relationships become
more idiosyncratic as they move to more intimate stages. There seems to be an
interplay of both differences and similarities in intercultural relationships. The
differences are a given, and the challenge can be to discover and build on the
similarities—common interests, activities, beliefs, or goals.

Negative stereotyping often comes into play in intercultural relationships.
As we discussed in Chapter 5, stereotypes are a way of categorizing and processing information but are detrimental when they are negative and are held
rigidly. Sometimes people must work to get information that can counteract
the stereotype. Navita Cummings James (2000), a communication scholar,
describes the beliefs and stereotypes about white people passed along to her
from her family:

- Whites can be violent and treacherous.
- Whites have an inferiority complex that compels them to "put down"
  blacks and other minorities.
- White men are arrogant, and white women are lazy.
- "Good" whites are the exception.

Young people often encounter disapproval for interethnic relationships, sometimes from both sides. Thomas Matthew Pilgrim and Robert Brown, from Athens, Georgia, are good friends. They describe how they got together and how they each get some static from their respective friends and family.

Matthew: *Ask anybody in Athens about me and Robert, they'll say that we are always together. I'm 15. He's 17. We think just alike, act just alike and dress just alike. If he wasn't black and if I wasn't white, people could think that we were brothers. A brother in every sense of the word.*

I'm part Mexican. I'm probably the only white person in Athens with their hair braided. I just did it because it's long; it's hard to keep up with. Most of the people I know are black or Mexican. As far as I know they don't have a problem with me. But there's always got to be an odd person that has to say something. One woman said, "Look, white boy, why you got your hair braided?" I just stopped caring what people think about me. [My] family are just really big ———. All they like are people with the same skin as them. But race doesn't matter to me and my sister. And Robert and the other people I hang with don't care that I'm white. They were who I stuck with when I first moved here two and a half years ago. They took to me and really helped me. He's my best friend.

Robert: *I was going to fight him at first. I'm not going to lie. The homeboys I used to hang around with were like, "Hey man, look at that white boy." But my friend Jason knew Matt, so it was cool. I asked him his name. I told him mine. We started chilling from there. All my friends are black except for Matthew. It'd be about 30 of us and Matt. . . . He fits right in with me. He acts like everybody else that I hang around with. I don't care that he's white. If you want to find me, you look for Matt. Every day, all day, we hang out. We play basketball, beat each other up, listen to rap. We have fun. . . .*

Source: "'Hometown Homeboys,' What They Were Thinking About Race," *New York Times Magazine*, special issue (How Race Is Lived in America), July 16, 2000, p. 26.

More importantly, James goes on to describe how she did not let these stereotypes become "an intellectual prison of my self identity or beliefs about Whites" (p. 45). Through intercultural relationships and effort, her beliefs evolved and the stereotypes diminished. She learned that race is not a predictor of intelligence but that income and opportunities are. She learned that all people, regardless of color, deserve to be treated with dignity and respect. And she made definite choices about how to relate to others and to cultivate a variety of friends, and not merely African Americans.

Another challenge in intercultural relationships involves the anxiety that people often experience initially. Some anxiety is present in the early stages of

> *My growing up and my being raised . . . there was all kind of problems out there in the open for black people. And it would be very easy to hate a white person. And at home I didn't sense that hate. I sensed an understanding of what was going on, a dislike for what was going on, but not hate for the individual. And I think I've always had an open mind. My dad had several white friends that would come by and sit around and eat and laugh and talk.*

Source: Wilson, in P. C. Rosenblatt et al., *Multiracial Couples: Black and White Voices* (Thousand Oaks, CA: Sage, 1995), p. 44.

any relationship, but the anxiety is greater in intercultural relationships. Anxiety arises from concern about possible negative consequences. We may be afraid that we'll look stupid or that we'll offend someone because we're unfamiliar with that person's language or culture. Differences in age do not usually evoke such anxiety, but differences in physical ability, class, or race are likely to—at least initially. For example, a student describes his experience of being on a soccer team with players from Kenya, Jamaica, Egypt, and Mexico:

> *In our first meeting, we were to get acquainted with everyone and introduce ourselves. At the end of the meeting, we all stood around talking—reducing anxiety. Eventually, our conversations were directed toward self-disclosure and relating our experiences. I believe this helped me prepare for more experiences along this line.*

The level of anxiety may be higher if one or both parties have negative expectations based on a previous interaction or on stereotypes (Stephan & Stephan, 1992). In contrast, intercultural interactions in which one or both parties have few negative expectations and no negative prior contact probably have less anxiety.

Writer Letty Cottin Pogrebin (1987) emphasizes that intercultural relationships take more "care and feeding" than do those relationships between people who are very similar. Intercultural relationships are often more work than in-group relationships. A lot of the work has to do with explaining—explaining to themselves, to each other, and to their respective communities.

First, in some way, conscious or unconscious, we ask ourselves, What is the meaning of being friends with someone who is not like me? Am I making this friend out of necessity, for my job, or because everyone I'm around is different from me in some way? Am I making this friend because I want to gain entry into this group for personal benefit? Because I feel guilty?

Second, we explain to each other. This is the process of ongoing mutual clarification, one of the healthiest characteristics of intercultural relationships. It is the process of learning to see from the other's perspective. For example, Judith discovered that, even when she thought she was being very indirect with her Japanese students, they still thought she was being rather direct. In this way, Judith came to understand that others can interpret events and conversation in very different ways.

395

Communication plays a key role in intercultural relationships. These intercultural relationships can change who you are and how you see the world. Our student Jessica went to New Zealand:

What an amazing experience. Not only did I get to stay with a family that had three girls, one my age, but I also learned about the Maoris, the first people to inhabit New Zealand. I developed a lifelong relationship with my host family and relished learning the difference and similarities between our cultures. I have fond memories of sitting up late at night drinking tea, not coffee, with my New Zealand mother. We would talk for hours. This was a powerful learning experience.

Although my experiences have for the most part been overseas, I feel they have opened a window for me. My worldview has gone from just me to phenomenally huge. I see things from other people's point of view; I actually try to see things in a different light. I have my experiences with people from other cultures to thank.

—Jessica

Third, people who cross boundaries often have to explain this to their respective communities. Thus, your friends may question your close relationship with someone who is much older or is of a different ethnicity. This may be especially true for those who date someone from a different culture. For example, one of our students recounted how his friend terminated an intercultural relationship because of his parents' attitudes:

My Jewish friend was dating a Christian girl he met during his freshman year in college. He proposed marriage when they both graduated last year. But throughout their relationship, the parents of my friend let it be known that they were not happy with the fact that they were dating. My friend and his girlfriend are no longer seeing one another. My friend has told me he believes the parents' disapproval of the relationship was one of the reasons for their eventual split.

Historically, the biggest obstacles to boundary-crossing friendships have come not from minority communities, but from majority communities (McCullough, 1998). Those in the majority (e.g., whites) have the most to gain by maintaining social inequality and are less likely to initiate boundary-crossing friendships. In contrast, minority groups have more to gain. Developing intercultural relationships can help them survive—economically, professionally, and personally.

Finally, in intercultural relationships, individuals recognize and respect the differences. In these relationships, we often have to remind ourselves that we can never know exactly what it's like to walk in another person's shoes. Furthermore, those in the majority group tend to know less about those in minority groups than vice-versa. As Pogrebin (1992) stated, "Mutual respect, acceptance, tolerance for the faux pas and the occasional closed door, open discussion and patient mutual education, all this gives crossing friendships—when they work at all—a special kind of depth" (p. 318). Perhaps this is especially true of interracial relationships in the United States. Pat, an African American woman, describes the importance of honesty and openness in her relationship with her friend Rose, who is white:

> *"Rose is one of the few White women that I have an honest, direct relationship with. . . . She is very aware that I am a Black woman and she is a White woman. . . . I care about her very deeply. . . . And I am committed to our friendship and I respect her a whole lot. . . . I like her values. I like how she thinks about people, about nature, her integrity and her principles. . . . It is her willingness to make race her issue." (quoted in McCullough, 1998, p. 193)*

THINKING DIALECTICALLY ABOUT INTERCULTURAL RELATIONSHIPS

Researcher Leslie A. Baxter (1993) suggests that a dialectical model explains the dynamics of relationships. She and her colleagues have identified several basic dialectical tensions in relationships: novelty–predictability, autonomy–connection, and openness–closedness (Baxter & Montgomery, 1996). That is, we can simultaneously feel the need to be both connected and autonomous in relationships with our parents, friends, and romantic partners. We may also feel the need simultaneously for novelty and predictability and the need to be open and yet private in our relationships. According to one study, Taiwanese students in close relationships experience these same dialectical tensions (Chen, Drzewiecka, & Sias, 2001). We can extend the notion of dialectical tensions to encompass the entire relational sphere (Chen, 2002; Martin, Nakayama, & Flores, 2002). Let's see how each of these dialectics work.

Personal–Contextual Dialectic

Intercultural relationships are both personal and contextual. There are aspects of the relationship that are personal—consistent from situation to situation—but context also plays a huge role in how intercultural relationships are developed and maintained. For example, are there contexts where you would be more or less comfortable in an intercultural relationship? How do your family, your church, your religious friends react to intercultural relationships? Studies have shown that the number-one predictor of whether individuals engage in intercultural dating is the diversity of their social networks—that is, if you are in contexts where there is diversity, it is more likely you will meet and go out with people from other ethnic/racial backgrounds (Clark-Ibanez & Felmlee, 2004).

Even who we are attracted to is largely determined by cultural contexts. Notions of attractiveness are defined for us and reinforced by what we see on TV and film and in other media. The standard of beauty for American women seems to be white and blond, and at least one study states that 90% of models in U.S. women's magazines are white (Frith, Shaw, & Cheng, 2005). This trend was noticed by one of our students:

> *I stopped by an airport newsstand and was struck by the similarity of the covers on the popular magazines displayed there (e.g., Vanity Fair, Cosmopolitan, Self). Out of the 24 magazines, 19 had a white model with long blond hair on their covers! Two magazines had Caucasian brunettes, and two covers featured nonwhite women (one was Jennifer Lopez, the other Oprah Winfrey—on the cover of her O magazine).*

At the same time, Asian and Asian American women are often portrayed in popular culture texts and discourses as erotic, exotic, and submissive and thus highly attractive to white men (Root, 2001). One young man, Shane, described his attraction to Asian women:

> *I think they're so exotic. Really, what concerns me about the girl is the eyes, and Asian women have beautiful eyes, the form and the shape of them. It's a plus for me. I had another Asian girlfriend before. And I like their skin color, tannish, not just white, white, white. A girl with color. It's just different; it's more sexual, it's not just like plain Jane. ("Talking About Race," 2000, p. 59)*

This kind of attraction has spawned an entire business of mail-order Asian brides. Communication scholar Rona Halualani (1995) analyzed how these businesses perpetuate and market stereotypes of Asian women as idealized wives—submissive, sexual, and eager to please men. In contrast, Asian men are often stereotyped in ways that downplay their masculinity (Eng, 2001).

Of course, we all want to believe we choose our relational partners outside of the influences of these social discourses. We all want to believe we fell in love with this man or this woman because he or she is "special." Yet if we want to understand the problems and dynamics of intercultural communication, we must be attentive to these large contextual discourses about racial and sexual identities and realize there is the tension of both personal and contextual forces in any intercultural relationship.

Differences–Similarities Dialectic

similarity principle A principle of relational attraction suggesting that individuals tend to be attracted to people they perceive to be similar to themselves.

cognitive consistency Having a logical connection between existing knowledge and a new stimulus.

According to the **similarity principle,** we tend to be attracted to people who we perceive to be similar to ourselves, and evidence indicates that this principle works for many cultural groups (Osbeck & Moghaddam, 1997; Tan & Singh, 1995). Finding people who agree with our beliefs confirms our own beliefs and provides us with **cognitive consistency** (if we like ourselves, we'll probably like others who share our views). In fact, we may explicitly seek partners who hold the same beliefs and values because of deep spiritual, moral, or religious conviction. In intercultural relationships, in contrast, we may be attracted to persons who are somewhat different from ourselves. The differences that form the basis of attraction may involve personality traits and may contribute to complementarity or balance in the relationship. An introverted individual may seek a more outgoing partner, or a spendthrift may be attracted to an individual who is more careful with money. Some individuals are attracted to people simply because they have a different cultural background. Intercultural relationships present intriguing opportunities to experience new ways of living in and looking at the world.

Most of us seek a balance between novelty and predictability in our relationships. Research shows that the most successful relationships have a balance of differences and similarities (Luo & Klohnen, 2005). In intercultural relationships especially, it is important to consider differences and similarities at the same time. Tamie, a student from Japan, explains how this dialectic works in her relationship with her roommate/friend Hong-Ju, a Korean graduate student:

> *We are both women and about the same age—30. Both of us are pursuing a Ph.D. degree and aspire to become successful professional scholars and educators. When we cook in our apartment, there are several common foods (e.g., rice, dried seaweed) while our eating styles may be different (e.g., Hong-Ju's cooking tends to include more spicy food than mine). We also share some common cultural values (e.g., importance of respect for elders). Yet Hong-Ju is married (a long-distance marriage), and I am single. Finally, we both consider ourselves as "not so typical" Korean or Japanese women. Hong-Ju's long-distance marriage and my staying single even in my 30s are usually considered as nontraditional in our respective countries. Eventually, this "nontraditionalness" creates in both of us a shared and proud sense of identity and bond.*

Cultural–Individual Dialectic

Communication in intercultural relationships is both cultural and individual, that is, idiosyncratic. We have described various cultural differences that exist in value orientations, in both nonverbal and verbal communication. Although we have provided some generalizations about how various cultural groups differ, it is important to remember that communication is both cultural and individual. Tamie describes how she deals with this cultural–individual dialectic in her classroom teaching:

> *I have become very aware of cultural differences between U.S. classrooms and Japanese classrooms. In terms of my teaching style, I have noticed myself delivering the course content in a more linear, straightforward, fast-paced manner than I would in Japan. Therefore, there is definitely a certain cultural expectation that I am aware of as I teach in the U.S. However, I am also aware that there are unique individual styles and preferences among U.S. students—some students are outspoken and comfortable in speaking up; others take more time before speaking up, as they reflect and think more holistically. So this cultural–individual dialectic is always at work in my intercultural teaching experience here in the U.S.*

Privilege–Disadvantage Dialectic

We have stressed the importance of (and the difficulty of understanding) power and power differentials in intercultural relationships. People may be simultaneously privileged and disadvantaged, or privileged in some contexts and disadvantaged in others. For example, Laura, a bilingual university student, feels at a greater advantage in settings in which conversations take place in Spanish and English than she does in all-English settings. Her friends who speak only English probably feel the opposite. People in more powerful positions in particular need to be sensitive to power differentials, which may be less obvious to them.

Static–Dynamic Dialectic

This dialectic suggests that people and relationships are constantly in flux, responding to various personal and contextual dynamics. Intercultural relationships are no different in this regard. When Judith first met her friend Patricia (a third-generation, Mexican American, older student), Patricia was single and had just transferred to Arizona State University from a community college. At that time, both were living alone (Judith was in a commuter marriage), but both were close to their families. Patricia is now married, has a daughter, and has almost completed her graduate education. In this context, Judith and Patricia cannot respond to each other as the people they were five years ago but must respond to each other as they are now. Changes occur very slowly sometimes, but we need to remind ourselves that relationships are both static and dynamic.

History/Past–Present/Future Dialectic

Rather than trying to understand relationships by examining the relational partners alone, it is helpful to consider the contexts in which relationships occur. Often, this means the historical context. As noted in Chapter 4, cultural groups have different relationships with each other; some of these relationships are more positive and others more negative. For example, the historical and continuing hostility between the United States and Cuba means that each cultural group has fewer opportunities to meet people from the other nation and thus fewer opportunities to develop relationships. One student, John, gives his views on the past–present dialectic:

> *I don't feel as if people should feel guilty about what their family, ethnic group, or country did in the past, but they should definitely empathize with those their ancestors have hurt, understand what they did, understand the implications of what they did, and understand how the past (whether we have ties to it or not) greatly affects the present.*

INTERCULTURAL RELATIONSHIPS

As with other topics, there are three communication approaches to studying intercultural relationships, and each makes a unique contribution to our understanding of how we develop and maintain relationships across differences. The social science approach identifies cross-cultural differences in how relationships are defined, initiated, and developed. The interpretive approach explores in depth the nature of these relationships and the role communication plays. The critical approach emphasizes the influence of various contexts—institutional, political, and historical—in facilitating and/or discouraging the development and maintenance of intercultural relationships.

Social Science Approach: Cross-Cultural Differences

The social science approach identifies various cross-cultural differences in relationships—including notions of friendships and the initiation and development of relationships.

Differences in Notions of Friendship   What are the characteristics of a friend? How do notions of friendship vary across cultures? To some people, a friend is someone to see or talk with occasionally, someone to do things with—go to a movie, discuss interests, maybe share some problems. This person might be one of many friends. If the friend moves away, the two people might eventually lose contact, and both might make new friends. Other people, however, view friendship much more seriously. For them, a friendship takes a long time to develop, includes many obligations (perhaps lending money or doing favors), and is a lifelong proposition.

Friendships are seen in very different ways around the world. For example, in most Western cultures, these relationships are seen as mostly voluntary and spontaneous, in contrast to family or work relationships. Although our friendships may be more constrained than we think (we do form relationships with people who are often very similar to ourselves), nonetheless, we enter into them voluntarily (Bell & Coleman, 1999).

Cultural differences in notions about friendships are related to ideas discussed earlier—ideas about identity and values. In societies that stress values like individualism and independence, as is the case in most Western cultures, it makes sense to view friendship and romance as voluntary relationships. However, people who view the self always in relation to others—that is, collectivists—hold a notion of friendship that is also less individual oriented and less spontaneous (Carrier, 1999). For example, in China, where the value of collectivism is very strong, friendships are long term and involve obligations:

> The meaning of friendship itself differs from the American version. Chinese make few casual, short-term acquaintanceships as Americans learn to do so readily in school, at work, or while out amusing themselves. Once made, however, Chinese friendships are expected to last and to give each party very strong claims on the other's resources, time and loyalty. (Gates, 1987, p. 6)

Friendship in China cannot be understood without attention to an important related concept, ***guanxi***—"relationships of social connection built on shared identities such as native place, kinship or attending the same school" (Smart, 1999, p. 120). It is through *guanxi* that things get done (e.g., jobs acquired or bureaucratic snafus resolved), often "through the back door." Although "connections" are important in the United States, they are not viewed in so positive a light. Here, one should not have to resort to connections to get something done.

guanxi A Chinese term for relational network

In China, in contrast, being able to get something done through connections, or *guanxi*, is seen as very positive, and so these relationships are purposefully cultivated. *Guanxi* is not the same thing as friendship, but friendship provides an acceptable base on which *guanxi* can be built (Smart, 1999).

This emphasis in China on cultivating close relationships, filled with obligations (and always open to *guanxi*), can be a bit overwhelming to people from Western cultures, but it can also be rewarding. A prominent journalist, Fox Butterfield (1982), who spent many years in China, describes these rewards:

> *Friendship in China offered assurances and an intimacy that we have abandoned in America; it gave the Chinese psychic as well as material rewards that we have lost. We ourselves did feel close to the Wangs [their Chinese friends], but as Westerners, the constant gift giving and obligations left us uneasy. (p. 47)*

Differences in Relational Development Cultural differences often come into play in the very beginning stages of relational development, in initial interactions. Different cultural rules govern how to regard strangers. In some cultural communities, all strangers are viewed as sources of potential relationships; in others, relationships can develop only after long and careful scrutiny. For example, in traditional German Mennonite society, strangers, especially those outside the religious group, are regarded with suspicion and not as potential friends. In contrast, many U.S. Americans are known to disclose personal information in very public contexts. One international student observes,

> *One thing that was very different from what I was used to in Iceland was that people, even people that I didn't know at all, were telling me their whole life stories, or so it felt like. Even some women at the checkout line at the super-market were talking about how many times they had been married or divorced or about the money they had, which, in my culture, we are not used to just telling anyone about.*

The renowned communication scholar Dean Barnlund (1989), along with his colleagues, found many differences in relational development in their students in Japanese and U.S. colleges. Students in both countries were asked about their interactions with strangers and friends and about their views on friendship and more intimate relationships. The U.S. American students were more open and receptive to strangers; they talked to strangers in many different contexts—perhaps at a bus stop, in line at the grocery store, or in classes. In contrast, the Japanese students talked to significantly fewer strangers than did U.S. Americans over the same period.

More recently, communication scholar Pei-Wen Lee studied intercultural friendships that arise in a third culture, a culture that is not home to either of the friends. She notes that "the third cultural context serves as a significant backdrop with rules, norms, and events to which the intercultural dyad can relate and refer during their interactions" (2008, p. 66). The influence of a third culture complicates the **stage model** for intercultural friendships but can serve as a useful background for building these friendships.

stage model The view that relationships develop in predictable phases over time.

SOME INTERESTING CULTURAL VARIABLES IN RELATIONSHIPS

Brazil: To be invited to a Brazilian's home is an honor. Guests are expected to stay for many hours rather than stop for a brief visit.

China: Face-saving is extremely important in China. Chinese always avoid embarrassing situations and help one another save face and retain self-respect.

France: When French greet people, they tend to be formal. Titles such as Monsieur, Madame, and Mademoiselle are often used. If they know the person, they may give the traditional kiss by the cheek/air.

Spain: The Spanish often invite guests to their home out of courtesy. One should wait until the host insists to accept the invitation.

Germany: Germans tend to be formal. They do not use first names unless they know the person very well.

Egypt: Always use titles such as Doctor or Professor to address these professionals.

Kenya: The Kenyan socialize at the end of the meal, not before the meal.

Greece: Avoid overpraising any item in a Greek home because the host may feel obligated to present it as a gift later.

Source: M. Mancini, *Selling Destinations: Geography for the Travel Professional*, 4th ed. (Clifton Park, NY: Thomson/Delmar Learning, 2003).

Friendships As relationships develop in **intimacy,** friends share more personal and private information.

intimacy The extent of emotional closeness.

Over a half century ago, Kurt Lewin (1948), a renowned psychologist, conducted a classic cross-cultural study in self-disclosure whose findings still hold true today. Lewin proposed that the personal/private self can be modeled as three concentric circles representing three areas of information we share with others. The first circle is an outer boundary that includes superficial information about ourselves and our lives—our general interests, our daily life, and so on. The middle circle includes more personal information—perhaps our life history, our family background, and so on. Then there is the inner core, which includes very personal and private information, some of which we share with no one. These spheres of information may correspond with the phases in relational development. Thus, in the exploratory stage, people exchange some personal information, and in the stability phase, they may disclose more intimate information.

According to Lewin, there is the most variation in the extent to which the outer area is more or less permeable. For example, for many European Americans, the outer boundary is highly permeable; they may disclose a wide range of relatively superficial information with many people, even those they don't know well, in many contexts. The middle, or second, area is less permeable; this information is shared with fewer people and in fewer contexts. And information in the

I n some societies, the development of relationships is intricately related to issues of status and formality. Communication scholar Wintilo Garcia explains how these issues are expressed in Mexican Spanish.

The Mexican use of the Spanish words tu *and* usted *signals the immediacy and status of the relational partners.* Tu *is the informal application of the pronoun* you. *It is common that individuals refer to their friends, family members, or children by this form of the word. The word* usted *is the formal form of the pronoun* you. *Cultural norms and rules require individuals to use this form when addressing new acquaintances, older people, professional (white-collar) people, and people who possess some sort of power. . . . In Mexico, as relationships become more intimate, the form of address changes. This often occurs over time where people who were once referred to by* usted *will later be referred to by* tu. *. . . Usually this transformation is initiated by the person who holds a perceived higher class. This is reasonable because high class individuals are perceived to possess more power in the relationship. In Mexico, the usual request phrase from the high class player is* tuteame *(interpreted as* you *"tu" me), which implies a desire for relational equality. In order for this request to be fulfilled, relational players must negotiate the pattern of communication. . . . For example, if a student normally addresses professors by the title* Doctor G *and* Doctor T, *it implies a status and class difference. In general, to change this form of address, the professor must initiate the request.*

Source: Wintilo Garcia, "Respeto: A Mexican Base for Interpersonal Relationships," in *Communication in Personal Relationships Across Cultures,* edited by W. B. Gudykunst, S. Ting-Toomey, and T. Nishida (Thousand Oaks, CA: Sage, 1996), pp. 137–155.

inner area is shared with very few. In contrast, for many other cultural and ethnic groups, the outer boundary is much more closed. International students in the United States often remark that U.S. students seem superficial. That is, U.S. students welcome interaction with strangers and share information of a superficial nature—for example, before class or at a party. When some international students experience this, they assume they are moving into the exploratory "friend" phase (the middle circle), only to discover that the U.S. student considers the international student to be merely an acquaintance. A student from Singapore explains,

I learned in the first couple months that people are warm yet cold. For example, I would find people saying "Hi" to me when I'm walking on campus or asking me how I am doing. It used to make me feel slighted that even as I made my greeting back to them, they were already a mile away. Then when real interaction occurs— for example, in class—somehow I sense that people tend to be very superficial and false. Yet they disclose a lot of information—for example, talking about personal relationships, which I wasn't comfortable with. I used to think that because of such self-disclosure you would share a special relationship with the other person, but it's

Traditionally, when studying other cultures, people focus on the differences, appreciating and respecting them. However, the dialectic that includes differences and similarities takes this process one step further. It not only expresses the importance of respecting differences but also points up the basic human needs and wants we all possess. In our multicultural society, it is important to recognize the similarities among ourselves.

It is apparent that most cultures share some common bonds. Human emotions are the same throughout the world. Knowing that someone laughs, cries, and is scared the same as you creates an empathy that is important to understanding other cultures. This point of view allows us to form bonds and brings us closer to the people of the other culture.

Emotions are universal, and being able to see someone as you see yourself can lead to a deep respect and appreciation for the other person. Using this dialectic myself, I have already begun to blur the lines that divide me from people of other cultures. Where I once might have been scared or nervous to approach someone different, I am now curious to see how the person is the same. It is a very rewarding feeling to break down these barriers and become enlightened by someone of a different culture. I've learned that the physical differences that at first seem so apparent begin to fade away as people of different cultures communicate with one another. No matter where we come from, what our language or skin color, we all bleed red, and that makes us the same.

—Danielle

not so because the same person who was telling you about her personal relationship yesterday has no idea who you are today. Now I have learned to not be offended or feel slighted by such incidents.

It's probably more accurate to say that what most people in the world consider simply a "friend" is what a U.S. American would consider a "close friend." A German student explains that in Germany people are hardly able to call somebody a friend, even if they have known that person for more than a year. Only if they have a "special emotional relationship" can they call the person a friend (Gareis, 1995, p. 128). For most U.S. Americans, the "special emotional relationship" is reserved for a so-called good or close friend.

Mary Jane Collier conducted a study with these three groups and Asian Americans in which she investigated conversational rules in close friendships (Collier, 1996). Again, she found many similarities in how these groups thought about close friendship. However, she also found some differences. For instance, Latino/a, Asian American, and African American students said that it took, on average, about a year to develop a close friendship; European Americans felt that it took only a few months. She also found differences in what each group thought was important in close friendships: "Latinos emphasized relational support, Asian Americans emphasized a caring, positive exchange of ideas, African Americans emphasized respect and acceptance and Anglo [European] Americans emphasized recognizing the needs of individuals" (p. 315). Clearly, such distinctions affect how people of different cultural groups develop friendships.

There also are cultural differences in how much nonverbal expression is encouraged. Again, according to Barnlund's and other studies, U.S. Americans expressed much more intimacy nonverbally than did the Japanese respondents (Nishida, 1996).

romantic relationships
Intimate relationships that comprise love, involvement, sharing, openness, connectedness, and so on.

Romantic Relationships   Some intimate relationships develop into **romantic relationships.** Several studies have compared the development of these types of intimate relationships across cultures. For example, communication researcher Gao Ge (1991) compared romantic heterosexual relationships among Chinese and U.S. American young people. Based on interviews with students about their romantic relationships, she identified common themes of openness, involvement, shared nonverbal meanings, and relationship assessment. However, there were some variations between the two groups. The U.S. American students emphasized the importance of physical attraction, passion, and love, which Gao interprets as a reflection of a more individualistic orientation. In contrast, the Chinese students stressed the importance of their partners' connectedness to their families and other relational connections, reflecting a more collectivistic orientation.

In another study, Gao (2001) compared intimacy, passion, and commitment in Chinese and U.S. American heterosexual romantic relationships. Based on her previous research and on cultural values, she predicted that intimacy and passion would be higher for U.S. couples, given that passion and intimacy are more individually centered relationship goals. She also predicted that commitment—a more collectivistic relational value—would be higher for Chinese couples. She found that passion *was* significantly higher in U.S. American couples than in Chinese couples but that the amount of intimacy and commitment did not vary cross-culturally. This may mean that intimacy is a universal dimension of romantic relationships, but the finding about commitment is more puzzling. Gao speculates that this finding may be related to the fact that all the couples in her study were in advanced stages of serious relationship, at which time commitment is more universally expected. Her hypothesis about commitment may have applied to couples in earlier stages in their relationships.

This was confirmed in a similar study comparing North American, Japanese, and Russian beliefs about romantic love. In this study, North Americans emphasized romantic love, passionate love, and love based on friendship more than did the Japanese or Russians. Other, more collectivistic cultural groups emphasized the acceptance of the potential mate by family members and commitment over romantic or passionate love (Sprecher et al., 1994).

Research on the development of romantic relationships in the United States has focused on the importance of the individual's autonomy. Togetherness is important as long as it doesn't interfere too much with a person's freedom. Being open, talking things out, and retaining a strong sense of self are seen as specific strategies for maintaining a healthy intimate relationship. This emphasis on autonomy—trying to balance the needs of two "separate" individuals—in relationships can be difficult. Also, extreme individualism makes it challenging for either partner to justify sacrificing or giving more than she or he is receiving. All of this leads to fundamental conflicts in trying to reconcile personal freedom with relational obligations (Dion & Dion, 1988). In fact, one study found that people who held extremely individualistic orientations experienced less sense of love, care, trust, and physical attraction toward their partners in romantic relationships (Dion & Dion, 1991). These problems are less common in collectivistic societies.

Interpretive Approach: Communicating in Intercultural Relationships

Now that we have considered the contributions of the social science research, let's turn our attention to more in-depth examination of how we communicate across cultural differences. As we've noted, intercultural relationships may be very similar to intracultural relationships. However, there may be some unique characteristics that can guide our thinking about communicating in these relationships.

Based on interviews with U.S. and Japanese students who were friends, researcher Sandra Sudweeks and colleagues (1990) identified competence, similarity, involvement, and turning points as characterizing important aspects of intercultural relationships. For example, the students talked about the importance of linguistic and cultural competence. At first, language was a common issue. Even when people speak the same language, they sometimes have language difficulties that can prevent relationships from flourishing. The same holds true for cultural information. Dissimilarity may account for the initial attraction, but these students mentioned the importance of finding some *similarity* in their relationships that transcended the cultural differences. For example, they looked for a shared interest in sports or other activities. Or they were attracted by similar physical appearance, lifestyle, or attitude. Sometimes shared religious beliefs can help establish common bonds (Graham, Moeai, & Shizuru, 1985).

Relationships take time to develop; students interviewed by Sudweeks and colleagues mentioned how important it was that the other person make time for the relationship. This is one aspect of involvement. Intimacy of interaction is another element, as are shared friendship networks. According to the study, sharing the same friends is more important for Japanese students than for U.S. American students because the Japanese students had left their friendships behind.

Finally, the students mentioned significant occurrences that were related to perceived changes in the relationship—turning points that moved the relationship forward or backward. For example, asking a friend to do a favor or to share an activity might be a turning point. The students remarked that if the other person refused, the relationship often didn't develop beyond that point. However, a turning point of understanding—**self-disclosure**—may move the relationship to a new level.

self-disclosure Revealing information about oneself.

Another communication scholar, Brenda J. Allen (2000), gives us an example of a turning point. She describes her relationship across sexual orientation lines with a colleague in her department:

We found that we had similar ideas about issues, activities and improvement on our own critical thinking skills in the classroom. . . . [We] were both baby boomers from the Midwest, only months apart in age. We also came from lower-class families, and religion played a strong role in our childhood. (p. 179)

Allen describes the turning point in their relationship when her friend revealed that she was gay: "As a heterosexual I had never before given much thought to sexual orientation or gays 'coming out of the closet.' Thanks to Anna, I have become far more sensitive and enlightened" (p. 180).

The process of dealing with differences, finding similarities, and moving beyond stereotypes and prejudice is summed up by a U.S. American student talking about her relationship with a Singaporean friend:

"We just had different expectations, different attitudes in the beginning, but at the end we were so close that we didn't have to talk about it. . . . After we erased all prejudices, that we thought the other person has to be different, after we erased that by talking, we just understood each other." (quoted in Gareis, 1995, p. 136)

Intercultural Work Relationships   For many people, work is the place where they encounter the most diversity—working with people from different religions, generations, language backgrounds, ethnicity, races, and nationality. These encounters may be face-to-face or mediated—through telephone or computer. Understanding this diversity is especially important as organizations move from an assimilationist perspective ("Hire the quota and let them assimilate to us") to a more integrative perspective. One leading diversity expert refers to the latter as "foxhole diversity," the view that if the enemy is all around, you need people in the foxhole with you to support you; you need to cut through the superfluous and think about what skills and expertise your foxhole colleagues really need to possess as job requirements, not just what you'd prefer. We may prefer that our co-workers look like us and have the same language and religious background, but these preferences are not the same as the requirements for the job (Chozick, 2005). And more and more organizations are seeing the bottom-line payoff for a truly diverse workforce in a global economy—moving beyond concerns of women and minorities to concerns of generational differences, the pressures on gays and lesbians who have to hide part of their lives, and challenges in incorporating disabled workers (Hymowitz, 2005).

So the challenge in the workplace is to get along with people who may be very different, and some of the work relationships may turn into friendships, as one of our students reported:

At my job in the Memorial Union, I work with students of all ethnicities, races, and nationalities. At first I was kind of intimidated, but I've found that I've got to know some of them, since work issues always provide an easy topic to discuss and some of the discussions have led to more socializing. While I can't say these are among my closest friends, I probably wouldn't have had the chance to meet so many different people if I weren't working at this job.

Power, of course, often comes into play because most work relationships are within a hierarchy. There are subordinate–superior relationships and peer relationships, and the nature of the relationship constrains the interaction. If your boss tells you your hairstyle violates company policy, that's one thing. If your office mate, your company peer, tells you the photos on your desk offend her, that's something else. There is more room for negotiation and discussion.

It is difficult when race, ethnicity, and class are all part of the hierarchy—as is common in the tourist and restaurant business. The experience of one of our students is quite common:

In the restaurant where I work, all the servers (like me) are female and white, and all the busboys and kitchen help are Latino, who mostly speak Spanish, and the two bosses are white males—who make everyone speak English when they're around. I kind of like to practice my Spanish a little in talking with the Latino workers, and I have a pretty good relationship with them. Some of the other servers really refuse to speak Spanish.

Because there is a hierarchy, the busboys and kitchen help must speak English—even if the server can speak Spanish whenever she feels like practicing her Spanish.

Intercultural Relationships Online   As we noted in Chapter 1, more and more people are using new technologies to communicate. The first and perhaps the most important impact of new communication technologies, particularly for young people, is the opportunities they provide for developing and maintaining relationships. Through social networking sites (SNSs) like Facebook, e-mail, instant messaging (IM), and Twitter, we can stay in touch with old friends, maintain almost constant contact with current friends, and find new friends. By some accounts, people spend more time on SNSs than any other online activity (Hampton, Goulet, Rainie, & Purcell, 2011; Zickuhr, 2010).

These new media technologies present us with enormous opportunities to communicate and develop relationships with people who are very different from us. We can communicate with people in other countries as easily as talking to our next-door neighbors. One of our students, Mariana, described her experience of getting to know Charlotte, a Finnish student, during a virtual team project in one of her classes:

Although we're separated by oceans and many miles, we share the same daily activities and understand each other quite well. What I enjoyed most about this experience was that even after this project, Charlotte and I will be friends. We've already contacted each other on Facebook and sent messages. Besides focusing on the course project, I've gotten to know a lot about my partner's studies in school and her personal life.

This increased use of new media also leads us to speculate how online relationships differ from offline relationships and whether it is easier or more difficult to communicate across cultures online. The answers to these questions seem to be dialectical. Online communication is both similar to and different from offline relationships, and communication technologies like the Internet and social media both facilitate and inhibit the development of intercultural relationships. For example some online communication (e-mail, instant messages, text messages) facilitates intercultural encounters in that it filters out much of the information we base first impressions on—physical attractiveness, gender, age, and race. While we may find it helpful to have information about people's characteristics, this information also sometimes causes prejudice and discrimination. For example, when Mariana and Charlotte communicated during the class project, they didn't know each other's height, race, or age—unless they chose to tell each other. Thus, some of our new media interactions may be freer of the tendency to stereotype or discriminate against someone based on those physical characteristics. People can develop solid online relationships, not based on physical attributes or attractiveness, and by the time online friends meet in person, these **line of sight** data don't matter much; the result can be close, lasting relationships (McKenna, Green, & Gleason, 2002). Of course this doesn't really address the problem of prejudices based on physical appearance. As scholar Radhika Gajjala points out,

line of sight Information about other people's identity based upon visible physical characteristics.

> *Why should it be wonderful for women and colored people to be able to hide who they are and to be able to disguise their gender, race, and culture in favor of passing as Caucasian? Why must we be ashamed of being women or colored or both? What's wrong with being colored? What's wrong with being a woman? (p. 84)*

A number of studies show that online relationships are very similar to offline relationships; they conclude that using new communication technologies do not weaken relationships, nor do they act as poor substitutes for face-to-face contact. Instead, individuals use various media to connect with different social networks (Boase, 2008). For example, people use mobile phones to stay in contact with people they already know well, and they use social media (Facebook, Twitter) to expand and maintain their social networks—getting to know, or reestablishing "dormant" relationships—and more and more, they are using social networking sites to stay in touch with local friends (Hampton et al., 2011; Kim, Kim, Park, & Rice, 2007).

How does online communication affect existing relationships? It allows us to be in almost constant contact. In a recent book, media expert Sherry Turkle (2011) challenges us to reexamine our assumptions about technology being the answer to intimacy and connections. She thinks that, although we are constantly in contact with each other—in fact, *tethered* to our technology—we sometimes choose technologies that merely substitute for human intimacy. She offers these examples as proof: Adults would rather e-mail, co-workers would rather leave voicemail messages, and teenagers would rather text. These technologies give us control over our relationships and actually distance us from others; as she puts it, "Technology makes it easy to communicate when we wish and to disengage at will" (p. 13). It's supposedly an efficient way to manage our time and relationships in our busy, hectic lives. As an example of how these new technologies can affect intergenerational relationships, Turkle (2011) describes the experience of Ellen, working in Paris, who used Skype to connect with her grandmother in Philadelphia. Twice a week they would talk for an hour. But, unbeknownst to her grandmother, Ellen was multitasking during the conversation—typing away on her keyboard answering e-mails. So it wasn't a *real* connection because Ellen wasn't really present. And Ellen reportedly felt guilty about her actions.

Communication scholar Ping Yang (2012) investigated intercultural online communication of college students and discovered that their encounters could be described by several dialectics. One dialectic was digital privilege/marginalization. The students reported that they experienced some privilege in these online encounters because of the fluidity and flexibility of online identities, as well as the suspension of prejudgment based on nonverbal cues. This was particularly true for ethnic and racial minority students. According to Claudia, "Interaction online is somewhat anonymous [and this] can be an advantage. Since people don't know [what] the person they are talking to looks like, it is harder to make a judgment based on their ethnicity or how they look." Although e-mails, computer, and the Internet play a vital role in the lives of many U.S. students, those from other cultural groups or world regions may not enjoy the same opportunity and comfort levels using them.

Another dialectic was trust/suspicion. The students explained that the use of some linguistic symbols and special cues facilitated the expression of their cultural selves. One student, Lisa, explained that she uses Yiddish phrases when conversing with Jewish peers online and that creates a bond and trust. At the same time, students described how online communication could also hinder the way they expressed who they were and sometimes created a climate of suspicion. As one student, Lena, said, "it's difficult to fully trust that they tell you about themselves to be true;" another said that in chat rooms, "it is easy to polish, overstate, or fake one's identity in these places," thus leading to some suspicion in online encounters (Yang, 2012, p. 119).

Language differences also create a dialectic for online interaction and intercultural relationships—both facilitating and hindering intercultural communication. The asynchronicity of some online communication allows nonnative speakers more time to compose a message and to decode and respond than is true to face-to-face interaction—thus facilitating communication. However, at the same time, language differences can lead to possible misunderstanding of specific words and phrases and humor online can often be misunderstood—thus inhibiting intercultural communication.

Understanding humor in a language often requires a sophisticated understanding of subtle nuances; irony, sarcasm, and cynicism in online communication across cultures should be approached with great caution (St. Amant, 2002). And when humor is misunderstood, it often takes complicated explanations to clarify, as one communication professor discovered:

> *One of the classmates in my online course made a remark, meant to be slightly sarcastic and humorous, about one of the group projects he was involved in for our*

course. However, the remark was perceived by some of the international members of his group to be in poor taste. Some thought it very rude and insulting. Others just found it childish. It took almost half the semester to figure out what had gone wrong, why the remark was misunderstood and to get things back on a good footing. I can't imagine it would have taken even half that long if the interaction had been face-to-face instead of on the Internet.

Sometimes problems caused by language differences are exacerbated because one or both interactants may not be aware of the problem, because confusion or misunderstanding is generally shown nonverbally—by a quizzical look or a raised eyebrow. Online communicators may have to work a little harder to make sure they understand each other and to give the other some leeway in expressing different cultural values and communication styles.

What happens when low-context and high-context communicators interact online? Because e-mail and text messages filters out almost all contextual cues (tone of voice, eye gaze, facial expression, etc.), scholars speculate that conversations between low- and high-context communicators might be difficult online (Olaniran, 2012). The low-context communicator might be very comfortable being direct about feelings and opinions, whereas the high-context communicator might feel rather constrained by online communication. When misunderstandings occur, it might be especially difficult to identify the source of misunderstanding and resolve it (Snyder, 2003).

For example, a Korean colleague who teaches at an American university reported that she often feels constrained in e-mail conversations with her U.S. colleagues. Having a preference for high-context communication, she finds the direct, low-context style of her colleagues a bit off-putting. This is especially true when they discuss sensitive issues through e-mail, and her colleagues ask her to give an explicit opinion that might conflict with others' opinions. She reports that she sometimes doesn't respond to these e-mail messages or tries to carry on the discussion with them face-to-face where contextual, nonverbal cues are available to her.

Another possible issue for high- and low-context communication differences concerns identity information. For many high-context cultures, background information of the speaker is part of the contextual information needed to understand and respond to a message, and, as we explained earlier, in text-based online encounters, the cues essential for determining identity (age, status, etc.) and context-related expectations are missing. The lack of identity and contextual cues may cause individuals in some cultures to be reluctant to engage in online communication. As St. Amant (2012, p. 82) explains:

Such hesitation seems particularly acute in high-context cultures where knowing how to communicate effectively is connected to knowing what that specific context/setting is. Without the cues commonly used to identify persons in—and thus the context of—a given situation, individuals from such cultures tend to remain silent. Such silence, in turn, can limit the sharing of essential information out of concern that doing so might violate expectations of credible communication in that context. (p. 82)

Of course, being reserved or quiet in online encounters can have implications for how one is perceived—particularly by those with low-context communication preferences. St. Amant goes on to explain that these factors are particularly problematic for intercultural relationships in global business settings because more organizations are using online media and virtual teams in internationally distributed projects.

Similarly, what are the challenges when someone from a high-power distance culture communicates from a low-power distance culture? The high-power person might be uncomfortable with the informality and relative disregard for hierarchy expressed by the low-power distance person. And depending on preference for face-saving strategies, it might be difficult to discuss communication differences, with interactants choosing different ways to protect or save theirs or the other person's face.

Intercultural Dating   Why do people date others from different cultural backgrounds? Probably for the same reasons we form any intercultural relationship. We are attracted to them, and the relationship offers benefits—increased knowledge about the world and the breaking of stereotypes. This has been the experience of Peiting, a Tawainese American dating Paul, a Danish exchange student: "Dating Paul offers me this whole new perspective of life as a Caucasian and a Dane." Also, she encounters ideas that differ from those of most of her U.S. American friends: "We'll talk for hours about American films, about Danish government, even about variations in our countries attitudes toward drinking" (quoted in Russo, 2001).

Several decades ago, researcher Phillip E. Lampe (1982) investigated interethnic dating among students attending a college in Texas. He discovered that the reasons students gave for dating within and outside their own ethnic group were very similar: They were attracted to the other person, physically and/or sexually. In contrast, the reasons students gave for not dating someone within or outside their own ethnic group were very different. The main reason for not dating *within* the ethnic group was lack of attraction. However, the reasons for not dating *outside* the ethnic group were not having an opportunity to do so and not having thought about it. Lampe interpreted this distinction in responses as reflecting the social and political structure of U.S. American society. That is, most individuals, by the time they reach adolescence, have been taught that it is better to date within one's ethnic and racial group and probably have had very little opportunity to date interethnically.

Have things changed since Lampe's study? It does seem that they have, that U.S. Americans today are much more open to intercultural relationships. For example, in one survey, 77% of those surveyed said it's all right for blacks and whites to date each other—up from 48% who felt this way in 1987. The young are the most accepting; 91% of people questioned who were born after 1976 said that interracial dating is acceptable—compared to 50% of the oldest generation (Taylor, Funk, & Craighill, 2006). This survey showed that attitudes are more tolerant, but do people's behaviors match their attitudes? The results of our own study show that, in some instances, patterns of intercultural dating

ANTI-MISCEGENATION LAWS

Laws prohibiting interracial marriage span most of the history of the United States and began before the United States was an independent nation.

Miscegenation laws, in force from the 1660s through the 1960s, were among the longest lasting of American racial restrictions. They both reflected and produced significant shifts in American racial thinking. Although the first miscegenation laws had been passed in the colonial period, it was not until after the demise of slavery that they began to function as the ultimate sanction of the American system of white supremacy. They burgeoned along with the rise of segregation and the early twentieth-century devotion to "white purity." At one time or another, 41 American colonies and states enacted them; they blanketed western as well as southern states. (Pascoe, pp. 48–49)

These laws functioned to mark interracial sex and marriage as illegal and unacceptable. Why was it so important to protect whiteness (as opposed to blackness, etc.)? How does this history affect the demographic character of the United States today?

Source: P. Pascoe, "Miscegenation law, court cases, and ideologies of 'race' in twentieth-century America," *Journal of American History*, *83* (1996), 44–69.

have not changed a great deal and confirm that individual dating experiences and societal contexts are still closely related (Martin, Bradford, Chitgopekar, & Drzewiecka, 2003). Like Lampe's respondents, about 60% of our respondents said they had dated interculturally, with Mexican Americans doing so more frequently than African Americans or whites. Many of the remaining 40% gave the same reasons as respondents in Lampe's study for not dating interculturally: They had no desire or no opportunity. So, even though Lampe's study was conducted in the early 1980s, the same conditions seem to hold, at least in some parts of the United States, particularly for African Americans and whites. The reality remains that most Americans live, go to school, and worship in segregated groups (Logan, Stults, & Farley, 2004). And this was certainly true in our study, as 80% of the white students said they grew up in all-white neighborhoods.

We also found that the social context and past experiences were a strong influence on whether young people dated interculturally. Not surprisingly, those who did date interculturally were more likely to have grown up in ethnically diverse neighborhoods and to have more ethnically diverse acquaintances and friends. In addition, they came from families in which other family members had dated interculturally. This suggests that family attitudes play a big role. Indeed, other studies confirm that families often instill negative attitudes regarding interracial friendships or romantic relationships (Moore, 2000). And these attitudes are learned at a very young age. As Derryck, a young black child said, when asked about his relationship with his white friend, "Black and white kids can be friends

> S ame-sex couples can get married in some places around the world, but these marriages are not recognized by U.S. immigration law. Some nations do recognize same-sex relationships for immigration purposes.
>
> *Binational couples refers to couples in which the partners come from differ-ent countries. Although 16 nations around the world allow their citizens to sponsor their same-sex partners for immigration benefits, unfortunately, the United States does not recognize our relationships for immigration purposes. Because of the Defense of Marriage Act, which defines marriage as between a man and a woman, even same-sex couples which have been legally mar-ried in Massachusetts, Canada, the Netherlands, or Belgium will not be able to immigrate based on their marriage. Every day we hear from desperate couples, forced to choose between the partner they love and the country they love, which is why we are fighting to change the immigration law and end this discrimination.*
>
> Source: "Immigration Equality." Retrieved May 13, 2008, from www.immigrationequality. org/template.php?pageid=2.

with each other, if you're in the same class. But they can't get married, because they don't match. They can't have a kid together" ("Talking About Race," 2000, p. 47). Interracial friendships may be more accepted in elementary school, but they are less accepted in teenage years (Graham & Cohen, 1997).

Finally, whether individuals date interculturally may also depend on the region of the country in which they grow up. A study conducted in California, for example, showed a slightly higher incidence of intercultural dating there than we found in our study (Tucker & Mitchell-Kernan, 1995). As the 2000 census shows, there is more diversity in the West and Southwest. Given what we know about the influence of context on interpersonal relationships, we would expect more diverse schools and neighborhoods, and thus more opportunity for inter-cultural contact in these areas.

There are other factors that do not clearly explain intercultural dating pat-terns. In a recent study of Internet personal ads, Shauna Wilson and her col-leagues (2007) found that blacks who knew they did or did not want children were more willing to date other blacks than blacks who were unsure if they wanted children. Also, blacks in the West were less willing to date other blacks than those living in other parts of the country. Also, black smokers were less willing to date other blacks. It isn't clear how these variables are related to inter-cultural dating. They call for more research to better understand these patterns.

Permanent Relationships In spite of substantial resistance to intercultural (especially interracial) romantic relationships, increasing numbers of people are marrying across racial and ethnic lines, so much so that scholar Maria P. P. Root (2001) says we are in the midst of a "quiet revolution." Who is most likely to

FIGURE 10-2   Freedom to Marry is one of the organizations that is working to secure same-sex marriage rights nationwide in the United States. It is also working to overturn the federal Defense of Marriage Act. (© *The McGraw-Hill Companies, Inc./ Christopher Kerrigan, photographer*)

intermarry in the United States? According to Root, women (except for black women) intermarry more than men. Also, older rather than younger people tend to intermarry, except where similar-size groups live in proximity to one another. For example, in Hawaii, California, and Arizona, younger persons are more likely to intermarry. In addition, later generations of immigrants have higher rates of intermarriage than earlier ones. (See Figure 10-2.)

Why are the rates of intermarriage so low for certain groups? The answer has to do with various contextual issues related to gender and social status. For example, there are fewer objections to Asian American–white than to black–white marriages. Gender stereotypes come into play in that Asian women are, even now, viewed as traditionally feminine, subservient, and obedient, as well as petite—making them attractive as partners for white men. This has led to increasing numbers of Asian American women intermarrying. The same is true for Latinas and Native American women, but not black women. As Root observes, blackness for them still has caste connotations, which means they are partnered in intermarriages less than any other group. White women, in contrast, intermarry more frequently.

The larger social discourses on interracial relationships should not be ignored. Columnist Hoyt Sze (1992) notes,

Most people describe their reasons for intermarriage in terms of romantic love. Mariel, a 24-year-old Chicana raised in a suburb of Los Angeles, reflected on what influenced her decision to marry her black husband and how fortunate she was that her family approved.

I was really active in La Raza *and feel committed to my people, so I always thought I would marry a Chicano guy. I love my older brothers and even thought I might marry one of their friends. When I went away to college. . . . I was just exposed to so many people. My political ideals didn't change. But I met my husband in my second year. He was very supportive of my commitments. We just started doing things together, studying, talking, going to parties. He fit in well with my friends and I liked his friends. It was like we would go to parties and there were all sorts of people there and I'd find I always had more in common with him than just about anyone in a room. We had really good talks. And music. We both loved music and movies. So one thing led to another. I tried to talk myself out of my feelings for him, thinking I should just keep it as good friends, but then I thought, "Shouldn't the man I marry be my best friend?" My family liked him. I mean, like, if my brothers didn't like him, this would have been real hard. They have a lot of influence on me even though I make up my own mind. We talked a lot about what it meant to marry someone different than your own cultural background. But I realized I didn't have to give up my commitment to my people. We believed in the same issues. Now it might have been different if he was white. I'm not sure how that would have gone over.*

Source: M. P. P. Root, *Love's Revolution: Interracial Marriage* (Philadelphia: Temple University Press, 2001), pp. 7–8.

Naturally, people outmarry [marry outside their racial group] for love. But we must ask ourselves how much of this love is racist, unequal love. Unfortunately, interracial love is still inextricably linked to colonialism. How else does one explain the disproportional rates at which Asian American women and African American men marry out? Is it just a coincidence that the mainstream media objectify the same groups as "exotic-erotic" playthings? I know that Asian American men and African American women aren't fundamentally lacking in attractiveness or desirability. (p. 10)

If we try to understand romantic love only on the interpersonal level, how might we explain the high rates of outmarriage by some groups and not others?

In any case, the current trend to intermarry may change things. As the rates of intermarriage continue to increase, these families will produce more children who challenge the current race and gender stereotypes, and the structural barriers to intermarriage will be eroded (Lee & Edmonston, 2005). As Root (2001) observes, "Intermarriage has ripple effects that touch many people's lives. It is a symbolic vehicle through which we can talk about race and gender and reexamine our ideas about race" (p. 12). And the fact is that younger people do have more tolerant attitudes about intermarriage. Although intermarriage will not solve all intercultural problems, the increasing numbers of multicultural people will have a positive impact.

What are the major concerns of couples who marry interculturally? One study compared experiences of inter- and intracultural couples. Their concerns, like those of dating couples, often involved dealing with pressures from their families and from society in general. An additional issue involved raising children. Sometimes these concerns are intertwined. Although many couples are concerned with raising children and dealing with family pressures, those in intercultural marriages deal with these issues to a greater extent. They are more likely to disagree about how to raise the children and are more likely to encounter opposition and resistance from their families about the marriage (Graham, Moeai, & Shizuru, 1985).

Writer Dugan Romano (1997) interviewed couples in which one spouse came from another country to identify challenges of these international marriages. Some are common problems faced by most couples, including friends, politics, finances, sex, in-laws, illness and suffering, and children. But some issues are exacerbated in these intercultural marriages; these involve values, eating and drinking habits, gender roles, attitudes regarding time, religion, place of residence, stress, and ethnocentrism.

Of course, every husband and wife develop their own idiosyncratic way of relating to each other, but intercultural marriage poses consistent challenges. Romano also points out that most couples have their own systems for working out the power balance in their relationships, for deciding who gives and who takes. She identifies four styles of interaction: submission, compromise, obliteration, and consensus. Couples may adopt different styles depending on the context.

The **submission style** is the most common. In this style, one partner submits to the culture of the other partner, abandoning or denying his or her own. The submission may occur in public, whereas in private life the relationship may be more balanced. Romano points out that this model rarely works in the long run. People cannot erase their core cultural background, no matter how hard they try.

In the **compromise style,** each partner gives up some of his or her culturally bound habits and beliefs to accommodate the other person. Although this may seem fair, it really means that both people sacrifice things that are important to them. For example, the Christian who gives up having a Christmas tree and celebrating Christmas for the sake of a Jewish spouse may eventually come to resent the sacrifice.

In the **obliteration style,** both partners deal with differences by attempting to erase their individual cultures. They may form a new culture, with new beliefs and habits, especially if they live in a country that is home to neither of them. This may seem to be the only way for people whose backgrounds are completely irreconcilable to survive. However, because it's difficult for people to completely cut themselves off from their own cultural backgrounds, obliteration is not a viable long-term solution.

submission style A style of interaction for an intercultural couple in which one partner yields to the other partner's cultural patterns, abandoning or denying his or her own culture. (Compare with **compromise style, consensus style,** and **obliteration style.**)

compromise style A style of interaction for an intercultural couple in which both partners give up some part of their own cultural habits and beliefs to minimize cross-cultural differences. (Compare with **consensus style, obliteration style,** and **submission style.**)

obliteration style A style of interaction for an intercultural couple in which both partners attempt to erase their individual cultures in dealing with cultural differences. (Compare with **compromise style, consensus style,** and **submission style.**)

The style that is the most desirable, not surprisingly, is the **consensus style,** which is based on agreement and negotiation. It is related to compromise in that both partners give and take, but it is not a trade-off; rather, it is a win-win proposition. Consensus may incorporate elements of the other models. On occasion, one spouse might temporarily "submit" to the other's culture or temporarily give up something to accommodate the other. For example, while visiting her husband's Muslim family, a Swiss wife might substantially change her demeanor, dressing more modestly and acting less assertive. Consensus requires flexibility and negotiation. Romano stresses that couples who are considering permanent international relationships should prepare for the commitment by living together, spending extended time with the other's family, learning the partner's language, studying the religion, and learning the cuisine. The couple should also consider legal issues like their own and their children's citizenship, finances and taxation, ownership of property, women's rights, and divorce.

Sexualities and Intimate Relationships   Most of the discussion so far was derived from research on heterosexual friendships and romantic relationships. Much less information is available about gay and lesbian relationships. What we know is that these relationships are a fact of society: homosexuality has existed in every society and in every era (Chesebro, 1981, 1997).

What we know about gay and lesbian relationships is often in contrast to the "model" of heterosexual relationships. Gay and lesbian relationships may be intracultural or intercultural. Although there are many similarities between gay/lesbian and straight relationships, they may differ in several areas, including the roles of same-sex friendships and cross-sex friendships and the relative importance of friendships.

Same-sex friendship relationships may have different roles for gay and straight males in the United States. Typically, U.S. males are socialized toward less self-expression and emotional intimacy. Most heterosexual men turn to women for emotional support; often, a wife or female romantic partner, rather than a same-sex friend, is the major source of emotional support.

This was not always the case in the United States, and it is not the case today in many countries, where male friendship often closely parallels romantic love. In India, for example, "men are as free as women to form intimate friendships with revelations of deep feelings, failures, and worries and to show their affection physically by holding hands" (Gareis, 1995, p. 36). Same-sex friendships and romantic relationships both may involve expectations of undying loyalty, deep devotion, and intense emotional gratification (Hammond & Jablow, 1987). This seems to be true as well for gay men, who tend to seek emotional support from gay male friendships (Sherrod & Nardi, 1988). However, this differentiation doesn't seem to hold for straight women and lesbians, who more often seek intimacy through same-sex friendships. That is, they seek intimate friendships with women more than with men.

There is frequently a clear distinction between "lover" and "friend" for both gays and lesbians similar to the "incest taboo" among a family of friends (Nardi, 1992, p. 114). Close friendships may play a more important role for gays than

consensus style
A style of interaction for an intercultural couple in which partners deal with cross-cultural differences by negotiating their relationship. (Compare with **compromise style, obliteration style,** and **submission style.**)

for straights. Gays and lesbians often suffer discrimination and hostility from the straight world (Nakayama, 1998), and they often have strained relationships with their families. For these reasons, the social support from friends in the gay community can play a crucial role. Sometimes friends act as family. As one young man explains,

> *"Friends become part of my extended family. A lot of us are estranged from our families because we're gay and our parents don't understand or don't want to understand. That's a separation there. I can't talk to them about my relationships. I don't go to them; I've finally learned my lesson: family is out. Now I've got a close circle of good friends that I can sit and talk to about anything. I learned to do without the family." (quoted in Nardi, 1992, p. 110)*

Many of the issues in heterosexual romantic relationships apply to gay/lesbian couples as well. However, some relational issues, especially those pertaining to permanence and relational dissolution, are unique to gay partners.

In the United States, there is little legal recognition of permanent gay and lesbian relationships. At the time of this writing, Connecticut, Iowa, Massachusetts, New Hampshire, New York, Vermont, and the District of Columbia issue marriage licenses to same-sex couples. California, Delaware, Hawaii, Illinois, Nevada, New Jersey, Oregon, Rhode Island, Washington, and the District of Columbia offer state-level spousal rights to same-sex couples. Colorado, Maine, and Wisconsin offer some spousal rights to same-sex couples. Maryland recognizes same-sex marriages from elsewhere, but does not issue same-sex marriage licenses. Most U.S. states prohibit same-sex marriage (see page 422). In fact, many states have passed laws stating that only marriages between a man and a woman will be recognized (Neil, 2005). The federal government also has passed the Defense of Marriage Act, which allows states to not recognize same-sex marriages registered in other states. These political and legal actions have implications for the development and maintenance, as well as the termination, of gay and lesbian relationships in the United States.

Some countries, however, formally recognize same-sex relationships and thereby create different social conditions for gay and lesbian relationships (Fish, 2005). Same-sex relationships, like heterosexual relationships, are profoundly influenced by the cultural contexts in which they occur. For example, Vietnam does not stipulate that marriage must be between members of the opposite sex ("Mariage Vietnamien Lesbien," 1998), and King Sihanouk has supported gay marriages in Thailand ("Cambodian King Backs Gay Marriage," 2004). In the Netherlands, Belgium, Spain, South Africa, Canada, and Norway, gay and lesbian couples are allowed to marry with all the same legal rights and responsibilities as heterosexual spouses (Knox, 2005). In many European countries (and also Australia and New Zealand), gay relationships are recognized as legal "partnerships"; in some of these countries (e.g., Denmark, Finland, Iceland, Norway, and Sweden), same-sex couples are provided rights similar to those enjoyed by married couples. In other countries (Czech Republic, France, Germany, Luxembourg, Norway, Sweden, and Switzerland) the rights of these partnerships pertaining to health and medical benefits and financial rights (such as tax status

I had a friend who was lesbian and with whom I used to work at a car dealership. In class, we talked about the theory that we are attracted by dissimilarities, but only after we interact with the dissimilar person. I can relate to this theory. When I first met Yvette, I was nervous and wasn't sure whether I wanted to become friends with her. Before I even met her, I made fun of her behind her back, along with my other co-workers. It was only after I got to know her that I realized a person's sexuality is insignificant in developing a relationship. I was threatened by what I didn't understand or know.

After I got to know Yvette, I came to appreciate our differences. She has become a real friend and confidante. I found her sexuality to be not only interesting but refreshingly different. I met her girlfriend and went out to dinner with them. Because I have allowed myself to let down my barriers with her, it has become easier to let down my barriers with other people whose culture is different from mine. However, sometimes I still make the mistake of patronizing on the basis of dissimilarities without fully getting to know the person. This is something I have a feeling we all need to work on!

—Shannon

and inheritance) are more restricted (ABC News Online, 1999; Cole, 2001; Fish, 2005; see also www.ilga-europe.org/europe/issues/marriage_and_partnership). However, in many places in the world, the social contexts are much more problematic for gay partners in permanent relationships.

Regardless of one's position on the desirability of gay and lesbian marriage, it is important to understand the implications for same-sex relationships, which include issues of dissolution. The dissolution of heterosexual relationships often is delayed because of family and societal pressures, religious beliefs, child custody battles, and so on. However, some gay relationships probably terminate much earlier because they are not subject to these pressures. This also may mean that even though they are shorter lived, gay and lesbian relationships are happier and more mutually productive (Bell & Weinberg, 1978).

We should also note that in some countries, the negative feelings about gays and lesbians are very high, making same-sex relationships difficult, if not impossible. In Cameroon, homosexuality is a crime, and there have been a number of arrests of gay men. In this country, gay men risk a prison term of five years, because same-sex activities are unlawful ("Cameroun," 2011). Even more repressive is Iran, where three men were executed for homosexuality in September 2011. They were hung and their executions "specifically refer to sections 108 and 110 of the Iranian penal code. Section 108 defines sodomy under Iran's interpretation of Sharia law and the latter rules that the punishment for lavat is death" (Taylor, 2011). Under these conditions, same-sex relationships are undertaken with great risk, as the anti-gay attitudes are institutionalized under the law.

MARRIAGE EQUALITY & OTHER RELATIONSHIP RECOGNITION LAWS

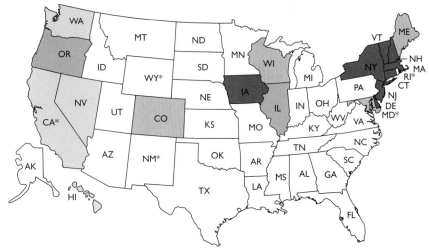

 State issues marriage licenses to same-sex couples (6 states and the District of Columbia): *Connecticut (2008), District of Columbia (2010), Iowa (2009), Massachusetts (2004), New Hampshire (2010), New York (2011, effective July 24, 2011) and Vermont (2009).*

 State recognizes marriages by same-sex couples legally entered into in another jurisdiction (1 state): *Maryland (2010).*

 Statewide law providing the equivalent of state-level spousal rights to same-sex couples within the state (9 states and Washington, DC): *California* (domestic partnerships, 1999, expanded in 2005), Delaware (civil unions, effective Jan. 1, 2012), Hawaii (civil unions, effective Jan. 1, 2012) Illinois (civil unions, 2011), Nevada (domestic partnerships, 2009), New Jersey (civil unions, 2007), Oregon (domestic partnerships, 2008), Rhode Island (civil unions, 2011) and Washington (domestic partnerships, 2007/2009).*

 Statewide law providing some statewide spousal rights to same-sex couples within the state (3 states): *Colorado (designated beneficiaries, 2009), Maine (2004), and Wisconsin (domestic partnerships, 2009).*

* California: Same-sex marriages that took place between June 16, 2008 and Nov. 4, 2008 continue to be defined as marriages. On Oct. 12, 2009, Gov. Schwarzenegger signed into law a bill that recognizes out-of-jurisdiction same-sex marriages that occurred between the June to Nov. 2008 time frame as marriages in California, and all other out-of-jurisdiction same-sex marriages as domestic partnerships.

* Maine: Gov. John Baldacci signed marriage equality legislation May 6, 2009. However, the new law was repealed by a ballot measure in November 2009.

* Maryland: does not have a registry but does provide certain benefits to statutorily defined domestic partners. Also, in 2010, the Maryland Attorney General issued an advisory opinion declaring that the state can recognize out-of-jurisdiction marriages.

*New Mexico: In Jan. 2011, the New Mexico Attorney General issued an advisory opinion declaring that the state can recognize out-of-jurisdiction same-sex marriages. At this time, it is unclear what affect this opinion will have.

* Wyoming: On June 6, 2011, the Wyoming Supreme Court decided *Christensen v. Christensen*, ruling that Wyoming trial courts have the ability to hear divorce proceedings terminating same-sex marriages created in other jurisdictions.

Source: www.hrc.org/documents/Relationship_Recognition_Laws_Map.pdf.

Critical Approach: Contextual Influences

It is important to consider intercultural relationships in the contexts in which they emerge—whether the contexts are supportive or whether they discourage intercultural relationships. Let's examine several of these contextual influences: family and neighborhood, educational and religious institutions, and historical and political contexts.

Family and Neighborhood Contexts   According to Dodd and Baldwin (2002), the first place we learn about communication adaptability and receptivity—how to respond to those who are different and how to respond to new situations—is in the family. Did your family encourage you to seek out intercultural relationships? Did your parents have a culturally diverse set of friends? And some types of relationships are more accepted that others. For example, parents may encourage children to develop friendships across religious, racial, and class lines but discourage romantic relationships with members of these same groups. Parents often play an important role in who their children date—particularly for daughters. In a recent study, it was found that women were much more likely than men to mention pressure from family members as a reason that interethnic dating would be difficult. As one Latina said,

> It would be hard . . . because my parents wouldn't agree with it and neither would my Hispanic friends. They've all told me not to mix blood. Stay with your own. (Clark-Ibanez & Felmlee, 2004, p. 300)

Even more important than what parents say is what they do. In this same study, it was the diversity of parents' friendship network, not the parents' attitudes, that determined the likelihood of the child's dating interethnically. Those whose parents had diverse friends were more likely to date interethnically than those whose parents had less diverse friends.

The diversity of one's neighborhood also has a great influence on whether one forms intercultural friendships. Here, the proximity principle comes into play. That is, we are more likely to be attracted to and form relationships with those we see often. How diverse was your childhood neighborhood?

Religious and Educational Contexts   Institutions like schools and churches/synagogues can play a huge part in promoting or discouraging intercultural friendships. It was not that long ago that some colleges banned interracial dating, and an often quoted statistic is that the most segregated hour of the week is Sunday morning—when Christians are in church. At the same time, religious institutions can provide much-needed support. One interracial couple found support by participating in a series of workshops for interracial families sponsored by their church:

> I think that being in this community helps us a lot . . . being in interracial family workshops, those kind of things; . . . it's an injection for us and that we value. And being able to expose ourselves to different types of interracial families. . . . I feel very interested and involved and somewhat knowledgeable and interested in the various

There are many Internet resources for those seeking international marriages. Think about the power relationships created in these marriages. Is this how you would want to meet your husband or wife? How would this work differently for same-sex relationships?

Mail-Order Relationships

Type	Nationality Specified	Website	Gender	Race	Power
International Female	Filipino	www .theatavist .com/	This site focuses on relationship building between Western men and Filipina women. There are discussion forums and links to international dating services.	From the site: "I have met so many men with an obsession for Filipina women that I have wondered exactly what it is men seem to find so alluring. Is there some single definitive quality that we can reach consensus on?"	Privileges white Western men who get to choose from a large number of Filipina women.
International Female	Russian and Ukrainian	www .anastasia-international .com/newest .html	The sexuality of the women is a primary focus of the photos.	The race of the women is not "featured." In fact, most of the women appear to accentuate their American characteristics.	"Romance tours" are a feature of this site. In these tours, men travel to the Ukraine where women compete for their affection.
International Male	Diverse with an emphasis on the Ukraine	www .aloving husband.com /index.php? page=index	The occupations of the men are featured along with their interests.	Not a focus of the site. However, the language issue seems to be a major one as translation is always available for site users.	There is a lack of information on the potential dynamics of the relationships.

adoption controversies that are going on and noticing again in this community the various levels of interracial activity. (Rosenblatt, Karis, & Powell, 1995, p. 271)

From very recent research, it appears that *integrated* religious institutions and educational institutions provide the best opportunities for intercultural friendships and the best environment to improve attitudes about interracial marriage (Johnson & Jacobson, 2005). For example, a study of six California State University campuses found that the students on these campuses interacted equally, in interracial and intraracial encounters (Cowan, 2005). These campuses are very diverse; no one ethnic or racial group is a majority. On the other hand, neighborhoods and work contexts do not seem to provide opportunities for the *type* of contact (intimate, friendly, equal status interaction) that clearly facilitates intercultural friendships (Johnson & Jacobson, 2005). Having ethnically varied friends has more of an influence on the propensity to engage in an interethnic romance than does being in a diverse social environment in general. "The role of friends is particularly important, perhaps because an individual is most likely to be introduced to a partner by a common friend, and because social approval from one's friends is a potent predictor of relationship stability" (Clark-Ibanez & Felmlee, 2004, p. 301).

Historical and Political Contexts   As noted in Chapter 4, history is an important context for understanding intercultural interactions and relationships. Many U.S. men in military service during various wars have returned to the United States with wives whom they met and married while stationed abroad. And many of the servicemen who experienced such intercultural relationships argued successfully against miscegenation laws, or laws that prohibited interracial marriages.

An example of the role that history and politics can play in intercultural communication can be seen in the experiences of William Kelly (2006), a communication scholar who lived in Japan for many years. He recounts his experiences when he first went to Japan to teach English 25 years ago. There were few U.S. Americans in Japan, and they were treated with great deference. In retrospect, he realizes that he was quite arrogant in his view of the Japanese:

I expected Japanese to assimilate to my culture. I also felt superior to them. Due to their culture, I believed that Japanese would never reach the goals of individual freedom, rational thought in daily life and speaking English like a U.S. American. Therefore they would always remain aspiring U.S. Americans, not capable of achieving equality. (p. 15)

His relationship with the Japanese can best be understood in the context of the history of U.S.–Japanese relations. As we learned in Chapter 1, Asians in the United States were treated very badly in the late 18th and early 19th centuries. (Remember the Oriental Exclusion Act of 1882 as well as the Johnson-Read Act of 1924, which severely restricted Japanese immigration to the United States.) Then came World War II and the internment of Japanese Americans, followed by the U.S. occupation of Japan. As a result, in the 1960s, 1970s, and 1980s, although the Japanese deferred to U.S. economic and political superiority, there was restrained resentment, and sometimes outright racism, toward

My aunt is full-blooded Mexican and her husband is full-blooded middle-Eastern. They have been married for about twelve years, and have three beautiful children. Despite many cultural differences, their relationship keeps going strong.

One such difference is the language barrier. She only spoke Spanish, while he spoke Arabic and English. At the beginning of their relationship a friend translated for them in order to understand each other. A year later they got married and my aunt had to learn English to communicate with him and his family, while also trying to learn Arabic. Another difference was their religion. She is Catholic and he is Christian. Together, they have to cope with each other and educate their children. They have learned from each others' culture and are trying to take a little bit of both and combine it for their kids.

—Amilia

U.S. Americans living in Japan. For example, in the 1980s, U.S. Americans in Japan could not enter certain establishments, obtain loans, or have the same jobs as Japanese. This example reveals the importance of the material and the symbolic realm in understanding culture. Kelly explains,

> *It was the material conditions of white U.S. power and privilege that led me to assume a stance of superiority in relation to the Japanese people I encountered. The communication grooves that I unthinkingly entered when I began living in Japan were the outcome of a colonial relationship between the United States and Japan. (p. 15) Japanese racial discrimination against whites has often been a defensive measure to keep members of a powerful nation within well-defined spheres. The goal has been to maintain a private area of Japanese people where the overbearing Western presence was absent and where Japanese could be "themselves." (pp. 16–17)*

Over the years, Kelly developed a different way of relating to Japanese. This came about primarily as a result of his encounters with U.S. Americans in Japan who were truly respectful of the Japanese. They learned Japanese, had many Japanese friends, and tried to adapt to the Japanese way of life—thereby achieving a more equal power balance. Eventually, he says, he was able to reach a level of understanding that accepted both similarities and differences between Japan and the United States. Kelly points out that his efforts to communicate with Japanese people in a truly respectful manner were assisted by the diminishing of the unequal power relations between the United States and Japan:

> *By the 1990s, there were many Japanese who had experienced the West that were no longer so positive about Westerners, and especially Americans. They expected white people to learn the Japanese language and communicate in a more Japanese way. . . . Many Japanese had gone overseas to work or study and there was less of an inferiority complex among Japanese towards white Americans. European Americans had been very gradually losing their place of privilege. (p. 18)*

All this points to the effect of power on hierarchical relations of communication. Although power does not determine communication patterns in any simple causal sense, it does have an impact on the direction communication takes within intercultural relations. Although U.S.–Japanese communication is still affected in numerous ways by the legacy of the U.S. occupation of Japan, increased economic power has given the Japanese people a new sense of pride.

There are other examples of how colonial histories framed relationships. The British, for example, constructed myriad intercultural relationships, recognized or not, within the lands they colonized. Writer Anton Gill (1995), in his book *Ruling Passions*, discusses various ways in which the colonialists tried to engage in or to avoid intercultural relations, as well as the legacy of interracial children left in their wake. He was concerned with British social policies in the colonies, particularly as they related to offspring, who were often unwanted and abandoned.

The dialectical tension rests, on the one hand, in the social, political, and economic contexts that make some kinds of intercultural relationships possible and, on the other hand, in the desires and motives of the partners involved. There are no easy explanations for whom we meet, when we meet them, and under what conditions we might have a relationship. Different cultural groups have different demographics, histories, and social concerns. Scholar Harry Kitano and his colleagues (1984) discuss some of these issues for Asian Americans. Scholars Robert Anderson and Rogelis Saenz (1994) apply the demographics of Mexican American communities to argue for the importance of larger structural factors—such as proximity—in understanding interracial marriage.

INTERNET RESOURCES

www.lovingday.org/
This website is dedicated to the legal histories of interracial relationships. There is an interactive map of the United States that gives a visual feel for interracial legislation. The site contains stories of interracial couples and their trials and triumphs. Most importantly, the site works to promote June 12 as "Loving Day" in commemoration of the 1967 decision in *Loving* v. *Virginia* that formally legalized interracial marriage.

www.npr.org/templates/story/story.php?storyId=10184979
This is an NPR podcast about negotiating intercultural relationships. The experts provide practical advice with an academic foundation for couples dealing with the tribulations of intercultural issues. The podcast is part of a series of NPR productions revolving around culture.

www.uscis.gov/portal/site/uscis
The U.S. Citizenship and Immigration Services has laws that regulate international relationships (whether marriage, adoption, family members, and so on). Because of the Defense of Marriage Act, the United States does not recognize same-sex marriages from nations where it is legal (e.g., Argentina,

Belgium, Canada, South Africa). Compare this with Australia's new changes to its laws: www.immi.gov.au/legislation/key-changes/2009/same-sex-relationships.htm. Look at the ways that these rules construct "families."

www.interfaithfamily.com/ix.php?tid=IF.RL.IR
This is a web resource designed for Jewish families seeking help negotiating intercultural and interfaith relationships. The inclusion of faith makes this an intercultural topic with added complications. Please note that the articles are written with the idea that the readers are Jewish.

www.hrw.org/audio/2010/11/29/senegals-gay-men-suffer-violence
www.hrw.org/features/forbidden-gays-and-lesbians-burundi
Listen to these stories about gay life in Burundi and Senegal. How do different societies create conditions that make gay relationships difficult or impossible? Should others respect these conditions as cultural differences? Or should others pressure these nations to change?

SUMMARY

- Through relationships, we acquire specific and general knowledge, break stereotypes, and acquire new skills.

- Special challenges of intercultural relationships include coping with differences, tending to stereotype, dealing with anxiety, and having to explain ourselves to others.

- There are six dialectics of intercultural relationships: personal–contextual, differences–similarities, cultural–individual, privilege–disadvantage, static–dynamic, and history/past–present/future.

- There are three communication approaches to understanding intercultural relationships: social science, interpretive, and critical.

- The social science approach emphasizes the individual role in relationships and identifies various cross-cultural differences in notions of friendship and how relationships are developed and maintained.

- The interpretive perspective provides in-depth descriptions of various types of intercultural relationships.

- Intercultural relationships often include competence, similarity, involvement, and turning points.

- Online relationships are both similar to and different from RL (real-life) relationships. Language and communication-style differences can be exacerbated in online communication.

- Relationships at work are characterized by hierarchy and sometimes varying attitudes toward power.

- In gay and lesbian relationships, friendship and sexual involvement are not mutually exclusive.

- Intercultural dating and marriage are increasingly common; however, interracial relationships are still often disapproved of by families and by society.
- Intercultural marriages face challenges of family and societal disapproval and issues of child rearing.
- The critical perspective emphasizes the role of institutions, politics, and history in intercultural relationships.
- Family, schools, and religious institutions can either hinder or discourage intercultural relationships.

DISCUSSION QUESTIONS

1. What are some of the benefits of intercultural relationships?
2. What factors contribute to our forming relationships with some people and not with others?
3. How is the development of intercultural relationships different from that of intracultural relationships?
4. What challenges do intercultural couples face when they decide to make their relationships permanent?
5. What are the advantages of taking a dialectical perspective on intercultural relationships?

 Go to the self-quizzes on the Online Learning Center at www.mhhe.com/ martinnakayama6 to further test your knowledge.

ACTIVITIES

1. *Intercultural Relationships.* List all of your friends to whom you feel close. Identify any friends on the list who are from other cultures. Answer the following questions, and discuss your answers with other class members.
   a. Do people generally have more friends from their own culture or from other cultures? Why?
   b. In what ways are intercultural friendships different from or similar to friendships with people from the same culture?
   c. What are some reasons people might have for not forming intercultural friendships?
2. *Friendship Dialectics.* Choose one friend who is different from you. Describe a situation or situations in which you experienced the dialectics discussed in this chapter. (*Hint:* Think of the ways in which the two of you are both similar and different—age, gender, background, interests, personality, and so on. Think of the ways your relationship has both changed and stayed the same—attitudes, experiences, interests, and so on.)

KEY WORDS

cognitive consistency (398)	intercultural relationships (391)	romantic relationships (406)
compromise style (418)	intimacy (403)	self-disclosure (407)
consensus style (419)	line of sight (410)	similarity principle (398)
guanxi (401)	obliteration style (418)	stage model (402)
	relational learning (392)	submission style (418)

 The Online Learning Center at www.mhhe.com/martinnakayama6 features flashcards and crossword puzzles based on these terms and concepts.

REFERENCES

ABC News Online. (1999, October 14). France grants equal legal rights to gay couples. *Australian Broadcasting Corporation.*

Allen, B. J. (2000). Sapphire and Sappho: Allies in authenticity. In A. Gonzalez, M. Houston, & V. Chen (Eds.), *Our voices: Essays in culture, ethnicity and communication* (3rd ed., pp. 179–183). Los Angeles: Roxbury.

Anderson, R. N., & Saenz, R. (1994). Structural determinants of Mexican American intermarriage, 1975–1980. *Social Science Quarterly, 75*(2), 414–430.

Barnlund, D. S. (1989). *Communication styles of Japanese and Americans: Images and reality.* Belmont, CA: Wadsworth.

Baxter, L. A. (1993). The social side of personal relationships: A dialectical perspective. In S. Duck (Ed.), *Social context and relationships* (pp. 139–165). Newbury Park, CA: Sage.

Baxter, L. A., & Montgomery, B. (1996). *Relating: Dialogues and dialectics.* New York: Guilford Press.

Bell, A. P., & Weinberg, M. S. (1978). *Homosexualities: A study of diversity between men and women.* New York: Simon & Schuster.

Bell, S., & Coleman, S. (1999). The anthropology of friendship: Enduring themes and future possibilities. In S. Bell & S. Coleman (Eds.), *The anthropology of friendship* (pp. 1–20). New York: Berg.

Boase, J. (2008). Personal networks and the personal communication system. *Information, Communication & Society, 11*(4), 490–508.

Butterfield, F. (1982). *Alive in the bitter sea.* Toronto: Bantam Books.

Cambodian king backs gay marriage. (2004, February 20). BBC News. Accessed at http://news.bbc.co.uk/2/hi/asia-pacific/3505915.stm.

Cameroun: Quatre nouvelles arrestations pour homosexualité. *Têtu.* Retrieved September 10, 2011, from www.tetu.com/actualites/international/cameroun-quatre-nouvelles-arrestations-pour-homosexualite-20060._

Carrier, J. G. (1999). People who can be friends: Selves and social relationships. In S. Bell & S. Coleman (Eds.), *The anthropology of friendship* (pp. 21–28). New York: Berg.

Chen, L. (2002). Communication in intercultural relationships. In W. B. Gudykunst & B. Mody (Eds.), *Handbook of international and intercultural communication* (pp. 241–258). Thousand Oaks, CA: Sage.

Chen, T. C.-C., Drzewiecka, J. A., & Sias, P. M. (2001). Dialectical tensions in Taiwanese international student friendships. *Communication Quarterly, 49,* 57–66.

Chesebro, J. W. (Ed.). (1981). *Gayspeak: Gay male and lesbian communication.* New York: Pilgrim Press.

Chesebro, J. W. (1997). Ethical communication and sexual orientation. In J. M. Makau & R. C. Arnett (Eds.), *Communication ethics in an age of diversity* (pp. 126–154). Bloomington: University of Illinois Press.

Chozick, A. (2005, November 14). Beyond the numbers. *Wall Street Journal,* p. R4.

Clark-Ibanez, M. K., & Felmlee, D. (2004). Interethnic relationships: The role of social network diversity. *Journal of Marriage and Family, 66,* 229–245.

Cole, D. (2001, July 31). Germany opens door to gay marriage. *Agence Presse.* www.gfn.com/archives/story.phtml?sid=9975.

Collier M. J. (1996). Communication competence problematics in ethnic friendships. *Communication Monographs, 63,* 314–346.

Cowan, G. (2005). Interracial interactions of racially diverse university campuses. *Journal of Social Psychology, 14,* 49–63.

Desnos, M. (2008, May 2). La France rejette un marié gay. *Le Journal du dimanche au quotidien.* Retrieved May 2, 2008, from www.lejdd.fr/cmc/societe/200818/la-france-rejette-un-marie-gay_114517.html.

Dion, K. K., & Dion, K. L. (1991). Psychological individualism and romantic love. *Journal of Social Behavior and Personality, 6,* 17–33.

Dion, K. L., & Dion, K. K. (1988). Romantic love: Individual and cultural perspectives. In R. Sternberg & M. Barnes (Eds.), *The psychology of love* (pp. 264–289). New Haven, CT: Yale University Press.

Dodd, C. H., & Baldwin, J. R. (2002). The role of family and macrocultures in intercultural relationships. In J. N. Martin, T. K. Nakayama, & L. A. Flores (Eds.), *Readings in intercultural communication* (2nd ed., pp. 279–289). Boston: McGraw-Hill.

Eng, D. L. (2001). *Racial castration: Managing masculinity in Asian America.* Durham, NC: Duke University Press.

Fahrenthold, D. A. (2005, October 2). Connecticut's first same-sex unions proceed civilly. *The Washington Post,* p. A3.

Farrell, E. (2005, February 4). More students plan to work to help pay for college. *Chronicle of Higher Education,* pp. A1, A34.

Fiebert, M. S., Nugent, D., Hershberger, S. L., & Kasdan, M. (2004). Dating and commitment choices as a function of ethnicity among American college students in California. *Psychological Reports, 94,* 1293–1300.

Fish, E. (2005). The road to recognition: A global perspective on gay marriage. *Harvard International Review, 27,* 32–35.

Frith, K., Shaw, P., & Cheng, H. (2005). The construction of beauty: A cross-cultural analysis of women's magazine advertising. *Journal of Communication, 55,* 56–70.

Gajjala, R. (2004). Negotiating cyberspace/negotiating RL. In A. Gonzalez, M. Houston, & V. Chen (Eds.), *Our voices: Essays in culture, ethnicity and communication* (4th ed., pp. 63–71). Los Angeles: Roxbury.

Gao, G. (1991). Stability of romantic relationships in China and the United States. In S. Ting-Toomey & F. Korzenny (Eds.), *Cross-cultural interpersonal communication* (pp. 99–115). Newbury Park, CA: Sage.

Gao, G. (2001). Intimacy, passion, and commitment in Chinese and U.S. American romantic relationships. *International Journal of Intercultural Relations, 25,* 329–342.

Gareis, E. (1995). *Intercultural friendship: A qualitative study.* Lanham, MD: University Press of America.

Gates, H. (1987). *Chinese working-class lives.* Ithaca, NY: Cornell University Press.

Gill, A. (1995). *Ruling passions: Sex, race and empire.* London: BBC Books.

Graham, J. A., & Cohen, R. (1997). Race and sex factors in children's sociometric ratings and friendship choices. *Social Development, 6,* 355–372.

Graham, M. A., Moeai, J., & Shizuru, L. S. (1985). Intercultural marriages: An intrareligious perspective. *International Journal of Intercultural Relations, 9,* 427–434.

Gudykunst, W. B., & Matsumoto, Y. (1996). Cross-cultural variability of communication in personal relationships. In W. B. Gudykunst, S. Ting-Toomey, & T. Nishida (Eds.), *Communication in personal relationships across cultures* (pp. 19–56). Thousand Oaks, CA: Sage.

Halualani, R. T. (1995). The intersecting hegemonic discourses of an Asian mail-order bride catalog: Pilipina "oriental butterfly" dolls for sale. *Women's Studies in Communication, 18*(1), 45–64.

Hammond, D., & Jablow, A. (1987). Gilgamesh and the Sundance Kid: The myth of male friendship. In H. Brod (Ed.), *The making of masculinities: The new men's studies* (pp. 241–258). Boston: Allen & Unwin.

Hampton, K. N., Goulet, L. S., Rainie, L., & Purcell, K. (2011). Social networking sites and our lives. Pew Internet & American Life Project. Retrieved July 22, 2011, from www.pewinternet.org/Reports/2011/Technology-and-social-networks.aspx.

Harris, T. M., & Kalbfleisch, P. J. (2000). Interracial dating: The implications of race for initiating a romantic relationship. *Howard Journal of Communications, 11,* 49–64.

Hymowitz, C. (2005, November 14). The new diversity. *Wall Street Journal,* pp. R1, R3.

Jacobson, C. K., & Johnson, B. R. (2006). Interracial friendship and African Americans' attitudes toward interracial marriage. *Journal of Black Studies, 36,* 570–584.

James, N. C. (2000). When Miss America was always white. In A. González, M. Houston, & V. Chen (Eds.), *Our voices: Essays in culture, ethnicity and communication* (3rd ed., pp. 42–46). Los Angeles: Roxbury.

Johnson, B. R., & Jacobson, C. K. (2005). Context in contact: An examination of social settings on Whites' attitudes toward interracial marriage, *Journal of Social Psychology, 68,* 387–399.

Jones, S. (2011, August 19). Upurea closing because of same-sex couple's immigration issues. *The Journal Times.* Retrieved September 11, 2011, from www.journaltimes.com/news/local/article_955d2546-cab8-11e0-80be-001cc4c002e0.html.

Kelly, W. E. (2006). Applying a critical metatheoretical approach to intercultural relations: The case of U.S.–Japanese communication. *China Media Research, 2*(4), 9–21.

Kim, H., Kim, G. J., Park, H. W., & Rice, R. E. (2007). Configurations of relationships in different media: FtF, email, instant messenger, mobile phone, and SMS. *Journal of Computer-Mediated Communication, 12,* 1183–1207.

Kitano, H. H. L., Yeung, W.-T., Chai, L., & Hatanaka, H. (1984). Asian-American interracial marriage. *Journal of Marriage and the Family, 56,* 179–190.

Knox, N. (2005, August 11). Religion takes a back seat in Western Europe, *USA Today,* p. 01A.

Lampe, P. (1982). Interethnic dating: Reasons for and against. *International Journal of Intercultural Relations, 6,* 115–126.

Lee, P.-W. (2008). Stages and transitions of relational identity formation in intercultural friendship: Implications for Identity Management Theory. *Journal of International and Intercultural Communication, 1,* 51–69.

Lee, S. M., & Edmonston, B. (2005). New marriages, new families: U.S. racial and Hispanic intermarriage. *Population Bulletin, 60*(2), 3–36.

Lewin, K. (1948). Some social psychological differences between the United States and Germany. In G. Lewin (Ed.), *Resolving social conflicts.* New York: Harper.

Lochhead, C. (2011, August 9). S.F. gay married couple loses immigration battle. *San Francisco Chronicle.* Retrieved September 11, 2011, from http://articles.sfgate.com/2011-08-09/bay-area/29866637_1_marriage-act-immigration-equality-immigration-benefits.

Logan, J. R., Stults, B. J., & Farley, R. (2004). Segregation of minorities in the Metropolis. *Demography, 41,* 1–22.

Luo, S., & Klohnen, E. C. (2005). Assortative mating and marital quality in newlyweds: A couple-centered approach. *Journal of Personality and Social Psychology, 88,* 301–326.

McKenna, K. Y. A., Green, A. S., & Gleason, M. E. J. (2002). Relationship formation on the Internet: What's the big attraction? *Journal of Social Issues, 58,* 9–31.

Mariage vietnamien lesbien. (1998, May). *Illico,* 32–33.

Martin, J. N., Bradford, L. J., Drzewiecka, J. A., & Chitgopekar, A. S. (2003). Intercultural dating patterns among young white U.S. Americans: Have they changed in the past 20 years? *Howard Journal of Communications, 14,* 53–73.

Martin, J. N., Nakayama, T. K., & Flores, L. A. (2002). A dialectical approach to intercultural communication. In J. N. Martin, T. K. Nakayama, & L. A. Flores (Eds.), *Readings in intercultural communication* (2nd ed., pp. 3–13). Boston: McGraw-Hill.

McCullough, M. W. (1998). *Black and White women as friends: Building cross-race friendships.* Cresskill, NJ: Hampton Press.

McKenna, K. Y. A., Green, A. S., & Gleason, M. E. J. (2002). Relationship formation on the Internet: What's the big attraction? *Journal of Social Issues, 58,* 9–31.

Mercer, K. (1994). *Welcome to the jungle.* New York: Routledge.

Moore, R. M. (2000). An exploratory study of interracial dating on a small college campus. *Sociological Viewpoints, 16,* 46–64.

Nakayama, T. K. (1998). Communication of heterosexism. In M. L. Hecht (Ed.), *Communication of prejudice* (pp. 112–121). Thousand Oaks, CA: Sage.

Nardi, P. M. (1992). That's what friends are for: Friends as family in the gay and lesbian community. In K. Plummer (Ed.), *Modern homosexualities: Fragments of lesbian and gay experience* (pp. 108–120). New York: Routledge.

Neil, M. (2005). Same-sex benefits bind. *ABA Journal, 91,* 22–24.

Nishida, T. (1996). Communication in personal relationships in Japan. In W. B. Gudykunst, S. Ting-Toomey, & T. Nishida (Eds.), *Communication in personal relationships across cultures* (pp. 102–121). Thousand Oaks, CA: Sage.

Olaniran, B. A. (2012). Exploring cultural challenges in e-learning. In P. H. Cheong, J. N. Martin, & L. P. Macfadyen (Eds.), *New media and intercultural communication: Identity, community and politics* (pp. 61–74). New York: Peter Lang.

Osbeck, L. M., & Moghaddam, F. M. (1997). Similarity and attraction among majority and minority groups in a multicultural context. *International Journal of Intercultural Relations, 21,* 113–123.

Pogrebin, L. C. (1987). *Among friends.* New York: McGraw-Hill.

Pogrebin, L. C. (1992). The same and different: Crossing boundaries of color, culture, sexual preference, disability, and age. In W. B. Gudykunst & Y. Y. Kim (Eds.), *Readings on communicating with strangers* (pp. 318–336). New York: McGraw-Hill.

Romano, D. (1997). *Intercultural marriage: Promises and pitfalls* (2nd ed.). Yarmouth, ME: Intercultural Press.

Root, M. P. P. (2001). *Love's revolution: Interracial marriage.* Philadelphia: Temple University Press.

Rosenblatt, P. C., Karis, T. A., & Powell, R. D. (1995). *Multiracial couples: Black and white voices.* Thousand Oaks, CA: Sage.

Russo, R. (2001, February 9). Intercultural relationships flourish despite differences. *The (Georgetown) Hoya.*

Sherrod, D., & Nardi, P. M. (1988). *The nature and function of friendship in the lives of gay men and lesbians.* Paper presented at the annual meeting of the American Sociological Association, Atlanta.

Shibazaki, K., & Brennan, K. (1998). When birds of a different feathers flock together: A preliminary comparison of intra-ethnic and inter-ethnic dating relationships. *Journal of Social and Personal Relationships, 15,* 248–256.

Smart, A. (1999). Expression of interest: Friendship and *quanxi* in Chinese societies. In S. Bell & S. Coleman (Eds.), *The anthropology of friendship* (pp. 119–136). New York: Berg.

Snyder, G. (2003, May). Teams that span time zones face new work rules. Stanford Business. Website of Stanford Graduate School of Business. Accessed at www.gsb.stanford.edu/news/bmag/sbsm0305/feature_virtual_teams.shtml.

Sprecher, S., Aron, A., Hatfield, E., Cortese, A., Potapova, E., & Levitskaya, A. (1994). Love: American style, Russian style, and Japanese style. *Personal Relationships, 1,* 349–369.

St. Amant, K. (2012). Culture, context, and cyberspace: Rethinking identity and credibility in international virtual teams. In P. H. Cheong, J. N. Martin, & L. P. Macfadyen (Eds.), *New media and intercultural communication: Identity, community and politics* (pp. 75–92). New York: Peter Lang.

St. Amant, K. (2002). When cultures and computers collide: Rethinking computer-mediated communication according to international and intercultural communication expectations. *Journal of Business and Technical Communication, 16,* 196–214.

Stephan, W., & Stephan, C. (1992). Reducing intercultural anxiety through intercultural contact. *International Journal of Intercultural Relations, 16,* 89–106.

Sudweeks, S., Gudykunst, W. B., Ting-Toomey, S., & Nishida, T. (1990). Developmental themes in Japanese–North American relationships. *International Journal of Intercultural Relations, 14,* 207–233.

Sze, H. (1992, July 24). Racist love. *Asian Week,* pp. 10, 24.

Talking about race. (2000, July 16). *New York Times Magazine,* special issue (How Race Is Lived in America).

Tan, D., & Singh, R. (1995). Attitudes and attraction. *Personality and Social Psychology Bulletin, 21,* 975–986.

Taylor, J. (2011, September 7). Iran executes three men for sodomy. *The Independent.* Retrieved September 10, 2011, from www.independent.co.uk/news/world/middle-east/iran-executes-three-men-for-sodomy-2350671.html.

Taylor, P., Funk, C., & Craighill, P. (2006). Guess who's coming to dinner?: 22% of Americans have a relative in a mixed-race marriage. Pew research report. Retrieved December 12, 2008, from http://pewsocialtrends.org/assets/pdf/interracial.pdf.

Tucker, M. B., & Mitchell-Kernan, C. (1995). Social structure and psychological correlates of interethnic dating. *Journal of Social and Personal Relationships, 12,* 341–361.

Turkle, S. (2011). *Alone together: Why we expect more from technology and less from each other.* New York: Basic Books.

Wilson, S. B., McIntosh, W. D., & Insana, S. P., II. (2007). Dating across race: An examination of African American Internet personal advertisements. *Journal of Black Studies, 37,* 964-982.

Yancy, G. (2002). Who interracially dates: An examination of the characteristics of those who have interracially dated. *Journal of Comparative Family Studies, 33,* 177–190.

Yang, P. (2012). Who am I in virtual space? A dialectical approach to students' online identity expression. In P. H. Cheong, J. N. Martin, & L. P. Macfadyen (Eds.), *New media and intercultural communication: Identity, community and politics* (pp. 109–122). New York: Peter Lang.

Zickuhr, K. (2010, December 16). *Generations 2010.* Pew Internet & American Life Project. Retrieved July 23, 2011, from www.pewinternet.org/Reports/2010/Generations-2010.aspx.

CULTURE, COMMUNICATION, AND CONFLICT

CHAPTER OBJECTIVES

After reading this chapter, you should be able to:

1. Define and describe characteristics of intercultural conflict.

2. Be able to discuss three approaches—social science, interpretive, and critical—to studying conflict.

3. Be able to identify five types of interpersonal conflict.

4. Explain the role of cultural values, family influences, gender, and ethnicity in interpersonal conflict.

5. Be able to discuss some of the contexts that contribute to social conflict.

6. Explain some strategies for dealing with conflict.

7. Be able to distinguish productive from destructive conflict.

8. Describe characteristics and advantages of mediation.

The need to understand intercultural conflict seems more important now than ever. One thing we can be sure of is that conflict is inevitable. Conflicts are happening all around the world, as they always have, and at many different levels: interpersonal, social, national, and international. For example, at the interpersonal level, friends or romantic partners may disagree about their relationship between themselves or with friends and family. Interpersonal conflicts can be intergenerational. You may disagree with your parents about where to attend college, or what you spend your money on, or where to live in the summer. These conflicts can have varying outcomes. Recently, older people in Britain, irritated about young people loitering in their neighborhood, used a device known as "Mosquito" that can only be heard by children and young people, which angered the young people (High pitched sound used to deter teenagers, 2008). Kenji, a Japanese American student from Alabama, had conflicts with her dad—with more serious consequences. When he found out she was gay, he threw her out of the house and still refuses to see her (Kramer, 2011).

Conflicts can also happen on a societal level. For example, various groups in the United States engage in conflict based on deeply held value differences; some feel that health care is a right that should be afforded to everyone for the good of the society in general, and others feel that it is an individualistic privilege that each person is responsible to obtain. As we've noted earlier, there are also strong feelings that lead to societal conflict around immigration issues. Some U.S. Americans believe that children of undocumented immigrants should not have access to educational opportunities (e.g., scholarships, internships) that are typically reserved for U.S. citizens—that doing so only rewards the illegal actions of their parents. Others believe that these children and young people should not be denied opportunities because of the actions of their parents (see Figure 11-1, p. 441).

An example of international conflict is current U.S.–Pakistan relations. While some Pakistanis were happy to see Osama bin Laden gone, the Pakistani government—already feeling humiliated by drone attacks against Taliban on Pakistani territory—are still angry that they were not notified in advance of the plan to kill bin Laden. They retaliated by denying visa requests for U.S. agents to enter Pakistan. American officials then arranged for the Pakistan embassy in Washington, D.C., to independently issue visas. Pakistan then leaked the name of the CIA station chief in Pakistan, forcing him to resign; the U.S. retaliated with news stories pointing fingers for the leak at Pakistani intelligence personnel; and so on and so on. "Anti-Americanism, always high, is soaring" (America and Pakistan: Stuck with you, 2011, p. 44).

Conflicts in one country can spill into neighboring countries. For example, the uprisings in Libya (North Africa) resulted in a great number of Libyans, as many as 1.5 million, fleeing across the Mediterranean to Italy—where they are met with hostility and anti-immigrant attitudes. Recently, violence erupted in the little town of Rosarno in southern Italy. After African farmworkers protested systematic anti-immigrant discrimination and the shooting of two farmworkers by local Italian youth, mobs of Italians attacked the farmworkers. Within 24 hours, most had fled the town, and seven were sent to the hospital to recover from beatings and gunshot wounds (Immigration in Italy, 2011).

As you can see from these examples, conflict is not simply a matter of disagreement. Conflict among cultural groups can escalate into tragedies that stretch across generations and continents. Pakistan and America, Italy and North African countries have complicated historical relationships. How can people overcome conflict and put it behind them? How can families and individuals restore relationships after hurtful interpersonal conflict? There are no easy answers to these questions, but we must consider them as part of our understanding of intercultural conflict.

Understanding intercultural conflict is especially important because of the relationship between culture and conflict. That is, cultural differences can cause conflict; once conflict occurs, cultural backgrounds and experience influence how individuals deal with it. Culture can shape what people consider valuable (like moral and religious beliefs) and worth fighting for; it can shape official positions taken and interpretations of others' actions. Sometimes conflicts arise not due to differences in values or morals, but just because someone is "different." For example, a recent report found that men in the military were often being bullied, even raped, because they were different in some way (in accent or from a particular region of the country) (Duell, 2011). Or consider that the targets of bullying and harassment in high school and college campuses often differ from the majority of students in some way. On the other hand, there are many reasons for conflicts, and serious disagreements or even violence can arise between people who are very similar in background (e.g., family members) or who share similar cultural traditions (Greek and Turkish Cypriots). We need to say upfront that intercultural conflict is an extremely complex topic.

As with other topics in this textbook, we use our tripartite framework (social science, interpretive, and critical) to examine and understand intercultural conflict. The social science approach focuses on how cultural differences cause conflict and influence the management of the conflict, primarily on the interpersonal level. The other two approaches—interpretive and critical—focus more on intergroup relationships and on cultural, historical, and structural elements as the primary sources of conflict. These three approaches emphasize different aspects of the individual–contextual dialectic and the need to view conflict on all three levels: the interpersonal, societal, and international.

We first define what we mean by conflict and intercultural conflict and then describe each of the three approaches. We conclude the chapter with practical suggestions for understanding and improving our intercultural conflict skills.

CHARACTERISTICS OF INTERCULTURAL CONFLICT

Conflict is usually defined as involving a perceived or real **incompatibility** of goals, values, expectations, processes, or outcomes between two or more **interdependent** individuals or groups. The complexity of intercultural conflict can be seen in the current debate, introduced in Chapter 7, on whether or not Muslim women should be allowed to wear veils in public. This has been a major issue in France, where a no-veil policy has been instituted. In the United States, the issue

conflict The interference between two or more interdependent individuals or groups of people who perceive incompatible goals, values, or expectations in attaining those ends.

incompatibility Incapable of existing harmoniously.

interdependent Mutually dependent.

gained national attention over the question of whether women could wear veils while driving or posing for their driver's license photo. These conflicts have roots in the history of Christian–Muslim relations and U.S/French–Arab/Muslim countries relations—histories characterized by domination on the part of the United States and colonization on France's part and by hostility and resentment on the part of some Muslims and Arabs. There are also gender issues involved. Some political leaders see the veil as a symbol of oppression of women, while others, including some women, see it as a symbol of religious devotion (Wolf, 2008).

The point here is that there is no reason to seek a single source for conflict. By taking a dialectical approach to thinking about conflict, you can see how various forces—economic, social, political, religious—may all play different roles at different times. Yet, when confronted with such conflicts, how should society respond? How should you respond?

What are the characteristics of **intercultural conflict?** How does intercultural conflict differ from other kinds of conflict? One unique characteristic is that intercultural conflicts tend to be more ambiguous than intracultural conflict. Other characteristics involve language issues and contradictory conflict styles.

intercultural conflict
Conflict between two or more cultural groups.

Ambiguity

There is often a great deal of ambiguity in intercultural conflicts. We may be unsure of how to handle the conflict or of whether the conflict is seen in the same way by the other person. And the other person may not even think there is a conflict. A student, Tabbetha, reported an ongoing conflict at work with one of her co-workers, an older gentleman, in the customer service department. She thinks the co-worker doesn't like her very much and they frequently disagree about how to handle certain customer complaints. Part of the problem is that she doesn't really get what is going on between them—she's not sure if it's her age, her gender, or if he's having a bad time in his personal life.

Language

Issues surrounding language may be important to intercultural conflict. One student, Stephanie, described a situation that occurred when she was studying in Spain. She went to an indoor swimming pool with her host family sisters. Being from Arizona, she was unaccustomed to swimming in such cold water, so she went outside to sunbathe. Her "sisters" asked her why she didn't swim with them. Stephanie explains,

> *At that point I realized they thought I should really be with them. . . . I didn't know how to express myself well enough to explain to them. . . . I tried, but I don't think it worked very well. So I just apologized. . . . I did basically ignore the conflict. I would have dealt with it, but I felt I did not have the language skills to explain myself effectively, so I did not even try. . . . That is why I had such a problem, because I could not even express what I would have liked to.*

MEDIA COVERAGE OF INTERNATIONAL CONFLICTS

Which intercultural conflicts are you most familiar with? The Israel–Palestine conflict? Are you aware of the many conflicts in Africa—for example, in Sudan? Somalia? Nigeria? Professor Matt Evans (2010) at Pennsylvania State University says there is a good reason we know more about some conflicts than others.

In his research, he found that during a 12-day period when there were 36 *The New York Times* news stories devoted to fighting between Arabs and Israelis in the town of Jenin (with 75 casualties), there were only 22 *The New York Times* stories on all the countries in Africa combined. Eighty-five percent of the stories were less than 500 words, and one-third were less than 100 words. He concludes that because of this, "dozens of conflicts, thousands of deaths and massive humanitarian crises, in an area thousands of times the size of Israel . . . received no attention" (p. 227). Perhaps even more important, he goes on to show how this disproportionate coverage has real consequences—it leads to "inconsistent foreign policy priorities and in many cases, a failure to anticipate significant foreign conflicts and crises" (p. 227).

Source: M. Evans, "Framing International Conflicts: Media Coverage of Fighting in the Middle East," *International Journal of Media and Cultural Politics*, 6(2) (2010), 209–228.

When individuals don't know the language well, it is very difficult to handle conflict effectively. At the same time, silence is not always a bad thing. Sometimes it provides a "cooling off" period, allowing things to settle down. Depending on the cultural context, silence can be very appropriate.

Contradictory Conflict Styles

Intercultural conflict also may be characterized by a combination of orientations to conflict and conflict management styles. Communication scholar Sheryl Lindsley (1999) interviewed managers in *maquiladoras*—sorting or assembly plants along the Mexican–U.S. border—and found many examples of conflict. For example, Mexican managers thought that U.S. managers were often rude and impolite in their dealings with each other and the workers. The biggest difference between U.S. Americans and Mexicans was in the way that U.S. Americans expressed disagreement at management meetings. One Mexican manager explained,

> *When we are in a meeting together, the U.S. American will tell another manager, "I don't like what you did." . . . Mexicans interpret this as a personal insult. They have a difficult time understanding that U.S. Americans can insult each other in this way and then go off and play golf together. . . . Mexicans would be polite, perhaps tell the person in private, or make a suggestion, rather than confronting. (quoted in Lindsley, 1999, p. 158)*

Why are some cultures more prone to conflicts, whereas others have a low incidence of conflict? Anthropologist Marc Howard Ross (2011) spent many years investigating this question in many different countries. He concludes that in some cultures, conflict tends to be minimized and dealt with constructively; in other cultures, conflicts abound. What makes the differences?

Ross thinks that the reasons are both structural and psychocultural (child-rearing practices, socialization, cultural values). He finds that low-conflict societies share common characteristics: interpersonal practices that build security and trust, a preference for joint problem solving, and a strong link between individual and communities. He describes how Norway exemplifies a low-conflict society.

Norwegians are socialized to avoid conflict, learning early in life that overt aggression is unacceptable and emotional self-control over negative feelings is important. In fact, Norway has a national policy to combat bullying and violence in schools and requires peer mediation and conflict resolution education in all public schools (Johannessen, 2007). There are few aggressive models in the popular culture—newspapers do not sensationalize crime, television features little violence and no boxing, and films are controlled. For example, *E.T.* was considered too violent for children under age 12 (Ross, 1993). In addition, there are high levels of parental nurturance and supervision.

There are also extensive "moralnets"—people who provide support to individuals in times of need, such as extended family, friends, and neighbors. A strong collective sense of responsibility is expressed in a variety of ways, including an emphasis on equality, attentiveness to community norms, and conformity and participation. Norway's low rate of violence predictably explained the horror felt by Norwegians after the senseless murder of children at a summer camp in July 2011 by an anti-immigrant gunman and does suggest that even in very peace-loving countries, individuals can deviate from the cultural norm (Zhang, 2011).

Sources: M. H. Ross, *The culture of conflict: Interpretations and interests in comparative perspective.* (New Haven, CT: Yale University Press, 1993a); M. H. Ross, "Reflections on the Strengths and Limitations to Cross-Cultural Evidence in the Study of Conflict and Its Mitigation," *Cross-Cultural Research*, *45*(1), (2011), 82–96.

As Lindsley points out, the conflict between the Mexican and U.S. American managers in their business meetings needs to be understood as a dialectical and "layered" process in which individual, dyadic, societal, and historical forces are recognized.

THE SOCIAL SCIENCE APPROACH TO CONFLICT

Perhaps if everyone agreed on the best way to view conflict, there would be less of it. But the reality is that different orientations to conflict may result in more conflict. In this section, which takes a social science approach, we identify cultural influences in approaches to conflict, different types of conflict, and different strategies and tactics for responding to conflict.

A key question is this: Is open conflict good or bad? That is, should conflict be welcomed because it provides opportunities to strengthen relationships? Or should it be avoided because it can only lead to problems for relationships and groups? Another key question is this: What is the best way to handle conflict when it arises? Should individuals talk about it directly, deal with it indirectly, or avoid it? Should emotions be part of the conflict resolution? Are expressions of emotions viewed as showing commitment to resolving the conflict at hand? Or is it better to be restrained and solve problems by rational logic rather than emotional expressiveness? Also consider the following questions: How do we learn how to deal with conflict? Who teaches us how to solve conflicts when they arise? How we answer all of these questions depends in large part on our cultural background and the way we were raised.

Cultural Values and Conflict

One general way to understand cultural variations in intercultural conflict resolution is to look at how cultural values influence conflict management. Face negotiation theory links cultural values to facework and conflict styles (Ting-Toomey, 2005). **Facework** refers to specific communication strategies we use to "save" our own or another person's face and is a universal concept; how we "do" facework varies from culture to culture and influences conflict styles. Communication scholar Ting-Toomey and her colleagues have conducted a number of studies showing that people from individualistic societies tend to be more concerned with saving their own face than another person's, so they tend to use more direct conflict management styles (Ting-Toomey & Oetzel, 2000, 2002).

In contrast, people from collectivistic societies tend to be more concerned with preserving group harmony and with saving the other person's face (and dignity) during conflict. They may use a less direct conversational style; protecting the other person's face and making him or her look good is considered a skillful facework style. These face concerns lead them to use a more accommodating conflict style (Ting-Toomey & Oetzel, 2002). However, some evidence indicates that not all collectivistic societies prefer indirect ways of dealing with conflict. How someone chooses to deal with conflict in any situation depends on the type of conflict and the relationship she or he has with the other person (Cai & Fink, 2002; Ting-Toomey, 2005). For example, Kaori, a Japanese student, recounted a conflict she had with her U.S. American friend, Mara, when the two were working together on a sorority project. Mara seemed to take a very competitive, individualistic approach to the project, saying things like, "I did this on the project," or referring to it as "my project." Kaori became increasingly irritated and less motivated to work on the project. She finally said to Mara, "Is this your project or our project?" Mara seemed surprised, tried to defend herself, and eventually apologized; the two women then continued to work on the project and put the conflict behind them. This example is supported by a study that showed that while Japanese young people said they would avoid conflict with strangers or

facework Communication strategies used to "save" our own or someone else's "face," or public image.

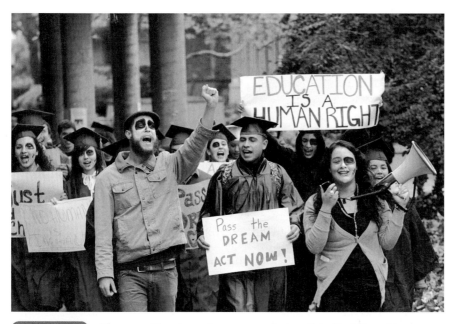

FIGURE 11-1   After marching through campus and a handful of buildings, Napa Valley College students make their way back to the plaza in front of the McCarthy Library while protesting the delayed passage of the Dream Act in Washington. If passed, the legislation would allow immigrant children who were brought into the country before they were 16, have lived in the United States for five years, and have completed a high school diploma to earn citizenship after finishing two years of college or military service. (© Jorgen Gulliksen/Zuma Press/Corbis)

acquaintances, like Kaori, they were more willing to deal openly with conflict and work through conflicts with ingroup members like close friends (Cole, 1996).

Family Influences

Most people deal with conflict in the way they learned while growing up—their default style. A primary influence is our family background; some families prefer a particular conflict style, and children come to accept this style as normal. For example, the family may have settled conflict in a direct, engaging manner, with the person having the strongest argument (or the biggest muscle) getting his or her way, and preserving his or her own self-esteem, rather than helping the other person "save face." Or, we may prefer to sacrifice our own self-esteem in order to preserve the relationship.

Sometimes, people try very hard to reject the conflict styles they saw their parents using. For example, suppose that Maria's parents avoided open conflict and never discussed what was bothering them. Their children learned to avoid conflict and become very uncomfortable when people around them use a more expressive style of conflict management. Maria has vowed she will never deal

Types of Conflict

There are many different types of conflict, and we may manage these types in different ways. Communication scholar Mark Cole (1996) conducted interviews with Japanese students about their views on conflict and found most of the same general categories as those identified in the United States. These categories include the following:

- *Affective conflict* occurs when individuals become aware that their feelings and emotions are incompatible. For example, suppose someone finds that his or her romantic love for a close friend is not reciprocated. The disagreement over their different levels of affection causes conflict.

- *A conflict of interest* describes a situation in which people have incompatible preferences for a course of action or plan to pursue. For example, one student described an ongoing conflict with an ex-girlfriend: "The conflicts always seem to be a jealousy issue or a controlling issue, where even though we are not going out anymore, both of us still try to control the other's life to some degree. You could probably see that this is a conflict of interest." Another example of a conflict of interest is when parents disagree on the appropriate curfew time for their children.

- *Value conflict*, a more serious type, occurs when people differ in ideologies on specific issues. For example, suppose Mario and Melinda have been dating for several months and are starting to argue frequently about their religious views, particularly as related to abortion. Melinda is pro-choice and has volunteered to do counseling in an abortion clinic. Mario, a devout Catholic, is opposed to abortion under any circumstances and is very unhappy about Melinda's volunteer work. This situation illustrates value conflict.

- *Cognitive conflict* describes a situation in which two or more people become aware that their thought processes or perceptions are incongruent. For example, suppose Marissa and Derek argue frequently about whether Marissa's friend Jamal is paying too much attention to her; Derek suspects that Jamal wants to have a sexual encounter with Marissa. Their different perceptions of the situation constitute cognitive conflict.

- *Goal conflict* occurs when people disagree about a preferred outcome or end state. For example, suppose Bob and Ray, who have been in a relationship for 10 years, have just bought a house. Bob wants to furnish the house slowly, making sure that money goes into the savings account for retirement, whereas Ray wants to furnish the house immediately, using money from their savings. Bob's and Ray's individual goals are in conflict with each other.

with conflict that way with her own children and has tried very hard to use other ways of dealing with conflicts when they do arise in her family. It is important to realize that people deal with conflict in a variety of ways and may not have the same reasons for choosing a certain style (Koerner & Fitzpatrick, 2006).

Conflicts arise for many reasons. Religion is a common cause of conflict in intercultural relationships. Note how this student dealt with religious differences in her marriage.

I just recently got married. I am Caucasian, and my husband is Hispanic. He comes from a large, traditional family. My family background does not include many specific traditions. His family is very religious, and I grew up virtually without religion. When I became pregnant, his family told me that the baby would be baptized Catholic and raised Catholic. They also told me that they did not view our marriage as being legitimate (because we were not "married in God's eyes," that is, the Catholic Church). This was hard for me to deal with at first. I felt that I was being pressured to become someone I wasn't. But I agreed to go to church and learn Catholicism.
—Stacy

Family conflict can also arise from generational differences in immigrant families that reflect intercultural differences. In Europe, Muslim immigrant girls are sometimes harassed or punished by their families for being too Western. For example, Latifa Ahmed, 25, arrived in the Netherlands from Morocco when she was 8. As she grew older, her family turned against her because she preferred to be with her Dutch classmates. "They were bad, they were infidels, I was told," she said. "My parents and my brothers started hitting me." Ahmed, who lived at home until she was 23, said, "I was going crazy from all the fights and the lies, but I was afraid to run away and lose my family" (Simon, 2005).

Other immigrant families may have conflicts over arranged marriages, dating, and other cultural expectations that may highlight differences between the country of origin and the new homeland.

Intercultural Conflict Styles

Given cultural background and values as well as family influences, how do people specifically respond to conflict situations? Conflict expert Mitchell Hammer (2005) has systematically investigated this topic and proposes a four-style framework, based on two primary dimensions (direct/indirect and emotional expressiveness/restraint). Let's see how this works.

Direct and Indirect Conflict Approaches This **direct/indirect approach** to conflict is similar to the direct/indirect language dimension we discussed in Chapter 6. There it was applied specifically to language use, whereas here it represents a broader conflict resolution approach. Some cultural groups think that conflict is fundamentally a good thing; these groups feel that it is best to approach conflict very directly, because working through conflicts constructively results in stronger, healthier, and more satisfying relationships. Similarly, groups

direct approach
A view that the best way to deal with conflict is to use precise and specific language.

indirect approach
A view that best way to approach conflict is to use vague and nonspecific language.

443

that work through conflict can gain new information about members or about other groups, defuse more serious conflict, and increase group cohesiveness (Putnam, 2006).

People who take this approach concentrate on using very precise language. While they may not always feel comfortable with face-to-face conflict, they think that it's important to "say what's on your mind" in a conflict situation. The goal in this approach is to articulate the issues carefully and select the "best" solution based on an agreed-upon set of criteria. However, many cultural groups view conflict as ultimately destructive for relationships and do not think that a direct approach to conflict resolution is useful. For example, many Asian cultures, reflecting the influence of Confucianism and Taoism, and some religious groups in the United States see conflict as disturbing the peace. For instance, most Amish think of conflict not as an opportunity for personal growth, but as a threat to interpersonal and community harmony. When conflict does arise, the strong spiritual value of **pacifism** dictates a non-resistant response—often avoidance or dealing with conflict very indirectly (Kraybill, 2001).

Also, these groups think that when members disagree they should adhere to the consensus of the group rather than engage in conflict. In fact, members who threaten group harmony may be sanctioned. One writer gives an example of a man from the Maori culture in New Zealand who was swearing and using inappropriate language in a public meeting:

> *A woman went up to him, laying her hand on his arm and speaking softly. He shook her off and continued. The crowd now moved back from him as far as possible, and as if by general agreement, the listeners dropped their gaze to their toes until all he could see was the tops of their heads. The speaker slowed, faltered, was reduced to silence, and then sat down. (Augsburger, 1992, p. 80)*

These people tend to approach conflict rather indirectly. They concentrate on the meaning that is "outside" the verbal message and tend to be very careful to protect the "face" of the person with whom they disagree. They may emphasize vagueness and ambiguity in language and often rely on third parties to help resolve disagreements. The goal in this approach is to make sure that the relationship stays intact during the disagreement. For example, they may emphasize the past history of the disputants and try to build a deeper relationship that involves increased obligation toward each other.

Emotional Expressiveness/Restraint Approaches A second broad approach to conflict management concerns the role of emotion in conflict. People who value intense and overt displays of emotions during discussion of disagreement rely on the **emotionally expressive approach.** They think it is better to show emotion during disagreement than to hide or suppress feelings; that is, they show emotion through expressive nonverbal behavior and vocalization. They also think that this outward display of emotions means that one really cares and is committed to resolving the conflict. In fact, one's credibility is based on the ability to be expressive.

pacifism Opposition to the use of force under any circumstances.

emotionally expressive approach A view that the best way to deal with conflict is by overt displays of feeling.

On the other hand, people who believe in the **restraint approach** think that disagreements are best discussed in an emotionally calm manner. For these people, it's important to control and internalize one's feelings during conflict and to avoid nonverbal emotion. They are uncomfortable with emotional expression and think that such expressions may hurt others. People who use this approach think that relationships are made stronger by keeping one's emotions in check and protecting the "face" or honor of the other person. Credibility is demonstrated by maintaining tight control over one's emotions.

restraint approach A view that the best way to deal with conflict is by hiding or suppressing feelings and emotion.

These two approaches to conflict resolution reflect different underlying cultural values involving identity and preserving self-esteem and "face." In the more individualistic approach that sees conflict as good, the concern is with individuals preserving their own dignity. The more communal approach espoused by both Amish and Asian cultures and by many other collectivist groups is more concerned with maintaining harmony in interpersonal relations and preserving the dignity of others. For example, in classic Chinese thought, social harmony is the goal of human society at all levels—individual, family, village, and nation (Oetzel, Arcos, Mabizela, Weinman, & Zhang, 2006).

It is possible to combine these approaches and come up with four different conflict resolution styles that seem to be connected to various cultural groups: the discussion style, the engagement style, the accommodating style, and the dynamic style (Hammer, 2005).

The **discussion style** combines the direct and emotionally restrained approaches and emphasizes a verbally direct approach for dealing with disagreements—to "say what you mean and mean what you say." People who use this style are comfortable expressing disagreements directly but prefer to be emotionally restrained. This style is often identified as the predominant style preferred by many white Americans, as well as by Europeans, Australians, and New Zealanders

discussion style combines the direct and emotional restrained approaches to conflict.

The **engagement style** emphasizes a verbally direct and confrontational approach to dealing with conflict. This style views intense verbal and nonverbal expression of emotion as demonstrating sincerity and willingness to engage intensely to resolve conflict. It has been linked to some African Americans and southern Europeans (France, Greece, Italy, Spain), as well as to some people from Russia and the Middle East (Israel). This approach is captured in the Russian proverb, "After a storm, fair weather; after sorrow, joy."

engagement style combines the direct and emotional expressive approaches to conflict.

The **accommodating style** emphasizes an indirect approach for dealing with conflict and a more emotionally restrained manner. People who use this style may be ambiguous and indirect in expressing their views, thinking that this is a way to ensure that the conflict "doesn't get out of control." This style is often preferred by American Indians, Latin Americans (Mexicans, Costa Ricans), and Asians. This style may best be expressed by the Swahili proverb, "Silence produces peace, and peace produces safety," or by the Chinese proverb, "The first to raise their voice loses the argument." In this style, silence and avoidance may be used to manage conflict. For example, the Amish would prefer to lose face or money rather than escalate a conflict, and Amish children are instructed to turn the other cheek in any conflict situation, even if it means getting beat up by the neighborhood bully.

accommodating style combines the indrect and emotional restrained manner.

intermediary In a formal setting, a professional third party, such as a lawyer, real estate agent, or counselor, who intervenes when two parties are in conflict. Informal intermediaries may be friends or colleagues who intervene.

mediation The act of resolving conflict by having someone intervene between two parties.

Individuals from these groups also use **intermediaries**—friends or colleagues who act on their behalf in dealing with conflict. For example, a Taiwanese student at a U.S. university was offended by the People's Republic of China flag that her roommate displayed in their room. The Taiwanese student went to the international student advisor and asked him to talk to the U.S. American student about the flag. People who think that interpersonal conflict provides opportunities to strengthen relationships also use **mediation**, but mainly in formal settings (lawyers, real estate agents, therapists), which we will discuss later in the chapter. It is often difficult for people who are taught to use the discussion or engaging style to see the value in the accommodating style or in nonviolent approaches. They see indirectness and avoidance as a sign of weakness. However, millions of people view conflict as primarily "dysfunctional, interpersonally embarrassing, distressing and as a forum for potential humiliation and loss of face" (Kim, 2002, p. 63). With this view of conflict, it makes much more sense to avoid direct confrontation and work toward saving face for the other person.

dynamic style combines the indirect and emotional expressive approaches to conflict.

The **dynamic style** uses an indirect style of communicating along with a more emotionally intense expressiveness. People who use this style may use strong language, stories, metaphors, and use of third-party intermediaries. They are comfortable with more emotionally confrontational talk and view credibility of the other person grounded in their degree of emotional expressiveness. This style may be preferred by Arabs in the Middle East.

Cautions About Stereotyping   As with any generalization, however, it must be remembered that all conflict resolution styles can be found in any one cultural group, and while cultural groups tend to prefer one style over another, we must be careful not to stereotype. Also, these cultural differences may depend on a number of factors, including (1) whether regions have been historically homogeneous and isolated from other cultures, (2) the influence of colonization, and (3) the immigration history of different cultural groups. For example, there is much more African influence in the Caribbean (compared to Central and Latin America), resulting in a more direct and emotionally expressive approach (engagement style) than in Mexico—where people maintain a more indirect and emotionally restrained approach (accommodation style). And there is great variety within the cultures on the African continent, accounting for tremendous variation in conflict resolution styles (Hammer, 2005).

It is also important to recognize that people deal with conflict in a variety of ways for a variety of reasons. Conflict specialists William Wilmot and Joyce Hocker (2010) warn that we should not think of preferred styles as static and set in stone. Rather, they suggest that purely individual styles really do not exist because we are each influenced by others in interaction. Therefore, our conflict management styles are not static across settings and relationships (see the Student Voice box). For example, people may use a discussion style at work and accommodating style at home, or they may use an accommodating style at work and an engagement style at home. And they may use different styles with different partners. For instance, with co-workers, individuals may tend to collaborate and work through conflict issues in a more direct way; with the boss, they may tend to employ more

When I was back home in Singapore, my parents never really taught me about how to deal with conflict. I was never encouraged to voice my opinions, and, I guess because I'm a girl, sometimes my opinions are not highly valued. I think society also taught me to maintain harmony and peace, and that meant avoiding conflict. I practiced silence and had to learn quietly to accept the way things are at school and especially at work.

When I first came to the United States, I tried to be more vocal and to say what was on my mind. But even then I would restrain myself to a point where I couldn't help it any longer, and then I would try to come across as tactfully as possible. I used to think about when I was back in Singapore, when I dealt with conflict in such a way: If I could not remove the situation, then I would remove myself from the situation. But now, after learning to be more independent, more vocal, and more sure of myself, I know that I can remain in the situation and perhaps try to resolve some if not all of it.
—Jacqueline

accommodating strategies. In addition, our styles often change over the course of a conflict and over the life span. For example, individuals who tend to avoid and accommodate may learn the benefits of engaging and working through conflicts.

Gender, Ethnicity, and Conflict Styles

Our gender and ethnicity may influence how we handle conflict. Some research shows that men and women do tend to behave in stereotypical ways in some contexts: Men using a more engagement conflict style, whereas women use a more accommodating style (Brewer, Mitchell & Weber, 2002; Cai & Fink, 2002; Davis, Capobianco, & Kraus, 2010). This may reflect the fact that in many cultures, women are socialized to focus on relationships and to be more accommodating and indirect in their interaction, while men are socialized to be more competitive. However, it may be that these gender behaviors are context-specific. Some research shows that the pattern may be reversed in heterosexual, romantic relationships—women tend to engage in more negative (competitive) conflict strategies, and men tend to avoid conflict with their romantic partners (Messmen & Mikesell, 2000).

Ethnicity may also influence conflict style. At least one study showed that Asian and Latino Americans tended to use accommodating and third-party conflict styles more than African Americans and that Asian Americans also tended to use more accommodating conflict tactics than European Americans (Ting-Toomey, Yee-Jung, Shapiro, Garcia, Wright, & Oetzel, 2000).

The relationship among ethnicity, gender, and conflict management is even more complex. Do males and females of different ethnic backgrounds prefer different ways of dealing with conflict? Researcher Mary Jane Collier (1991) investigated this issue in a study in which she asked African American, white

At my work, I have learned to be somewhat of a "chameleon" in adapting to different cultural styles of conflict. I supervise a number of workers, a mixture of collectivists and individualists—some from Mexico, Mexican Americans, and white U.S. Americans. I have learned to play to each person's cultural style, soften them up for my suggestions on how to solve the conflict. With the collectivists, people from Mexico, it takes a little time for them to open up to me. I have to build a relationship before they start to resolve the conflict. Since I've figured this out, they have been more cooperative with me in dealing with conflict issues. With the individualists, they come right out and tell me what's wrong, but I still play to their emotional style and make them feel comfortable, calm them down so that we can move on with the resolution process.
—Mike

American, and Mexican American students to describe conflicts they had had with close friends and the ways they dealt with the conflicts. She also asked them what they should (and should not) have said and whether they thought that males and females handle conflict differently.

Collier found that male and female ethnic friends differed in their ideas about the best ways to deal with conflict. African American males and females offered generally similar descriptions of a problem-solving approach (integration style) as appropriate behavior in conflict management. (One friend said, "I told him to stay in school and that I would help him study." Another explained, "We decided together how to solve the problem" [p. 147].) The males tended to emphasize that appropriate arguments should be given, information should be offered, and opinions should be credible, whereas the females generally emphasized appropriate assertiveness without criticism. (One man complained, "She pushed her own way and opinion and totally disregarded mine" [p. 147].) Some of these findings seem to contradict earlier studies comparing African American and white communication styles. These contradictions might be related to differences among the groups studied (e.g., comparing working-class African Americans and middle-class whites). Furthermore, because these studies are based on very small samples, we should interpret their findings tentatively.

White males and females generally seemed to focus on the importance of accepting responsibility for their behavior. Males in particular mentioned the importance of being direct. (They used expressions like "getting things in the open" and "say right up front" [p. 145].) Females talked about the importance of concern for the other person and the relationship, and for situational flexibility. (One woman explained, "She showed respect for my position and I showed respect for hers" [p. 146].)

Mexican American males and females tended to differ in that males described the importance of talking to reach a mutual understanding. (One man wanted to "make a better effort to explain." Another said that he and his partner "stuck to the problem until we solved it together" [p. 147].) Females described several kinds of appropriate reinforcement of the relationship. In general, males and females in all groups described females as more compassionate and concerned with feelings, and males as more concerned with winning the conflict and being "right."

It is important to remember that, whereas ethnicity and gender may be related to ways of dealing with conflict, it is inappropriate (and inaccurate) to assume that any one person will behave in a particular way because of his or her ethnicity or gender.

INTERPRETIVE AND CRITICAL APPROACHES TO SOCIAL CONFLICT

Both the interpretive and critical approaches tend to emphasize the social, cultural, and historical aspects of conflict. In these perspectives, conflict is far more complex than the ways that interpersonal conflict is enacted. It is deeply rooted in cultural differences in these contexts. Further, a dialectical perspective requires a more complex consideration of types and contexts of conflict.

Social conflict arises from unequal or unjust social relationships. Consider, for example, the recent uprisings of immigrant youths in Europe. In the fall of 2005, riots began in a suburb of Paris—*Clichy-sous-Bois*—and spread throughout the nation to more than 300 cities (Mandonnet, Pelletier, Pontaut, & Rosso, 2005). Again in 2007, there were more riots; *The Economist* reported that "over two nights of violence, they torched scores of cars and rubbish bins, a police station, a nursery school, a library, shops, a car dealer and a McDonald's" (Le Paris flambé, 2007).

More recently, in the summer of 2011, riots erupted in Tottenham, North London, and soon spread south and east to many more areas, where hundreds of "thugs ran riot across the city, looting shops and setting fires to building and vehicles . . . police were pelted with fireworks and petrol bombs, patrol cars were smashed while other vehicles and building were set alight" (Hughes & Whitehead, 2011). How do we understand this conflict? A social science approach may view the conflicts as stemming from cultural differences (generational, ethnic, racial, religious), and these differences certainly play a role.

That is, some experts say it's just hooliganism pure and simple: young undisciplined looters lashing out against society. And some point out the religious element, describing the conflict as rooted in Islamic discontent with the West, particularly in France, because many of the rioters come from Islamic backgrounds. And in both France and England, many of the rioters were ethnic and racial minorities. In France, it was primarily the children and grandchildren of North African immigrants, in London "most are young, male and many are black" (After the riots: The knees jerk, 2011). However, the interpretive and critical perspectives suggest that we look beyond cultural differences to economic, political, and historical contexts and underscore the point that disputes are often more complicated than they first appear. We can invoke the various dialectics to illuminate the complexity of this conflict.

I used to work part-time in a restaurant. One time, a large group of German tourists visited the restaurant and had a long leisurely meal. When I gave them the bill, they protested, thinking I had added a 15% tip to the bill because they were tourists, not realizing that it was company policy when serving large groups. Even though I was pretty angry, I was much more accommodating when dealing with this group in the restaurant (maybe because they were foreigners) than I would have been in a more social context. I thought the tourists were rude, but I tried to practice good listening skills and took more of a problem-solving approach than I would have otherwise.
—Nikki

The rioting in both England and France started with those economically marginalized in society (i.e., the common denominator in both countries): the perpetrators come from poor neighborhoods. *The Economist* suggests that in France "[a] much greater contributor than Islam to the malaise in the suburbs is the lack of jobs" and that in London, soaring property prices push the middle class into "ever-edgier" neighborhoods (Rennie, 2011, p. 54). On the other hand, to exclude other explanations is to insult the poor people who didn't riot (i.e., most of them).

In addition to economic marginalization, many ethnic and racial minorities feel excluded from French and English society. Unlike the United States and Canada, where there is an expression (not always realized) that anyone can become American or Canadian, immigrants in France, particularly of African heritage, can never really become French; they remain forever on the societal periphery:

> [t]he French believe that multiculturalism would only privilege individuals by association with their ethnic, religious or racial roots. There is no such concept as Algerian French. By contrast, one can be Chinese Canadian and still be considered a full citizen. Before immigrants to Canada become equal in the economic sense, their culture is already considered equal in the theoretical sense. The one helps lead to the other. (Smith, 2005)

For these reasons, the rioting points to deep social and cultural conflict. In England and France, officials had warned of tensions in many neighborhoods; as long as these cultural groups remain marginalized, alienated, and largely unemployed, these cultural conflicts are likely to continue.

Some believe this kind of violence is one of the few ways that society can be provoked into interrogating social inequities and begin the long process of changing any society. While there are no easy solutions to these conflicts, both England and France are working to change the economic and cultural conditions underlying the social conflict; there have been infusions of cash, renovations of housing estates that ring the big cities, and messages of inclusion to the heavily Muslim and ethnic population in the *banlieues* (On the streets, again, 2007). The point here is that there is no reason to seek a single source for conflict. In a sense, then, the economic contexts, the cultural identities and belongingness, and the political and religious contexts all work together to shape these conflicts. By taking a dialectical approach to thinking about these riots, you can see how these various forces—economic, social, political, religious—may all play different roles simultaneously.

Social Movements

Some conflict may be motivated by a desire to bring about social change. In **social movements**, individuals work together to bring about social change. They often use confrontation as a strategy to highlight the injustices of the present system. So, for example, when African American students in Greensboro, North Carolina, sat down at white-only lunch counters in the 1960s, they were pointing out the injustices of segregation. Although the students were nonviolent, their actions drew a violent reaction that, for many people, legitimized the claims of injustice. The women's suffrage movement of the early 20th century is another example of a social movement, a mass effort to win women the right to vote in the United States. Many similar contemporary social movements give meaning to conflicts. These include movements against racism, sexism, and homophobia and movements in support of animal rights, the environment, free speech, and civil rights. College campuses are likely locations for much activism.

social movements
Organized activities in which individuals work together to bring about social change.

However, experts note that activism on U.S. campuses today is very different from the politically charged, often violent activism of the 1960s. College students are still involved in social movements; on many campuses there are booths, flyers, posters, and speakers focused on a variety of issues—genocide in Darfur, Islam-fascism, cruelty to animals, environmental concerns, abortion concerns. However, students now don't seem to push the limits of protest, perhaps because they have access to a variety of channels for spreading their messages—including social media like Facebook, Twitter, and blogging, where there is a tremendous amount of political activism (Gordon, 2011).

Many interpersonal conflicts arise and must be understood against the backdrop of large-scale social movements designed to change contemporary society. For example, Jacqueline, from Singapore, is annoyed by U.S. Americans who comment on how well she speaks English because English is her first language even though she is ethnically Chinese. She used to say nothing in response; now sometimes she retorts, "So is yours," reflecting her struggle against the stereotype that Asians cannot speak English. In this context, the social movement against racism gives meaning to the conflict that arises for Jacqueline.

There is, of course, no comprehensive list of existing social movements. They arise and dissipate, depending on the opposition they provoke, the attention they attract, and the strategies they use. As part of social change, social movements need confrontation to highlight the perceived injustice.

Confrontation, then, can be seen as an opportunity for social change. In arguing for a change, Dr. Martin Luther King, Jr. (1984) emphasized the importance of nonviolent confrontation:

Nonviolent resistance is not a method for cowards; it does resist. . . . [It] does not seek to defeat or humiliate the opponent, but to win his friendship and understanding. The nonviolent resister must often express his protest through noncooperation or boycotts, but he realizes that these are not ends themselves; they are merely means to awaken a sense of moral shame in the opponent. (pp. 108–109)

This type of confrontation exposes the injustices of society and opens the way for social change. Although nonviolence is not the only form of confrontation employed by social movements, its use has a long history—from Mahatma Gandhi's struggle for India's independence from Britain, to the civil rights struggle in the United States, to the struggle against apartheid in South Africa. In each case, images of violent responses to nonviolent protesters tended to legitimize the social movements and delegitimize the existing social system. For example, in the 1950s and 1960s, the televised images of police dogs attacking schoolchildren and riot squads turning fire hoses on peaceful protesters in Birmingham, Alabama, swung public sentiment in favor of the civil rights movement.

Some social movements have also used violent forms of confrontation. Groups such as Action Directe in France, the Irish Republican Army, Earth First, and independence movements in Corsica, Algeria, Kosovo, and Chechnya have all been accused of using violence. As a result, they tend to be labeled as terrorists rather than mere protesters. Even the suggestion of violence can be threatening to the public. For example, in 1964, Malcolm X (1984) spoke in favor of civil rights: "The question tonight, as I understand it, is 'The Negro Revolt and Where Do We Go From Here?' or 'What Next?' In my little humble way of understanding it, it points toward either the ballot or the bullet" (p. 126). Malcolm X's rhetoric terrified many U.S. Americans, who then refused to give legitimacy to his movement. To understand communication practices such as these, it is important to study their social contexts. Social movements highlight many issues relevant to intercultural interaction.

Historical and Political Contexts

Most of us recall the childhood saying "Sticks and stones may break my bones, but words will never hurt me." In fact, we know that derogatory words can be a powerful source of conflict. The force that many derogatory words carry comes from their historical usage and the history of oppression to which they refer. As we noted in Chapter 4, much of our identity comes from history. It is only through understanding the past that we can understand what it means to be members of particular cultural groups. For example, understanding the history of Ireland helps give meaning to Irish American identity.

In Kyrgyzstan, a nation in Central Asia, conflicts between the Uzbeks and the Kyrgyz (two different ethnic groups) broke out in 2010. These ethnic conflicts took place in Osh, which is a part of the fertile Fergana Valley, near the Uzbekistan border. Ethnic clashes are not new to this area, but "the clashes are the worst ethnic violence to hit southern Kyrgyzstan since 1990, when several hundred people were killed. Kyrgyzstan was then part of the Soviet Union, which sent in troops to quell the unrest" (Demytrie, 2010).

The historical context is an important part of understanding this conflict. The Fergana Valley is inhabited primarily by Uzbeks, Krygyz, and Tajiks. This fertile valley has been culturally diverse for thousands of years and has seen the influx of peoples from Europe and Asia. More recently, under the Soviet Union, the valley was divided by the establishment of three Soviet Socialist Republics: Uzbekistan, Tajikistan, and Krygyzstan, whose borders split the valley but did not follow along the lines where the ethnic groups lived. Once the Soviet Union collapsed, and the republics became independent, the ethnic composition of these new nations became more significant. Because of this history, "the valley remains an ethnic patchwork, and minority enclaves, like that of the Uzbeks in Osh, have been scenes for violence" (Schwirtz, 2010).

So the violence that broke out between the two ethnic groups in 2010 was embedded in a long history of tensions between these ethnic groups—tensions that go back hundreds of years, but which have been exacerbated by creating national borders and independent nations that put various ethnic groups together in imbalanced ways. The thousands of refugees and the many people who died in the conflict create a new history that will be difficult to easily overcome in the future. Indeed, some observers believe that there is an even larger political context that prevents a more responsible government from arising in Kyrgyzstan: "outside powers, particularly Russia and China, who covet the region's extensive natural resources of natural gas and hydro power, and the US, with its base in Kyrgyzstan, show little interest in fostering more responsible rule" (Tran, 2010).

These dynamics are at work all around the world. Historical antagonisms become part of cultural identities and practices that place people in positions of conflict. Whether in the Middle East, Northern Ireland, Rwanda, Uganda, Nigeria, Sri Lanka, East Timor, Kosovo, or Chechnya, these historical antagonisms lead to various forms of conflict. (See Figure 11-2.)

When people witness conflict, they often assume that it is caused by personal issues between individuals. By reducing conflict to the level of interpersonal interaction, we lose sight of the larger social and political forces that contextualize these conflicts. People are in conflict for reasons that extend far beyond personal communication styles.

MANAGING INTERCULTURAL CONFLICT

Productive Versus Destructive Conflict

One way to think about conflict across cultures is in terms of what is more or less successful conflict management or resolution. Given all of the variations in how people deal with conflict, what happens when there is conflict in intercultural relationships?

Scholar David Augsburger (1992) suggests that productive intercultural conflict is different from destructive conflict in four ways. First, in productive conflict, individuals or groups narrow the conflict in terms of definition, focus, and issues. In destructive conflict, they escalate the issues or negative attitudes.

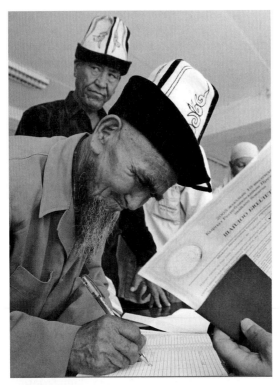

FIGURE 11-2   An elderly Kyrgyz man receives his ballot at a polling station in Bas-Bulak village, 700 km (430 miles) south of the capital, Bishkek. Krygyzstan held presidential elections that the West had urged should be free and fair to add legitimacy to a new leadership installed after a "People's Revolution" in March. (© *Gleb Garanich/Reuters/Corbis*)

For example, if a partner says, "You never do the dishes" or "You always put me down in front of my friends," the conflict is likely to escalate. Instead, the partner could focus on a specific instance of being put down.

Second, in productive conflict, individuals or groups limit conflict to the original issue. In destructive conflict, they escalate the conflict from the original issues, with any aspect of the relationship open for reexamination. For example, guests on talk shows about extramarital affairs might initially refer to a specific affair and then expand the conflict to include numerous prior arguments.

Third, in productive conflict, individuals or groups direct the conflict toward cooperative problem solving. For example, a partner may ask, "How can we work this out?" In contrast, in destructive conflict, strategies involve the use of power, threats, coercion, and deception. For example, an individual might threaten his or her partner: "Either you do what I want, or else." Finally, in productive conflict, individuals or groups trust leadership that stresses mutually satisfactory outcomes. In destructive conflict, they polarize behind single-minded and militant leadership.

Competition Versus Cooperation

As you can see, the general theme in destructive conflict is competitive escalation, often into long-term negativity. The conflicting parties have set up a self-perpetuating, mutually confirming expectation. "Each is treating the other badly because it feels that the other deserves to be treated badly because the other treats it badly and so on" (Deutsch, 1987, p. 41).

How can individuals and groups promote cooperative processes in conflict situations? The general atmosphere of a relationship will promote specific processes and acts (Deutsch, 1973). For instance, a *competitive* atmosphere will promote coercion, deception, suspicion, and rigidity and lead to poor communication. In contrast, a *cooperative* atmosphere will promote perceived similarity, trust, and flexibility and lead to open communication. The key is to establish a positive, cooperative atmosphere in the beginning stages of the relationship or group interaction. It is much more difficult to turn a competitive relationship into a cooperative one once the conflict has started to escalate.

Essential to setting a cooperative atmosphere is exploration. Whereas competition often relies on argumentation, cooperation relies on exploration. Exploration may be done in various ways in different cultures, but it has several basic steps. The parties must first put the issue of conflict on hold and then explore other options or delegate the problem to a third party. They must also give up blaming and persuasion in favor of exploration of new ideas or positions (Wilmot & Hocker, 2010).

However, exploration does not have to be logically consistent or rational. As Augsburger (1992) points out, "Exploration can be provocative, speculative, and emotional" (p. 61). It should encourage individuals to think of innovative and interesting solutions to the conflict at hand. For example, Bill and David were having an ongoing disagreement about a project they were working on, and their relationship was becoming more and more strained. One day, Bill spontaneously suggested that they go out to eat together and really talk about the problem. David was surprised because they did not normally socialize—their relationship revolved around work. They talked about the problem, spent some time getting to know each other, and found they had some things in common. Although the problem didn't magically go away, it became easier to manage. Bill's spontaneous invitation to talk helped facilitate the resolution of the conflict.

Dealing with Conflict

There are no easy answers in dealing with intercultural conflict. Sometimes, we can apply the principles of dialectics; other times, we may need to step back and show self-restraint. Occasionally, though, it may be more appropriate to assert ourselves and not be afraid of strong emotion. Here, we offer seven suggestions for dealing with conflict:

1. Stay centered and do not polarize.
2. Maintain contact.
3. Recognize the existence of different styles.

4. Identify your preferred style.

5. Be creative and expand your style repertoire.

6. Recognize the importance of conflict context.

7. Be willing to forgive.

Let's look at these guidelines in more detail.

Stay Centered and Do Not Polarize   It's important to move beyond traditional stereotypes and either-or thinking. David Augsburger (1992) elaborates on this approach to dealing with conflict:

> *Immediately challenge the intrusion of either-or thinking, traditional stereotypes, and reductionistic explanations of the other's motives as simple while seeing your own as complex. Sustain the conflicting images of reality, one from the antagonist and one of your own, in parallel co-existence within your mind. Be open to a third, centered perspective that may bring a new synthesis into view. (p. 66)*

The parties involved must practice self-restraint. It's okay to get angry, but it's important to move past the anger and to refrain from acting out feelings. For example, Jenni and her co-worker both practiced self-restraint and stayed centered in a recent disagreement about religion. Jenni explains,

> *My friend is a devout Catholic, and I am a devout Mormon. She asked me about where we get some of our doctrine and how it relates to the Bible. We never really solved our differences, but compromised and "agreed to disagree." This was necessary to keep our friendship and respect as co-workers. I felt bad that she couldn't see the points I was coming from. I do think it turned out for the best, though, because we don't feel tension around each other.*

Maintain Contact   This does not mean that the parties have to stay in the conflict situation—sometimes it's necessary to step away for a while. However, the parties should not cut off the relationship. Rather, they should attempt a dialogue rather than isolate themselves from each other or engage in fighting. **Dialogue** differs from conversation in that it assumes the transformative power of speaking and being understood; it involves listening and speaking, not to persuade, but to clarify—even to clarify and truly understand an opposing viewpoint. Quality dialogue is attentive, careful, and full of feeling (Wilmot & Hocker, 2010).

dialogue Conversation that is slow, careful, full of feeling, respectful, and attentive.

Dialogue is possible only between two persons or two groups whose power relationship is more or less in balance. Dialogue offers an important opportunity to come to a richer understanding of intercultural conflicts and experiences.

Our student John experienced an intercultural conflict in an accounting class in which his maintaining contact paid off. He was placed in a group with three Japanese students who were all friends. He recalls:

> *Right from the beginning things were quite awkward; their mathematics abilities far exceeded mine. After only two days, they had met twice without me and completed part of the assignment. I had been left out of the decision-making process.*

Did you know that the third Thursday of October is Conflict Resolution Day? In many conflicts, mediation can be helpful in reaching a solution or compromise. This is an international celebration organized by the Association for Conflict Resolution.

Reproduced with permission from the Association for Conflict Resolution (ACR). www.ACRnet.org.

Rather than avoiding the problem, however, he decided to invite them all over to his house to talk about the project. Everyone was able to loosen up and discuss what had gone wrong, and the conflict was handled productively: "Although I was unhappy with the way things went during the earlier parts of the project, the end result was three new acquaintances and an A in accounting."

Recognize the Existence of Different Styles Conflict is often exacerbated because of the unwillingness of partners to recognize management style differences. The heart of the question is how to reconcile these different styles, particularly when dealing with difficult issues like interracial relations, gay and lesbian rights, abortion rights, and so on. One approach is to "maintain civility," stressing that when contentious issues arise, it's most productive to be polite, respectful, and maybe even avoid direct confrontation. As we've discussed earlier, this approach would be very accepted among many cultural groups. However, some Western scholars contend that this emphasis on civility actually constructs barriers to productive understanding and reinforces the very inequality and injustice it portends to address (Mayo, 2002; Mindell, 1995). Mayo says that civility works precisely because it maintains the distance it initially appears to bridge—and is not the way people build close relations. For example, if gay and lesbian students or other minority students complain about homophobia on campus, they may be seen being "uncivil"—making an issue of something that, in polite society, ought to be ignored. Mayo and others advocate a more direct, expressive style—suggesting that we should not be afraid of "incivility" and anger, rather it is in moments of listening to and giving space to angry voices that conflicts can be resolved and hurt feelings soothed (Mindell, 1995).

An example that illustrates these different styles occurred during a Diversity, Racism, and Community meeting in Compton, Los Angeles. There were many diverse community groups in attendance and the atmosphere was tense, when a middle age white man spoke confidently and gently about all the experience he had with multicultural groups and how he did not like anger. A young black man said he thought the white man didn't know what he was talking about. The white man ignored him and finally the black man stood up and spoke vehemently about his experiences of discrimination in the local community and his disappointments at not being listened to. The white man turned his body away, repeatedly saying he was open to anyone but refusing to talk to an "angry" person.

The multiracial facilitating team pointed out the contrasting assumptions underlying the behavior of the two men: different conflict styles and perceptions. The white man thinking that one needs to be calm to debate, the black man perceiving the white's man style (civility and calmness) as communicating a hidden message: don't upset me about issues that aren't mine. The engaging style demonstrated by the black man was that one can be emotional and rational in dealing with conflict, and, in fact, one *should* be emotional about topics one really cares about (Mindell, 1995).

This particular combination of differing but complementary styles often results in damaged relationships and frozen agendas—the rational/avoiding–emotional/confronting "dance." Other combinations may be problematic but less overtly damaging. For example, two people with assertive emotional styles may understand each other and know how to work through the conflict. Likewise, things can work if both people avoid open conflict, particularly in long-term committed relationships (Pike & Sillars, 1985). Jointly avoiding conflict does not necessarily mean that it goes away, but it may give people time to think about how to deal with the conflict and talk about it.

Identify Your Preferred Style   Although people may change their way of dealing with conflict based on the situation and the type of conflict, most tend to

CAN THE INTERNET REDUCE INTERCULTURAL CONFLICT?

Israeli Jews and Palestinians are engaged in an ongoing conflict that has made it difficult for them to communicate with each other in face-to-face situations. Some have turned to computer-mediated communication (CMC) as one way to communicate across these geographic, cultural, and historical divides. Because CMC offers the opportunity for Israeli Jews to communicate with Palestinians, two communication scholars, Donald Ellis of the University of Hartford and Ifat Maoz of the Hebrew University of Jerusalem, studied high school students' interactions to discover if the Internet could help reduce intercultural conflict. They found that

- Arguments are stunted. "There is no convergence or progress toward elaborated argument" (p. 301).
- Lack of dialogue. Because the participants do not engage with each others' assertions, the "participants immediately diverge, and there is a deafening silence with respect to developing and converging sequences" of arguments (p. 301).
- Jointly constructed points of view do not develop. The participants were more focused on controlling the discussion, rather than mutually building a common perspective.
- Participants tended to directly challenge each other and the "challenges are more intense and emotional" (p. 303).

While CMC can help put cultural groups into contact who might not otherwise communicate with each other, this communication medium does not necessarily solve intercultural conflict.

Source: C. G. Ellis and I. Maoz (2007), Online Argument Between Israeli Jews and Palestinians, *Human Communication Research, 33:* 291–309.

use the same style in most situations. For example, Tom and Judith both prefer an avoiding style. If we are pushed into conflict or feel strongly that we need to resolve a particular issue, we can speak up for ourselves. However, we both prefer more indirect means of dealing with current and potential conflicts. We often choose to work things out on a more personal, indirect level.

It is also important to recognize which conflict styles "push your conflict button." Some styles are more or less compatible; it's important to know which styles are congruent with your own. If you prefer a more confronting style and you have a disagreement with someone like Tom or Judith, it may drive you crazy.

Be Creative and Expand Your Style Repertoire If a particular way of dealing with conflict is not working, be willing to try a different style. Of course, this is easier said than done. As conflict specialists William Wilmot and Joyce Hocker (2010) explain, people often seem to get "frozen" into a conflict style. For example, some people consistently deny any problems in a relationship, whereas others consistently escalate small conflicts into large ones.

There are many reasons for getting stuck in a conflict management style, according to Wilmot and Hocker. The style may have developed during a time when the person felt good about himself or herself—when the particular conflict management style worked well. Consider, for example, the high school athlete who develops an aggressive style on and off the playing field, a style that people seem to respect. A limited repertoire may be related to gender differences. Some women get stuck in an avoiding style, whereas some men get stuck in a confronting style. A limited repertoire also may come from cultural background—a culture that encourages confronting conflict or a culture (like Judith's and Tom's) that rewards avoiding conflict. A combination of these reasons is the likely cause of getting stuck in the use of one conflict management style. For example, even though Tom and Judith prefer an avoiding style, we have occasionally found it effective to be more assertive and direct in intercultural conflicts in which the dominant communication style was more confrontational.

In most aspects of intercultural communication, adaptability and flexibility serve us well—and conflict communication is no exception. This means that there is no so-called objective way to deal with conflict. Many times, as in other aspects of relationships, it's best simply to listen and not say anything. One strategy that mediators use is to allow one person to talk for an extended time while the other person listens.

Recognize the Importance of Conflict Context   As noted earlier in this chapter, it is important to understand the larger social, economic, political, and historical contexts that give meaning to many types of conflict. Conflict arises for many reasons, and it is misleading to think that all conflict can be understood within the interpersonal context alone. For example, when one student, George, went home for a family reunion, everyone seemed to be talking about their romantic relationships, spouses, children, and so on. When George, who is gay, talked about his own partner, George's uncle asked why gay people had to flaunt their lifestyle. George reacted angrily. The conflict was not simply between George and his uncle; it rests in the social context that accepts straight people talking frequently and openly about their relationships but that does not validate the same discussion of romantic relationships from gay people. The same talk is interpreted differently because of the social context.

People often act in ways that cause conflict. However, it is important to let the context explain the behavior as much as possible. Otherwise, the behavior may not make sense. Once you understand the contexts that frame the conflict, whether cultural, social, historical, or political, you will be in a better position to understand and conceive of the possibilities for resolution. For example, Savina, who is white, was shopping with her friend Lashieki. The employee at the cash register referred to someone as "that black girl," and Lashieki, who is African American, demanded, "Why did they have to refer to her as that black girl?" Lashieki's response can only be understood by knowing something about the context of majority–minority relations in the United States. That is, whites are rarely referred to by color, whereas people of color are often defined solely on the basis of race.

Be Willing to Forgive   A final suggestion for facilitating conflict is to consider forgiveness. This means letting go of—not forgetting—feelings of revenge.

Teaching forgiveness between estranged individuals is as old as recorded history; it is present in every culture and is part of the human condition. In fact, recent research suggests that both revenge and forgiveness are instinctual and universal among humans and both have developed as adaptive mechanisms in human evolution (McCullough, 2008).

At the same time, forgiveness is also a basic human instinct that has also served humans well. And it is not always bad to retaliate when someone has done us a great wrong . . . but not helpful to hold a grudge forever. At a very fundamental level, forgiveness ensures that we get along with both family and close friends and helps establish and maintain cooperative relationships with nonrelatives, and, overall, forgiveness is the best strategy for human beings in the long term—it can deliver freedom from fear and freedom to resume normal, peaceful relations. In fact, it is in our self-interest to forgive. Psychologists point out that blaming others and feeling resentment lead to a victim mentality and may actually lead to stress, burnout, and physical problems. Forgiveness, on the other hand, can lead to improved physical health (Waldron & Kelley, 2008).

As cooperation and group level evolve, revenge and forgiveness are not on opposite sides, they are on the same team. You can't be easy-going all the time, you can't be vengeful and spiteful all of the time. . . . "In social dilemmas that pit the short-term gains of selfishness against the long-term gains of cooperation, evolution favors the organism that can be vengeful when necessary, that can forgive when necessary, and that has the wisdom to know the difference" (p. 87).

There are several models of forgiveness—most include an acknowledgement of feelings of hurt and anger and a need for healing. Communication scholars Vince Waldron and Doug Kelley (2008) propose a dialectical approach to forgiveness, particularly applicable because forgiveness is a complex process, often with many contradictions. They identify four dialectical tensions: (1) remembering versus forgetting (it may be good to forget the transgression while, at the same time in some relationships, it may be productive to remember so as not to get involved in repeat of conflict), (2) heart versus mind (tension between strong emotional response to conflict and sometimes needing to engage a more intellectual, cognitive approach to forgiveness), (3) trust versus risk (forgiveness is sometimes a process of rebuilding trust and reducing future relational risk; and (4) mercy versus justice (perhaps the most fundamental dialectic; trying to let go of hostile feelings, extending mercy to the transgressor and, at the same time, a letting go of a desire for revenge and retribution).

In a dialectical forgiveness loop, forgiveness is seen as socially constructed and based in communication. If someone is in a stressed relationship, he or she can create actions and behaviors that make forgiveness seem real, balancing these dialectical tensions; then he or she can communicate this to the other person, enabling the relationship to move forward. It is easier to forgive when one can see the offender as someone who is careworthy, valuable and safe and when the vengeful impulse has been satisfied to some degree, perhaps knowing that an offender has been punished. So an important part of apologizing and asking for forgiveness may be compensation and some measure of restorative justice.

The importance of compensation in preventing violent revenge and encouraging forgiveness can't be overstated. Cross-cultural studies of premodern cultures found that many had developed compensation strategies and forgiveness rituals for quelling revenge, which often included accepting "blood money" as an alternative to killing a murderer or one of his or her relatives, as well as compensations and gift exchanges (McCullough, 2008). A final important component in the forgiveness process for criminals and offenders is restoring justice. Restorative justice conferences are extremely effective at reducing the desire for revenge and fostering forgiveness. "They give people the chance to process the traumatic experience and talk to their offenders in a safe nonthreatening way" (McCullough, 2008, p. 177). "The restorative justice movement is another great example of an institution that brings out people's best selves in the aftermath of conflict and violence. . . it works because it enables people to use their evolved moral intuitions to address the pain of crime in the mega-societies in which most of us live . . ." (pp. 179–180).

Civil wars that end in forgiveness and reconciliation have four processes: redefine affected people's identities, implement countless small actions, process of public "truth," justice short of revenge (legal consequences, amnesty, reparations) (McCullough, 2008). An example of forgiveness on a national level involves the National Sorry Day and the Journey of Healing, which serve to acknowledge and apologize for the wretched treatment of Aboriginals by non-Aboriginal Australians. Another example is the Truth and Reconciliation Commission in South Africa, formed to investigate and facilitate the healing of racial wounds as a result of apartheid. The committee hears stories of the atrocities that were committed, but the ultimate goal is forgiveness, not revenge (Henderson, 1999).

Forgiveness may take a long time. It is important to distinguish between what is forgiveness and what is not, because false forgiveness can be self-righteous and obtrusive; it almost nurtures past transgression. As writer Roxane Lulofs (1994) explains, forgiveness is not

> *simply forgetting that something happened. It does not deny anger. It does not put us in a position of superiority. It is not a declaration of the end of all conflict, of ever risking again with the other person (or anybody else). It is not one way. . . . We do not forgive in order to be martyrs to the relationship. We forgive because it is better for us and better for the other person. We forgive because we want to act freely again, not react out of past pain. . . . [It] is the final stage of conflict and is the one thing that is most likely to prevent repetitive, destructive cycles of conflict. (pp. 283–284, 289)*

Mediation

Sometimes two individuals or groups cannot work through conflict on their own. They may request an intermediary, or one may be assigned to intervene.

It is not easy to forgive, but Kari Huus reports how a victim of a vicious hate crime forgave his attacker and even tried to save his attacker from the death penalty sentence:

It was a widely reported story. As Huus describes it, just after the 9/11 terror attacks, Mark Stroman, a self-styled "Arab Slayer," killed two Asian immigrants and shot another, Rais Bhuiyan, at close range. Stromon walked into the store where Bhuiyan was working, asked him where he was from and then shot him in the face. Bhuiyan, a Bangladeshi immigrant, spent years recovering and is now blind in one eye. He worked tirelessly to collect signatures on a petition to reduce Stroman's death penalty sentence to a life sentence. He explained that his religious beliefs as a Muslim told him to forgive: "I've had many years to grow spiritually. . . . I'm trying my best not to allow the loss of another human life. I'll knock on every door possible."

While lawyers and others often seek clemency for an accuser, it is very unusual to have a victim ask for clemency for his or her attacker. Though the Texas Prison Board eventually denied his request, Bhuiyan's actions have inspired others through his website, "World without Hate," with a stated mission: "to live in a better and peaceful world, to break the cycle of hate and violence. . . . forgiveness is the key." Bhuiyan says he has received a lot of support from all over the world, including relatives of the two victims who were killed by Stroman.

Source: Huus, K. (2011, June 3). A Victim of 9/11 Hate Crime Now Fights for his Attacker's Life. Retrieved from www.msnbc.msn.com/id/43241014/ns/us_news-crime_and_courts/

In some societies, these third parties may be rather informal. In Western societies, though, they tend to be built into the legal and judicial system. For example, lawyers or counselors may act as mediators to settle community or family disputes.

Contemporary Western mediation models often ignore cultural variations in conflict processes. Fortunately, more scholars and mediators are looking at other cultural models that may work better in intercultural conflicts. Augsburger (1992) suggests that the culturally sensitive mediator engages in conflict transformation (not conflict resolution or conflict management). The conflict transformer assists disputants to think in new ways about the conflict—for example, to transform attitudes by redirecting negative perceptions. This requires a commitment by both parties to treat each other with goodwill and mutual respect. Of course, this is often much easier said than done. Behavior can be transformed by limiting all action to collaborative behavior; this can break the negative cycle but requires a commitment to seek a noncoercive process of negotiation even when there has been intense provocation. For example, in the recent Northern Ireland agreement, mediation resulted in commitment by most people to change the vision of Northern Ireland, in spite of horrendous provocation on the part of some extremists.

onflict specialist David Augsburger identifies six key Western assumptions—conflict myths—and notes their inadequacies in intercultural settings.

1. **People and problems can be separated cleanly; interests and positions can be distinguished sharply.** *In most cultures of the world, equal attention must be given to both person and problem, to relationship and goals and to private interests as well as public positions if a creative resolution is to be reached.*

2. **Open self-disclosure is a positive value in negotiations. An open process of public data shared in candid style is assumed necessary for trust.** *"Open covenants, openly arrived at," Woodrow Wilson insisted, as did Harry Truman, were the basis for setting up the United Nations. However, the real negotiation is done in corridors or behind closed doors, and is announced publicly when agreements have been reached. Virtually nothing of any substance is agreed on in the official public UN debates.*

3. **Immediacy, directness, decisiveness, and haste are preferred strategies in timing.** *The Western valuation that time is money can press the negotiator to come to terms prematurely. Many different cultures find that the best way to reach an agreement is to give the matter sufficient time to allow adjustments to be made, accommodations to emerge, and acceptance to evolve and emerge. Believing that "time is people," they are in less haste to reach closure.*

4. **Language employed should be reasonable, rational, and responsible.** *In some cultures, deprecative language, extreme accusations and vitriolic expressions are used as a negotiating power tactic.*

5. **No is no and yes is yes (an affirmation is absolute, a negation final).** *In some cultures, one does not say no to an offer; requests are not phrased to elicit negations; when an offer is affirmed, the real meanings are weighed and assessed carefully.*

6. **When an agreement is reached, implementation will take care of itself as a logical consequence.** *The agreements negotiated may mean different things to parties in a reconciliation. Built-in processes, ongoing negotiations, open channels for resolving problems as they arise in ongoing interpretation, and circumstances that would warrant renegotiation are all useful elements for ensuring ongoing success.*

Source: D. Augsburger, *Conflict Mediation Across Cultures* (Louisville, KY: Westminster/John Knox Press, 1992), pp. 206–208.

Traditional societies often use mediation models based on nondirect means. The models vary but share many characteristics. Whereas North American mediation tends to be more formal and structured, involving direct confrontation and communication, most traditional cultural models are more communally based, with involvement by trusted leaders. Indirect communication is preferred in order to permit individuals to save face. In addition, the process is more dynamic, directed toward resolving tension in the community—the responsibility of the disputants to their larger community is central (Augsburger, 1992, p. 204).

Augsburger provides the example of mediation in the Gitksan Nation, in northwest British Columbia, where mediation of disputes begins with placement of the problem "in the middle of the table." Everyone involved—including those in authority and the witnesses—must make suggestions in a peaceful manner until they come to a decision all can live with. Even conflicts ending in murder are resolved in this consensus-oriented fashion. For instance, "land would be transferred as compensation to help deal with the pain of the loss. The murderer might be required to give up his or her name and go nameless for a period to show respect for the life taken" (p. 213). Eventually, however, the land or anything else that was given up would be returned, "when the pain has passed and time has taken care of the grief" (p. 213). Augsburger points out that this traditional communal approach to mediation is based on collectivistic beliefs that make individualistic solutions to conflicts unacceptable.

Contemporary mediators have learned some lessons from the traditional non-Western models, and mediation is used increasingly in the United States and other countries to resolve conflicts. Mediation is advantageous because it relies on the disputing parties' active involvement in and commitment to the resolution. Also, it represents the work of all involved, so it's likely to be more creative and integrative. Finally, mediation is often cheaper than adversarial legal resolution (Wilmot & Hocker, 2010).

INTERNET RESOURCES

http://hammerconsulting.org/
www.youtube.com/watch?v=s3-Zmj3sTt8&feature=related
The first link is to a website of a for-profit consulting firm, based on Dr. Mitch Hammer's work in intercultural conflict resolution. The website describes the research results and validation studies that led to the development of the Intercultural Conflict Styles inventory, as well as a list of relevant resources and also organizations that have used the program. The second link is a presentation about the conflict resolution program explained on the first website.

http://mediationchannel.com/
This is a great blog maintained by conflict mediation professional Diane Levin. The blog has interesting entries on new media items like *Cool Stuff on the Web*, *Self Awareness Tools*, and *Police Officer's Dilemma* (a video game that tests the effect of racial bias on decisions to shoot). Browse the website for a variety of mediation guides founded in good academic literature. There is even a section with advice in case you want to pursue a career in conflict mediation!

www.mideastweb.org/timeline.htm
The whole Mideast website contains valuable information about conflict and progress in the Middle East. However, this timeline is especially valuable in trying to understand the context of current conflicts. Information here details key moments in the Arab-Israeli conflict from over 3,000 years ago to the present. Many of these events and issues form an invisible context for current conflicts and negotiations. It is worth considering what histories inform other cultural conflicts around the world.

www.usip.org/mediation/index.html
This is the website of the U.S. Institute of Peace. Its focus is on international policy. There are a lot of great resources on this site, including reviews of practitioners and detailed descriptions of the group's efforts in hotspots like Iraq and Haiti. Within the site, www.usip.org/library/ is an organized and useful compilation of resources for researchers.

SUMMARY

- Conflict is defined as involving a perceived or real incompatibility of goals, values, expectations, processes, or outcomes between two or more interdependent individuals or groups.
- Intercultural conflict may be characterized by ambiguity, language issues, and contradictory conflict management styles.
- The social science approach focuses on how cultural differences cause conflict and influence the management of the conflict, primarily on the interpersonal level.
- The five types of conflict are affective conflict, conflict of interest, value conflict, cognitive conflict, and goal conflict.
- There are four intercultual conflict styles—discussion, engagement, accommodating, and dynamic.
- The choice of conflict style may be impacted by cultural values, family influences, gender, and ethnicity.
- Interpretive and critical approaches to conflict emphasize intergroup and social conflict and emphasize contexts of conflict.
- Social movements are one approach to social change and often involve conflict or confrontation.
- Conflict can be productive or destructive.
- Some strategies for conflict resolution include staying centered, maintaining contact, recognizing the existence of different conflict management styles, identifying a preferred style, being creative and expanding one's conflict style repertoire, recognizing the importance of conflict context, and being willing to forgive.
- Transforming methods of mediation are commonly used in many cultures.

DISCUSSION QUESTIONS

1. How does the "conflict as opportunity" orientation differ from the "conflict as destructive" orientation?
2. Why is it important to understand the context in which intercultural conflict occurs?
3. How are conflict strategies used in social movements?

4. How does an attitude of forgiveness facilitate conflict resolution?

5. What are some general suggestions for dealing with intercultural conflict?

 Go to the self-quizzes on the Online Learning Center at www.mhhe.com/
martinnakayama6 to further test your knowledge.

ACTIVITIES

Cultures in Conflict. For this assignment, work in groups of four. As a
group, select two countries or cultural groups that are currently in conflict
or that have historically been in conflict. In your group, form two pairs.
One pair will research the conflict from the perspective of one of the two
cultural groups or countries; the other pair will research the conflict from
the perspective of the other group or country. Use library and community
resources (including interviews with members of the culture if possible).
Outline the major issues and arguments. Explore the role of cultural values
and political, economic, and historical contexts that may contribute to the
conflict. Be prepared to present an oral or written report of your research.

KEY WORDS

accommodating
    style (445)
conflict (436)
dialogue (456)
direct approach (443)
discussion style (445)
dynamic style (446)

emotionally expressive
    approach (444)
engagement style (445)
facework (440)
incompatibility (436)
indirect approach (443)
intercultural conflict (437)

interdependent (436)
intermediaries (446)
mediation (446)
pacifism (444)
restraint approach (445)
social movements (451)

 The Online Learning Center at www.mhhe.com/martinnakayama6 features
flashcards and crossword puzzles based on these terms and concepts.

REFERENCES

After the riots: The knees jerk. (2011, August 20).
    The Economist, 400(8747), 13–14.

America and Pakistan: Stuck with you. (2011, March
    4). The Economist, *398*(8723), 44–46.

Augsburger, D. (1992). *Conflict mediation across cultures.*
    Louisville, KY: Westminster/John Knox Press.

Balmforth, R. (2008, February 20). Seven under inves-
    tigation for Paris suburb riots. *Reuters.* Retrieved,
    May 10, 2008, from www.reuters.com/article/
    worldNews/idUSL2077366820080220?page
    Number=1&virtualBrandChannel=0.

Brewer, N., Mitchell, P., & Weber, N. (2002). Gender
    role, organizational status, and conflict management

styles. *The International Journal of Conflict Manage-
    ment, 13*(1), 78–94.

Cai, D. A., & Fink, E. L. (2002). Conflict style
    differences between individualists and collectivists.
    Communication Monographs, 69, 67–87.

Cole, M. (1996). *Interpersonal conflict communication in
    Japanese cultural contexts.* Unpublished dissertation,
    Arizona State University, Tempe.

Collier, M. J. (1991). Conflict competence within
    African, Mexican, and Anglo American friendships.
    In S. Ting-Toomey & F. Korzenny (Eds.), *Cross-
    cultural interpersonal communication* (pp. 132–154).
    Newbury Park, CA: Sage.

Davis, M., Capobianco, S., & Kraus, L. (2010). Gender differences in responding to conflict in the workplace: Evidence from a large sample of working adults. *Sex Roles, 63*(7/8), 500–514.

Demytrie, R. (2010 June 13). Tens of thousands flee ethnic violence in Krygyzstan. *BBC News.* Retrieved August 26, 2011, from www.bbc.co.uk/news/10304165. www.bbc.co.uk/news/10304165.

Deutsch, M. (1973). *The resolution of conflict: Constructive and destructive processes.* New Haven, CT: Yale University Press.

Deutsch, M. (1987). A theoretical perspective on conflict and conflict resolution. In D. Sandole & I. Sandole-Staroste (Eds.), *Conflict management and problem solving* (pp. 38–49). New York: New York University Press.

Duell, M. (2011, April 4). "I was in middle of the viper's pit." *Dailymail.co.uk.* Retrieved August 30, 2011, from www.dailymail.co.uk/news/article-1373270/Male-male-sexual-assault-soldiers-increases-Greg-Jeloudov-reports-gang-rape.html.

Forbes, G. B., Collinsworth, L. L., Zhao, P., Kohlman, S., & LeClaire, J. (2011). Relationships among individualism-collectivism, gender, and ingroup/outgroup status, and responses to conflict: A study in China and the United States. *Aggressive Behavior, 37*(4), 302–314.

Gordon, J. (2011, July 24). What happened to college protests? *Saturday Night Magazine.* Retrieved August 30, 2011, from www.snmag.com/MAGAZINE/Features/What-Happened-to-College-Protests.html.

Hammer, M. R. (2005). The Intercultural Conflict Style Inventory: A conceptual framework and measure of intercultural conflict approaches. *International Journal of Intercultural Relations, 29,* 675–695.

Henderson, M. (1999). *Forgiveness: Breaking the chain of hate.* Wilsonville, OR: Book-Partners.

High-pitched sound used to deter teenagers. (2008, February 14). *ABC News* (Australian Broadcasting Corporation). Retrieved May 9, 2008 from www.abc.net.au/news/stories/2008/02/14/2162976.htm.

Hughes, M., & Whitehead, T. (2011, August 8). London riots: Police lose battle as lawlessness erupts. *telegraph.co.uk.* Retrieved August 25, 2011, from www.telegraph.co.uk/news/uknews/crime/8690199/London-riots-police-lose-battle-as-lawlessness-erupts.html.

Immigration in Italy: Southern misery (2010, January 16). *The Economist, 394*(8665), 50.

Johannessen, H. (2007). Norway's commitment to conflict resolution education. *Conflict Resolution Quarterly, 25*(1), 93–100.

Kim, M-S. (2002). *Non-Western perspectives on human communication.* Thousand Oaks, CA: Sage.

Koerner, A. F., & Fitzpatrick, M. A. (2006). Family conflict communication. In J. G. Oetzel & S. Ting-Toomey (Eds.), *The Sage handbook on conflict communication: Integrating theory, research, and practice* (pp. 159–183). Thousand Oaks, CA: Sage.

Kramer, S. (2011, May 20). "Coming out": Gay teenagers, in their own words. *The New York Times online.* Retrieved August 23, 2011, from www.nytimes.com/2011/05/23/us/23out.html?_r=1.

King, M. L., Jr. (1984). Pilgrimage in nonviolence. In J. C. Albert & S. E. Albert (Eds.), *The sixties papers: Documents of a rebellious decade* (pp. 108–112). New York: Praeger. (Original work published 1965)

Kraybill, D. (2001). *The riddle of Amish culture.* Baltimore, MD: Johns Hopkins University Press.

Le Paris flambé. (2007, November 29). *The Economist.* Retrieved May 11, 2008, from www.economist.com/world/europe/displaystory.cfm?story_id=10225005.

Lindsley, S. L. (1999). A layered model of problematic intercultural communication in U.S.-owned *maquiladoras* in Mexico. *Communication Monographs, 66,* 145–167.

Lulofs, R. S. (1994). *Conflict: From theory to action.* Scottsdale, AZ: Gorsuch Scarisbrick.

Malcolm X. (1984). The ballot or the bullet. In J. C. Albert & S. E. Albert (Eds.), *The sixties papers: Documents of a rebellious decade* (pp. 126–132). New York: Praeger. (Original work published 1965)

Mandonnet, E., Pelletier, E., Pontaut, J.-M., & Rosso, R. (2005, November 10–16). Pourquoi la France brûle. *L'Express International,* pp. 22–28.

Mayo, C. (2002). The binds that tie: Civility and social difference. *Educational Theory, 53*(2), 169–180.

McCullough, M. E. (2008). *Beyond revenge: The evolution of the forgiveness instinct.* San Francisco: Jossey-Bass.

Messman, S. J., & Mikesell, R. I. (2000). Competition and interpersonal conflict in dating relationships. *Communication Reports, 13,* 21–34.

Mindell, A. (1995). *Sitting in the fire: Large group transformation using conflict and diversity.* Portland, OR: Lao Tse Press.

Oetzel, J. G., Arcos, B., Mabizela, P., Weinman, A. M., & Zhang, Q. (2006). Historical, political, and spiritual factors of conflict: Understanding conflict perspectives and communication in the Muslim world, China, Colombia, and South Africa. In J. G. Oetzel & S. Ting-Toomey (Eds.), *The Sage handbook on conflict communication: Integrating theory, research, and practice* (pp. 549–575). Thousand Oaks, CA: Sage.

On the streets again. (2007, November 28). *The Economist.* Retrieved May 11, 2008, from www.economist.com/world/europe/displaystory. cfm?story_id=10204344.

Pike, G. R., & Sillars, A. L. (1985). Reciprocity of marital communication. *Journal of Social and Personal Relationships, 2,* 303–324.

Putnam, L. L. (2006). Definitions and approaches to conflict and communication. In J. G. Oetzel & S. Ting-Toomey (Eds.), *The Sage handbook on conflict communication: Integrating theory, research, and practice* (pp. 1–32). Thousand Oaks, CA: Sage.

Rennie, D. (2011, August 2011). Bagehot: The transportation option. *The Economist, 400*(8747), 54.

Ross, M. H. (2011). Reflections on the strengths and limitations to cross cultural evidence in the study of conflict and its mitigation. *Cross-Cultural Research, 45*(1), 82–96.

Ross, M. H. (1993). *The culture of conflict: Interpretations and interests in comparative perspective.* New Haven, CT: Yale University Press.

Schwirtz, M. (2010, June 13). Ethnic rioting ravages Kyrgyzstan. *The New York Times.* Retrieved August 26, 2011, from www.nytimes.com/2010/06/14/world/asia/14kyrgyz.html.

Ting-Toomey, S., & Oetzel, J. G. (2002). Cross-cultural face concerns and conflict styles: Current status and future directions. In W. B. Gudykunst & B. Mody (Eds.), *Handbook of international and intercultural communication* (2nd ed., pp. 141–163). Thousand Oaks, CA: Sage.

Ting-Toomey, S., Yee-Jung, K. K., Shapiro, R., Garcia, W., Wright, T. J., & Oetzel, J. G. (2000). Ethnic/cultural identity salience and conflict styles in four U.S. ethnic groups. *International Journal of Intercultural Relations, 24,* 47–81.

Tran, M. (2010, June 14). War in Kyrgyzstan: What is causing the violence? *The guardian.* Retrieved August 26, 2011, from www.guardian.co.uk/world/2010/jun/14/kyrgyzstan-conflict-background.

Waldron, V. R., & Kelley, D. L. (2008). *Communicating forgiveness.* Thousand Oaks, CA: Sage.

Wilmot, W. W., & Hocker, J. L. (2010). *Interpersonal conflict* (8th ed.). New York: McGraw-Hill.

Wolf, N. (2001, September 4). Veiled sexuality meshes with Muslim values. *The Japan Times,* p. 15.

Zhang H. (2011, July 27). Norwegians filled with "Oslove." *ChinaDaily.com.* Retrieved August 25, 2011, from www.chinadaily.com.cn/cndy/2011-07/27/content_12989357.htm.

CHAPTER 12

STRIVING FOR ENGAGED AND EFFECTIVE INTERCULTURAL COMMUNICATION

CHAPTER OBJECTIVES

After reading this chapter, you should be able to:

1. Identify and describe four individual components of competence.

2. Explain how various contexts influence individual intercultural competence.

3. Describe the importance of applying knowledge about intercultural communication.

4. Describe the various ways one can enter into intercultural dialogue.

5. Identify strategies for building coalitions across cultures.

6. Understand the relationship between social justice and intercultural competence.

7. Identify and describe specific strategies for working for social justice.

8. Explain the role of forgiveness in intercultural communication.

9. Identify several challenges for future intercultural communication.

Now that we are nearing the end of our journey through this textbook, you might ask, How do you really know whether you are a good intercultural communicator? We have covered a lot of topics and discussed some ideas that will help you be a better communicator. But you can't learn how to be a good communicator merely by reading books. Just as in learning to be a good public speaker or a good relational partner, it takes experience. In this chapter, we want to leave you with some specific ideas and suggestions for improving your skills in communicating across cultures.

We can approach intercultural competence in several ways. We begin this chapter with the social science approach, identifying specific components of competence: motivation, knowledge, attitudes, behaviors, and skills. We then turn to interpretive and critical approaches, emphasizing the contextual issues in competence. Finally, we continue our dialectical perspective, combining individual and contextual elements to offer specific suggestions for improving intercultural relations by building alliances and coalitions across cultures.

THE COMPONENTS OF COMPETENCE

What are the things we have to know, the attitudes and behaviors, to make us competent communicators? Do we have to be motivated to be good at intercultural communication? Intercultural communication scholars have been investigating these questions for many years (Chen & Starosta, 1996). Scholars taking a social science perspective have identified four basic components, or building blocks, of intercultural competence: motivation, knowledge, attitudes, and behaviors (Wiseman, 2002). We present these components here because we think they serve as a useful starting point. However, interpretive and critical scholars remind us that we need to contextualize these components (Collier, 1998, 2005). We need to ask ourselves, Who came up with these components? Are they applicable to everyone? For example, if a group of Native American scholars came up with guidelines for what it takes to be interculturally competent, would these guidelines apply to other cultural groups? Do the same competencies work in every context? Again, it is useful to remember our dialectical perspective. Intercultural communication competence may rely on individual competence, but context is also important. Let's look first at the individual components.

Social Science Perspective: Individual Components

Motivation   Perhaps the most important dimension of communication competence is **motivation.** If we aren't motivated to communicate with others, it probably doesn't matter what other skills we possess. We can't assume that people always want to communicate. This is a difficult idea to wrestle with, especially for those of us who have dedicated our lives to studying and understanding intercultural communication. And yet, motivation is an important aspect of developing intercultural competence.

motivation As an individual component of intercultural communication competence, the desire to make a commitment in relationships, to learn about the self and others, and to remain flexible.

Why might people not be motivated to engage in intercultural communication? One reason is that members of large, powerful groups often think they don't need to know much about other cultures; there is simply no incentive. In contrast, people from less powerful groups have a strong incentive to learn about and interact with more powerful groups. For example, female managers in corporations are motivated to learn about and adjust to the dominant male norms, Latinos/as are motivated to learn European American norms, and visitors overseas are motivated to learn about and adjust to the norms of foreign cultures. The survival of these less powerful groups often depends on members' motivation to succeed at intercultural interaction (Johnson, 2006).

Sometimes people can *become* motivated to learn about other cultures and to communicate interculturally. For example, the events of 9/11 motivated many U.S. Americans to become more aware of how U.S. worldviews and behavior, on both a personal and a political level, are intertwined with those in other cultures and countries. The increasing levels of violence in the world among religious groups has also motivated people to reach out to those in other cultures. One recently formed group, Women Against War, was started by two women, an Israeli Arab and an Israeli Jew; together they have organized activities and events to advocate for peace and more understanding in Israel. As one of the founders said, "we don't want to see any citizens on both sides killed because of an avoidable war. There is no sense in that" ("Women Demand Peace," 2008).

A second reason that people aren't motivated is because intercultural communication can be uncomfortable. As discussed previously, anxiety, uncertainty, and fear are common aspects of intercultural interactions. And yet, moving out of our "communication comfort zone" often leads to insights into other individuals, groups, and cultures. One of our students, Kati, explains,

> *I think that you learn the most by traveling and/or making a conscious effort to interact with those in another culture or nation or race. Especially being thrust outside of your "comfort zone" (most Americans never get out of their comfort zone) will force you to see the diverse beauty and differences in other cultures.*

Sometimes people do not address delicate intercultural issues out of fear—fear of being isolated from friends and family members who may be prejudiced and not motivated themselves. In one study, college students said they censored their communication in class discussions about race because they were afraid their comments would be taken as offensive, racist, or ignorant; they were afraid of being attacked or yelled at, and they didn't want to be perceived as "trying to prove" they weren't racist (Harris, Miller, & Trego, 2004). Tatum (1997) points out that this fear, and the resulting silences, have huge costs to us as individuals and for our society. Individually, when we are not motivated to reach out across cultural divides, we suffer from distorted perception (we don't really know how individuals from other cultures may view us or a particular situation) and a lack of personal growth. On the societal level, when we are not motivated to embrace other cultures and other ways of thinking and behavior, our organizations suffer from a loss of productivity and human potential (not everyone gets the opportunity to contribute ideas).

The following anecdote illustrates how complicated intercultural communication can be. It concerns a well-intentioned individual trying to be sensitive to one group (Native Americans) but inadvertently ignoring the feelings and sensibilities of another (Japanese).

I participated in a week-long cross-cultural seminar last summer in which the participants were from a mix of domestic and international cultural groups. On the first day, as an icebreaker, we took turns introducing the person to the left. There were several international students, including an older Japanese woman, who had a little trouble with English. She introduced her partner in halting English but made only one mistake; she said that her partner (a white American woman) was "Native American." She meant to say that her partner was born in America, but her English wasn't quite fluent.

Immediately, one of the other members of the group raised her hand and said, "I have an ouch," and proceeded to tell the group how important it was that we be honest and tell others when things were bothering us. She said, further, that it bothered her that this woman had been called a Native American when she was not. She emphasized how important it was that people be labeled accurately. She meant well. But the Japanese woman was mortified. She was embarrassed about her English to begin with, and she was really embarrassed at being singled out as being incorrect in her language. She did not say anything at the time. None of the rest of us in the group knew how distressed she was. As soon as the session was over, she went to the workshop leaders and asked to be transferred out of the group.
—Mary

Third, motivation is lacking in contexts in which historical events or political circumstances have resulted in communication breakdowns. For example, it is understandable, given the history of animosity in the Middle East, that Israeli and Arab students would not be motivated to communicate with each other. It is also understandable why a Serbian student would not want to room with a Croatian student, or why a Greek Cypriot would not want to forge a friendship with a Turkish Cypriot, given that these two ethnic communities have been engaged in one of the most protracted international disputes of all time.

To use an example closer to home, many blacks and whites in the United States are not motivated to forge friendships with each other. This may be partly due to social pressure. One study investigated why so few whites have black friends and why the interracial marriage rate is so low between whites and blacks. The researchers analyzed data from three separate ethnographic interview studies of whites and blacks and concluded that lack of interracial friendships is not because of lack of interracial contact. They found that 90% of the whites interviewed grew up in white-only neighborhoods, but even those who grew up in racially mixed neighborhoods and went to racially mixed schools and had the opportunity to form close relationships with African Americans failed to do so. Those who did have black friends as adolescents tended to not maintain these friendships as adults. The researchers conclude that it is not only the social isolation from blacks that prevents whites from forming close friendship. Rather, the limited interaction is a result of "white habitus"—shared negative attitudes about blacks or blaming blacks for not trying harder to make friends with them, and an "oblivion about the racial components of their own socialization" (Bonilla-Silva, Embrick, Ketchum, & Saenz, 2004).

The point here is that it doesn't matter how good a communicator you are if you are not motivated to use those communication skills. For some people, the first step in developing intercultural communication competence may be to examine their motivation to reach out to others who are culturally different.

knowledge As an individual component of intercultural communication competence, the quality of knowing about oneself (that is, one's strengths and weaknesses), others, and various aspects of communication.

Knowledge   The **knowledge** component comprises various cognitive aspects of communication competence; it involves what we know about ourselves and others and about various aspects of communication. Perhaps most important is **self-knowledge**—knowing how you may be perceived as a communicator and what your strengths and weaknesses are. How can you know what these are?

Acquiring self-knowledge is a long and sometimes complicated process. It involves being open to information coming in many different ways. A white student describes her growing awareness of what it means to be white in the United States after listening to Chicano and African American guest speakers:

self-knowledge Related to intercultural communication competence, the quality of knowing how one is perceived as a communicator, as well as one's strengths and weaknesses.

> *They each spoke about their experiences that they have had [with others prejudging them]. . . . We discover our white identity by listening to others. We hear these hardships that they have had to endure and we realize that we never have had to experience that. You learn a lot about yourself that way. . . . By listening to our guests speak today, I realized that sometimes other ethnicities might not view my culture very highly.*

We often don't know how we're perceived because we don't search for this information or because there is not sufficient trust in a relationship for people to reveal such things. **Other-knowledge,** or knowledge about how other people think and behave will also help you be a more effective communicator. However, learning about others in only abstract terms can lead to stereotyping. It is often better to learn through relational experience, as this student did:

other-knowledge Related to intercultural communication competence, knowledge about how people from other cultures think and behave that will also help you be a more effective communicator.

> *My friend Jack told me a couple of years ago that he was gay, and we have had many discussions on . . . what it means to be gay. A few years ago I didn't take a stance on whether it was right or wrong to be gay, and if anyone made a joke I would laugh. Now that I gained experience from Jack, I respect his way of life and would always support him. This point is valid because the more one experiences things with other people from different backgrounds, the more one will be able to respect and understand other people.*

Of course, we can't know everything about all cultures or develop relationships with people from all cultural groups, so it's important to develop some general knowledge about cultural differences. For example, in this book, we have described cultural variations in both verbal and nonverbal communication.

To avoid stereotyping, perhaps it is better simply to be aware of the range in thought and behavior across cultures, and not to assume that because someone belongs to a particular group, he or she will behave in a particular way.

Linguistic knowledge is another important aspect of intercultural competence. Awareness of the difficulty of learning a second language helps us appreciate the extent of the challenges that sojourners and immigrants face in their new cultural contexts. Also, knowing a second or third language expands our communication repertoire and increases our empathy for culturally different individuals. For example, as Judith struggles through her conversational Spanish class, she is reminded again of how difficult it is to accomplish ordinary things in a second language. And when she sits in class and worries that the instructor might call on her, she is reminded of the anxiety of many international students and immigrants trying to navigate a new country and language.

> **linguistic knowledge** Knowledge of other languages besides one's native language or of the difficulty of learning a second or third language.

Attitudes   Many **attitudes** contribute to intercultural communication competence, including tolerance for ambiguity, empathy, and nonjudgmentalism.

Tolerance for ambiguity refers to the ease in dealing with situations in which much is unknown. Whether we are abroad or at home, interacting with people who look different from us and who behave in ways that are strange to us requires a tolerance for ambiguity. When Judith was studying Spanish in Mexico recently, she was struck by the range of attitudes of her fellow students from the United States. Some seemed very tolerant of the classroom procedures in Mexico, but others seemed to want the classes to be run as they would be in the States.

> **attitudes** An individual's dispositions or mental sets. As a component of intercultural communication competence, attitudes include tolerance for ambiguity, empathy, and nonjudgmentalism.

Tolerance for ambiguity is one of the most difficult things to attain. As mentioned previously, people have a natural preference for predictability; uncertainty can be disquieting. Nick, an exchange student in Mexico, discusses how tolerance and language ability are particularly important—and problematic—in stressful situations:

> **tolerance for ambiguity** The ease with which an individual copes with situations in which a great deal is unknown.

> *I had lost my wallet in the marketplace and asked my wife to wire money to me. I couldn't figure out which Western Union location (there are many) I was supposed to go to to pick up my money. I finally went to the central post office, only to be told that my money had been delivered somewhere else—and I couldn't understand where. I was frustrated, tired and worried—and my language skills were deteriorating rapidly! Fortunately, I pulled myself together, tried to be patient, and joked with the postal workers. It took six hours to get my money, but by the end of the day, I had my money and had made some new friends at the post office!*

Empathy refers to the ability to know what it's like to "walk in another person's shoes." Empathic skills are culture bound. We cannot really view the world through another person's eyes without knowing something about his or her experiences and life. To illustrate, suppose a U.S. American and a Japanese have been introduced and are conversing. The Japanese responds to the U.S. American's first remark with a giggle. The U.S. American feels pleasurable empathic sensations and makes an impulsive comment, indicating a congenial, accepting reaction. However, the Japanese observer now feels intensely uncomfortable. What the U.S. American doesn't realize is that the giggle may not mean that the Japanese is feeling pleasure. Japanese often giggle to indicate embarrassment

> **empathy** The capacity to "walk in another person's shoes."

In his book *Last Watch of the Night*, Paul Monette points out that it is important to recognize the many forms of intolerance most of us experience as we grow up. This excerpt is from a speech he gave at the Library of Congress during National Book Week. The writer he refers to, Urvashi Vaid, is a lesbian who has written about issues of tolerance. Think about how the intolerance around you may affect you and how difficult it is sometimes to be tolerant of the many diversities you encounter.

Most of our families do the very best they can to bring us up whole and make us worthy citizens. But it's a very rare person who manages to arrive at adulthood without being saddled by some form of racism or sexism or homophobia. It is our task as grownups to face those prejudices in ourselves and rethink them. The absolute minimum we can get out of such a self-examination is tolerance, one for another. We gay and lesbian people believe we should be allowed to celebrate ourselves and give back to the larger culture, make our unique contributions—but if all we get is tolerance, we'll take it and build on it.

We don't know what history is going to say even about this week, or where the gay and lesbian revolution is going to go. But we are a revolution that has come to be based very, very strongly on diversity. We have to fight like everyone else to be open in that diversity; but I love Urvashi Vaid's idea that it's not a matter of there being one of each on every board and every faculty and every organization. It's a matter of being each in one. You'll pardon my French, but it's not so hard to be politically correct. All you have to do is not be an ——.

Source: Paul Monette, *Last Watch of the Night* (New York: Harcourt Brace, 1994), pp. 122–123.

and unease. In this case, the U.S. American's "empathy" is missing the mark. In this sense, empathy is the capacity to imagine oneself in another role, within the context of one's cultural identity.

Intercultural communication scholars have attempted to come up with a more culturally sensitive view of empathy. For example, Ben Broome (1991, 1993) stresses that to achieve empathy across cultural boundaries, people must forge strong relationships and strive for the creation of shared meaning in their interpersonal encounters. However, because this is difficult to achieve when people come from very different cultural backgrounds, Broome suggests that this shared meaning must be seen as both provisional and dynamic, that understanding is not an all-or-nothing proposition. In addition, cross-cultural empathy must integrate both thinking and feeling—we must try to understand not only what others *say* (content) but also how they *feel* (empathy). Finally, he reminds us that to achieve cross-cultural empathy, we must seek to understand the context of both others' lived experiences and the specific encounters.

Magoroh Maruyama (1970), an anthropologist-philosopher, agrees that achieving cross-cultural empathy and trying to see the world exactly as the other person sees is very difficult. She describes the process as **transpection,** a postmodern phenomenon that often involves trying to learn foreign beliefs, assumptions, perspectives, and feelings in a foreign context. Transpection, then, can be achieved only with practice and requires structured experience and self-reflection.

Communication scholar Milton Bennett (1998) suggests a "Platinum Rule" ("Do unto others as *they themselves* would have done unto them") instead of the Golden Rule ("Do unto others as *you* would have done unto you") (p. 213). This, of course, requires movement beyond a culture-bound sympathy or empathy for others.

Achieving **nonjudgmentalism** is much easier said than done. We might like to think that we do not judge others according to our own cultural frames of reference, but it is very difficult not to do so. One of our colleagues recalls being at a university meeting at which a group of Icelandic administrators and a group of U.S. American faculty were discussing implementing a study-abroad exchange program. The Icelandic faculty were particularly taciturn, and our colleague wanted to lighten up the meeting a little. Eventually, however, she realized that the taciturnity probably reflected different norms of behavior. She had unknowingly judged the tenor of the meeting based on her own style of communication.

The **D.I.E. exercise** is helpful in developing a nonjudgmental attitude (Wendt, 1984). It involves making a distinction between description (D), interpretation (I), and evaluation (E) in the processing of information. Descriptive statements convey factual information that can be verified through the senses (e.g., "There are 25 chairs in the room" and "I am 5 feet tall"). Interpretive statements attach meaning to the description (e.g., "You must be tired"). Evaluative statements clarify how we feel about something (e.g., "When you're always tired, we can't have any fun together"). Only descriptive statements are nonjudgmental.

This exercise can help us recognize whether we are processing information on a descriptive, interpretive, or evaluative level. Confusing the different levels can lead to misunderstanding and ineffective communication. For example, if I think a student is standing too close to me, I may interpret the behavior as "This student is pushy," or I may evaluate it as "This student is pushy, and I don't like pushy students." However, if I force myself to describe the student's behavior, I may say to myself, "This student is standing 8 inches away from me, whereas most students stand farther away." This observation enables me to search for other (perhaps cultural) reasons for the behavior. The student may be worried about a grade and may be anxious to get some questions answered. Perhaps the student is used to standing closer to people than I am. Or perhaps the student really is pushy.

It is impossible to always stay at the descriptive level. But it is important to know when we are describing and when we are interpreting. Most communication is at the interpretive level. For example, have you ever been set up for a blind date and asked for a description of the person? The descriptions you

transpection
Cross-cultural empathy.

nonjudgmentalism
Free from evaluating according to one's own cultural frame of reference.

D.I.E. exercise A device that helps us determine if we are communicating at a descriptive, interpretive, or evaluative level. Only descriptive statements are nonjudgmental.

might get (e.g., tall, dark, handsome, nice, kind, generous) are not really descriptions; rather, they are interpretations that reflect individual and cultural viewpoints (Wendt, 1984).

Behaviors and Skills   Behaviors and skills are another component of intercultural competence. What are the most competent behaviors? Are there any universal behaviors that work well in all cultural contexts? At one level, there probably are. Communication scholar Brent D. Ruben devised a list of universal behaviors that actually includes some attitudes. These behaviors are a display of respect, interaction management, ambiguity tolerance, empathy, relational rather than task behavior, and interaction posture (Ruben, 1976, 1977; Ruben & Kealey, 1979).

Some general behaviors seem applicable to many cultural groups and contexts (Koester & Olebe, 1988; Olebe & Koester, 1989). Notably, these skills become problematic when we try to apply them in specific ways. For example, being respectful works well in all intercultural interactions, and many scholars identify this particular skill as important (Collier, 1988; Martin & Hammer, 1989). Notably, how one expresses respect behaviorally may vary from culture to culture and from context to context. For example, European Americans show respect by making direct eye contact, whereas some Native Americans show respect by avoiding eye contact. We address the importance of context more fully in the next section.

It is not enough to know how competent behaviors vary from culture to culture, one needs to be able to put that knowledge into practice by demonstrating those behaviors appropriately. Let's see how this works. In one study, Mitch Hammer and his colleagues evaluated the effectiveness of a cross-cultural training program for Japanese and U.S. American managers in a joint venture (a steel company) in Ohio. One goal was to determine if the managers' intercultural communication skills had improved significantly. The research team used a general behavioral framework of communication competence that included the following dimensions: immediacy, involvement, other orientation, interaction management, and social relaxation (Hammer, Martin, Otani, & Koyama, 1990). The two groups (Japanese managers and U.S. American managers) rated these dimensions differently. The U.S. Americans said that the most important dimension was involvement (how expressive one is in conversation), whereas the Japanese managers said that the other orientation (being tuned in to the other person) was most important. The researchers also judged how well each group of managers adapted to the other group's communication style. They videotaped the interaction and asked Japanese raters to judge the U.S. American managers on how well they adapted to the Japanese style, and vice-versa. For example, good interaction management for the Japanese meant initiating and terminating interaction and making sure everyone had a chance to talk; for U.S. Americans, it meant asking opinions of the Japanese, being patient with silence, and avoiding strong disagreement and assertive statements. As this example shows, intercultural communication competence means being able to exhibit or adapt to different kinds of behaviors, depending on the other person's or group's cultural background.

unconscious incompetence When one communicates without adapting their communication style and not thinking about why it may not be effective.

conscious incompetence When one is aware that interaction is not going well, but doesn't understand why

conscious competence When one is aware that interaction is going well and understands why.

unconscious competence When interaction is going well, but one doesn't have to think about why, as the various aspects of intercultural communication are being used unconsciously.

William Howell (1982), a renowned intercultural scholar, investigated how top CEOs made decisions. He found, to his surprise, that they did not follow the analytic process prescribed in business school courses—analysis of cost, benefits, and so on. Rather, they made decisions in a very holistic way. Howell emphasized that intercultural communication is similar, that only so much can be gained by conscious analysis, and that the highest level of communication competence requires a combination of holistic and analytic thinking. He identified four levels of intercultural communication competence: (1) unconscious incompetence, (2) conscious incompetence, (3) conscious competence, and (4) unconscious competence.

Unconscious incompetence is the "be yourself" approach, in which we are not conscious of differences and do not need to act in any particular way. Sometimes this works. However, being ourselves works best in interactions with individuals who are very similar to us. In intercultural contexts, being ourselves often means that we're not very effective and don't realize our ineptness.

At the level of **conscious incompetence,** people realize that things may not be going very well in the interaction, but they are not sure why. Most of us have experienced intercultural interactions in which we felt that something wasn't quite right but couldn't quite figure out what it was. This describes the feeling of conscious incompetence.

As instructors of intercultural communication, we teach at a conscious, intentional level. Our instruction focuses on analytic thinking and learning. This describes the level of **conscious competence.** Reaching this level is a necessary part of the process of becoming a competent communicator. Howell would say that reaching this level is necessary but not sufficient.

Unconscious competence is the level at which communication goes smoothly but is not a conscious process. You've probably heard of marathon runners "hitting the wall," or reaching the limits of their endurance. Usually, inexplicably, they continue running past this point. Communication at the unconscious competent level is like this. This level of competence is not something we can acquire by consciously trying to. It occurs when the analytic and holistic parts are functioning together. When we concentrate too hard or get too analytic, things don't always go easier.

You've probably had the experience of trying unsuccessfully to recall something, letting go of it, and then remembering it as soon as you're thinking about something else. This is what unconscious competence is—being well prepared cognitively and attitudinally, but knowing when to "let go" and rely on your holistic cognitive processing.

While it is useful to acquire knowledge about how competent behaviors vary from culture to culture, as in the cross-cultural training program just described, this analytical knowledge may not be sufficient. A renowned communication scholar, William Howell, suggested that the most competent intercultural communicators are those who consciously acquire knowledge, but who also strive for an "unconscious competence" (see Point of View box).

GLOBAL KIDS

Parents often try to raise their children to be prepared to meet the challenges of the contemporary era. As we move into a more global economy, is the United States raising children who are multilingual and able to work and live in international, multicultural environments? According to the U.S. State Department, there are 102,183,989 active U.S. passports (http://travel.state.gov/passport/ppi/stats/stats_890.html). Out of a total population of about 312 million (www.census.gov), this means about 33% of U.S. Americans have an active passport.

Today, some parents want to raise global children—children who are comfortably multilingual and multicultural—by raising them in other countries. Some send their children to immersion schools, where they learn another language and culture. Others move overseas so that their children are raised with and comfortable in another culture and language. Jim Rogers moved his family from New York City to Singapore so that his children would be fluent in Mandarin. He says, "I'm trying to prepare my children for the future, for the 21st century. I'm trying to prepare them as best I can for the world as I see it" (qtd. in Miller, p. 48). When Clifford Levy was stationed in Moscow, he sent his three children to a Russian school. Although they did not speak Russian at first, they quickly learned Russian and Russian culture. This decision made all the difference in their Russian experiences: "Their fluency and familiarity with the culture unlocked doors everywhere. On a long train ride to Estonia, they befriended a middle-aged construction executive and his wife, a doctor, who were from southern Russia. The couple set out black bread, pickled vegetables and smoked fish for the kids, and everyone sat there snacking and chatting for hours" (Levy).

How well-prepared are you to be a global citizen in the 21st century? As you see the changes happening around you in the world economy, how would you raise your children differently from how you were raised?

Sources: C. J. Levy, "My family's experiment in extreme schooling," *The New York Times*, September 2011. Retrieved September 24, 2011, from www.nytimes.com/2011/09/18/magazine/my-familys-experiment-in-extreme-schooling.html?pagewanted=1&_r=1&sq=russian school&st=cse&scp=3; L. Miller, "How to raise a global kid," *Newsweek*, July 25, 2011, pp. 48–50.

Interpretive Perspective: Competence in Contexts

As we have stressed throughout this book, an important aspect of being a competent communicator is understanding the context in which communication occurs. Intercultural communication happens in many contexts. An interpretive perspective reminds us that a good communicator is sensitive to these contexts. (See Figure 12-1.)

Consider how definitions for competence may vary from one cultural context to another. In one research project we asked European American and Latino students to identify nonverbal behaviors that they thought would be competent in various contexts. The Latino students placed importance on approachability behaviors (e.g., smiling, laughing, pleasant facial expression) in *task* contexts.

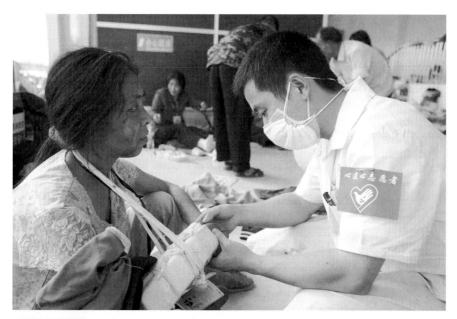

FIGURE 12-1   Intercultural competence in medical contexts may involve getting to know the cultural identities of patients—taking time to understand cultural barriers and showing interest in the patient's cultural background. (© *Ryan Pyle/Corbis*)

In contrast, non-Latino students reported that it was more important to exhibit these behaviors in *social* contexts (Martin, Hammer, & Bradford, 1994). These results probably reflect the importance in the Latino community of establishing personal rapport with those they work with (e.g., smiling, laughing), which sets a good "atmosphere." In contrast, non-Latino white cultural patterns often include a strong distinction between work and social relationships. Laughing and smiling—behaviors that typically communicate liking—are expected in pleasant social situations; however, one need not like a person one works with and therefore, in a task situation, it is not necessarily important to smile, laugh, and so forth in order to accomplish a joint task.

Another study examined intercultural communication competence in medical contexts (Rosenberg, Richard, Lussier, & Abdool, 2006). Using the framework described earlier (motivation, attitudes, behaviors), researchers examined (through observation and in-depth interviews) the degree to which the Canadian physicians were competent in their intercultural communication with immigrant patients. They found that intercultural competence in this context involved getting to know the cultural identities of their patients, something that most physicians did not think was essential in their job. Those physicians who were most competent took time to understand cultural barriers, showed interest in patient's cultural background, realized that some medical practices might not be culturally appropriate, and identified a similarity between themselves and their patients. Their patients described their satisfaction with these physicians, saying, "She knows me; she knows my family" or "She's a woman too, so she can understand" (p. 244).

What about intercultural communication competence in mediated contexts? As we've discussed in earlier chapters, the lack of nonverbal cues (behaviors that communicate a liking and positive attitude toward the other and that establish one's identity) are absent in computer-mediated communication. Perhaps this requires slightly different (or additional) skills—especially involving issues of identity and language expression. First, consider how different cultures value identity expression. For example, some cultural groups place high importance on knowing the identity of a person before entering into relationships. Since much of our identity is expressed nonverbally (how we look and our conversational style), mediated conversations pose challenges. Identity is also expressed verbally, through communication style and humor (not always easily translatable across cultures and particularly difficult in cyberspace). Identity expression can also involve bragging—not viewed positively in all cultures (St. Amant, 2002). A final note about language—mediated contexts can actually facilitate communication between persons not sharing a native language, since they have more time to interpret and understand the other (the text/words are durable), as well as time to phrase their own messages (Osman & Herring, 2007). It is probably a good idea to use humor sparingly, since it is even more difficult to translate in cyberspace and is viewed in different ways in various cultures.

We have emphasized that *many* contexts can influence intercultural communication. For instance, by focusing only on the historical context, you may overlook the relational context; by emphasizing the cultural context, you may be ignoring the gender or racial contexts of the intercultural interaction; and so on. It may seem difficult to keep all of these shifting contexts in mind. However, by analyzing your own intercultural successes and failures, you will come to a better understanding of intercultural communication.

Another aspect of context is the communicator's position within a speech community. Reflect on your own social position in relation to various speech communities and contexts. For example, if you are the only woman in a largely male environment or the only person of color in an otherwise white community, you may face particular expectations or have people project motivations onto your messages. Recognizing your own relation to the speech community and the context will help you better understand intercultural communication.

Critical Perspective: Competence for Whom?

A critical perspective reminds us that individuals' competence may be constrained by the political, economic, and historical contexts. Intercultural communication scholar Mary Jane Collier (1998) reflects,

> *I have come to see that competence, a central issue in my early work, is a construct that is based on implicit privilege. . . . Relevant questions from postcolonial critics include, "Competence and acceptance from whom? Who decides the criteria? Who doesn't? Competent or acceptable on the basis of what social and historical context?" (p. 142)*

Early research on communication competence, conducted largely by white researchers and using data from white respondents, failed to take into account issues of power differentials in understanding competence. Later research, based on data from a variety of ethnic and racial groups, expanded the definition and concept of competence to include issues of stereotyping, powerlessness, and authenticity (Martin, Hecht, & Larkey, 1994). The point is that powerful groups are not likely to focus on these issues, and yet they must be taken into consideration when trying to understand the dimensions of competence. For example, African Americans report that they use stronger, more assertive, aggressive and divergent strategies not identified in previous competence studies in order to be effective in interethnic interactions (Martin, Hecht, Moore, & Larkey, 2001).

For another example, characteristics of effective communication for women in the United States have changed dramatically in the last 50 years. In the 1960s, an "effective" female communicator was expected to be rather passive (both verbally and nonverbally), indirect, and nurturing. Assertive women met with disapproval and sanctions. Today, the "effective" female is expected to behave rather differently from this. As the 21st century unfolds, there is a broader range of acceptable behaviors that define competence for females. They may be unassertive in some contexts, but they are also free, and even expected, to be more assertive in many contexts. Similarly, effective black communicators in the 1960s were expected to be nonassertive in verbal and nonverbal style. Blacks like Muhammad Ali who went against these expectations were severely sanctioned. In short, we need to understand that notions of communication competence depend on specific social, political, and historical contexts. And we need to question who is setting these standards.

Regarding the problematizing of "competence," consider the goals of intercultural interaction: Why do we want to be competent? Because we enjoy interacting with individuals whose backgrounds are different from our own? Is it because we want to sell products, or because we want to convert people to our religion? Because we want to change the world? Or bring about social justice? It is worth examining our own and others' goals in intercultural encounters and to ask whose interests are being served.

These are important questions raised by the critical perspective that force us to rethink intercultural communication competence. Indeed, you now have the skills to push your own thinking about intercultural communication—both strengths and weaknesses—as they help and hinder your ability to communicate.

APPLYING KNOWLEDGE ABOUT INTERCULTURAL COMMUNICATION

Now that we have taken you down the path of intercultural communication, we would like to conclude with specific suggestions for becoming better intercultural communicators. Our dialectical approach recognizes the important role of individual skills *and* contextual constraints in improving intercultural relations. The dialectical perspective also emphasizes the relational aspects of intercultural communication. Perhaps the first step in applying our knowledge to intercultural communication is to recognize the connectedness of humans and the importance of dialogue.

Entering into Dialogue

To recognize and embrace our connectedness even to people who are different from us, we have to engage in true dialogue. A central notion of dialogue is sharing and reciprocity. Communication scholars Starosta and Chen (2005) suggest that a focus on mutual *listening*, instead of talking, forms the core of successful intercultural dialogue. How to do this? A "sharing of narratives" is one metaphor:

> *We come to the world with a master narrative that explains what things are, which ones count for what, what is good or bad about them, and we "braid" these accounts of fact and value into a somewhat coherent personal web of meaning. (p. 277)*

Starosta and Chen go on to suggest that a good intercultural listener exchanges narrative accounts to expand his or her repertoire of possibilities in explaining the world—and this interest and skill is built on a foundation of openness, curiosity, and empathy.

An Eastern model of listening is also useful here. Japanese scholar Ishii (1984) models intercultural communication as listening. In this model, the effective intercultural communicator, sensitive to the other, thinks *carefully* before speaking and delivers a message that is never threatening or condemnatory and one that appears open to multiple possible interpretations. The listener hears the message, considers it, reconsiders it, trying on different possible interpretations—trying to understand the speaker's possible intent. When the listener believes she has understood the point being made, she frames a response, again in a non-threatening manner. You can see that ambiguity is a feature of such listening, which may seem contradictory to other guidelines for competent communication that extol being clear and concise. Perhaps this points to a dialectical view. Intercultural dialogue may have to be clear *and* somewhat ambiguous.

But how can we *really* hear the voices of those who come from cultures very different from our own—and especially those who have not been heard from? As you think about all the messages you hear every day, the most obvious voices and images are often the most privileged. To resist the tendency to focus only on the loudest, most obvious voices, we should strive for "harmonic discourse." This is discourse in which all voices "retain their individual integrity, yet combine to form a whole discourse that is orderly and congruous" (Stewart, 1997, p. 119).

Any conciliation between cultures must reclaim the notion of a voice for *all* interactants. In intercultural contexts, there are two options for those who feel left out—exit or expression. When people feel excluded, they often simply shut down, physically or mentally abandoning the conversation. When this happens, their potential contributions—to some decision, activity, or change—are lost. Obviously, the preferred alternative is to give voice to them. People's silence is broken when they feel that they can contribute, that their views are valued. And those who have historically been silenced sometimes need an invitation. Or those who have a more reserved conversation style may need prompting, as was the case with this traveler from Finland:

> *I was on a business trip in England with some colleagues. We visited universities, where we were shown different departments and their activities. The presenters*

There are many small interventions we might make in everyday life to change what we take for granted. Note how this student has learned to use intercultural relationships as a part of her antiracism struggle.

I am beginning to see the long-term benefits of intercultural relationships: acquiring knowledge about the world, breaking stereotypes, and acquiring new skills. I did not have any stereotypes of Brazilians before I met Anna, but I tell all my family and friends about her, so if any of them had any prior stereotypes, they may think differently now. I have also found that when you are friends with a person of a different culture, it tends to promote some sort of peace and unity in some small way. If I am with someone of a different culture, people are less likely to make racial remarks of any kind in front of them. For example, a co-worker of mine often tells jokes about gay or black people in front of workers that are white and seemingly heterosexual. When I bring a friend into work or go out with work friends that are of a different culture (Spanish, Ukrainian, or Brazilian), he will not tell these jokes. Although my friends are not even of the culture that he makes fun of, I think he is not sure of how his jokes will go over with people he sees as being "ethnic." Regardless, the jokes stop, and that is a step toward preventing racial discrimination.
—Michele

spoke volubly, and we, in accordance with Finnish speaking rules, waited for our turn in order to make comments and ask questions. However, we never got a turn; neither had we time to react to the situations.

In sum, one way to become a more competent communicator is to work on "dialogue" skills by trying to engage in true dialogue. It's important to work on speaking and listening skills. A second step is to become interpersonal allies with people from other cultures.

Becoming Interpersonal Allies

The dialectical approach involves becoming allies with others for better intergroup relations. But we need a new way to think about multiculturalism and cultural diversity—one that recognizes the complexities of communicating across cultures and that addresses power issues. Otherwise, we can get stuck within a competitive framework: If we win something, the other person or group loses, and we can *only* win if others lose. This kind of thinking can make us feel frustrated and guilty.

The goal is to find a way in which we can achieve equitable unity despite holding many different and contradictory truths, a unity based on conscious coalition, a unity of affinity and political kinship, in which we all win.

How can we do this? We first identify what **intercultural alliances** might look like. Communication scholar Mary Jane Collier (1998) interviewed many

intercultural alliances
Bonds between individuals or groups across cultures characterized by a shared recognition of power and the impact of history and by an orientation of affirmation.

485

people in intercultural friendships and identified three issues that characterize intercultural alliances. The first has to do with power and privilege: Intercultural friends recognize and try to understand how ethnic, gender, and class differences lead to power and try to manage these power issues.

In their study of college students, Chesler, Peet, and Sevig (2003) described how difficult it is to understand power issues in interracial relationships. Their findings are based on interviews with white college students. They found that most students came to college with little experience in interracial relations and were generally unaware or held negative attitudes toward racial issues, or even saw themselves as victims, as described by one young man:

> *I think white males have a hard time because we are constantly blamed for being power-holding oppressors, yet we are not given many concrete ways to change. Then we just feel guilty or rebel. (p. 227)*

Through educational and personal experiences, some did come to understand privilege, but it is often a difficult process. As we discussed in Chapter 5, it involves a phase of feeling guilty and paralyzed. As one student described it, "I was horribly liberal-guilt ridden, paralyzed, I was totally blowing every little minor interaction that I had with people of color way out of proportion. . . . I saw how hard it was for me to stop doing that and start being more productive" (p. 227).

Understanding and acknowledging one's privilege, as Collier notes, is often necessary in intercultural friendships. This student describes this acknowledgment:

> *I learned that being white, [there are] so many privileges that I didn't even know of . . . like loans from the bank, not being stopped by the police and other things me and white kids can get away with. I had not noticed the extent to which white privilege has affected and continues to affect many aspects of my everyday life. I thought "I" had accomplished so much, but how much of where I am is due to my accumulated privilege, my family, economic status, school advantages? (Chesler et al., 2003, p. 227)*

Being on two different sides of the power issue can challenge individuals in intercultural relationships. For example, Eleanor, an African American woman, and her friend Mairead, who is white, describe how they negotiate this issue in their own relationship. Often the only African American participating in discussions of race, Eleanor says she gets tired of "educating white girls" about racism. Mairead recognizes the problem of unwittingly saying or doing racist things and "hurting my friend." This is not merely a matter of benign faux pas, but is an ongoing source of oppression for black women, something with far deeper implications than simply saying the right thing in a social situation involving equals (McCullough, 1998, p. 83). Eleanor sometimes needs to withdraw from her white friends to restore herself. For her part, Mairead recognizes that she needs to educate herself about issues of racism. And the two women realize that negotiating time-out from a friendship or time to work on personal issues alone is one aspect of intercultural friendship in a racially segregated society.

Collier's (1998) second component of intercultural alliances has to do with the impact of history: Intercultural friends recognize that people from historically powerful groups view history differently than do those who belong to less

My roommate is from Poland; we are allies. We have similar traits in common. We also study the same major. Having the same course of study really helps us understand one another as it takes a certain type of personality to be successful. Understanding what it takes to be a good intercultural ally is indeed a learning process. There are many things that my Polish roommate does that I disagree with. But because he is from another culture I learn to understand what makes him unique and different. I have shared many meals with his extended family and even had him translate a Polish television show. I have met and enjoy being around his Polish friends.
—David

powerful groups. As we learned in Chapter 4, history often plays an important part in intercultural interactions. One of our colleagues describes how she and her friend Michael had very different views on history:

I was always amazed at how often my friend Michael talked about his relatives' experience during the Holocaust—even though his family wasn't directly involved. He was constantly told as he was growing up that prejudice against Jews could easily lead to another holocaust—and that he always had to be vigilant against anti-Semitism. For me, not being Jewish, I used to get impatient with him, but after learning more about the history and getting to know Michael better, I realize that this is an important part of who he is, and I've actually learned a lot from him about the experiences of a group of people that I knew little about. And I appreciate that side of him better.

History also plays a part in black–white relationships. We're often struck by how, in discussions about race in our classes, white students go to great lengths to affirm that they aren't racist, often telling stories about friends and family members—who, unlike them, are racist. They seem to want to be absolved of past or present responsibilities where race was concerned. And whites expect persons of color to communicate in ways that are friendly, comfortable, and absolving. In this case, true dialogue for whites involves a genuine commitment to listening, to not being defensive, and to recognizing the historical contexts that impact us all. True intercultural friends accept rather than question others' experiences, particularly when historical inequities and power issues are involved. They recognize the importance of historical power differentials and affirm others' cultural experiences even when this calls into question their own worldviews.

Collier's (1998) third component of intercultural alliances has to do with orientations of affirmation. Intercultural friends value and appreciate differences and are committed to the relationship even when they encounter difficulties and misunderstandings. For example, our student Shara comes from a cultural background that emphasizes commitment to family and family obligations. Her friend Kati has very little contact with her parents and siblings. They aren't estranged; they just aren't close. Kati would like to spend time with Shara on holidays, but Shara always spends holidays with her family, who live in another state. This issue has caused tension between the two over the years. But they each realize that these different values are important aspects of their identities. And in complex and dialectical ways, they learn from each other. Shara sometimes envies Kati for her relative freedom and lack of family obligations. But she also feels sorry for Kati that she doesn't have the kind of family support to back her up when she needs help. Similarly, Kati envies Shara's relationships with her large extended family and all the activities and help they provide. But she also sometimes feels sorry for Shara that she never seems to have any time for herself.

Building Coalitions

As we have emphasized throughout this book, many identities and contexts give meaning to who you really are. That is, your identities of gender, sexual orientation, race, region, religion, age, social class, and so on gain specific meaning and force in different contexts. Coalitions can arise from these multiple identities. There are many good examples, such as the Seeds of Peace project (see p. 493), which brings together Jewish and Palestinian young people to work toward peace and harmony. Other local coalitions work to promote dialogue between blacks and whites, and between gays and straights.

Some contexts that arise in the future may cause you to rethink many of your identities. The rhetoric that people use to mobilize coalitions may speak to you in various ways. As you strive to build better intercultural relations, you may need to transcend some of your identities, as the workers in Hawaii did, or you may reinforce other identities. These shifting identities allow you to build coalitions among seemingly different peoples, to foster positive intercultural relationships for a better world.

Coalitions, which are built of multiple identities, are never easy to build. In the process, you may find that some of your own identities feel neglected or injured. Part of the process is the commitment to work through these emotional blows, rather than simply withdrawing to the safety of older identities. Work your way to a richer, more meaningful life by navigating between safety and stability, and change.

Social Justice and Transformation

As we near the end our journey, we would like to refer back to our ethical challenge in the first chapter—the responsibility that comes with the acquisition of intercultural knowledge and insights. As we noted then, this educational experience is not just transformative for you, the individual, but should also benefit the larger society and other cultural groups in the increasingly interdependent world.

The first step in working for social justice is acknowledging that oppression and inequities exist—as we have tried to point out, cultural differences are not just interesting and fascinating, they exist within a hierarchy in which some are privileged and set the rules for others (Allen, 2004).

Social inequities are sometimes manifested in work contexts. For example, workplace bullying—the ill treatment and hostile behavior toward people at work—has recently become a topic of interest to organizational communication scholars. Bullying behaviors range from the most subtle, even unconscious, incivilities to the most blatant, intentional emotional abuse and in some instances are targeted at others explicitly based on race/ethnicity. A recent study explored the connection between workplace bullying and racism for Asian Americans, African Americans, Latinos, and whites (Fox & Stallworth, 2005). The researchers found that while laws and norms no longer condone overtly racist behaviors, the workplace provides many opportunities for "subtle, even unconscious manifestations of racism, including neglect, incivility, humor, ostracism, inequitable treatment and other forms of 'micro-aggression'" (p. 439). Their results showed that experiences with general bullying were similar (and surprisingly frequent) across the four racial/ethnic groups; 97% of the respondents had experienced some type of general bullying. Members of the three ethnic minority groups reported higher instances of bullying based on race/ethnicity than whites. Many of the reported incidents involved a supervisor or occurred with the knowledge of supervisors. The instances were often subtle, seemingly relatively innocuous behaviors by themselves, but when delivered incessantly, the cumulative effects on the victims are of an unimaginable magnitude, leading to a general decrease in confidence in the organization and lack of confidence in the possibility of addressing or resolving the issues.

Starosta and Chen (2005) point out that intercultural listening should be followed by application. Dialogue should ultimately set things right that have been wrong. Good listening "promotes intercultural and interracial harmony, the amelioration of poverty, the introduction of justice, and mutual respect and harmony" (p. 282).

Johnson (2006) gives the following very concrete suggestions for working toward social justice and personal transformation.

1. Acknowledge that trouble exists. There are many obstacles to doing this. Many involved in oppression—those at the top—deny it, trivialize, call it something else, or blame those who are oppressed.

2. Pay attention. We have given you many suggestions for how to "pay attention," including intercultural listening. Johnson points out that there is a great deal of literature available representing many marginalized "voices," but these are rarely heard. For this reason, he suggests it is a good idea not to rely on the media for meaningful analysis of social oppression and inequalities—there is little money to be made from the stories of the powerless. While the media often give play to people of color who criticize affirmative action, or women who criticize feminism, there is little attention given to serious discussions of gender and violence, or class and race issues.

3. Do something. The more you pay attention to privilege and oppression, the more you'll see opportunities to do something.

   Make noise, be seen. Stand up, volunteer, speak out, write letters, sign petitions, show up. Every oppressive system feeds on silence.

POINT *of* VIEW

In outlining specific ways in which white people can fight racism, Paul Kivel lists questions they can ask to better understand specific contexts in which they live and work.

WORKPLACE

1. *What is the gender, race and class composition in your workplace? Which groups hold which positions?*

2. *Who, by race, gender and class, has the power to make decisions about hiring, firing, wages and working conditions in your workplace? Who gets promoted and who doesn't?*

3. *Is hiring non-discriminatory? Are job openings posted and distributed? Do they attract a wide variety of applicants? Are certain groups excluded? Does the diversity of your workplace reflect the diversity of the wider community?*

4. *Are there "invisible" workers, people who cook, clean or do maintenance, for example, who are not generally noticed or paid well?*

5. *What is the racial composition of the people who actually own your workplace? Who makes money from the profits of your work?*

RELIGION

1. *What is your religious upbringing?*

2. *What did you learn about people of color in Sunday school or sermons? About Jewish people?*

3. *Was your religious community all white? Was the leadership of your religious organization all white?*

Find little ways to withdraw supports from paths of least resistance. You can start with yourself—by not laughing at racist or heterosexist jokes, or objecting to others' jokes.

> *I remember the first time I met my sister's boyfriend and he made a disparaging reference to gay people, I knew I had to say something. I objected in a nice way, and we ended up talking for hours. I think he had just never thought about it very much and we're good friends to this day, although we disagree on almost every political and social issue!*

> *Dare to make people feel uncomfortable, beginning with yourself.* Ask your professors how many people of color are on the college's communication faculty. Ask why administrators at your children's schools are white men and why the teachers and secretaries are women. You might think this doesn't make much difference, but it can. . . . And discomfort is unavoidable. One student describes her discomfort: "I love movies, and now I point out all the instances of racist and

4. *What attitudes were expressed about people of color through discussion of missionary work, charity or social problems?*

5. *What do you know about the history of resistance to racism in your religious denomination?*

HOME AND FAMILY

1. *Were people of color and racism talked about in your childhood home? Think about particular incidents when it was. Was there tension around it? What was the general tone? Who initiated discussions and who resisted them?*

2. *Was there silence in your home on issues of racism or anti-Semitism? What did you learn from the silence?*

3. *As a child, what stories, TV shows or books influenced you the most in your attitudes about people of color? What do you carry with you from that exposure?*

4. *Talk with your partner, housemates and friends about [racial] issues. Notice the whiteness of your surroundings out loud to family and friends. This needn't be done aggressively or with great anger. You don't need to attack other people. Ask questions, notice things out loud, express your concerns and give other people room to think about and respond to what you say.*

5. *If you did a room-by-room assessment of your home today, would you find a diversity of images and items? If the answer is no, what do you and other family members lose because of that lack? How does it contribute to racial prejudice and discrimination?*

Source: Paul Kivel, *Uprooting Racism: How White People Can Work for Racial Justice* (Gabriola Island, BC: New Society Publishers, 1996), pp. 182–183, 199, 222.

homophobic humor in movies. My friends think I'm nuts, but they humored me, and now they're starting to point them out to me."

Actively promote change in how systems are organized around privilege. (See the Point of View box beginning on page 490 with Kivel's lists of questions to ask in the workplace, in houses of worship, and within the home and family.)

Don't keep it to yourself. Work with other people—build interpersonal alliances and build coalitions, as discussed earlier. Join organizations dedicated to change the systems that produce privilege and oppression. Most college and university campuses have student organizations that work on issues of gender, race, and sexual orientation. A list of such organizations follows.

National Association for the Advancement of Colored People (NAACP)

National Organization for Women (NOW)

National Conference for Community and Justice

National Gay and Lesbian Task Force

B ruce Feiler, a journalist recounts, how conflict turns to coalition and cooperation in the immediate aftermath of the Egypt uprising in the 2011 Arab Spring:

In the tiny village of Sol, which is south of Cairo, there was conflict between Christians and Muslims. Apparently, a Christian man and Muslim woman were in a romantic relationship, which led to an altercation between the families and the woman's father was killed. The Christian man sought refuge in a church, and there were rumors that he was using black magic against Muslims. At that point a crowd of Muslims went to the church and set it on fire—an act of revenge. The scene seemed set for escalating religious violence, so familiar in these contexts.

However, this time something extraordinary happened. A group of Christians and Muslims who had been working together during the revolution came to the town, held reconciliation discussions and public meetings. During the uprisings earlier, this group had worked together to protect the houses of worship of Muslims, Christians, and Jews from opposing religious groups who wished them harm. In Sol, a popular televangelist, Amr Khaled, "Islam's Billy Graham," told a crowd "My message here today for Muslims and Christians is, Let's be one hand." The military rebuilt the church and the group is trying to be an example to other countries where Muslims and Christians live side by side.

Source: B. Feiler, "Faith in the Arab Spring," *Time.com*, June 6, 2011. Retrieved August 19, 2011, from www.time.com/time/magazine/article/0,9171,2074093,00.html.

The Southern Poverty Law Center

The National Organization of Men against Sexism

National Urban League

There are also many opportunities on the Internet. Conhaim (2004) points out the many web-based projects through which Internet users can participate in online dialogues, gain insights into many different global cultures, and work for social justice. See the Internet Resources, section at the end of this chapter.

One important area where intercultural communication can be productively applied is **community engagement.** Many different organizations are interested in community engagement, such as the Centers for Disease Control, to advance their organizational missions (see the Point of View box on CDC community engagement on page 495).

community engagement Active engagement with communities to improve the lives of those in that particular group, by working together.

Forgiveness

Sometimes the cultural divide simply seems too huge. Sometimes there are grievances perpetrated by one cultural group upon another or by one individual on another that are so brutal as to make the suggestions listed above sound hollow and idealistic. What can we say to the widow of Daniel Pearl, the *Wall Street Journal* writer who was brutally murdered in Pakistan? He and his wife were known for promoting intercultural understanding in their personal and professional lives. Or to Pauline Mitchell, the mother of Fred Martinez, a Native American who was brutally murdered because he was *nadleeh* (a Native American term meaning "two spirited—with spirit of both male and female"). His mother described the horror of his death: "He'd been chased, beaten with a rock. He had been left to bleed, with a fractured skull, alone in the dark in a little canyon. . . ."

We would like to return to the notion of forgiveness we introduced in Chapter 11. Although limited and problematic, forgiveness is an option for promoting intercultural understanding and reconciliation. As we noted, forgiveness is more than a simple rite of religious correctness; it requires a deep intellectual and emotional commitment during moments of great pain. It also requires a letting go, a moving on, a true transformation of spirit.

Forgiveness has been likened to a train. People get on the train but must make various stops before forgiveness becomes a way off. The trick is not to miss your stop. And perhaps we might remember these cautionary words from Philip Yancy, an award-winning Christian author who writes about grace and forgiveness in the face of atrocities and brutality: "The only thing harder than forgiveness is the alternative" (quoted in Henderson, 1999, p. 176).

McCullough poses the question: "So if you set out to build 'the forgiving society' a society in which forgiveness flourishes and revenge is ever more infrequent what sorts of conditions and institutions would you need to put in place? And what kind of society would you end up with?" (p. 180). His answer is strongly related to the contact hypothesis that we discussed in Chapter 4. That is, leaders must construct conditions of contact among groups that lead to decategorization and recategorization, opportunities to develop intimate positive knowledge of each other, and provide superordinate goals that foster cooperation. For example, the Seeds of Peace program, started about 15 years ago, is trying to encourage the right kinds of contact. Seeds of Peace is a summer camp where adolescents from warring groups and countries are chosen by their education ministries on the basis of their leadership potential to participate in the camp. The entire agenda is structured around activities that help campers "develop durable friendships with people from the other side, appreciation and respect for the concerns that keep the conflict going and firm conviction that a peaceful and respectful coexistence is possible" (p. 200). The goal is simple: by building up a reserve of new positive experiences, these young leaders can use them as a sort of psychological buffer to help them undo the vicious ingroup–outgroup revenge that they will return to after camp.

The Amish are another group of people that try very hard to foster a life of forgiveness and peaceful relations—persecuted to the point of extinction in Europe in the 17th century, they came to America and settled. As Michael McCullough describes it, the Amish had 400 years to prepare their response to what happened on October 2, 2006, when a gunman entered a one-room Amish schoolhouse in Nickel Mines, Pennsylvania, sent the young male students and adults out of the school, tied up 10 girl students and then shot and killed 5, wounded 5 more, and then shot himself. As soon as it happened, those in the community who knew the Amish well, told reporters at the scene that the Amish would find a way to forgive the killer. As Mennonite scholar Donald Kraybill, describes it, "the blood was hardly dry on the bare, board floor of the West Nickel Mines School when Amish parents sent words of forgiveness to the family of the killer who had executed their children" (Kraybill, 2006, C01).

Amish aren't the only ones; many famous proponents of peace and forgiveness—Martin Luther King, Jr., Mahatma Ghandi, Desmond Tutu—are motivated by deep religious beliefs concerning forgiveness. However, the link between religion and forgiveness is tricky. As Michael McCullough (2008) points out, religion can motivate forgiveness (as described earlier), but also revenge. The great monotheistic religions of the world (Christianity, Judaism, and Islam) have perpetrated great violence on others in the name of religion. While many religious people say they disapprove of revenge in theory, there have been many studies that show their true feelings. A 2004 study showed that conservative U.S. Americans with strong religious beliefs were nearly 3 times more likely (than Americans with lower religiousity) to believe that Muslim Americans' movement should be monitored by the government, 50% more likely to think that the United States should be able to detain terrorists indefinitely, and 50% more likely to think that Islam encourages violence more than other religions. Christian beliefs seem to motivate people to be tough not only on terrorists but also on the millions of American Muslims who've done absolutely nothing wrong (Nisbet & Shanahan, 2004). In another study, people who made frequent donations to their churches (a measure of devoutness) administered higher levels of shock to their provokers than did the infrequent donors, even when statistically controlling for age, gender, and other measures of religious behavior (Greer, Berman, Varan, Bobrycki, & Watson, 2005).

Perhaps a useful way to look at the role of religions is to see them as strong viable forces—capable of great good and also violence. "Religions are here for the foreseeable future and religious groups are going to keep doing exactly what they please, largely shaped by their perceptions of their self-interest. . . . We can either ignore religion's power to shape forgiveness and revenge to our peril or else we can try to understand that power and work with it. . . . We shouldn't let misplaced optimism cause us to expect anything more, but we shouldn't let unwarranted pessimism cause us to strive for anything less" (McCullough, 2008, p. 223).

The future of our world may well rest on our ability to control revenge and promote forgiveness. As we suggested in Chapter 11, scholar McCullough is convinced that we humans have an instinct for both, but is optimistic because we are an adaptive species. We have proved that we can adapt quickly to respond to challenges in the environment; we have also shown that we can learn to do the right thing—to learn where and when to seek revenge and when to forgive—by watching those who demonstrate forgiveness—leaders, teachers, parents—and finally, we are cooperative creatures and "we've already organized into very large groups called nation-states, perhaps the next evolutionary transition will result in a lasting bond of cooperation among the world's nations" (p. 234). We must believe that it is possible "as the bad people of the world get angrier, more organized and better funded, we really do have to worry about what the desire for revenge might be capable of doing to our world" (p. 225).

The Centers for Disease Control and Prevention (CDC) have identified core principles of their community engagement. As you have seen throughout the course of this book, intercultural understanding requires a wide range of knowledge about cultural groups, from history to politics to cultural patterns. This approach connects well with the experience of the CDC. For example, they note:

> *Become knowledgeable about the community in terms of its economic conditions, political structures, norms and values, demographic trends, history, and experience with engagement efforts. Learn about the community's perceptions of those initiating the engagement activities.*

It is important to note that they ask that you be self-reflexive about the image of your group in that community. As we noted earlier, intercultural communication is not simply about studying others.

Another principle focuses on understanding cultural diversity:

> *All aspects of community engagement must recognize and respect community diversity. Awareness of the various cultures of a community and other factors of diversity must be paramount in designing and implementing community engagement approaches.*

If you find yourself with a community engagement project, it will require that you pull together all of your intercultural communication skills. You may find the complete CDC guidelines to be helpful.

Source: Centers for Disease Control and Prevention, *Principles of Community Engagement*, 2nd ed. (Atlanta: CDC/ATSDR Committee on Community Engagement, June 2011). Retrieved September 24, 2011, from www.atsdr.cdc.gov/communityengagement/pdf/PCE_Report_508_FINAL.pdf.

WHAT THE FUTURE HOLDS

Predicting the future is impossible, of course, but we can be sure that the world that we live in tomorrow will be very different from the world we live in today. At the time of this writing, the King of Saudi Arabia has announced that women will be allowed to vote in local elections and run for office, but women will still not be allowed to drive (Fleischman, 2011). Brazil's new president, Dilma Vana Rousseff, is a woman (Margolis, 2011). Yet, forced marriages and "honor killings" are occurring to women in the United Kingdom and the United States (Goldberg, 2011). The situation of women around the world is both improving and not improving. Even after watching a video of a public whipping of a Sudanese woman, Toni Morrison remains hopeful: "Nevertheless, the abused-animal life so many women are required to live is being challenged. The lasting response I had watching that video is the most important. You did not crouch or kneel or assume a fetal position. You shouted. You fell. But you kept rising" (2011, p. 43).

The global economic situation remains troubling. The European Union is desperately trying to save the euro by working to help Greece overcome its debt problems, but debt issues in other countries (Italy, Spain, Portugal) may bring down the euro (Fighting for its life, 2011; Profligacy is not the problem, 2011). Some have suggested that the United States might make the financial bailout for Europe (Schoen, 2011).

The International Monetary Fund predicts that China will be the largest economy in the world by 2016 (Becoming number one, 2011). Will U.S. Americans be upset that they are no longer number 1? What will this mean for the world? Are you ready? What other changes will we be facing in the future?

Osama bin Laden was killed by the U.S. military, although some ask if he became irrelevant before that, as he did not solve problems of poverty, social inequality, unemployment, and other social problems (Greeley, 2011). Political tensions between Pakistan and the United States are high after the United States accused Pakistan of helping terrorists attacking the U.S. embassy in Afghanistan (Khalilzad, 2011). Tensions between the United States and Pakistan will influence intercultural relations in the future, as the Obama administration takes a hard stance.

In December 2010, a Tunisian street vendor set himself on fire to protest harassment and is widely seen as the catalyst for the "Arab Spring" (Blight & Pulham, 2011). The spread of protests across the Arab world—where unhappiness over corruption, unemployment, and other issues—has many asking what will replace these older governments. Will they be more democratic? When will the brutal repression in Syria end? Palestine has asked the United Nations to recognize the Palestinian state, but its unsuccessful bid does not mean the end of the ongoing issues in this part of the world (Q & A, 2011). What is the future of intercultural tensions and relations in this area of the world? What role will the United States play?

In military terms, the United States is embarking on more and more overseas operations. Although not the primary reason for their assignments overseas, U.S. soldiers can play important roles in foreign relations as cultural ambassadors. Culturally insensitive soldiers can also wreak havoc on the image of the United States abroad, as happened in Afghanistan when U.S. soldiers used burnt corpses as propaganda, leading to an extremely negative reaction from the Islamic world. As part of this effort in enhancing intercultural contact, "American forces receive some cultural sensitivity training before arriving here, but with new troops rotating through every 7 to 12 months, the instruction can be spotty and inconsistent" (Schmitt, 2006, p. 7). Thus, the military has distributed laminated wallet-sized cultural guides to help the soldiers avoid negative encounters (see the Point of View box on page 498).

In political terms, the rise of anti-Americanism is an increasing challenge for U.S. Americans. Although many U.S. Americans became aware of the French anti-Americanism in the wake of their disagreement over the invasion of Iraq, anti-Americanism is a worldwide phenomenon and certainly not a recent perspective (Ross & Ross, 2004). U.S. Americans may focus on the French, but rising anti-Americanism in Latin America, particularly Venezuela, and other areas around the world should not be overlooked. Whether or not you agree with the reasons for anti-Americanism—and these reasons are not the same around the world—you should know the reasons that people may feel this way. Without understanding the

FIGURE 12-2   In February 2008, Australian Prime Minister Kevin Rudd formally apologized to the "stolen generations," the thousands of indigenous children who were forcibly removed from their families and communities between 1910 and 1970, as part of a government "assimilation" program. These children were placed in foster homes and institutions, resulting in many being sexually abused and/or forced into unpaid labor. Rudd said, "In saying we are sorry, and deeply sorry, we remind ourselves that each generation lives in ignorance of the long-term consequences of its actions." How might forgiveness function to overcome this horrible chapter in Australian history? (© William West/AFP/Getty Images)

reasons for anti-American feelings, it is difficult to engage in meaningful intercultural dialogue.

Similarly, in the context of this new global world, with its emerging national security concerns, anti-Americanism, global economic relations, and political challenges, U.S. Americans may need to rethink their easy isolation in a monolingual society. "The disinclination of Americans to learn foreign languages is a running joke in Europe. But it's a serious matter for federal officials who cited both security needs and the quest for global competitiveness in announcing the $114 million National Security Language Initiative. The plan calls for students to begin studying 'critical need' foreign languages, including Arabic, Farsi and Chinese, as early as kindergarten" (Kingsbury, 2006, p. 35). This emphasis on learning foreign languages may benefit the United States as a whole in many ways, aside from national security and global economics, including intercultural understanding. But what will happen to those U.S. Americans who do not learn other languages? What will their economic futures look like? Will they be left behind in this new competitive environment?

Finally, we should also note that many communities are looking to their past to begin the long process of reconciliation by recognizing the reasons for the inequalities that persist (see Figure 12-2). Wilmington, North Carolina, where

INTERCULTURAL TRAINING FOR U.S. AMERICAN SOLDIERS IN AFGHANISTAN

This writer lists suggestions U.S. soldiers are given to help them avoid negative encounters with Afghan citizens.

- *Do not walk in front of someone at prayer.*
- *Do not ask a Muslim if he is a Sunni or Shiite.*
- *Identify, show respect to, and communicate with elders. Work with elders to accomplish your mission.*
- *Do not unnecessarily humiliate men by forcing them onto the ground in front of their families.*
- *Males may never ask a man about his wife, daughters, or sisters. Females can.*
- *Do not yell or use profanity. It is a sign of weakness, poor upbringing, and lack of discipline.*
- *When a guest, do not focus complimentary comments on your host's possessions, as he/she will feel culturally obligated to give them to you.*
- *Do not stare at women, touch them, or try to shake a woman's hand (unless she extends her hand first).*
- *Do not react negatively if Afghan men kiss, embrace, or hold hands. This is polite behavior in Afghan society.*
- *Speak about your families. Afghans like to know you have them.*
- *If you are eating something, offer to share.*
- *Dress modestly. Do not wear shorts. Men should not go shirtless.*

Source: E. Schmitt, "A Man Does Not Ask a Man About His Wife," *The New York Times*, January 8, 2006, Section 4, p. 7.

a race riot occurred that had far-reaching consequences is one such place, and the state of North Carolina has commissioned a study of this history. "On the heels of Florida's investigation into the 1923 Rosewood Massacre, Oklahoma's inquiry into the 1921 Tulsa Race Riot, and the centennial of the Port City's tragic event in 1898, the General Assembly in 2000 enacted legislation calling for the creation of a commission to examine the riot and to develop a historical record" (Wilmington Race Riot Commission, 2005, p. 5). The Wilmington race riot was an "uprising engineered by white supremacists who unseated a government that had been elected by an alliance that included black citizens and white progressives. Scores of black citizens were killed during the uprising—no one yet knows how many—and prominent blacks and whites were banished from the city under threat of death. White supremacists hijacked the state government, stripped black citizens of the right to vote and brought black political participation to a close" (Staples, 2006, p. 13). Although called a riot, it might also be thought of as a coup d'état or an armed insurrection that led to the overthrow of a democratically elected government (with no response from the state or federal government). The economic development of the black community threatened many whites who wreaked havoc and destroyed some of these communities in the United States. In Wilmington, when "the full scope of what the plotters had in mind became clear, black people by the hundreds left the city, taking their ideas and commercial energies elsewhere. The city has yet to recover from the exodus" (p. 13).

How we face these past events, how they help us understand the ways that history has changed us, and what we can do to face these past injustices are an important part of rebuilding intercultural relations and intercultural under-standing. What other states are willing to examine their pasts? How might this historical honesty be helpful in intercultural communication?

There are no easy answers to what the future holds. But it is important to think dialectically about these issues, to see the dialectical tensions at work throughout the world. For example, a fractured, fragmented Europe is in dialec-tical tension with a unified Europe. We can see the history/past–present/future dialectic at work here. The fragmented Europe returns to its historical roots, but the unified Europe represents a forward-looking attempt to deal with the global economy. As a unifying force, a global economy also creates fragmentation.

The task of this book has been to help you begin to think dialectically, to begin to see the many contradictions and tensions at work in the world. Under-standing these contradictions and tensions is key to understanding the events themselves. We acknowledge that there are no easy answers to the challenge of intercultural communication, but we hope we have given you the groundwork to begin your own intercultural journeys.

Continue to push yourself to see the complexities of life, and you will have taken an important step toward successful intercultural communication. Have the confidence to engage in intercultural communication, but be aware that there is always more to learn.

INTERNET RESOURCES

http://friendshipthrougheducation.org/ptpi.htm
This website, People to People International, which started after September 11, provides many resources for cyber dialogue and educational collaboration, primarily for elementary and high school children. Students can get pen pals and work on collaborative projects.

www.ciee.org
The Council on International Educational Exchange (CIEE) offers information about overseas study and work programs (including volunteering and teaching) for young people on its website, with resources for individuals, employers, communities, and educational institutions.

www.laetusinpraesens.org/links/webdial.php
This website links to different kinds of dialogue groups (intercultural, interfaith, etc.); resources on how to start such groups; and articles, books, and frameworks for understanding and implementing dialogue groups.

www.globalexchange.org/
The website of Global Exchange, a membership-based international human rights organization "dedicated to promoting social, economic, and environmental justice around the world," provides news on current global issues, organizes "reality tours" that take participants on education tours to various regions of the world, and offers opportunities to get involved in efforts to build international partnerships and affect change.

www.culturelink.org/dbase/links.html
Culturelink lists worldwide cultural "E-resources" on its site. They include intergovernmental organizations, national institutions, research institutions, art organizations, and publications.

www.stthomas.edu/cilce/default.html
This web page shows the work of the Center for Intercultural Learning and Community Engagement at the University of St. Thomas in St. Paul, Minnesota. There are resources listed for students, faculty/staff, and the community. There is also information on the kinds of work they are doing.

www.eycb.coe.int/eycbwwwroot/index.asp?language=eng&url=/ eycbwwwroot/eng/LINKS_TO.ASP
This website provides a number of useful references to European educational Internet resources on key intercultural issues. Websites are collected under the following themes: intercultural learning, nonformal learning, participation, minorities, conflict resolution, human rights, and human rights education.

SUMMARY

- Intercultural communication competence is both individual and contextual.
- Social science research has identified four individual components of intercultural communication: motivation, attitudes, behaviors, and skills.
- The levels of competence are unconscious incompetence, conscious incompetence, conscious competence, and unconscious competence.
- Interpretive and critical perspectives emphasize the importance of contextual constraints on individual intercultural competence.
- Applying knowledge about intercultural communication includes entering into dialogue, becoming interpersonal allies, building coalitions, and working for social justice and personal transformation.
- Forgiveness is an option when transgression of one cultural group on another is too brutal to understand.
- The future holds global challenges for intercultural communication in political, military, and economic contexts.

DISCUSSION QUESTIONS

1. In what ways is the notion of intercultural competence helpful? In what ways is it limiting?

2. How can you be an interpersonal ally? How do you know if you are being an ally?

3. How might you better assess your unconscious competence and unconscious incompetence?

4. How might the European Union affect the United States?

5. How does your own social position (gender, class, age, and so on) influence your intercultural communication competence? Does this competence change from one context to another?

 Go to the self-quizzes on the Online Learning Center at www.mhhe.com/martinnakayama6 to further test your knowledge.

ACTIVITIES

1. *Global Trends and Intercultural Communication.* Identify and list global trends that are likely to influence intercultural communication in the future. Reflect on the contexts and dialectics that might help you better understand these trends.

2. *Roadblocks to Communication.* Identify and list some of the biggest roadblocks to successful intercultural communication in the future. In what ways will the increasingly global economy be a positive or negative factor in intercultural communication?

3. *Strategies for Becoming Allies.* In a dialogue with someone who is culturally different from you, generate a list of ways that each of you might become an ally of the other. Note the specific communication strategies that will help you become each other's allies.

KEY WORDS

attitudes (475)
community engagement (492)
conscious competence (479)
conscious incompetence (479)
D.I.E. exercise (477)

empathy (475)
intercultural alliances (485)
knowledge (474)
linguistic knowledge (475)
motivation (471)
nonjudgmentalism (477)
other-knowledge (474)

self-knowledge (474)
tolerance for ambiguity (475)
transpection (477)
unconscious competence (479)
unconscious incompetence (479)

 The Online Learning Center at www.mhhe.com/martinnakayama6 features flashcards and crossword puzzles based on these terms and concepts.

REFERENCES

Allen, B. J. (2004). *Difference matters: Communicating social identity*. Long Grove, IL: Waveland Press.

Arnett, R. C. (1997). Communication and community in an age of diversity. In J. M. Makau & R. C. Arnett (Eds.), *Communication ethics in an age of diversity* (pp. 27–47). Chicago: University of Illinois Press.

Barnett, R. C. (2005). Ageism and sexism in the workplace. *Generations, 29*(30), 25–30.

Becoming number one. (2011, September 24). Special Report: The World Economy. *The Economist*, p. 5.

Bennett, M. J. (1998). Overcoming the Golden Rule: Sympathy and empathy. In M. J. Bennett (Ed.), *Basic concepts in intercultural communication: Selected readings* (pp. 191–214). Yarmouth, ME: Intercultural Press.

Blight, G., & Pulham, G. (2011, September 2). Arab spring: An interactive timeline of Middle East protests. *The Guardian*. Retrieved October 1, 2011, from www.guardian.co.uk/world/interactive/2011/mar/22/middle-east-protest-interactive-timeline.

Bonilla-Silva, E., Embreck, D. G., Ketchum, P. R., & Saenz, R. (2004). Where is the love?: Why whites have limited interaction with blacks. *Journal of Intergroup Relations, 1*, 24–38.

Broome, B. J. (1991). Building shared meaning: Implications of a relational approach to empathy for teaching intercultural communication. *Communication Education, 40*, 235–249.

Broome, B. J. (1993). Managing differences in conflict resolution: The role of relational empathy. In D. J. D. Sandole & H. van der Merwe (Eds.), *Conflict resolution theory and practice: Integration and application* (pp. 97–111). Manchester, England: Manchester University Press.

Chen, G.-M. (2005). A model of global communication competence. *China Media Research 1*(1), 3–11.

Chen, G.-M., & Starosta, W. J. (1996). Intercultural communication competence: A synthesis. In B. R. Burleson (Ed.), *Communication yearbook, 19* (pp. 353–383). Thousand Oaks, CA: Sage.

Chesler, M. A., Peet, M., & Sevig, T. (2003). Blinded by whiteness: The development of white college students' racial awareness. In A. W. Doane & E. Bonilla-Silva (Eds.), *White out: The continuing significance of racism* (pp. 215–230). New York: Routledge.

Collier, M. J. (1988). A comparison of conversations among and between domestic culture groups: How intra- and intercultural competencies vary. *Communication Quarterly, 36*, 122–144.

Collier, M. J. (1998). Researching cultural identity: Reconciling interpretive and postcolonial perspectives. In D. V. Tanno & A. González (Eds.), *Communication and identity across cultures* (pp. 122–147). Thousand Oaks, CA: Sage.

Collier, M. J. (2002). Intercultural friendships as interpersonal alliances. In J. N. Martin, T. K. Nakayama, & L. A. Flores (Eds.), *Readings in intercultural communication: Experiences and contexts* (pp. 301–310). Boston: McGraw-Hill.

Collier, M. J. (2005). Theorizing cultural identification: Critical updates and continuing evolution. In W. B. Gudykunst (Ed.), *Theorizing about intercultural communication* (pp. 235–256). Thousand Oaks, CA: Sage.

Conhaim, W. W. (2004, November). The Global Net: Part II. *Information Today, 21*(10), 41–42.

Cose, E. (1993). *The rage of a privileged class*. New York: HarperCollins.

Deetz, S., Cohen, D., & Edley, P. P. (1997). Toward a dialogic ethic in the context of international business organization. In F. L. Casmir (Ed.), *Ethics in intercultural communication* (pp. 183–223). Mahwah, NJ: Lawrence Erlbaum.

Early, P. S., & Ang, S. (2003). *Cultural intelligence: Individual interactions across cultures*. Stanford, CA: Stanford University Press.

Fighting for its life. (2011, September 17). *The Economist*, pp. 73–74.

Fleischman, J. (2011, September 25). Saudi Arabia to allow women to vote. *Los Angeles Times*. Retrieved October 1, 2011, from http://articles.latimes.com/2011/sep/25/world/la-fg-saudi-women-vote-20110926.

Fox, S., & Stallworth, L. E. (2005). Racial/ethnic bullying: Exploring links between bullying and racism in the US workplace. *Journal of Vocational Behavior, 66*, 438–456.

Goldberg, M. (2011, September 26). Marry—or else. *Newsweek*, pp. 48–51.

Greeley, B. (2011, May 9–15). Why Bin Laden lost. *Bloomberg Businessweek*, pp. 7–9.

Greer, T., Berman, M., Vara, V., Bobrycki, L., & Watson, S. (2005). We are a religious people; we are a vengeful people. *Journal of the Scientific Study of Religion, 44*, 45–57.

Hammer, M. R., Martin, J. N., Otani, M., & Koyama, M. (1990, March). *Analyzing intercultural competence: Evaluating communication skills of Japanese and American managers*. Paper presented at the First Annual Intercultural and International Communication Conference, California State University, Fullerton.

Harris, T. M, Miller, A. N., & Trego, A. (2004). A co-cultural examination of community building in the interracial communication classroom. *Journal of Intergroup Relations, 31*, 39–63.

Henderson, H. (1999). *Forgiveness: Breaking the chain of hate*. Wilsonville, OR: Book-Partners.

Howell, W. (1979). Theoretical directions in

intercultural communication. In M. Asante, E. Newmark, & C. Blake (Eds.), *Handbook of intercultural communication.* Beverly Hills, CA: Sage.

Howell, W. S. (1982). *The empathic communicator.* Belmont, CA: Wadsworth.

Imahori, T., & Lanigan, M. L. (1989). Relational model of intercultural communication competence. *International Journal of Intercultural Relations, 13,* 269–286.

Ishii, S. (1984). *Enryo-sasshi* communication: A key to understanding Japanese interpersonal relations. *Cross Currents, 11,* 49–58.

Johnson, A. G. (2006). *Privilege, power, and difference.* New York: McGraw-Hill.

Khalilzad, Z. (2011, October 3). Our deceitful "friends." *Newsweek,* p. 4.

Kingsbury, A. (2006, January 16). Untying U.S. tongues. *U.S. News & World Report,* p. 35.

Koester, J., & Olebe, M. (1988). The behavioral assessment scale for intercultural communication effectiveness. *International Journal of Intercultural Relations, 12,* 233–246.

Kraybill, D. B. (2006, October 8). Forgiving is woven into life of Amish. Op Ed page, *The Philadelphia Inquirer,* p. C01. Retrieved August 28, 2008, from http://infoweb.newsbank.com.ezproxy1.lib.asu.edu/iw-search/we/InfoWeb?p_product=AWNB&p_theme= aggregated5 &p_action=doc&p_docid=11A70D2BE9EAD1D8&d_ place=PHIB&f_ subsection=sCURRENTS&f_issue=2006-10-08&f_ publisher=.

Margolis, M. (2011, September 26). Don't mess with Dilma. *Newsweek,* pp. 36–40.

Martin, J. N., & Hammer, M. R. (1989). Behavioral categories of intercultural communication competence: Everyday communicators' perceptions. *International Journal of Intercultural Relations, 13,* 303–332.

Martin, J. N., Hammer, M. R., & Bradford, L. (1994). The influence of cultural and situational contexts on Hispanic and non-Hispanic communication competence behaviors. *Communication Quarterly, 42,* 160–179.

Martin, J. N., Hecht, M. L., & Larkey, L. K. (1994). Conversational improvement strategies for interethnic communication: African-American and European perspectives. *Communication Monographs, 61,* 236–255.

Martin, J. N., Hecht, M. L., Moore, S., & Larkey, L. (2001). An African American perspective on conversational improvement strategies. *Howard Journal of* Communications, *12,* 1–28.

Maruyama, M. (1970). *Toward a cultural futurology.* Paper presented at the annual meeting of the American Anthropological Association, published by the Training Center for Community Programs, University of Minnesota, Minneapolis.

McCullough, M. E. (2008). *Beyond revenge: The evolution of the forgiveness instinct.* San Francisco: Jossey-Bass.

McCullough, M. W. (1998). *Black and White women as friends: Building cross-race friendships.* Cresskill, NJ: Hampton Press.

Nisbet, E. C., & Shanahan, J. (2004). *MRSG special report: Restrictions on civil liberties, views of Islam, and Muslim Americans.* Ithaca, NY: Media and Society Research Group. Retrieved May 5, 2008, from www.comm.cornell.edu/msrg/report1a.pdf.

Olebe, M., & Koester, J. (1989). Exploring the cross-cultural equivalence of the behavioral assessment scale for intercultural communication. *International Journal of Intercultural Relations, 13,* 333–347.

Osman, G., & Herring, S. (2007). Interaction, facilitation, and deep learning in cross-cultural chat: A case study. *Internet and Higher Education, 10,* 125–141.

Profligacy is not the problem. (2011, September 17). *The Economist,* pp. 74–75.

Q & A: Palestinian bid for full membership at the UN (2011, September 24). *BBC News.* Retrieved October 1, 2011, from www.bbc.co.uk/news/world-middle-east-13701636.

Rosenberg, E., Richard, C., Lussier, M-T., & Abdool, S. N. (2006). Intercultural communication competence in family medicine: Lessons from the field. *Patient Education and Counseling, 61*(2), 236–245.

Ross, A., & Ross, K. (Eds.). (2004). *Anti-Americanism.* New York: New York University Press.

Ruben, B. D. (1976). Assessing communication competency for intercultural adaptation. *Group and Organization Studies, 1,* 334–354.

Ruben, B. D. (1977). Guidelines for cross cultural communication effectiveness. *Group and Organization Studies, 2,* 470–479.

Ruben, B. D., & Kealey, D. J. (1979). Behavioral assessment of communication competence and the prediction of cross-cultural adaptation. *International Journal of Intercultural Relations, 3,* 15–47.

Ruth, J. L. (2007). *Forgiveness: A legacy of the West Nickel Mines Amish School.* Scottdale, PA: Herald Press.

Schmitt, E. (2006, January 8). A man does not ask a man about his wife. *The New York Times,* Section 4, p. 7.

Schoen, J. W. (2011, September 16). US taxpayers could be hook for Europe bailout. *MSNBC.* Retrieved October 1, 2011, from http://bottomline.msnbc.msn.com/_news/2011/09/16/7795342-us-taxpayers-could-be-on-hook-for-europe-bailout.

St. Amant, K. (2002). When cultures and computers collide: Rethinking computer-mediated communication according to international and intercultural communication expectations. *Journal of Business and Technical Communication, 16,* 196–214.

Staples, B. (2006, January 8). When democracy died in Wilmington, N.C. *The New York Times*, Section 4, p. 13.

Starosta, W. J., & Chen, G.-M. (2005). Intercultural listening: Collected reflections, collated refractions. In W. J. Starosta & G.-M. Chen (Eds.), *Taking stock in intercultural communication: Where to now?* (pp. 274–285). Washington, DC: National Communication Association.

Stewart, L. P. (1997). Facilitating connections: Issues of gender, culture, and diversity. In J. M. Makau & R. C. Arnett (Eds.), *Communication ethics in an age of diversity* (pp. 111–125). Chicago: University of Illinois Press.

Tatum, B. (1997). *Why are all the Black kids sitting together in the cafeteria?* (pp. 193–206). New York: Basic Books.

Touraine, A., Dubet, F., Hegedus, Z., & Wieviorka, M. (1981). *Le pays contre l'Etat: Luttes occitanes.* Paris: Editions du Seuil.

Wendt, J. (1984). D.I.E.: A way to improve communication. *Communication Education, 33,* 397–401.

Wilmington Race Riot Commission. (2005, December 15). 1898 Wilmington Race Riot Report—Draft. Raleigh: North Carolina Department of Cultural Resources. Available at www.ah.dcr.state .ne.us/1898-wrrc/report/report.htm.

Wiseman, R. L. (2002). Intercultural communication competence. In W. B. Gudykunst & B. Mody (Eds.), *Handbook of international and intercultural communication* (2nd ed., pp. 207–224). Thousand Oaks, CA: Sage.

Women demand peace in the Middle East. Salon.com. Retrieved May 10, 2008, from /www.salon .com/mwt/broadsheet/2006/08/09/kopty/.

Wood, J. T. (1997). Diversity in dialogue: Commonalities and differences between friends. In J. M. Makau & R. C. Arnett (Eds.), *Communication ethics in an age of diversity* (pp. 5–26). Chicago: University of Illinois Press.

Credits

[page 8, Figure 1-2: "Population by race and ethnicity, actual and projected: 1960-2050"] Copyright © 2008 by The Pew Research Center. Reprinted with permission; [page 17, text] Excerpts from *U.S. Religious Landscape Survey*. Copyright © 2008 by The Pew Forum on Religion and Public Life. Reprinted with permission; [page 21, text] J. Watts, excerpt from "China Chops Nike Ad; Multinational Apologizes After Outcry" from *The Guardian* (December 8, 2004): 15. Copyright © 2004 by Guardian News and Media Ltd. Reprinted with permission; [page 30, text] Jessica Stark, excerpt from "Rice research shows Starbucks logo redesign could prove beneficial to company" (Press Release, Rice University News and media Relations, (January 6, 2011). Copyright © 2011 by Rice University. Reprinted with the permission of Rice University/Office of News and Media Relations; [pages 34-35, text] Benjamin Feinberg, excerpt from "What Students Don't Learn Abroad" from *The Chronicle Review* (May 2, 2000): B20. Reprinted with the permission of the author; [pages 58-59, text] Ann Hartnell, excerpts from "The Disneyfication of New Orleans," guardian.co.uk (August 28, 2008). Copyright © 2008 Guardian News Service, Ltd. Reprinted with permission; [pages 89, 94–95, text] Mary Jane Collier, Radha S. Hegde, Wen Shu Lee, Thomas K. Nakayama, and Gust A. Yep, excerpts from "Dialogue on the Edges: Ferment in Communication and Culture" in *Transforming Communication About Culture*, edited by M. J. Collier. Copyright © 2002 by Sage Publications, Inc. Reprinted by permission of Sage Publications, Inc; [page 95, text] Fox News Latino, excerpt from "Arizona State University Valedictorian is an Undocumented Immigrant" (May 13, 2011). Copyright © 2011 Fox News Network LLC. Reprinted with permission; [pages 103-104, text] John Engle, excerpt from "Culture's Unacknowledged Iron Grip" from *Chronicle of Higher Education* (February 2, 2007): B16. Reprinted with the permission of the author; [page 108, Table 3-3: "Hofstede Value Orientations"] Adapted from G. Hofstede and G. J. Hofstede, *Cultures and Organizations: Software of the Mind, Second Edition*. Copyright © 2004 by Geert Hofstede BV. Reprinted with permission; [page 140, text] B. McGrory, excerpt from "Centuries of interruption and a history rejoined" from *The Boston Globe* (May 11, 2011): A1, A9. Copyright © 2011 by The Boston Globe. Reprinted with the permission of The Boston Globe c/o the Copyright Clearance Center; [page 154, text] Gretchen Parker, "Dealing with Issues of Race in America" from *Tampa Tribune* (March 30, 2008). Copyright © 2008. Reprinted with permission of The Tampa Tribune; [page 188, text] J. Rosen, excerpt from "Victim of McDonald's beating speaks out; transgender woman says attack was a 'hate crime'." from *The Baltimore Sun* (April 24, 2011). Copyright © 2011 by The Baltimore Sun. Reprinted with permission of The Baltimore Sun Media Group. All Rights Reserved; [page 195, text] Peggy McIntosh, excerpt adapted from "White Privilege and Male Privilege: A Personal Account of Coming to See Correspondences through Work in Women's Studies" (Working paper 185, Wellesley College Center for Research on Women, 1988). Copyright © 1988. Reprinted with permission; [page 197, Figure 5-2: "Are Blacks Better Off Now Than Five Years Ago?"] Copyright © 2010 by The Pew Research Center. Reprinted with permission. Reprinted with permission; [page 203, text] Henry Chu, excerpt from "Tennis star may bring shine back to Serbia's tarnished reputation" from *The Los Angeles Times* (June 5, 2011). Copyright © 2011 The Los Angeles Times. Reprinted by permission; [page 242, Table 6-2: "Co-Cultural Communication Orientations"] From Mark Orbe, *Constructing Co-Cultural Theory: An Explication of Culture, Power, and Communication*. Copyright © 1998 by Sage Publications, Inc. Reprinted with the permission of Sage Publications, Inc.; [page 253, text] Laurel Delaney, excerpt from "8 Global Marketing Gaffes" (2002) from MarketingProfs.com. Copyright © 2002 by MarketingProfs LLC. Reprinted with the permission of Laurel Delaney, President, Global TradeSource Ltd.; [page 261, text] Stuart Silverstein, excerpt from "Conversing is No Simple Matter for the Bilingual" from *Los Angeles Times* (November 15, 2007). Copyright © 2007 The Los Angeles Times. Reprinted with permission; [page 264, text] Harumi Befu, excerpt from "English Language Intellectual Imperialism and Its Consequences" from *Newsletter: Intercultural Communication* 37 (June 2000): 1. Reprinted with the permission of the Intercultural Communication

Name Index

Subject Index